Introduction
to Sociology

Henry L. Tischler
Framingham State College

Phillip Whitten
Bentley College

David E. K. Hunter
Yale University

Introduction to Sociology

Second Edition

Holt, Rinehart and Winston
New York Chicago San Francisco Philadelphia Montreal
Toronto London Sydney Tokyo Mexico City Rio de Janeiro Madrid

Publisher   Robert Woodbury
Acquisitions Editor   Lucy Rosendahl
Assistant Editor   Lucy Macmillan Stitzer
Senior Project Editor   Françoise Bartlett
Art Director   Louis Scardino
Designer   Caliber Design Planning, Inc.
Production Manager   Annette Mayeski
Photo Researcher   Cheryl Mannes
Portfolio Researcher   Christine Pullo
Cover: Gerard Fromanger. *Sienne-Paris-Sienne, 1983.* "Allegro" series.
Fresco, 6′4⅜″ × 33′8″.
Collection Cité Judiciaire,
Draguignan, France.

Credits are on page 573.

**Library of Congress Cataloging in Publication
Data**

Tischler, Henry L.
  Introduction to sociology.

  Bibliography: p. 558
  Includes indexes.
  1. Sociology.   I. Whitten, Phillip.
  II. Hunter, David E.   III. Title.
HM51.T625   1986   301   85-8444

ISBN 0-03-002707-1

Copyright © 1983, 1986 by CBS College
  Publishing

Address correspondence to:
383 Madison Avenue
New York, NY 10017

6 7 8 9   32   9 8 7 6 5 4 3 2

CBS COLLEGE PUBLISHING
Holt, Rinehart and Winston
The Dryden Press
Saunders College Publishing

Some seek credit when none is due,
Others do not get the credit they deserve.
This book is dedicated to Linda H. Tischler,
My wife, friend, and writing partner.

H.L.T.

Preface

The first edition of *Introduction to Sociology*, published in 1983, met with wide acceptance. We were gratified by the enthusiastic response to the book received from professors representing a diversity of colleges and universities. Only three years have elapsed since the writing of the first edition, but research and theory in many areas of sociology have advanced so rapidly that the current edition incorporates findings from over one hundred post-1980 publications. We have included in this new edition many of your comments and suggestions.

In the second edition we demonstrate the vitality, interest, and utility associated with the study of sociology. Examining society, social institutions, and social processes is an exciting and absorbing undertaking. Our goal is not to make sociologists of our readers (although if that is an outcome we will be delighted) but rather to show how sociology applies to many areas of life and how it is used in day-to-day activities. In meeting this objective we focused on two basic ideas: first, sociology as a rigorous scientific discipline; and second, that a basic knowledge of sociology is essential for understanding social interactions in many different settings, whether they are oriented to a work or social environment. In order to understand society, we need to understand how society shapes people—and how people in turn shape society. We need to develop a new way of understanding the world we have been experiencing for so many years.

Major Changes in This Edition

We have received a good deal of feedback from professors and students on the first edition. Based on that information we have incorporated a number of major changes into this edition. They include the following:

1. While all chapters have been revised and updated, five chapters have been extensively rewritten. They are Chapters 9, "Deviance and Criminal Behavior"; 11, "Racial and Ethnic Minorities"; 13, "Marriage, Family, and Alternative Lifestyles"; 16, "The Economy"; and 19, "Population and Demography."

2. Chapter 5, "Social Interaction and Social Structure," has been reorganized for a more logical flow and to make it easier for students to learn the subject.

3. The four types of boxes in each chapter represent one of the truly unique aspects of this book. They give us a chance to introduce the most current material, are very interesting to the students, and show the importance of sociology in today's world. Fifty-five of the eighty boxes are new. We have replaced those for which more current material was available and those that had limited appeal.

4. "Rules, Sanctions, and Social Control" and "Persuasion and Protest" are two new black & white portfolios that have been added to replace previous portfolios.

5. Instead of bowing to popular usage we have renamed the sex roles chapter gender roles. The chapter deals with the social, psychological, and cultural attributes of masculinity and femininity. Therefore, the term "gender roles" is more appropriate than "sex roles," which refers to biological distinctiveness.

6. Finally, every aspect of this book has been thoroughly reviewed in order to ensure that we are presenting the most accurate and current material.

Organization

A primary concern of ours has been to provide a comprehensive text that is both highly readable and interesting. Part One introduces the sociological perspective and the methods of sociological research. Part Two examines the individual in society, focusing on the social and cultural forces that shape individual and social behavior. Part Three looks at social structure and social organization, exploring such topics as small groups and formal organizations, communities, society, and social control and deviant behavior. Part Four considers social inequality, examining social stratification, race and ethnic relations, and gender roles. Part Five moves to the major social institutions: the family, religion, education, the economy, and the political system. Part Six views social change that results from social movements and collective behavior, population shifts, and modernization.

The chapters together build from a micro- to a macro-level analysis of society, with each part introducing increasingly more comprehensive factors necessary for a broad-based understanding of social organization. Great care has been taken to structure the book in such a way as to permit flexibility in the presentation of the material. Each chapter is self-contained and, therefore, may be taught in any order.

A Comparative Approach

Sociology is a highly organized discipline shaped by several theoretical perspectives, or schools of thought. It is not merely the study of social problems or the random voicing of opinions. No single perspective is given greater emphasis; a balanced presentation of both functionalist theory and conflict theory is supplemented whenever possible by the symbolic interactionist viewpoint.

The book also has a strong cross-cultural orientation. Sociology is concerned with the interactions of people wherever and whenever they occur. It would be shortsighted, therefore, to concentrate on only our own society. Often, in fact, the best way to appreciate our own situation is through comparison with other societies. We use our cross-cultural focus as a basis for comparison and contrast with U.S. society.

In addition, the historical dimension has been introduced to provide background to the growth and development of the field of sociology. Although sociologists do not usually approach issues historically, sociological study suffers when its focus is too heavily on the present. Most current social situations have historical roots and, in turn, serve as the roots for future events.

Learning Aids

The primary objective of a textbook is to provide clear information in a format that promotes learning. *Introduction to Sociology* contains six specific elements designed to aid learning.

Photo Portfolios Six unique photographic essays—three in full color—enhance each major section of the text and highlight the theme of each part. The photo essays dramatize real-life cultures, themes, or events such as Mexican-American farm laborers as an American subculture; the vast variety of symbols associated with the U.S. flag; and the different faces of collective behavior.

Running Glossary Key terms are defined in the margins of the text, at the points where they occur. This format allows the student to concentrate on the contents of the chapter without having to locate a glossary item in a remote section of the book. All glossary items appear in the index and for easy identification are boldfaced on the pages where they appear.

Chapter Outline Each chapter opens with an outline of the subject headings in the chapter, making it possible for the instructor to organize the material in an orderly manner. This format also serves as an important aid to facilitate student review.

Illustrations All graphs, drawings, and photographs were carefully chosen to amplify and enhance the subject matter of every chapter.

Chapter Summary Student review is reinforced by the end-of-chapter summaries of most significant topics and ideas covered in the text.

For Further Reading An incentive for further study and a source for research assignments are the annotated references at the end of each chapter.

Features

The book presents the following features that provide current information and sidelights on the text presentation. Every chapter includes the following special elements:

Using Sociology Sociological research is applied to understanding social issues, such as "Why Do People Join Cults?" "Group Interaction in the Airplane Cockpit," and "Gentrification and Homelessness."

Popular Sociology Sociological issues are viewed as seen in the popular media. Among the issues examined are "What Happened to the Student Radicals?" "Can a Man Change His Race?" and "Women in Male-Dominated Professions: The Unfinished Revolution."

Case Study Issues or events that relate to the subject matter of each chapter are explored in depth. Controversial topics that have been reported on or debated in the sociological literature are covered, such as "Is It Ethical to Lie to Your Research Subjects?" "Women in Prison," and "China's Last Word on Children: One."

Focus on Research Current research studies are summarized. Among those presented are "Protecting Yourself During a Violent Crime," "Punks, Hippies, and Middle-Class Values: A Comparison," and "The Mystery of Child Prodigies."

Supplementary Materials

A broad array of supplementary materials to accompany the text is designed to make teaching and learning more effective. *Introduction to Sociology* is accompanied by a complete, convenient, and carefully conceived package: an Instructor's Manual, Student Study Guide, Test Bank, Computerized Test Bank, and CLEAR.

The Instructor's Manual parallels the contents of the text. For each chapter it offers teaching objectives, a list of key terms, and lecture notes.

The Study Guide, like the Instructor's Manual, is organized into chapters that cor-

respond to the text. Each chapter includes a synopsis, learning objectives, key terms, matching exercises, multiple choice questions, true or false questions, and completion questions. Answers to the questions appear at the end of each chapter.

The Test Bank contains 2,000 multiple choice items (100 per chapter). Each item is preceded by a block of codes that gives the correct answer, text page reference, and indication whether the item tests knowledge or applications.

A Computerized Test Bank on floppy disk is also available. Users can construct tests of up to 200 items selected from the printed Test Bank.

Finally, an expanded version of the well-known, innovative CLEAR (Computerized Learning and Review in Sociology) program by George H. Conklin of North Carolina Central University is available to qualified adopters of this text. CLEAR is a series of interactive lessons for microcomputers designed to help students apply and analyze recent data related to major issues in sociology. Each year CLEAR has been improved. This year it is better than ever, with new lessons, simulations, and easier on-screen instructions. The User's Guide that accompanies CLEAR includes many assignment suggestions and enables professors with no computer experience to use the program effectively.

Acknowledgments

Anyone who has written an introductory textbook realizes that at various points a project of such magnitude becomes a team effort, with many people devoting enormous amounts of time to ensure that the final product is as good as it can possibly be.

The manuscript was reviewed and commented on by professors from a wide variety of institutions. We would like to thank the following for their thoughtful reading of the chapters:

Roger Basham, College of the Canyons; Brent Bruton, Iowa State University; Walter Clark, St. Louis Community College, Florissant Valley; Mary Beth Collins, Central Piedmont Community College; David Flanagan, Central Piedmont Community College; Mike Fuller, St. Louis Community College, Florissant Valley; Theodore Groat, Bowling Green University; Roger Little, University of Illinois; Greg Matoesian, William Woods College; Earl Mead, Los Angeles Pierce College; David O' Brian, University of Akron; Chuck Osborne, University of South Carolina; Fred Pampel, University of Iowa; Barry Pearlman, Community College of Philadelphia; Philip Reichel, University of Northern Colorado; John V. Salmon, Triton College; Jackie Scherer, Oakland University; Doug Schocke, Northern Virginia Community College, Annandale; Carol Sloane, John C. Calhoun Community College; Vme Edom Smith, Northern Virginia Community College, Manassas; and Richard Sweeney, Modesto Junior College.

Many people at Holt, Rinehart and Winston provided valuable assistance to this project. Earl McPeek ushered this project through many difficult stages and managed to keep it on schedule despite a variety of obstacles. It was a privilege to have his support and assistance. We would also like to thank Bob Woodbury for his involvement and concern with this book.

We are also grateful to Lucy Rosendahl, Françoise Bartlett, Cheryl Mannes, Annette Mayeski, Louis Scardino, Lucy MacMillan Stitzer, and John Yarley for their efforts in making this book possible.

H. L. T.
P. W.
D. E. K. H.

Contents in Brief

Contents

Preface   vii

Contents

Introduction
to Sociology

The Study
of Society

■ ■ ■ ■ ■ ■ ■ ■

Part One

1 The Sociological Perspective

Each of us has a way of looking at the world, a perspective that we use to understand the world around us. In trying to answer questions about our own identity and about the actions and reactions of others, we usually rely on information gathered from our experiences, our backgrounds, or the types of people with whom we identify. Although we accept the premise that individuals are unique, we tend to categorize or even stereotype people in order to interpret and predict behavior and events.

☐ Sociology as a Point of View

Is this individual perspective adequate for bringing about an understanding of ourselves and society? Even though our individual perspectives may serve us quite well in our day-to-day lives, sociologists would answer that they are not enough for understanding the broader picture. In order to do that, we must know something of the society in which we live, of the social processes that affect us, and of the typical patterns of interaction in which we engage. **Sociology** is the scientific study of human society and social interactions. The main focus of sociology is the group, not the individual. Sociologists attempt to understand the forces that operate throughout society—forces that mold individuals, shape their behavior, and thus determine social events.

For example, if you were asked to go to a major-league baseball game and to prepare a report on your observations of the spectators at that game, your notes might contain comments about the woman next to you who carefully recorded each play on a scorecard, the man behind you who seemed more interested in the offerings of the food vendors than in the game, and the young boy several rows away who wore an oversized mitt in the hope of catching a foul ball. Sociologists, on the other hand, would more likely be interested in the age, socioeconomic level, and ethnic background of the crowd and the ball players as well. They might want to compare the background and behavior of spectators at a baseball game with the characteristics of spectators at a tennis match and ask such questions as: Are there differences? If so, what kinds and why?

While studying sociology you will be asked to look at the world a little differently than you usually do. Because you will be looking at the world through other people's eyes—using new perspectives—you will start to notice things you may never have noticed before. When you look at life in a middle-class suburb, for instance, what do you see? How does your view differ from that of a poor slum resident? How does the suburb appear to a recent immigrant from the Soviet Union or Cuba or Haiti? How does it appear to a burglar? Finally, what does the sociologist see?

Sociology asks you to broaden your perspective on the world. You will start to see that the reason people act in markedly different ways is not because one person is "sane" and another is "crazy." Rather it is because they all have different perceptions of what is going on in the world. These different perceptions of reality produce many different lifestyles, and different lifestyles in turn produce different perceptions of reality. In order to understand other people, we must begin to look at the world from a perspective that is broader than one based only on our own individual experiences.

The Sociological Imagination

C. Wright Mills (1959) described the sociological imagination as the realization that there are different levels on which social events can be perceived and interpreted. People often interpret social events on the basis of their individual experiences, whereas sociologists look for *relationships* among these individual experiences in order to understand the broader forces in society. For example, some individuals are unable to hold jobs because they suffer from intellectual, emotional, or physical handicaps. If only these people were jobless in our society, our unemployment would be solely a matter of individual troubles—personal traits that cause affected individuals serious financial problems. But this is not the case. In recent years some 7 to 8 percent of all able-bodied workers in the United States have been unable to find jobs. In the inner cities this figure rises to over 30 percent, and among black and Hispanic teenagers it is well over 50 percent during the summer months (Dumanoski, 1981). Clearly there are forces at work that produce these conditions—forces that have little to do with the personal traits of the individuals affected by them. In addition, unemployment and the people who are unemployed have an affect on many social structures, including their families, the economy, business, and even crime rates. The sociological imagination would view unemployment as a social issue created by and, in turn, affecting social, cultural, economic, and political forces—in addition to any other factors affecting the situation.

Alcoholism is another personal problem to which several social perspectives can be applied. Almost six million Americans are chronic alcoholics—that is, addicted to drinking alcohol consistently and in such amounts that it interferes with their job performance, their interpersonal relations, and their psychological and physical functioning. Although each alcoholic personally makes the decision to take each drink—and each suffers the pain of addiction—to think of alcoholism as being merely each alcoholic's personal problem is to misunderstand the issue. Sociologists want to know about the social bases of alcoholism. They want to know who drinks excessively, when they drink, where they drink, and under what conditions they drink. Sociologists also want to know the social costs of chronic drinking—costs in terms of families torn apart, jobs lost, children severely abused and neglected; in terms of highway accidents and deaths; in terms of drunken quarrels leading to violence and to murder. Noting the startling increase in heavy alcohol use by adolescents over the last 10 years and the rapid rise of chronic alcoholism among women, sociologists ask: At this moment in history, what forces are at work to account for these patterns?

The sociological imagination focuses on every aspect of society and every relationship among individuals. It studies the behavior of crowds at ball games and racetracks; shifts in styles of dress and popular music; changing patterns of courtship and marriage; the emergence and fading of different lifestyles, political movements, and religious sects; the distribution of income and access to resources and services; decisions made by the Supreme Court, by congressional committees, and by local zoning boards; and so on. Every detail of social existence is food for sociological thought and relevant to sociological analysis.

The broad spectrum of areas into which sociology delves is reflected in the number of articles related to sociological subjects that appear in the mass media—newspapers, magazines, books, and television and radio programs. From predictions and analyses of voting behavior of various groups such as blacks, women, and union members, to reports on school busing and why it works in some places and not in others, to surveys of people's attitudes and opinions on different issues—the popular media are full of stories based on sociology (see Popular Sociology: "What's Happening to American Families?").

It is necessary to exercise caution when interpreting media polls and reports on studies because many of them do not use acceptable sociological methodology (see Chapter 2). Reports in the media may be used as a source for finding out what basic information has been learned from research, as a springboard for thinking about what further studies are needed, and for searching for patterns among events. Media reports should not be viewed as sociological gospel.

In addition, the potential for sociology to be put to use—applied to the solution of "real-world" problems—is very great. Proponents of the idea of applied sociology believe the work of sociologists can and should be used to help bring about an understanding of, and perhaps even guidelines for changing, the complexities of modern society. The demand for applied sociology is growing, and many sociologists work directly with government agencies or private businesses in an effort to apply sociological knowledge to real-world problems. For example, they might investigate such questions as how the building of a dam on a particular site will affect the residents of the area, how busing to integrate schools affects the children involved, why voters select one candidate over another, how a company can boost employees' morale, and how relationships among administrators, doctors, nurses, and patients affect hospital care.

sociology The scientific study of human society and social interactions.

POPULAR SOCIOLOGY
What's Happening to American Families?

One feature used by many mass circulation magazines to attract readers is questionnaires and surveys. These may range from self-tests, which enable readers to rate their attitudes toward social issues, need for status or achievement, values in life, and so on, to surveys on topics of current interest that are sent in to the publication for analysis. You have probably seen these questionnaires in many national magazines. Most of them concern topics that are sociological in nature. The following is one of the more extensive examples of this type of popular sociology.

An example of a magazine questionnaire that received a wide distribution is one that appeared in the fall of 1982 in *Better Homes and Gardens* on the subject of the American family—one of the institutions studied extensively by sociologists. Readers were asked to send the completed questionnaire back to the publisher. The results were tabulated, and an analysis appeared in two 1983 issues. The questionnaire generated a high level of interest, as evidenced by the 201,320 replies and the more than 10,000 people who wrote letters, which were included with the replies.

The questionnaire had two separate parts, divided by topics. The first part, containing 62 questions, was designed to assess what readers thought was happening to family life in America. The second part, containing 64 questions, was designed to measure and assess the current state of the family. The following is a sample of the types of questions asked in the survey and the answers:

Do you feel that the American family is in trouble?

Yes   80%
No   20%

In your marriage, which of the following reasons for staying married are the strongest?

(Check no more than three.)

Love	75%
Companionship	52%
Children's welfare and security	28%
Emotional security	18%
Religion	14%
The comforts of home	13%

Others in descending order: Financial security, sex, have learned to tolerate the marriage, fear of living alone.

If you had it to do over, would you choose to marry your present spouse?

Yes	81%
No	13%
No, would not marry at all	6%

There are more women with families in the working world than ever before. Do you think this has had a detrimental effect on family life?

Yes   69%
No   30%

A brief statistical profile of the people who responded to the poll showed that 72 percent had attended or graduated from college; 89 percent were married; 43 percent had children 12 and under; and 26 percent had children 13 to 18 years old. The median family income was $33,462, and 85 percent of the people were home owners. All of these figures were significantly higher than the national average. In that light, the important point the readers often overlooked was that the answers were coming from a group that was not representative of the American population as a whole. The views expressed were strictly those of *Better Homes and Gardens* readers who were willing to fill out a questionnaire and mail it in.

The typical respondent was a married, well-educated, middle-class female parent—someone with a strong personal interest in the well-being of the American family. As a whole, the respondents perceived their own families as reassuringly sound—loving, stable, and basically happy. The recurring self-image that evolved from the responses was one of a traditional, closely knit family with a strong belief in God, firm discipline, and the importance of work, education, and thrift.

This confident image of the respondents' own families contrasted sharply with their perceptions of other families. An astonishing 80 percent of the respondents stated that family life in America was in trouble. The greatest threats were given as absence of religious/spiritual foundation (33 percent), inattentive parents (26 percent), divorce (22 percent), and moral decay (20 percent).

A section of the questionnaire dealt with the issue of children. When the respondents were asked if they had it to do over, how big their family would be, 78 percent would have had the same number or more children; 10 percent would have had them later; 8 percent would have had fewer; and 6 percent would have chosen not to have children. Some of the other questions and responses were as follows:

Overall, how satisfied are you with the way your children are "turning out"?

Very satisfied	48%
Mostly satisfied	44%
Not satisfied	5%

Do you think your teenager(s) share your basic beliefs and values about marriage, family, sex, religion, and the like?

Yes	79%
No	14%

As a whole, American families appear to be holding on to those values they believe to be the most important to their way of life—belief in God; stable marriages; and loving, respectful, self-contained families. At the same time, they are altering their views on values they believe are no longer appropriate or necessary—the role of women, family size, premarital sex (among people who are in love and intend to marry).

Individual families see themselves as bastions of traditional values against outside forces—such as television and the movies with their overemphasis on sex and violence—and other, less strong families—those without a religious or spiritual foundation—and

inattentive parents as threats to the American family.

Source: "What's Happening to American Families?" *Better Homes and Gardens* (September, 1982), pp. 29–32; (October, 1982), pp. 29–32; (July, 1983), pp. 24–36; (August, 1983), pp. 15–33. □

The answers to these questions have practical applications. The growing demand for sociological information provides many new career areas for sociologists (see Using Sociology: "Careers in Sociology").

Indeed, the sociological imagination looks at all types of human behavior patterns, discerning unseen connections among events, noting similarities in the actions of individuals with no direct knowledge of one another, and finding subtle forces that mold people's actions. Like a museum-goer who draws back from a painting in order to see how the separate strokes and colors form subtly shaded images, sociologists stand back in their imagination from individual events in order to see why and how they occurred. In so doing, they discern patterns that govern our social existence.

Sociology and Science

Sociology is commonly described as one of the social sciences. **Science** refers to a body of systematically arranged knowledge that shows the operation of general laws. It also refers to the logical, systematic methods by which that knowledge is obtained. Because we live and interact with other people every day, we all are interested in our relationships with other people. We also listen to or read reports about what is going on in the world. From all of this we form common-sense ideas about the world around us, but this does not make us sociologists. Unfortunately, our ideas do not always provide a reliable picture of social reality. Common-sense ideas result from personal observations, opinions, hearsay, and media reports—all of which can be misleading. Common sense, in fact, can create a barrier to understanding human social life because we tend to believe what we want to

believe, to see what we want to see, and to accept as fact whatever appears to be logical, without further investigation. A true understanding of how social life operates must be based on facts and not on common sense. Sociologists strive to gather and analyze facts in an objective fashion, which is why sociology is a science (see Case Study: "Sociology: Science versus Common Sense").

In addition to the issue of common sense, sociologists encounter a number of other problems if their research either contradicts or supports what others believe to be the case. For example, Table 1.1 presents us with a number of possibilities, each producing a problem for the sociologist. In the first box, we note that if a sociologist studies an issue that has a set of assumptions that are widely accepted and then proves that it is actually true, he or she will be accused of engaging in futile research exploring the obvious. In the second box, we note that if, instead, the research proves that a widely rejected assumption is true, the sociologist will then be accused of being a charlatan and presenting false information. In the third box, we see that if a sociologist investigates a view that is widely believed to be true and then shows that it is actually untrue, he or she will be accused of being a heretic who refuses to accept what everyone knows is true. In the fourth box, we see that if a sociologist proves that a widely rejected view is really untrue, he or she will once again be accused of being a fool wasting effort on obvious untruths.

---

science A body of systematically arranged knowledge that shows the operation of general laws. The term also refers to the logical, systematic methods by which that knowledge is obtained.

USING SOCIOLOGY
Careers in Sociology

As in many other fields, the job market for a recent graduate with a degree in sociology is limited. Sociology majors must plan their academic careers carefully and be prepared to use an imaginative, resourceful, and aggressive approach to obtain a job to which they can apply the specialized knowledge acquired in school. An overview of possible careers in sociology will help clarify those areas that offer the best opportunities.

Teaching remains the primary field in which the overwhelming majority of sociologists seek and find employment. Because of the keen competition for job openings, a Ph.D. degree is almost essential for anyone applying for a teaching position in sociology beyond the high-school level. With the number of college-age students declining, teaching positions currently are scarce, despite the popularity of sociology courses. The college-age population is expected to rise in the late 1980s, but longer-range projections cannot yet be made.

After teaching, nonacademic research jobs employ the greatest number of sociologists. These positions are found in public agencies—federal, state, and local; in private research institutes supported by government, corporate, and foundation grants; and in the research departments of private corporations. An area that has seen a significant upsurge of activity in recent years is evaluation research—the assessment of the impact of a particular policy or program on the area of concern. Laws requiring environmental impact studies of all large-scale federal projects and installations have contributed greatly to the need for evaluation specialists.

Careers in applied sociology also exist at policymaking and administrative levels, particularly in the health services and law enforcement fields. For example, a sociologist working for a community health center can provide essential data on the population groups being served and on the sociological aspects of the distribution of health needs within the community. A sociologist working in a prison system can devise methods for alleviating the social problems that result from confinement and overcrowding.

A solid foundation in a particular field of sociological study—such as the family, the urban community, education, organizational behavior, industrial or occupational sociology—may be helpful in obtaining a specialized position. In addition, certain expanding fields draw many of their practitioners from sociology graduates, including demographers, who compile and analyze population data; methodologists, who design and assess research procedures; and human ecologists, who investigate the structure and organization of a community in relation to its environment.

The sociology major can also consider diverse career possibilities in which, although the title is not defined as "sociologist," a background in sociology may be relevant to obtaining the position and performing the tasks involved in the job. Examples of such career possibilities are

Affirmative action coordinator
Community planner
Correctional officer
Counselor (alcoholism, drug abuse, career, handicapped, etc.)
Environmental analyst
Equal opportunity specialist
Grants officer
Labor relations specialist
Marketing researcher
Personnel manager
Probation officer
Public information specialist

Many sociologists engage in social research. These researchers are revising a questionnaire.

Rehabilitation counselor
Resident director
Social service worker

Many of these positions require a minor or some course work in another field such as political science, psychology, ecology, law, or business. They offer opportunities for a student to combine two or more interests.

Many types of businesses outside the academic world and government agencies may offer career opportunities for sociologists. Some possibilities are

Advertising (writers/researchers)
Banking (researchers for determining community financial needs and viability)
Foundations (grants analysts)
Insurance companies (demographers)
Publishing (writers and editors)

As the American Sociological Association observed in its pamphlet *Careers in Sociology,* few fields have as broad a scope and relevance as does sociology. Yet its career potential is just beginning to be tapped. Sociology majors must choose their courses intelligently, both within and outside their field, in order to build a solid academic foundation. They should keep informed about career trends, including the development of new types of careers in sociology, by reading relevant articles in the sociological journals and in *Occupational Outlook Quarterly,* published by the U.S. Bureau of Labor Statistics. Finally, when the time comes to seek a job, they must be prepared to search carefully and intensively for a position that will be the first step in building a successful, satisfying career. ☐

TABLE 1.1 *The Sociological Dilemma*

		If a Sociologist Investigates an Issue That Is	
		Widely Accepted	*Widely Rejected*
If the Results Prove That the Assumptions Were	Actually True	*1* The sociologist is engaged in futile research exploring the obvious.	*2* The sociologist is a charlatan presenting false information.
	Actually Untrue	*3* The sociologist is someone who has an axe to grind and refuses to accept what everyone knows is true.	*4* The sociologist is an idiot who explores things that are obviously untrue.

Source: Robert K. Merton, "Notes on Problem-Finding in Sociology." In Robert K. Merton, Leonard Broom, and Leonard S. Cottrell, Jr., *Sociology Today: Problems and Prospects* (New York: Basic Books, 1959), pp. xv–xvi, n. 5. Also Michael S. Bassis, Richard J. Gelles, and Ann Levine, *Sociology,* 2d ed. (New York: Random House, 1984), p. 13.

Science is only one of the ways in which human beings study the world around them. Unlike other means of inquiry that depend on a logical discussion of abstract concepts such as religion or philosophy, science for the most part limits its investigations to things that can be observed directly or that produce directly observable events. Things that can be observed in this way are termed empirical entities; therefore, one of the basic features of science is **empiricism.** For example, theologians might discuss the role of faith in producing "true happiness"; philosophers might deliberate over what happiness actually encompasses; but sociologists would note, analyze, and predict the consequences of such measurable items as job satisfaction, the relationship between income and stated contentment, and the role of social class in the incidence of depression.

Sociology as a Social Science

The **social sciences** consist of all those disciplines that apply scientific methods to the study of human behavior. Although there is some overlap, each of the social sciences has its own areas of investigation. It is helpful to understand each of the social sciences and to examine sociology's relationship to them.

Cultural Anthropology Cultural anthropology is the social science most closely related to sociology. The two have many theories and concepts in common, and they often overlap each other. The main difference is in the groups they study and the research methods they use. Sociologists tend to study groups and institutions within large, modern, industrial societies, using research methods that enable them rather quickly to gather specific information about large numbers of people. In contrast, cultural anthropologists often immerse themselves in another society for a long

empiricism An approach to knowledge that relies on evidence from things that can be observed directly or that produce directly observable events. One of the fundamental features of science is empiricism, or the *empirical method.*

social sciences All those disciplines that apply scientific methods to the study of human behavior. The social sciences include sociology, cultural anthropology, psychology, economics, history, and political science.

CASE STUDY
Sociology: Science versus Common Sense

Because people are involved with society and culture all their lives, they often believe they know a great deal about social relationships. It's simply common sense, they say. However, the common-sense approach to social knowledge often leads to distortions, misinterpretations, and falsehoods. Having "experience with" something does not necessarily produce scientific knowledge about this something, even though "experience with" something may have built up a store of common-sense ideas.

Although Mr. Jones may have had considerable experience with upper-class people, it does not necessarily follow that he has scientific knowledge about them. On another level the fact that Mrs. Jones has had experience with electric refrigerators does not make her an electrical engineer. She may in fact have had years of experience with refrigerators without ever really understanding much about refrigeration. Nor is Mrs. Jones necessarily an authority on mechanics just because she has had long experience with cars. The fact that an individual has had considerable experience with a minority group—say, Native Americans—does not mean that person's understanding of them is scientific. Evidence indicates that individuals with much experience with certain groups of people may believe many things about their behavior that are contrary to scientific findings. It is likewise true that having had extensive experience with yourself does not mean that you have scientific knowledge of yourself.

Common sense often contains many beliefs that are false according to scientific information. At one time it was widely believed that the world was flat; this, however, did not make the world flat. That people have believed something for years and acted accordingly does not make the belief scientifically true. The fact that at one time people believed the average female—because of her "innate inferiority"—could not do college work as well as the average male did not prove the biological inferiority of the female.

Sociology is not the same as common sense. Sociology falls into the category of a science. Its goal is to gain an understanding of human interaction—of why human beings relate one to another the way they do—through use of the scientific method. Sociologists provide scientific checks for common sense.

While common sense is often vague, oversimplified, and frequently contradictory, sociology as a science attempts to be specific, to qualify its statements, and to prove its assertions. Upon closer inspection, we find that the proverbial words of wisdom rooted in common sense are often illogical. Why, for example, should you "look before you leap" if "he who hesitates is lost"? How can "absence make the heart grow fonder" when "out of sight, out of mind"? Why should "opposites attract" when "birds of a feather flock together"? Sociologists as scientists would attempt to qualify these statements by specifying, for example, under what conditions "opposites tend to attract" or "birds of a feather flock together."

The distinction between common sense and sociological sense becomes clearer when we look at how sociologists would reinterpret some of our best-known maxims. We may remember being told as children at bedtime some version of the "early to bed, early to rise makes a man healthy, wealthy, and wise" maxim and accepting it at face value. The sociologist may agree with such advice but still ask, "How is this premise supported?" or "What proof is there on this issue?" Common sense tells us that the promise of health, wealth, and wisdom is worth going to bed early for. After scientific investigation, however, the sociologist might conclude that "early to bed and early to rise probably indicates unskilled unemployment." In this same revised sense, "If Detroit had meant people to walk, it would have manufactured shoes," or "Waste not and there will be no work."

Studying human interactions scientifically is a unique experience. To have had many nonscientific experiences with people does not qualify a person as a scientific student of human interactions. While common sense gleaned from personal experience may help us in certain types of interactions, it will not help us understand why and under what conditions these interactions are taking place. Sociology as a science is oriented toward gaining knowledge about why and under what conditions they do take place, thus to understand human interactions better.

Source: Glenn M. Vernon, *Human Interaction: An Introduction to Sociology* (New York: Ronald Press, 1965), pp. 204–206. □

period of time, trying to learn as much as possible about that society and the relationships among its people. Thus, anthropologists tend to focus on the culture of small, preindustrial societies.

Psychology Psychology is the study of brain functioning, mental processes, and individual behavior. It is concerned with such issues as motivation, perception, cognition creativity, mental disorders, and personality. More than any other social science, psychology uses laboratory experiments. Psychology and sociology overlap in a subdivision of each field known as *social psychology*—the study of how human behavior is influenced and shaped by various social situations. Social psychologists study such issues as how individuals in a group solve problems and reach a consensus or what factors might produce nonconformity in a group situation. For the most part, however, psychology studies the individual, and sociology studies groups of individuals, as well as society's institutions.

Economics   Economics studies the creation, distribution, and consumption of goods and services. Economists have developed techniques for measuring such things as prices, supply and demand, money supplies, rates of inflation, and employment. The economy, however, is just one part of society. It is each individual in society who decides whether to buy an American car or a Japanese import, whether she or he is able to handle the mortgage payment on a dream house, and so on. Whereas economists study price and availability factors, sociologists are interested in the social factors that influence the resulting economic behavior. Is it peer pressure that results in the buying of the large flashy car, or is it concern about gas mileage that leads to the purchase of a small, fuel-efficient import? What social and cultural factors contribute to the differences in the portion of income saved by the average wage earner in different societies? What are the implications of the richest 1 percent of the American population owning 24 percent of all assets in the nation? These are examples of the questions sociologists seek to answer.

History   History looks at the past in an attempt to learn what happened, when it happened, and why it happened. Sociology also looks at historical events within their social contexts to discover why things happened and, more importantly, to assess what their social significance was and is. Historians provide a narrative of the sequence of events during a certain period and may use sociological research methods to try to learn how social forces have shaped historical events. Sociologists, on the other hand, examine historical events to see how they influenced later social situations. Historians focus on individual events—the American Revolution or slavery—and sociologists generally focus on phenomena such as revolutions or the patterns of dominance and subordination that exist in slavery. They try to understand the common conditions that contribute to revolution or slavery wherever they occur. Let us consider the subject of slavery in the United States. Traditionally, historians might focus on when the first slaves arrived or how many slaves there were in 1700 or 1850 and the conditions under which they lived. Sociologists and modern social historians would use these data to ask many questions: What were the social and economic forces that shaped the institution of slavery in the United States? How did the Industrial Revolution affect slavery? How has the experience of slavery affected the black family? and so on. Although history and sociology have been moving toward each other over the last 20 years, each discipline still retains a somewhat different focus: sociology on the present, history on the past.

Political Science   Political science concentrates on three major areas: political theory, the actual operation of government, and, in recent years, political behavior. In its emphasis on political behavior, political science overlaps with sociology. One of the few distinctions that can be made is that whereas sociologists are primarily interested in how the political system affects other institutions in society, political scientists may devote more attention to the forces that shape political systems and theories for understanding these forces. However, both disciplines are trying to learn more about why people vote the way they do, why they join political movements, how the mass media are changing political parties and processes, and so on.

Social Work   Much of the theory and research methods of social work are drawn from sociology and psychology, but social work focuses to a much greater degree on application and problem solving. The disciplines of sociology and social work are often confused with each other. The main goal of social work

1.1
Auguste Comte 1798–1857

Born in the French city of Montpellier on January 19, 1798, Auguste Comte grew up in the period of great political turmoil that followed the French Revolution of 1789–1799.

Early in his school years Comte began to hate the Emperor Napoleon and dreamed of a revival of the revolutionary spirit of liberty. Comte was an excellent student—and a troublemaker. His mathematics teacher was the only member of the faculty who made a strong impression on him and influenced him to take the exams for the *École Polytechnique*. Placing fourth among those who took the exam, Comte moved to Paris and entered the school in 1814.

Soon after Comte entered the school, Napoleon was defeated and exiled from France, and the Bourbon king Louis XVIII took the throne. By this time Comte was beginning to feel that he belonged at the school and strove not only to graduate with high honors but also to be retained as a teacher after he completed his studies. As the leader of his class in scholarship, Comte also led in unruly behavior. This time, however, his hatred was directed against the reestablished monarchy, compared with which, it seemed to him, even Napoleon's rule was better. When Napoleon returned in 1815, the school greeted him enthusiastically, and Comte was one of his leading supporters.

Despite Napoleon's defeat at Waterloo 100 days later and the re-restoration of the monarchy under Louis XVIII, calm prevailed at the school, and Comte returned to his studies and his insubordinate ways. Then, in April, 1816, when six students protested against the school's examination methods and faced punishment, the entire student body rallied around them, and the governor closed the school for reorganization. Because only those students who had behaved were eligible for readmission, Comte was out.

In August, 1817, Comte met Henri Saint-Simon and became his secretary and eventually his close collaborator. Saint-Simon, who was to have a major and lasting influence on Comte's life, was attracted to the young man's brilliant and methodical mind. Under Saint-Simon's influence Comte converted from an ardent advocate of liberty and equality to a supporter of an elitist conception of society. During their association the two men collaborated on a number of essays, most of which contained the seeds of Comte's major ideas. Their alliance came to a bitter end in 1824, when Comte broke with Saint-Simon for both financial and intellectual reasons.

Then, hoping to establish some security in his personal life, he married Caroline Mannis, whom he had known for several years, and devoted himself to explaining his positive philosophy—the application of the methods used by the natural sciences toward the creation of a science to study and codify the history and workings of society.

He began giving lectures in his home in April, 1826, and they were attended by a number of illustrious men, but he suffered a serious mental collapse after giving only three. He was treated in a hospital for a while and released but fell into a state of deep depression and even tried to commit suicide. His slow recovery did not permit him to resume his lectures until 1829. Soon members of almost every branch of the scientific community began to ridicule him for his attempts to codify all of the sciences into one grandiose system.

Financial problems, lack of academic recognition, and marital difficulties combined to force Comte further into a shell, and he reached the point that for reasons of "cerebral hygiene" he decided that he would no longer read any scientific work related to the fields about which he was writing. Living in isolation at the periphery of the academic world, Comte concentrated his efforts between 1830 and 1842 on writing his major work, *Cours de Philosophie Positive,* in which he coined the term *sociology.*

As a result of the publication of the *Cours,* Comte began to acquire a few admirers, including John Stuart Mill, who went so far as to arrange for a number of his British followers to send Comte money. On the negative side, his wife left him for good soon after the *Cours* was published. Alone and still fighting for recognition and an academic appointment. Comte experienced a drastic change in his life in 1844, when he met and fell in love with Clothilde de Vaux. Although she died of tuberculosis soon after they met, Comte vowed to devote the rest of his time on earth to her memory. He thus began writing *Le Système de Politique Positive,* which proclaimed the importance of emotion over intellect and of feelings over ideas and established the Religion of Humanity based on universal love. Published between 1851 and 1854, the *Système* lost Comte his few remaining followers—including Mill, who could not support the idea that love was the answer to all the problems of the time.

Undisturbed by this loss, Comte concentrated on building his new religion, of which he named himself High Priest. He began preaching the virtues of submission and the necessity for order and spent the rest of his life trying to gain converts. In his frenzy he even sought to court the powerful in the world including the Czar Nicholas, the grand vizier of the Ottoman Empire, and the head of the Jesuits.

A few days after the February Revolution of 1848, Comte founded his Société Positiviste, which became the center for his teaching and finally attracted a group of devoted disciples who came together not only because of his intellect but also to love and be loved in return. He died on Septembert 5, 1857. □

---

is to help people directly with their problems, and the aim of sociology is to understand why the problems exist. Social workers provide help for individuals and families who have emotional and psychological problems or who experience difficulties that stem from poverty or other ongoing problems that are rooted in the structure of society. They also organize community groups to tackle local issues such as housing problems and try to influence policymaking bodies and legislation. Sociologists provide many of the theories and ideas that can be used to help others. Although sociology is not social work, it is a useful area of academic concentration for those interested in entering the helping professions.

Goals, Theories, and Methods: Science and Sociology

Science has two major goals: (1) to describe particular things or events and (2) to propose and test general principles that explain those things or events. Most scientists would add that scientific study should lead to accurate predictions of future events. As a science, sociology shares these goals: Like all sciences, however, sociology is rooted in certain theoretical orientations and uses specific methods for developing and testing its ideas. These theories and methods were formulated in response to the historical climate in which sociology emerged as a distinct discipline. Therefore, in order to understand the sociological perspective, we should know something of its history.

□ The Development of Sociology

It is hardly an accident that sociology emerged as a separate field of study in Europe during the nineteenth century. That was a time of turmoil, a period in which the existing social order was being shaken by the growing Industrial Revolution and by violent uprisings against established rulers (the American and French revolutions). People were also affected by the impact of discovering how others lived as a result of world exploration and colonization and by the declining power of the church and religion to impose its views of right and wrong on whole nations. A new social class of industrialists and business people was emerging to challenge the rule of the feudal aristocracies. Many peasants became industrial workers. Tightly knit communities, held together by centuries of tradition and well-defined social relationships, were strained by dramatic changes in the social environment. Factory cities began to replace the rural estates of nobles as a center for society at large. People with different backgrounds were brought together under the same factory roof to work for wages instead of exchanging their services for land and protection. Families now had to protect themselves, to buy food rather than grow it, and to pay rent for their homes. These new living and working conditions led to the development of an industrial, urban lifestyle, which, in turn, produced new social problems.

Karl Marx 1818–1883

Karl Marx was born of Jewish parents on May 5, 1818, in Trier, Germany. The year before Karl's birth his father, Heinrich, a lawyer, descended from a line of rabbis, converted to the Lutheran faith. As a Jew, Heinrich had been threatened with the loss of his legal practice. He had no contacts with the synagogue and regarded conversion as an expedient act with little moral significance; so the young Marx never felt any tensions as a result of the family's minority status. He did, however, recognize and feel repelled by his father's subservience to government authority and fear of people in positions of power. Nonetheless, this did not have any detrimental effect on the development of strong intellectual bonds between father and son.

In 1838 Marx entered the University of Berlin to study law. There he became involved with a group of marginal academics who were radical, antireligious, and bohemian. As a result of their influence Marx abandoned law for philosophy and aspired to become a philosophy professor. His hopes were soon dashed when his friend from the group, Bruno Bauer, who had promised him a position at the University of Bonn, was dismissed from that faculty because of his antireligious, liberal views.

Faced with an uncertain future, Marx accepted a position in Cologne as a writer and then editor-in-chief for a liberal-radical paper. The articles he wrote about the plight of the peasants and the poor in the Moselle wine region attracted a great deal of attention, and within a year and a half the paper was suppressed.

Out of work and with no prospects once again, Marx married Jenny von Westphalen, to the dismay of her family, who viewed him as a social inferior. Unable to find employment in Germany because of his reputation as a radical, Marx took his wife to Paris in 1843.

He immediately took up the study of the reformist and socialist theorists and the British economists of the time, all of whose writings had been unavailable in Germany. Most importantly he met Friedrich Engels, with whom he formed a lifelong friendship and partnership. Engels had become a socialist after witnessing the terrible conditions of the working class. Converted by Engels to socialism, Marx began writing for socialist papers.

Expelled from Paris in 1845 because of these writings, Marx moved to Brussels, Belgium, where he became a leader in the international revolutionary movement. He was asked to write an official declaration of the beliefs of the German Workers' Educational Association, a socialist group, and, using material prepared by Engels, drafted *The Communist Manifesto,* an analysis of the history of society as the history of class struggle and a call for revolutionary action.

When the 1848 revolution broke out in Germany, Marx returned to his homeland, where he assumed the editorship of another radical newspaper. The revolution failed, however, and once again Marx was forced into exile, finally settling with his family in London, where he was to remain more or less permanently for the rest of his life.

Believing that a worker's revolution was imminent, Marx spent the first few years in London writing his most brilliant pamphlets and waiting for the fight to begin. As the years passed, he began to realize a revolution would not take place as soon as he had expected. He lived in complete poverty, often pursued by debt collectors, without a place to live, and beset with family illness and even death (three of his children died of malnutrition). If it had not been for Engels' financial help, the entire family probably would have perished.

Despite these wretched conditions Marx never stopped writing. He spent most of his time at the British Museum, doing research on what was to become the first volume of *Das Kapital,* which was published in 1867. (The remaining two volumes of this work were completed and published by Engels after Marx's death.) In 1863 the formation of an international federation devoted to changing the economic system, called the International, provided Marx with the vehicle for which he had been waiting. He wrote the inaugural address of the International and soon led it.

Under Marx's direction the International became a powerful movement, and it appeared that he finally had achieved the union of socialist theory and revolutionary practice that he had formulated during the lonely, isolated years. However, his dream soon was shattered when in 1871 the French arm of the International suffered a bloody defeat and its exiled leaders began fighting among themselves. The British trade unionists feared association with the French terrorists, and attempts were made to oust Marx as leader of the International. To avoid losing control, Marx transferred the seat of the International to the United States, where his followers were still dominant. This marked the beginning of the end, for in 1876 the International disbanded in Philadelphia.

Although very ill, Marx spent the remaining years of his life a famous man, consulted by socialists from all over Europe. His death on March 14, 1883, drew little public notice, however, and his funeral was attended by only a few friends and socialist representatives. □

Many people were frightened by what was going on and wanted to find some way of understanding and dealing with the changes that were taking place. The need for a systematic analysis of society coupled with acceptance of the scientific method resulted in the emergence of sociology. Henri Saint-Simon (1760–1825) and Auguste Comte (1798–1857) were among the pioneers in the science of sociology.

Roots of Sociology

Saint-Simon and Comte rejected the lack of empiricism in the social philosophy of the day. Instead they turned for inspiration to the methods and intellectual framework of the natural sciences, which they perceived as having led to the spectacular successes of industrial progress. They set out to develop a "science of man" that would reveal the underlying principles of society much as the sciences of physics and chemistry explained nature and guided industrial progress.

Auguste Comte (see Box 1.1: "Auguste Comte 1798–1857") devoted a great deal of his writing to describing the contributions that he expected sociology would make in the future. He was much less concerned with defining sociology's subject matter than with showing how it would improve society. Although Comte was reluctant to specify subdivisions of sociology, he did identify two major areas that sociology should concentrate on: social statics—the study of how the various institutions of society are interrelated, focusing on order, stability, and harmony—and social dynamics—the study of complete societies and how they develop and change over time. Comte believed all societies move through certain fixed stages of development, eventually reaching perfection (as exemplified in his mind by industrial Europe). The idea of a perfect society, however, no longer is accepted by sociologists today.

Classical Theorists

During the nineteenth century sociology developed rapidly under the influence of four scholars of highly divergent temperaments and orientations. Despite their differences in aims and theories, however, these men—Karl Marx, Herbert Spencer, Émile Durkheim, and Max Weber—were responsible for shaping sociology into a relatively coherent discipline.

Karl Marx (1818–1883) Because the name Karl Marx (see Box 1.2: "Karl Marx 1818–1883") triggers thoughts of communism, those who are unfamiliar with his writings often think of him as a revolutionary proponent of the political and social system we see in the Soviet Union today. Yet Marx was not a Russian, and although he was committed to social change, he did not espouse the type of government and social structure that we now see in those countries that today are labeled communist.

Marx lived during a period when the overwhelming majority of people in industrial societies were poor. This was the early period of industrialization in such nations as England, Germany, and the United States. Those who owned and controlled the factories and other means of production exploited the masses who worked for them. The rural poor were forced or lured into cities where employment was available in the factories and workshops of the new industrial economies.

In this way the rural poor were converted into an urban poor. In the United States, children some as young as five or six years old, were employed in the cotton mills of the South. They worked 12 hours a day at the machines, six and seven days a week (Lipsey and Steiner, 1975), and received only a subsistence wage. The "iron law of wages"—the philosophy that justified paying workers only enough money to keep them alive—prevailed during this early period of industrialization. Meanwhile, those who owned the means of production possessed great wealth, power, and prestige. Marx tried to understand the institutional framework that produced such conditions and looked for a means to change it in order to improve the human condition.

Marx stated that the entire history of human societies may be seen as the history of class conflict: the conflict between those who own and control the means of production and those who work for them—the exploiters and the exploited. He believed that ownership of the means of production in any society determines the distribution of wealth, power, and even ideas in that society. The power of the wealthy is derived not just from their control of the economy but from their control of the political, educational, and religious institutions as well. According to Marx, capitalists construct and enforce laws that serve their interests and act against the interests of workers. Their control over all institutions enables them to create ideologies that justify to the workers the worth of the institutions. These economic, political, and religious ideologies make the masses loyal to the very institutions that are the source of their exploitation and that also are the source of the wealth, power, and prestige of the ruling class. Thus, the prevailing ideologies of any society are those of its dominant group.

Marx predicted that capitalist society eventually would be polarized into two broad classes—the capitalists and the increasingly impoverished workers. Intellectuals like himself would show the workers that the capitalist institutions of production were the source of exploitation and poverty. Gradually, the workers would become unified and organized, and then through revolution they would take over control of the economy. The means of production would then be owned and controlled by the workers in a workers' socialist state. Once the capitalist elements of the society had been eliminated, the government would wither away. Pure communism would evolve—a society in which people may work according to their ability and take according to their need. For Marx the seeds of societal conflict and social change through revolution would come to an end once the means of production no longer were privately owned.

Today we see that capitalist societies did not become polarized into two classes. In retrospect it is clear that the government was not simply a tool of the capitalist classes; rather, it often intervened to regulate many of the excesses of capitalism. Unions were legalized and integrated into the capitalist economy and the political system, giving their members a legal, legitimate means through which they could benefit from the capitalist system. Contrary to Marx's predictions, revolutions did not take place in the industrialized Western nations where most people have been freed from worrying about their basic subsistence needs. Rather, communist revolutions occurred in nations that were mostly agrarian—the Soviet Union, China, Cuba, and Vietnam, for example.

Marx's interests focused on the stresses and strains of society. His perspective thus is often called *conflict theory,* of which he is considered to be the major contributor. From his point of view, the social order of society is determined by the control exercised by a dominant group over subordinate groups through control of social institutions. The subordinate groups in a stable society tend to be socialized in conformity with the prevailing ideologies of the institutions. Marx's conflict theory is thought to be as applicable to communist nations as it is to capitalist nations. In communist nations, it is the Communist party that is the source of control over the economy and other institutions.

Herbert Spencer *(1820–1903)* Herbert Spencer was a largely self-educated Briton who had a talent for synthesizing information. In 1860 he undertook the work of organizing all human knowledge into one system. The result was his *Principles of Sociology* (1876, 1882), the first sociology textbook. Unlike Comte, Spencer was precise in defining the subject matter of sociology. He included in the field of sociology the study of the family, politics, religion, social control, work, and stratification.

It was Spencer who first introduced the term *evolution* into the literature of science in his *First Principles* (1860–1862). By evolution Spencer meant change from simple to complex forms. He viewed societies as constantly evolving from primitive to industrial and saw society as analogous to a living organism. He argued that just as the individual organs of a living creature are interdependent and ultimately must be understood in terms of their specialized contributions to the living whole, so, too, the various component structures of society are interdependent. They serve specialized functions necessary to ensure society's survival as an integrated entity.

Spencer's ideas became part of a doctrine that came to be known as **Social Darwinism.** According to this view, people who were not successful in the environment of an industrializing society were really inferior specimens of humanity. Lack of success was seen as an example of individual inferiority and in no way related to societal barriers (such as racism) created by others. Spencer reasoned from Darwin's theory of the survival of the fittest that people who could not successfully compete in the industrial world were poorly adapted to their environment and therefore inferior.

> Darwin's theory that the process of evolution resulted primarily from conflict and competition among the species, which culminated in the survival of the fittest and the disappearance of the unfit, had a great attraction to those who believed in the inequality of racial thinking. With the concept of the survival of the fittest, it could now be claimed that the inferior races were those that were unable to compete in the white world. Those who lost out in the struggle for existence were inferior specimens who were poorly adapted to their environment. The survivors were clearly of superior stock. (Berry and Tischler, 1978)

Dominant groups accepted Social Darwinism because it served as a justification for their control over institutions. It enabled them to oppose reforms or social welfare programs, which they viewed as interfering with nature's plan to do away with the unfit. Social Darwinism thus became a justification for the repression and neglect of U.S. blacks following the Civil War. It also justified policies that had resulted in the decimation of North American Indian populations and the complete extinction of the native people of Tasmania (near Australia) by white settlers (Fredrickson, 1971).

The history of Social Darwinism has led many scholars to disregard Spencer's original contributions to the discipline of sociology. However, many of the standard concepts and terms still current in sociology today were formulated by Spencer first, and their use derives directly from his works.

Émile Durkheim (1858–1917)　A student of law, philosophy, and social science, Émile Durkheim (see Box 1.3: "Émile Durkheim 1858–1917") was the first professor of sociology at the University of Bordeaux, France. Whereas Spencer wrote the first textbook of sociology, it was Durkheim who produced the first true sociological study. Durkheim's work moved sociology fully out of the realm of social philosophy and charted the discipline's course as a social science.

Durkheim believed that individuals are exclusively the product of their social environment, that society shapes people in every possible way. In order to prove his point, Durkheim decided to study suicide. He believed that if he could take what was perceived to be a totally personal act and show that is was patterned by social factors rather

Social Darwinism　A doctrine and social movement that uses—or, more correctly, misuses—Darwin's theory of evolution to justify existing forms of social organization. Reasoning from Darwin's theory of the survival of the fittest, Social Darwinism claims that those people who cannot successfully compete in the industrial world are poorly adapted to their environment and, therefore, inferior. The idea actually was formulated by Herbert Spencer and has been used to justify social inequality and the repression and neglect of various groups.

1.3
Émile Durkheim 1858–1917

Born at Epinal—a commune on the Moselle River in the French province of Lorraine—on April 15, 1858, Émile Durkheim was brought up in an Orthodox Jewish community, which was insulated from the larger society.

Durkheim experienced two major historical events in his early teens that proved to be significant influences on both his intellectual and social development. The French defeat in the Franco-Prussian War of 1870–1871 and the infamous and bloody Paris Commune of 1871 led to his passionate involvement in the workings of French society and the French nation. Ultimately Durkheim broke away from his Jewish roots by declaring himself an agnostic. He directed his frugal and disciplined upbringing to a secular (nonreligious) search for civic morality to replace the dominant religious values.

The three years Durkheim spent at the Ecole Normale Supérieure in Paris were by far his most formative. Although Durkheim is not noted as a classical thinker, he was nevertheless a prodigious reader and dedicated to scientific instruction and the search for a secular morality. Above all else was his drive to establish sociology as a legitimate scientific study following the lead of Comte and others. Another of his major concerns was the increasing significance of individualism in modern society. He viewed the emergence of a new secular social order dominated by individualistic ideals as futile. Related to this, Durkheim was interested in the sources and nature of moral authority. Regardless of the politics of social change, he believed that certain moral values played a major role in the public's acceptance of change. Finally, Durkheim wanted to apply his scientific knowledge of society in a practical way—namely, using his system of sociology as a means of providing moral direction for society.

Perhaps the biggest academic influences on his life and writings came from two of his teachers at the Ecole: the historian Fustel de Coulanges and the philosopher Emile Boutroux. De Coulanges taught him the value of critical and methodical historical research—that is, viewing history systematically, uninfluenced by one's own personal, religious, or social values. Boutroux first led Durkheim to the works of Comte and pointed out that unique properties of any subject exist within each level of scientific analysis.

Durkheim taught philosophy in several provincial schools after graduating from the Ecole in 1882. He spent 1885 and 1886 in Germany studying contemporary methods of research and in-struction in social philosophy. His experiences in Germany helped him solidify his academic philosophies and sense of social reality. The papers and critical reviews he published on German social thought led to an appointment as lecturer in social science and education at the University of Bordeaux in 1887. The same year Durkheim married Louise Dreyfus.

Durkheim stirred up as much controversy as support concerning his views of society, which is probably why he remained at the University of Bordeaux for so long. This was the most productive period in his life. In four years he published *The Division of Labor* (1893), his Latin thesis on Montesquieu (1893), *The Rules of Sociological Method* (1894), and *Suicide* (1897), in addition to numerous critiques and articles. While at Bordeaux he also lectured on the history of socialism, believing, unlike Marx, that profound change was the result of long-term social reform.

In 1896 Durkheim received France's first full professorship in social science at the University of Bordeaux. With public interest in sociology growing, he helped found in 1897 the review journal *L'Année Sociologique.* One of Durkheim's main goals was to bring together the conceptual elements of the specialized social sciences and the scientific methodologies with which to study them. The objectives of *L'Année,* which occupied most of Durkheim's time until the outbreak of World War I, were to analyze the sociological literature and related works that appeared throughout Europe. *L'Année* published many reviews on the sociology of religion, which became Durkheim's major interest toward the end of his career. The insights he gained from these reviews and from a course in religion that he taught at Bordeaux were published in 1912 as *The Elementary Forms of Religious Life* and ultimately led him to revise all of his previous research.

After 15 years at Bordeaux, Durkheim was offered and accepted a position as lecturer in education at the Sorbonne in 1902, although he was not named professor until 1906. His chair was changed to one of education and sociology in 1913, when he was directed to teach a class on the history and theory of French education.

Toward the end of 1915, Durkheim's only son, André, was killed during the Serbian Retreat. This proved to be a devastating blow, as the young man had already started to follow closely in his father's sociological footsteps. Durkheim suffered a stroke in 1916 from which he never really recovered, and he died on November 15, 1917. Although he had published most of his classic studies during his lifetime, much of his work in the form of written lectures was published posthumously. □

than exclusively by individual mental disturbances, he would be able to verify his view.

In order to approach the study scientifically, Durkheim collected massive statistical data on suicides. His systematic, empirical research showed that suicide, which appears to be purely an individual act, is in fact strongly influenced by social processes—the nature of the individual's involvement with others (Durkheim, 1897). This study of suicide set both the tone and standard for future sociological studies (see Focus on Research: "The Social Origins of Suicide").

Durkheim's interests were not limited to suicide. His mind ranged over the entire spectrum of social activities. He published studies on *The Division of Labor in Society* (1893) and *The Elementary Forms of the Religious Life* (1917). In both these works he drew on what was known about nonliterate societies, following the lead of Comte and Spencer in viewing them as evolutionary precursors of the contemporary industrial societies of Europe.

Because Durkheim was primarily interested in how society molds the individual, he focused on the forces that hold society together—that is, on the functions of various social structures. This point of view, often called the *functionalist theory* or *perspective* remains today one of the dominant approaches to the study of society.

Max Weber (1864–1920)   Max Weber (see Box 1.4: "Max Weber 1864–1920") was one of the founders of academic sociology. Unlike Marx, who was not only an intellectual striving to understand society but a revolutionary conspiring to overturn the capitalist social sys-

tem, Weber was much more an academic attempting to understand human behavior than a revolutionary who sought change. Weber believed the role of the intellectual should be simply to describe and explain what is true, whereas Marx believed that the scholar also should tell people what they ought to do. Much of the work of Weber is an attempt to clarify, criticize, and modify the works of Marx. For that reason we shall discuss Weber's ideas as they relate to and contrast with those of Marx.

Marx believed that ownership of the means of production resulted in the control of wealth, power, and ideas in a society. Weber showed that economic control does not necessarily result in prestige and power. For example, the wealthy president of a chemical company whose toxic wastes have been responsible for the pollution of the local water supply might have very little prestige in the community. Moreover, the company's board of directors may well deprive the president of real power.

Although Marx maintained that the control of production inevitably results in the control of ideologies, Weber stated that the opposite may happen: ideologies sometimes influence the economic system. When Marx called religion "an opiate to the people," he was referring to the ability of those in control to create an ideology that would justify the exploitation of the masses. Weber, however, showed that religion could be a belief system that contributed to the creation of new economic conditions and institutions. In *The Protestant Ethic and the Spirit of Capitalism* (1904–1905), Weber tried to demonstrate how the Protestant Reformation of the seventeenth century provided an ideology that gave religious justification to the pursuit of eco-

FOCUS ON RESEARCH
The Social Origins of Suicide

Émile Durkheim's study of Suicide *(1897) is a classical example of sociological research and analysis.*

Durkheim began with a theory—that the industrialization of Western society was undermining the social control and support that communities had historically provided for individuals. Industrialization forced or induced individuals to leave rural communities for urban areas, where there was usually greater economic opportunities. The anonymity and impersonality of urban areas, however, caused many people to become isolated from both family and friends. In addition, in industrial societies people are frequently encouraged to aspire to goals that are often unclearly defined and difficult to attain. Suspecting that this trend would have an impact on the suicide rate and wishing to prove the importance of sociology by demonstrating how what was believed to be a totally personal act, suicide, was in fact a product of social forces, Durkheim refined his theory to state that suicide rates are influenced by the degree of solidarity or integration in society. He believed that low levels of solidarity—which involve more individual choice, more reliance on self, and less adherence to group standards—would mean high rates of suicide.

In order to test his idea Durkheim narrowed his focus and decided to study the suicide rates of Catholic versus Protestant countries. He assumed the suicide rate in Catholic countries would be lower than in Protestant countries be-

cause Protestantism emphasized the individual's relationship to God over community ties. He then compared the suicide records in Catholic and Protestant countries, communities, and provinces in Europe to see if he were right. The results of these comparisons supported his theory by showing the probability of suicide to be higher in Protestant than in Catholic communities.

Recognizing that his results did not necessarily prove his theory, because the fact that Catholics had lower suicide rates than Protestants could be based on factors other than solidarity, Durkheim proceeded to test other groups. Reasoning that married people would be more integrated into a group than single people, people with children more than people without children, non-college-educated people more than college-educated people (because college tends to break group ties and encourage individualism), and Jews more than non-Jews, Durkheim tested each of these groups, and in each case his theory held up.

Then, characteristic of the scientist that he was, Durkheim extended his theory by identifying three types of suicide—egoistic, altruistic, and anomic—that take place under different types of conditions.

Egoistic suicide comes from low solidarity, an underinvolvement with others. Durkheim argued that loneliness and a commitment to personal beliefs rather than group values can lead to egoistic suicide. He found that single and divorced people had higher suicide rates than did married people and that Prot-

estants, who tend to stress individualism, had higher rates of suicide than did Catholics.

Altruistic suicide derives from a very high level of solidarity, an overinvolvement with others. The individual and the moral order are so close that the person is willing to die for the sake of the community. This type of suicide, Durkheim noted, still exists in the military as well as in societies based on ancient codes of honor and obedience. Perhaps the best-known examples of altruistic suicide come from Japan: the ceremonial rite of *segguku*, in which a disgraced person rips open his own belly, and the *kamikaze* attacks by Japanese pilots at the end of World War II.

Anomic suicide results from a sense of disorientation and a lack of values experienced when people lose their social moorings. A person may know what goals to strive for but not have the means of attaining them, or a person may not know what goals to pursue. Durkheim found that times of rapid social change or economic crisis are associated with high rates of anomic suicide.

Durkheim's study was noteworthy not only because it proved that the most personal of all acts, suicide, is in fact a product of social forces, but also because it was one of the first examples of a scientifically conducted, sociological study. Durkheim systematically posed theories, tested them, and drew conclusions that led to further theories. He also published his results for everyone to see and criticize. □

nomic success through rational, disciplined, hard work. This ideology, called the Protestant Ethic, ultimately helped transform northern European societies from feudal agricultural to industrial capitalist.

On the other hand, Weber also predicted that science—the systematic, rational description, explanation, and manipulation of the observable world—would lead to a gradual demythologizing and disenchantment of the

1.4
Max Weber 1864–1920

Max Weber was born in Erfurt, Germany, on April 21, 1864. His Protestant parents placed a high value on education, culture, and national pride.

A prodigious learner, Weber was torn between his role as a scholar—separated from but observing of society—and the self-serving lifestyle of a gentleman. His whole life was troubled by inner tensions and conflict stemming from less than favorable family relations. Weber's father was very much part of the German political establishment—a city councilor in Berlin, a magistrate in Erfurt, and an important member of the National Liberation party that was closely aligned with Bismarck. Although flexible in political affairs, Weber's father ran a disciplined, authoritarian household.

His mother's religious commitments and Calvinist sense of sacrifice had little in common with her husband's pleasure-seeking lifestyle and cold, cruel efficiency. This apparent conflict in personality was the main source of tension between father and son; yet young Max identified more with his father than with his mother.

Weber entered the University of Heidelberg to study law but also developed a keen interest in economics, philosophy, and Roman history. He joined his father's dueling fraternity, making many beer-drinking friends. His free-wheeling ways angered his pious mother, who feared Weber would follow in his father's footsteps. Once again the young man was faced with a choice—scholarly pursuits or personal indulgence—and in 1883, after three terms at Heidelberg, he left for a year of military service in Strasbourg. Here he came under the influence of his aunt and uncle, Hermann and Ida Baumgarten. They were like parents to Weber with one significant difference—they treated him as an intellectual peer. Freeing himself from the hedonist model of his father, Weber identified more with his uncle, who became his political and intellectual mentor for nearly ten years.

Weber soon fell in love with his cousin, Emmy Baumgarten. Their six-year engagement was tenuous at best, due to Emmy's frail mental and physical health, and Weber finally broke it off.

At the end of his military training in the fall of 1884, Weber returned to the University of Berlin to resume his studies. As a student, living with and financially dependent on his parents, Weber came under the influence of many different professors. He took his law exam in 1886 and became a junior lawyer in the Berlin courts, all the while continuing his studies. The influence of one of his closest advisers, historian Theodor Mommsen, can be seen in Weber's Ph.D. thesis (1889) on the history of medieval businesses and in his postdoctoral work on Roman agrarian history, published in 1891. Shortly after completing the latter study Weber took on a second job as an instructor at the University of Berlin.

The laborious and disciplined rigors of his academic and professional careers eased up in 1893, when Weber married Marianne Schnitger, a cousin on his father's side, and was offered a full professorship in economics at the University of Freiberg. In 1896 he was called back to the University of Heidelberg to succeed his former economics professor, Karl Knies.

This was a very productive time for Weber, and everything seemed to be going his way. But in 1898 all the inner tensions and conflicts growing out of family difficulties—his guilt feelings over his engagement to one cousin and marriage to another, the different role models presented by his father, uncle, mother, and aunt, and his chronic overwork characterized by a passionate involvement in both political and scholarly affairs—finally caught up with him. Shortly after his father died, Weber suffered a complete breakdown. For nearly five years he was unable to work or even read. When it became apparent that he would never lecture again, Weber resigned his chair at Heidelberg.

Returning to his studies in 1903 Weber focused mainly on methods of social research but also became involved in the political developments of the day. This period was another major turning point in Weber's life. In 1910 he cofounded, with sociologists Georg Simmel and Ferdinand Tönnies, the German Sociological Society.

The outbreak of World War I seemed to reinspire Weber's nationalist roots. He volunteered for service in the administration of military hospitals until retiring in 1915. His experience provided the firsthand knowledge he needed for formulating his principles of bureaucratic systems. For the rest of his life Weber was politically active, publishing many

papers and becoming a founding member of the German Democratic party. During this period he began what may be one of his most significant works, *Economics and Society,* which contained many of the definitions and basic principles needed for a general science of social behavior.

Weber developed pneumonia in early June, 1920, and died on June 14. He never finished his introduction to sociology, but what he did write was published posthumously and has since become the backbone of modern-day sociology as we know it today. □

---

population and hence to a gradual turning away from religion. The apparent decline in the influence of organized religion in the highly industrialized societies seems to support Weber's prediction. (We shall look at this question more deeply in Chapter 14.)

Weber also was interested in understanding the development of bureaucracy as the means by which people and material resources could be organized for the pursuit of specific goals. Whereas Marx saw capitalism as the source of control, exploitation, and alienation of human beings and believed that socialism and communism would ultimately bring an end to this exploitation, Weber believed that bureaucracy would characterize both socialist and capitalist societies. He anticipated and feared the domination of individuals by large bureaucratic structures. As he foresaw, our modern industrial world, both capitalist and socialist, is now ruled by bureaucracies—economic, political, military, educational, and religious. Given the existing situation, it is easy to appreciate Weber's anxiety. As he put it,

> . . . each man becomes a little cog in the machine and, aware of this, his one preoccupation is whether he can become a bigger cog. . . . The problem which besets us now is not: how can this evolution be changed?—for that is impossible, but what will become of it. (Quoted in Coser, 1977)

American Developments

Sociology has its roots in Europe. But America is the home of twentieth-century sociology, for it is in this country that its goals and methods were refined.

The first president of the American Sociological Society was Lester Ward (1841–1913), who saw in sociology the means for the scientific promotion of social progress. He was followed in this position by William Graham Sumner (1840–1910), an Episcopal priest whose interest in anthropology led him to emphasize the tremendous variability of customs, values, and behavior from one society to another. He published his findings in *Folkways* (1906), which for many years was an extremely influential work.

Whereas Ward and Sumner influenced the direction of sociology through their impressive individual efforts, the University of Chicago provided a context in which a large number of scholars and their students could work closely together to refine their views of the discipline. It was there that the first graduate department of sociology in America was founded in the 1890s. From the 1920s to the 1940s the so-called Chicago school of sociologists led American sociology in the study of communities, with particular emphasis on urban neighborhoods and ethnic areas. Many of America's leading sociologists from this period were members of the Chicago school, including Robert E. Park, W. I. Thomas, and Ernest W. Burgess. Most of these men were Protestant ministers or sons of ministers, and as a group they were deeply concerned with social reform.

Perhaps the single most influential American sociologist was Talcott Parsons (1902–1979). He presided over the Department of Social Relations at Harvard University from the 1930s until he retired in 1973. Parsons' early research was quite empirical,

Robert K. Merton has been responsible for furthering the development of functionalist theory.

but he later turned to the philosophical and theoretical side of sociology. In *The Structure of Social Action* (1937) Parsons presented English translations of the writings of European thinkers, most notably Weber and Durkheim. In his best-known work, *The Social System* (1951), Parsons portrayed society as a stable system of well-ordered, interrelated parts. His viewpoint elaborated on Durkheim's functionalist perspective.

Contemporary sociologist Robert K. Merton also has been an influential proponent of functionalist theory. He is concerned with understanding the structures and functions of social systems whatever their forms. In his classic work, *Social Theory and Social Structure* (1968), first published in 1949, Merton spelled out the functionalist view of society. One of his main contributions to sociology was to distinguish between two forms of social functions—manifest functions and latent functions. By **social functions** Merton meant those social processes that contribute to the ongoing operation or maintenance of society.

The manifest function of the clock at the top is to tell time. The clock at the bottom has the same manifest function, but in addition, it has the latent function of imparting status.

social function A social process that contributes to the ongoing operation or maintenance of society.

Manifest functions are the intended and recognized consequences of those processes. For example, one of the manifest functions of going to college is to obtain knowledge, training, and a degree in a specific area. **Latent functions** are the unintended or not readily recognized consequences of such processes. Therefore, college may also offer the opportunity of making lasting friendships and finding potential marriage partners.

Under the leadership of Parsons and Merton, sociology in America moved away from a concern with social reform and adopted a so-called value-free perspective. This perspective, which was advocated by Max Weber, requires description and explanation rather than prescription: people should be told what is, not what should be. As critics of Parsons and Merton point out, however, interpretations of what exists may differ depending on the perspective from which reality is viewed and on the values of the viewer (Gouldner, 1970; Lee, 1978; Mills, 1959).

☐ Theoretical Perspectives

Scientists need a set of working assumptions to guide them in their work. These assumptions suggest which problems are worth investigating and offer a framework for interpreting the results of studies. Such sets of assumptions are known as **paradigms.** They are models for explaining events that provide frameworks for the questions that generate and guide research. Of course, not all paradigms are equally valid, even though at first they seem to be. Sooner or later, some will be found to be rooted in fact, whereas others will remain abstract and unusable, finally to be discarded. We shall examine those paradigms that have withstood the scrutiny of major sociologists.

Functionalism

Functionalism, or **structural functionalism,** as it is often called, is rooted in the writings of Spencer and Durkheim and the work of such scholars as Parsons and Merton. Functionalists view society as a system of highly interrelated structures or parts that function or operate together rather harmoniously.

Functionalists analyze society by asking what each different part of society contributes to the smooth functioning of the whole. For example, we may assume the education system serves to teach students specific subject matter. However, functionalists might also note that it acts as a system for the socialization of the young and as a means for producing conformity. The education system acts as a gatekeeper to the rewards society offers to those who follow the rules.

From the functionalist perspective, society appears quite stable and self-regulating. Much like a biological organism, society is normally in a state of equilibrium or balance. Most of a society's members share a value system and know what to expect from one another.

The best-known proponent of the structural-functionalist perspective was Talcott Parsons. He, more than anyone else, helped develop this viewpoint in sociology. His theory centered on the view that there were interrelated social systems consisting of the major areas of social life, such as the family, religion, education, politics, and economics. These systems were then analyzed according to the functions they performed for society as a whole and for one another.

Functionalism is a very broad theory in that it attempts to account for the complicated interrelationships of all the elements that make up human societies, including the complex societies of the industrialized (and industrializing) world. In a way it is impossible to be a sociologist and not be a functionalist, because most parts of society do serve some stated or unstated purpose. Functionalism is limited in one regard, however: the preconception that societies normally are in balance or harmony makes it difficult for proponents of this view to account for how social changes come about.

A major criticism of functionalist theory is that it has a very conservative bias. That is, if all the parts of society fit together smoothly, we can assume that the social system is working well. Conflict is then seen as something that disrupts the essential orderliness of the social structure and produces disequilibrium between the parts and the whole.

Conflict Theory

The forces of social change lie at the core of **conflict theory**; which is rooted in the work of Marx and other social critics of the nineteenth century. For the conflict theorists, social change pushed forward by social conflict is the normal state of affairs. Static periods are merely temporary way stations along the road. Social order results from dominant groups making sure that subordinate groups are loyal to the institutions that are the dominant groups' sources of wealth, power, and prestige. The dominant groups will use coercion, constraint, and even force to help control those people who are not voluntarily loyal to the laws and rules they have made. Marx and his contemporaries saw the main source of conflict as the struggle among social classes for access to, and control over, the means of production and the distribution of resources. Indeed, much of the nineteenth century in Europe was characterized by such struggles, which frequently resulted in violence and political upheaval.

Modern conflict theory has been refined by such sociologists as C. Wright Mills (1959), Ralf Dahrendorf (1958), Randall Collins (1975, 1979), and Lewis Coser (1956) to reflect the realities of contemporary society. Mills and Dahrendorf do not see conflict as confined to class struggle. Rather, they view it as applicable to the inevitable tensions that arise between groups: parents and children, suppliers and producers, producers and consumers, professional specialists and their clients, environmentalists and industrialists, unions and employers, the poor and the materially comfortable, and minority and majority ethnic groups (and among minority groups as well). Members of these groups have both overlapping and competing interests, and their shared needs keep all parties locked together within one society. At the same time the groups actively pursue their own ends, thus constantly pushing the society to change in order to accommodate them.

Conflict theorists are concerned with the issue of who benefits from particular social arrangements and how those in power maintain their positions and continue to reap benefits from them. In this sense Randall Collins sees the conflict perspective as an attempt to study how those in power maintain and enlarge their sphere of influence over many aspects of the social structure, including values and beliefs. The ruling class is seen as a group that spreads certain values, beliefs, and social arrangements in order to enhance its power and wealth. The social order then reflects the outcome of a struggle among those with unequal power and resources.

Another conflict perspective has been expressed by Lewis Coser. Coser's view incorporates aspects of both functionalism and conflict theory, seeing conflict as an inevitable element of all societies and as both functional and dysfunctional for society. Conflict between two groups tends to increase their internal cohesion. For example, competition between two divisions of two computer companies to be the first to produce a new product may draw the members closer to each other as they strive to reach the desired goal. This feeling might not have occurred had it not been for the sense of competition, as the conflict itself becomes a form of social interaction. Conflict could also lead to cohesion by causing two or more groups to form alliances against a common enemy. For example, a po-

manifest function One of two types of social functions identified by Robert Merton referring to an *intended* and recognized consequence of a social process.

latent function One of two types of social functions identified by Robert Merton referring to an unintended or not readily recognized consequence of a social process.

paradigm A basic model for explaining events that provides a framework for the questions that generate and guide research.

functionalism (structural functionalism) One of the major sociological theories, it views society as a system of highly interrelated parts that operate (function) together rather harmoniously. This theory analyzes society by asking what function is served by each part of society. Functionalism is useful in studying human societies, but it is less useful in attempting to account for social change.

conflict theory One of the major sociological theories, it views society as being in a constant state of social conflict with only temporarily stable periods. Rooted in the works of Karl Marx, modern conflict theory has been refined and applied to a wide variety of conflicts that occur in society. Conflict theory is useful in studying social conflict and change.

TABLE 1.2   Comparison of Functionalist and Conflict Theory

Functionalist Theory	Conflict Theory
1. The various parts of society are interdependent and functionally related.	1. Society is a system of accommodations among competing interest groups.
2. Each part of the social system contributes positively to the continued operation of the system.	2. The social system may at any time become unbalanced because of shifts in power.
3. The various parts of the social system fit together harmoniously.	3. The various parts of the social system do not fit together harmoniously.
4. Social systems are highly stable.	4. Social systems are unstable and are likely to change rapidly.
5. Social life is governed by consensus and cooperation.	5. Social life involves conflict because of differing goals.
6. Functionalist sociologists are concerned with the role each part of society contributes to the smooth functioning of the whole.	6. Conflict sociologists are concerned with who benefits from particular social arrangements.
7. Social order is achieved through cooperation.	7. Social order is achieved through coercion and even force.

litical contest may cause several groups to unite in order to defeat a common opponent.

Conflict perspectives are often criticized for concentrating too much on conflict and change and too little on what produces stability in society. They are also criticized for being too ideologically based and making little use of research methods or objective statistical evidence. The conflict theorists counter that the complexities of modern social life cannot be reduced to statistical analysis, that doing so has caused many sociologists to become detached from their object of study and removed from the real causes of human problems.

Both functionalist and conflict theories are descriptive and predictive of social life. Each has its strengths and weaknesses, and each emphasizes an important aspect of society and social life. Table 1.2 compares the approaches of functionalist and conflict theory.

Symbolic Interactionism

Human beings are unique in that most of what they do with one another has meaning beyond the concrete act. The theory of **symbolic interactionism,** as developed by George Herbert Mead (1863–1931), is concerned with the meanings that people place on their own and one another's behavior. According to Mead, people do not act or react automatically but carefully consider and even rehearse what they are going to do. They take into account the other people involved and the situation in which they find themselves. The expectations and reactions of other people greatly affect each individual's actions. In addition, people give things meaning and act or react on the basis of these meanings. For example, when the flag of the United States is raised, people stand because they see the flag as representing their country.

Because most human activity takes place in social situations—in the presence of other people—we must fit what we as individuals

Conflict theorists see conflict as an essential element of all societies. At times this conflict may result in violent confrontations.

do with what other people in the same situation are doing. We go about our lives with the assumption that most people share our definitions of basic social situations. This agreement on definitions and meanings is the key to human interactions in general, according to symbolic interactionists. For example, a staff nurse in a mental hospital unlocking a door for an inpatient is doing more than simply enabling the patient to pass from one ward to another. He or she also is communicating a position of social dominance over the patient (within the hospital) and is carrying a powerful symbol of that dominance—the key. The same holds true for a professor writing on a blackboard or a company vice-president dictating to a secretary. Such interactions, therefore, although they appear to be simple social actions, also are laden with highly symbolic social meanings. These symbolic meanings are intimately connected with our understanding of what it is to be and to behave as a human being. This includes our sense of self; how we experience others and their views of us; the joys and pains we feel at home, at school, at work, and among friends and colleagues; and so on.

Ethnomethodology

Many of the social actions we engage in on a day-to-day basis are quite commonplace events. They tend to be taken for granted and rarely are examined or considered. Harold Garfinkel (1967) has proposed that it is important to study the commonplace. Those things we take for granted have a tremendous hold over us because we accept their demands without question or conscious consideration. **Ethnomethodology** seeks to discover and describe the sets of rules or guidelines that individuals use to initiate behavior, respond to behavior, and modify behavior in social settings. For ethnomethodologists, all social interactions are equally important because they all provide information about a society's unwritten rules for social behavior, the shared knowledge of which is basic to social life.

Garfinkel asked his students to participate in a number of experiments in which the researcher would violate some of the basic understandings among people. For example,

when a conversation is held between two people, each assumes that certain things are perfectly clear and obvious and do not need further elaboration. Examine the following conversation and notice what happens when one individual violates some of these expectations:

BOB: That was a very interesting sociology class we had yesterday.

JOHN: How was it interesting?

BOB: Well, we had a lively discussion about deviant behavior, and everyone seemed to get involved.

JOHN: I'm not certain I know what you mean. How was the discussion lively? How were people involved?

BOB: You know, they really participated and seemed to get caught up in the discussion.

JOHN: Yes, you said that before, but I want to know what you mean by lively and interesting.

BOB: What's wrong with you? You know what I mean. The class was interesting. I'll see you later.

Bob's response is quite revealing. He is puzzled and does not know whether or not John is being serious. The normal expectations and understandings around which day-to-day forms of expression take place have been challenged. Still, is it not reasonable to ask for further elaboration of certain statements? Obviously not when it goes beyond a certain point.

Another example of the confusion brought on by the violation of basic understandings was shown when Garfinkel asked his students to act like boarders in their own homes. They were to ask whether they could use the phone, take a drink of water, have a snack, and so on. The results were quite dramatic:

symbolic interactionism A sociological theory that is concerned with the meanings people place on their own and one another's behavior.

ethnomethodology The study of the sets of rules or guidelines people use in their everyday living practices. This approach to social relations provides information about a society's unwritten rules for social behavior, and no behavior is too small for its scrutiny. Ethnomethodology would look at, for example, why people in our society all face front in an elevator, frequently glancing at the floor indicator.

Family members were stupefied. They vigorously sought to make the strange actions intelligible and to restore the situation to normal appearances. Reports were filled with accounts of astonishment, shock, anxiety, embarrassment, and anger and with charges by various family members that the student was mean, inconsiderate, selfish, nasty, or impolite. Family members demanded explanations: What's the matter? What's gotten into you? Did you get fired? Are you sick? What are you being so superior about? Why are you mad? Are you out of your mind or are you stupid? One student acutely embarrassed his mother in front of her friends by asking if she minded if he had a snack from the refrigerator. "Mind if you have a little snack? You've been eating little snacks around here for years without asking me. What's gotten into you?" (Garfinkel, 1972)

Ethnomethodology seeks to make us more aware of the subtle devices we use in creating the realities to which we respond. These realities are often more inside us than they are outside us. Ethnomethodology addresses questions about the nature of social reality and how we participate in its construction.

In Japanese culture, bowing is a way of showing respect.

Dramaturgy

People create impressions, and others respond with their own impressions. Erving Goffman (1959, 1963, 1971) concluded that a central feature of human interaction is impression formation—the attempt to present oneself to others in a particular way. Goffman believed that much human interaction can be studied and analyzed on the basis of principles derived from the theater. This approach, known as **dramaturgy,** states that in order to create an impression, people play roles, and their performance is judged by others who are alert to any slips that might reveal the actors' true character. For example, a job applicant at an interview tries to appear composed, self-confident, and capable of handling the position's responsibilities. The interviewer is seeking to find out whether the applicant is really able to work under pressure and perform the necessary functions of the job.

Most interactions require some type of playacting in order to present an image that will bring about the desired behavior from others. Dramaturgy sees these interactions as governed by planned behavior designed to enable an individual to present a particular image to others.

Symbolic interaction and its various offshoots have been criticized for paying too little attention to the larger elements of society. Interactionists respond that societies and institutions are made up of individuals who interact with one another and do not exist apart from these basic units. They believe that an understanding of the process of social interaction will lead to an understanding of larger social structures. In actual fact interactionists still have to bridge the gap between their studies of social interaction and those of the broader social structures. Nevertheless, symbolic interactionism does complement functionalism and conflict theory in important ways and gives us profound insights into how people interact.

☐ Theory and Practice

It is sociological theory that gives meaning to sociological practice. The mere assembling of countless descriptions of social facts may keep bookbinders busy, but it has no scientific value, just as personal experiences are inadequate for an understanding of society as a whole. If we rely only on our own experiences, we are like the blind men of Hindu legend trying to describe an elephant: the first man, feeling its trunk, asserted, "It is like a snake"; the second, trying to reach around the beast's massive leg argued, "No, it is like a tree"; and the third, feeling its powerful side, disagreed, saying, "It is more like a wall." In a small way, each man was right, but not one of them was able to understand or describe what the whole elephant was like. So, too, with sociology. Only when data are collected within the conceptual framework of a theory—in order to answer the specific questions growing out of that theory—is it possible to draw conclusions and make valid generalizations. This is the ultimate purpose of all science.

Theory without practice (research to test it) is at best poor philosophy, not science, and practice uninformed by theory is at best trivial and at worst a tremendous waste of time and resources. Therefore, in the next chapter we shall move from theory to practice—to the methods and techniques of social research.

☐ Summary

Although each of us has a personal perspective that we use to interpret the world around us, this perspective is not adequate to the task of the sociologist, whose goal is to try to understand the forces that operate throughout society: forces that mold individuals, shape their behavior, and thus determine social events. The focus of sociology is the group and not the individual. To achieve their goals, sociologists rely on the sociological imagination—the realization that there are a number of levels on which social events can be perceived and interpreted.

Common-sense ideas often interfere with the study of sociology. We tend to believe what we want to believe, to see what we want to see, and to accept as fact whatever appears to be logical. Sociologists strive to gather and analyze facts in an objective fashion. Sociologists are often presented with a no-win situation. Either they are criticized for studying the obvious, or they may be ridiculed for presenting information that refutes popular belief.

Sociology is one of the social sciences, which encompass all those disciplines that apply scientific methods to the study of human behavior. Although there is some overlap in goals and procedures, each of the social sciences has its own areas of concern. Cultural anthropology, psychology, economics, history, political science, and social work all have some things in common with sociology, but each is distinct in its overall objectives, theories, and methods.

The science of sociology began to emerge during the nineteenth century—a time of dramatic social change. In an effort to understand the effects of the Industrial Revolution on the fabric of society and on the lifestyle of individuals, scholars such as Henri Saint-Simon and Auguste Comte turned to the methods of the natural sciences to reveal the underlying principles of society.

Karl Marx, Herbert Spencer, Émile Durkheim, and Max Weber used a variety of approaches to try to make sense and science of the phenomenon of social change.

Marx believed that the entire history of human societies could be viewed as a history of class struggle—the conflict between those who own and control the means of production and those who work for them. He believed not only in investigating social problems but also in working to change the social system.

Spencer was the first to define the subject matter of sociology. Although he has been criticized for his adherence to Social Darwinism, his original contributions to the discipline still form the basis for many of today's standard concepts.

Durkheim, believing individuals are exclusively the product of their social environment, set out to prove his point through the study of suicide. He identified three major types of suicide: altruistic, egoistic, and anomic. All types, he stated, were a result of some type of social influence.

dramaturgy The study of the roles people play in order to create a particular impression in others.

Weber was interested in understanding rather than changing human behavior and interaction. He challenged Marx on many of his ideas and proposed that ideologies could influence groups and that power over the means of production did not automatically lead to power in other areas.

It was in the twentieth-century United States that the goals and methods of sociology were refined under the leadership of the Chicago school and such other distinguished sociologists as Talcott Parsons and Robert Merton.

Scientists need theories to guide their work, and as scientists, sociologists have developed several theoretical perspectives from which to view social events. Functionalism sees society as a system of highly interrelated structures that work together harmoniously, whereas conflict theory regards society as being pushed forward by the struggle between classes for control over the means of production and distribution of resources. Modern conflict theorists such as C. Wright Mills and Ralf Dahrendorf do not see conflict as confined to class struggle. Rather, they view it as applicable to the inevitable tensions that arise in families, businesses, racial groups, and a variety of other settings. Symbolic interactionism is concerned with the meanings people place on their own and one another's behavior. This perspective looks beyond the concrete act itself to the symbolic meanings of the act. Ethnomethodology tries to discover and describe unwritten rules that guide the behavior of individuals and groups in society, and dramaturgy looks at the roles people play in order to create a desired impression among others.

☐ For Further Reading

ANDRESKI, STANISLAV. *The Social Sciences as Sorcery*. New York: St. Martin's Press, 1972. A criticism of the state of the art of social scientific research and theory by a leading European sociologist. Andreski writes in an elegant and humorous style, yet never fails to penetrate to the heart of an issue. Of special value are the chapters "Manipulation Through Description," "Smoke Screen of Jargon," "Hiding Behind Methodology," and "Quantification as Camouflage." Andreski is also concerned with documenting Herbert Spencer's contributions to sociology.

BART, PAULINE, and LINDA FRANKEL. *The Student Sociologist's Handbook*. 3rd ed. Chicago: Scott, Foresman, 1981. This is a very useful guide for the beginning sociology student, presenting information on sociological perspectives, research and resource materials, and techniques for writing research papers.

BERGER, PETER L. *Invitation to Sociology: A Humanistic Perspective*. Garden City, N.Y.: Doubleday, 1963. A classic work presenting the sociological perspective on the world.

CUZZORT, RAY P., and EDITH W. KING. *Twentieth Century Social Thought*, 3rd ed., New York: Holt, Rinehart and Winston, 1980. A well-written, well-organized introduction to the thinkers whose ideas have shaped modern social thought. Among them are Karl Marx, Émile Durkheim, Max Weber, George Herbert Mead, Pitirim Sorokin, Robert Merton, David Riesman, C. Wright Mills, Howard Becker, Peter Berger, Erving Goffman, and Harold Garfinkel.

GOULDNER, ALVIN W. *The Coming Crisis of Western Sociology*. New York: Equinox Books (Avon), 1970. A review of major approaches to sociological theory leading to a thoughtful examination of the difficulties facing the discipline. Of special value is the author's discussion of the social responsibilities facing sociologists in today's political world.

HUBER, BETTINA J. *Embarking upon a Career with an Undergraduate Sociology Major*. Washington, D.C.: American Sociological Association, 1982. A booklet that contains practical advice on how to use the knowledge obtained as a sociology major.

INKELES, ALEX. *What Is Sociology?* Englewood Cliffs, N.J.: Prentice-Hall, 1964. In this brief but comprehensive book, the student will find a survey of sociology's history, approaches, and schools of thought.

LEE, ALFRED MCCLUNG. *Sociology for Whom?* New York: Oxford University Press, 1978. A leading figure in the tradition of humanistic sociology deals directly with the question that his title poses. Sociology, he answers, is for the people. Lee rejects the idea of value-free sociology and sees his discipline as a liberating weapon against many kinds of tyrannies—political, economic, and psychological. This is a book about the social responsibility of sociologists.

MILLS, C. WRIGHT. *The Sociological Imagination.* New York: Oxford University Press, 1959. A discussion of sociological theory, including an attack on the concept of value-free sociology. Talcott Parsons comes in for rough treatment, and the use of sociological jargon to obscure fuzzy thinking or an author's unacknowledged political values is exposed.

2 Doing Sociology: Research Methods

"Love leads to marriage." Suppose you were given that statement as a subject for sociological research. How would you proceed to gather data to prove or disprove it? After reading Chapter 1, you would know that you could not approach this proposition on the basis of your personal experience and perceptions; rather, you would have to approach the subject scientifically.

☐ Sociological Research

Science has two main goals: (1) to describe in detail particular things or events and (2) to propose and test general principles by means of which these things or events can be understood. To begin your research project, then, you would have to define "love." This in itself would pose a serious problem, as to this day people are still grappling with the question "How do you know when you are in love?" We may define love as an intense emotional state in which positive feelings for another person are present. We would then have to find some way of determining whether this condition exists. Next we would decide whether love had to be present between both people in the possible union. You may already have noticed that it may be too difficult here to achieve the level of precision necessary for a useful research project. However, if we could accurately define our terms and provide details to clarify our descriptions, we could then begin to test the statement we proposed.

In this chapter we shall examine some of the methods used by scientists in general—and sociologists in particular—to collect data in order to test their ideas. This investigative process involves trial and error and, in some respects, resembles what a detective does when trying to solve a crime (see Using Sociology: "The Sociologist as Detective").

Posing Questions

Scientists ask questions and seek to answer them—but not all questions can be answered. For instance, there is no way to discover what would happen if Napoleon had beaten the British at Waterloo or whether there is life after death. The first is a question for historical speculation and the second for theological

cal or philosophical debate. If you turned the opening statement in this chapter into a question—Does love lead to marriage?—you might find that it, too, is unanswerable. Even after arriving at a careful definition of your terms and a detailed description of love, you might discover that the question cannot be answered empirically.

An **empirical question** is one that can be answered by observation and analysis of the world as it is known. To ask how many students in the class have an A average or how widespread the problem of child abuse is, is to ask an empirical question. In order to begin to turn the statement about love into an empirical question, we thus would have to ask: How do we measure the existence of love?

Scientists pose empirical questions in order to collect information to add to what already is known and to test hypotheses. Hypotheses are statements about relationships among things or events. In order to be useful they must be empirical—that is, provable or disprovable in terms of things or events that can be observed directly or indirectly. For example, suppose you were interested in investigating students' study habits. First, you would need to decide what it was about their habits you wished to investigate; that is, you would have to formulate an empirical question. Perhaps you might ask: Is there a relationship between study habits and grades earned? Then this question would have to be stated as an empirical hypothesis or statement. For example, it could be phrased either as the longer students study, the better their grades will be or as A-average students have study habits that differ from those of B-average students. These hypotheses can be tested because all their variables are empirical, in that both grades and study behavior can be observed and recorded.

In the language of science, hypotheses are most useful if their terms are defined opera-

empirical question A question that can be answered by observation and analysis of the world as it is known. Philosophical questions ("What is the best form of government?") or theological questions ("How many angels can dance on the head of a pin?") are not empirical questions.

USING SOCIOLOGY
The Sociologist as Detective

There actually is a great deal of similarity between what a detective does in attempting to solve a crime and what a sociologist does in answering a research problem. The following example shows how much of a similarity there really is.

There is great similarity between how a detective tries to solve a crime and what a sociologist does in answering a research problem.

In the course of their work, both detectives and sociologists must gather and analyze information. For detectives, the object is to identify and locate criminals and to collect enough evidence to ensure that their identification is correct. Sociologists, on the other hand, develop theories and methods to help them understand social behavior. Although their specific goals differ, both sociologists and detectives formulate theories and develop methods in order to answer two general questions: "Why did it happen?" and "Under what circumstances is it likely to happen again?"—that is, to explain and predict.

To test their theories, detectives and sociologists rely on empirical evidence and logical modes of analysis as well as on their imagination. Both employ observation techniques, interviews, experiments, and other empirical methods to test the validity of their theories. Nevertheless, there are differences in their methods of gathering and analyzing information, and each can profit from techniques developed by the other.

In investigating a crime, detectives interview victims, witnesses, informants, and suspects. They compare their interviews with physical evidence that they gather in order to piece together a consistent account of what took place and to determine whether the people they interviewed were telling the truth. They may conduct an experiment to see whether a crime could have occurred in the way suggested by the accounts and the physical evidence. Finally, the detectives may discern a pattern from several cases involving crimes of the same sort.

Theory The stereotype of the detective who asks for "just the facts" is inaccurate, for detectives are always working with and testing theory. In any investigation, a detective would be at a loss for questions to ask without at least a rudimentary theory. For instance, in homicide cases, the first people generally contacted by the detectives are the friends, relatives, or acquaintances of the victim. Behind such investigative procedures is the theory that most homicides are committed by people who are socially close to the victim.

Similarly, sociologists develop theories that lead them to ask certain questions and not others, and these questions in turn lead them to notice certain "facts" and not others. For example, Durkheim's theory of anomic suicide led him to examine suicide rates in various countries in terms of each country's dominant religion. Religion was a fact to be noticed. In Goffman's examination of mental hospitals (1961a), on the other hand, the focus of his theory on the social world of patients in a mental hospital as they developed and sustained it led him to ignore the issue of what bearing their religious backgrounds had on their being committed. Problems rele-

vant to certain theories are not relevant to others, and certain questions are relevant to certain problems and not to others. The facts that are located in research stem from the researcher's theory.

Central to theories and research are concepts, in that they direct the researcher to "see" the world in certain terms and configurations. Concepts provide the crucial link between theory and research, because they tell the researcher what is of theoretical interest and what to look for. If a theory states, for example, that there is a relationship between associations and criminal behavior, the researcher will not look at head shapes, economic position, or family size but will concentrate on with whom criminals associate.

Detectives' investigations are also guided by certain concepts. The concept of "motive," for example, plays a central role in many investigations. Assuming that people are generally rational, detectives attempt to identify those who would benefit from a crime. This conceptual view leads them to certain people as possible suspects and away from others.

Evidence Just as theories direct researchers to facts and give meaning and relevance to facts, so facts in turn give validity and shape to theories. And because sociology, like detecting, is an empirical enterprise, sociological theories require evidence for them to be considered valid, just as detectives' theories do.

Beginning with a hypothesis, the researcher gathers concrete evidence either to substantiate or disprove it. For example, detectives may hypothesize that the butler was responsible for the murder of the lord of the manor. Before they can arrest him, however, they must find evidence to show that there is a "prob-able cause" for considering him a suspect.

Similarly, sociologists must prove their hypotheses. For example, in attempting to discover whether there is a relationship between amount of education and income, the sociologist might hypothesize that the more education an individual has, the greater his or her income will be. The sociologist gathers evidence to prove or disprove this hypothesis, not by showing that one person with a college degree has a larger income than another person with less education does, but by comparing several persons' average amount of education with their average income. Thus, instead of working with single cases, sociologists typically work with several cases.

We can think of the social researcher as a detective investigating social phenomena.

Source: Excerpted and adapted from William B. Sanders, *The Sociologist as Detective* (New York: Praeger, 1976), pp. 1–5.

---

tionally. An **operational definition** is a statement of the features that describe the things that are being investigated. To continue the example about investigating differences in study habits between A-average students and B-average students, you would have to define: (1) the observable behaviors that you would count as studying, (2) how often the behaviors would have to be repeated to count as habits, and (3) how you would establish the cutoff line between A-average and B-average students. Then your terms would be defined operationally.

Research, however, is rarely that simple. To illustrate its complexity, let us consider a social issue of great national concern—child abuse. In order to investigate child abuse, we must first give it an operational definition. The first person to describe what he called the "battered child syndrome" was Ambroise Tardieu, a professor of legal medicine in Paris. In 1860 he published an account of 32 autopsies on children who had been fatally battered by beating or burning (Kempe and Kempe, 1978). Later reports defined abuse in terms of X-ray photographs of children's bones (Caffey, 1946; Kempe et al., 1962). Some children, including infants, when X-rayed to determine the extent of an injury, were found to have had several previously broken bones. Knowing that only abnormal treatment could account for the presence of so many broken bones in these young children, doctors concluded that the children must have been beaten or otherwise abused. The presence of unaccountably broken bones in a child, then, came to be taken as an operational definition of child abuse.

In recent years child abuse has been given a wider definition. Unexplained and untreated wounds, repeated bruising, multiple burns, and such severe neglect that death is threatened all are commonly recognized symptoms of child abuse. Lately the concept of abuse has been expanded still further to include what has come to be called emotional abuse (Gesmone, 1972; Martin, 1976; Kempe, 1978).

Based on this information, the first step confronting a sociologist who wants to study child abuse is to choose an operational definition appropriate to the planned study. For instance, one recent study defined child abuse as consisting of physical violence and willful injury, physical and emotional neglect, emotional mistreatment, and sexual exploitation (Kempe and Kempe, 1978). Each of these terms would have to be explained operationally before the definition could be used for research.

The next step is to decide exactly what we want to learn about child abuse. There are many questions that might be asked. How

operational definition A statement of the empirical (observable) features that describe the things being investigated.

widespread is it in the United States? Does the incidence vary according to social class, geographical region, or ethnic group? Do parents who abuse their children have certain psychological traits in common? Do such parents have in common certain childhood experiences? How does abuse affect children's development? Does it affect all aspects of development equally? When one child in a family is abused, are all the other children? If not, why not? Are there ways in which social agencies can prevent or intervene effectively in cases of child abuse?

Reviewing Previous Research

Which questions are the "right" questions? Although there are no inherently correct questions, some are better suited to investigation than are others. First the researcher must learn as much as possible about the studies already done on the subject. Next the researcher must choose a perspective from which to study the subject.

The more we know about previous research on the subject, the better we can plan a project and the more valuable it is likely to be. In the case of child abuse, for example, both a lot and very little are known. Estimates of how widespread it is in America differ because studies use different operational definitions of abuse. Further, laws requiring the reporting of child abuse and designating the kinds of records that must be kept differ from state to state. Finally, there may be biases among those who identify and report its presence. Physicians often may be reluctant to identify the presence of child abuse among their white middle- and upper-class patients, but will note it readily among lower-class blacks and Hispanics (Parke and Collmer, 1975). Nevertheless, one thing is clear: child abuse is widespread, and the figures indicating its incidence are constantly getting larger. For example, between 1968 and 1972, the reported cases of child abuse jumped from 721 to 30,000 in Michigan, from 4,000 to 40,000 in California, and from 10 to 30,000 in Florida (Kempe and Kempe, 1978). More recently, in interpreting the results of a study in Denver by C. H. Kempe and his colleagues, one research team calculated the incidence of

actual physical abuse at 2 percent of the entire population, and as many as 18 percent of the population showed signs of damagingly abnormal parenting practices (Ferholt, Hunter, and Leventhal, 1978).

Most research on child abuse has focused on parents from low socioeconomic groups, even though many social workers and other health professionals maintain that child abuse also is present among middle-class families. Therefore, much of what is known about child abuse may be seriously distorted by the fact that it has been studied primarily in the context of poverty, and it is well known that poverty itself can exert an overwhelming influence on people's behavior. Perhaps more might be learned about the origins and expressions of child abuse if it were studied among groups of comfortable means. The point is, a researcher should examine what studies have already been done on a subject before planning a new project.

Choosing a Research Perspective

After reviewing the previous research on a subject, the sociologist must decide how to approach the issue. For example, early research on child abuse focused on the parents—on what sorts of people abuse their children. Later, factors of social environment were considered. More recent work emphasizes the view that parents and children are part of an interactive system and that in order to understand abuse, it is necessary to look at the behavior of both parents and children.

All these approaches are valid, but each will lead researchers to ask different questions and thereby seek different information. Choosing a perspective is analogous to working a jigsaw puzzle in that the overall picture or design is envisioned before the pieces are put together. As each piece of the puzzle is picked up, it is examined carefully to see where it fits. If a piece is placed incorrectly, the other pieces will not fall into place, and if some pieces are missing, the picture will not be complete. Thus it is important that a sociologist choose a viewpoint with care and identify it so that others can assess the research in terms of it. In the end we stand to learn most about a particular social phenomenon when it is investigated from a number of different theoretical points of view.

Developing Hypotheses

A **hypothesis,** to be more precise than we have been so far, is a testable statement about the relationships between two or more empirical variables. A **variable** is anything that can change (vary). The number of highway deaths on Labor Day weekends, the number of divorces that occur each year in the United States, the amount of energy the average American family consumes in the course of a year, the daily temperature in Dallas, the number of abused children in Boston or in Knoxville, Tennessee—all these are variables. The following are not variables: the distance from Los Angeles to Las Vegas, the altitude of Denver, and the number of children who were abused in Ohio in 1981. These are fixed, unchangeable facts.

Hypotheses involve statements of causality or association. A **statement of causality** says that something brings about, influences, or changes something else. "Smoking causes cancer" is a statement of causality. A **statement of association,** on the other hand, says that changes in one thing are related to changes in another but that one does not necessarily cause the other. For example, if you were studying the relationship between poverty and street crime, you might find, in general, the greater the level of poverty was, the higher the rate of street crime in a given area would be. However, because research has shown that a majority of poor people do not commit crimes, you cannot say poverty is the only cause of crime. You can only say, at most, that poverty is associated with crime.

Often hypotheses propose relationships between two different kinds of variables—a dependent variable and an independent variable. A **dependent variable** changes in response to changes in the independent variable. An **independent variable** changes for reasons that have nothing to do with the dependent variable. For example, someone interested in studying child abuse might propose the following hypothesis: parents who live in cities are more likely to abuse their children than are parents who live in the country. In this hypothesis the independent variable is the location: some parents live in the city, some live in the country, but presumably their choice of where to live is not influenced by whether they abuse their children. The dependent variable is the presence of abuse, because it is possible that parents may abuse their children more or less depending on where they live. If research shows that child abuse (the dependent variable) is indeed more frequent among urban parents than among rural parents, the hypothesis probably is correct. If there is no difference in the incidence of child abuse among urban and rural parents—or if it is higher among rural parents—then the hypothesis is not supported by the data. Keep in mind that proving a hypothesis false can be scientifically useful: it eliminates unproductive avenues of thought and suggests other, more productive approaches to understanding a problem.

Even if research shows a hypothesis may be correct, that does not mean the independent variable necessarily produces or causes the dependent variable. For example, if it turns out that there is more child abuse in the city than in the country, we still do not know why. There may be ethnic differences between city and country populations with very different attitudes toward child-rearing practices, or one group may be much poorer or more socially isolated than the other.

hypothesis A testable statement about the relationship between two or more empirical variables.

variable Anything that can change (vary). There are two kinds of variables: dependent and independent.

statement of causality A proposition that one thing brings about, influences, or changes something else. "Cigarette smoking causes lung cancer" is a statement of causality.

statement of association A proposition that changes in one thing are related to changes in another but that one does not necessarily cause the other.

dependent variable A variable that changes in response to changes in the independent variable.

independent variable A variable that changes for reasons that have nothing to do with the dependent variable. In the statement, "Cigarette smoking causes lung cancer," cigarette smoking is the independent variable, and lung cancer is the dependent variable.

PORTFOLIO I
The Fabric of Society

Sociology is the scientific study of human society and the social interactions that emerge among people. The main focus of sociology is the group rather than the individual. Sociologists attempt to understand the forces that operate throughout society—forces that mold individuals, shape their behavior, and thus determine social events.

All of us are members of society, and we may also be members of specific subcultures. We often feel we understand a great deal about society because of our continuing experiences within it. However, these experiences are limited to a specific social group, and we may not realize how different the norms and values of other groups in society might be from our own. The Masai warriors have their own unique culture, one with a specific set of norms, values, and beliefs. This cultural background will differ markedly from that of the owner of a Rolls Royce or that of the girls in a Brownie troop.

Sociologists realize that we become social beings through our interactions with others. We develop primary relationships with members of our family and close friends. We develop secondary relationships with those with whom we interact on a less intimate basis—at work, in organizations, and in public transactions. All these relationships combine to become part of the socialization process that shapes us into the people we are.

Sociology asks us to broaden our perspective of the world. It enables us to begin to understand that the reason people act in markedly different ways is that they have different perceptions of what is going on in the world. These different perceptions of reality produce many different lifestyles, and different lifestyles in turn produce different perceptions of reality. In order to understand other people, we must begin to look at the world from a perspective that is broader than that based on only our own experiences.

Every society has a specific culture. Cross-cultural influence, illustrated by these Masai warriors, is an important means of cultural change. Children learn the expectations and rules of their culture through socialization by their family, school, the mass media, and groups, such as the Cub Scouts and Brownies. Socialization continues into adulthood and is influenced by the norms and values of even the informal groups to which the individual belongs.

Social movements, population trends, urbanization, mechanization, robotics, and ecological events are some of the elements that have determined social change. The vitality of a society is dependent upon the course of its social change. Change is inevitable, but its direction is determined by each of us.

Designing a Research Project

Once the empirical hypotheses have been developed, the researcher must design a project in which they can be tested. This is a difficult task, one that frequently causes scholars much trouble. If a research design is faulty, it may be impossible to conclude whether the hypotheses are true or false, and the whole project will have been a waste of time, resources, and effort.

A research design must provide for the collection of all necessary and sufficient data to test the stated hypotheses. The important word here is "test." The researcher must not try to prove a point; rather, the goal is to test its validity. For example, if we want to know what traits generally characterize parents who abuse their children, we would not interview research subjects solely from among parents who have been identified as abusers. This would be a mistake because the traits these subjects have in common might not be significantly different from the traits most people share—hardly a useful finding. In order to prove that the shared traits of the abusing parents are significantly different from those shared by nonabusing parents, it is necessary to design the project to include a group of nonabusing parents for comparison. Such a comparison group is frequently used in research—especially in experiments. (We shall discuss experiments and other approaches to sociological research in greater detail later in this chapter.)

A research design should also guard against the collection of unnecessary information, because this wastes time and money. For example, to understand the personality traits of abusing parents, it is not necessary to interview the parents of every abused child. What is crucial is that enough parents be interviewed to make the study useful. Data collection, an apparently straightforward task, has its own peculiar problems, and specific methods have been devised to address them.

Collecting Data

Beginning researchers assume that once a research project has been designed, collecting the data is a simple matter. Nothing could be further from the truth. Those who have been through data collection subscribe to Murphy's law: everything that can go wrong will go wrong! Subjects forget appointments, interviewers fail to obtain critical information, investigators get mugged, film is somehow overexposed, videotapes are erased, data cards get lost, and so on and on, sometimes seemingly without end.

There are two basic ways sociologists gather data about human social behavior: (1) by observing the way people actually behave and (2) by asking people about their behavior, attitudes, and beliefs. A researcher can use one or both of these methods. Naturally, different methods yield different results. For example, a sociologist interested in voting behavior in presidential elections would have found, by actually observing how individuals vote (method 1), that 60.7 percent of voters in 1972 cast their ballots for Richard Nixon. However, surveys (method 2) conducted in 1973 and again in 1974 yielded different results. In the 1973 survey, conducted shortly after Nixon's inauguration, almost 70 percent of those surveyed said they had voted for the president. In the later survey, taken just after Nixon had resigned in disgrace, fewer than 50 percent of those surveyed claimed to have voted for Nixon. Both surveys produced results that differed from the actual voting behavior—and also from one another. Sociologists would not say that any of these results are wrong, however. Rather, they would propose hypotheses to explain the differences among them, and they might design research projects to test these hypotheses.

One of the most serious problems in data collection is **researcher bias:** the tendency for researchers to select data that support, and to ignore data that seem to go against, their hypotheses. We are not referring here to deliberate cheating, as in the case of Cyril Burt's statements on the genetic basis of intelligence discussed in Box 2.1: "A Social Scientific Hoax." Rather, we are speaking here of human frailty, of the subjective nature of data gathering and how susceptible it is to unintended distortion. Examples of this kind of bias often can be found in the popular media.

researcher bias The tendency for researchers to select data that support their hypothesis and to ignore data that appear to contradict it.

2.1
A Social Scientific Hoax

The history of science is replete with examples of frauds. Some of these were quickly discovered and forgotten, and others have damaged the reputations of individuals or even entire fields of study. But perhaps the hoax that has had the most devastating consequences for the social sciences was the IQ fraud perpetrated by the British psychologist Sir Cyril Burt.

Over a period of 60 years, beginning in 1912, Burt published a great many books and articles "proving" that intelligence is largely inherited. The basis of this so-called proof was his analysis and comparison of some 53 pairs of identical twins who had been orphaned and raised apart.

Though Burt's work was attacked by sociologists, anthropologists, and geneticists, he was defended by his fellow psychologists and in 1946 was knighted for his service to British education. When he died in 1971, at the age of 88, colleagues called him "a born nobleman" and "a man of Renaissance proportions." The *London Times* eulogized him, stating: "For over forty years he had been the leading figure in . . . the application of psychology to education and the development of children, and to the assessment of mental qualities."

In 1969, when Arthur Jensen published an article in the *Harvard Education Review* in which he implied that blacks are innately less intelligent than whites, he acknowledged his great debt to Burt by citing 10 of Burt's studies. It now is known that all 10 studies were fraudulent. Apparently Burt was so convinced that intelligence was determined mainly by a person's genetic endowment and that upper-class Britons were the most generously endowed of all that he simply invented the existence of pairs of twins raised in different environments to prove his point.

Burt's prestige was so great that it was not until five years after his death that accusations of fraud were raised publicly. It was then discovered that no one except Burt's colleague, a Ms. Conway, had ever seen any of the twins who figured in Burt's studies. After an investigation it turned out that Ms. Conway never existed.

Why Burt—a man of undoubted intelligence and ability—spent a lifetime deliberately publishing fraudulent studies is a question to which no one really knows the answer. Whatever the reason, the fraud Burt perpetrated has had an incalculably negative impact on thousands, perhaps even millions, of young children. In Britain Burt's research was used to develop a national education policy that "tracked" youngsters from a very early age and systematically excluded many of them from obtaining the necessary skills that would lead them up the social and economic ladder. In the United States Burt's studies were cited over and over again as a justification for shifting federal funds away from day care and Head Start programs. Many programs were closed down, and thousands of children were deprived of what might have been enriching educational experiences. □

Recently, for instance, a 15-year-old girl wrote a letter to "Ask Beth," a columnist in the *Boston Globe* who answers teenagers' questions on love, sex, drugs, school, and so on:

> Dear Beth:
> I'm 15 and like very much a boy who is 20. He has liked me for three years, but I never told him how I felt until three weeks ago. The only problem is my parents don't like the idea of my going with someone so much older. Should I stay with him or break it up? Remember, I love him a lot.
>
> —Stacy
> (*Boston Globe*, October 3, 1980)

Beth answered by supporting Stacy's parents, noting that it can be hard for a young girl to resist pressures from an older boy. "I'm not saying every 20-year-old wants to sleep with every girl friend," she wrote, "but it is only natural to expect a man of more maturity to desire a more intense relationship than most 15-year-olds do." To drive the point home Beth added, "The fact is, the majority of girls who get pregnant by mistake have boyfriends older than they are." Beth did not produce any statistics to support her statement—though it is, in fact, true. However, her statement is totally irrelevant. Why? Because in our society, almost *all* girls have boyfriends who are older than they are (Conger, 1980). In this case Beth's bias led to a subtle distortion in her use of the facts.

The problem of bias looms especially large in social research, in which scholars often have strong feelings about the issues they are investigating. In studying child abuse, for example, pediatricians and others collecting data on this problem may find it difficult to report obvious child abuse in middle-class families who appear similar in background and status to their own family. Conversely, investigators may be vulnerable to seeing abuse when assessing families that are lower class or of ethnic groups dissimilar to their own (Parke and Collmer, 1975).

Researcher bias often takes the form of a self-fulfilling prophecy. A researcher who is strongly inclined toward one point of view may communicate that attitude through questions and reactions in such a way that the subject fulfills the researcher's expectations. Most often this phenomenon is seen in the classroom where a teacher, treating a child as an intellectually inferior, elicits from that child behavior that conforms to the teacher's view (Rosenthal and Jacobson, 1966). Researchers in sociology can also fall into this trap and pull the subjects in with them. For example, a researcher who is trying to prove an association between poverty and antisocial behavior might question low-income subjects in a way that would indicate a low regard for their social attitudes. The subjects, perceiving the researcher's bias, might react with hostility and thus fulfill the researcher's expectations.

One of the standard means for dealing with research bias is to use **blind investigators,** who do not know whether a specific subject belongs to the group of actual cases being investigated or to a comparison group. For example, in a study on the causes of child abuse, the investigator looking at the children's family background would not be told which children had been abused and which were in the nonabused comparison group. Sometimes **double-blind investigators** are used. They are kept uninformed not only of the kinds of subjects (case subjects or comparison group subjects) they are studying but also of the hypotheses being tested. This eliminates any tendency on their part to find cases that support—or disprove—the research hypothesis.

Sampling

Sampling is a research technique through which investigators study a manageable number of people, called a **sample,** selected from a larger population or group. If the procedures are carried out correctly, the sample will show, in equivalent proportion, the significant variables that characterize the population as a whole. In other words, the sample will be representative of the larger population, and the findings of the research thus will generalize to the larger group. Such a sample is called a **representative sample,** and failure to achieve a representative sample is called **sampling error.** Suppose you wanted to sample the attitudes of the American public on some issue such as military spending or federal aid for abortions. You could not limit your sample to only New Yorkers or Republicans or Catholics or blacks or home owners. These groups do not represent the nation as a whole, and any findings you came up with would contain a sampling error.

How do researchers make sure their samples are representative? The basic technique is to use a **random sample**—to select subjects so that each individual in the population has

blind investigator A researcher who does not know whether a specific subject belongs to the group of actual cases being investigated or to a comparison group. Using a blind investigator helps eliminate researcher bias.

double-blind investigator A researcher who does not know either the kind of subject being investigated or the hypothesis being tested.

sampling A research technique that allows investigators to study a manageable number of people (a sample), selected from a larger population.

sample A manageable number of people selected for study from a larger population.

representative sample A sample or subgroup of a population that is representative of the larger population from which it is drawn. If a sample is representative, the research findings about it are generalizable to the larger group.

sampling error The failure to select a representative sample.

random sample A technique of selecting subjects so that each individual in the population has an equal chance of being chosen. By using random samples, sociologists make sure that the samples are representative of the larger society.

an equal chance of being chosen. For example, if we wanted a random sample of all college students in the United States, we might choose every fifth or tenth or hundredth person for a comprehensive list of all college students registered in this country. Or we might assign each student a number and have a computer pick a sample randomly. However, there is a possibility that simply by chance, a small segment of the total college student population would fail to be represented adequately. This might happen with Native American students, for instance, who make up less than 1 percent of college students in America. For some research purposes this might not matter, but if ethnicity is an important aspect of the research, it would be important to make sure Native American students were included.

The method used to prevent certain groups from being under- or overrepresented in a sample is to choose a **stratified random sample.** With this technique the population being studied is first divided into two or more groups (or strata) such as age, sex, or ethnicity. A simple random sample is then taken within each group. Finally, the subsamples are combined (in proportion to their numbers in the population) to form a total sample. In our example of college students, the researcher would identify all ethnic groups represented among college students in America. Then the researchers would calculate the proportion of the total number of college students represented by each group and draw a random sample separately from each ethnic group. The number chosen from each group should be proportional to its representation in the entire college student population. The sample would still be random, but it would be stratified for ethnicity.

Analyzing Data and Drawing Conclusions

It is not unusual for a sociological research project to result in hundreds of thousands of individual pieces of information. By itself this vast array of data has no particular meaning; research data become meaningful only when they are analyzed. One important device to aid in the analysis of data is the table, which is explained in Box 2.2: "How to Read a Table."

In its most basic sense, **analysis** is the process through which large and complicated collections of scientific data are organized so that comparisons can be made and conclusions drawn. For example, a sociologist might collect many case histories of children who have been abused or mistreated in a wide variety of ways: left unattended for long periods of time, seldom spoken to or played with, not fed adequately, not protected from environmental danger such as lead paint or traffic, beaten repeatedly resulting in bad bruises and broken bones, burned with cigarettes, sexually used by family members, and so on. The analyst must find ways to organize such data into useful categories so that the kinds of relationships that exist between the categories of data can be determined. In this way the hypotheses that are the core of the research can be tested, and new hypotheses can be formulated for further investigation.

Modern sociologists use a wide variety of statistical techniques to analyze their data. Some of these techniques are described in Box 2.3: "Basic Statistical Tools: Mean, Median, and Mode." However, we want to caution against an overreliance on statistical methodology. To say that a finding has statistical significance does not necessarily mean that this finding is important. **Statistical significance** is only a mathematical statement about the probability that some event or relationship is not due to chance alone. It has meaning (and thus importance) only to the extent that it has relevance to the context of the research and to the world as we understand it. For example, a British study found a statistically significant relationship between (1) the presence of emotional depression in mothers of young children, and (2) where they lived in their apartment buildings. The higher the apartment floor was, the greater the incidence of depression was. Alone, this finding is not important because it does not seem to be relevant to anything we know about depression. However, if we know that few of these apartment buildings have elevators, and if we imagine the difficulty of negotiating two, three, or four flights of stairs with one or more youngsters several times a day, we can construct a new hypothesis: the higher up in an apartment building a parent with a young child lives, the less likely the parent is to go outside with the child. And then another hypothesis suggests itself: the more a parent is confined to the apartment with a young child, the greater is the stress of parenthood and hence the likelihood of emotional depression. In this context the research findings acquire meaning as well as statistical significance.

This example also illustrates a very important aspect of scientific research—namely, the analysis of data raises new questions and leads to further investigation.

Scientists usually are careful in drawing conclusions from their research. One of the purposes of drawing conclusions from data compiled in the course of doing research is to be able to apply the information gathered to other, similar situations. Problems thus may develop if there are faults in the research design. For example, the study must show **validity**—that is, the study must actually test what it was intended to test. If you want to say that one event is the cause of another, you must be able to rule out other explanations to show that your research is valid. Suppose you conclude that marijuana use leads to heroin addiction. You must show that it is marijuana use and not some other factor that leads to heroin addiction.

The study must also demonstrate **reliability**—that is, the findings of the study must be repeatable, true not just for the particular conditions of the initial research. To demonstrate reliability we must show that research can be **replicated**—repeated for the purpose of determining whether initial results can be duplicated. Suppose you conclude from a study that whites living in racially integrated housing projects, who have contact with blacks in the project, have more favorable attitudes toward them than do whites living in racially segregated housing projects. If you or other researchers carry out the same study in housing projects in various cities throughout the country and get the same results, then the study is reliable.

Posing New Questions

It is highly unlikely that any single piece of research will provide all the answers to a given question. In fact, good research frequently leads to the discovery of unanticipated information that needs further research in order to be understood. One of the pleasures of research is that ongoing studies keep opening up new perspectives and posing further questions that require originality and creativity in the design of fresh research to answer them. For example, research has shown that strong negative parental feelings directed at young children can cause some children to stop growing, even though they receive more than adequate nutrition (Ferholt et al., 1978). This raises more questions than it answers. Why do negative feelings have a physical effect on some children but not on others? How is parental hatred communicated to a child? How does a child's experience of being hated affect the child emotionally? What are the connections between emotional experience and physiological processes? How is the so-called growth hormone regulated? What other hormones (chemical substances that control bodily processes) are involved in growth? How closely are mind and body interconnected? For raising such questions this research is exciting, even though it is not yet conclusive.

Sharing Results

Research that goes unreported is wasted. Scientific progress is made through the accumulation of research that tests hypotheses and contributes to the ongoing process of bettering our understanding of the world. Therefore, it is usual for agencies that fund research to insist that scientists agree to share their findings.

stratified random sample A statistical technique to make sure that all significant groups in a society are represented in a sample in proportion to their numbers in the larger society.

analysis The process through which scientific data are organized so that comparisons can be made and conclusions drawn.

statistical significance A mathematical statement about the probability that some event or relationship is not due to chance alone.

validity The ability of a research study to test what it was designed to test.

reliability The abillity to repeat the findings of a research study.

replication Repetition of the same research procedure for the purpose of determining whether earlier results can be duplicated.

2.2

How to Read a Table

Statistical tables are used frequently by sociologists both to present the findings of their own research and to study the data of others. We will use the accompanying table to outline the steps to follow in reading and interpreting a table.

1. *Read the title.* The title tells you the subject of the table. This table presents data on life expectancy in various countries for people of both sexes and of different ages.

2. *Check the source.* At the bottom of a table you will find its source. In this case the source is the *United Nations Demographic Yearbook* for 1978. Knowing the source of a table can help you decide whether the information it contains is reliable. It also tells you where to look to find the original data and how recent the information is. In our example the source is both reliable and recent. If the source were the 1958 *Yearbook,* it would be of limited value in telling you about life expectancy in those countries today. Improvements in health care, control of epidemic diseases, or national birth-control programs all are factors that may have altered life expectancy drastically in several countries since 1958. Likewise, consider a table of data about the standard of living of black people in South Africa. If its source were an agency of the South African government (which might be trying to "prove" how well-off blacks are in that country), you might well be skeptical about the reliability of the information in the table.

3. *Look for headnotes.* Many tables contain headnotes directly below the title. These may explain how the data were collected, why certain variables (and not others) were studied, why the data are presented in a particular way, whether some data were collected at different times, and so on. In our table on life expectancy the headnote explains that the numbers in the table refer to the average number of additional years a person can expect to live at a given age.

4. *Read the labels or headings for each row and column.* The labels will tell you exactly what information is contained in the table. It is essential that you understand the labels—both the row headings on the left and the column headings at the top. Here the row headings tell you the names of the countries being compared for life expectancy. The column headings are broken down into two groups: males and females. For each group, life expectancy at several ages is given. Note the units being used in the table. In this case the units are years. Often the figures represent percentages or rates. Many population and crime statistics are given in rates per 100,000 people.

5. *Examine the data.* Suppose you want to find the life expectancy of a 20-year-old man in the United States. First look down the row at the left until you come to "United States." Then look across the various columns under "Males" until you find "20." Reading across you discover that on average, a 20-year-old man in the United States can expect to live another 50.8 years. By contrast, a 20-year-old woman can look forward to another 58.1 years.

6. *Compare the data.* Compare the data in the table both horizontally and vertically. Suppose you want to find in which country males can expect to live longest from birth. Looking down the "Males 0" column we find that males born in Sweden can expect to live longest—72.1 years. Among these ten nations United States males rank fourth be-

Expectation of Life by Age and Sex for Selected Countries

| | Average Future Lifetime in Years at Stated Age | | | | | | | | | | | |
| | Males | | | | | | Females | | | | | |
Country	0	1	10	20	40	60	0	1	10	20	40	60
Burma	40.8	49.8	45.5	36.8	21.1	10.6	43.8	51.6	47.0	38.3	23.7	12.4
Canada	69.3	69.8	61.2	51.7	33.2	17.0	76.4	76.6	67.9	58.2	39.0	21.4
Guatemala	48.3	52.5	51.3	43.2	28.1	14.8	49.7	53.4	52.8	44.6	29.2	14.7
India	41.9	48.4	45.2	36.9	22.1	11.8	40.6	46.0	43.8	35.6	22.4	12.9
Israel	70.3	71.1	62.5	53.1	34.5	17.4	73.9	74.5	65.9	56.1	36.9	19.2
Kenya	46.9	52.6	51.0	43.0	28.3	14.5	51.2	56.6	54.1	45.7	30.3	15.7
Poland	66.8	68.0	59.4	49.8	31.6	15.5	73.8	74.6	66.0	56.2	37.0	19.3
Sweden	72.1	71.9	63.2	53.5	34.7	17.7	77.7	77.3	68.5	58.7	39.4	21.3
Syria	54.5	60.7	56.4	47.4	30.5	15.2	58.7	64.1	59.5	50.5	33.3	17.3
United States	68.7	68.9	60.3	50.8	32.6	16.8	76.5	76.6	67.9	58.1	39.0	21.8

Source: Adapted from *United Nations Demographic Yearbook* (1978).

hind Sweden, Israel, and Canada. A boy born in Burma has the shortest life expectancy—only 40.8 years.

Now suppose you wanted to compare the life expectancy at birth of men versus women. Look down the "Males 0" and "Females 0" columns. We find that in nine of the ten countries in the table women can expect to live longer than men. Only in India is a man's life expectancy (at birth) longer than a woman's.

7. *Draw conclusions.* Draw conclusions about the information in the table. After examining the data in the table, you might conclude that women generally live longer than men do. You might also conclude that a person born in a relatively devel-oped country (Canada, Israel, Poland, Sweden, United States) is likely to live much longer than is someone born in a poorer nation (Burma, Guatemala, India, Kenya, Syria).

8. *Pose new questions.* The conclusions you reach might well lead to new questions that could prompt further research. Why, you might want to know, do women tend to live longer than men? Why do Indian women have shorter life expectancies than Indian men do until age 40, after which, like their sisters in the rest of the world, they can expect to live longer? Why does the gap in life expectancy between the rich and poor nations at birth (24.9 years) narrow by age 1 (19.3 years)? ☐

Scientists generally publish their findings in technical journals. However, an increasing number of popular and semiscientific publications report on research findings. It is especially important that research in sociology and the other social sciences be made available to the public, because much of this research has a bearing on social issues and public policies.

Unfortunately, the general public is not always cautious in interpreting research findings. Special-interest groups, politicians, and others who have a cause to plead are quick to pick up research findings and generalize from them—frequently distorting them beyond recognition. This is especially likely when the research focuses on something of national or emotional concern (see Popular Sociology: "Stripteasers—A Six-Year History of Public Reaction to a Study"). It is therefore important to check out such popular reports by going back to the original research—or at least to discussions of the research by the investigators themselves.

☐ Sociological Research Methods

There are three main methods of research used by sociologists: surveys, participant observation, and experiments. Each has its own advantages and limitations. Therefore, the choice of one or the other of these methods depends on the questions the researcher hopes to answer.

Surveys

A **survey** is a research method in which a population, or a portion thereof, is questioned in order to reveal specific facts about itself. Surveys are used when it is desirable to discover the distribution and interrelations of certain variables among large numbers of people. The largest survey in the United States takes place every 10 years when the government makes its census. In theory, at least, a representative of every family and every unmarried adult responds to a series of questions about his or her circumstances. From the answers it is possible to construct a picture of the social and economic facts that characterize the American public at one point in time. Such a view, which cuts across a population at a given time, is called a **cross-sectional study.** Surveys, by their nature, usually are cross-sectional. If the same population is surveyed two or more times at certain intervals, a comparison of cross-sectional research can give a picture of changes in variables over time. Research that investigates a population over

survey A research method in which a population or a sample is studied in order to reveal specific facts about it. Surveys are used to discover the distribution of certain variables among large numbers of people.

cross-sectional study A view of the social and economic facts that cut across and characterize a population at a given point in time. Surveys, by their nature, usually are cross-sectional.

2.3

Basic Statistical Tools: Mean, Median, and Mode

Sociologists often summarize their data by calculating central tendencies or averages. Actually, there are three different types of averages used by sociologists: the mean, the median, and the mode. Each type is calculated differently, and each can result in a different figure.

Suppose you are studying a group of 10 college students and you find that their verbal SAT scores were as follows:

450	690	280	450	760
540	520	450	430	530

You might want to report the information only in this form. More likely, however, you would want to give some indication of the central tendency of the ten SAT scores.

The mean is what is commonly called the average. To calculate the mean, you add up all the figures and divide by the number of items. In our example the SAT scores add up to 5,100. Dividing by 10 gives a mean of 510.

The median is the figure that falls midway in a series of numbers—there are as many numbers above it as below it. Because we have 10 scores—an even number—in our example, the median is the mean (the average) of the fifth and sixth figures, the two numbers in the middle. To calculate the median, rearrange the data in order from the lowest to highest (or vice versa). In our example you would list the scores as follows: 280, 430, 450, 450, 450, 520, 530, 540, 690, 760. The median is 485—midway between the fifth score (450) and the sixth score (520).

The mode is the number that occurs most often in the data. In our example the mode is 450.

The three types of averages are used for different reasons, and each has its advantages and disadvantages. The mean is most useful when there is a narrow range of figures, as it has the advantage of including all the data. It can be misleading, however, when there are one or two scores much higher or lower than the rest. The median can be useful because it does not allow extreme figures to distort the central tendency. The mode is used when the researcher wants to show which number occurs most often. Its disadvantage is that it does not give any idea of the entire range of data. Sociologists thus often state the central tendency in more than one form in order to present their findings more accurately. □

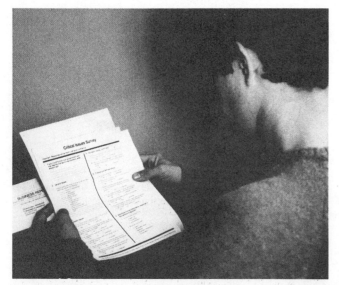

Surveys are used to reveal specific facts about a population.

a period of time is called **longitudinal research.**

To return to the problem of child abuse, most studies thus far have been cross-sectional survey research and have produced one consistent finding: abuse, neglect, and parental deprivation are repeated in families generation after generation (Kempe and Kempe, 1978). This is an important finding because, among other things, it suggests that abuse-prevention programs should be directed at such families before child abuse reappears in the youngest generation.

It is not necessary to survey every member of an entire population. Surveying many thousands of people can be quite expensive and time-consuming, and as we mentioned above, it is possible to choose a representative sample of subjects that will yield a fairly accurate picture of the distribution of variables

POPULAR SOCIOLOGY
Stripteasers—a Six-Year History of Public Reaction to a Study

We have discussed how sociological research can be used (and in some cases abused) by different groups or special interests within a society. Academic studies are often generalized or used selectively by groups or individuals to support certain motives. This frequently results in a misinterpretation and distortion of the facts. Because much of the research in sociology has an effect on public policies, it is essential that the complete reports be made available to the public. The mass media coverage of a study about stripteasers is a classic illustration of how social scientific research can be blown out of proportion and thus misinterpreted by the general public.

In September, 1969, at the Annual Meeting of the American Sociological Association, James K. Skipper, Jr., and Charles McCaghy presented a paper on deviant behavior, "Stripteasers: The Anatomy and Career Contingencies of a Deviant Occupation." Both men had hopes that it would be accepted by the academic community as a modest contribution to the knowledge of deviant behavior and that it would be looked upon favorably enough to become part of the published literature on the subject. Their expectations were more than met.

Although the whole study was reported in a series of published papers, the authors were caught completely unaware by both the academic and the nonacademic interest, curiosity, and controversy their study generated. There are few recorded reports of public reactions to behavioral science research, especially when that research has no explicit public policy implications. Because of that, Skipper wrote a paper, the purpose of which was to present some of the public reaction to his and McCaghy's study in order to better understand the popular culture of the age in which we live. In the pa-

per, from which the material in this box is drawn. Skipper classified into five areas the events and widespread media coverage that occurred as a result of the study.

1. *The sensationalism principle.* If a social scientific study is novel and related to sex, it is likely that its scholarly value may be ignored or forgotten in comparison with aspects of the study that lend themselves to sensationalism. The immediate media coverage focused on two passages in the paper, which evidently were easy to sensationalize, and completely ignored the scientific value of the research. The first passage concerned the physical characteristics of the strippers:

> In terms of body types, the strippers' measurements showed considerable variation. However, compared to the average American woman between the ages of 20 and 30, and even Playboy Playmates of the Month, the strippers were taller, heavier, with large hips, and had extremely well-developed busts, several approaching astronomical proportions.

The second passage that the press highlighted concerned the strippers' relationships with their fathers:

> Although our data are not complete in all cases, there is a clear indication that at least 60 percent of the girls came from broken and unstable homes where they received little attention and affection. A characteristic feature was the absence of the father from the home, or, if he was present, his disintegrating influence on the family relationships.

Headlines on the various stories illustrate the way in which these two passages were sensationalized: "Study Finds Stripper Outpoints Wife" (*Cleveland Plain Dealer*, September 3, 1969), "Profs Discover Strippers Have Big Busts" (*New York Post*, Sep-

tember 3, 1969). "Strippers Lacked Tender Care from Fathers" (*Cleveland Plain Dealer*, September 25, 1971).

Skipper concluded that the principle of sensationalism involves a selective process. The criterion is not the scientific value of academic papers or how other scientists may evaluate them but their human interest and attractiveness to a large audience. In the case of stripteasers it was the novelty of the study and its sexual content that were used by the press to lure the reader's interest. Objective reporting seemed to take a back seat to the sensational value.

2. *The erotic principle.* Public response to the study was as varied as the newspaper headlines reporting it. If a social scientific study is novel and related to sex, it is likely to become a subject of intense curiosity and humor by some individuals and a subject of intense ridicule and scorn by others.

There were many humorous aspects to the erotic interest and curiosity in the study, although they did not seem funny at the time. Several days after the study was presented, the authors received a "Losers of the Day" award from a major midwestern radio station. Columnists around the country poked fun by reporting on dedicated sociologists who were "expanding science's front," "pioneer researchers who laid bare exciting facts," and "front row peeper professors." With tongue in cheek, one man wrote that it must have been exhaustive research discovering strippers are "big-busted broads." Another columnist stated that if he had known you could get paid for such work and make headlines to boot, he would have changed his occupation long ago. Morrie Ryskind, a Pulitzer Prize-winning dramatist, pointed out in his column that although the authors stated they investigated the background characteristics of strippers, they must have also been interested in the strippers' foregrounds.

3. *The Evergreen principle.* If there is nothing else to talk or write about, evergreen material may be utilized and it will be just as valuable as the day it was discovered. When asked when the report on the stripteaser study would appear, a local Cleveland television reporter replied, "I don't know. With this type of material it really doesn't matter—today, tomorrow, next week, next month, next year—it is Evergreen, man, Evergreen!" And thus the Evergreen principle. If a social scientific study is novel and related to sex, its newsworthiness to the mass media is not likely to be tied to any time-space framework, medium, or form of usage.

On a time basis under the category of "reporting" news, most of the coverage took place within three days of the study's presentation. In terms of space, it was covered throughout North America, parts of Latin America, Europe, and perhaps elsewhere, primarily through newspaper accounts. The extent of initial broadcast media coverage is not known, but most reports that appeared were in the form of a final, 15-second, humorous, human interest story rather than straight reporting.

The beauty of evergreen material to those in the mass media is that it does not have to be used im-

mediately. Newspaper and magazine columnists wrote about the study one to three years after it was originally presented and generally for their own purposes, to poke fun at and make light of the results.

4. *The instant expert and expert-by-association principle.* If a social scientific study investigates a previously unexplored subject, the researchers are likely to be considered instant experts in both that area and, by some means of association, in related or semirelated areas of study.

Somewhat predictably the authors received many letters asking for advice on sexual problems, including some from current and former strippers. A medical journal even asked them to answer a reader's question about whether nude dancers are sexually aroused by their own performance. Quite unexpectedly, however, the authors were asked to serve as sex counselors for college students and as advisers to a campus lesbian group. These are just a few examples of the public reaction that occurred shortly after the study was reported. Whether or not intentionally, the authors were portrayed by the mass media as experts on stripteasers and a host of other related areas. To some extent this attitude still exists today.

5. *The conversation piece principle.* Finally, if a social scientific study is novel and concerns sex, it is likely to have appeal to a variety of individuals and may be used as a topic of conversation in a variety of social

situations. Since the authors first presented their paper, they have met and talked with hundreds of sociologists at conventions, conferences, college campuses, and cocktail parties, taught numerous sociology classes, and presented guest lectures and seminars in medical sociology to different groups of behavioral scientists and members of the health professions. Regardless of the circumstances, almost inevitably they were faced with the same request: "Now tell us about stripteasers."

What began as a small contribution to sociological knowledge in the area of deviant behavior ended up producing some major and quite unanticipated consequences as a result of the media's involvement. The generalizations presented here may make these consequences more understandable, if not more predictable, and all convey a part of the popular culture in which we live. At the same time, the fact that stripteasers as a topic of information draw such wide attention in almost any group is also a commentary on present-day American culture.

Source: Excerpted from James K. Skipper, Jr., "Stripteasers: A Six-Year History of Public Reaction to a Study." In Leonard Cargan and Jeanne H. Ballantine (eds.), *Sociological Footprints: Introductory Readings in Sociology* (Boston: Houghton Mifflin, 1979), pp. 12–18. By permission of James K. Skipper, Jr.

among a population as a whole. However, it is crucial that a sample be chosen with care. In 1936, for instance, *Literary Digest* magazine wanted to predict the outcome of the United States' presidential election. Using telephone directories and automobile registration lists to recruit subjects, its pollsters gathered some two million responses from people all across the nation and found the Republican candidate Alfred E. Landon held a large lead over

the Democratic candidate. Based on this poll the *Digest* confidently predicted Landon's victory. Who was Alfred E. Landon? He was the candidate who was buried in the landslide vote for Franklin D. Roosevelt.

However, the outcome of the election was not entirely a surprise. A young pollster by the name of George Gallup forecast the results accurately. He realized that although the *Literary Digest's* sample was large, it was not representative of the nation's population because it contained a major sampling error. In the Depression years, only the well-to-do could afford telephones and automobiles, and the well-to-do were likely to vote for a Republican. The majority of Americans, however, supported the New Deal policies proposed by the Democrats. Gallup's sample was much smaller but far more representative of the American public than that of the *Literary Digest,* which never really recovered after its disastrous adventure in journalistic sociology.

As we have already stated, the *Literary Digest's* mistake was one of sampling error. In 1980 Richard Link, writing in *Public Opinion,* showed how a little data analysis could have saved the *Literary Digest* a great deal of embarrassment in spite of the error in sampling. The October 31, 1936, issue of the magazine reported both the 1936 poll results and how the same respondents voted in 1932. By using the actual 1932 vote, the editors of the *Digest* could have adjusted the 1936 data and "awarded" the electoral votes of each state to the candidate with the higher adjusted vote.

Link used California as an example. In 1932 the *Digest* found that 46.8 percent of California voters planned to vote Democratic. In fact, the actual California vote that year was 61 percent Democratic—14.2 percent higher than the poll predicted. The 1936 *Literary Digest* poll found that 46.3 percent of Californians planned to vote Democratic. By using the 1932 results to adjust the 1936 data, the *Digest* could have predicted that the Democratic vote would be over 60 percent. This would have moved California into the Democratic column—where, in fact, California wound up in the general election.

Using this method, a total of 19 states would have been moved from the Republican to the Democratic side of the ledger, whereas no states would have moved the other way. The result would have been accurate prediction by the *Literary Digest* of Roosevelt's landslide victory.

A problem that often arises with surveys of people's attitudes is that they may miss important feelings that lie behind the attitudes. For example, columnist Abigail Van Buren polled her readers on their reaction to a letter

Harry Truman enjoying the 1948 election headline that erroneously announced his defeat. Contrary to public opinion polls, Truman defeated Dewey by 114 electoral votes.

signed by "Tired in Lincoln, Nebraska" they said, "At age 50 and after 30 years of marriage, I would like to forget about sex altogether." Out of a total of 227,606 responses, 114,005 agreed with "Tired," and 113,601 disagreed (*Los Angeles Times,* August 23, 1980).

Although those statistics are interesting, they do not tell us nearly as much about people's attitudes as do some of the letters that accompanied the "votes." A 53-year-old woman wrote, "I'm also tired. Tired of living with a slob. I have to nag my husband to shower and use a deodorant. I don't think he knows where his toothbrush is. So if he can live without a toothbrush, I can live without sex."

Because survey research usually deals with large numbers of subjects in a relatively short time, investigators are not able to capture the full richness of feelings, attitudes, and motives underlying people's responses. They usually gather this kind of information through interviewing. An **interview** consists of a con-

longitudinal research A research technique in which a population is studied at several intervals over a relatively long period of time.

interview A conversational research technique in which all questions are carefully worked out in order to obtain specific information.

versation between two (or occasionally more) individuals in which one party attempts to gain information from the other(s) by asking a series of questions. Sociologists use interviews for three purposes: (1) to explore a subject in order to identify important variables and relationships and to develop hypotheses, (2) as a research tool to obtain core data, and (3) as a supplementary research tool to follow up unexpected findings or to pursue certain issues in greater depth (Kerlinger, 1973).

It would, of course, be ideal to gather exactly the same kinds of information from each research subject. One way researchers attempt to achieve this is through interviews in which all questions are carefully worked out to get at precisely the information that is wanted. Sometimes subjects also are forced to choose from among a limited number of responses to the questions (as in multiple-choice tests). This process results in very uniform data that are easily subjected to statistical analysis.

A research interview entirely predetermined by a questionnaire (or so-called interview schedule) that is followed rigidly is called a **structured interview.** Structured interviews tend to produce uniform or replicable data that can be elicited time after time by different interviewers. The use of this method, however, may also allow useful information to "slip into the cracks" between the predetermined questions. For example, a questionnaire being administered to parents who have abused their children might ask many questions about family background, child-rearing practices, and so on. Only late in the study might it occur to investigators that only one child may be abused in a family with several children and that it would be useful to know what variables distinguish that child from the others in the family. Were all the children wanted and planned? Did the parents feel differently after the birth of the abused child than they felt after the birth of the others? Which child in the sequence of children came to be abused? Were there unusual circumstances in the family occurring around the birth of the abused child (for instance, was the main breadwinner unemployed)? If such questions were not built into the questionnaire from the beginning, it is impossible to recover this "lost" information later in the process when its importance may become apparent.

One technique that can prevent this kind of information loss is the **semistructured,** or **open-ended, interview,** in which the investigator asks a list of questions but is free to vary them or even to make up new questions on topics that take on importance in the course of the interview. This means that each interview will cover those topics important to the research project but, in addition, will yield additional data that are somewhat different for each subject. Analyzing such diverse and complex data is difficult, but the results are often rewarding.

Interviewing is a complex, time-consuming art. One way to get around interviewing is to distribute questionnaires directly to the subjects and ask them to fill them in and return them. This is the way our government conducts much of its census. It is perhaps the least expensive way of doing social research, but it is often difficult to assess the quality of data obtained in this manner. For example, people may not answer honestly or seriously for a variety of reasons: they may not understand the questions, they may fear the information will be used against them, and so on. But even data gained from personal interviews may be unreliable. The authors know of one study in which student-interviewers were embarrassed to ask subjects preassigned questions on sexual habits. So they left these questions out of the interviews and filled them in themselves afterward. In another study, follow-up research found that the subjects had consistently lied to the interviewers.

Participant Observation

Participant observation requires that researchers enter into a group's activities and also observe the group members at the same time. Unlike the usual practice in survey research, participant observers do not take a sample of the group they are studying. Rather, they attempt to get to know all the members of the group personally to whatever degree this is possible. This research method generally is used to study relatively small groups over an extended period of time. The intention is to obtain a detailed portrait of the way of life of the group, to observe individual and group behavior, and to interview selected informants. Much more than does survey research, participant observation depends for its success on the nature of the relationship that develops between the researchers and research subjects. The closer and more trusting the relationship is, the more information will be revealed to the researcher—especially the kinds of personal information that often are crucial if the research is to be successful.

One of the first and still most famous studies employing the technique of participant observation was a study of Cornerville, a lower-class Italian neighborhood in Boston. William Foote Whyte moved into the neighborhood and lived there for three years with an Italian family. He published his results in a book called *Street Corner Society* (1943). All the information for the book came from his field notes, which described the behavior and attitudes of the people whom he came to know by living with them for an extended period of time and participating in their day-to-day activities. The book primarily focuses on the behavior and lifestyle of two groups of young men with whom Whyte became friendly—the "corner boys" and the "college boys." Several years after Whyte's study, Herbert Gans conducted a participant observation study, published as *The Urban Villagers* (1962), of another Italian neighborhood in Boston. The picture Gans drew of the West End was broader than Whyte's study of Cornerville. Gans included descriptions of the family, work experience, education, medical care, relationships with social workers, and other aspects of life in the West End. Although he covered a wider range of activities than Whyte, his observations were not as detailed.

On rare occasions, participant observers hide their identities while doing research. They join groups under false pretenses as did Leon Festinger and his students when they studied a religious group preaching the end of the world and the arrival of flying saucers to save the righteous (Festinger, Riecken, and Schacter, 1956). However, most sociologists consider this to be unethical. It is better for participant observers to be honest about their intentions and work together with their subjects to create a situation that is satisfactory to all concerned. By declaring their positions at the outset, sociologists can then ask appropriate questions, take notes, and carry out research tasks without fearing the risk of detection.

Participant observation has a highly subjective aspect. In fact, some scholars reject it because different researchers often produce different results. However, this method has the virtue of revealing the social life of a group in far more depth and detail than would a survey or use of interviews alone. The participant observer who is able to establish good rapport with subjects is likely to uncover information that would never be revealed to a survey taker. It is important to keep in mind, however, that participant observers are in a difficult role. They are constantly torn between the need to become trusted and, therefore, also emotionally involved participants in the group's life, and the need to remain a somewhat detached observer striving for scientific objectivity.

Experiments

The most precise research method available to sociologists is the controlled **experiment.** In a controlled experiment, inside or outside a laboratory, it is possible to make observations while recording information in detail.

structured interview A research interview determined entirely in advance and followed rigidly. This type of interview produces replicable data.

semistructured (open-ended) interview A research interview in which the investigator asks a list of questions but is free to vary them or make up new ones that become important during the course of the interview. This technique can obtain information that might be missed in a structured interview, but analyzing such interviews can be difficult.

participant observation A research technique in which the investigators enter into a group's activities while, at the same time, they study the group's behavior. This method usually is used to study a small group over a relatively long period of time.

experiment A research technique in which it is possible to have greater control over all the variables of the study. Laboratory experiments are appropriate for studying interaction in small groups, but most of the issues of interest to sociologists cannot be studied in the laboratory.

Under these circumstances, it is possible to have more control over the variables of the study.

Because of their precision, experiments are an attractive means of doing research. Many researchers have used experiments to study patterns of interaction in small groups under different conditions such as stress, fatigue, limited access to information, and pre-structured channels of communication among group members. For example, in order to study the effects of group pressure on an individual's judgment, Solomon Asch (1951) chose to use a controlled experiment. His subjects were shown a pair of white cards. On one card was a single black vertical line. On the other card were three black vertical lines of different lengths. The subject's task was to judge which of the three lines exactly matched the standard line on the other card. It was an easy task because two of the lines were considerably longer or shorter than the standard line. When the subjects made their judgments alone without group pressure, they almost never made an error. But when the subjects were placed in a group made up of Asch's associates, who were given the same task and instructed to make an incorrect choice purposely, many subjects conformed to group pressure even when the choice made by the group was obviously wrong. By controlling the

experiment through the use of associates, Asch was able to study the effects of group pressure on the individual. This could not have been done as easily outside a controlled situation because there would have been no way of setting up the correct situation.

Although experimentation is appropriate for small-group research, most of the issues that interest sociologists cannot be investigated in totally controlled situations. Social events do not lend themselves easily to study in controlled experiments because many social events cannot be controlled. For these reasons experiments remain the least-used research method in sociology. However, surveys and participant observation, the most frequently used methods, often are vulnerable to researchers' values, attitudes, and experiences—a problem of continuing concern to sociologists.

☐ Objectivity and Ethics in Sociological Research

Max Weber believed that the social scientist should describe and explain what is rather than prescribe what should be. His goal was a value-free approach to sociology. More and more sociologists today, however, are admitting that completely value-free research may not be possible.

Objectivity

Sociology, like any other science, is molded by factors that impose values on research. Gunnar Myrdal (1969) lists three such influential factors: (1) the scientific tradition within which the scientist has been educated, (2) the cultural, social, economic, and political environment within which the scientist is trained and engages in research, and (3) the scientist's own temperament, inclinations, interests, concerns, and experiences. These factors are especially strong in sociological research because the researcher usually is part of the society being studied.

Does this mean that all science—and sociology in particular—is hopelessly subjective? Is objectivity in sociological research an impossible goal? There are no simple answers to these questions. The best sociologists can do is to strive to become aware of the ways in

Margaret Mead conducted participant observation research in a variety of settings. Here she is with a member of the Manus tribe of the Admiralty Islands.

which these factors influence them and to make such biases explicit when sharing the results of their research. We think of this as disciplined, or "objective," subjectivity, and it is a reasonable goal for sociological research. Another problem of bias in sociological research relates to the people being studied rather than to the researcher themselves. The mere presence of investigators or researchers may distort the situation and produce unusual reactions from the people being studied by making them feel special because they were selected to be studied. When subjects feel special or privileged, they may behave in different ways than they would under normal circumstances, which would lead to biased results (see Focus on Research: "The 'Hawthorne Effect' ").

Ethical Issues

In 1919 Franz Boas, the father of American anthropology, incurred the anger of the United States government by publicly denouncing spying done under the guise of social research. Boas's criticism did not result in any changes, however. During the intervening years social scientists have continued to engage in research projects that—with or without their knowledge—are used for political purposes by governments. Project Camelot, organized in 1964, is an example of government-controlled research that backfired on its planners.

The aim of that project, as described by the United States Army, was "to devise procedures for assessing the potential for internal war within national societies." It sought to "predict and influence politically significant aspects of social change in . . . Latin American countries" and "to identify . . . actions which a government might take to relieve conditions which are assessed as giving rise to a potential for internal war." In plain English, the army wanted to know how to predict revolutions in Latin America and how to nip them in the bud.

The complete story of Project Camelot has been detailed by Irving Louis Horowitz in *The Rise and Fall of Project Camelot* (1976). It started with a budget of some $6 million and the army's recruitment of some top social scientists in the United States. According to Horowitz,

these participants saw themselves as "reformers" with an opportunity to influence government policy, to help eradicate poverty, and to "educate" the army. None actually believed, however, that the army would act on their policy recommendations. Enticed by the lure of almost limitless funds, the social scientists simply ignored the ethical issue of how their research would be used.

Project Camelot never really got off the ground. News of the project and the source of its funding were leaked to newspapers in Chile, and a loud hue and cry erupted immediately throughout South America. Both the State Department and Congress, unwilling to risk the nation's already strained relations with our neighbors to the south, pressured the army to cancel the project. Only a year after it was conceived, Project Camelot was aborted.

The issue of ethics in social research is not confined to such spectacular cases. All research projects raise fundamental questions. In whose interest is the research? Who will benefit from it? How might people be hurt? To what degree do subjects have the right to be told about the research design, its purposes, and possible applications? Who should have access to and control over research data after a study is completed—the agency that funded the study, the scientists, the subjects? Should research subjects have the right to participate in the planning of projects? Is it ethical to manipulate people without their knowledge in order to control research variables? To what degree do researchers owe it to their subject not to invade their privacy and to keep secret (and, therefore, not report anywhere) things that were told them in strict confidence? What obligations do researchers have to the society in which they are working? What commitments do researchers have to supporting or subverting a political order? Should researchers report to legal authorities any illegal behavior discovered in the course of their investigations? Is it ethical to expose subjects to such risk by asking them to participate in a study?

In the 1960s the federal government began to prescribe regulations for "the protection of human subjects." These regulations force scientists to think about one central is-

FOCUS ON RESEARCH
The "Hawthorne Effect"

In the process of conducting research on the effect of lighting and other environmental factors on the morale of workers in a midwestern plant, the researchers ended up with what is now a classic study of research itself. The reactions of the members of the group being studied clearly demonstrated one of the difficulties that may be encountered in sociological research—changes in the behavior of research subjects as a result of their knowledge that they are being studied.

It all began quite innocently. In the mid-1920s officials of the Western Electric Company in Hawthorne, Illinois, wanted to know whether improving the lighting on their assembly lines would raise worker productivity. Sure enough, work output increased when brighter lighting was provided. But then the output continued to increase, even when the lights were dimmed again! The puzzled officials decided to consult some experts, and they called in a team of social scientists.

The researchers designed a carefully worked out study, selecting six experienced female workers from the Western Electric production line and placing them in a separate room where their work could be observed in detail. Then they began to change working conditions by manipulating the experimental variables: lighting and temperature were increased and decreased, the length and number of work and rest periods were varied, the arrangement of tasks was changed around, even holidays and pay were altered. Meanwhile, careful records were kept of the women's work output and their morale. After several years the researchers were puzzled. The worker's morale and productivity had risen steadily and independently of changes in their work conditions whether good or bad. After every manipulation of a variable, the productivity went up somewhat but then settled back into the more stable, rising curve of regular increase.

The researchers finally discovered what had caused these results. First, they had artificially created a small group that was more homogeneous with regard to sex, age, and education than was the production line as a whole. Second, two of the women had already been friends when the group was started, and it was they who selected the other women to form the group. This contributed to the creation of a special group whose members were more likely to develop feelings of friendship and intimacy with each other than would a work group that developed "naturally" on the assembly line.

Most importantly, however, the very act of choosing the women and placing them in a separate room set them off from the other workers and made them feel special. The researchers concluded that as a result of these factors the women not only became motivated to perform well in order to reflect credit on their group but also were motivated to cooperate with the company management, who treated them so specially, in meeting their goals.

Source: Fritz J. Roethlisberger and William J. Dickson, *Management and the Worker* (Cambridge, Mass.: Harvard University Press, 1939). ☐

---

sue: how to judge and balance the intellectual and societal benefits of scientific research against the actual or possible physical and emotional costs paid by the people who are being studied. This issue arises in at least three types of situations.

The first situation concerns the degree of permissible risk, pain, or harm. Suppose a study that temporarily induces severe emotional distress promises significant benefits. The researcher may justify the study. However, we may wonder whether the benefits will be realized or whether they justify the potential dangers to the subjects, even if they are volunteers who know what to expect and when all possible protective measures have been taken.

A second dilemma is the extent to which subjects should be deceived in a study. It is now necessary for researchers to obtain, in writing, the "informed consent" of the people they study. Questions still arise, however, about whether the subjects were informed about the true nature of the study and whether, once informed, they could freely decline to participate (for a further discussion of deceiving research participants, see Case Study: "Is It Ethical to Lie to Your Research Subjects?").

A third problem in research studies concerns the disclosure of confidential or personally harmful information. Is the researcher entitled to delve into people's personal lives? What if the researcher uncovers some information that should be brought to the attention of the authorities? Should confidential information be included in a published study (Gans, 1979)?

Every sociologist must grapple with these

CASE STUDY
Is It Ethical to Lie to Your Research Subjects?

The ideal in the relationship between scientist and research participant is that of openness and honesty. Deliberate lying in the interest of manipulating the participant's perceptions and actions goes directly against this ideal. Yet often the choice appears to be between carrying out such deception and abandoning the research. The following excerpt presents three of the more common situations in which deception may be employed.

Deception to conceal the true purpose of the research. In some research situations the sociologists may believe that a description of their hypothesis will distort the research participants' behavior. An example comes from a study of the effects of the expectations by teachers on gains in IQ of children in their classes. Twenty percent of the children in each of 18 classrooms were identified as having scored high on a test designed to predict academic "blooming" or intellectual gain. This was false; these children had been selected at random. Results showed the predicted bloomers increasing in IQ significantly more than equally able comparison children. Clearly, such a study with its sweeping implications for education would have been impossible had the teachers not been deceived.

Deception to conceal the true function of the research participants' actions. Many studies have been carried out with the general aim of discovering whether subjects convince themselves in the process of giving arguments for a position they do not believe in or extolling the virtues of a product that they know is of little value. Considerable evidence is available that this happens, but there is much disagreement as to why. In one of the experiments attempting to solve this puzzle, the investigators succeeded in getting a group of college students to believe that they were thinking up arguments in favor of a program they opposed, namely, to send other college students to the Soviet Union for four years in order to study the Soviet system of government and the history of communism. The researchers accomplished this by representing themselves as staff members of the U.S. State Department (or, alternately, the Soviet Embassy) who needed the arguments for a pamphlet. Their purpose in doing this was to direct the students' attention away from the effect of this activity on their own opinions.

Deceptions similar to the preceding are regularly practiced by social scientists in order to engage research participants in actions counter to their opinions. Investigators have devised various misleading reasons for engaging them on the production of oral or written counterattitudinal arguments, such as participation in debates in which they represent the side opposed to their own position.

Other deceptions to conceal the true function of the participant's actions take the form of announcing that the participant is interacting with one other person—usually a peer—when in fact the "other person" is the experimenter or a confederate of the experimenter or even a computer! The purpose of such deception is to present the research participant with a *standardized experience* and *one that can be varied in a controlled manner along a discussion being studied.*

Deception to conceal the experiences the research participant will have. In many studies research participants cannot be told in advance about the critical experiences they are to have. Instead they must be led to encounter this experience as a natural unplanned development. One example comes from an experiment in which the research participants were to be induced to lie to a second person. It was hypothesized that people who received a large bribe to lie would feel less need to reduce the dissonance between their beliefs and their public "lie" than would those who lied for a trivial bribe. The latter presumably would be under more pressure to reconcile their own beliefs with the untruthful account they gave to a second person. Since telling the participants what was in store for them would have completely changed the nature of their experience in the experiment, the investigator decided to recruit persons instead for a study of "measures of performance."

With few, if any, exceptions, social scientists regard deception of research participants as a questionable practice to be avoided if at all possible. It diminishes the respect due to others and violates the expectations of mutual trust upon which organized society is based. When the deceiver is a respected scientist, it may have the undesirable effect of modeling deceit as an acceptable practice. Conceivably, it may contribute to the growing climate of cynicism and mistrust bred by widespread use of deception by important public figures. Obviously planned deception of research subjects presents the sociologist with a serious ethical dilemma.

Source: Louise H. Kidder, *Research Methods in Social Relations,* 4th ed. (New York: Holt, Rinehart and Winston, 1981), pp. 384–385 (references omitted). ☐

questions and find answers that apply to particular situations. However, two general points are worth noting. The first is that social research rarely benefits the research subjects directly. Benefits to subjects tend to be indirect and delayed by many years—as when new government policies are developed to correct problems discovered by researchers. Second, most subjects of sociological research belong to groups with little or no power. It is hardly an accident that poor people are the most studied, rich people the least. Therefore, research subjects typically have little control over how research findings are used, even though such applications may affect them greatly. This means that sociologists must accept responsibility for the fact that they have recruited research subjects who may be made vulnerable as a result of their cooperation. It is important that researchers establish safeguards limiting the use of their findings, protecting the anonymity of their data, and honoring all commitments to confidentiality made in the course of their research.

Nevertheless, it is useful for human beings to seek to understand themselves and the social world in which they live. Sociology has a great contribution to make to this endeavor, both in promoting understanding for its own sake and in providing social planners with scientific information with which well-founded decisions can be made and sound plans for future development adopted. However, sociologists must also shoulder the burden of self-reflection—of seeking to understand the role they play in contemporary social processes and at the same time of assessing how these social processes affect their findings (Gouldner, 1970).

☐ Summary

To attain the goals of science—describing things or events in accurate detail and proposing and testing general principles that explain these things and events—scientists usually begin by asking questions. Empirical questions are ones that can be answered by observation and analysis of the world as it is known. Such questions are often asked in order to test hypotheses—statements about relationships among things or events—which are useful only if their terms are defined operationally.

Before beginning a project the researcher must first try to find out as much as possible about the work that has already been done on the subject. The next step is to choose a perspective and develop a hypothesis.

In developing a hypothesis the researcher should keep in mind the difference between a statement of causality and a statement of association: an event may be caused by another event, or it may merely be related to another event. Hypotheses often propose a relationship between a dependent variable and an independent variable. A dependent variable changes in response to changes in the independent variable, and an independent variable changes for reasons that have nothing to do with the dependent variable. Once the hypotheses have been developed, the researcher designs a project in which they can be tested.

When researchers collect data, they must be on the alert for any distortions that may arise from researcher bias or sampling error. The first problem is sometimes avoided by the use of blind investigators, the second by the use of a representative sample. A sampling error can occasionally be overcome by weighting the results of a survey. Researchers can ensure a representative sample through the technique of choosing a random sample. A further refinement of the technique is choosing a stratified random sample.

After the data have been collected, the researcher analyzes the many pieces of information and then determines what conclusions can be drawn. It is important to make clear whether research findings are generalizable—that is, applicable to the wider society because the research population adequately reflects the characteristics of the wider society.

There are three research methods used by sociologists: surveys, participant observation, and experiments. A survey is a research method in which a population is studied in order to reveal specific facts about it. The survey can be conducted through the use of questionnaires or interviews. An interview can be structured or semistructured (open-ended).

Participant observation requires that researchers enter into a group's activities and observe the behavior of the group's members. Although some participant observers conceal their identities while doing research, most sociologists argue that this tactic is unethical.

An experiment is carried out in a controlled situation that permits close observation through the use of videotape or other recording instruments. Although laboratory experiments are an attractive means of doing research, sociologists seldom use them because most of the issues that interest sociologists cannot be investigated within the confines of a laboratory.

Although sociologists strive for objectivity in their research, a completely value-free approach may be impossible; however, it is a goal toward which all social scientists strive. All scientists bring to bear on their work their cultural, social, economic, political, and educational backgrounds as well as their interests, concerns, and personalities.

Of major concern to social scientists is the question of ethics in research. In whose interest is the research? Who will benefit from it? Will anyone be hurt? While struggling to answer these questions, researchers must also keep in mind that social research rarely benefits the subjects directly and that most subjects of sociological research belong to groups with little or no power. These conditions place an added responsibility on researchers to protect their subjects.

☐ For Further Reading

BABBIE, EARL R. *The Practice of Social Research,* 3rd ed. Belmont, Calif.: Wadsworth, 1983. A readable text that presents the basic logic and ideal techniques of sociological inquiry. All of this is presented in the context of research realities, showing the compromises that have to be made.

DENZIN, NORMAN K. *The Research Act: A Theoretical Introduction to Sociological Methods.* Hawthorne, N.Y.: Aldine, 1978. The various sociological research methods are presented with a particular emphasis on nonstatistical approaches such as participant observation.

GREER, SCOTT A. *The Logic of Social Inquiry.* Chicago: Aldine, 1962. A discussion of the basic assumptions underlying the field of sociology and its major research methods. Greer explores the issue of objectivity in sociological research.

HOROWITZ, IRVING LOUIS. *Constructing Theory.* New York: Praeger, 1979. An examination of the relationship between social policy and social research. The book uses actual case studies as examples, including Project Camelot.

HUFF, DARRELL. *How to Lie with Statistics.* New York: Norton, 1954. An entertaining as well as instructive book. Huff explains some of the many ways in which statistics can be used to mislead or deceive.

KATZER, JEFFREY, KENNETH H. COOK, and WAYNE W. COUCH. *Evaluating Information: A Guide for Users of Social Science Research,* 2d ed. Reading, Mass.: Addison-Wesley, 1982. A text which guides the reader through the use and evaluation of research results.

KUHN, THOMAS S. *The Structure of Scientific Revolutions,* 2d ed. Chicago: University of Chicago Press, 1966. In this important work Kuhn explains how scientific research methods and concepts are developed, how knowledge accumulates under a particular approach, and how, ultimately, concepts and perspectives are replaced.

LABOVITZ, SANFORD, and ROBERT HAGEDORN. *Introduction to Social Research,* 2d ed. New York: McGraw-Hill, 1975. A brief, concise introduction to the major research methods of social science.

MYRDAL, GUNNAR. *Objectivity in Social Research.* New York: Pantheon, 1969. A short and personal reflection on the possibility and challenge of achieving objectivity in social research by the Swedish author of one of the classic studies of race relations in the United States—An American Dilemma

SJOBERG, GIDEON (ed.). *Ethics, Politics and Social Research.* Cambridge, Mass.: Schenkman, 1967. An excellent collection of case studies dealing with ethical issues in social research.

The Individual in Society

■ ■ ■ ■ ■ ■ ■ ■

Part Two

3

Culture

In 1830 the British exploring vessel *Beagle* reached Tierra del Fuego, at the southern tip of South America. The crew of the *Beagle* represented the most highly developed industrial society of the time, whereas the Fuegian Indians were members of one of the simplest New World societies. The captain of the *Beagle* thus decided to take back with him four Fuegian Indians, in the hope of educating them and eventually returning them to their community, so that they could introduce "civilized cultural" ways.

The four were reduced to three after one contracted smallpox. These three included two men, Jemmy and York, and one woman, Fuegia Basket. The three spent one year with a minister near London who taught them the English language and culture. They were even granted an audience with King William IV, who gave them a variety of gifts representative of the industrial age. At the end of 1831 the *Beagle* sailed back to South America carrying the three Anglicized Fuegian Indians and Charles Darwin. Darwin was very impressed with the experiment, which seemed to have supplanted one set of cultural ways with another.

Once they reached Tierra del Fuego, Jemmy, York, and Fuegia Basket were dropped off. York was met by his mother and several brothers. Darwin noted,

> The meeting was less interesting than that between a horse, turned out into a field, when he joins an old companion. There was no demonstration of affection; they simply stared for a short time at each other; and the mother immediately went to look after her canoe.

Darwin and the crew then departed, expecting the cultural transformation of the community to begin under the leadership of the three Fuegian Indians.

A year later Darwin and the crew of the *Beagle* again returned to the area. Soon a canoe paddled by Jemmy approached. Darwin had been enormously impressed by Jemmy's Anglicized manner acquired during his year in England. However, Darwin now noted that Jemmy was

> . . . a thin haggard savage, with long disordered hair, and naked, except a bit of blanket around his waist. We did not recognize him till he was close to us; . . . We had left him plump, fat, clean, and well dressed;—I never saw so complete and grievous a change.

Over the years further information about the three showed that the experiment in cultural change had failed. Jemmy eventually instigated the massacre of six missionaries who had come to the area; York was murdered after he killed another man; and Fuegia Basket returned to her previous cultural ways (Farb, 1978).

The failure of this experiment demonstrates to us how deeply ingrained the cultural customs and beliefs are that have been transmitted to us since birth as members of a society.

☐ The Concept of Culture

In the nineteenth century, anthropologists, inspired by Darwin's work on evolution, began to describe the complex rules of behavior, linguistic structures, and other aspects of the lives of primitive peoples. Old assumptions that these peoples were living a life in pure nature, or as "noble savages" were discarded. It was recognized that all human societies had complex ways of life, which differed greatly from one society to another. These ways came to be referred to as *culture*, and in 1871 Edward Tylor gave us the first definition of the concept that to this day remains one of the most widely quoted. Culture, he noted, "is that complex whole which includes knowledge, belief, art, law, morals, custom, and other capabilities and habits acquired by man as a member of society" (Tylor, 1958). Robert Bierstadt then simplified Tylor's definition by stating, "Culture is the complex whole that consists of all the ways we think and do and everything we have as members of society" (Bierstadt, 1974).

Most definitions of culture emphasize certain features. Namely, culture is shared; it is acquired, not inborn; the elements make up a complex whole; and it is transmitted from one generation to the next (Sagarin, 1978).

We will define **culture** as all that human beings learn to do, to use, to produce, to know, and to believe as they grow to maturity and

Cultural diversity is seen in these two vastly different modes of transportation found in Egypt.

live out their lives in the social groups to which they belong. Culture is basically a blueprint for living in a particular society. In common speech, people often refer to a "cultured person" as someone with an interest in the arts, literature, or music, suggesting that the individual has a highly developed sense of style or aesthetic appreciation of the "finer things." To sociologists, however, every human being is "cultured." All human beings participate in a culture, whether they are Harvard educated and upper class, or illiterate and living in a primitive society. Culture is crucial to human existence.

When sociologists speak of culture, they are referring to the general phenomenon that is a characteristic of all human groups. However, when they refer to *a* culture, they are pointing to the specific culture of a particular group. In other words, all human groups have a culture, but it often varies considerably from one group to the next. Take the concept of time, which we accept as entirely natural. To Westerners, time "marches on" steadily and predictably, with past, present, and future divided into units of precise duration (minutes, hours, days, months, years, and so on). In the

culture of the Sioux Indians, however, the concept of time simply does not exist apart from ongoing events: nothing can be early or late—things just happen when they happen. For the Navajo Indians, the future is a meaningless concept—immediate obligations are what count. For natives of the Pacific island of Truk, however, the past has no independent meaning—it is a living part of the present. These examples of cultural differences in the perception of time point to a basic sociological fact—each culture must be investigated and understood on its own terms before it is possible to make valid cross-cultural comparisons (Hall, 1981).

In every social group, culture is transmitted from one generation to the next. Unlike other creatures, human beings do not pass on many behavioral patterns through their genes. Rather, culture is taught and learned through social interaction.

culture All that human beings learn to do, to use, to produce, to know, and to believe as they grow to maturity and live out their lives in the social groups to which they belong.

In some cultures adults believe infants should be left to "cry it out." In others infants are picked up and soothed when they seem unhappy or uncomfortable.

Culture and Biology

Human beings, like all other creatures, have basic biological needs. We must eat, sleep, protect ourselves from the environment, reproduce, and nurture our young—or else we could not survive as a species. In most other animals, such basic biological needs are met in more or less identical ways by all the members of a species. This is a result of inherited behavior patterns or instincts, which are unlearned and specific for a given species as well as universal for all members of that species. Thus instinctual behaviors, such as the web spinning of specific species of spiders, are constant and do not vary significantly from one individual member of a species to another. This is not true of humans, whose behaviors are highly variable and changeable, both individually and culturally. It is through culture that human beings acquire the means to meet their needs. For example, the young, or larvae, of hornets or yellow jackets are housed in paper-walled, hexagonal chambers that they scrape against with their heads when hungry and are immediately fed, by workers, tiny bits of undigested insect parts (Wilson, 1975). Neither the larvae nor the workers learns these patterns of behavior: they are instinctual. In contrast, although human infants cry when hungry or uncomfortable, the responses to those cries vary from group to group and even from person to person. In some groups, infants are breast-fed; in others, they are fed prepared milk formulas from bottles; and in still others they are fed according to the mother's preference. Some groups breast-feed children for as long as 5 or 6 years; others for no more than 10 to 12 months. Some mothers feed their infants on demand—whenever they seem to be hungry; other mothers hold their infants to a rigid feeding schedule. In some groups, infants are picked up and soothed when they seem unhappy or uncomfortable. Other groups believe that infants should be left to "cry it out." In the United States, mothers differ in their approaches to feeding and handling their infants, but most are influenced by the practices they have observed among members of their families and their social groups. Such habits, shared by the members of each group, express the group's culture. They are learned by group members and are kept more or less uniform by social expectations and pressures.

Culture Shock and Ethnocentrism

Every social group has its own specific culture, its own way of seeing, doing, and making things, its own traditions. Some cultures are quite similar to one another; others are very different. When individuals travel abroad to countries with cultures that are very different from their own, the experience can be quite upsetting. Meals are scheduled at different times of day, "strange" or even "repulsive" foods are eaten, and the traveler never quite knows what to expect from others or what others in turn may expect. Local customs may seem "charming" or "brutal." Sometimes travelers are unable to adjust easily to a foreign culture; they may become anxious, lose their appetites, or even feel sick. Sociologists call these reactions **culture shock** to describe what happens when people have a difficult time adjusting to a new culture that differs markedly from the one they are used to. Many Peace Corps workers experienced culture shock when they were sent to developing nations. Those who made the best cultural adaptation to a preindustrial culture often experienced reverse culture shock upon returning to the United States. Culture shock can be a problem for sociologists who wish to study foreign countries or social groups whose lifestyles are very different from those in their own country. (Anthropologist Napoleon Chagnon describes a personal experience of culture shock in the Case Study: "Culture Shock—the Ya̧nomamö.")

Culture shock can also be experienced within a person's own society. Picture the army recruit fresh from civilian life and having to adapt to a whole new set of behaviors, rules, and expectations in basic training—a new cultural setting.

People often make judgments about other cultures according to the customs and values of their own, a practice sociologists call **ethnocentrism**. Thus, for example, an American might call the floor of a Guatemalan peasant's home filthy because it is constructed of packed dirt or believe that the family organization of the Watusi (of East Africa) is immoral because it allows a husband to have several wives. Ethnocentrism can lead to prejudice and discrimination and can become quite ugly when it results in the repression or domination of one group by another. Immigrants, for instance, often encounter hostile ethnocentrism when their manners, dress, eating habits, or religious beliefs, differ markedly from those of their new neighbors. Because of this hostility and because of their own ethnocentrism, immigrants often establish their own communities in their adopted country.

Sociologists recognize that social groups and cultures must be studied and understood on their own terms before valid comparisons can be made. This perspective is termed **cultural relativism**, a position that frequently is taken to mean that social scientists never should judge the relative merits of any group or culture. This is not the case. Cultural relativism is an approach to doing objective cross-cultural research. It does not require researchers

to abdicate their personal standards. In fact, good social scientists will take the trouble to spell out exactly what their standards are so that both the researchers and the readers will be alert to possible bias in their studies. Cultural relativism requires that behaviors and customs be viewed and analyzed within the context in which they occur. The packed-dirt floor of the Guatemalan house should be noted in terms of the culture of the Guatemalan peasant, not in terms of suburban America. Researchers, however, may find that dirt floors contribute to the incidence of parasites in young children and may, therefore, judge such construction to be less desirable than wood or tile floors.

☐ Components of Culture

The concept of culture is not easy to understand, perhaps because every aspect of our social lives is an expression of it and also because familiarity produces a kind of nearsightedness toward our own culture, making it difficult for us to take an analytical perspective toward our everyday social lives. Sociologists find it helpful to break down culture into two separate components: material culture (having and using objects) and nonmaterial culture (doing, thinking, and feeling).

Material Culture

Material culture consists of human technology—all the things human beings make and use from small hand-held tools to sky-

---

culture shock The reaction people may have when encountering cultural traditions different from their own. As people attempt to adapt to a new set of behaviors, rules, and expectations in a new cultural setting, they may become anxious and upset.

ethnocentrism The tendency to judge other cultures in terms of one's own customs and values.

cultural relativism An approach to doing cross-cultural research that requires social scientists to view and analyze behaviors and customs within the context in which they occur. It does not require researchers to abdicate their personal standards but to spell them out.

material culture All the things human beings make and use, from small hand-held tools to skyscrapers: human technology.

CASE STUDY
Culture Shock—The Yąnomamö

Every society has its own culture, its own way of viewing the world. Some cultures—like those of the United States and Canada—are quite similar. Others are very different. Sociologists use the term culture shock *to describe the upset and the disorienting feelings people experience when they enter a culture that is different from their own. In this case study Napoleon A. Chagnon, an American anthropologist, describes his own culture shock when he first met the Yąnomamö in November, 1964 and how he had to assume attitudes and behaviors that, ideally, he preferred not to adopt, in order to cope with the normative demands of their culture, which was completely alien to him.*

These men of the Yąnomamö tribe are about to depart for a raid on another village.

The Yąnomamö (the word is pronounced "Yah-no-mama" and is nasalized) are South American Indians who live in southern Venezuela and northern Brazil. There are about 10,000 Yąnomamö living in some 125 villages. When Chagnon first visited them, from 1964 to 1966, they had had almost no contact with the outside world. The Yąnomamö are known as "the fierce people" because of the importance aggression and fighting play in their culture. Each village is in a constant state of warfare with others. Men often beat their wives and engage in chest-pounding duels and club fights with one another.

At first Chagnon found the going rough. It took him months, for example, to learn that the Yąnomamö had deliberately lied to him when he asked questions about their kinship. Indeed, they invented phony names for everyone in the village, as each tried to outdo the other in coming up with the most ridiculous name.

Eventually, Chagnon became good friends with the Indians. On a trip in 1975 he was amused when one Yąnomamö reflected about his first visit: "I remember when you first came to live with us," he reminisced. "We could really intimi-

date and trick you then and make you give away vast quantities of valuable goods for almost nothing and convince you that it was a fair bargain." He laughed aloud and sighed: "Those days are gone, for . . . you have become just like . . . you know how to trade. You have become a Yąnomamö."

But it was not so easy or pleasant. Here Chagnon describes his first enounter with the Yąnomamö:

My first day in the field illustrated to me what my teachers meant when they spoke of "culture shock." I had traveled in a small, aluminum rowboat propelled by a large outboard motor for two and a half days. . . . We arrived at the village, Bissaai-teri, about 2:00 P.M. and docked the boat along the muddy bank at the [end] of the path used by the Indians to fetch their drinking water. It was hot and muggy, and my clothing was

soaked with perspiration. It clung uncomfortably to my body, as it did thereafter for the remainder of the work. The small, biting gnats were out in astronomical numbers, for it was the beginning of the dry season. My face and hands were swollen from the venom of their numerous stings. In just a few moments I was to meet my first Yąnomamö, my first primitive man. What would it be like? . . . Would they like me? This was important to me; I wanted them to be so fond of me that they would adopt me into their kinship system and way of life. I was determined to become a member of their society. My heart began to pound as we approached the village and heard the buzz of activity within the circular compound. . . .

The entrance to the village was covered over with brush and dry palm leaves. We pushed them aside to expose the low opening to the village. The excitement of meeting my first Indians was almost unbearable as I duck-waddled through the low passage into the village clearing.

I looked up and gasped when I saw a dozen burly, naked, filthy, hideous men staring at us down the shafts of their drawn arrows! Immense wads of green tobacco were stuck between their lower teeth and lips making them look even more hideous, and strands of dark green slime dripped or hung from their noses. We arrived at the village while the men were blowing a hallucinogenic drug up their nose. The mucus is always saturated with the green powder and the Indians usually let it run freely from their nostrils. My next discovery was that there were a dozen or so vicious, underfed dogs snapping at my legs, circling me as if I were going to be their next meal. I just stood there holding my notebook, helpless and pathetic. Then the stench of the decaying vegetation and filth struck me and I almost got sick. I was horrified. What sort of welcome was this for the person who came here to live with you and learn your way of life, to become friends with you? They put their weapons down when they recognized [my companion] and returned to their chanting, keeping a nervous eye on the village entrances. . . .

[By evening,] I had not eaten all day, I was soaking wet from perspiration, the gnats were biting me, and I was covered with red pigment, the result of a dozen or so complete examinations I had been given by as many burly Indians. These examinations capped an otherwise grim day. The Indians would blow their noses into their hands, flick as much of the mucus off that would separate in a snap of the wrist, wipe the residue into their hair, and then carefully examine my face, arms, legs, hair, and the contents of my pockets. I asked Mr. Barker how to say "Your hands are dirty"; my comments were met by the Indians in the following way: They would "clean" their hands by spitting a quantity of slimy tobacco juice into them, rub them together, and then proceed with the examination. . . .

The thing that bothered me most was the incessant, passioned, and aggressive demands the Indians made. It would become so unbearable that I would have to lock myself in my mud hut every once in a while just to escape from it: Privacy is one of Western culture's greatest achievements. But I did not want privacy for its own sake; rather, I simply had to get away from the begging. Day and night for the entire time I lived with the Yąnomamö I was plagued by such demands as: "Give me a knife, I am poor!"; "If you don't take me with you on your next trip to Widokaiya-teri I'll chop a hole in your canoe!"; "Don't point your camera at me or I'll hit you!" "Share your food with me!"; "Take me across the river in your canoe and be quick about it!"; "Give me a cooking pot!"; "Loan me your flashlight so I can go hunting tonight!"; "Give me medicine . . . I itch all over!"; "Take us on a week-long hunting trip with your shot gun!"; and "Give me an axe or I'll break into your hut when you are away visiting and steal one!" And so I was bombarded by such demands day after day, months on end, until I could not bear to see an Indian.

It was not as difficult to become calloused to the incessant begging as it was to ignore the sense of urgency, the impassioned tone of voice, or the intimidation and aggression with which the demands were made. It was likewise difficult to adjust to the fact that the Yąnomamö refused to accept "no" for an answer until or unless it seethed with passion and intimidation—which it did after six months. Giving in to a demand always established a new threshold; the next demand would be for a bigger item or favor, and the anger of the Indians ever greater if the demand was not met. I soon learned that I had to become very much like the Yąnomamö to be able to get along with them on their terms: sly, aggressive, and intimidating. . . .

Source: Excerpted from Napoleon A. Chagnon, *Yąnomamö: The Fierce People,* 2d ed. (New York: Holt, Rinehart and Winston, 1977), pp. 4–10, 140–143. ⬜

---

scrapers. Without material culture our species could not long survive, for material culture provides a buffer between humans and their environment. Using it, human beings can protect themselves from environmental stresses, as when they build shelters and wear clothing to protect themselves from the cold or from strong sunlight. Even more important, humans use material culture to modify and exploit the environment. They build dams and irrigation canals, plant fields and forests, convert coal and oil into energy, and transform ores into versatile metals. Using material culture, our species has learned to cope with the most extreme environments and to survive and even to thrive on all continents and in all climates. Human beings have walked on the floor of the ocean and on the surface of the moon. No other creature can do this: none has our flexibility. Material culture has made human beings the dominant life form on earth.

nonmaterial culture The totality of knowledge, beliefs, values, and rules for appropriate behavior that specifies how a people should interact and how they may solve their problems.

USING SOCIOLOGY
Space: The Hidden Dimension

The use of personal space between these two Arab men would make most Americans feel uncomfortable.

In his study of space, The Hidden Dimension, *Edward T. Hall found that an understanding of the amount of space people need around them in different societies can lead to a better understanding of intercultural relations. By examining different people's needs for space, it is possible to reveal hidden cultural frames that determine the way they act and live. More specifically, Hall has discovered how a comprehension of space may help to explain why, after more than two thousand years of contact, Westerners and Arabs still do not understand each other. The following is only a brief excerpt from Hall's work dealing with space, but it gives some idea of how differing cultural patterns make it harder for people to understand and therefore to interact successfully with one another. As people begin to learn and understand more about these divergent cultural patterns, both from firsthand experience and from researchers like Hall, interactions on personal, business, and political levels may be facilitated and enhanced.*

Americans follow an unwritten rule concerning public behavior. As soon as an individual stops or is seated in a public place, a small, invisible sphere of privacy that is considered inviolate swells around the person. The size will vary with the degree of crowding, the age, sex, and importance of the person, and the general surroundings. Anyone who enters this zone and stays there is intruding. In order to overcome this personal-space barrier, a person who intrudes for a specific purpose, will usually acknowledge the intrusion by beginning with a phrase like "Pardon me, but can you tell me . . . ?"

On the other hand, pushing and shoving in public places is a characteristic of Middle Eastern culture, a characteristic that, unlike the attitude in Western cultures, is not considered a rude behavior. For the Arab, there is no such thing as an intrusion of space in public. Occupying a given spot does not give you any special rights to that area at all. If, for example, person A is standing on a street corner and person B wants that spot, it is perfectly all right for person B to try to make person A uncomfortable enough to move.

Another silent source of friction between Americans and Arabs concerns the manners and rights of the road. In general, we tend to defer to the bigger, more powerful, and faster vehicle. Pedestrians walking along a road may be annoyed by a speeding car but will still step aside. They know that because they are moving they do not have the right to the space around them that they may have if they were standing still.

It appears that the reverse is true with Arabs, who apparently take on rights to space as they move. For someone else to move into a space an Arab is also moving into is a violation of the Arab's rights. Though it may be irritating to Americans when someone cuts them off on the highway, it is also a very common behavior. Such an act is infuriating to an Arab. In fact, it is Americans' treatment of moving space that makes the Arabs call them aggressive and pushy.

Arabs have a completely different set of assumptions regarding the body and the rights associated with it than do Westerners. Certainly the Arab tendency to shove and push one another in public and to feel and pinch women in public conveyances would not be tolerated by Westerners. Arabs do not have any concept of a private zone outside the body. In the Western world, the person is synonymous with an individual inside a skin, and in many places the skin and even the clothes are inviolate. You need permission to touch if you are strangers. For the Arab, however, the location of the person in relation to the body is quite different. The person exists somewhere down inside the body, protected from touch. Touching the outside of the body—skin and clothes—is not really touching the person.

Although Arabs do not mind being crowded by people, they hate to be hemmed in by walls. They avoid partitions because they do not like to be alone. When searching for a home, Arabs look for plenty of unobstructed space in which to move around. Because physical privacy is relatively unknown in the Arab world, their way to be alone with their thoughts is simply to stop talking. To the Arab, if you are not with people, you are deprived of life. Arab behavior in regard to their own real estate is apparently an extension of, and consistent with, their approach to the body.

The sense of smell occupies a prominent place in Middle Eastern life. To the Arab, good smells are pleasing and a way of being involved with each other. To smell one's friends is desirable and to deny them your breath is interpreted as an act of shame. So it is that Americans, trained as they are not to breathe in people's faces, automatically communicate shame to the Arabs.

These few simple observations of Hall's, if applied by those Westerners and Arabs who come into regular contact, should help dispel some of the discomfort or even disgust that often results when people from divergent cultures are forced to interact.

Source: Excerpted and adapted from Edward T. Hall, *The Hidden Dimension* (New York: Doubleday, 1966). □

The construction of shelters is a reflection of material culture. Types of shelters, however, may vary considerably, as the contrast between the houseboats and skyscrapers of Hong Kong illustrates.

Nonmaterial Culture

Nonmaterial culture is the totality of knowledge, beliefs, values, and rules for appropriate behavior (norms) that specifies how a people should interact and how they may solve their problems. Nonmaterial culture is ordered through the institutions of the family, religion, education, economy, and government. Most people acquire culture through these institutions.

Whereas the elements of material culture are things that have a physical existence (they can be seen, touched, and so on), the elements of nonmaterial culture are the ideas associated with their use. Although engagement rings and birthday flowers have a material existence, they also reflect attitudes, beliefs, and values that are part of our culture. There are rules for their appropriate use in specified situations. Nonmaterial culture is separated into two categories: normative culture and cognitive culture.

Normative Culture   **Normative culture** consists of the rules for doing things. **Norms** are central elements of normative culture. They are rules of behavior that are agreed upon and shared within a culture to prescribe limits of acceptable behavior. They define "normal"

expected behavior in a given situation and help human beings achieve organization and predictability in their lives. For example, Americans do not have to wonder which side of the street they should drive on every time they get into their cars—nor do the British. The American norm is to drive on the right; the British drive on the left. One behavior is no better or more correct than the other. Each is correct within its culture. In Using Sociology: "Space: The Hidden Dimension," Edward T. Hall examines the differences between Arab and American perceptions of personal space and the misunderstandings that may arise because of these differences.

Mores (pronounced more-ays) are strongly held norms that usually have a moral connotation and are based on the central values of the culture. Violations of mores produce strong negative reactions, which are often supported and expressed through the legal system. Desecration of a church or temple, sexual molestation of a child, rape, murder, incest, and child beating all are violations of American mores.

Not all norms command such absolute conformity. Much of day-to-day life is governed by traditions, or **folkways**, which are norms that permit a rather wide degree of individual interpretation as long as certain limits are not overstepped. People who violate folkways are seen as peculiar or possibly eccentric, but rarely do they elicit strong public response. For example, a wide range of dress is now acceptable in theaters and restaurants. A man may wear clothes ranging from a business suit, shirt, and tie to informal jeans, open-necked shirt, and sweater. A woman may

normative culture One of the two categories of nonmaterial culture. Normative culture consists of the rules people follow for doing things. Norms, mores, and folkways are the central elements of normative culture.

norms Specific rules of behavior that are agreed upon and shared within a culture to prescribe limits of acceptable behavior.

mores Strongly held norms that usually have a moral connotation and are based on the central values of the culture.

folkways Norms that permit a rather wide degree of individual interpretation as long as certain limits are not overstepped. Folkways change with time and vary from culture to culture.

POPULAR SOCIOLOGY
Cultural Differences in International Gift Giving

Whether you're celebrating the closing of a multimillion dollar international business deal or meeting an old pen pal in Paris, it is important to consider cultural differences in gift giving. A little research could save you and the recipient of your gift the embarrassment that can result from unwittingly violating cultural norms.

Want to thank your Japanese hostess for a lovely dinner? Flowers are always a thoughtful gift. But be careful. If you choose to send chrysanthemums, be sure to specify ones with 15 petals, not 16. The one-petal-larger version is used in the imperial family crest and should not be used commercially.

Such subtle cultural differences can make international gift giving a source of anxiety or embarrassment to well-meaning travelers. American businessmen and women often find themselves in situations in which a gift is required. To help them avoid missteps that could result in lost business, the Parker Pen Company has published a guide to appropriate gifts throughout the world. The following are some of the rules that potential gift givers should be aware of:

Arab Countries Don't give gifts on first meeting an Arab businessman, as they may be interpreted as bribes.

Don't give liquor, as the Muslim culture prohibits alcohol. Don't ever give a gift for a business contact's wife—or wives. In fact, don't even ask about the family. That's personal business and has no place in the office. Above all, don't look longingly at something belonging to your Arab host. His culture requires that he then give it to you.

China A very acceptable gift in China is to stage a banquet for your host. But this is tricky business. There are four levels of banquets in China, and it is important that the American host give one of the same degree of lavishness as would be presented to him by his Chinese host. The American host should also know how to give a toast and how to use chopsticks. If you decide to pass on the idea of a banquet, a good bottle of brandy or something associated with your home state might be nice. Above all, don't give a clock, for in China, that is considered bad luck.

Latin America Color is important in Latin America. Be careful not to give anything that is black or purple, as they are the colors associated with the Lenten season. Also, don't give knives or handkerchiefs. The former connotes the end of a friendship; the latter is associated with sad-

ness. Small, American-made home appliances are appropriate, and gifts for the family are always appreciated.

France It's bad form in France to give a gift on the first encounter. Wait for the next visit. Then the gift should be something to compliment the Frenchman's intelligence, but nothing too personal. If you're invited to a French home for dinner, take flowers. But don't take chrysanthemums—even with 15 petals—as French consider them flowers for mourning.

Japan The Japanese are maniacal gift givers. Gift giving is so prevalent in the Japanese culture that they often practice something called *taraimawashi*. This involves giving a gift of something utterly useless that the recipient can then give to someone else, who in turn can then pass it on. The recipient of a gift should not open it in front of the giver. The Japanese like brand-name gifts, but they don't like anything depicting foxes or badgers. "The fox," says the guide, "is a symbol of fertility; the badger, cunning." Neither would be appropriate from a business acquaintance.

Source: Based on "Business Abroad: A Guide for Giving," *New York Times,* December 6, 1981, sec. 3, p. F-23. □

---

choose a cocktail dress and high-heeled shoes or, like the man, the casual-jeans look. However, extremes in either direction will cause a reaction. Many establishments limit the extent of informal dress: signs may specify that no one with bare feet or without a shirt may enter. On the other hand, a person in extremely formal attire might well attract attention and elicit amused comments in a fast-food restaurant.

Good manners in our culture also show a range of acceptable behavior. A man may or may not open a door or hold a coat for a woman, who may also choose to open a door or hold a coat for a man—all four options are acceptable behavior and cause neither comment nor other negative reactions from people.

These two examples illustrate another aspect of folkways: they change with time. Not too long ago a man was *always* expected to hold a door open for a woman, and a woman was *never* expected to hold a coat for a man.

Folkways also vary from one culture to another. In the United States, for example, it is customary to thank someone for a gift. Not to do so is to be ungrateful and ill-mannered. However, this is not a universal folkway, as anthropologist Richard Lee (1969a,b) discovered one Christmas when he attempted to give an ox to his hosts, the !Kung San, a nomadic people in southern Africa. Far from being grateful, the !Kung ridiculed the gift, deriding the ox as dead on its feet—a wreck. The !Kung, Lee learned, take the sharing of food for granted. Indeed, it is basic to their way of life. If people thank someone for doing what is "natural," they feel it could lead to vanity or a swelled head. So the !Kung deliberately downplay the value of gifts (for a further discussion of how folkways affect gift giving, see Popular Sociology: "Cultural Differences in International Gift Giving").

Having said that norms are rather specific expectations about social behavior, we must now modify that statement somewhat. True, people learn such expectations along with the rest of their culture, but there is room for what might be called "slippage" in each person's interpretation of these norms, room for individual approaches to enacting them. That is because there are what sociologists call norms and what they call statistical norms, or real norms, which are in effect different ways of looking at norms.

Ideal norms are expectations of what people should do under perfect conditions. These are the norms we first teach our children. They tend to be simple, making few distinctions and allowing for no exceptions. "Drivers stop at red lights" is an ideal norm in American society. So is the norm that a marriage will last "until death do us part."

In reality, however, nothing about human beings is ever that dependable. For example, if you interviewed Americans about how drivers respond to red lights, you would get answers something like this: "Ideally, drivers should stop at red lights. But in actual fact, drivers sometimes run red lights. So even though you can pretty much count on a driver

stopping for a red light, it pays to be careful. And if it looks like a driver isn't gonna stop for a light, better play it safe and slow down." In other words, people recognize that drivers usually do feel they should stop when a traffic light is red, but they also acknowledge that as things really are, there are times when a driver will not stop for a red light. The driver may be in a hurry, drunk, upset, or simply not paying attention. Norms expressed in this way—with qualifications and allowances for differences in individual behavior—are what sociologists call **real norms**, and they specify how people actually behave. They reflect the fact that people's behavior is a function not only of norm guidance but also of situational elements, as exemplified by the driver who does not always stop at a red light if no car appears to be coming from the other direction.

The concepts of ideal and real norms are useful for distinguishing between mores and folkways. For mores the ideal and the real norms tend to be very close, whereas for folkways they can be much more loosely connected: our mores say *thou shalt not kill* and really mean it, but thou might forget to follow folkways and neglect to say thank you without provoking general outrage. More important, the very fact that a culture legitimizes the difference between ideal and real expectations allows the individual room to interpret norms to a greater or lesser degree according to his or her own personal disposition.

Cognitive Culture **Cognitive culture**, the thinking component of culture, consists of shared beliefs and knowledge of what the world is like—what is real and what is not, what is

ideal norms Expectations of what people should do under perfect conditions. The norm that marriage will last "until death do us part" is an ideal norm in American society.

real norms Norms that allow for differences in individual behavior. Real norms specify how people actually behave, not how they should behave under ideal circumstances.

cognitive culture The thinking component of culture consisting of shared beliefs and knowledge of what the world is like—what is real and what is not, what is important and what is trivial.

Ahmed's Boat

The following situation described by Moshe Rubinstein provides an excellent example of contrasting values between American culture and Arab culture.

> One summer my wife and I became acquainted with an educated, well-to-do Arab named Ahmed in the city of Jerusalem. Following a traditional Arabic dinner one evening, Ahmed decided to test my wisdom with his fables. One of them caught me in a rather awkward setting. "Moshe," he said as he put his fable in the form of a question, "imagine that you, your mother, your wife, and your child are in a boat, and it capsizes. You can save yourself and only one of the remaining three. Whom will you save?" For a moment I froze, while thoughts raced through my mind. Did he have to ask this of all questions? And in the presence of my wife yet? No matter what I might say, it would not be right from someone's point of view, and if I refused to answer I might be even worse off. I was stuck. So I tried to answer by thinking aloud as I progressed to a conclusion, hoping for salvation before I said what came to my mind as soon as he posed the question, namely, save the child.
>
> Ahmed was very surprised. I flunked the test. As he saw it, there was one correct answer and a corresponding rational argument to support it. "You see," he said, "you can have more than one wife in a lifetime, you can have more than one child, but you have only one mother. You must save your mother!"
>
> I told the story to a class of one hundred freshmen and asked for their responses. Sixty would save the child, and forty the wife. When I asked who would save his mother, there was a roar of laughter. No one raised his hand. They thought the question was funny. They were also quite amazed to learn of Ahmed's response.
>
> A group of about forty executives whom I addressed on problem solving and decision making responded as follows: More than half would save the child, less than half would save the wife. One reluctantly raised his hand in response to "Who would save his mother?" (I believe he had an accent. . . .) I promised the group to send the mothers sympathy cards.
>
> The executives were apparently impressed by the story because, at a dinner party that followed the lectures, Ahmed's question was ringing all over the place. Across the table from me sat one of the course instructors and his wife. Both came from Persia and spent the last seven years in the United States. She wanted to know what the conversation about mother, wife, child was all about. Her husband related the story, and she came up with a response immediately: "Of course I would save my mother, you have only one mother." Here her values were a perfect match to Ahmed's culture. But then she turned to her husband and added: "I hope you won't do that." The influence of new values in the USA, or did she mean specifically her mother-in-law . . . ?
>
> Most of our friends reacted as if it was natural to save the child. One, an artist, said that she would probably drown before she could ever decide what to do. . . .

Source: Moshe Rubinstein, *Patterns of Problem Solving* (Englewood, N.J.: Prentice-Hall, 1975), pp. 1–2. □

---

important and what is trivial. The beliefs need not even be true or testable as long as they are shared by a majority of the people. Cognitive culture is like a map in that it is a representation of the world around us. Think of a scout troop on a hike in the wilderness. The troop finds its way by studying a map showing many of the important features of the terrain. The scouts who use the map share a mental image of the area as it is represented by the map. Yet just as maps differ, each perhaps emphasizing different details of the terrain or using different symbols to represent them, so do cultures differ in the ways in which they represent the world. It is important not to confuse any culture's representation of reality with what ultimately is real—just as a map is not the actual terrain it charts.

Values are a culture's general orientations toward life—its notions of what is good and bad, what is desirable and undesirable. Values themselves are abstractions. They can best be found by looking for the recurring patterns of behavior that express them. Values are not the same in every culture (see Box 3.1: "Ahmed's Boat"). In American middle-class culture, individual freedom, democracy, the success orientation, work ethic, and the commitment to progress, monogamy, and heterosexuality are strongly held values (Williams, 1970). In contrast, traditional Hopi Indian culture stressed being cooperative, tranquil, and in harmony with nature (Thompson, 1950).

Relationship of Material and Nonmaterial Culture

Material culture and nonmaterial culture are very closely related. People produce and use things the way their cognitive culture instructs them to. Living side by side, culturally different groups may produce and use very different things. In Israel, for example, Bedouin nomads live in felt tents, whereas their farming neighbors live in concrete prefabricated apartments.

It would be wrong, however, to think of material culture simply as the expression of cognitive culture. Once created, material culture can result in changes in a people's cognitive culture. Thus, for instance, the invention of the plow and irrigation ditches were relatively modest achievements in themselves, but the development of agriculture helped make possible the rise of civilization as we know it. Computers originally were developed simply as a means to perform high-speed calculations, but within a generation's time they have contributed to previously undreamed-of developments in the sciences, the arts, and even philosophy.

☐ Culture and Adaptation

Over time cultures adjust to the demands of the environment. Although **environmental determinism**—the belief that the environment dictates cultural patterns—is no longer accepted, there must be some degree of "fit" between environment and culture. Whereas other animal species must rely on the long, slow process of evolution in order to adapt to their environment, culture has allowed humans to adapt to many different habitats and become the most flexible species on earth. In Arctic regions, generation after generation of animal life developed the fur, feathers, and fat layers necessary to survive. In the deserts only those life forms that could cope with intense heat and little water have remained.

Adaptation to the environment among other animal species is a slow biological process. Among human beings, it is a relatively fast series of developments in knowledge, behavior, and toolmaking. For example, the hammock allows air to circulate freely around the sleeper; surely it was no accident that it was invented and used by tropical peoples. Using culture, humans do not simply adapt to their environment, they also change it.

Human Evolution: Biological and Cultural

Because most of human behavior is not instinctive but is learned (see Chapter 4) and depends on culture, much can be learned about human development by tracing the evolution of culture.

The earliest evidence of culture found thus far is in Africa. In Tanzania, Kenya, and Ethiopia, fist-sized stone tools have been found dating from 1.5 to 2.9 million years ago. These are very simple tools made by knocking several flakes off pieces of flint to produce an implement with which animals could be killed and butchered. The creatures that produced these tools stood upright and walked on their hind legs as we do, were between 4 and 5 feet tall, and weighed between 80 and 150 pounds. However, their heads were still very apelike.

These ancestors of ours subsisted on a varied diet of plants and small game, and there is evidence that they also were able to hunt larger animals. In order to protect themselves against dangerous meat-eating predators and to be successful in activities such as big-game hunting, these ancestors must already have developed some form of communication system and social organization. (This is a reasonable assumption, as modern apes and monkeys, our closest primate relatives, also live in organized social groups.)

Sometime between 1 and 1.5 million years ago our immediate ancestors—called *Homo*

values A culture's general orientations toward life—its notion of what is good and bad, what is desirable and undesirable.

environmental determinism The belief that the environment dictates cultural patterns.

A Neanderthal man, with his weapons in hand, is about to leave his cave in search of game.

erectus—evolved. *Homo erectus* resembled the modern human in all respects except for its head, which still was quite primitive. The jaws were large, the eyes protected by heavy ridges, the forehead still slanted sharply back. However, the brain had grown significantly. It averaged 1,000 cubic centimeters, which is a little over two-thirds that of modern humans.

Homo erecti were very versatile. Their bands moved out of the tropics and subtropics, venturing forth across the vast expanses of Africa, Europe, and Asia as far north as Germany in Europe and Peking in China. They lived in caves and skin huts on windswept plains, braving cold winters in their pursuit of big game—mammoth, horse, rhinoceros, deer, and oxen. *Homo erecti* lived in nomadic, well-organized bands, and their tools and weapons were well adapted to the different environments they inhabited.

Human culture and subsistence activities changed significantly around 70,000 years ago. By this time the Neanderthal, an early form of our own species, had already been in existence for several hundred thousand years. The cultural changes that came about at this time seem to have been in response to human populations moving ever farther north, right up to the ice-age glaciers. Here humans became even more skillful hunters than their ancestors were. Stone tools were made in a new process that involved shaping a piece of flint carefully before the final tool was split off. The process resulted in the production of a great variety of specialized tools including spear points. But the most dramatic cultural developments were in other areas. There is evidence that Neanderthals practiced crude surgery, cared for the aged and crippled, and buried their dead according to rituals that included tying corpses into a fetal position, sprinkling them with red powder, placing offerings of food beside them, and sometimes even covering them with flower petals (Solecki, 1971). This evidence suggests that Neanderthal people were intelligent, devel-

Art forms began to emerge in southern Europe around 25,000 B.C.

oped strong feelings for each other, and had ideas about death and possibly even about an afterlife.

By 35,000 to 40,000 years ago, stone-tool technology had reached its highest stage of development. Tool kits featured many forms of choppers, scrapers, chisels, points, and blades. In southern Europe, beginning around 25,000 B.C., we find the emergence of sophisticated art forms: engravings, wall paintings, abstract designs, and even three-dimensional sculptures of animals and humans. Hunter-gatherers—nomadic people who moved around in small groups living off whatever game or plants they happened to come upon—were responsible for these advances. It was bands of these versatile and creative hunter-gatherers that crossed the last frontiers into Australia and the Americas (where they arrived probably around 40,000 years ago).

By 10,000 B.C. the agricultural revolution was beginning, and on this base civilizations were built—societies that were to push forward the evolution of culture at an ever-accelerating pace. As the agricultural revolution progressed, the remaining hunting and gathering bands were driven into increasingly marginal territories, where their lifestyles were doomed to extinction.

Mechanisms of Cultural Change

Cultural change takes place at many different levels within a society. Some of the radical changes that have taken place often become obvious only in hindsight. When the airplane was invented, few people could visualize the changes it would produce. Not only did it markedly decrease the impact of distance on cultural contact, but it also had an enormous impact on such areas as economics and warfare.

It is generally assumed that the number of cultural items in a society (including everything from toothpicks to structures as complex as government agencies) has a direct relation to the rate of social change. A society that has few such items will also tend to have few innovations. As the number of cultural items increases, so do the innovations, as well as the rate of social change. For example, an inventory of the cultural items—from tools to religious practices—among the hunting and gathering Shoshone Indians totals a mere three thousand. Modern Americans who also inhabit the same territory in Nevada and Utah are part of a culture with items numbering well into the millions. Social change in American society is proceeding rapidly, while Shoshone culture, as revealed by archeological excavations, appears to have changed scarcely at all for thousands of years.

Two simple mechanisms are responsible for cultural evolution: innovation and diffusion. **Innovation** is the source of all new **culture traits**—that is, items of a culture such as tools, materials used, beliefs, values, and typical ways of doing things. Innovation takes place in several different ways, including recombining in a new way elements already available to a society (invention), discovering new concepts, finding new solutions to old problems, and devising and making new material objects.

Diffusion is the movement of culture traits from one culture to another. It almost inevitably results when people from one group or society come into contact with another, as when immigrant groups take on the dress or manners of already established groups and in turn contribute new foods or art forms to the dominant culture. However, rarely does a trait diffuse from one culture into another without being modified in some way so that it fits better in its new context. This process of modification, called **reformulation**, can be seen in the transformation of black folk-blues into commercial music such as rhythm and blues and rock 'n roll. Or, consider moccasins—the machine-made, chemically waterproofed, soft-soled cowhide shoes (with or without thongs)—which today differ from the Native American originals and usually are worn for recreation and not as a part of basic dress, as they originally were. Sociologists would say, therefore, that the culture trait of moccasins was reformulated when it diffused from Native American culture to the culture of industrial America.

Culture as an Adaptive Mechanism

Culture probably has been part of human evolution since the time, some 15 million years ago, when our ancestors first began to live on the ground. As we have stressed throughout this chapter, humans are extraordinarily flexible and adaptable. This adaptability, however, is not the result of our being biologically fitted to our environment; in fact, human beings are remarkably unspecialized. We do not run very fast, jump very high, climb very well, or swim very far. But we are specialized in one area: we are culture producing, culture transmitting, and culture dependent. This unique specialization is rooted in the size and structure of the human brain and in our physical ability both to speak and to use tools.

Culture, then, is the primary means by which human beings adapt to the challenges of their environment. Thus, using enormous machines we strip away layers of the earth to extract minerals, and using other machines we transport these minerals to yet other machines, where they are converted to a staggering number of different products. Take away all our machines and American society would cease to exist. Take away all culture and the human species would perish. Culture is as much a part of us as our skin, muscles, bones, and brains.

Cultural lag results when new patterns of behavior emerge even though they conflict with traditional values.

Adaptation is the process by which human beings adjust to changes in their environment. Adaptation can take two different forms: specialization and generalized adaptability. Most cultures make use of both these means. **Specialization** involves developing ways of doing things that work extremely well in a particular environment or set of circumstances. For example, the Inuit (Eskimo) igloo is a specialized way of building a shelter. It works in the Arctic but would fail miserably in the Sahara desert or in a Florida swamp. An American brick apartment building also is specialized. It is fine where the ground is solid and bricks can be delivered by truck or train, but in swamps, deserts, or where people must move around a great deal in order to subsist, the brick apartment building is of no use whatsoever.

Generalized adaptability involves developing more complicated yet more flexible ways of doing things. For example, industrial society has very elaborate means of transportation, including trucks, trains, planes, and ships. Industrialized transportation is complex, much more so than, say, the use of camels by desert nomads. At the same time, industrial transportation is a much more flexible transportation system, adaptable to every climate on earth. As such, it displays the quality of generalized adaptability as long as our environment continues to provide enough resources to meet its needs. Should we ever run out of rubber, metals, oil, and the other resources necessary for the operation of this technology, suddenly it will have lost its adaptive value. Then the camel might look like a very tempting means of transportation, and our "adaptable" technology would be as overspecialized as the dinosaur, with about the same probability of survival.

Cultural Lag

Although the diverse elements of a culture are interrelated, some may change rapidly and others lag behind. Thus, new patterns of behavior may emerge, even though they conflict with traditional values. William F. Ogburn (1964) coined the term **cultural lag** to describe this phenomenon. Ogburn observed that technological change (material culture) typically is faster than changes in nonmaterial

culture—a culture's norms and values—and technological change often results in cultural lag. Consequently, stresses and strains among elements of a culture are more or less inevitable. For example, many Americans still believe that the husband should be the principal source of income in the family, even though currently more than half of all married women work. Because more and more machines substitute mechanical strength for physical strength, women can now be employed in jobs traditionally held by men. Our society's ideas about women's roles and rights, however, have not kept pace with these technological changes; the women's movement is an attempt to close this gap. Or, consider the warning recently issued to commuters between Kuala Lumpur, the capital of Malaysia, and the town of Port Kelang. Workers building a modern bridge apparently consulted local religious leaders, who declared that human heads were needed to appease dangerous spirits during the construction, and commuters were alerted that

innovation One of the two mechanisms responsible for cultural evolution. Innovation is the source of all new cultural traits.

cultural traits Items of a culture such as tools, materials used, beliefs, values, and typical ways of doing things.

diffusion One of the two mechanisms responsible for cultural evolution. Diffusion is the movement of cultural traits from one culture to another. It almost inevitably results when people from one group or society come into contact with people from another.

reformulation The process in which traits passed from one culture to another are modified to fit better in their new context.

adaptation The process by which human beings adjust to the changes in their environment through specialization and generalized adaptability.

specialization One of the two forms of adaptation. Specialization is developing ways of doing things that work extremely well in a particular environment or set of circumstances. The Inuit Eskimo igloo, for example, is a specialized way of building a shelter.

generalized adaptation One of the two forms of adaptation. Generalized adaptation is developing more complicated yet flexible ways of doing things. Industrial transportation displays the quality of generalized adaption.

cultural lag A situation that develops when new patterns of behavior conflict with traditional values. Cultural lag may occur when technological change (material culture) is more rapid then are changes in norms and values (nonmaterial culture).

FOCUS ON RESEARCH
The International Language of Gestures

Few travelers would think of going abroad without taking along a dictionary or phrase book to help them communicate with the people in the countries they visit. Although most people are aware that gestures are the most common form of cross-cultural communication, they do not realize that the language of gestures can be just as different, just as regional, and just as likely to cause misunderstanding as the spoken word can.

After a good meal in Naples, a well-meaning American tourist expressed his appreciation to the waiter by making the "A-okay" gesture with his thumb and forefinger. The waiter was shocked. He headed for the manager. The two seriously discussed calling the police and having the hapless tourist arrested for obscene behavior in a public place.

What had happened? How could such a seemingly innocent and flattering gesture have been so misunderstood?

While we all recognize the differences in language and even colloquial phrases between countries, few of us are aware that the meaning of gestures may vary remarkably from culture to culture. Take the "A-okay" symbol, for example. In American culture it is used confidently in public by everyone from astronauts to politicians to signify that "everything is fine." In France and Belgium, however, it means "You're worth zero," while in Greece and Turkey it is an insulting or vulgar sexual invitation. And in parts of southern Italy, it is an offensive and graphic reference to a part of the anatomy. Small wonder that the waiter was shocked.

There are, in fact, dozens of gestures that take on totally different meanings as you move from one country to another. Is "thumbs up" always a positive gesture? It is in the United States and in most of western Europe. And when it was displayed by the Emperor of Rome, the upright thumb gesture spared the lives of gladiators in the Coliseum. But don't try it in Sardinia and Northern Greece. There the gesture means the insulting phrase, "Up yours."

The same naivete that can lead Americans into trouble in foreign countries also may work in reverse. After paying a call on Richard Nixon, Soviet leader Leonid Brezhnev stood on a balcony at the White House and saluted the American public with his hands clasped together in a gesture many people interpreted as meaning "I am the champ," or "I won." What many Americans perceived as a belligerent gesture was really just the Russian gesture for friendship.

In an attempt to decode the various meanings of gestures around the world, three researchers have compiled a dictionary of emblems (those physical acts that can fully take the place of words in a given culture). To do this, the researchers asked a group of people from each culture they studied if they had a gesture for a variety of phrases, such as "That's good," "He's a homosexual," or "Yes." When 10 to 15 people gave similar responses, the researchers felt they had identified a culture's emblem for that phrase.

Using this procedure, they catalogued three types of emblems:

Popular emblems have the same or similar meanings in several cultures. The side-to-side motion meaning "no" is typical.

Unique emblems have a specific meaning in one culture, but none elsewhere. For example, a Frenchman likes to put a fist around the tip of his nose and twist it to signify, "He's drunk." No other culture uses that gesture.

Multimeaning emblems are those which have one meaning in one culture and a totally different meaning in another. For example, the thumb inserted between the index and third fingers is an invitation to have sex in Germany, Holland, and Denmark, but in Portugal and Brazil it is a wish for good luck or protection.

The number of emblems in use varies considerably among cultures, from fewer than 60 in the United States to more than 250 in Israel. The Israelis' large number of emblems can be partially explained by the presence in their culture of many recent immigrants, all of whom bring their own large emblem vocabularies with them. In addition, since emblems are helpful in military operations where silence is essential, and all Israelis serve in the armed forces, military service provides both the opportunity and the need to learn new emblems.

The kind of emblems used also varies considerably from culture to culture. Some cultures have large numbers of gestures for insults, while others are heavy on emblems for sex or hunger.

Finally, gestures may even be used as a form of secret code by which members of one culture can communicate unbeknownst to others. In 1968, for example, the crew of an American ship, the *Pueblo,* was captured by the North Koreans. After the members of the crew had been forced to confess crimes against the People's Republic of Korea, the PRK supplied a photo to the international press to prove that the crewmen were in good health, and their confessions unforced. Three of the men, however, showed the insulting middle-finger gesture, indicating contempt for their captors and giving lie to their confessions.

Source: Paul Ekman, Wallace V. Friesen, and John Bear, "The International Language of Gestures," *Psychology Today,* May, 1984, pp. 64–69. ☐

headhunters had been busy trying to supply them.

Other instances of cultural lag have considerably greater and more widespread negative effects. Advances in medicine have led to lowered infant mortality and greater life expectancy, but there has been no corresponding rapid worldwide acceptance of birth control methods. The result is a potentially disastrous population explosion—our planet may not be able to support all the people who are being born and who are living longer.

☐ The Symbolic Nature of Culture

Our discussion so far has stressed several qualities of culture: it is *learned*, it is *shared*, and it is *adaptive*. There is yet a fourth quality of culture, which is equally important: culture is *symbolic*.

All human beings respond to the world around them. They may decorate their bodies, make drawings on cave walls or canvases, or mold likenesses in clay. These all act as symbolic representations of their society. All complex behavior is derived from the ability to use symbols for people, events, or places. Without the ability to use symbols, culture could not exist.

Signs, Symbols, and Culture

What does it mean to say that culture is symbolic? In order to answer this we first must distinguish between signs and symbols. **Signs** are objects or things that can represent other things because they share some important quality with them. A clenched fist can be a sign of anger, because when people are angry they may use their fists to beat one another. Wrinkling one's nose can be a sign that something is undesirable because that is what people do when something smells bad (for a discussion of cultural variations in the interpretation of signs, see Focus on Research: "The International Language of Gestures"). The communication systems of many animal species consist of more or less complicated systems of signs. For example, a worker bee returning to its hive can communicate accurately to other bees the location

The symbols displayed in this road sign stand for things simply because people agree that they do.

of pollen-rich plants, by performing a complicated dance. Careful research by the German biologist Karl von Frisch (1967) showed that this is accomplished when the bee, in effect, acts out a miniature version of its flight. The direction of the dance is the direction of the flight, and the duration of the dance is proportional to the distance of the pollen-rich flowers from the hive. Most important, a bee can dance only to communicate where pollen is to be found, not about anything else, such as imminent danger from an approaching bear.

Symbols are objects that, like signs, represent other things. However, unlike signs, symbols need not share any quality at all with whatever they represent. Symbols stand for things simply because people agree that they do. Hence, when two or more individuals agree

signs Objects or things that can represent other things because they share some important quality with them. A clenched fist, for example, can be a sign of anger because fists are used in physical arguments.

symbols Objects that represent other things. Symbols need not share any of the qualities of whatever they represent and stand for things simply because people agree that they do. When two or more people agree about the things a particular object represents, that object becomes a symbol by virtue of its shared meaning for those people. Symbols are a matter of cultural convention.

about the things a particular object represents, that object becomes a symbol by virtue of its shared meaning for those individuals. When Betsy Ross sewed the first American flag, she was creating a symbol.

The important point about the meanings of symbols is that they are entirely arbitrary, a matter of cultural convention. Each culture attaches its own meanings to things. Thus, in the United States mourners wear black to symbolize their sadness at a funeral. In the Far East people wear white. In this case the symbol is different but the meaning is the same. On the other hand, the same object can have different meanings in different cultures. Among the Sioux Indians the swastika (a cross made with ends bent at right angles to its arms) was a religious symbol; in Nazi Germany its meaning was political.

Looking at culture from this point of view, we would have to say that all aspects of culture—nonmaterial and material—are **symbolic.** Thus, culture may be said to consist of shared patterns of meanings expressed in symbols (Geertz, 1973). This means that virtually everything we say and do and use as group members has some shared meaning beyond itself. For example, wearing lipstick is more than just coloring one's lips; smoking a cigarette is more than just filling one's lungs with smoke; and wearing high-heeled shoes is more than just trying to be taller. All these actions and artifacts are part of American culture and are symbolic of sexuality and adulthood, among other things. Even a person's clothes and home—material possessions—are not only means of protection from the environment; they are also symbolic of that person's status in the social class structure. An automobile for many people is more than just a means of transportation—it is symbolic of their socioeconomic status.

Language and Culture

Of all symbols, words are the most important. Using the symbols of language, humans organize the world around them into labeled cognitive categories and use these labels to communicate with one another. Language, therefore, makes possible the teaching and sharing of cognitive and normative culture. It provides the principal means through which culture is transmitted and the foundation on which the complexity of human thought and experience rests.

Language allows humans to transcend the limitations imposed by their environment and biological evolution. It has taken tens of millions of years of biological evolution to produce human beings. On the other hand, in a matter of decades, cultural evolution has made it possible for us to travel to the moon. Biological evolution had to work slowly through genetic changes, but cultural evolution works quickly through the transmission of information from one generation to the next. In terms of knowledge and information, each human generation, because of language, is able to begin where the previous one left off. Each generation does not have to begin anew, as is the case in the animal world.

It is important that we remember that culture is selective: in each culture some aspects of the world are viewed as important and others are virtually neglected. The language of a culture reflects this **selectivity** in its vocabulary and even in its grammar. Therefore, as children learn a language, they are being molded to think and even to experience the world in terms of one particular cultural perspective.

This view of language and culture, known as the **Sapir-Whorf hypothesis,** argues that the language a person uses determines his or her perception of reality (Whorf, 1956; Sapir, 1961). This idea caused some alarm among social scientists at first, for it implied that people from different cultures never quite experience the same reality. Although more recent research has modified this extreme view, it remains true that different languages classify experiences differently—that language is the lens through which we experience the world. The prominent anthropologist Ruth Benedict (1961) pointed out, "We do not see the lens through which we look."

The category corresponding to one word and one thought in language A may be regarded by language B as two or more categories corresponding to two or more words or thoughts. For example, we have only one word for water but the Hopi Indians have two words—*pāhe* (for water in a natural state) and *kēyi* (for water in a container). On the other hand, the Hopi have only one word to cover every thing or being that flies, except birds. Strange as it may seem to us, they call a flying insect, an airplane, and a pilot by the same word. Inuit (Eskimos) must find it very odd indeed to learn that we have only one word for snow. For them falling snow, slushy snow, loose snow, hard-packed snow, wind-driven snow, and so on clearly are different, and the Inuit language uses different words for each of them. In contrast, the ancient Aztecs of Mexico used only one word for cold, ice, and snow. Verbs also are treated differently in different cultures. In English we have one verb *to go*. In New Guinea, however, the Manus language has three verbs—depending on direction, distance, and whether the going is up or down.

A little bit closer to home, consider today's urban American youngsters, who casually use many words and expressions pertaining to technology. Technological terms even are used to describe states of mind—*tuned in* or *tuned out, turned on* or *turned off,* for instance. This use of language reflects the preoccupation of American culture with technology. In contrast, many Americans are at a loss for words when they are asked to describe nature: varieties of snow, wind, or rain; kinds of forests; rock formations; earth colors and textures; vegetation zones. Why? Because these things are not of great importance in urban American culture.

The translation of one language into another often presents problems. Direct translations are often impossible because (1) words may have a variety of meanings and (2) many words and ideas are culture-bound and are not natural to another culture.

An extreme example of the first type of these translation problems occurred near the end of World War II. After Italy and Germany had surrendered, the Allies sent Japan an ultimatum to surrender also. Japan's premier responded that his government would *mokusatsu* the surrender ultimatum. *Mokusatsu* could be interpreted to mean "to consider" or "to take notice of." The premier meant it to mean the government would consider the

surrender ultimatum. The English translators, however, interpreted it to mean "to take notice of" and assumed that Japan had rejected the ultimatum. This belief that Japan was unwilling to surrender led to the atomic bombing of Hiroshima and Nagasaki. Most likely the bombing would still have taken place even with the other interpretation, but this example does demonstrate the problems in translating words and ideas from one language into another (Samovar, Porter, and Jain, 1981).

These examples demonstrate the uniqueness of language. No two cultures represent the world in exactly the same manner, and this cultural selectivity or bias is expressed in the form and content of a culture's language.

☐ Do Animals Have Culture?

All human beings have culture. It is the foundation on which all human achievements rest and is perhaps the defining characteristic of our species. But do animals have culture too? Only a short time ago most scholars would have answered "no," but in the last decade or so several kinds of research have challenged this view. For example, Jane van Lawick-Goodall (1971) discovered that chimpanzees living in nature not only use tools but produce them first and then carry them to where they will use them. These chimps break twigs off trees, strip them of leaves and bark, then carry them to termite mounds where after wetting them with spit, they poke them into tunnels and pull them out again all covered with delicous termites ready to be licked off. Sea otters search out flat pieces of rock and, while floating on their backs, place them on their stomachs and crack shellfish open against them.

symbolic A term used to describe the meanings that group members assign to things. Lipstick, for example, is used to color the lips and is also symbolic of sexuality and adulthood.

selectivity A process that defines some aspects of the world as important and others as unimportant. Selectivity is reflected in the vocabulary and grammar of language.

Sapir-Whorf hypothesis A hypothesis that argues that the language a person uses determines his or her perception of reality.

3.2
Apes and Language

Language is often cited as perhaps the major behavioral difference between humans and animals. It is said we possess language, whereas animals do not. For years scientists reported that animals used their calls simply to announce their identity, sex, species, location, and readiness to fight or mate. Some scientists claimed that it is all animals need to express, as life in the wild is simple. Or is it? Could it be that animals use symbols in other ways that we have overlooked? Is it possible to find the roots of human language in animal language?

A number of experiments—the earliest dating back to the mid-1960s—have shown that apes are able to master some of the most fundamental aspects of language. Apes, of course, cannot talk. Their mouths and throats simply are not built to produce speech, and no ape has been able to approximate more than four human words. However, efforts to teach apes to communicate by other means have met with a fair amount of success.

The first and most widely known experiment in ape language research began in 1966, under the direction of Alan and Beatrix Gardner of the University of Nevada, with a chimpanzee named Washoe. This experiment consisted of teaching to Washoe American Sign Language (ASL), the hand-gesture language used by deaf people. Washoe learned over 130 distinct signs and was able to ask for food, name objects, and make reference to her environment. The Gardners replicated their results with four other chimpanzees.

Today Washoe lives with four other signing chimpanzees at Central Washington University under the direction of Roger and Debbie Fouts. She now has an adopted son named Loolis. Loolis is not being taught any signs by humans, and the Fouts are observing him to see whether he will acquire signs from the other chimps. To date he has learned 41 signs.

Another female chimp, Lana, has been taught to communicate by pressing different-shaped buttons in a particular series to obtain a desired goal. These buttons represent individual words, and Lana has mastered quite a few of them. She can even distinguish among nouns, verbs, adjectives, and adverbs.

One of the most successful experiments involves a female gorilla named Koko. Francine Patterson has been working with Koko for the last 13 years. Koko uses approximately 400 signs regularly and another 300 occasionally. She also understands several hundred spoken words (so much

Washoe makes the sign for ball, one of hundreds of distinct signs she has learned using American Sign Language.

so that Patterson has to spell such words as "candy" in her presence). In addition Koko also invents signs or creates sign combinations to describe new things. She tells Patterson when she is happy or sad, refers to past and future events, defines objects, and insults her human companions by calling them such things as "dirty toilet," "nut," and "rotten stink."

Koko has taken several IQ tests, including the Stanford-Binet, and scores just below average for a human child—between 85 and 95 points. However, as Patterson points out, the IQ tests have a cultural bias toward humans, and the gorilla may be more intelligent than the test indicates. For example, one item instructs the child: "Point to two things that are good to eat." The choices are a block, an apple, a shoe, a flower, and an ice cream sundae. Reflecting her tastes, Koko pointed to the apple and the flower. She likes to eat flowers and has never seen an ice cream sundae. The answer therefore was quite right for Koko but was wrong for a human and so was scored as incorrect.

Patterson claims that Koko uses signs to swear, gossip, rhyme, and lie. If she is right, then these findings represent the most sophisticated results anyone has ever achieved with an ape.

Recently, however, some social scientists have raised serious questions as to whether apes truly are using language (Terrace et al., 1979; Greenberg, 1980). They argue that although apes can acquire large vocabularies, they cannot produce a sentence and are not using the equivalent of human language. For now the implications of language use by apes remains unresolved, and the evidence continues to mount on both sides. □

Drawing by Cem. © 1961. The New Yorker Magazine, Inc.

Communicating through hand signals.

Then there is the still-controversial research suggesting that primates such as chimpanzees, gorillas, and orangutans can be taught to communicate by using sign language and even symbols (see Box 3.2: "Apes and Language") and that they can invent sentences they never have been taught. Although this is not full human speech, such behavior does seem to show some of the general qualities of language such as knowing that specific things (hand signals and plastic shapes) can "stand for" other things and that such symbols must be used in certain sequences and not in others—that is, they must be used grammatically. However, some investigators doubt that these apes use grammatical rules, and they feel that many of the apes' responses are not spontaneous; they may be triggered by cues given by the researcher or teacher working with the ape (Terrace et al., 1979).

Language and the production and use of tools are central elements of nonmaterial and material culture. So does it make sense to say that culture is limited to human beings? Although scientists disagree in their answers to this question, they do agree that humans have refined culture to a far greater degree than have any other animals and also that humans depend on culture for their existence much more completely than do any other creatures.

☐ Subcultures

In order to function, every social group must have a culture of its own—its own goals, norms, values, and typical ways of doing things. As Thomas Lasswell (1965) pointed out, such a group culture is not just a "partial or miniature" culture. It is a full-blown, complete culture in its own right. Every family, clique, shop, community, ethnic group, and society has its own culture. Hence, every individual participates in a number of different cultures at the same time or in sequence in the course of a day. Meeting social expectations of various cultures is often a source of considerable stress for individuals in complex, heterogeneous societies like ours. Many college students, for example, find that the culture of the campus varies significantly from the culture of their family or neighborhood. At home they may be criticized for taking on new ways, for having crazy ideas, or for giving up good, traditional values. On campus they may be pressured to open up their minds and experiment a little or to reject old-fashioned values.

Sociologists use the term **subculture** to refer to the distinctive lifestyles, values, norms, and beliefs of groups that nevertheless participate in the culture of a whole society. The concept of subculture originated in studies of juvenile delinquency and criminality (Sutherland, 1924), and in some contexts the *sub* in *subculture* still has the meaning of "inferior." However, sociologists increasingly use *subculture* to refer to the cultures of discrete population segments within a society (Gordon, 1947). The term is primarily applied to the culture of ethnic groups (Italian-Americans, Jews, Native Americans, and so on) as well as to social classes (lower or working, middle, upper, and so on). Certain sociologists reserve the term *subculture* for marginal groups—that is, for groups that differ significantly from the so-called dominant culture.

Some theorists, stressing the adaptive function of culture, view subcultures as specialized approaches to solving the particular problems faced by specific groups (Cohen, 1955). For example, they note that chronic unemployment or underemployment among inner-city residents evokes criminal behavior that is reinforced by social interactions and eventually becomes normal for certain inner-city groups. Once this happens, a deviant subculture has begun to flourish.

Types of Subcultures

Several groups have been studied at one time or another by sociologists as examples of subcultures. These can be classified roughly as follows.

Ethnic Subcultures Especially in America, many immigrant groups have maintained their group identities and sustained their traditions while at the same time adjusting to the demands of the wider society. Though originally these were distinct and separate cul-

tures, they have become American subcultures in the context of our society.

Occupational Subcultures Certain occupations seem to involve people in a distinctive lifestyle even beyond their work. For example, New York's Madison Avenue has come to stand not only for the advertising industry but also for a somewhat frantic, success-oriented, fashion-conscious way of life. Construction workers, police, entertainers, and many other occupational groups involve people in distinctive subcultures.

Religious Subcultures Certain religious groups, though continuing to participate in the wider society, nevertheless practice lifestyles that set them apart. These include Christian evangelical groups, Mormons, Muslims, Jews, and many religious splinter groups.

Political Subcultures Small, marginal political groups may so involve their members that their entire way of life is an expression of their political convictions. Often these are so-called left-wing and right-wing groups that reject much of what they see in American society but remain engaged in the society by their constant efforts to change it to their liking.

Geographical Subcultures Large societies often show regional variations in culture. America has several geographical areas known for their distinctive subcultures. For instance, the South is known for its leisurely approach to life, its broad dialect, and its hospitality. The North is noted for "Yankee ingenuity," commercial cunning, and a crusty standoffishness. California, or "the Coast," is known for its trendiness and ultrarelaxed or "laid-back" lifestyle. And New York stands as much for an anxious, elitist, arts-and-literature-oriented subculture as for a city.

Social Class Subcultures Although social classes cut horizontally across geographical, ethnic, and other subdivisions of society, to some degree it is possible to discern cultural differences among the classes. Sociologists have documented that linguistic styles, family and household forms, and values and norms ap-

Hasidic Jews have a distinct subculture that sets them apart from society at large.

plied to child rearing are patterned in terms of social class subcultures.

Deviant Subcultures   As we mentioned above, sociologists first began to study subcultures as a way of explaining juvenile delinquency and criminality. This interest has expanded to include the study of a wide variety of groups that are marginal to society in one way or another and whose lifestyles clash with that of the wider society in important ways. Some of the deviant subcultural groups studied by sociologists include prostitutes, strippers, swingers, pool hustlers, pickpockets, drug users, and various kinds of criminals.

Counterculture as Subculture

In 1960 Milton Yinger used the term *contra-culture* to refer to those normative systems that contain as a primary element opposition to, or conflict with, the values of the wider society. He further suggested that such a culture can be understood only by reference to the relationships of the participants to the surrounding society. Sociologists now generally use the term **counterculture** to refer to the phenomenon Yinger was describing, perhaps as a result of the success of Theodore Roszak's book *The Making of a Counter-Culture* (1969).

Sociologists have described a series of recent American countercultures that include the beatniks of the 1940s and 1950s, the hippies of the early and mid-1960s, and the so-called drug culture of the late 1960s and 1970s. But the counterculture that seems to have been the most interesting one of all because of its high visibility and social impact was called simply the *Counter-culture*. Its most noted chroniclers were Roszak and Philip Slater (1970).

The Counter-culture was a complex phenomenon whose roots grew in the soils of previous countercultures but whose impetus came from the civil rights movement and opposition to the war in Vietnam. Drugs (especially marijuana) were an important part of it, and so was an odd mixture of Marxist politics, cynicism, and irreverence. Opposition to the seemingly mindless worship of technology was also a prominent feature. As Slater pointed out, central to the Counter-culture was a feeling of alienation and isolation, the feeling of estrangement from American society. Participants in the Counter-culture—mostly young people in their teens and twenties—longed for community and involvement and set about trying to create their own new social processes and institutions to meet these needs: communal living, cooperative food markets, experimental colleges and free universities, political groups and parties, and alternative (underground) newspapers. Bob Dylan, the Beatles, the Rolling Stones, and others provided the Counter-culture with some of its guiding sentiments. Paul Goodman's *Growing Up Absurd* (1962) advanced its social criti-

subculture The distinctive lifestyles, values, norms, and beliefs of discrete population segments within a society.

counterculture A term used to refer to those normative systems that contain as a primary element opposition to, or conflict with, the values of the wider society.

Bob Dylan and his music were representative of the Counter-culture of the 1960s and 1970s.

cisms, Herbert Marcuse's *Eros and Civilization* (1955) its combination of despair and sense of urgency to change things, and R. D. Laing's *The Politics of Experience* (1967) its sense that one had to be insane to be healthy in this crazy world.

The Counter-culture did indeed influence mainstream American culture: its attitudes toward sexuality and interpersonal relationships, authority, war and peace, and the rights of individuals were profoundly changed. After years of Counter-culture protests, the majority of Americans came to oppose the war in Vietnam, and the United States withdrew. The music and casual dress of the Counter-culture became the accepted style within the larger society (witness the designer blue-jean craze). The Counter-culture's emphasis on personal growth and development became part of the American ethic of the 1970s and 1980s, along with many other attitudes and values of

the Counter-culture that have had an effect on American society.

On the whole, however, the Counter-culture was not successful in its aim of radically transforming the basic values of the dominant culture. Perhaps one reason for its lack of success was the fact that in many important ways, members of the Counter-culture actually shared many of the significant underlying values of the dominant culture. One such value is the expectation of rapid success—a value that is constantly fed by the mass media, particularly by advertising. When antiwar demonstrations did not end the war quickly, many members of the Counter-culture gave up and withdrew from the mainstream of society. As the years passed, ironically, many reappeared as full-fledged members of the same prosperous communities in which they had been raised and had rejected earlier.

☐ Universals of Culture

In spite of their individual and cultural diversity, their many subcultures and counter-cultures, human beings are members of one species with a common evolutionary heritage. Therefore, people everywhere must confront and resolve certain common, basic problems such as maintaining their group organization and overcoming difficulties originating in their social and natural environments. To resolve such problems, our species has developed certain forms or patterns that are found in all cultures and, therefore, are called **cultural universals.**

Among those universals that fulfill basic human needs are the division of labor; the incest taboo, marriage, and the family; rites of passage; and ideology. It is important to keep in mind that although these *forms* are universal, their specific *contents* are particular to each culture.

The Division of Labor
Many primates live in social groups in which it is typical for each adult group member to meet most of his or her own needs. The adults find their own food, prepare their own sleeping places, and, with the exception of infant care, mutual grooming, and some defense-

Many members of the Counter-culture have reappeared as prosperous members of the communities they rejected earlier. On the left is Jerry Rubin in the 1960s as a scruffy antiestablishment Yippie leader. On the right we see him today as a Wall Street stockbroker.

related activities, they generally fend for themselves (DeVore, 1965; Kummer, 1971).

This is not true of human groups. In all societies—from the simplest bands to the most complex industrial nations—groups divide the responsibility for completing necessary tasks among their members. This means that humans constantly must rely on one another; hence they are the most cooperative of all primates (Lancaster and Whitten, 1980).

The variety of ways in which human groups divide up their tasks and choose the kinds of tasks they undertake reflects differences in environment, history, and level of technological development. Yet there are certain commonalities in the division of labor. All cultures distinguish between females and males and between adults and children, and these distinctions are used to organize the division of labor. Thus, in every society there are adult-female tasks, adult-male tasks, and children's tasks. In the last two decades in America, these role distinctions have been changing quite rapidly, a topic we shall explore in Chapter 12.

The Incest Taboo, Marriage, and the Family

All human societies regulate sexual behavior. Sexual mores vary enormously from one culture to another, but all cultures apparently share one basic value: sexual relations between parents and their children are to be avoided. (There is evidence that some primates also avoid sexual relations between males and their mothers.) In most societies it is also held to be wrong for brothers and sisters to have sexual contact (notable exceptions being the brother-sister marriages among royal families in ancient Egypt and Hawaii, and among the Incas of Peru). The term for sex within families is **incest,** and because in most

cultural universals Forms or patterns for resolving the common, basic, human problems that are found in all cultures. Cultural universals include the division of labor, the incest taboo, marriage, the family, rites of passage, and ideology.

incest The term used to describe sexual relations within families. Most cultures have strict taboos against incest, which is often associated with strong feelings of horror and revulsion.

cultures very strong feelings of horror and revulsion are attached to incest, it is said to be forbidden by **taboo.**

The presence of the incest taboo means that individuals must seek socially acceptable sexual relationships outside their families. All cultures provide definitions of who is or is not an acceptable candidate for sexual contact. They also provide for institutionalized marriages—ritualized means of publicly legitimizing sexual partnerships and the resultant children. Thus, the presence of the incest taboo and the institution of marriage results in the creation of families. Depending on who is allowed to marry whom—and how many spouses each person is allowed to have—the family will differ from one culture to another. However, the basic family unit consisting of husband, wife, and children (called the nuclear family) seems to be a recognized unit in almost every culture, and sexual relations among its members (other than between husband and wife) are almost universally taboo. For one thing, this helps keep sexual jealousy under control. For another, it prevents the confusion of authority relationships within the family. But perhaps most important, the incest taboo ensures that family offspring will marry into other families, thus recreating in every generation a network of social bonds among families that knits them together into larger, more stable social groupings.

All cultures have rites of passage which recognize stages through which individuals pass in the course of their lives.

Rites of Passage

All cultures recognize stages through which individuals pass in the course of their lifetimes. Some of these stages are marked by biological events, such as appearance of menstruation in girls. However, most of these stages are quite arbitrary and culturally defined. All such stages—whether or not corresponding to biological events—are meaningful only in terms of each group's culture.

Rarely do individuals just drift from one such stage to another; every culture has standardized rituals marking each transition. These rituals are called **rites of passage.** The most widespread—if not universal—rites of passage are those marking the arrival of puberty (often resulting in the individual's taking on adult status), marriage, and death. Typical rites of passage celebrated in American society include baptisms, bar and bas mitzvahs, confirmations, major birthdays, graduations, showers (for brides-to-be), stag parties (for grooms-to-be), wedding ceremonies and receptions, major anniversaries, retirement parties, and funerals and wakes. Such rituals accomplish several important things, including helping the individual achieve a sense of social identity, mapping out the individual's life course, and aiding the individual in making appropriate life plans. Finally, rites of passage provide people with a context in which to share common emotions, particularly with regard to events that are sources of stress and intense feelings such as marriage and death.

Ideology

A central challenge that every group faces is how to maintain its identity as a social unit. One of the most important ways that groups accomplish this is by promoting beliefs and values to which group members are firmly committed. Such strongly held beliefs and values, called **ideologies,** are the cement of social structure.

Ideologies are universal in that they are found in every culture. Some are religious, referring to things and events beyond the perception of the human senses. Others are more secular—that is, nonreligious and concerned with the everyday world. In the end all ideologies rest on untestable ideas that are rooted in the basic values and assumptions of each culture. There is a story (Geertz, 1973) about a researcher who challenged the assertion of a native of India that the world is supported on the back of an elephant. "Well," he snorted, "what's the elephant standing on?"

"He's standing on the back of a turtle," came the confident reply.

"And what's the turtle standing on?"

"From there"—the Indian smiled—"it's turtles . . . turtles all the way down."

Even though ideologies rest on untestable assumptions, their consequences are very real. They give direction and thrust to our social existence and meaning to our lives. The power of ideologies to mold people's passions and behavior is well known. History is filled with both horrors and noble deeds people have performed in the name of some ideology: thirteenth-century Crusaders, fifteenth-century Inquisitors, pro–states rights and pro–union forces in nineteenth-century America, abolitionists, prohibitionists, trade unionists, nazis and fascists, communists, segregationists, civil rights activists, feminists, consumer activists, environmentalists. These and countless other groups have marched behind their ideological banners, and in the name of their ideologies they have changed the world, often in major ways.

☐ Culture and Individual Choice

Very little of human behavior is instinctual or biologically programmed. In the course of human evolution, culture gradually was substituted for genetic programming as the source of instructions about what to do, how to do it, and when it should be done. This means that humans have a great deal of individual freedom of action—probably more than any other creature.

However, as we have seen, individuals' choices are not entirely free. By being born into a particular society with a particular culture, every human being is presented with a limited number of recognized or socially valued choices. Every society has means of training and of social control that are brought to bear on each person, making it difficult for

individuals to act or even think in ways that deviate too far from their culture's norms. In order to get along in society, people must keep their impulses under some control and express feelings and gratify needs in a socially approved manner at a socially approved time. This means that human beings inevitably feel somewhat dissatisfied, no matter to which group they belong (Freud, 1930).

Coming to terms with this central truth about human existence is one of the great tasks of living. Perhaps it is especially important to consider at the present time, for a society that sets out to meet all personal needs is doomed to failure. Sociology, therefore, has an opportunity to make a contribution to setting goals for the future, for only if these goals are grounded solidly on the nature of society and culture will it be possible to make realistic plans that have a chance of succeeding in the long run.

☐ Summary

Modern sociologists define culture as being all that humans learn to do, to use, to produce, to know, and to believe as they live out their lives in the social groups to which they belong. Although all human groups have culture, it often varies considerably from one group to another.

Whereas other animals rely on instincts to take care of their biological needs, the human animal relies on culture, which is taught and learned through social interaction. Interaction between and among cultures can result in unpleasant or amusing misunderstandings because of ethnocentrism. Being exposed to a culture that is quite different from one's own can produce culture shock. When sociologists study various cultures, they must view them objectively and perceive their customs in the context of the situation in which they

taboo The prohibition against a specific action. Incest taboos are found in most cultures.

rites of passage Standardized rituals that mark the transition from one stage of life to another.

ideologies Strongly held beliefs and values to which group members are firmly committed and which cement the social structure.

occur. Such a perspective is called cultural relativism.

The concept of culture is best understood when it is separated into two components: material culture and nonmaterial culture.

Material culture consists of all the things that human beings learn to use and produce. Humans use material culture to modify and exploit the environment. Because of their ability to control and fit into the environment, human beings have prevailed as the most flexible species on earth.

One part of nonmaterial culture is normative culture, which includes norms, mores, and folkways. Norms are rules of behavior that are agreed upon and shared within a culture. They define normal behavior. Mores define moral behavior, and folkways (or conventions) reflect custom and habit. Ideal norms are expectations of what people should do if conditions were perfect, and statistical norms provide qualifications and allowances for differences in individual behavior.

Another aspect of nonmaterial culture is cognitive culture, the shared conceptions of what the world is like—what is real, important, and correct. Included in this conception are values, a culture's orientations toward life, its notions of what is good and what is bad.

Innovation and diffusion are responsible for our cultural evolution. Innovation, comprising invention and discovery, is the source of all new culture traits, such as tools and materials, beliefs and values. Diffusion is the movement of culture traits from one culture to another. When, as sometimes happens, the material culture surges forward, the normative culture does not always keep up. This results in cultural lag.

Culture is learned, shared, adaptive, and symbolic. Symbols are objects that represent other things but need not share any quality with what they represent. Signs, on the other hand, can represent other things because they share some important quality with them. Of all the symbols in human culture, words are the most important because they enable us to organize the world into labeled cognitive categories and use these labels to communicate with one another.

The term *subculture* is used to refer to the distinctive lifestyles, values, norms, and beliefs of smaller groups that participate in the culture of a whole society. Subcultures have been categorized as ethnic, occupational, religious, political, geographical, social, and deviant. *Counterculture* is the label used to identify those normative systems that contain as a primary element opposition to, or conflict with, the values of the wider society.

Certain forms and patterns that are found in all cultures are termed cultural universals. Those universals that directly promote the organization of group life are the division of labor; the incest taboo, marriage and the family; rites of passage; and ideology.

☐ For Further Reading

BENEDICT, RUTH. *Patterns of Culture*. Boston: Houghton Mifflin, 1961 (orig. 1934). A classic study of the ways that culture shapes personality and behavior. The book compares three cultures, each dominated by one ruling motivation: the Zuñi Indians of New Mexico, the Kwakiutl of British Columbia, and the Dobu of Melanesia.

GEERTZ, CLIFFORD. *The Interpretation of Cultures*. New York: Basic Books, 1973. An absorbing collection of essays by a leading anthropologist. Rich in detail and full of lively insights, these essays show a social thinker at work examining the patterns of meaning embedded in the symbols of culture.

GORDON, MILTON M. (ed). Special Issue, "America as a Multicultural Society," *Annals of the American Academy of Political and Social Science* **454** (March, 1981), pp. 1–205. An examination of some of the major religious and ethnic subcultures in the United States.

HALL, EDWARD T. *The Dance of Life*. New York: Anchor Press/Doubleday, 1984. In this book time is treated as a language, as an organizer of activities, a synthesizer and integrator, as well as a special message system revealing how people really feel about one another.

———— *Beyond Culture*. New York: Doubleday, 1981.   An insightful discussion of recent research in communication among people in various cultures.

HARRIS, MARVIN. *Cultural Materialism*. New York: Random House, 1979.   An important book by a major social theorist. Harris, an anthropologist, attempts to show that his theory of cultural materialism stressing the adaptive role of culture is the best theory available for the study of human social life.

KROEBER, A. L., and CLYDE KLUCKHOHN. *Culture*. New York: Vintage Books, 1952.   A critical review of over 100 definitions of culture from the literature of social science. Although some core elements appear in virtually all definitions, the definitions vary greatly depending on their intended purposes and their authors' theoretical orientations.

MEAD, MARGARET. *Sex and Temperament in Three Primitive Societies*. New York: Morrow, 1963 (orig. 1936).   A fascinating study of the lives of three primitive tribes in New Guinea: the gentle Arapesh, the fierce Mundugumor, and the graceful Tchambuli. In this classic work Mead suggests that many masculine and feminine characteristics are not based on fundamental differences between the sexes but reflect the cultural conditioning of different societies.

Natural History magazine. Published by the American Museum of Natural History, New York.   A monthly magazine for the layperson. Several articles in each issue describe different aspects of cultures around the world.

SCHNEIDER, LOUIS. *The Sociological Way of Looking at the World*. New York: McGraw-Hill, 1975.   A discussion of the sociological perspective with particular emphasis on the concept of culture.

SUMNER, WILLIAM GRAHAM. *Folkways*. New York: NAL, 1960 (orig. 1906).   Sumner's theory of the emergence of norms and their cultural functions. This is a classic work on customs, folkways, and mores.

WILLIAMS, ROBIN M. *American Society: A Sociological Interpretation*, 3rd ed. New York: Knopf, 1970.   A thoughtful analysis of the norms and values of American culture and their impact on social life. Williams presents a set of characteristically American values.

YINGER, J. MILTON. *Countercultures: The Promise and the Peril of a World Turned Upside Down*. New York: Free Press, 1982.   An examination of groups and social movements that subscribe to values and norms contrary to those of the dominant society.

4 Socialization and Development

Few things in this world are as helpless as a newborn human infant. Certain reflexes are present—grasping, toe curling, sucking, startling, and crying—but muscular control is poor. It cannot roll over, move from one place to another, or even raise its head. Its limbs are weak. Unless it is fed, kept warm, and protected by others, an infant will quickly die.

If we were asked to choose a design for species survival, we would probably find these characteristics less than ideal. If we were asked to design a species that would not only survive but take over as the dominant life form on a planet, we might be inclined to reject the creature described above. This would be particularly true if we were told that in addition to its weaknesses at birth, the human being takes longer to develop and to mature than most other animals do.

□ Becoming a Person: Biology and Culture

A macaque monkey reaches maturity in 4 to 6 years, a chimpanzee in 6 to 10, but a human being takes 10 to 15 years to reach sexual maturity and usually even longer to come of age socially. This long period of dependency allows children time to learn things they need to know in order to care for themselves and become members of society. The long and complicated processes of social interaction through which a child learns the intellectual, physical, and social skills needed to function as a member of society is called **socialization.** It is through socialization experiences that children learn the culture of the society into which they have been born. It is in the course of this process that each child slowly acquires a **personality**—that is, the patterns of behavior and ways of thinking and feeling that are distinctive for each individual. Contrary to popular wisdom, nobody is a born business genius, a criminal, or a leader. These things all are learned as part of the socialization process.

Nature versus Nurture: A False Debate

Every human being is born with a set of inherited units of biological material called **genes.** Half are inherited from the mother, half from the father. No two people have exactly the same genes, except for identical twins. Genes are made up of complicated chemical substances, and a full set of genes is found in each body cell. Scientists still do not know how many different genes a human being has, but certainly they number in the tens of thousands.

What makes genes so special is that they influence the chemical processes in our bodies and even control some of these processes completely. For example, such things as blood type, the ability to taste the presence of certain chemicals, and some people's inability to distinguish certain shades of green and red are completely under the control of genes. Most of our body processes are not controlled solely by genes, however, but are the result of the interaction of genes and the environment (physical, social, and cultural). Thus, how tall you are depends on the genes that control the growth of your legs, trunk, neck, and head and also on the amount of protein, vitamins, and minerals in your diet. Genes help determine your blood pressure, but so do the amount of salt in your diet, the frequency with which you exercise, and the amount of stress under which you live.

For over a century, sociologists, educators, and psychologists have argued about which is more important in determining a person's qualities: inherited characteristics (nature) or socialization experiences (nurture). After Charles Darwin (1809–1882) published *On the Origin of Species* in 1859, human beings were seen to be a species similar to all the others in the animal kingdom. Because most animal behavior seemed to the scholars of that time to be governed by inherited factors, they reasoned that human be-

socialization The long and complicated processes of social interaction through which a child learns the intellectual, physical, and social skills he or she needs to function as a member of society.

personality The patterns of behavior and ways of thinking and feeling that are distinctive for each individual.

genes The set of inherited units of biological material with which each individual is born.

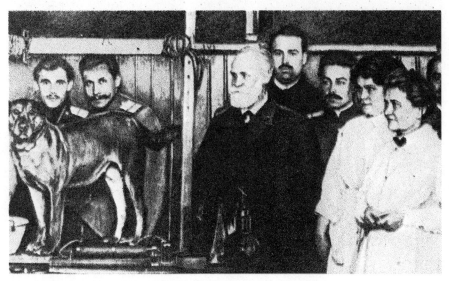

The idea of conditioning behavior emerged from Ivan Pavlov's experiments in which he was able to get a dog to salivate whenever a bell was rung.

havior similarly must be determined by **instincts**—biologically inherited patterns of complex behavior. Instincts were seen to lie at the base of all aspects of human behavior, and eventually over 10,000 human instincts were catalogued by researchers (Bernard, 1924).

Then, at the turn of the century, a Russian scientist named Ivan Pavlov (1834–1936) made a startling discovery. He found that if a bell were rung just before dogs were fed, eventually they would begin to salivate at the ringing of the bell itself, even when no food was served. The conclusion was inescapable: so-called instinctual behavior could be molded or, as Pavlov (1927) put it, *conditioned*. Dogs could be taught to salivate. Pavlov's work quickly became the foundation on which a new view of human beings was built—one that stressed their infinite capacity to learn and be molded. The American psychologist John B. Watson (1878–1958) taught a little boy to be afraid of a rabbit by startling him with a loud noise every time he was allowed to see it. What he had done was to link a certain reaction (fear) with an object (the rabbit) through the repetition of the experience. He also claimed that if he were given complete control over the environment of a dozen healthy infants, he could train each one to be whatever he wished—doctor, lawyer, artist, merchant, even beggar or thief (Watson, 1925). Among certain psychologists, **conditioning** became the means through which they explained human behavior.

Sociobiology The debate over nature versus nurture has taken a new turn with the emergence of sociobiology. The discipline of **sociobiology** tries to use biological principles to explain the behavior of all social beings, both animal and human. For example, when an especially harsh and prolonged winter leaves an Inuit (Eskimo) family without food supplies, they must break camp and quickly find a new site in order to survive. Frequently an elderly member of the family, often a grandmother, who may slow down the others and require some of the scarce food, will stay behind and face certain death. From the viewpoint of a sociobiologist such as Edward O. Wilson (1975, 1979), this would be an example of altruism, which might ultimately have a biological component.

Wilson believes that behavior can be explained in terms of the ways in which individuals act to increase the probability that their genes and the genes of their close relatives will be passed on to the next generation. Proponents of this view, known as sociobiologists, believe that social science will one day be a mere subdivision of biology. Sociobiologists would claim that the grandmother, in sacrificing her own life, is improving her kin's chances of survival. She has already made her productive contribution to the family. Now the younger members of the family must survive to ensure the continuation of the family and its genes into future generations.

Many researchers disagree with the sociobiological viewpoint. Biologist/geologist Stephen Jay Gould (1976) proposed another, equally plausible scenario, one that discounts the existence of a particular gene programmed for altruism. He perceives the grandmother's sacrifice as an adaptive cultural trait. (It is widely acknowledged that culture is a major adaptive mechanism for humans.) Gould posits that the elders remain behind because they have been socially conditioned from earliest childhood to the possibility and appropriateness of this choice. They grew up hearing the songs and stories that praised the elders who stayed behind. Such self-sacrificers were the greatest heros of the clan. Families whose elders rose to such an occasion survived to celebrate the self-sacrifice, but those families without self-sacrificing elders died out.

Wilson nonetheless makes several major concessions to Gould's viewpoint, acknowledging that among human beings, "the intensity and form of altruistic acts are to a large extent culturally determined" and that "human social evolution is obviously more cultural than genetic." However Wilson insists that the underlying motivation remains genetic, no matter how it is altered or reinforced by cultural influences.

Gould agrees that human behavior has a biological, or genetic, base. He does, however, distinguish between genetic determinism (the sociobiological viewpoint) and genetic potential. What the genes prescribe is not necessarily a particular behavior but the capacity to develop certain behaviors. Although the total array of human possibilities is inherited, which of these numerous possibilities a particular person displays depends on his or her experience in the culture.

Although both nature and nurture are important, the debate over the relative contribution of each continues. However, just as a winter snowfall is the result of both the temperature and the moisture in the air, so must the human organism and human behavior be understood in terms of both genetic inheritance and the effects of environment. **Nurture**—that is, the socialization experience—is as essential a part of "human nature" as are our genes. It is from the interplay between genes and environment that each human being emerges.

Deprivation and Development

Some unusual events and interesting research indicate that human infants need more than just food and shelter if they are to function effectively as social creatures.

Extreme Childhood Deprivation   In the winter of 1799, hunters in Aveyron, southern France, captured a boy who was running naked through the forest. He seemed to be about 11 years old and apparently had been living alone in the forest for at least 5 or 6 years. He appeared to be thoroughly wild and was subsequently exhibited in a cage from which he managed to escape several times. Finally, he was examined by "experts" who found him to be an incurable "idiot." But a young doctor, Jean Itard, thought differently. He believed that the boy's wild behavior, lack of speech, highly developed sense of smell, and poor visual attention span all were the result of having been deprived of human contact. He took the boy into his house, named him Victor, and tried to socialize him. He had little success. Although Victor slowly learned to wear clothes, to speak and write a few simple words, and to eat with a knife and fork, he ignored human voices unless they were associated with

---

instincts Biologically inherited patterns of complex behavior.

conditioning The molding of behavior through a series of repeated experiences that link a desired reaction with a particular object or event.

sociobiology A theory that explains behavior as the ways in which individuals act to increase the probability that their genes and the genes of their close relatives will be passed on to the next generation.

nurture The entire socialization experience.

food, developed no relationships with people other than Dr. Itard and the woman who cared for him, and died at the age of 40 (Itard, 1932; Shattuck, 1980).

Psychologist Bruno Bettleheim (1967) believes that children such as Victor are really autistic—that is, they have never developed the capacity to relate to others in a human way because of a prolonged early period of deprivation. The case of Anna sheds more light on this subject.

Anna had the misfortune of being born illegitimately to the daughter of an extremely disapproving family. Her mother tried to place Anna with foster parents, was unable to do so, and therefore brought her home. In order to quiet the family's harsh criticisms, the young mother hid Anna away in a room in the attic, where she could be out of sight and even forgotten by the family. Anna remained there for almost six years, ignored by the whole

Isolation in childhood denies the individual the chance to become a socialized member of society. The story of Victor was depicted in the film *The Wild Child.*

family, including her mother, who did the very minimum to keep her alive. Finally, Anna was discovered by social workers. The 6-year-old girl was unable to sit up, to walk, or to talk. In fact, she was so withdrawn from human beings that at first she appeared to be deaf, mute, and brain damaged. However, after she was placed in a special school, Anna did learn to communicate somewhat, to walk (awkwardly), to care for herself, and even to play with other children. Unfortunately, she died at the age of 10 (Davis, 1940).

A more recent case is that of a girl named Genie who for most of her life had been tied down, kept out of contact with others, and beaten. When she was removed from her home at age 13, she was poorly nourished and unable to speak or even stand upright. After four years of good care Genie had learned some social skills, was able to take a bus to school, had begun to express some feelings toward others, and had achieved the intellectual development of a 9-year-old (Curtiss et al., 1977).

These examples of extreme childhood isolation point to the fact that none of the behavior we think of as typically human arises spontaneously. Humans must be taught to stand up, to walk, to talk, even to think. Human infants must learn to have feelings for others and must see evidence that other people care for them—that is, they need to develop **social attachments.** This seems to be a basic need of all primates, as the research by Harry F. Harlow shows.

In a series of experiments with rhesus monkeys, Harlow and his coworkers demonstrated the importance of body contact in social development (Harlow, 1959; Harlow and Harlow, 1962). In one experiment, infant monkeys were taken from their mothers and placed in cages where they were raised in isolation from other monkeys. Each cage contained two substitute mothers: one was made of hard wire and contained a feeding bottle; the other was covered with soft terry cloth but did not have a bottle. Surprisingly, the baby monkeys spent much more time clinging to the cloth mothers than to the wire mothers, even though they received no food at all from the cloth mothers. Apparently the need to cling to and to cuddle against even this miserable substitute for a real mother was more important to them than being fed.

Human infants develop social attachments when they learn to have feelings for others and see that others care for them.

Other experiments with monkeys have confirmed the importance of social contact in behavior. Monkeys raised in isolation *never* learn how to interact with other monkeys or even how to mate. If placed in a cage with other monkeys, they either withdraw or become violent and aggressive—threatening, biting, and scratching the others.

Monkeys who are raised without affection make wretched mothers themselves. After being artificially impregnated and giving birth, such monkeys either ignored their infants or displayed a pattern of behavior described by Harlow as "ghastly."

> When an infant attempted to make contact with its mother, she would literally scrape it from her body and abuse it by various sadistic devices. The mother would push the baby's face against the floor and rub it back and forth. Not infrequently, the mother would encircle the infant's head with her jaws, and in one case an infant's skull was crushed in this manner. (*Science News*, 1972)

Most times the researchers were able to stop the battering and abuse, but in a few instances the mothers were so violent that the infants were killed before the researchers could intervene. For obvious ethical reasons, similar experiments have never been carried out with human babies.

As with all animal studies, we must be very cautious in drawing inferences for human behavior. After all, we are not monkeys. Yet Harlow's experiments show that without socialization, monkeys do not develop normal social, emotional, sexual, or maternal behavior. Because human beings rely on learning even more than monkeys do, it is likely that the same is true of us.

It is obvious that the human organism needs to acquire culture to be complete; it is very difficult, if not impossible, for children who have been isolated from other people from infancy onward to catch up. They apparently suffer permanent damage, although human beings do seem to be somewhat more adaptable than were the rhesus monkeys studied by Harlow.

Infants in Institutions   Studies of infants and young children in institutions confirm the view that human beings' developmental needs include more than the mere provision of food and shelter. Psychologist René Spitz (1945) visited orphanages in Europe and found that in those dormitories where children were given routine care but were otherwise ignored, they were slow to develop and were withdrawn and sickly. In sociological language these children's needs for **affiliation** (meaningful interaction with others) were not met.

More recently, 75 children in an American institution were studied (Provence and Lipton, 1962). The infants who received minimal physical care but were otherwise neglected in their first year of life became severely retarded socially and emotionally. Although they improved when they were given

social attachments The emotional bonds that infants form with others that are necessary for normal development. Social attachments are a basic need of human beings and all primates.

affiliation Meaningful interaction with others.

USING SOCIOLOGY
Childhood Socialization and Day Care Centers

A variety of demographic and social changes have produced a demand for day care centers. The children in these centers encounter a fair amount of primary socialization by individuals other than their parents. A variety of opinions have been expressed about the effect that this type of socialization will have on children during their early years.

Individuals born between 1945 and 1957 are said to be part of the baby-boom generation. That is, they were born during a period in our history when we saw a steadily rising birth-rate. These same people are now forming the families of today. The baby-boomers have fewer children than families did in the past, but even so, there are so many of them that the actual number of births has been increasing in recent years. For example, there were 15.6 million preschoolers in 1977, and it is projected there will be 19.2 million in 1990.

The mothers who were born between 1945 and 1957 are far more likely to be working when their children are preschoolers than were women in the past. Forty-seven percent of the women in this category are working today, as opposed to only 20 percent who did so in 1960. Meanwhile Grandma has moved to a retirement area, and the woman next door, who in the past may have taken in children, now has a full-time job herself. Small wonder then that the number of parents who put their preschoolers in group care centers has more than doubled in the last 20 years.

Attempting to cash in on this phenomenon is an enterprise known as Kinder-Care, started in 1969 by Robert Mendel. Mendel saw it as an opportunity "to bring child care out of antiquity, as McDonald's did with the hamburger or Holiday Inns did with the motel." As with Mc-

Donald's, this company has been able to add standardization and centralization to something that in the past may have been a mom-and-pop operation. Mendel's ability to change the need for such a service based on the sociological changes that were taking place has made Kinder-Care an enormously successful company. However, is this type of high-volume, profit-oriented child care serving the children as well as traditional child rearing did?

Sociologists and psychologists have been able to answer this question by noting that just as all parenting is not uniformly good, neither is all day care mediocre. High-quality day care can be a suitable substitute for home parenting. According to one review of infant day care by Kagan, Kearsley, and Zelago,

> with regard to the possibility of adverse effects, there appears to be little or no pervasive empirical research evidence thus far indicating that infant day care experience is likely to have unfavorable developmental consequences. This is a valid generalization whether one considers the child's intellectual development, affectional relationships between child and mother, or subsequent peer relationships and responsiveness to adult socialization influences.

There seems to be little doubt that good-quality day care is not a problem. The problems arise in centers where the staff is underpaid, where there is a high staff turnover, and where there is a high worker–child ratio. For example, a teacher with a college degree and a teaching certificate will start at Kinder-Care at the minimum wage and will average just over $7,000 for a full year's work. At some centers the staff turnover is consequently quite high. Kinder-Care staffs its centers according to

state-mandated ratios, which for infants in Connecticut is 1 to 4. In Alabama it is 1 to 6, and in Ohio it is 1 to 8. For 3-year-olds, some states allow a ratio of 1 worker to 15 children.

Lois Hoffman (1974) raised another interesting point about working women and day care. If a mother is employed and her child is in a group care setting, is she providing a different model of behavior for the children in the family? We would assume that the children in such a family would have a different idea of what a woman's role in society is. This would be particularly important to women who have daughters, as research has shown that the daughters of working women see the world in a less sex-stereotypical fashion than do daughters of nonworking women. They have a higher regard for their own sex and a greater sense of competence. As Hoffman concludes,

> for girls, maternal employment seems to contribute to a greater admiration of the mother, a concept of the female role which includes less restriction and a wider range of activities, and a self-concept which incorporates these aspects of the female role.

Because day care is now becoming a reality for a large segment of the nation's preschoolers, the issue that needs to be addressed is how to make it a positive socialization experience. Clearly this requires well-trained staff and a properly supervised environment. Given that type of environment, there need be no fear of damaging experiences, and we shall perhaps even see a decrease in sex-role stereotyping.

Sources: Louis W. Hoffman, "The Effects of Maternal Employment on the Child: A Review of the Research," *De-*

velopmental Psychology **10** (1974), pp. 204–228. J. Kagan, R. B. Kearsley, and P. R. Zelago, "The Effects of Infant Day Care on Psychological Development" (Paper presented at the meeting of the American Association for the Advancement of Science, Boston, 1976). Myron Magnet, "What Mass-Produced Child Care Is Producing," *Fortune,* November 28, 1983, pp. 157–174. Caryl Rivers, Rosalind Barnett, and Grace Baruch, *Beyond Sugar and Spice* (New York: Putnam's, 1979), pp. 82–96. ☐

more attention or when they were brought back into their families, they continued to show some long-lasting emotional problems. Like Harlow's monkeys, they found it difficult to form relationships with others, and they were unable to control their aggressive impulses adequately.

As these studies show, human infants need more than just food and shelter if they are to grow and develop normally. Every human infant needs frequent contact with others who demonstrate affection, who respond to attempts to interact, and who themselves initiate interactions with the child. Infants also need contact with people who find ways to interest the child in his or her surroundings and who teach the child the physical and social skills and knowledge that are needed to function. In addition, in order to develop normally, children need to be taught the culture of their society—to be socialized into the world of social relations and symbols that are the foundation of the human experience (see Using Sociology: "Childhood Socialization and Day Care Centers").

☐ The Concept of Self

Every individual comes to possess a social identity by occupying culturally and socially defined positions—called **statuses**—in the course of his or her socialization. This social identity changes as the person moves through the various stages of childhood and adulthood recognized by the society. New statuses are occupied; old ones are abandoned. Picture a teenage girl who volunteers as a "candystriper" in a community hospital. She leaves that position to attend college, joins a sorority, becomes a premedical major, and graduates. She goes to medical school, completes an internship, becomes engaged, and then enters a program for specialized training in surgery. Perhaps she marries; possibly she has a child. All along the way she is moving through different social identities, often assuming several at once. When, many years later, she returns to the hospital where she was a teenage volunteer, she will have an entirely new social identity: adult woman, surgeon, wife (perhaps), mother (possibly).

The above description of the developing girl was from the outside, the way that other members of the society experience her social transitions, or what sociologists would call changes in her **social identity.** But what of the person herself? How does this human being who is growing and developing physically, emotionally, intellectually, and socially experience these changes? Is there something constant about a person's experience that allows one to say, "I am that changing person—changing, but yet somehow the same individual?" In other words, do all human beings have personal identities separate from their social identities? Most social scientists believe that the answer is yes. This changing yet enduring personal identity is called the **self.**

The self develops when the individual becomes aware of his or her feelings, thoughts, and behaviors as separate and distinct from those of other people. This usually happens at a young age when children begin to realize that they have their own history, habits, and needs and begin to imagine how these might appear to others. By adulthood the concept

---

statuses The culturally and socially defined positions occupied by individuals throughout their lifetime.

social identity The statuses that define an individual. Social identity is determined by how others see us.

self The personal identity of each individual that is separate from his or her social identity.

of self is fully developed. Most researchers would agree that the concept of self includes (1) an awareness of the existence, appearance, and boundaries of one's own body (you are walking among the other members of the crowd, dressed appropriately for the occasion, and trying to avoid bumping into people as you chat), (2) the ability to refer to one's own being by using language and other symbols ("Hi, as you can see from my name tag, I'm Harry Hernandez from Gonzales, Texas."), (3) knowledge of one's personal history ("Yup, I grew up in Gonzales. My folks own a small farm there, and since I was knee-high to a grasshopper I've wanted to study farm management."), (4) knowledge of one's needs and skills ("I'm good with my hands all right, but I need the intellectual stimulation of doing large-scale planning."), (5) the ability to organize one's knowledge and beliefs ("Let me tell you about planning crop rotation. . . ."), (6) the ability to organize one's experiences ("I know what I like and what I don't like."), and (7) the ability to take a step back and look at one's being as others do, to evaluate the impressions one is creating, and to understand the feelings and attitudes one stimulates in others ("It might seem a little funny to you that a farmer like me would want to come to a party for the opening of a new art gallery. Well, as far back as I can remember, I always kinda liked looking at pictures, and now that I can afford to indulge myself, I thought maybe I'd get me some of my own.") (see Cooley, 1909; Erikson, 1964; Gardner, 1978; Mead, 1934).

Theories of Development

Among the scholars who have devised theories of development, Charles Horton Cooley, George Herbert Mead, Sigmund Freud, and Erik Erikson stand out because of the contributions they have made to the way sociologists today think about socialization. Cooley and Mead saw the individual and society as partners. They were symbolic interactionists (see Chapter 1) and as such believed that the individual develops a self solely through social relationships—that is, through interaction with others. They believed that all our behaviors, our attitudes, even our ideas of self, arise from our interactions with other people. Hence they were pure environmentalists in that they believed that social forces rather than genetic factors shape the individual.

Freud, on the other hand, tended to picture the individual and society as enemies. He saw the individual as constantly having to yield reluctantly to the greater power of society, to keep internal urges (especially sexual and aggressive ones) under strict control.

Erikson presented something of a compromise position. He thought of the individual as progressing through a series of stages of development that express internal urges, yet are greatly influenced by societal and cultural factors.

Charles Horton Cooley (1864–1929) Cooley believed that the self develops through the process of social interaction with others. This process begins early in life and is influenced by such primary groups as the family. Later on, peer groups become very important as we continue to progress as social beings. Cooley believed that each of us develops a sense of self through a three-stage process known as the **looking-glass theory.** First, we imagine how our actions appear to others. Second, we imagine how other people judge these actions. Finally, we make some sort of self-judgment based on the presumed judgments of others. In effect, other people become a mirror or looking glass for us (1909).

In Cooley's view, therefore, the self is entirely a social product—that is, a product of social interaction. Each individual acquires a sense of self in the course of being socialized and continues to modify it in each new situation throughout life. Cooley believed that the looking-glass self constructed early in life remains fairly stable and that childhood experiences are very important in determining our sense of self throughout our lives.

One of Cooley's principal contributions to sociology was his observation that although our perceptions are not always correct, what we believe is more important to determining our behavior than is what is real. This same idea was also expressed by sociologist W. I. Thomas (1928) when he noted, "If men define situations as real, they are real in their

During Mead's play stage children begin to imitate behavior and also formulate role expectations.

consequences." If we can understand the ways in which people perceive reality, then we can begin to understand their behavior.

George Herbert Mead (1863–1931) Mead was a philosopher and a well-known social psychologist at the University of Chicago. His work led to the development of the school of thought called symbolic interactionism (described in Chapter 1). Mead built on Cooley's ideas, tracing the beginning of a person's awareness of self to the relationships between the caregiver (usually the mother) and the child (1934). At some point, children realize that they are separate from the caregiver who comes and goes regardless of the child's wishes, and that it is possible to influence the behavior of the caregiver. Through trial and error, infants discover how the caregiver responds to such things as crying, gurgling, squirming, and so on, and is able to get the caregiver to provide food, cuddles, dry diapers, and so on. This trial-and-error process leads the child to develop those gestures that are recognized and responded to by the caregiver (and by others

who are immediately important to the child). In this way the child builds a repertoire of what Mead called **significant symbols**—that is, those gestures (frowns, pouts, screams, smiles, and eventually words) that have meaning in terms of the culture of the people caring for the child. These symbols, Mead argued, are the basis of social existence. Eventually children acquire language and refer to themselves symbolically, thus learning self-awareness. At that point each child is a full, social person separate from but in interaction with others.

Mead believed that the self develops in three stages (1934). The first or *preparatory*

looking-glass theory A theory developed by Charles Horton Cooley to explain how individuals develop a sense of self through interaction with others. The theory has three stages: (1) we imagine how our actions appear to others, (2) we imagine how other people judge these actions, and (3) we make some sort of self-judgment based on the presumed judgments of others.

significant symbols The repertoire of gestures that have meaning in terms of a particular culture.

PORTFOLIO II
The Amish

The Old Order Amish are a separate subculture within American society. As such, they have norms, values, and beliefs that differ widely from those of the larger society. The Amish believe that any intrusion by modern society into their lifestyle will result in the ultimate destruction and disappearance of their culture and community. They therefore reject modern conveniences, forbid radios, movies, and television, and have their own school system which ends with the eighth grade. They neither smoke nor drink and have a uniquely austere style of dress.

These followers of Jacob Amman first came to the United States in 1717 when a schism developed in the Anabaptist movement in Switzerland. Today most Amish are found in Pennsylvania, Ohio, and Indiana. There are no longer any Amish in Europe.

The Amish practice shunning, or "meidung," as a form of social control. Anyone guilty of a major violation of the accepted values is subject to social ostracism, and if this does not correct the behaviors, the members of the community will completely ignore and isolate the guilty party. They will not eat with, talk to, or carry on business with the offender. Shunning has proven an effective method of controlling unacceptable behavior.

The values and norms of Amish culture have remained constant since the Amish first established communities in America in the early 1700s. Most Amish are farmers, although some now work in factories and in the construction business. The Amish reject modern conveniences, including automobiles, preferring horse-drawn transportation.

Amish women "visit" at a local farmers' market while the men attend an auction, where one young man has bought a pair of skis. Most socializing seems to take place while individuals are attending to practical matters, such as buying farm implements at auction or purchasing produce at market.

Due to the 1972 Supreme Court decision ruling that mandatory attendance at public schools is a violation of the First Amendment of the Constitution, children can now attend Amish schools. When not in school, most children help their parents with farm work.

stage is characterized by the child's imitating the behavior of others, which prepares the child for learning social-role expectations. In the second or *play stage* the child has acquired language and begins not only to imitate behavior but also to formulate role expectations: playing house, cops and robbers, and so on. In this stage the play will feature many discussions among playmates about the way things "ought" to be. "I'm the boss," a little boy may announce. "The daddy is the boss of the house." "Oh no," his friend might counter, "Mommies are the real bosses. . . ." In the third or *game stage* the child learns that there are rules that specify the proper and correct relationship among the players. For example, in a baseball game there are rules that apply to the game in general as well as to a series of expectations about how each position should be played. During the game stage, according to Mead, we learn the expectations, positions, and rules of society at large. Throughout life, in whatever position we occupy, we must learn the expectations of the various positions with which we interact as well as the expectations of the general audience, if our performance is to go smoothly.

Thus, for Mead the self is rooted in, and begins to take shape through, the social play of children and is well on its way to being formed by the time the child is 8 or 9 years old. Therefore, like Cooley, Mead regarded childhood experience as very important to charting the course of development.

Sigmund Freud (1856–1939) Freud was a pioneer in the study of human behavior and the human mind. He was a doctor in Vienna, Austria, who gradually became interested in the problem of understanding mental illness. Once he turned his attention to this area, he charted new pathways of scholarship and thought, and today he is regarded as one of the most creative and original thinkers of the nineteenth and twentieth centuries.

Over his lifetime, Freud developed a body of thought about the mind that is called **psychoanalysis.** (The same term is used to refer to the form of treatment Freud developed to treat patients suffering from mental illnesses.) Psychoanalysis rests on two basic hy-

Sigmund Freud (1856–1939).

potheses: (1) Psychic determinism, or the view that every human act has a psychological cause or basis. Because no human behavior comes about as the result of chance, "slips" of the tongue, moments of clumsiness, and unexpected moods all are explainable as events in the person's mind. (2) The existence of the unconscious, or the view that people are aware of only a small part of the thoughts and feelings that exist in their minds.

In Freud's view, the self has three separately functioning parts: the id, the superego, and the ego. The **id** consists of the drives or instincts that Freud believed every human being inherits but for the most part remain unconscious. Of these instincts two are most important: the aggressive drive and the erotic

psychoanalysis A body of thought developed by Sigmund Freud that rests on two basic hypotheses: (1) every human act has a psychological cause or basis, and (2) every person has an unconscious mind.

id In Freudian theory, one of the three separately functioning parts of the self. The id consists of the unconscious drives or instincts that Freud believed every human being inherits.

or sexual drive (called **libido**). Every feeling derives from these two drives. The **superego** is the internal censor. It is not inherited biologically, like the id, but is learned in the course of a person's socialization. The superego keeps trying to put the brakes on the id's impulsive attempts to satisfy its drives (the so-called **pleasure principle**). Another way to describe this is to say that the superego in each of us represents society's norms and moral values as learned primarily from our parents. So, for instance, the superego must hold back the id's

TABLE 4.1 *Erikson's Stages of Development Toward Maturity*

Stage	Age Period	Characteristic to Be Achieved	Major Hazards to Achievement
Trust versus mistrust	Birth to 1 year	Sense of trust or security—derived from affection and gratification of needs	Neglect, abuse, or deprivation of consistent and appropriate love in infancy; harsh or early weaning
Autonomy versus shame and doubt	1 to 4 years	Sense of autonomy—children viewing themselves as individuals in their own right, apart from their parents, although dependent upon them	Conditions that interfere with the child's achieving feeling of adequacy or learning skills such as walking
Initiative versus guilt	4 to 5 years	Sense of initiative—period of vigorous reality testing, imagination, and imitation of adult behavior	Overly strict discipline, internalization of rigid ethical attitudes that interfere with the child's spontaneity and reality testing
Industry versus inferiority	6 to 12 years	Sense of duty and accomplishment—laying aside fantasy and play, undertaking real tasks, developing academic and social competencies	Excessive competition, personal limitations, or other conditions that lead to experiences of failure, resulting in feelings of inferiority and poor work habits
Identity versus role confusion	Adolescence	Sense of identity—clarification in adolescence of who one is and what one's self is	Cultural and personal factors combined with failure of society to provide clearly defined roles and standards; formation of cliques that provide clear but not always desirable roles and standards
Intimacy versus isolation	Young adulthood	Sense of intimacy—ability to establish close personal relationships with members of both sexes	Cultural and personal factors that lead to psychological isolation or to formal rather than warm personal relations
Generativity versus stagnation	30s to 50s	Parental sense—productivity and creativity for others as well as self	Failure to master developmental tasks, resulting in egocentric, nonproductive person
Integrity versus despair	60+	Sense of integrity—acceptance of the dominant ideals of one's culture, sense of past, present, and future, and meaning of life	Lack of tradition, consistent values, support from culture leaves much for the individual to work out; many unable to find meaning in life or accept limitations

unending drive for sexual expression (Freud, 1920, 1923). The id and superego, then, are eternally at war with each other. Fortunately, there is a third functional part of the self that tries not only to mediate in the eternal conflict between id and superego but also to find socially acceptable ways for the id's drives to be expressed. This part of the self, which constantly is evaluating social realities and looking for ways to adjust to them, is called the **ego.** For example, the ego finds socially appropriate sexual partners with whom the individual can discharge sexual drives. Thus, just as the id works on the pleasure principle, the ego works on the **reality principle** (Freud, 1920, 1923).

Freud pictured the individual as constantly in conflict: the instinctual drives of the id (essentially sex and aggression) push for expression, while at the same time the demands of society set certain limits on the behavior patterns that will be tolerated. Even though the individual needs society, society's restrictive norms and values are a source of ongoing discontent (Freud, 1930). Freud's theories suggest that society and the individual are enemies, with the latter yielding to the former reluctantly and only out of compulsion.

Erik H. Erikson (1902–   ) In 1950 Erikson, an artist-turned-psychologist who studied with Freud in Vienna, published an influential book called *Childhood and Society* (1963). In it he built on Freud's theory of development but added two important elements. First, he stressed that development is a lifelong process and that a person continues to pass through new stages even during adulthood. Second, he paid greater attention to the social and cultural forces operating on the individual at each step along the way.

In Erikson's view, human development is accomplished in eight separate stages (see Table 4.1). Each stage amounts to a crisis of sorts brought on by two factors: biological changes in the developing individual and social expectations and stresses. At each stage the individual is pulled in two opposite directions to resolve the crisis. In normal development the individual resolves the conflict

Erik H. Erickson (1902–   ).

experienced at each stage somewhere toward the middle of the opposing options. For example, very few people are entirely trusting, and very few trust nobody at all. Most of us are able to trust at least some other people and thereby form enduring relationships while at the same time staying alert to the possibility of being misled.

libido One of the two basic instincts of the id. According to Freud, the libido controls the erotic or sexual drive.

superego In Freudian theory, one of the three separately functioning parts of the self. The superego consists of society's norms and values, learned in the course of a person's socialization, that often conflict with the impulses of the id. The superego is the internal censor.

pleasure principle A Freudian principle that explains the id's impulsive attempts to satisfy its drive for sexual expression.

ego In Freudian theory, one of the three separately functioning parts of the self. The ego tries to mediate in the conflict between the id and the superego and to find socially acceptable ways for the id's drives to be expressed. This part of the self constantly evaluates social realities and looks for ways to adjust to them.

reality principle A Freudian principle that explains the ego's attempts to adjust to the socially appropriate demands of the real world.

According to Erik Erickson, the period between birth and age one is a time when the desired outcome is that the child develop a sense of trust or security, derived from affection and the gratification of needs.

Erikson's view of development has proved to be useful to sociologists because it seems to apply to many societies. In a later work (1968) he focused on the social and psychological causes of the "identity crisis" that seems to be so prevalent among American and European youths. Erikson's most valuable contribution to the study of human development has been to show that socialization continues throughout a person's life and does not stop with childhood. There is indeed development after 30—and after 60 and 70 as well. The task of building the self is lifelong; it can be considered our central task from cradle to grave. We construct the self—our identity—using the materials made available to us by our culture and our society.

Daniel Levinson (1920–   ) A fascinating blend of sociology and psychology has taken place in the area of adult development. Through research in this field we have come to recognize that there are predictable age-related developmental periods in the adult life cycle, just as there are in the developmental cycles for children and adolescents. These periods are marked by a concerted effort to resolve particular life issues and goals.

Important research in this area has been done by Daniel Levinson and his colleagues (1978). Levinson recruited 40 men, aged 35 to 45, from four occupational groups: factory workers, novelists, business executives, and academic biologists. Each subject was interviewed several times during a two- to three-month period and again, if possible, in a follow-up session two years later.

From this study Levinson developed the foundation of his theory. He proposed that adults are periodically faced with new but predictable developmental tasks throughout their life and that working through these challenges is the essence of adulthood. Levinson believes the adult life course is marked by a continual series of building periods, followed by stable periods, and then followed again by periods in which attempts are made to change some of the perceived flaws in the previous design.

Levinson's model describes the periods in the adult life cycle:

I. EARLY ADULT PERIOD (age 18 to 22)
   Leaving the family of origin is the major task of this period. A great deal of energy is expended in trying to reduce dependence on the family for support or authority. Peer support often becomes critical to this task.

II. GETTING INTO THE ADULT WORLD (age 22 to 28)
   This period is marked by the exploration and beginning commitment to adult roles, responsibilities, and relationships. Career advancement may become a major focal point. This period produces an initial life structure including marriage and occupation. The individual may also form a *dream* that serves as a guiding force and provides images of future life structures.

III. AGE 30 TRANSITIONAL PERIOD (age 28 to 32)
   At this point the individual begins to per-

ceive some of the "flaws" in his or her initial life structure and sets out to correct them. Divorce and job changes are common during this period. This is a time of internal instability, in which many aspects of the individual's life are questioned and examined.

IV. SETTLING DOWN (age 33 to 40)
Having reworked some of the aspects of one's life during the previous period, the individual is now ready to seek order and stability. There is a strong desire for achievement and an earnest attempt to make the dream a reality. The individual wants to "sink roots."

V. AGE 40 TRANSITIONAL PERIOD (age 38 to 42)
This is a major transitional period and represents the turning point between young and middle adulthood. The individual starts to see a difference between the dream and the reality of his or her life, leading to a great deal of soul searching. Divorce and career changes once again become real possibilities. The individual may start to give up certain aspects of the dream and become less achievement and advancement oriented.

VI. BEGINNING OF MIDDLE ADULTHOOD (age mid-40s)
The previous period of turmoil has produced a greater acceptance of oneself. The individual is less dominated by the need to win or to achieve external rewards and more concerned with enjoying his or her life and work. The individual also has a greater concern for other people than before.

Levinson did not study people beyond age 45, though he does believe that the developmental process continues throughout the entire life course. The model is particularly interesting to sociologists because it shows us what a close relationship there is between individual development and one's position in society at a particular time.

Dimensions of Human Development

Clearly, the development of the self is a complicated process. It involves many interacting

Jean Piaget (1896–1980).

factors, including the acquisition of language and the ability to use symbols. There are three dimensions of human development tied to the emergence of the self: cognitive development, moral development, and gender identity.

Cognitive Development For centuries most people assumed that a child's mind worked in exactly the same way as an adult's mind does. The child was thought of as a miniature adult who was simply lacking information about the world. Swiss philosopher and psychologist Jean Piaget (1896–1980) was instrumental in changing that view, through his studies of the development of intelligence in children. His work has been significant to sociologists because the processes of thought are central to the development of identity and, consequently, to the ability to function in society.

Piaget found that children move through a series of predictable stages on their way to logical thought, and some never attain the most advanced stages. From birth to age 2, the sensorimotor stage, the infant relies on touch and the manipulation of objects for information about the world, slowly learning about cause and effect. At about the age of 2, the child begins to learn that words can be symbols for objects. In this, the preoperational stage of development, the child cannot yet see the world from another person's point of view.

The operational stage is next and lasts from the age of 7 to about the age of 12. During this period the child begins to think with some logic and can understand and work with numbers, volume, shapes, and spatial relationships. With the onset of adolescence, the child progresses to the most advanced stage of thinking—formal logical. People at this stage are capable of abstract, logical thought and can develop ideas about things that have no concrete reference, such as infinity, death, freedom, and justice. In addition, they are able to anticipate possible consequences of their acts and decisions. Achieving this stage is crucial to developing an identity and an ability to enter into mature interpersonal relationships (Piaget and Inhelder, 1969).

Moral Development Every society has a **moral order**—that is, a shared view of right and wrong. Without moral order a society would soon fall apart. People would not know what to expect from themselves and one another, and social relationships would be impossible to maintain. Therefore, the process of socialization must include instruction about the moral order of an individual's society.

The research by Lawrence Kohlberg (1969) suggests that not every person is capable of thinking about morality in the same way. Just as our sense of self and our ability to think logically develop in stages, our moral thinking develops in a progression of steps as well. To illustrate this, Kohlberg asked children from a number of different societies (including Turkey, Mexico, China, and the United States) to resolve moral dilemmas such as the following: A man's wife is dying of cancer. A rare drug might save her, but it costs $2,000. The man tries to raise the money but can come up with only $1,000. He asks the druggist to sell him the drug for $1,000, and the druggist refuses. The desperate husband then breaks into the druggist's store to steal the drug. Should he have done so? Why or why not?

Kohlberg was more interested in the *reasoning* behind the child's judgment than in the answer itself. Based on his analysis of this reasoning, he believed that changes in moral thinking progress step by step through six qualitatively distinct stages (although most people never go beyond stages 3 or 4):

Stage 1: Orientation toward punishment. Those who thought the man should steal (pros) said he could get into trouble if he just let his wife die. Those who said he should not steal (cons) stressed that he might be arrested for the crime.

Stage 2: Orientation toward reward. The pros said that if the woman lived, the man would have what he wanted. If he got caught in the act of stealing the drug, he could return the drug and would probably be given only a light sentence. The cons said that the man should not blame himself if his wife died; and if he got caught, she might die before he got out of jail so he would have lost her anyway. Stealing just would not pay.

Stage 3: Orientation toward possible disapproval by others. The pros observed that nobody would think the man was bad if he stole the drug but that his family would never forgive him if his wife died and he had done nothing to help her. The cons pointed out that not only would the druggist think of the man as a criminal, but the rest of society would, too.

Stage 4: Orientation toward formal laws and fear of personal dishonor. The pros said that the man would always feel dishonored if he did nothing and his wife died. The cons said that even if he saved his wife by stealing, he would feel guilty and dishonored for having broken the law.

Stage 5: Orientation toward peer values and democracy. The pros said that failure to steal the drug would cost the man his peers' respect because he would have acted out of fear rather than out of consideration of what was the logical thing to do. The cons countered that the man would lose the respect of the community if he were caught because he would show himself to be a person who acted out of emotion rather than according to the laws that govern everybody's behavior.

Stage 6: Orientation toward one's own set of values. The pros focused on the man's conscience, saying he would never be able to live with himself if his wife died and he had done nothing. The cons argued that although others might not blame the man for stealing the drug, in doing so he would have failed to live up to his own standards of honesty.

Kohlberg has found that although these stages of moral development correspond roughly to other aspects of the developing self, most people never progress to stages 5 and 6. In fact, Kohlberg subsequently dropped stage 6 from his scheme because it met with widespread criticism that he could not deny. It was felt by critics that stage 6 was elitist and culturally biased. Kohlberg himself could find no evidence that any of his long-term subjects ever reached this stage (Muson, 1979). At times people regress from a higher state to a lower one. For example, when Kohlberg analyzed the explanations that Nazi war criminals of World War II gave for their participation in the systematic murder of millions of people who happened to possess certain religious (Jewish), ethnic (gypsies), or psychological (mentally retarded) traits, he found that none of the reasons were above stage 3 and most were at stage 1—"I did what I was told to do, otherwise I'd have been punished" (Kohlberg, 1967). However, many of these war criminals had been very responsible and successful people in their prewar lives and presumably in those times had reached higher stages of moral development. In his experiments where he has tried to create "Just Communities," Kohlberg has put his research to use by attempting to teach moral order in schools and penal institutions in the United States.

Gender Identity   One of the most important elements of the sense of self is our view of ourselves resulting from our sex—what sociologists call **gender identity.** Certain aspects of gender identity are rooted in biology. Males tend to be larger and stronger than females are, but females tend to have better endurance than males do. Females also become pregnant and give birth to infants and (usually) can nurse infants with their own milk. However, gender identity is mostly a matter of cultural definition. There is nothing inherently male or female about a teacher, a pilot, a carpenter, or a typist other than what our culture tells us. As we shall indicate in Chapter 12, gender identity and "sex roles" are far more a matter of nurture than of nature.

☐ Early Socialization in American Society

Children are brought up very differently from one society to another. Each culture has its own child-rearing values, attitudes, and practices. No matter how children are raised, however, each society must provide certain minimal necessities to ensure normal development. The infant's body must, of course, be cared for. But more than that is required. Children need speaking social partners (some evidence suggests that a child who has received no language stimulation at all in the first five to six years of life will be unable ever to acquire speech [Chomsky, 1975]). They also need physical stimulation; objects that they can manipulate; space and time to explore, to initiate activity, and to be alone; and finally, limits and prohibitions that organize their options and channel development in certain culturally specified directions (Provence, 1972).

Every society provides this basic minimum care in its own culturally prescribed ways. A variety of agents are used to mold the child to fit into the society. Once again, these agents vary from culture to culture. Here we consider some of the most important agents of socialization in American society.

The Family

For young children in most societies—and certainly in American society—the family is

---

moral order A society's shared view of right and wrong.

gender identity The view of ourselves resulting from our sex. Gender identity is one of the most important elements of the sense of self.

Each family socializes its children to its own particular version of that society's culture.

the primary world for the first few years of life. Children's earliest social relationships are with family members. Because the young child has few experiences outside the family, the family's values, norms, ideals, and standards are accepted by the child uncritically as correct—indeed, as the only way things could possibly be. Even though later experiences lead children to modify much of what they have learned within the family, it is not unusual for individuals to carry into the social relationships of adult life the role expectations that characterized the family of their childhood. It is hardly insignificant that we joke about such things as a newlywed wife not being able to cook her husband's favorite meal as well as his mother did or that the daughter of a stereotypical Jewish mother is herself destined to become one.

Every family, therefore, socializes its children to its own particular version of the society's culture. In addition, however, each family exists within certain subcultures of the larger society: it belongs to a geographical region, a social class, one (or two) ethnic groups, and possibly a religious group or other subculture. Families differ with regard to how important these factors are in determining their lifestyle and their child-rearing practices. For example, some families are very deeply committed to an ethnic identification such as black, Hispanic, Chinese, Native American, Italian American, Polish American, or Jewish. Much of family life may revolve around participation in social and religious events of the community and may include speaking a language other than English.

There is also evidence that social class influences the ways in which children are raised in America. There is a great deal of variation in socialization practices among the families of any given social class and also much overlapping of practices from one class to another. Certain patterns of child rearing do seem to characterize working-class parents, and others are typical of the middle class. One study (Kohn, 1969) found that working-class parents value cleanliness, neatness, obedience, and respectful behavior in their children more than do middle-class parents. The latter are less interested in the specifics of their children's behavior and are more concerned about the psychological factors that motivate their children. They want their children to be happy and curious and to learn self-control.

The School
The school is an institution intended to socialize children in selected skills and knowledge. In recent decades, however, the school has been assigned additional tasks. For instance, in poor communities and neighborhoods, school lunch (and breakfast) programs are an important source of balanced nutrition for children. There is also a more basic problem the school must confront. As an institution the school must resolve the conflicting values of the local community and of the state and regional officials whose job it is to deter-

mine what should be taught. For example, in many schools of the rural American South, the theory of evolution is not taught, even though it represents a body of knowledge that most American scholars accept as valuable and important. In other instances, education officials are able to ramrod curriculum changes into the classroom despite the complaints of parents, whose objections are dismissed as ignorant or tradition-bound.

The school has a function, often called the "hidden curriculum," beyond the transmitting of skills and knowledge. It is expected to expand the child's socialization across the narrow boundaries of family and community and instill a commitment to society as a whole. Toward this end pupils are required to recite the Pledge of Allegiance and to study civics and American history. Unfortunately, the school often socializes children into docile behavior by teaching them to sit quietly and passively and to absorb knowledge as it is presented to them by their teachers. In this way children learn to rely on "authorities" or "experts" to define what is or is not important. Argument and critical skepticism rarely are encouraged (Henry, 1963).

In coming to grips with their multiple responsibilities, many schools have established a philosophy of education that encompasses socialization as well as academic instruction. According to the philosophy adopted by one school, for instance, its aim is to help students develop to their fullest capacity, not only intellectually, but also emotionally, culturally, morally, socially, and physically. By exposing the student to a variety of ideas, the teachers attempt to guide the development of the whole student in areas of interests and ability unique to each. Students are expected to learn how to analyze these ideas critically and reach their own conclusions. The ultimate goal of the school is to produce a "well-integrated" person who will become socially responsible and a good neighbor and citizen. Two questions arise: Is such an ambitious, all-embracing educational philosophy working? And is it an appropriate goal for our schools?

In a way the school is a model of much of the adult social world. Interpersonal relationships are not based on individuals' love

Peer groups help adolescents to form a set of values and beliefs independent of those of their parents.

and affection for one another. Rather, they are impersonal and predefined by the society with little regard for each particular individual who enters into them. Children's process of adjustment to the school's social order is a preview of what will be expected as they mature and attempt to negotiate their way into the institutions of adult society (job, political work, organized recreation, and so on). Of all the socializing functions of the school, this may be the most important.

Peer Groups

Peers are individuals who are social equals. From early childhood until late adulthood we encounter a wide variety of peer groups. No one will deny that they play a powerful role in our socialization. Often their influence is greater than any other socialization source.

Within the family and the school, children are in socially inferior positions relative

peers Individuals who are social equals.

to figures of authority (parents, teachers, principals). As long as the child is small and weak, this social inferiority seems natural, but by adolescence a person is amost fully grown, and arbitrary submission to authority is not so easy to accept. Hence, many adolescents withdraw into the comfort of social groups composed of peers. In the United States, school-age children spend twice as much time with their peers, on the average, than they do with their parents (Bronfenbrenner, 1970).

Peer groups provide valuable social support for adolescents who are moving toward independence from their parents. As a consequence their peer-group values often run counter to those of the older generation. New group members are quickly socialized to adopt symbols of group membership such as styles of dress, use and consumption of certain material goods, and stylized patterns of behavior. It is ironic that although adolescents often proclaim their freedom from the conformity of their parents, within their peer groups they are themselves slaves to group fashion.

A number of studies have documented the increasing importance of peer-group socialization in America. One reason for this is that parents' life experiences and accumulated wisdom may not be very helpful in preparing young people to meet the requirements of life in a society that is changing constantly. Not infrequently adolescents are better informed than their parents are about such things as sex, drugs, and technology. In her study of the generation gap, Margaret Mead (1970) likened youth to pioneers exploring not a new land but rather a new time.

As the authority of the family diminishes under the pressures of social change, peer groups move into the vacuum and substitute their own morality for that of the older generation. Peer groups are most effective in molding the behavior of those adolescents whose parents do not provide consistent standards, a principled moral code, guidance, and emotional support (Baumrind, 1975; Elder, 1975). In fact, three decades ago sociologist David Riesman (1950) already thought that the peer group had become the single most powerful molder of many adolescents' behavior and that striving for peer approval had become the dominant concern of an entire American generation—adults as well as adolescents. He coined the term *other directed* for those who are so concerned with finding social approval, and he called the groups to which they belong the *lonely crowd*.

The Mass Media

It is possible that today Riesman would review his thinking somewhat. Over the past 25 to 30 years, the **mass media**—television, radio, magazines, films, newspapers—have become important agents of socialization in America. It is almost impossible in our society to escape from the images and sounds of television or radio; even in most private homes, especially those with children, the media are constantly visible and/or audible.

The mass media are an impersonal means of transmitting information to great numbers of people in a very short period of time. For the most part, the communication is one way, creating an audience that is conditioned to receive passively what is sometimes called the **mass culture** (Rosenberg and White, 1971), consisting of whatever news, messages, programs, or events are brought to them. Because young children are so impressionable and because in so many American households the television is used as an unpaid mechanical babysitter, social scientists have become increasingly concerned about the socializing role played by the mass media in our society.

Today 98 percent of all households in the United States have a television set. The average household has the television on for over seven hours each day. Most children become regular watchers of television between the ages of 3 and 6. One study concluded that by the time most people reach the age of 18, they will have spent more waking time watching television than doing anything else—talking with parents, spending time with friends, or even going to school (Liebert and Poulos, 1972). What effect does this have on children (see Focus on Research: "Value Socialization on Television")?

For one thing, today's children receive an enormous amount of information. They are instantly informed of new fads and styles, new activities, and new products such as the Cab-

FOCUS ON RESEARCH
Value Socialization on Television

Linda and Robert Lichter analyzed three decades of television programming and found that contemporary TV is laced with antiestablishment and antiauthority themes. The public is being socialized to a particular view of society through entertainment programming, as the following indicates.

A popular staple of television is the cops-and-robbers show. Few of us are aware of the subtle messages that are coming through in these shows. Criminals on prime time TV are usually middle- or upper-class white males over thirty. In fact, wealthy individuals are portrayed as criminals twice as often as those who are middle-class or poor. Why are the affluent breaking the law? According to the scriptwriters, it is an insatiable desire for more wealth. More than 75% of the crimes committed were acts of pure greed.

A reappearing example is the businessman whose selfish pursuit of profit leads him into illegal activity. These evil entrepreneurs range from the head of a multinational corporation who murders a competitor to the owner of a chemical company who illegally dumps toxic wastes and attempts murder to cover up his crime.

The Lichters found that on TV businessmen constitute the largest criminal group aside from professional gangsters. Almost one in four lawbreakers with identifiable occupations are businessmen or their underlings.

Another television evildoer is the pillar of the community. We are exposed to the doctor who runs a counterfeiting ring or the lawyer whose sideline is pornography. And finally the police themselves often turn out to be the criminals. One criminal in eight on television is drawn from the ranks of those sworn to uphold the law.

The criminals we hardly ever see on television are the juvenile delinquents or the youth gangs. We are rarely exposed to the culture of poverty that is directly or indirectly responsible for a great deal of crime.

When it comes to solving crimes private investigators were portrayed to be far more successful than the police. In fact, the success of private eyes was part of a broader trend involving the need for outside help or unorthodox means to enforce the law. Law enforcers who bent the rules were twice as likely to solve crimes as those who went by the book. Even more effective was the work of private citizens who as a group were actually more effective crime-stoppers than the private eyes.

Television programming manages to uphold the law without glorifying the law-enforcement establishment. The messages that come through are ones of political alienation, that public officials and the wealthy are often greedy and corrupt, and that only the modern-day Robin Hoods are successful in preserving the moral standards of our society.

Source: Linda Lichter and Robert Lichter, *Wall Street Journal,* January 6, 1984, p. 20. ☐

---

bage Patch dolls that swept the country in 1983 and 1984. There also are more and more shows specifically designed to instruct children—to supplement what they learn in school (or prepare preschoolers for school). Most young viewers of "Sesame Street," for instance, have learned to recite their ABC's, and children who watch a great deal of television may enter school somewhat better informed than those who do not.

Serious concerns have been raised about the impact of television and the other mass media on the development of America's youth. Groups of parents and consumers have questioned whether it is good to expose children (and adults) to an unending barrage of messages suggesting that only through the purchase of advertisers' products will they find satisfaction in their lives. There is also some evidence that the content of television shows can affect people's attitudes, values, and behavior (Wiebe, 1971). Television as a major factor in children's lives is illustrated by the case of a 6-year-old who, when asked if he had ever had bad dreams, answered, "Sure I do. But when that happens, I just flick to another channel."

The influence of television on behavior is of special concern to those who are worried

mass media Impersonal methods of communication, including television, radio, magazines, films, and newspapers, that have become some of society's most important agents of socialization.

mass culture The products of the mass media, including news, messages, programs, and events, that audiences passively receive.

about the increase of violent crime and aggression among children and who believe that the prevalence of violence depicted on TV and in films is one cause of this problem (Johnson, 1971). This concern led, in 1969, to a federal appropriation of $1 million to help study the problem. The research eventually led to a major report by the Surgeon General's Scientific Advisory Committee on Television and Social Behavior (1972). The information was fairly conclusive: televised violence does lead to aggressive behavior. In 1976 Jesse Steinfeld, then surgeon general of the United States, noted, "These studies and scores of similar ones make it clear to me that the relationship between televised violence and antisocial behavior is sufficiently proved to warrant immediate remedial action. . . ."

We need to know more about the socializing effects of the mass media on today's youth. Nobody who observes young people can fail to notice the constant presence of radios, tape decks, stereos, television sets, and magazines catering to their fads and interests. The socializing impact of mass media on America's youth is not very well understood, and research on these matters is difficult and expensive to carry out. As sociologist Paul Lazarsfeld (1971) observed, "What we do or hope for in regard to mass culture is based on value judgments." Vested interests and prejudices make the objective assessment of the impact of mass media on socialization very difficult indeed.

☐ Adult Socialization

A person's **primary socialization** is completed when he or she reaches adulthood. This means that adults have mastered the basic information and skills required of members of a society. They have (1) learned a language and can think logically to some degree, (2) accepted the basic norms and values of the culture, (3) developed the ability to pattern their behavior in terms of these norms and values, and (4) assumed a culturally appropriate social identity.

There is still much to learn, however, and there are many new social identities to explore. Socialization, therefore, continues during the adult years. However, **adult socialization** differs from primary socialization in two ways.

First, adults are much more aware than are young people of the processes through which they are being socialized. In fact, they deliberately engage in programs such as advanced education or on-the-job training in which socialization is an explicit goal. Second, adults often have more control over how they wish to be socialized and therefore can mobilize more enthusiasm for the process. Whether going to business school, taking up a new hobby, or signing up for the Peace Corps, adults can decide to channel their energy into making the most effective use of an opportunity to learn new skills or knowledge.

An important aspect of adult socialization is **resocialization,** which involves being exposed to ideas or values that in one way or another conflict with what was learned in childhood. This is a common experience for college students who leave their homes for the first time and encounter a new environment in which many of their family's cherished beliefs and values are held up to critical examination. Changes in religious and political orientation are not uncommon during the college years, which often lead to a time of stress for students and their parents.

Television has become an important agent of socialization. Most children become regular viewers of television between the ages of 3 and 6. "Sesame Street" is a program that attempts to educate as well as entertain.

Resocialization involves exposure to ideas and values that conflict with those learned in childhood. In this scene from the film *An Officer and a Gentleman* the new recruits are about to experience the culture and values of the army.

Erving Goffman (1961a) discussed the major resocialization that takes place in **total institutions**—environments such as prisons or mental hospitals in which the participants are physically and socially isolated from the outside world. Goffman noted several factors that make for effective resocialization. These include (1) isolation from the outside world, (2) spending all of one's time in the same place with the same people, (3) shedding individual identity by giving up old clothes and possessions for standard uniforms, (4) a clean break with the past, and (5) loss of freedom of action. Under these circumstances there usually is a major change in the individual along the lines prescribed by those doing the resocialization. This can also be seen in the methods used by various religious cults to indoctrinate their members. Group pressures start to become so strong that major personality changes take place, and new value systems replace the ones learned previously. Consequently, friends and family members may feel that they no longer recognize a person who has been resocialized (see Popular Sociology: "Moonies and the Unification Church").

There are many important issues involved in adult socialization, of which four will be discussed below: marriage and responsibility, parenthood, vocation, and aging.

Marriage and Responsibility

As Ruth Benedict (1938) noted in a now-classic article on socialization in America, ". . . our culture goes to great extremes in emphasizing contrasts between the child and the adult." We think of childhood as a time without cares, a time for play. Adulthood, on the other hand, is marked by work and taking up the burden

primary socialization The process by which children master the basic information and skills required of members of society.

adult socialization The process by which adults learn new statuses and roles. Adult socialization continues throughout the adult years.

resocialization An important aspect of adult socialization that involves being exposed to ideas or values that in one way or another conflict with what was learned in childhood.

total institutions Environments, such as prisons or mental hospitals, in which the participants are physically and socially isolated from the outside world.

POPULAR SOCIOLOGY
Moonies and the Unification Church

In 1977, Alan MacRobert of Boston's The Real Paper *decided to do a study of the Reverend Sun Myung Moon's Unification church, which had been receiving a lot of publicity. Reports were circulating about Moon's vast wealth and real estate holdings, about terror and brainwashing, deceptive fund-raising tactics, and the armies of young people selling flowers and candy at airports and parking lots. MacRobert chose to do his research from within the church as a participator-observer. He easily made contact and allowed himself to be invited to a weekend workshop/retreat. Much to his dismay as a journalist, what began for MacRobert as a simple investigative story evolved into a deeply shaking emotional experience. The tactics used by the Moonies, as they are called, to win converts closely resemble the resocialization tactics that sociologist Erving Goffman described as being used in total institutions.*

Many people think the Unification Church's recruiting methods are the most disturbing aspect of all its activities. Most recruits are first approached on the street. Because the Moonies' objective is to persuade the potential convert to go away to one of their weekend workshops, the techniques they use in this initial contact are designed to be highly persuasive. Love and emotion are the two themes emphasized throughout. Flattery and ego gratification are never-ending and difficult to resist. These calculated forms of manipulation finally convince many to go to the weekend workshop.

Once the young recruits have been lured away from their daily lives, the Moonies begin applying their resocializing techniques in earnest. Upon arriving at the retreat, the potential converts are met with balloons and a banner reading "Welcome Home Brothers and Sisters." Complete strangers stage a big hugging "welcome home" scene and, without thinking, the newcomers hug back.

Everybody has such an unself-conscious good time that even the most reluctant recruit is happy to join in. This lovefest is actually a subtle form of intimidation, calculated to make any nonparticipant conspicuous.

The Moonies plan their tightly controlled activities so that every minute of the 16- to 18-hour-long day is accounted for—no free time for recruits. It quickly becomes difficult to keep track of time, and by the day's end the new arrivals feel emotionally drained. The use of games, group sing-alongs, discussions, lectures, and prayers give such a strong sense of oneness or mission that most recruits feel intense guilt at the thought of leaving. They are never allowed to be alone or given time for private thoughts; a Moonie is always nearby ready to talk and draw them back into the group's activities. Little time is scheduled for sleep. After two or three days of such a grueling schedule the potential convert is confused and numb.

This constant physical and mental bombardment is exhausting, capable of wearing down the strongest resistance and leaving the young recruit open to suggestion. This is where the lectures and discussion groups come in, the Moonies' main methods of resocialization. Both can be extremely persuasive; their presentation is slick and controlled, questions and answers are subtly sidetracked, and the newcomers are effectively prevented from speaking with each other away from the group. As soon as a recruit manages to go off alone or with another newcomer, three Moonies appear, offering hot chocolate or tea and urging the strays to rejoin the main group.

The lecturers are touted as "very special" and are immaculately tailored and groomed—clear signs of authority. Interestingly, they are the only persons allowed to wear shoes in the house, which serves to rein-

force those special and authoritarian qualities, albeit subconsciously. All are well-trained, masterful speakers and begin their lectures with the look-what-the-church-has-done-for-me approach. They seek to make the new people feel guilt and terror about anything resembling self-interest, stressing the church's importance over all else, especially any relationships outside the group, whether they be with parents, friends, or lovers. This theme is repeated in the tightly controlled discussion groups through the negative reinforcement of traditional values, the discussion leader (a Moonie, of course) hedging on answers and evading questions from the group. The Moonie routine in discussions is to deflect all questions, let information about the group be doled out in bits and pieces to hold the recruits' interest, and maintain the image of a warm communal family with never a harsh word or putdown, a place where one can truly open one's heart. Because by now it has been made abundantly clear that mom, dad, and apple pie are all bad, the Moonie way is accepted as the only way by the young recruits, who are under the stress of mental and physical exhaustion. Resocialization is complete as the last vestige of their sense of detachment is swallowed up in the communal spirit.

At the end of the weekend, staff Moonies go into full swing with their sales pitch, trying to convince the recruits to sign up for the next step—another, longer workshop. Feelings of guilt are aroused when the recruits are told how heartbroken everyone will be if they leave. And if that doesn't work, the Moonies exploit the weaknesses of their young guests until the recruits feel they can't leave. For example, the father of a new recruit had died three months before the weekend workshop. It was repeatedly suggested to him that three is a mystical number and could only mean his father was trying to tell him something, namely, to go to the next workshop. The possibility was convincing enough to get him to go, although within a week he had returned to his normal life, harboring a strong distrust of the Moonies. Others, on the other hand, were convinced to stay and become active members.

Although the tactics used by the Moonies have been heavily criticized, the Moonies defend their position. They describe their program as simply being involved in getting people to rid themselves of a few old ideas and replace them with new ones.

Source: Alan M. MacRobert, "The Dark Side of the Moon," *The Real Paper* (March 5, 1977), and "The Moon Business," *The Real Paper* (April 9, 1977). □

---

of responsibility. One of the great adult responsibilities in our society is marriage.

Indeed, many of the traditional role expectations of marriage no longer are accepted uncritically by today's young adults. For both men and women choices loom large: How much should they devote themselves to a career, how much to self-improvement and personal growth, how much to a spouse? Ours is a time of uncertainty and experimentation. Even so, marriage still retains its primacy as a life choice for adults. Although divorce has become acceptable in most circles, marriage still is treated seriously as a public statement that both partners are committed to each other and to stability and responsibility.

Once married, the new partners must define their relationships to each other and in respect to the demands of society. This is not as easy today as it used to be when these choices largely were determined by tradition. Although friends, parents, and relatives usually are only too ready to instruct the young couple in the "shoulds" and "should nots" of married life, increasingly such attempts at socialization are resented by young people who wish to chart their own courses. One choice they must make is whether or not to become parents.

Parenthood as a Developmental Stage

Once a couple has a child, their responsibilities increase enormously. They must find ways to provide the care and nurturing necessary to the healthy development of their baby, and at the same time they must work hard to keep their own relationship intact, because the arrival of an infant inevitably is accompanied by stress. This requires a reexamination of the role expectations each partner has of the other, both as a parent and as a spouse.

Of course, most parents anticipate some stresses and try to resolve them even before the baby is born. Financial plans are made, living space is created, baby care is studied. Friends and relatives are asked for advice, and their future baby-sitting services are secured. However, not all the stresses of parenthood are so obvious. One that is frequently overlooked is the fact that parenthood is itself a new developmental phase.

The psychology of being and becoming a parent is extremely complicated. Already during the pregnancy both parents experience intense feelings—some expected, others quite surprising. Some of these feelings may even be very upsetting: for instance, the fear that one will not be an adequate parent or that one might even harm the child. Sometimes such feelings lead people to reconsider their decision to become parents.

The birth of the child brings forth new feelings in the parents, many of which can be traced to the parents' own experiences as infants. As their child grows and passes through all the stages of development we have described, parents relive their own development. In psychological terms parenthood can be viewed as a "second chance": adults can bring to bear all that they have learned in order to resolve the conflicts that were not resolved when they were children. For example, it might be possible for some parents to develop a more trusting approach to life while observing their infants grapple with the conflict of basic trust and mistrust (Erikson's first stage). Only some of this "reliving" will be experienced consciously, but it is an ongoing aspect of parenthood and can account for unexpected changes both in one's own self or in one's spouse (Anthony and Benedek, 1970).

CASE STUDY
Socialization to a Profession

As one enters a profession, a certain amount of socialization takes place. Not only must the newcomer be initiated into practices of that profession, but he or she also must be socialized to the values, common understandings, and shared interests of those already in the profession. In fact, many have suggested that the real factor that determines an individual's success in a profession is how well he or she has learned the dominant themes and ideology expressed by the practitioners of that profession. The following is an example of a woman's introduction into the profession of psychiatry.

Patricia Paddison is a psychiatric resident at Mount Sinai Hospital in New York City. She is officially a second-year postgraduate (PGY-2), but that is misleading. Like the majority of her 12 fellow residents, Paddison spent the previous year in a standard medical internship. Her PGY-2 experience represented her first extended exposure to psychiatry, and her full introduction to psychiatry was to last three years.

The transition from medicine to psychiatry is abrupt, dramatic, and usually unsettling. In medicine, when a patient has a defect, the physician's job is to fix it. There is a tremendous amount of security in that model. "In psychiatry, you may get the neurotransmitters under control with drugs, but then you still have to figure out what being mentally ill means to the patients and help them cope with it."

Suspended between art and science, psychiatry is characterized by extremes. The strict Freudians believe that developmental disruptions in childhood are the basis of adult psychological disorders. The pure biologists maintain that mental diseases are mainly a function of chemical imbalances. The behaviorists focus instead on a patient's behavior and seek ways to modify it, caring little about the Freudian or biological issues.

Pat Paddison and her fellow residents grappled with these theoretical issues in the course of their training. In practice, however, disparate treatment approaches coexisted peacefully on the wards. "Whatever works" was the unspoken guideline.

If the professional challenges that a PGY-2 faces are considerable—managing difficult patients, recognizing symptoms, making diagnoses, and learning to lead a team of nurses and support staff—so are the personal ones. The exposure to so much psychopathology often threatens the defenses of the residents themselves and brings their own conflicts to the surface. At the very least, it prompts most of them to look more deeply into themselves.

On the first day of her residency, Paddison reported to the nursing station. No one offered to point out her patients to her. Eventually she began walking from room to room, making her own introductions. Later in the morning, one of the nurses mentioned casually to Paddison that she would be expected to run a small group that afternoon. But she was not yet sure what a "small group" was, much less what running one entailed. She soon found out that groups are simply open-ended gatherings of the more verbal patients on the ward and the staff members in charge of treating them. But lead such a group? Trial by fire, Pat thought to herself. And sure enough, no sooner had the group begun than an animated, articulate patient challenged her.

"What are you, anyway?" the woman asked, verbalizing the anger that patients commonly feel when they are forced to accept a whole new set of doctors. "Are you a resident, a doctor, or what?"

"I'm a resident and a psychiatrist," Paddison answered, wondering whether she was giving an appropriate answer.

It was not long before Paddison found herself in a confrontation with the nursing staff. The testing of new residents by nurses is a predictable rite of passage. Residents come and go on the wards, but the nurses remain, in the front-line jobs. When patients attack, verbally or physically, nurses and aides, not doctors, are usually the victims. More seasoned and often more knowledgeable than beginning PGY-2s, nurses are understandably reluctant to take orders from them at first—or to trust their judgment.

The practice of having the least experienced doctors take care of patients so disturbed that they require hospitalization seems incongruous at first. As it happens, patients with acute symptoms often require the most straightforward treatment. The main issue is deciding what medications to prescribe and in what dosages. Insight-oriented psychotherapy requires much more training and subtlety, but it usually is not appropriate in a hospital setting, in which time is short and the patients are often too sick to step back and look inward, anyway.

It was about three months into her residency that Paddison was finally able to step back from her work. It began to dawn on her that she had set a very difficult course for herself. Working with patients in such acute distress—for whom there were rarely simple answers—took a subtler toll than had the long hours of her internship. She started to wonder, "Am I really helping these people?"

The absence of positive feedback was a frequent source of discussion among the residents. "Most people in medicine," Paddison observed, "are used to delaying gratification for a lot of years. After all that time in medical school, you assume you're going to get a payoff in the end. Then you come into psychiatry, start treating patients, and you feel like you're never appreciated. Every once in a while, a patient says something positive when he's ready to leave. But even that is an exception."

The right mix of empathy and professional detachment was a tricky issue for all the residents. It was all too easy to treat symptoms as if they were not attached to human beings. But it was not necessarily productive to become too personally involved with the patients, either.

Neutrality was the word most often used to describe the ideal therapeutic stance. Paddison rarely volunteered any personal information to a patient or exhibited any emotion besides attentive concern. "Patients have a natural curiosity about you, but it really does end up interfering in the end. You want to have a positive alliance with them, but you also want to keep it professional. You want to be personable, but not too personal."

If residents sometimes interpreted the concept of neutrality a bit too literally, there was an explanation for that. They were doing what they thought experienced psychiatrists do. The ability to show more of yourself would come later. Even then, psychotherapy is such a mystical process that you never know for sure what effect saying something is going to have on a patient. The right thing for a good but inexperienced resident to say may be nothing—on the grounds that if you cannot do any good, at least do not do any harm.

Source: Abridged and adapted from Tony Schwartz, "The Making of a Psychiatrist," *New York* magazine, February 28, 1984, pp. 32–43. □

Career Development: Vocation and Identity

Taking a job is more than finding a place to work. It means stepping into a new social context with its own statuses and roles, and it requires that a person be socialized to meet the needs of the situation. This may even include learning how to dress appropriately. For example, a young management trainee in a major corporation was criticized for wearing his keys on a ring snapped to his belt. "Janitors wear their keys," his supervisor told him. "Executives keep them in their pockets." The keys disappeared from his belt.

Aspiring climbers of the occupational ladder may even have to adjust their personalities to fit the job. In the 1950s and 1960s, corporations looked for quiet, loyal, tradition-oriented men to fill their management positions—men who wouldn't "upset the apple-cart" (Whyte, 1956)—and most certainly not women. Since the late 1960s, however, the trend has been toward recruiting men and women who show drive and initiative and a capacity for creative thinking and problem solving.

Some occupations require extensive resocialization (see Case Study: "Socialization to a Profession"). Individuals wishing to become doctors or nurses must overcome their squeamishness about blood, body wastes, genitals, and the inside of the body. They must also accept the undemocratic fact that they will receive much of their training while caring for poor patients (usually ethnic minorities). More well-to-do patients receive care mostly from fully trained personnel.

The armed forces use basic training of recruits to socialize them to obey orders without hesitating and to accept killing as a necessary part of their work. For many people such resocialization can be quite painful. It is not unusual for those undergoing such experiences to become confused and depressed and to question whether they have chosen the right occupation. Some drop out; others eventually stop resisting and accept the values of their teachers. In retrospect the pain and confusion of their resocialization process may even seem amusing.

Aging and Society

In many societies age itself brings respect and honor. Older people are turned to for advice, and their opinions are valued because they reflect a full measure of experience. Often older people are not required to stop their productive work simply because they have reached a certain age. Rather, they work as long as they are able to, and their tasks may be modified to allow them to continue to work virtually until they die. In this way people maintain their social identities as they grow old—and their feelings of self-esteem as well.

This is not the case in the United States. Most employers retire their employees arbitrarily once they have reached age 70, and social security regulations restrict the amount of nontaxable income that retired persons may earn.

The American family is not ordinarily prepared to accommodate an aging parent who is sick or whose spouse has recently died. Apartment rents are high, and the cost of an extra room may be more than the family can afford. Most suburban houses are not designed to meet the needs of the elderly. In the typical split-level house, for example, none of the bedrooms is at the same level as the kitchen or living room, and the family room frequently is down a flight of stairs. As a result, those older people who have trouble moving around or caring for themselves often find themselves with no choice but to live in homes for the aged and nursing homes. They have little access to their families and are deprived of the pleasure of seeing their grandchildren grow up. (The grandchildren also are deprived of the pleasure of getting to know their grandparents.)

This means that late in life, many people are forced to acquire another social identity. Sadly, it is not a valued one but, rather, one of social insignificance (de Beauvoir, 1972). This can be very damaging to older people's self-esteem, and it may even hasten them to their graves. The last few years have seen some attempts at reform to address these issues. Age discrimination in hiring is illegal, and some companies have extended or eliminated arbitrary retirement ages. However, the problem will not be resolved until the elderly achieve once again a position of respect and value in American culture.

Even though aging is itself a biological process, becoming old is a social and cultural one: only society can create a "senior citizen." From infancy to old age both biology and culture play important parts in determining how people develop over the course of their lives.

☐ Summary

Socialization is that long and complicated process of social interaction through which children learn the intellectual, physical, and social skills they need to function as a member of society. Through socialization experiences, children learn the culture of the society into which they have been born. During this process each child acquires a personality—the patterns of behavior and ways of thinking and feeling that are distinctive for each individual.

The long-standing debate over nature versus nurture has taken a new turn with the emergence of sociobiology. The discipline of sociobiology tries to use sociological principles to explain the behavior of all social beings, both animal and human.

Studies of extreme childhood deprivation have shown that humans need more than just food and shelter in order to develop into fully functioning social beings. Every individual acquires a social identity by occupying culturally and socially defined positions. In addition, the individual acquires a personal identity called the self. Cooley, Mead, Freud, and Erikson developed theories of self that have been useful to sociologists in helping them view socialization. Cooley and Mead were symbolic interactionists who believed that the individual can develop only through social relationships. Freud saw the individual and society as enemies in a constant struggle, explaining this struggle through his concept of the id, ego, and superego. Erikson emphasized that development is a lifelong process and that even in adulthood, a person continues to pass through new stages. Levinson showed that there are predictable age-related developmental periods in the adult life cycle, just as there are in the developmental cycles for children and adolescents.

The work of Piaget has been important for sociologists because the processes of thought are central to the development of identity and therefore to the ability to function in society. Piaget found that children move through a series of predictable stages on their way to logical thought: from objects to symbols to concepts to logic. Kohlberg studied the moral development of individuals and proposed that it takes place in six stages. Most people never progress beyond stage 3 or 4, and those who do sometimes regress. In addition to the development of thought processes and moral orientation, the development of a gender identity is crucial to the sense of self.

The most important early socializing influences on the American child are the family, the school, peer groups, and the mass media. These factors have an impact on the concept of self as well as on the individual's interaction with others.

Adulthood marks the completion of primary socialization, but it does not mark the end of learning and developing. Often adults are required to go through a process of resocialization when they are exposed to ideas or values that conflict with what they learned in childhood. Among the important issues involved in adult socialization, marriage, parenthood, vocation choice, and aging stand out as pivotal points in adult development.

☐ For Further Reading

COX, HARVEY. *Turning East*. New York: Simon & Schuster, 1977. A fascinating and sympathetic account of some of the new Asian religions and the processes by which their young adherents are resocialized into their new faiths.

ERIKSON, ERIK H. *Childhood and Society*, rev. ed. New York: Norton, 1963. A theory of childhood socialization that uses a historical and cross-cultural approach and emphasizes the importance of the social environment. The book discusses Erikson's eight stages in the human life cycle and the crises confronting the individual at each stage.

FISCHER, DAVID HACKETT. *Growing Old in America*. New York: Oxford University Press, 1977. A sociological and historical look at aging in America—the social consequences of an extended life span, attitudes toward the elderly, and attitudes of the elderly toward themselves.

FREUD, SIGMUND. *Civilization and Its Discontents*. New York: Norton, 1962 (orig. 1930). Freud's classic work on the inherent conflict between society's demands on the individual (imposed during socialization) and the individual's own internal drives.

LEVIN, JACK, and WILLIAM C. LEVIN. *Ageism: Prejudice and Discrimination Against the Elderly*. Belmont, Calif.: Wadsworth, 1980. The authors document the ageism that pervades Western society. Similarities are pointed out among racism, sexism, and ageism and the common practice of blaming the victims for their dilemmas.

LEVINSON, DANIEL J., with CHARLOTTE N. DARROW, EDWARD B. KLEIN, MARIA H. LEVINSON, and BRAXTON MCKEE. *The Seasons of a Man's Life*. New York: Ballantine, 1978. A full account of a study that explores and explains the periods of personal development through which adults pass.

PIAGET, JEAN. *The Moral Judgment of the Child*. New York: Free Press, 1965. An examination of a problem that stands at the heart of society: How does a child distinguish right from wrong? For a concise account of Piaget's theory of cognitive development, see *The Psychology of the Child* (New York: Basic Books, 1969) by Piaget and his colleague, Barbel Inhelder.

ROSE, PETER I. (ed.) *Socialization and the Life Cycle*. New York: St. Martin's Press, 1979. An anthology dealing with various aspects of socialization throughout the life cycle.

SHATTUCK, ROGER. *The Forbidden Experiment: The Story of the Wild Boy of Aveyron*. New York: Farrar, Straus, & Giroux, 1980. This is an account of the wild boy who was discovered in France in 1799.

SPIRO, MELFORD. *Children of the Kibbutz*. rev. ed. Cambridge, Mass.: Harvard University Press, 1975. A look at what happens when the responsibility for raising a child lies not with the parents but with the entire social group. In this classic work Spiro examines the process of socialization and the development of personality among children raised on an Israeli *kibbutz*.

5 Social Interaction and Social Structure

Most human infants come into a world made up of several social groups and networks. They encounter a family, relatives of family members, friends of the family, community or tribe, ethnic or racial group, nation, and so on. Thus at birth, human infants enter a social environment that has preexisting and ongoing structures, values, and expectations. Through their interactions with others, the new arrivals survive, grow, and learn. From the beginning, human beings are social beings.

Human infants need people who will care for them, feed them, shelter them against the elements, and, perhaps most important, teach them. It is this teaching that contributes to both similarities and differences among individuals and among various cultural groups and societies. One person does not behave exactly like any other person, nor is any one family or group or society exactly like any other family or group or society.

A human being accustomed to the norms, values, and behavior patterns of one society might have a great deal of difficulty functioning effectively or surviving in a society whose patterns are different. There are no instincts to guide an American's behavior in Dakar or a Turk's behavior in Cleveland. Because such behaviors are learned as humans grow and develop within a society, they are of special interest to sociologists.

☐ What Social Interaction Is

When sociologists study human behavior, they are concerned primarily with its social aspects. In most situations, sociologists are interested in how people's behavior affects other people and in turn is affected by others. They look at the overt actions that produce responses from others as well the subtle cues that may result in unintended consequences. In this respect human social interaction is very flexible and quite unlike that of the more social animals.

Max Weber (1922) was one of the first sociologists to stress the importance of social interaction in the study of sociology. He argued that the main goal of sociology was to explain what he called *social action*. He used this term to refer to anything people are conscious of doing because of other people. Weber claimed that in order to interpret social actions, we have to put ourselves in the position of the people we are studying and try to understand their thoughts and motives. The German word Weber used for this is *Verstehen*, which can be translated as "sympathetic understanding."

It is easier to understand social actions than it is to understand social interactions. A **social action** involves one individual taking others into account before acting. A **social interaction** involves two or more people taking each other into account. It is the interplay between the actions of one individual and those of one or more other people. In this respect, social interaction is a central concept to understanding the nature of social life.

In this chapter we shall explain how sociologists investigate social interaction phenomena. We shall start with the basic components of social interaction, such as the goals, norms, contexts, and motivations that produce it. Next we shall examine how social interaction affects those involved in it. Then we shall look at social interactions in social groups. The web of all patterned social interactions in a society makes up its social organization. Finally, we shall describe the means by which society maintains its patterns of interaction through the social institutions that make social life possible and that ultimately make up the social structure. In other words, we shall start with social behavior at the most basic level and show how human beings are tied together into ever more complicated and abstract levels of interaction as we move outward from the individual to the society as a whole.

Components of Social Interaction

Can the picking up of a glass of sherry at a social event be thought of as a social interaction? A social interaction has four major components: (1) the ends or goals it is in-

social action Anything people are conscious of doing because of other people.

social interaction The interplay between the actions of one individual and those of one or more other people.

Often the goal of an action is not obvious to the outsider. What is the goal of this runner's action? Is it to win the race? to test his limits? to stay fit?

Goals and Motivations When a doctor taps your leg just below the kneecap, the lower portion of your leg is likely to jerk forward. This action is a normal reflex, a normal physical response. It is obviously not a social interaction, as it lacks both a goal and a motivation. Goals and motivations are closely related and often confused. The **goal** is the state of affairs one wishes to achieve. For many actions the goal may seem obvious: One eats to satisfy one's hunger, sleeps to rid one's body of fatigue, and runs for exercise. Even in such obvious cases, however, there can be more than one goal for an action. For example, one can eat to be polite to one's host as well as to satisfy hunger; one can sleep (perhaps with the aid of a pill) to get through a boring (or anxiety-producing) experience such as a transatlantic airplane flight as well as to eliminate fatigue; and one may run as much for the social prestige of being a marathoner as for the exercise itself. Therefore it is important to remember that social interactions often have less obvious goals that may or may not be related to the obvious goals.

A **motivation** is a person's wish or intention to achieve a goal. Hence, a behavior such as a reflex has no goal and consequently no motive. In our example the doctor's behavior does have a motive—the desire to find out whether the patient's reflexes are normal.

Social interactions may have numerous goals and a variety of motivations as well. For example, consider a young man running to catch a bus. His goal is to catch the bus, but his motivations may be quite complex: he may want to be on time for work; he may have seen one of his coworkers through the window; or he may run for the bus every morning because he needs the exercise.

The goals of a social interaction may often be obvious, though human motivations are often very complicated—so much so that we often are unaware of all the motivations that prompt us (see Case Study: "The Laugh-Makers" for a discussion of how comedians derive their humor from redefining, controlling, and manipulating social interactions).

tended to achieve; (2) the motivation for its being undertaken; (3) the situation or context within which it takes place; and (4) the norms or rules that govern or regulate it (Parsons and Shils, 1951). Hence, picking up a glass of sherry has a number of goals—refreshment, reduction of anxiety, interaction with others at a particular social event, conformity to the actions of these others, and the like. The context may be the opening of an art gallery. The norms governing such an event may dictate that not too much sherry be consumed and that it be consumed in an appropriate manner over a certain period of time. The motivation for the behavior may be to appear relaxed and to achieve the previously described goals. Let us examine more closely each of the components of a social interaction.

Contexts Where a social interaction takes place makes a difference in what it means. Edward

T. Hall (1974) identified three elements that, taken together, define the **context** of a social interaction: (1) the physical setting or place, (2) the social environment, and (3) the activities surrounding the interaction—preceding it, happening simultaneously with it, and coming after it. For example, consider a kiss, an interaction that can have many different meanings.

What is its physical setting—does it happen in the back seat of a parked car, in the bleachers of a football stadium, in the grand ballroom of the Plaza Hotel, on a Hawaiian beach, at the airport, in the living room, in the bedroom, or in a motel room? What is the social context—two teenagers alone, a married couple at a party, a father with his young son at a football game, a family welcoming a relative at the airport, a married couple at home, or a couple at a secret rendezvous? And then, what else is happening—is the kiss preceded by a handshake, a hug, a sigh? Is it accompanied by fondling, a pat on the back, laughter? Does it lead to another kiss, to a wink and a smile, to more fondling, to a wave good-bye? The context of an interaction is a complicated whole that consists of the various interrelated elements, as we can see from the above example. Without knowledge of these elements it is impossible to know the meaning of even the simplest interaction. It follows, then, that the context of an interaction is also closely tied to cultural learning.

For example, Germans and Americans treat space very differently. Hall (1969) noted that in many ways the difference between German and American doors gives us a clue about the space perceptions of these two cultures. In Germany public and private buildings usually have double doors that create a soundproof environment. Germans feel that American doors, in contrast, are flimsy and light, inadequate for providing the privacy that Germans require. In American offices doors are usually kept open; in German offices they are kept closed. In Germany the closed door does not mean that the individual wants to be left alone or that something is being planned that should not be seen by others. Germans simply think that open doors are sloppy and disorderly. As Hall explained it:

I was once called in to advise a firm that has operations all over the world. One of the first questions asked was, "How do you get the Germans to keep their doors open?" In this company the open doors were making the Germans feel exposed and gave the whole operation an unusually relaxed and unbusinesslike air. Closed doors, on the other hand, gave the Americans the feeling that there was a conspiratorial air about the place and that they were being left out. The point is that whether the door is open or shut, it is not going to mean the same thing in the two countries. (Hall, 1969)

The English, particularly those of the middle and upper classes, are at the opposite extreme from the Germans in their requirements for privacy. They are usually brought up in a nursery shared with brothers and sisters. The oldest has a room to himself or herself that is vacated when he or she leaves for boarding school. Children in England may never have a room of their own and seldom expect one or feel entitled to one. Even members of Parliament have no offices and often conduct their business in the open. The English are consequently puzzled by the American need for a secure place in which to work—an office. Americans working in England often are annoyed that they are not given an appropriately enclosed workplace (Hall, 1969) (see Using Sociology: "Communication and Body Movements" for a discussion of cultural differences in nonverbal behavior). These markedly different views of the use of space are culturally determined, and it is important to be aware of these differences in order to interpret correctly the context of an interaction.

Norms Human behavior is not random. It is patterned and, for the most part, quite predictable. What makes human beings act predictably in certain situations? For one thing,

goal The intended result of an action.

motivation A person's wish or intention to achieve a goal.

context The conditions under which an action takes place, including the physical setting or place, the social environment, and the other activities surrounding the action.

The Laugh-Makers

Comedians are capable of deflating pretentiousness, defying convention, tackling taboos, and transforming our anxieties into absurdities. They are rarely at a loss for the right words to turn a potential disaster into a howling success. Their success stems from an ability to redefine, control, or manipulate social interactions. Who are these people who can make us look at the same old thing in a new way, whose uninhibited behavior somehow helps us loosen up? What are funny people really like, and how do they get that way?

The individual who has been digging into the comedic character and personality the longest is Samuel S. Janus, who since 1967 has been interviewing professional comedians and probing their psyches. He has come to the conclusion that comedians all are graced with bright-average to genius-level intelligence, and that their divorce rate is the lowest in show business. Overall, he characterizes them as brilliant, angry, paranoiac, fearful, and depressed. But, he says, "They aren't depressed when they're working." To Janus, Abe Burrows's comment, "The comedian must practice his comedy in order to avoid destroying himself," tells it all. "They use their illness to make a lot of money," he says.

Not all researchers who have looked into the subject agree with Janus's somber view. Seymour and Rhoda Fisher conducted a four-year study comparing 43 professional stand-up comics and clowns with 41 professional actors. They did not find any elevated rates of psychopathology among the comedians, rather, in general, the comics appeared to conduct a constant internal debate as to whether they were devils or angels. Though they usually described themselves as wanting to help people, they seemed to indicate they were lacking in virtue. They seemed to be uncomfortable with their anger, which contrasted with the way they openly expressed anger in their humor. The comic is always saying a lot of unpleasant things to people and at the same time adding, "Don't take is seriously; it isn't so bad."

Waleed Salameh did a study comparing 20 stand-up comics with 20 artists and found the comedians to be more depressed than the average person was. They seemed, however, to have the emotional ability to make their depression into creative material.

Sociologist Graham Tomlinson notes that comedic performances on television may only last 5 to 10 minutes. Within that short span of time the comedian will deliver perhaps 25 punch lines. In other words, "The comedian will be notified 25 times about whether he has succeeded or not. Even professors professing and preachers preaching do not make themselves vulnerable with such frequency."

Why would anyone want to make himself or herself so vulnerable? Janus believes that early in life, comedians stumble on humor as a way of making people like them and then use it to get attention. The Fishers propose that "a major motive of comedians in conjuring up funniness is to prove they are not bad or repugnant."

Janus, Salameh, and the Fishers all agree on one thing: many comedians grow up in extremely deprived circumstances, and their early lives are marked by suffering. The Fishers say that a common element is a relatively nonmaternal, nonnurturing mother, who gave her young comic-to-be the impression that he should relieve her of her load. One of the major findings was that very early in their lives the comics were expected to take on tremendous responsibility. The Fishers suggest that a comic's fascination with the absurd may grow out of his mother's absurd expec-

A popular comedian with all age groups: Bill Cosby.

tations that he be an adult early in life.

In the Fishers' study, it was the mother who often was the rule enforcer, the aggressive critic. They think that some of the techniques that comedians develop are an attempt to establish a reconciliation with the mother. "They become very sensitive to her moods and learn to kid in a way to protect her. We found that the comedian uses humor to protect and comfort people. That becomes his role in the family. And one of the people he's trying particularly to protect is his mother."

It has also been found that those who see themselves as humorous also see themselves as dominant and aggressive. It is possible that the need to dominate is one of the precursors for humor development. The person in a group who is the initiator of humor is really in control of the social situation. Humor consequently becomes a very powerful means of control.

Being aggressive and maintaining control of a social situation are still considered masculine virtues, and so it should come as no surprise that humor behavior begins to diverge by sex early in the socialization process. Starting in grade school, boys seem to initiate humor and laugh more, whereas girls become more prone to respond and smile. Not only do little girls, at this time, start to express humor appreciation in a more restrained and "ladylike" manner; they also want to know that it is socially acceptable before they smile or laugh.

Source: Excerpted from Susan Witty, "The Laugh-Makers," *Psychology Today,* August 1983, pp. 22–29. □

there is the presence of **norms**—that is, rules for proper behavior that guide people in their interactions. Norms tell us the things we should both do and not do. In fact, our society's norms are so much a part of us that we often are not aware of them. In the United States our norms tell us that it is proper to drive on the right, to look at someone when speaking to him or her, and to stand up for the national anthem. Likewise, they tell us that when two people meet, one of the ways of greeting people is by shaking hands. Yet in most Asian countries, people have learned to bow to express this same idea.

We also have norms that guide us in how we present ourselves to others. We realize that how we dress, how we speak, and the objects we possess relay information about us. In this respect North Americans are a rather outgoing group of people. The Japanese have learned that it is a sign of weakness to disclose too much of oneself by overt actions. They are taught very early in life that touching, laughing, crying, or speaking loudly in public are not acceptable ways of interacting.

Not only can the norms for behavior differ considerably from one culture to another, but they also can differ within our own society. Conflicting interpretations of an action have been shown to exist among men and women in our society when a stranger joins them at a public table they may be using, such as in a library. It has been found that men prefer to position themselves across from others they like, whereas women prefer to position themselves next to someone they like (Byrne, 1971). On the basis of this information Fisher and Byrne (1975) reasoned that females thus would respond more negatively than males would to a side-by-side invasion of their personal space, and males would respond more negatively to face-to-face invasions.

An experiment was set up using males and females who were sitting alone in a library. An "invader" was sent to sit either across or next to the subjects. After five minutes, the invader left and an experimenter arrived to ask the subjects some questions. Regardless of the invader's sex, the males felt negatively about the invader when he or she sat across from them but did not seem to have those feelings about a side-by-side invader. The females responded negatively when the invader sat next to them but not when he or she sat across from them.

It was hypothesized this difference results from sex-role socialization in which males are taught to be relatively competitive and hence more sensitive to competitive cues. Sitting across from a male may tend to signal a competitive situation, and males tend to prefer a trusted or nonthreatening person in that location. Females were thought to be more sensitive to affiliative cues. Sitting adjacent to a female tends to be interpreted as an affiliative demand, and so females tend to respond negatively to this cue when the person occupying the seat is a stranger or someone with whom they do not wish to be intimate.

Sociologists thus need to understand the norms that guide people's behavior, as without this knowledge it is impossible to understand social interaction.

□ Types of Social Interaction

When two individuals are in each other's presence, they inevitably affect each other. They may do so intentionally, as when one person asks the other for change of a quarter, or they may do so unintentionally, as when

norms Rules for proper behavior that guide people in their interactions.

USING SOCIOLOGY
Communication and Body Movements

The amount of eye contact maintained between two parties varies from culture to culture and with the status of the individuals involved.

In recent years many researchers have focused our attention on how we communicate with one another by using body movements. This study of body movements is known as kinesics. *It attempts to examine how such things as slight head nods, yawns, postural shifts, and other nonverbal cues, whether spontaneous or deliberate, affect communication. The following is an examination of some of these.*

Many of our movements relate to an attitude that our culture has, consciously or unconsciously, taught us to express in a specific manner. In the United States, for example, we show a status relationship in a variety of ways. The ritualistic nonverbal movements and gestures in which we engage to see who goes through a door first or who sits or stands first are but a few ways our culture uses movement to communicate status. In the Middle East, status is underscored nonverbally by which individual you turn your back to. In Oriental cultures, the bow and backing out of a room are signs of status relationships. Humility might be shown in the United States by a slight downward bending of the head, but in many European countries this same attitude is manifested by dropping one's arms and sighing. In Samoa humility is communicated by bending the body forward.

The use of hand and arm movements as a means of communicating also varies among cultures. We all are aware of the different gestures for derision. For some European cultures it is a closing fist with the thumb protruding between the index and middle fingers. The Russian expresses this same attitude by moving one index finger horizontally across the other.

In the United States, making a circle with one's thumb and index finger while extending the others is emblematic of the word *OK*; in Ja-

pan it signifies "money," and among Arabs this gesture is usually accompanied by a baring of the teeth, and together they signify extreme hostility. In the United States we have learned that waving the hand and arm up and down is a symbol for good-bye or farewell. However, if we wave in this manner in South America, we are apt to discover that the recipient of this gesture is not leaving, but moving toward us. In many countries what we use as a sign of parting is a gesture that means "come."

Eye contact is another area in which some interesting findings have appeared. In the United States the following has been noted: (1) We tend to look at our communication partner more when we are listening than when we are talking. The search for words frequently finds us, as speakers, looking into space, as if to find the words imprinted somewhere out there. (2) The more rewarding we find our partner's message to be, the more we will look at him or her. (3) The amount of eye contact we try to establish with other people is determined in part by our perception of their status. Researchers claim that when we address someone we regard as having high status, we attempt a modest-to-high degree of eye contact. But

when we address a person of low status, we make very little effort to maintain eye contact. (4) We tend to feel discomfort if someone gazes at us for longer than 10 seconds at a time.

These notions of eye contact differ from those of other societies. In some Far Eastern cultures, for example, it is considered rude to look into another person's eyes during conversation. Arabs, on the other hand, because of their use of personal space, stand very close to their communication partners and stare directly into their eyes. For Arabs, the eyes are a key to a person's being, and looking deeply into another's eyes allows one to see another's soul.

A culture's male-female relationship also influences eye behavior. In many Asian cultures it is considered taboo for women to look straight into the eyes of males. Therefore, most Asian men, out of respect for this cultural characteristic, do not stare directly at women. This is in stark contrast with men in France who stare at women in public, as such a stare is an accepted cultural norm.

Source: Excerpted from Larry A. Samovar, Richard E. Porter, and Nemi C. Jain, *Understanding Intercultural Communication* (Belmont, Calif.: Wadsworth, 1981), pp. 166–173. □

Unfocused interactions occur simply because two or more people happen to be in each other's presence.

two people drift toward opposite sides of the elevator in which they are riding. Whether intentional or unintentional, they both represent types of social interaction.

Unfocused and Focused Interaction

Some interactions occur simply because two or more people happen to be in each other's presence. For example, two people in a doctor's waiting room cannot help noticing each other. Usually they will look at each other's clothing, posture, behavior, and other characteristics while at the same time adjusting their own behavior because they assume the other person is also doing the same thing. Sociologist Erving Goffman (1961b) called such actions, which have little by way of goals other than to catalogue other people and make a decent impression on them, **unfocused interaction**. Although such interaction is an ongoing, almost unconscious part of daily life, it is important because through it we monitor how others are reacting to what we are doing. With this constant stream of feedback we can adjust our behavior to try to achieve our goals.

Unfocused interactions were included in our discussion of ethnomethodology and dramaturgy in Chapter 1.

When two or more individuals agree (explicitly or implicitly) to sustain an interaction with one or more particular goals in mind, they are engaged in a **focused interaction** (Goffman, 1961b). People playing cards, watching home movies, or simply enjoying a conversation are involved in focused interaction (see Popular Sociology: "Why People Go to School Reunions"). Focused interactions are the basic building blocks of all social organization.

unfocused interaction An interaction that occurs simply because two or more people happen to be in each other's presence with the single goal of cataloguing people in the immediate environment and making a decent impression on them. Through this almost unconscious behavior we learn how others react to us and adjust our behavior to achieve our goals.

focused interaction A purposeful interaction between two or more individuals who have one or more particular goals in mind.

POPULAR SOCIOLOGY
Why People Go to School Reunions

After reluctantly attending his 10-year high school reunion, a social psychologist decided to conduct an informal study of a question that has intrigued many people: Why do people decide to attend or not attend their high school reunions, and how do they perceive the motivations of those who make the opposite decision?

Jack Sparacino was interested in finding out if those who attended a class reunion were different from those who chose not to attend. If the two groups were different, what determined these differences? Personality? Experiences in school? Current success or failure? To obtain answers, Sparacino sent questionnaires to former classmates of his who attended (116) and who did not attend (249) their 10-year high school reunion. Those who attended were asked why they went, what they had expected the reunion to be like, and what it was actually like. Those who did not go were asked why they had not attended and why they thought others did go. The respondents were asked to provide information on their subsequent education, occupation, and income and on their grades in school, who their friends had been, and who in the class had "functioned best." In addition, they were asked to fill out a two-page questionnaire on personality traits. Sparacino himself went through his old yearbook and compiled a list of extracurricular activities for each classmate.

The table presents the responses (in percentages) of 69 attenders and 80 nonattenders to the question: Why do people attend school reunions?

As the table shows, those who attended perceived their motivation for attending differently from those who did not attend. Nonattenders downplayed the desire to see old friends and gave considerably more attention to nostalgia and showing off than did the attenders. Of course, some of the attenders may have gone to show off, but they gave a more flattering response such as to see old friends. Actual and stated motivations often are not the same.

No significant personality differences were evident between attenders and nonattenders. More attenders (61 percent) were professionals than were nonattenders (44 percent), but income levels averaged out to about the same for both groups. However, there was a clear distinction between attenders and nonattenders in regard to degree of participation (extracurricular activities) and status (those rated high in "functional best") in high school. The evidence suggests that those who were the most successful in high school were the most apt to return for the reunion and not necessarily to flaunt recent success but often to relive earlier triumphs.

Source: Jack Sparacino, "The State of the Reunion," *Psychology Today* **14** (1) (June, 1980), pp. 80–81. □

Why Do People Attend School Reunions? *(percent giving each response)*

Nonattenders (N = 80)	Response	Attenders (N = 69)
37%	To see old friends	59%
37%	To learn what people have been doing	32%
13%	Curious (unspecified)	21%
12%	To see how others have changed	12%
27%	For nostalgia	3%
0%	For entertainment	8%
19%	To show off	3%

Types of Focused Interaction
Social interactions are not random but occur in predictable patterns. There are four basic types of focused social interaction: exchange, cooperation, conflict, and competition.

Exchange When people do something for each other with the express purpose of receiving a reward or return, they are involved in an **exchange**. Most employer–employee relationships are exchange relationships. The employee does the job and is rewarded with a salary. The reward in an exchange interaction, however, need not always be material; it can also be based on emotions such as gratitude. For example, if you visit a sick friend, help someone with a heavy package at the supermarket, or assist a blind person across a busy intersection, you probably will expect these people to feel grateful to you.

Without cooperation these basketball players would have trouble meeting their goal of winning the game.

Focused interactions involve two or more individuals who have particular goals in mind.

Sociologist Peter Blau pointed out that exchange is the most basic form of social interaction:

> Social exchange can be observed everywhere once we are sensitized . . . to it, not only in market relations but also in friendship and even in love. . . . Neighbors exchange favors; children, toys; colleagues, assistance; acquaintances, courtesies; politicians, concessions; discussants, ideas; housewives, recipes. (Blau, 1964)

Cooperation   A form of social interaction in which people act together to promote common interests or achieve shared goals is **co-operation**. The members of a basketball team pass to one another, block off opponents for one another, rebound, and assist one another to achieve a common goal—winning the game. Likewise, family members cooperate to promote their interests as a family—husband and wife both may hold jobs as well as share in household duties, and children may help out

by mowing the lawn and washing the dishes. College students often cooperate by studying together for tests. The United States and the Soviet Union cooperated in achieving a shared goal—an apparent reduction in the arms race and risk of global war—when they signed the first Strategic Arms Limitation Talks treaty.

Sociologists Robert A. Nisbet and Robert Perrin (1977) describe four types of cooperation: spontaneous, traditional, directed, and contractual. The oldest, most natural, and most common form of cooperation is **spontaneous cooperation**, which arises from the needs of a particular situation. For example, when subway passengers in New York saw a fellow passenger being robbed, they pursued and captured the robber, holding him until the police arrived. **Traditional cooperation**, which held together earlier (preindustrial) societies,

exchange An interaction involving one person doing something for another with the express purpose of receiving a reward or return.

cooperation A form of social interaction in which people act together to promote common interests or achieve shared goals.

spontaneous cooperation A form of cooperation that arises from the needs of a particular situation.

traditional cooperation A form of cooperation that is tied to custom and is passed on from one generation to the next, such as barn raising in the American farming communities.

carries the weight of custom and is passed on from one generation to the next. Examples of this form of cooperation are the barn raisings and quilting bees of American farming communities.

Modern societies rely less on traditional cooperation than on directed and contractual cooperation. **Directed cooperation** is a joint activity that is under the control of people in authority. It is planned in advance and requires leadership. When President John F. Kennedy announced that the United States would put a person on the moon before 1970, he initiated large-scale directed cooperation that achieved its goal. **Contractual cooperation** is also planned, but here people agree to cooperate in certain specified ways, with each person's obligations clearly spelled out. The authors of this text and the publisher signed a formal contract and met their specific obligations to produce the book you are now reading.

Conflict　In a cooperative interaction, people join forces to achieve a common goal. By contrast, people in **conflict** struggle with one another for some commonly prized object or value (Nisbet and Perrin, 1977). In a conflict relationship, a person can gain only at someone else's expense. Conflicts arise when people or groups have incompatible values or

when the rewards or resources available to a society or its members are limited. Thus, conflict always involves an attempt to gain or use power.

Because conflict often leads to unhappiness and violence, many people view it negatively. However, conflict appears to be inevitable in human society. A stable society is not a society without conflicts but one that has developed methods for resolving its conflicts by justly or brutally suppressing them temporarily. For example, Lewis Coser (1956, 1967) pointed out that conflict can be a positive force in society. The American civil rights movement in the 1950s and 1960s may have seemed threatening and disruptive to many people at the time, but it helped bring about important social changes that may have led to a greater social stability.

Coercion is a special kind of conflict that can occur when one of the parties in a conflict is much stronger than the other. The stronger party can impose its will on the weaker, as in the case of a parent using the threat of punishment to impose a curfew on an adolescent child. Coercion rests on force or the threat of force, but usually it operates more subtly.

Competition　The fourth type of social interaction, **competition**, is a form of conflict in which individuals or groups confine their conflict within agreed-upon rules. Competition is a common form of interaction in the modern world—not only on the sports field but in the marketplace, the education system, and the political system as well.

One type of relationship may span the entire range of focused interactions: an excellent example is marriage. Husbands and wives cooperate in household chores and responsibilities (an interaction discussed earlier). They also engage in exchange interactions. Married people often discuss their problems with each other—the partner whose role is listener at one time will expect the other spouse to provide a sympathetic ear at another time. Married people also experience conflicts in their relationship. A couple may have a limited amount of money set aside, and each may want to use it for a different purpose. Unless they can agree on a third,

Competition, whether on the race track or in the business world, is a common form of interaction.

mutually desirable use for the money, one spouse will gain at the other's expense, and the marriage may suffer. The husband and wife whose marriage is irreversibly damaged may find themselves in direct competition. If they wish to separate or divorce, their conflict will be regulated according to legal and judicial rules.

Through the course of a lifetime people constantly are involved in several types of social interaction because most of our time is spent in some kind of group situation. How we behave in these situations is generally determined by two factors—the statuses we occupy and the roles we play—which together constitute the main components of what sociologists call social organization.

☐ Components of Social Organization

Social organization consists of the patterned relationships that exist among individuals and groups. These relationships involve a variety of statuses and roles.

Statuses

Statuses are socially defined positions that people occupy in a group or society and in terms of which they interact with one another. Common statuses may pertain to religion, education, ethnicity, and occupation—for example, Protestant, college graduate, black American, and teacher. Statuses exist independent of the specific people who occupy them (Linton, 1936). For example, our society recognizes the status of race car driver. Many people occupy that status, including Al and Bobby Unser, Mario Andretti, Paul Newman, and Janet Guthrie. New racers are trained; old racers retire (or are killed). But the status, as the culture defines it, remains essentially unchanged. The same is true for all other statuses: occupational statuses such as doctor, computer analyst, bank teller, police officer, butcher, insurance adjuster, thief, and prostitute, and nonoccupational statuses such as son and daughter, jogger, friend, Little League coach, neighbor, gang leader, and mental patient.

It is important to keep in mind that from a sociological point of view, status does not refer—as it does in common usage—to the idea of prestige, even though different statuses often do contain differing degrees of prestige. In America, for example, research has shown that the status of Supreme Court Justice has more prestige than that of lawyer, which in turn has more prestige than does the status of sociologist (Hodge et al., 1964).

People generally occupy more than one status at a time. Consider yourself, for example: you are someone's daughter or son, a full-time or part-time college student, perhaps also a worker, a licensed car driver, a member of a church or synagogue, and so forth. Sometimes one of the multiple statuses a person occupies seems to dominate the others in patterning that person's life. Such a status is called a **master status**. For example, Ronald Reagan has occupied a number of diverse statuses: husband, father, lifeguard, sports announcer, actor, Air Force captain, governor of California, presidential candidate, and president of the United States. After January 20, 1981, however, his master status was that

directed cooperation A form of cooperation characterized by a joint effort that is under the control of people in authority such as the United States' effort to put a person on the moon.

contractual cooperation A form of planned cooperation in which each person's specific obligations are clearly spelled out, such as the agreement between an author and publisher to produce a book.

conflict The opposite of cooperation. People in conflict struggle with one another for some commonly prized object or value.

coercion A special kind of conflict that can occur when one of the parties in a conflict is much stronger than the others.

competition A form of conflict in which individuals or groups confine their conflict within agreed-upon rules.

social organization The patterned relationships that exist among individuals and groups. These relationships involve a variety of statuses and roles.

statuses Socially defined positions that people occupy in a group or society and in terms of which they interact with one another.

master status One of the multiple statuses a person occupies that dominates the others in patterning that person's life.

of president, as it governed his actions more than did any other status he occupied at the time. A person's master status will change many times in the course of his or her life cycle. Right now your master status probably is that of college student. Five years from now it may be graduate student, artist, lawyer, spouse, or parent. Figure 5.1 illustrates the different statuses occupied by a 35-year-old

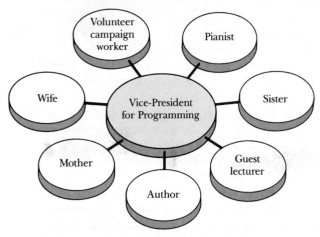

Figure 5.1 Status and Master Status Generally, each individual occupies many statuses at one time. The statuses of a female executive at a major television network include author, wife, mother, pianist, and so on. Other statuses could be added to this list. However, one status— vice-president for programming—is most important in patterning this woman's life. Sociologists call such a status a master status.

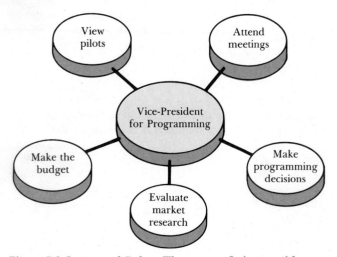

Figure 5.2 Status and Roles The status of vice-president for programming at a major television network has several roles attached to it, including attend meetings, make programming decisions, and so on.

woman who is an executive at a major television network. Although she occupies many statuses at once, her master status is that of vice-president for programming.

In some situations, a person's master status may have a negative influence on that person's life. For example, people who have followed what their culture considers a deviant lifestyle may find that their master status is labeled according to their deviant behavior. Those who have been identified as ex-convicts are likely to be so classified no matter what other statuses they occupy: they will be thought of as ex-convict–painters, ex-convict–machinists, ex-convict–writers, and so on. Their master status has a negative effect on their ability to fulfill the roles of the statuses they would like to occupy. Ex-convicts who are good machinists or house painters may find employers unwilling to hire them because of their police records.

Some statuses are conferred upon us by virtue of birth or other socially significant factors not controlled by our own actions or decisions. These are called **ascribed statuses,** and people occupy them regardless of their intentions. Certain family positions—daughter, son—are typical ascribed statuses, as are one's sex and ethnic or racial identity. Other statuses are occupied as a result of the individual's actions. These are called **achieved statuses**—student, professor, garage mechanic, race driver, hobo, artist, prisoner, bus driver, husband, wife, mother, or father.

Roles

Statuses alone are static—nothing more than social categories into which people are put. Roles bring statuses to life, making them dynamic. As Linton (1936) observed, you occupy a status but you play a role. **Roles** are the culturally defined rules for proper behavior that are associated with every status. Roles may be thought of as collections of rights and obligations. To return to our example of race car drivers, every driver has the *right* to expect other drivers not to try to pass when the race has been interrupted by a yellow flag because of danger. Turned around, each driver has the *obligation* not to pass other drivers under yellow-flag conditions. A driver also has a *right* to expect race committee members to enforce the rules and spectators to stay off the raceway. On the other hand, a driver has an *obligation* to the owner of the car to try hard to win.

In the case of our television executive, she has the *right* to expect to be paid on time, to be provided with good-quality scripts and staff support, and to make decisions about the use of her budget. On the other hand, she has the *obligation* to act in the best interests of the network, to meet schedules, to stay within her budget, and to treat her employees fairly. What is important is that all these rights and obligations are part of the roles associated with the status of vice-president for programming. They exist without regard to the particular individuals whose behavior they guide (see Figure 5.2).

A status may include a number of roles, and each role will be appropriate to a specific social context. For example, the president of the United States must be a host at diplomatic dinners, a leader at cabinet sessions, and a policy setter for his staff. Sociologists use the concept of role sets to explain this phenomenon.

Role sets All the roles attached to a single status are known collectively as a **role set.** However, not every role in a particular role set is enacted all the time. An individual's role behaviors depend on the statuses of the other people with whom he or she is interacting. For example, as a college student you behave one way toward other students and another way toward professors. Similarly, professors behave one way toward other professors, another way toward students, and yet a third way toward deans. So the role behavior we expect in any given situation depends on the pairs of statuses occupied by the interacting individuals. This means that role behavior really is defined by the rights and obligations that are assigned to statuses when they are paired with one another (see Figure 5.3). It would be difficult to describe the wide-ranging, unorganized assortment of role behaviors associated with the status of television vice-president for programming. Sociologists find it more useful to describe the specific behav-

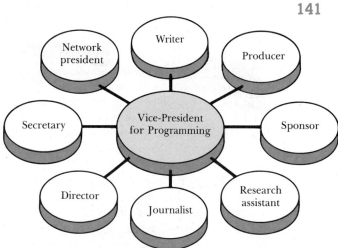

Figure 5.3 Role Sets People's role behaviors change according to the statuses of the other people with whom they interact. The female vice-president of programming will adopt somewhat different roles depending on the statuses of the various people with whom she interacts at the station: a writer, a journalist, her secretary, and so on.

ior expected of a network television vice-president for programming interacting with different people. Such a role set would include

vice-president for programming/network president
vice-president for programming/other vice-presidents
vice-president for programming/script writer
vice-president for programming/secretary
vice-president for programming/television star
vice-president for programming/journalist
vice-president for programming/producer
vice-president for programming/sponsor

The vice-president's role behavior in each case would be different, meshing with the role behavior of the individual(s) occupying the other status in each pairing (Merton, 1968).

ascribed statuses Statuses that are conferred on an individual at birth or on other occasions by circumstances beyond the individual's control, such as sex and ethnic identity.

achieved statuses Statuses that are occupied as a result of the individual's actions, such as lawyer, mother, or student.

roles Culturally defined rules for proper behavior associated with every status.

role sets All the roles attached to a single status.

Role Strain   Even though most people try to enact their roles as they are expected to, they sometimes find it difficult. When a single role has conflicting demands attached to it, individuals who play that role experience **role strain** (Goode, 1960). For example, the captain of a freighter is expected to be sure the ship sails only when it is in safe condition, but the captain also is expected to meet the company's delivery schedule, because a day's delay could cost the company thousands of dollars. These two expectations may exert competing pulls on the captain especially when some defect is reported, such as a malfunction in the ship's radar system. The stress of these competing pulls is not due to the captain's personality but rather is built into the nature of the role expectations attached to the captain's status. Therefore, sociologists describe the captain's experience of stress as role strain.

Role Conflict   An individual who is occupying more than one status at a time and who is unable to enact the roles of one status without violating those of another status is encountering **role conflict.**

Consider, for example, the role conflict faced by a high school teacher who must take on a part-time job as a used-car salesman in order to feed his family of six children. On the one hand is his status as an educator, a role model regarded highly by the community. On the other hand, in his status as a used-car salesman, he is viewed by some of his students and their parents as an inferior—if not with suspicion. To deal with this role conflict, the teacher may develop a variety of defense mechanisms such as rationalization ("The sales job is only temporary. I'll find something better soon.") and aggression toward the community. ("If this weren't such a cheap town, I'd make enough to feed my family.").

Or consider the problems faced by the woman who occupies at the same time the statuses of business executive, wife, and mother. In the status of business executive, the woman's role is to work long hours, entertain clients, and travel. As wife her role is to be a stimulating companion to her husband and help keep the household running smoothly. As mother she is expected to spend time with the children, go places with them, do things with them, and take pleasure in nurturing and teaching them. The people with whom she interacts in each status expect her to consider their needs first—clearly an impossible task.

As society becomes more complex, individuals occupy increasingly larger numbers of statuses. This increases the chances for role conflict, which is one of the major sources of stress in modern society.

Role Playing   The roles we play can have a profound influence on both our attitudes and our behavior. Playing a new social role often feels awkward at first, and we may feel we are just acting—pretending to be something that we are not. However, many sociologists feel that the roles a person plays are the person's only true self. Peter Berger's (1963) explanation of role playing goes further: the roles we play can transform not only our actions but ourselves as well.

> One feels more ardent by kissing, more humble by kneeling and more angry by shaking one's fist. That is, the kiss not only expresses ardor but manufactures it. Roles carry with them both certain actions and emotions and attitudes that belong to these actions. The professor putting on an act that pretends to wisdom comes to feel wise.

In an attempt to gauge the degree to which social roles affect attitudes and behavior, Stanford social psychologist Philip G. Zimbardo (1972) created his own prison. An ad was placed in a local newspaper asking for volunteers for an experiment. Two dozen young men described by Zimbardo as "mature, emotionally stable, normal intelligent college students" were selected. The students were paid $15 a day for their participation. Half were arbitrarily given the role of prisoner by a flip of a coin, and the other half were assigned the role of guard in the simulated prison.

Zimbardo allowed his guards to make up their own formal rules for maintaining law, order, and respect. The prisoners were treated like any other prisoners. Picked up at their homes by a city police officer, they were "searched, handcuffed, fingerprinted, and booked. . . ." They were then taken blindfolded to Zimbardo's jail where they were stripped, deloused, given a number and a uniform, and placed in a cell with two other "prisoners."

The experiment was expected to last for two weeks, but at the end of only six days Zimbardo had to stop it. It was no longer apparent to most of the subjects—or even to Zimbardo himself—where reality ended and the "artificial" roles began. Zimbardo explained:

> The majority had indeed become prisoners or guards, no longer able to clearly differentiate between role playing and self. There were dramatic changes in virtually every aspect of their behavior, thinking and feeling. In less than a week the experience of imprisonment undid (temporarily) a lifetime of learning; human values were suspended, self-concepts were challenged and the ugliest, most base pathological side of human nature surfaced. We were horrified because we saw some boys (guards) treat others as if they were despicable animals, taking pleasure in cruelty, while other boys (prisoners) became servile, dehumanized robots who thought only of escape, of their own individual survival and of their mounting hatred for the guards.
>
> We had to release three prisoners in the first four days because they had such acute situational traumatic reactions as hysterical crying, confusion in thinking and severe depression. Others begged to be paroled. By then . . . they had been so programmed to think of themselves as prisoners that when their request for parole was denied, they returned docilely to their cells. . . .
>
> About a third of the guards became tyrannical in their arbitrary use of power, in enjoying their control over other people. They were corrupted by the power of their roles and became quite inventive in their techniques of breaking the spirit of the prisoners and making them feel they were worthless. (Zimbardo, 1972)

The technique of role playing is often used to help people understand another person's attitude or behavior—to see the world from the other person's perspective. Often conflict can be resolved when we are made to stand in our adversary's shoes.

Role Enactment No two people are exactly alike in how they enact their roles. Some are skillful, others awkward; some enthusiastic, others reluctant; some happy, others ashamed; some involved, others detached. Therefore, although two individuals may occupy the same status, their behavior is not likely to be identical. People interpret the roles they enact through their own unique personalities, much as two actors bring to the stage very different interpretations of the same dramatic role. For example, Chris Evert-Lloyd and John McEnroe both are professional tennis players, but they enact their roles very differently. Evert-Lloyd shows little emotion, whether she is winning or losing. McEnroe, on the other hand, has been fined for his displays of anger and disgust and his arguments with umpires' decisions.

Statuses and roles, together with values and norms, are the basic threads that make up the fabric of society. As these elements vary, so, too, does the social structure that evolves.

☐ Institutions and Social Structure

Anyone who has traveled to foreign countries knows that different societies have different ways of doing things. The basic things that get done actually are quite similar—food is produced and distributed; people get married and have children; and children are raised to take on the responsibilities of adulthood. The vehicle for accomplishing the basic needs of any society is the social institution.

Social Institutions

Sociologists usually speak of five areas of society in which basic needs have to be fulfilled:

role strain The stress that results from conflicting demands within a single role.

role conflict The situation in which an individual who is occupying more than one status at the same time is unable to enact the roles of one status without violating those of another.

the family sector, the education sector, the economic sector, the religious sector, and the political sector. For each of these areas there are social groups and associations that carry out the goals and meet the needs of society. The behavior of people in these groups and associations is organized or patterned by the relevant **social institutions**—that is, the ordered social relationships that grow out of the values, norms, statuses, and roles that organize those activities that fulfill society's fundamental needs. Thus, economic institutions organize the ways in which society produces and distributes the goods and services it needs; educational institutions determine what should be learned and how it should be taught; and so forth.

Of all social institutions, that of the family is perhaps the most basic. A stable family unit is the main ingredient necessary for the smooth functioning of society. For instance, sexual behavior must be regulated and children must be cared for and raised to fit into society. Hence, the institution of the family provides a system of continuity from one generation to the next.

Although nothing in society is completely static, social institutions normally are among the most slowly changing aspects of any society. Thus, particular businesses may come and go, but basic economic institutions persist. Political power may change hands, but usually according to the rules and within the context of a society's political institution. It is important, therefore, to keep clear the distinction between the concept of group and the concept of institution. A **group** is a collection of specific, identifiable people. An **institution** is a system for organizing standardized patterns of social behavior. In other words, a group consists of people, and an institution is the standardized ways in which people do certain things. For example, when sociologists discuss *a* family (say the Smith family), they are referring to a particular group of people. When they discuss *the* family, they are referring to the family as an institution—a cluster of statuses and roles and values and norms that organize the standardized patterns of behavior that we expect to find within family groups. Thus, the family as an American institution typically embodies several master

statuses: those of husband, wife, and, possibly, father, mother, and child. It also includes the statuses of son, daughter, brother, and sister. These statuses are organized into well-defined, patterned relationships: Parents have authority over their children; spouses have a sexual relationship with each other (but not with the children); and so on. However, specific family groups may not conform entirely to the ideals of the institution. There are single-parent families, families in which the children appear to be running things, and families in which there is an incestuous parent–child relationship. Although a society's institutions provide what can be thought of as a "master plan" for human interactions in groups, *actual* behavior and *actual* group organization often deviate in varying degrees from this plan.

We should make it clear that in common speech there are several different uses of the term *institution* that could be confused with the sociological one we have presented. Sometimes the term is used to refer to an association like the Smithsonian Institution in our nation's capital. Sometimes—more popularly—it is applied to hospitals for mental patients or homes for the aged. In adjective form it is used to denote a style of architecture: cold, formal, "functional," large, impersonal, and without a trace of aesthetic virtue. In everyday speech each of these uses is valid, though sociologists confine their use of the term to the specific definition we have offered.

If we step back from a mosaic, the many multicolored stones are seen to compose a single, coordinated pattern or picture. Similarly, if we step back and look at society, the many actions of all its members fall into a pattern or series of interrelated patterns. These consist of social interactions and relationships expressing individual decisions and choices. These choices, however, are not random; rather, they are organized by the society's institutions. This "systematic ordering of social relations by acts of choice and decision" (Firth, 1963) is the **social organization** of society. In other words, social organization is the web of actual interactions among individuals and groups in society. As you might expect, social organization differs from one society to the next. It varies because social institutions also differ among societies. Thus, Islam allows a man to marry up to four wives at any given time, whereas in our society with its Judeo-Christian religious tradition, such plural marriage is not an acceptable family form.

Social Structure

Just as statuses and roles exist within ordered relationships to one another in the context of institutions, social institutions also exist in patterned relationships with one another in the context of society. All societies have their own patterning for these relationships, which is called the **social structure** of a society. For example, a society's economic and political institutions often are closely interrelated. So, too, are the family and religious institutions. Thus, a description of American social structure would indicate the presence of monogamy along with Judeo-Christian values and norms and the institutionalization of economic competition and of democratic political organizations.

Social structure tends to be the most stable aspect of society. The American social structure, however, may not be as static as that of many other societies. Our society is experiencing relatively rapid social change because of its complexity and because of the great variety in the types of people that are part of it. This complexity makes life less predictable because new values and norms being introduced from numerous quarters result in changes in both social organization and structure. For example, ideas about the behavior that should go along with female sex roles have changed considerably over the last decade or two. Not long ago it was assumed that most married women would not work but would stay home and attend to the rearing of children. Today the majority of American women are working outside the home, and views on what roles mothers should play in the lives of their children are in flux. The subtle effect of society's expectations of women's behavior and the need to change traditional views of women's roles are explored in Focus on Research: "Changing Sexual Stereotypes."

Using the concepts we have discussed in this chapter, sociologists study the ways in which individuals interact with one another

Women today are trying to resolve the issue of integrating their work and family roles.

as individuals and within gatherings and groups and the ways in which they organize themselves into the large mosaic that makes up modern society. The rest of this book consists of an extended analysis of these processes.

☐ Summary

Because human beings are born with few instincts, human infants need people who will care for them and teach them. It is through this teaching that cultural patterns develop and that societies differ from one another.

Social interaction involves two or more people taking each other into account. Although the goals of social interaction may often be obvious, the motivations may be quite obscure and complicated. Social interactions that have no goal other than the cataloguing of

social institutions The ordered social relationships that grow out of the values, norms, statuses, and roles that organize those activities that fulfill society's fundamental needs.

group A collection of specific, identifiable people.

institution A system for organizing standardized patterns of social behavior.

social organization The web of actual interactions among individuals and groups in society that defines their mutual rights and responsibilities and differs from society to society.

social structure The stable, patterned relationships that exist among social institutions within a society.

FOCUS ON RESEARCH
Changing Sexual Stereotypes

Despite recent changes in ideas about the behavior that should go along with the female sex role, many sex-role stereotypes persist. The research project described here suggests that the attitudes of the men a woman admires play an important role in shaping the self-image she chooses to project, as well as her behavior and performance.

Researchers Mark P. Zanna and Susan J. Pack wanted to determine if sex differences in behavior might, in part, be shaped by the expectations of desirable members of the opposite sex. Their investigation included both attitudinal and behavioral measures.

Eighty female undergraduates at Princeton University were selected as subjects. First they were given a battery of questionnaires to determine their self-image on a series of sex-role stereotypic traits and behaviors. Each subject was instructed to indicate to what extent she agreed with such statements as "I am the kind of person who is not at all dependent on other people . . . not at all aggressive . . . very career-oriented . . . very tender." Responses were made on a 6-point scale from "strongly disagree" to "strongly agree."

Next, each subject was paired with a male who fit either of two types: High Desirability—6 feet 1 inch tall, 21 years old, Princeton senior, unattached, owns a car, interested in sports; or Low Desirability—5 feet 5 inches tall, 18 years old, non-Princeton freshman, dating someone, no car, little interest in sports.

Each subject was also supplied with a questionnaire entitled "Opinion on Women," supposedly completed by her partner. A male whose responses indicated moderate or strong agreement with such statements as "the ideal woman would be very emotional . . . very home-oriented . . . very passive" was

identified as Traditional Stereotype in his image of the ideal woman. A male who moderately or strongly agreed with such statements as "the ideal woman would be very independent . . . very competitive . . . very ambitious" was classified as Untraditional Stereotype.

Each subject was asked to identify her partner as highly desirable or not and as traditional or untraditional to confirm the researchers' classifications. The result was four clearly demarcated categories of partners: High Desirability—Traditional Stereotype; High Desirability—Untraditional Stereotype; Low Desirability—Traditional Stereotype; Low Desirability—Untraditional Stereotype.

The subjects were then given another battery of questionnaires that included all the questions that had determined their self-images in regard to sex-role stereotypes on the initial test. They were told that their responses would be shown to their partners. The initial and retest scores were compared. Subjects paired with Low Desirability partners, whether they were identified as Traditional Stereotype or Untraditional Stereotype, showed almost no change in their scores on the self-image questions. Subjects coupled with High Desirability—Traditional Stereotype partners shifted their self-images toward a Traditional Stereotype. Subjects coupled with High Desirability—Untraditional Stereotype partners showed an even greater shift in their self-images toward the viewpoint of their partners.

Finally, the researchers wanted to determine how the subjects would perform on a simple intelligence test given the desirability and sexual stereotype views of their partners. The researchers knew that holders of traditional views do not expect females to perform well on such tests, whereas holders of untradi-

tional views do not share this negative bias. The subjects were told that their partners would not see their scores, so the results would be influenced by their own expectations, not any impression they wanted to make on their partners. Each subject was given 50 four-letter anagrams and told to unscramble as many as she could within five minutes.

Subjects who had been coupled with High Desirability—Untraditional Stereotype males attained the highest scores (a mean average of 44.25 out of a possible 50) on the anagram test. Subjects coupled with High Desirability—Traditional Stereotype males had the lowest scores (mean average 37.40). The subjects who had been coupled with Low Desirability partners, whether they held traditional or untraditional stereotypes, scored about midway between (Untraditional, 41.50; Traditional, 40.35), suggesting that Low Desirability partners had no influence on the scores.

Zanna and Pack concluded that people—females in this case—moderate their attitudes (as indicated in the change in the self-image questionnaire scores) and their behavior (as indicated by the anagram test scores) as a consequence of the impact of the attitudes of desirable others—males in this case—on one's own self-image. Of special interest was the finding that the women's attitudes and behavior was most apt to be affected by desirable men who held untraditional views on the female sex role. The women's movement should welcome this confirmation that society's expectations of women must change to reinforce women's positive self-image and support their improved performance in nontraditional roles.

Source: Mark P. Zanna and Susan J. Pack, "On the Self-Fulfilling Nature of Apparent Sex Differences in Behavior," *Journal of Experimental Social Psychology* **11** (1975), pp. 583–591. □

other people are called unfocused, whereas a sustained interaction with a goal in mind is called focused. The four basic types of focused interaction are exchange, cooperation, conflict, and competition.

Social organization consists of the patterned relationships that exist among individuals and groups. The relationships involve a variety of statuses and roles. Statuses consist of socially defined positions that people occupy in a group or society and in terms of which they interact with one another. Most people occupy more than one status at a time, but sometimes one status dominates the others. This is called a master status. The statuses that are conferred upon a person (usually at birth) are called ascribed statuses; those that are occupied as a result of an individual's actions are called achieved statuses.

Roles are the culturally defined rules for proper behavior associated with every status. A status may contain a number of roles, which collectively are known as a role set. When a single role has conflicting demands attached to it, people who play that role often experience role strain. When an individual is unable to enact the roles of one status without violating those of another status, role conflict results. The roles individuals play can have a dramatic influence on their attitudes and behavior. Deliberately playing the role of someone with whom we are in conflict can often help us resolve that conflict by letting us see the other person's point of view or experiencing that person's emotions. No two people are exactly alike in the way they enact their roles. The differences in role enactment are the result of differences in personality.

Social institutions consist of the ordered social relationships that grow out of the values, norms, statuses, and roles that organize the activities that fulfill society's basic needs. The patterned relationships among people in a society that grow out of the choices they make because of the society's institutions compose its social organization. The patterned relationships among a society's social institutions make up its social structure. Although social structure tends to be the most stable aspect of society, the American social structure has undergone relatively rapid change because of its complexity and because of the many types of people that are part of it.

☐ For Further Reading

BERGER, PETER L., and THOMAS LUCKMANN. *The Social Construction of Reality*. Garden City, N.Y.: Doubleday, 1966.   An evaluation of how our knowledge of everyday life and our interpretations of social reality are developed and maintained through social interaction.

BLUMER, HERBERT. *Symbolic Interactionism: Perspective and Method*. Englewood Cliffs, N.J.: Prentice-Hall, 1969.   An excellent summary of the symbolic interactionist perspective.

GOFFMAN, ERVING. *The Presentation of Self in Everyday Life*. New York: Doubleday (Anchor Books), 1959.   Goffman's classic statement of the dramaturgical approach to the study of social interaction. He employs the metaphor of the theatrical performance to explore the theme of human behavior in social situations and the way that we appear to others. Other important works by the same author on this topic include *Behavior in Public Places* (Free Press, 1963) and *Relations in Public* (Harper & Row, 1971).

HALL, EDWARD T. *The Silent Language*. New York: Doubleday (Anchor Books), 1959.   An excellent and entertaining introduction to nonverbal communication ("body language") and *proxemics*—the ways people use space to communicate with one another.

HOMAN, GEORGE. *Social Behavior: Its Elementary Forms*. Rev. ed. New York: Harcourt Brace Jovanovich, 1974.   A very readable and classic work that develops the exchange view of social interaction.

NISBET, ROBERT. *The Social Bond*. New York: Knopf, 1970.   An important functionalist analysis of society. Nisbet describes the "social bond" that links together society's different groups, statuses, roles, and institutions.

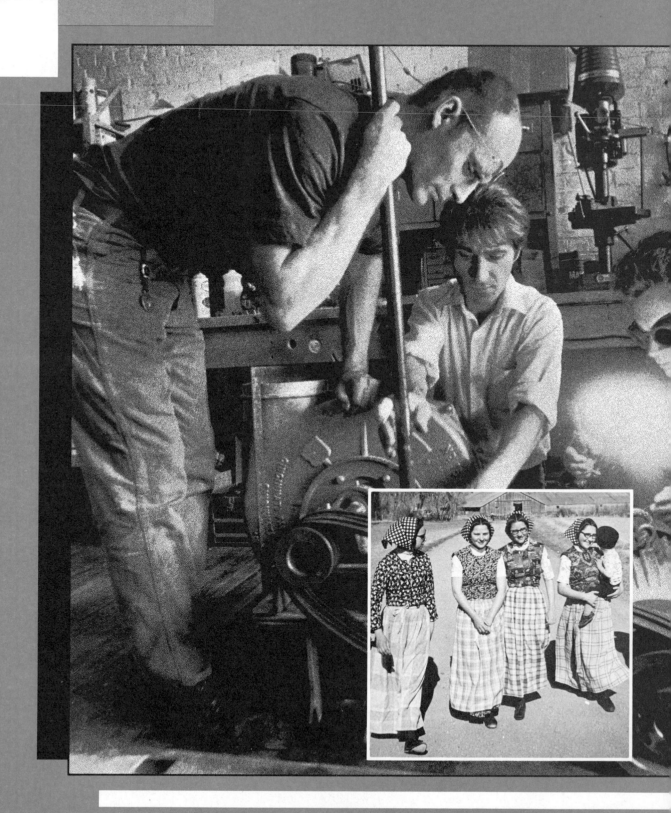

The Organization of Society

Part Three

6

Group Structures

"No man is an Iland, intire of it selfe . . . every man is a peece of the Continent, a part of the maine. . . ." John Donne, the poet who wrote these words more than 250 years ago, probably never dreamed of the size and complexity of modern society, but he did understand human beings' dependence on one another. From the smallest, personal groups of the family, friends, schoolmates, and work companions, to the large—often anonymous—groups of people who provide us with goods, services, and tax forms, we are involved with others.

In this chapter we shall be talking about our interactions with others and the effects that these associations have on our lives.

☐ The Nature of Groups

In common speech the word *group* is often used for almost any occasion when two or more people come together. In sociology, however, there are several terms we use for various collections of people, not all of which are considered groups. A **social group** consists of two or more people who interact recurrently in a patterned way and who recognize that they constitute a distinct social unit. For a social group to exist, the individuals must interact with one another according to established patterns in terms of the statuses and roles they recognize. The members develop expectations of proper behavior for people occupying different positions in the social group. The people have a sense of identity and realize they are different from others who are not members. Social groups have a set of values and norms that may or may not be similar to those of the larger society.

Our description of a social group contrasts with our definition of a **social aggregate,** which is made up of people who happen to be in the same place but share little else. Consider passengers riding together in one car of a train. They may share a purpose (getting to Des Moines) but do not interact or even consider their temporary association to have any meaning. It hardly makes sense to call them a group—unless something more happens. If it is a long ride, for instance, and

several passengers start a card game, the cardplayers will have formed a social group: they have a purpose, they share certain role expectations, and they attach importance to what they are doing together. Moreover, if the cardplayers continue to meet one another every day (say on a commuter train), they may begin to feel special in contrast with the rest of the passengers, who are "just riders."

A social group, unlike an aggregate, does not cease to exist when its members are away from one another. Members of social groups carry the fact of their membership with them and see the group as a distinct entity with specific requirements for membership. A social group has a purpose and is therefore important to its members, who know how to tell an "insider" from an 'outsider." It is a social entity that exists for its members apart from any other social relationships that some of them might share. Members of a group interact according to established norms and traditional statuses and roles. As new members are recruited to the group, they move into these traditional statuses and adopt the expected role behavior—if not gladly, then as a result of group pressure.

Consider, for example, a tenants' group that consists of the people who rent apartments in a building. Most such groups are founded because tenants feel a need for a strong, unified voice in dealing with the landlord on problems with repairs, heat, hot water, and rent increases. Many members of a tenants' group may never have met one another before; others may be related to one another; and some may also belong to other groups such as a neighborhood church, the PTA, a bowling league, or political associations. The group's existence does not depend on these other relationships for its existence, nor does it cease to exist when members leave the building to go to work or to go away on vacation. The group remains even when some tenants move out of the building and others move in. Newcomers are recruited, told of the group's purpose, and informed of its meetings; they are encouraged to join committees, take leadership responsibilities, and participate in the actions the group has planned. Members who fail to support the group action (such as withholding rent) will be pressured and criticized and may even receive threats of violence or be expelled from the group.

A social group also differs from a **statistical category,** which consists of people classified together because they share certain characteristics. If this similarity is unknown or unimportant to those in the category, it is not a social group. Involvement with others cannot develop unless one is aware of them. In this light Kurt Lewin (1948) made the following point:

> Similarity between persons merely permits their classification, their subsumption under the same abstract concept, whereas belonging to the same social group means concrete, dynamic interrelations among persons. A husband, a wife and a baby are less similar to each other, in spite of their being a strong natural group, than the baby is to other babies. . . .

If people are merely aware of one another, it is still not enough to make them a social group. We may be classified as Democrats, college students, upper class, or suburbanites. Yet for many of us who fall into these categories, there is no group. We may not be involved with the others in any patterned way that is an outgrowth of that classification. In fact, we personally may not even define ourselves as members of the particular category, even if someone else does.

Social groups can be large or small, temporary or long lasting: your family is a group, as is your bowling club, any association to which you belong, or the clique with which you "hang around." In fact, it is difficult for you to participate in society without belonging to a number of different groups.

In general, social groups, regardless of their nature, have the following characteristics: (1) permanence beyond the meetings of members—that is, even when members are dispersed, (2) means for identifying members, (3) mechanisms for recruiting new members, (4) goals or purposes, (5) social statuses and roles (that is, norms for behavior), and (6) means for controlling members' behavior.

The traits we have just described are features of many groups. A baseball team, a couple about to be married, a work unit, a weekly poker game, members of a family, or a town planning board all may be described as groups. Yet being a member of a family is significantly different from being a member of a work unit. The family is a primary group, whereas most work units are secondary groups.

Primary and Secondary Groups

The difference between primary and secondary groups lies in the kinds of relationships their members have with one another. Charles Horton Cooley (1909) defined **primary groups** as groups that are characterized by

> intimate face-to-face association and cooperation. They are primary in several senses, but chiefly in that they are fundamental in forming the social nature and ideas of the individual. The result of intimate association, psychologically, is a certain fusion of individualities in a common whole, so that one's very self, for many purposes at least, is the common life and purpose of the group. Perhaps the simplest way of describing this wholeness is by saying that it is a "we"; it involves the sort of sympathy and mutual identification for which "we" is the natural expression. (p. 23)

Cooley identified three basic primary groups: the family, children's play groups, and neighborhood or community groups.

Primary groups involve interaction among members who have an emotional investment

social group Two or more individuals who interact recurrently according to some pattern of social organization and who recognize that they constitute a distinct social unit.

social aggregate People who happen to be in the same place but share little else, such as passengers on the New York to Boston air shuttle.

statistical category People classified together because they share certain characteristics, such as college students.

primary group A group that is characterized by intimate face-to-face association and is basic to the development of the social self and the continued adjustment of its members. Primary groups involve interaction among members who have an emotional investment in one another and who interact as total individuals rather than through specialized roles.

in one another and in a situation, who know one another intimately and interact as total individuals rather than through specialized roles. For example, members of a family are emotionally involved with one another and know one another well. In addition, they interact with one another in terms of their total personalities, not just in terms of their social identities or statuses as breadwinner, student, athlete, or community leader.

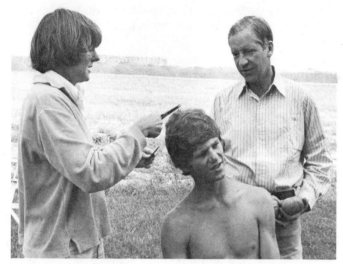

The family is one of the three basic primary groups in which members interact in direct, intimate, face-to-face association. Peer groups and neighborhood and community groups are other basic primary groups.

Many high school peer groups may be viewed as in-groups, because of the "we" feeling among their members.

A **secondary group** in contrast, is characterized by much less intimacy among its members. It usually has specific goals, is formally organized, and is impersonal. Secondary groups tend to be larger than primary groups, and their members do not necessarily interact with all other members. In fact many members often do not know one another at all; to the extent that they do, rarely do they know more about one another than about their respective social identities. Members' feelings about, and behavior toward, one another are patterned mostly by their statuses and roles rather than by personality characteristics. The chairman of the board of General Motors, for example, is treated respectfully by all General Motors employees—regardless of the chairman's sex, age, intelligence, habits of dress, physical fitness, temperament, or qualities as a parent or spouse. In secondary groups, such as political parties, labor unions, and large corporations, people *are* very much what they *do.* Table 6.1 outlines the major differences between primary and secondary groups.

In-groups and Out-groups

Some groups go a long way toward distinguishing between themselves and other groups. These distinctions may be based on unique racial, ethnic, religious, or social-class characteristics or on special interests, residential location, or unique common experiences. William Graham Sumner (1906) referred to this type of group as an **in-group**—a group that members use as a point of reference. Their definition of who they are is very closely linked to the in-group. There is a "we" feeling generated among the members of the group, who are immediately aware of those who do not belong—the "they" groups. For example, I am a member of the Lions Club, you are not; I am a Tri Delt, you are not; I live on the hill, you live in the valley; I am an alumnus of Harvard, you are not. Those who do not belong to the in-group are part of the **out-group,** which exists in the perceptions of in-group members and takes on a social reality as a result of behavior by in-group members who use the out-group as a negative point of reference. As an in-group member, you reject out-group people or at least do not think of

TABLE 6.1   Relationships in Primary and Secondary Groups

	Primary	*Secondary*
Physical Conditions	Small number Long duration	Large number Shorter duration
Social Characteristics	Identification of ends Intrinsic valuation of the relation Intrinsic valuation of other person Inclusive knowledge of other person Feeling of freedom and spontaneity Operation of informal controls	Disparity of ends Extrinsic valuation of the relation Extrinsic valuation of other person Specialized and limited knowledge of other person Feeling of external constraint Operation of formal controls
Sample Relationships	Friend–friend Husband–wife Parent–child Teacher–pupil	Clerk–customer Announcer–listener Performer–spectator Officer–subordinate
Sample Groups	Play group Family Village or neighborhood Work-team	Nation Clerical hierarchy Professional association Corporation

Source: Kingsley Davis, *Human Society* (New York: Macmillan, 1949).

them as having a standing equal to that of your in-group members. High school peer groups very often are quite invested in being in-groups, "putting down" those schoolmates who do not belong—that is, who are "out."

Characteristics of Groups

In order to function properly, all groups—both primary and secondary—must (1) define their boundaries, (2) choose leaders, (3) make decisions, (4) set goals, (5) assign tasks, and (6) control members' behavior.

Defining Boundaries   Group members must have ways of knowing who belongs to their group and who does not. Sometimes devices for marking boundaries are obvious symbols such as the uniforms worn by athletic teams, lapel pins worn by Rotary Club members, rings worn by Masons, and styles of dress. Other ways in which group boundaries are marked include the use of gestures (think of the special handshakes often used by many American blacks) and language (dialect differences often mark people's regional origin and social class). In some societies (including our own), skin color also is used to mark boundaries between groups. The idea of the British school tie that, by its pattern and colors, signals exclusive group membership, has been adopted

by businesses ranging from banking to brewing. Manufacturers Hanover Trust in New York gives its executives ties that sport the symbols of various currencies; the Anheuser-Busch brewery displays its brands of beer on neckwear for executives and friends.

Choosing Leaders   All groups must grapple with the issue of leadership. A **leader** is someone to whom others turn for guidance in their behavior. Group leadership depends on two things: (1) the type of group involved and (2) the situation of the group.

In some groups, such as large corporations, leadership is assigned to individuals by

secondary group A group that is characterized by an impersonal, formal organization with specific goals. Secondary groups are larger and much less intimate than are primary groups, and the relationships among members are patterned mostly by statuses and roles rather than by personality characteristics. Example: political parties.

in-group A group that members use as a point of reference. The identity of in-group members is very closely linked to their sense of belonging to the group.

out-group A group that exists in the perceptions of in-group members and takes on a social reality as a result of behavior by in-group members who use the out-group as a negative point of reference.

leader Someone to whom others turn for guidance in their behavior.

those in positions of authority. (Authority combines leadership and legitimized power—the ability to force people to act in certain ways.) In other groups, such as adolescent peer groups, individuals move into positions of leadership through the force of personality or through particular skills such as athletic ability, fighting, or debating. In still other groups, including organized clubs such as the Lions Club, leadership is awarded through the democratic process of nominations and voting.

Leadership need not always be held by the same person within a group. It can shift from one individual to another in response to problems or situations that the group encounters. In a group of factory workers, for instance, leadership may fall on different members depending on what the group plans to do—complain to the supervisor, head toward a tavern after work, or organize a picnic for all members and their families.

Politicians and athletic coaches often like to talk about individuals who are "natural leaders." Although attempts to account for leadership solely in terms of personality traits have failed again and again, personality factors may determine what kinds of leadership functions a person assumes. Researchers (Bales, 1958; Slater, 1966) have identified two types of leadership roles: (1) **instrumental leadership,** in which a leader actively proposes tasks and plans to guide the group toward achieving its goals, and (2) **expressive leadership,** in which a leader works to keep relations among group members harmonious and morale high. Both kinds of leadership are crucial to the success of a group. Sometimes both functions are fulfilled by one person, but often they are distributed among several group members. The individual with knowledge of the terrain who leads a group of airplane crash survivors to safety is providing instrumental leadership. The group members who think of ways to keep the group from giving in to despair are providing expressive leadership. The group needs both to survive.

There are three types of instrumental leaders: an **authoritarian leader** makes decisions and gives orders; a **democratic leader** attempts to encourage group members to reach a consensus; and a **laissez-faire leader** is a leader in name or title only and does little actively to influence group affairs. On the whole, Americans are biased toward democratic leaders. Much of this is due to an ideological opposition to authoritarian political systems. Indeed, in most situations a democratic style of leadership promotes greater satisfaction among group members and more effective group functioning than either the authoritarian or laissez-faire style does. However, there are certain group situations in which the authoritarian form of leadership is more effective than the democratic form. For example, when speed and efficiency are important, an authoritarian leader can be quite useful. As one researcher noted: "If the group is faced with a need for emergency action, then that leader behavior is most effective which is prompt and decisive and which is perceived by members as likely to remove quickly the threats in the situation. Authoritarian leadership is practically demanded under such circumstances" (Gibb, 1969) (for a discussion of authoritarian leadership among airline pilots, see Using Sociology: "Group Interaction in the Airplane Cockpit").

Making Decisions Closely related to the problem of leadership is the way in which groups make decisions. In many early hunting and food-gathering societies, important group decisions were reached by consensus—talking about an issue until everybody agreed on what to do (Fried, 1967). Today, occasionally, town councils and other small governing bodies operate in this way. Because this takes a great deal of time and energy, many groups opt for efficiency by taking votes or simply letting one person's decision stand for the group as a whole. Bales and Strodtbeck (1951) identified four stages in group decision making: (1) *orientation*—in which a situation that has disrupted the group's equilibrium is identified and information is gathered, (2) *evaluation*—in which the information is assessed and possible courses of action are proposed, (3) *decision*—in which the group chooses a course of action, and (4) *restoration of equilibrium*—in which the group once more takes up its normal activities.

Setting Goals   As we pointed out before, all groups must have a purpose, a goal, or a set of goals. The goal may be very general, such as spreading peace throughout the world, or it may be very specific, such as playing cards on a railroad train. Group goals may change. For example, the cardplayers might discover that they all share a concern about the use of nuclear energy and decide to organize a political-action group.

Assigning Tasks   Establishing boundaries, defining leadership, making decisions, and setting goals are not enough to keep a group going. In order to endure, a group must do something, if nothing more than ensure that its members continue to make contact with one another. Therefore, it is important that group members know what needs to be done and who is going to do it. This assigning of tasks in itself can be an important group activity—think of your family discussions about sharing household chores. By taking on group tasks, members not only help the group reach its goals but also show their commitment to one another and to the group as a whole. This leads members to appreciate one another's importance as individuals and the importance of the group in all their lives—a process that injects life and energy into a group.

Controlling Members' Behavior   If a group cannot control its members' behavior, it will cease to exist. For this reason, failure to conform to group norms is seen as dangerous or threatening, whereas conforming to group norms is rewarded—if only by others' friendly attitudes. Groups not only encourage but often depend for survival on conformity of behavior. A member's failure to conform is met with responses ranging from coolness to criticism or even ejection from the group. Anyone who has ever tried to introduce changes into the constitution of a club or to ignore long-standing conventions, such as ways of dressing, rituals of greeting, or the assumption of

designated responsibilities, probably has experienced group hostility.

Primary groups tend to be more tolerant of members' deviant behavior than are secondary groups (Lee, 1966). For example, families often will conceal the problems of a member who suffers from chronic alcoholism or drug abuse. Even primary groups, however, must draw the line somewhere, and they will invoke negative sanctions (see Chapter 9) if all else fails to get the deviant member to show at least a willingness to *try* to conform. When this does happen and primary groups finally act, their punishments can be far more severe or harsh than those of secondary groups. Thus, an intergenerational conflict in a family can result in the commitment of a teenager to an institution or treatment center.

Secondary groups tend to use formal, as opposed to informal, sanctions and are much more likely than primary groups are simply to expel, or push out, a member who persists in violating strongly held norms: corporations fire unsatisfactory employees, the army discharges soldiers who violate regulations, and so on.

Even though primary groups are more tolerant of their members' behavior, people tend to conform more closely to their norms than to those of secondary groups. This is because people value their membership in a primary group, with its strong interpersonal bonds, for its own sake. Secondary group

authority   A combination of leadership and legitimized power, which confers the ability to force people to act in certain ways.

instrumental leadership   A form of leadership in which a leader actively proposes tasks and plans to guide the group toward achieving its goals.

expressive leadership   A form of leadership in which a leader works to keep relations among group members harmonious and morale high.

authoritarian leader   A type of instrumental leader who makes decisions and gives orders.

democratic leader   A type of instrumental leader who attempts to encourage group members to reach a consensus.

laissez-faire leader   A type of instrumental leader who is a leader in name or title only and does little actively to influence group affairs.

Group Interaction in the Airplane Cockpit

Domineering bosses, timid subordinates, poor teamwork, failure in communication, and lack of priorities can cause trouble in any human organization. On the flight deck of an airplane they can have very serious consequences, leading to crashes and the loss of lives. Airlines are beginning to realize that flight safety is greatly influenced by how well the pilot and copilot work with each other.

"Slushy runway. Do you want me to do anything special for it or just go for it?" asked the copilot of Air Florida's flight 90 as he peered into a snowstorm at Washington National Airport.

"Unless you got anything special you'd like to do," quipped the plane's 34-year-old pilot. From that moment to the instant that the ice-laden Boeing 737 struggled into the air, straining for altitude, the copilot told the pilot four times that conditions were "not right" for takeoff. But the pilot took off anyway. Seconds later, Flight 90 came back down, hitting the Fourteenth Street Bridge before it slammed onto the ice covering the Potomac River and sank, killing 74 persons on the airplane, including the pilot, copilot, and four motorists on the bridge.

The National Transportation Safety Board, an independent federal agency that lists probable causes of civil-aviation, railroad, marine, and major highway accidents, decided that flight crew errors were the probable cause of the crash, including the decision to take off with snow and ice on the plane and the pilot's failure to stop the takeoff, despite warnings from the copilot that instrument readings indicated engine problems. The board also cited contributing factors, such as improper ground servicing by the airline, that had nothing to do with crew error.

Smooth, efficient, and decisive operation and interaction are important at all times in the cockpit of an airplane. A flight crew ought to perform synergistically; that is, it should function even better than the individuals composing it do. Close cooperation is especially difficult to achieve, though, in large airlines where many pilots and copilots bid for routes on the basis of seniority and therefore often fly with colleagues they have never seen before. The situation is not unlike assembling a football team with expert players who have never met and sending them right into a game. Although all the players would know what a pro set or blitz was, they would be handicapped by not knowing one another's capabilities.

The frequent use of pickup crews is not the only thing that contributes to accidents. The emotional makeup of the pilot and copilot and their relationship to each other and to the flight engineer can also be critical.

Records show that 70 percent of all civil-aviation incidents during a recent five-year period were attributable to human error, mainly when information was improperly transferred from one crew member to another or was not transferred at all. Human error pertains to how crew members communicate, how their personalities interrelate, how clearly they set lines of authority and adhere to them, and how their responsibilities are delegated.

The pilot, or captain, as he is known in the trade, is the authority figure for both the crew and the passengers, and he therefore plays the most important management role. The smiling, confident, gray-at-the-temples father image of a captain so dear to those who conjure up commercials—the chap exuding the wisdom of Solomon, the looks and certainty of Robert Redford, and the sure reflexes of Reggie Jackson—can have as real-life counterparts men who are aggressive and domineering to the point of being bullies. Captains like this

A U.S. Park Police helicopter crew member pulls a passenger from the ice-filled Potomac River after a jetliner crashed into the bridge in the background during takeoff.

may inhibit contributions from their copilots and engineers. Others may be so passive that their copilots either usurp their authority or are left wondering who would do what in an emergency.

Industry sources agree that very assertive, even domineering pilots outnumber the passive ones by a very wide margin. This may be because about 90 percent of all airline pilots come from the military, where a premium is placed on aggressiveness. It is also true that fighter pilots, as opposed to bomber and transportation pilots, either fly alone or in front of a radar operator in the back seat, and therefore tend to be aeronautical loners who can easily interpret assistance by another pilot as interference.

Another, more likely reason for the preponderance of overly aggressive captains has to do with most pilots' understanding that flying cannot be a democratic endeavor because of extremely short decision times. That being so, it is safe to assume that some captains believe that treating copilots with anything less than the firmest of hands invites arguments when time is desperately short. Reports abound with instances of captains' either ignoring their first officer's help or actually spurning it, as was the case when one copilot tried to correct a sloppy approach to Chicago's O'Hare International Airport. "I'll do what I want," the captain snapped. "You just look out the damn window."

The Aviation Safety Reporting System shows that of those pilots who reported communication problems as factors in incidents or accidents, 35 percent mentioned problems having to do with crew coordination, poor understanding, and division of responsibilities. Twelve percent cited a total lack of communication, sometimes because of acrimony arising out of role and personality conflicts, as in the O'Hare example. More than 15

percent said that information believed by one or more crew members to have been transferred was not, in fact, transmitted. Ten percent mentioned communication deficiency because of complacency—assumptions that everybody understood what was taking place, when they did not.

Robert L. Helmreich of the University of Texas says that a significant proportion of accidents arise from a failure to work well as a team. He goes on to say that if this is the case, then "the evaluation of *individual* performance may fail to capture the crucial dimensions of crew behavior in stressful situations."

Helmreich and his associates found two personality dimensions that they consider particularly relevant to flight crew performance: instrumentality, or goal orientation, and expressivity, or group orientation. "Macho" pilots generally have goal orientations that are high instrumental and low expressive. In the industry, macho pilots are considered problems. They tend to take risks, and they have more problems

working with women on the flight deck. In high-stress situations, they often ignore or overrule women.

"The authoritarian type may be generally disliked as a captain in normal operations," says Helmreich. "Such an individual may, on the other hand, take charge very effectively during emergencies, whereas the democratic leader might be highly valued during routine operations but find it more difficult to assume a strong leadership role when the situation demands it."

Because *individual* performance in emergencies might be expected to be handled better by the goal-oriented person, according to Helmreich, and because lack of teamwork causes accidents, the best captain is the one with both high-goal and group orientations. "Such individuals might be expected to be both competent in dealing with the technical aspects of the problem *and* attuned to the reactions of others."

Source: Abridged and excerpted from William E. Burrows, "Cockpit Encounters," *Psychology Today,* November 1982, pp. 43–47. □

membership is valued mostly for what it will do for the people in the group, not because of any deep emotional ties. Because primary group membership is so desirable, its members are more reluctant to risk expulsion by indulging in behavior that might violate the group's standards, or norms, than are secondary group members.

Usually group members will want to conform as long as the group is experienced as important. Solomon Asch (1955) showed just how far group members will go to promote group solidarity and conformity. In a series of experiments, he formed groups of eight people and then asked each member to match one line against three other lines of varying lengths (see Figure 6.1). Each judgment was announced in the presence of the other group members. The groups were composed of one real subject and seven of Asch's confederates,

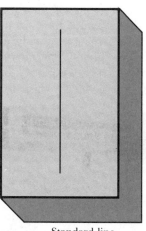 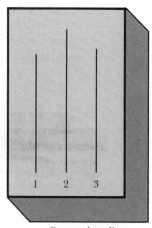

Standard line   Comparison lines

Figure 6.1 Group Pressure In Solomon Asch's experiment on conformity to group pressure, groups of eight students were asked to decide which of the comparison lines (right) was the same length as the standard line (left).

whose identity was kept secret from the real subject. The confederates had previously met with Asch and had been instructed to give a unanimous but incorrect answer at certain points throughout the experiment. Asch was interested in finding out how the individual who had been made a minority of one in the presence of a unanimous majority would respond. The subject was placed in a situation in which a group unanimously contradicted the information of his or her senses. Asch repeated the experiment many times. He found that 32 percent of the answers by the real subjects were identical with, or in the direction of, the inaccurate estimates of the majority. This was quite remarkable, because there were virtually no incorrect answers in the control groups that lacked Asch's accomplices, which rules out the possibility of optical illusion. What we have here is an instance in which individuals are willing to give incorrect answers in order not to appear out of step with the judgments of the other group members. Although groups must fulfill certain functions in order to continue to exist, they serve primarily as a point of reference for their members.

Reference Groups

Groups are more than just bridges between the individual and society as a whole. We spend much of our time in one group or another, and the impact that these groups have on us continues even when we are not actually in contact with the other members. The norms and values of groups to which we belong or with which we identify serve as the basis for evaluating our own and others' behavior.

A **reference group** sets and enforces standards of behavior and belief and provides a comparison point against which persons measure themselves and others. Often reference groups are categories with which we identify, rather than specific groups to which we belong. For example, a communcations major may identify with individuals in the media without having any direct contact with them. In this respect, anticipatory socialization is taking place, in that the individual may alter his or her behavior and attitudes toward those they perceive to be part of the group they plan to join in the future. For example, people who become bankers soon feel themselves part of a group—bankers—and assume ideas and lifestyles that help them identify with that group. They tend to dress in a conservative, "bankerish" fashion, even buying their clothes in shops that other bankers patronize to make sure they have the "right" clothes from the "right" stores. They join certain clubs and other organizations such as country clubs and alumni associations—so that they can mingle with other bankers and clients. Eventually the norms and values they adopted when they joined the bankers' group become internalized—they see and judge the world around them as bankers.

We can also distinguish between positive and negative reference groups. Positive reference groups are made up of people that we want to emulate. Negative reference groups provide a model that we do not wish to follow. Therefore, a writer may identify positively with those writers who produce serious fiction, while thinking of journalists who write for gossip publications as a negative reference group.

Even though groups are in fact composed of individuals, individuals are also created to a large degree by the groups to which they belong through the process of socialization (see Chapter 4). Of these groups, the small group usually has the strongest direct impact on an individual.

☐ Small Groups

The term **small group** is relative. It refers to the many kinds of social groups, such as families, peer groups, and work groups, that actually meet together and contain few enough members so that all members know one another. The smallest possible group contains only two members, and its technical label is **dyad.** An engaged couple is a dyad, as are the pilot and copilot of an aircraft. Dyads resist change in their group size: on the one hand, the loss of one member destroys the group, leaving the other member alone; but on the other hand, the addition of a third member, creating a **triad,** adds uncertainty because it introduces the possibility of two-against-one alliances and group pressure directed at one member.

Triads can sometimes be more adaptable than dyads can. However, on occasions they can be more unstable. "Two's company, three's a crowd" derived from this view. Triads are more stable in those situations when one member can help resolve quarrels between the other two. When three diplomats are negotiating offshore fishing rights, for example, one member of the triad may offer a concession that will break the deadlock between the other two. If that does not work, the third person may try to analyze the arguments of the other two in an effort to bring about a compromise. The formation of shifting pair-offs within triads can help stabilize the group. When it appears that one group member is weakening, one of the two paired members often will break the alliance and form a new one with the individual who had been isolated (Hare, 1976). This is often seen among groups of children engaged in games. In triads in which there is no shifting of alliances and the configuration constantly breaks down into two against one, the group will become unstable and may eventually break up. In Aldous Huxley's novel *Brave New World,* the political organization of the earth was organized into three eternally warring political powers. As one power seemed to be losing, one of the others would come to its aid in a temporary alliance, thereby ensuring worldwide political stability while also making possible endless warfare. No power could risk the total defeat of another because the other surviving power might then become the stronger of the surviving dyad.

As a group grows larger, the number of relationships within it increases, which often leads to the formation of **subgroups**—splinter groups within the larger group. Once a group has more than five to seven members, spontaneous conversation becomes difficult for the group as a whole. Then there are two solutions available: the group can split into subgroups (as happens informally at parties), or it can adopt a formal means of controlling communication (use of *Robert's Rules of Order,*

for instance). For these reasons, small groups tend to resist the addition of new members because increasing size threatens the nature of the group. In addition there may be a fear that new members will resist socialization to group norms and thereby undermine group traditions and values. On the whole, small groups are much more vulnerable than large groups are to disruption by new members, and the introduction of new members often leads to shifts in patterns of interaction and group norms.

The Study of Small Groups

Small groups are everywhere. More than a decade ago one researcher estimated that there were as many as four or five billion small groups functioning around the world (Mills, 1967). Sheer numbers, however, do not alone account for sociologists' interest in small groups.

Small Groups and the Course of History   It is important to understand how small groups function because they play an important part in determining the course of history. During the summer and fall of 1941, for example, the commander in chief of the U.S. Pacific Fleet, Admiral Husband Kimmel, received many warnings that war with Japan was imminent. He discussed these warnings with his staff but was assured again and again that his decision to ignore them was correct. As late as November 27, Admiral Kimmel received an official "war warning" from Washington, but because the message did not specifically mention the naval base at Pearl Harbor as a possible target of attack, Kimmel and the other officers in his in-group decided that no spe-

reference group A group that sets and enforces standards of behavior and belief and provides a comparison point against which persons measure themselves and others.

small group A relative term that refers to the many kinds of social groups that actually meet together and contain few enough members so that all members know one another.

dyad A small group containing two members.

triad A small group containing three members.

subgroups Splinter groups within the larger group.

Although there were a number of warnings of an attack on Pearl Harbor, those in charge refused to take defensive action.

cial defensive preparations were needed. On December 3, Kimmel was informed that Washington had intercepted a secret message from Tokyo to all Japanese diplomatic missions abroad ordering staff immediately to destroy their secret codes—a very strong sign of last-minute war preparations. Again Kimmel's group refused to take defensive action (such as sending out scout planes and dispersing the ships of the fleet anchored in the harbor). Finally, on December 6, the signs of war were too many to ignore, but by then Kimmel and his staff were paralyzed: they felt unable to choose among their few remaining options. On the next day the Japanese attacked Pearl Harbor with bombs and torpedos and succeeded in destroying or incapacitating much of the U.S. Pacific Fleet as it rode at anchor. The internal group processes that kept Kimmel and his staff from acting appropriately, even though they had more than enough information, is called **defensive avoidance** (or more popularly, "groupthink").

This same small-group process also characterized the administration of President Richard M. Nixon and eventually led to his downfall after the Watergate scandal (Janis and Mann, 1976). Clearly, it is important to understand under what conditions defensive avoidance emerges in small groups (especially in groups with important responsibilities) and to know how to intervene and bring such processes to a halt.

Small Groups and Society Small groups such as families, clubs, and peer groups are enduring and important elements of the social world. Sociologists study them because unless they did so, their theories of social action would be based on incomplete data. Small groups exhibit many of the characteristics of complete societies. The division of labor, decision making, leadership, ethical and moral systems, prestige rankings, myths, and many other aspects of social life can be studied in the microcosm of a small-group setting (Slater, 1966).

Small Groups and Experiments Because of their convenient size, small groups can be studied in the laboratory and their variables subjected to tight experimental control (see

Chapter 2). For example, it is possible to study how all-female groups compare with all-male groups in coping with stress and frustration or how limiting the distribution of information to certain arbitrary flow channels affects a group's ability to reach decisions.

Cohesiveness in Small Groups

One facet of small groups that is of particular interest to sociologists is the impact that group members have on one another. Recent research indicates that working on a task with several other people may, in fact, reduce individual effort (Latané, Williams, and Harkins, 1979). Although increases in group size may produce greater total output, the gains may not be as great as expected. They may even represent a clear example of the law of diminishing returns, as each of the people participating in a joint task expends less effort on it than would be the case if he or she worked alone (see Focus on Research, "The Causes and Consequences of Social Loafing"). The quality of interaction of group members and the cohesiveness that develops can determine the success of the group as a whole. An example of the importance of group cohesiveness can be found in an examination of morale in the military forces.

During World War II the American soldier's morale generally was high. Fighting, they took great risks, and when captured, they constantly sought to escape. In the 1960s in Vietnam, military morale sank to an all-time low. It finally reached the point at which some soldiers joined protest movements against the war—risking imprisonment rather than continuing to fight or to train others to fight. The use of drugs, including heroin, reached epidemic proportions, and many soldiers have testified that they were "high" for much of their active tour of duty—including the times they were out on patrol (Moskos, 1975).

What happened to American soldiers in the 20 to 25 years between World War II and Vietnam? Many things changed, of course. The issues and goals in World War II seemed much more clear-cut than they did in the war in Vietnam, and society as a whole backed military involvement in the war of the 1940s much more so than in that of the 1960s. But so-

In contrast to World War II, morale among soldiers during the war in Vietnam was extremely low.

ciologists have found another—perhaps even more powerful—difference. In World War II it was understood that soldiers generally stayed with the same unit to which they were originally assigned for the duration of the war. As a result each soldier knew that the sooner the war was won, the sooner he could return home. Also, because he would stay with the same unit until the war was over, a soldier quickly came to identify his own safety with the survival of the unit. The men ate, slept, and fought side by side for years. They went on leave together, read one another's mail from home, and formed close friendships. In other words, American fighting units in World War II became primary groups as well as ingroups—with commitment to and pride in their membership (Shils, 1950).

In Vietnam a soldier was assigned for a one- or two-year tour of duty. In all fighting units, the members came and went constantly, and each member had his own number of days left to stay. Group loyalties never could develop the way they did in World War II because each soldier worked desperately to play it safe so that he would survive until the

defensive avoidance An internal group process that keeps an in-group from acting appropriately despite the evidence before it; also known as "groupthink."

FOCUS ON RESEARCH
The Causes and Consequences of Social Loafing

Although small groups provide a convenient size for study, this does not necessarily mean that the experimental results will provide simple answers. The following experiments raise serious questions regarding commonly held beliefs about the effectiveness of small groups in terms of work performance.

More than 50 years ago, a German psychologist named Ringelmann performed a small-group study in which subjects were instructed to pull as hard as they could on a rope, alone and with one, two, and seven other people. A strain gauge was used to measure how hard each subject pulled in kilograms of pressure.

You might expect that three people pulling together on a rope would exert close to three times as much force as one person would and that eight people pulling together would exert nearly eight times as much force. But Ringelmann's results were strikingly different. When pulling one at a time, subjects averaged 63 kilograms of pressure. Groups of three people exerted a force of 160 kilograms, only two-and-a-half times the average individual performance. Groups of eight pulled 248 kilograms, less than four times the solo rate. Thus, the collective group performance, although increasing somewhat with group size, was substantially less than the sum of the individual efforts. As group size increased, average individual effort decreased.

Three researchers at Ohio State University, Bibb Latané, Kipling Williams, and Stephen Harkins, wanted to find out if Ringelmann's effect held true for other simple small-group tasks. They selected shouting and hand clapping as the tasks to be observed.

In the first of two experiments,

six subjects were seated in a semicircle in a soundproof laboratory. They were told that on a signal they were to clap or cheer as loudly as they could for 5 seconds. Each subject clapped and shouted twice alone, four times each in pairs and foursomes, and six times in groups of six. A sound-level meter recorded their performances in dynes/cm²— the physical unit of work involved in producing sound pressure.

The results showed that, as with rope-pulling, individual performance decreased as the size of the group increased. Alone, each subject's performance averaged 3.7 dynes/cm². In pairs, individual performance dropped to 2.6 dynes/cm². Foursomes averaged 1.8 dynes/cm² each; groups of six, 1.5 dynes/cm² each. The sound of 12 hands clapping is not even three times as intense as the sound of 2 hands clapping. The experimenters identified this tendency of individual performances to decrease as the number of coperformers increased as social loafing.

In their second experiment, the investigators wanted to exclude the influence of direct social interaction among the subjects. The format was similar to that of the first experiment, but each subject could not see or hear the other subjects. Instead, they heard recordings through earphones that led them to believe that they were shouting alone or with two or six other subjects.

As a whole, subjects in the second experiment shouted with considerably more intensity than did those in the first experiment. But individual performance levels still decreased as the apparent number fo participants increased. Hence, social loafing was not dependent on direct contact with other group

members.

The experimenters concluded that participation in groups can inhibit the productivity of individuals. People reduce their own exertions as group size increases. This finding fitted well with Latané's theory of social impact: if a person is the target of social forces, increasing the number of people in the target group diminishes the pressure on each individual because the impact is divided among the group members. In a group-performance situation, such as these experiments, in which the pressures to work come from outside the group (from the investigators) and individual outputs are not identifiable (only averaged), this division of impact will lead each individual to work less. In such group tasks, the amount of effort expended on group tasks decreases as the number of people in the group increases.

These findings in support of Ringelmann's effect and the concept of social loafing seem to violate both common stereotype and social organizational theory. Common stereotype holds that team participation leads to increased effort, that group morale and cohesiveness spur individual enthusiasm, that by pulling together groups can achieve any goal, that in unity there is strength. Organizational theory holds that, at least for simple, well-learned tasks, the presence of coworkers should facilitate performance. The contrary evidence of social loafing requires further thinking and investigation into small-group dynamics.

Source: Bibb Latané, Kipling Williams, and Stephen Harkins, "Many Hands Make Light Work: The Causes and Consequences of Social Loafing," *Journal of Personality and Social Psychology* **37** (6) (1979), pp. 822–832. □

POPULAR SOCIOLOGY
Networks in the 1980s

Modern technology and the massive amount of information present in contemporary society have led to the emergence of what are known as networks. *These networks are examples of primary and secondary groups that have formed as a result of a changing society. John Naisbitt explored this trend in his book* Megatrends.

Networks exist to foster self-help, to exchange information, to change society, to improve productivity and work life, and to share resources. They are structurerd to transmit information in a way that is quicker, more "high touch," and more energy efficient than any other process we know.

Simply stated, networks are people talking to one another, sharing ideas, information, and resources. The point is often made that networking is a verb, not a noun. The important part is not the network, the finished product, but the process of getting there—the communication that creates the linkages between people and clusters of people.

Networks are the sociological equivalent of technology. They provide a form of communication and interaction that is suitable for the information-rich future of the 1980s and beyond.

One of networking's great attractions is that it is an easy way to get information. Lipnack and Stamps list a variety of interesting examples of the networking phenomenon:

In Newton, Massachusetts, there is a local information network, called WARM LINES, that provides a service as mundane and critical as providing parents with the names of available babysitters.

In Denver, Colorado, you can join the Denver Open Network and gain access to a computerized file of over 500 other people with a variety of different interests: That's how one inventor found an investor to finance his new self-contained water system.

The National Women's Health Network in Washington, D.C., began in a typical networking fashion with a long-distance phone call between two friends concerned with improving women's health care. Since 1974 it has evolved into a national network of more than 500 health groups.

Thousands of similar networks exist, as well as millions more, to which all of us belong—the informal networks among friends, colleagues, discussion groups, community organizations—that never grow into the organization stage.

Although sharing information and contacts is their main purpose, networks can go beyond the mere transfer of data to the creation and exchange of knowledge. As each person in a network takes in new information, he or she synthesizes it and comes up with other, new ideas. Networks share these newly forged thoughts and ideas.

Source: Excerpted from John Naisbitt, *Megatrends* (New York: Warner Books, 1984), pp. 215–217. □

---

end of his tour. Whereas it is true that soldiers everywhere are motivated by a concern for their own survival, the way in which the U.S. armed forces were organized in Vietnam prevented the soldiers from identifying the survival of their fighting units as groups with their own survival (Moskos, 1975).

□ Large Groups: Associations

Although all of us probably would be able to identify and describe the various small groups to which we belong, we might find it difficult to follow the same process with the large groups that affect us. As patrons or employees of large organizations and governments, we function as part of large groups all the time. Thus, sociologists must study large groups as well as small groups in order to understand the workings of society.

Much of the activity of a modern society is carried out through large and formally organized groups. Sociologists refer to these groups as **associations.** These are purposefully created special-interest groups that have clearly defined goals and official ways of doing things (for an example of how these types of associations are changing in contemporary society, see Popular Sociology: "Networks in the 1980s"). Associations include such or-

associations Purposefully created special-interest groups that have clearly defined goals and official ways of doing things such as government agencies.

CASE STUDY
From Mafia to Cosa Nostra

If an association is to be successful, it must be able to adapt to changing conditions. In this case study, Robert T. Anderson describes how the old Mafia of Sicily changed from an intimate family association to the bureaucratic, highly organized Cosa Nostra of contemporary America.

Sicily has known centuries of inept and corrupt governments that have always seemed unconcerned about the enormous gap between the very rich minority and the incredibly poor majority. Whether from disinterest or from simple incapacity, governments have failed to maintain public order. Under these circumstances, local strong men, beyond reach of the government or in collusion with it, have repeatedly grouped together to seek out their own interest. They have formed, in effect, little extralegal principalities. A code of conduct, the code of *omertà*, justified and supported these unofficial regimes by linking compliance with a fabric of tradition that may be characterized as chivalrous. By this code, an "honorable" Sicilian maintained unbreakable silence concerning all illegal activities. To correct abuse, he might resort to feud and vendetta. But never would he avail himself of a governmental agency.

Known as "Mafias," these groups took root in the United States, where industrialization and urbanization have created a new kind of society. Can a preindustrial peasant institu-

tion survive unchanged in an urban, industrial milieu? May we not anticipate major modifications of structure and function under such circumstances? The available evidence on secret organizations—though regrettably incomplete, inconsistent, and inaccurate—suggests affirmative answers to both questions. The Mafia has survived, and it has bureaucratized.

Mafia formal organization seems at a turning point. The scale of operations is expanding. The face-to-face, familylike group is changing into a bureaucratic organization.

Recent decades in the United States have witnessed the acceleration of all aspects of modernization. Here, if anywhere, the forces of urbanization impinge upon group life. Although American criminals have always been quick to capitalize upon technological advances, no significant organizational innovation occurred until the repeal of prohibition in 1932, an event that abruptly ended much of the lucrative business of the underworld. Small face-to-face associations gave way over subsequent decades to the formation of regional, national, and international combines, a change in which American *mafiosi* participated.

Personnel now regularly specialize as professional gunmen, runners, executives, or adepts in other particular operations. Departmentalization was introduced and now

includes an organizational breakdown into subgroups, such as narcotics operations, gambling, the rackets, prostitution, and an enforcement department—the infamous Murder, Inc., with its more recent descendants.

The Mafia as a traditional type of formal organization has disappeared in America. Modern criminals refer to its successor as Cosa Nostra. "Our Thing." The Cosa Nostra is a lineal descendant of the Mafia, but it is a different kind of organization. Its goals are much broader, as it exploits modern cities and an industrialized nation. The real and fictive kinship ties of the old Mafia still operate among fellow Sicilians and Italians, but these ties now coexist with bureaucratic ones. The Cosa Nostra operates above all in new and different terms. This new type of organization includes elaboration of the hierarchy of authority: the specialization and departmentalization of activities; new and more pragmatic, but still unwritten, rules; and a more developed internal impartiality. Hence, in America, the traditional Mafia has evolved into a relatively complex organization that perpetuates selected features of the older peasant organization but subordinates them to the requirements of a bureaucracy.

Source: Excerpted and adapted from Robert T. Anderson, "From Mafia to Cosa Nostra," *American Journal of Sociology,* **71** (November, 1965), pp. 302–310. □

ganizations as government departments and agencies, businesses and factories, labor unions, schools and colleges, fraternal and service groups, hospitals and clinics, and clubs for various hobbies from gardening to antique collecting. Their goals may be very broad and general, such as helping the poor, healing the sick, or making a profit, or quite specific and

limited, such as manufacturing automobile tires, teaching people to speak Chinese, or treating skin diseases. They may range in size from a local garden club to American Telephone & Telegraph. Although an enormous variety of associations exist, they all are characterized by some degree of formal structure with an underlying informal structure (for an example of how an association operates even in the criminal sphere, see Case Study: "From Mafia to Cosa Nostra").

The Formal Structure

In order for associations to function, the work that must be accomplished is assessed and broken down into manageable tasks that are assigned to specific individuals. In other words, associations are run according to some type of **formal organizational structure** that consists of planned, highly institutionalized, and clearly defined statuses and role relationships (see Chapter 5). The formal organizational structure of large associations in contemporary society is best exemplified by the organizational structure called *bureaucracy*.

Consider a college or university. Fulfilling its main purpose of educating students requires far more than simply bringing together students and teachers. Funds must be raised, buildings constructed, qualified students and instructors recruited, programs and classes organized, materials ordered and distributed, grounds kept up, and buildings maintained. Messages need to be typed, copied, and filed; lectures must be given; and seminars must be led. To accomplish all these tasks the school must create many different positions: president, deans, department heads, registrars, public relations staff, grounds keepers, maintenance personnel, purchasing agents, secretaries, faculty, and students. Every member of the school has clearly spelled-out tasks that are organized in relation to one another: students are taught and evaluated by faculty, faculty are responsible to department heads or deans, deans to the president, and so on. Yet, underlying these clearly defined assignments are procedures that are never written down but are worked out and understood by those who have to get the job done.

The Informal Structure

Sociologists recognize that formal associations never operate entirely according to their stated rules and procedures. Every association has an **informal structure** consisting of networks of people who help out one another by "bending" rules and taking procedural shortcuts. No matter how carefully plans are made,

no matter how clearly and rationally roles are defined and tasks assigned, every situation and its variants cannot be anticipated. Sooner or later, then, individuals in associations are confronted with situations in which they must improvise and even persuade others to help them do so.

As every student knows, no school ever runs as smoothly as planned. For instance, "going by the book"—that is, following all the formal rules—often gets students tied up in long lines and red tape. Enterprising students and instructors find shortcuts. For example, a student who wants to change from Section A of Sociology 100 to Section E might find it very difficult or time-consuming to change sections ("add-and-drop") officially. However, it may be possible to work out an informal deal—the student stays registered in Section A but attends and is evaluated in Section E. The instructor of Section E then turns the grade over to the instructor of Section A who hands in that grade with all the other Section A grades—as if the student had attended Section A all along. The formal rules have been "bent," but the major purposes of the school (educating and evaluating students) have been served.

In addition, human beings have their own individual needs even when they are on "company time," and these needs are not always met by attending single-mindedly to assigned tasks. To accommodate these needs, people often try to find extra break time for personal business by getting jobs done faster than would be possible if all the formal rules and procedures were followed. To accomplish these ends, individuals in associations find it useful to help one another by "covering" for one another, "looking the other way" at strategic moments, and offering one another useful information about office politics, people, and procedures. Gradually the reciprocal

formal organizational structure The planned, highly institutionalized, and clearly defined statuses and role relationships that characterize associations.

informal structure The structure within an association that is made up of networks of people who help one another by "bending" rules and taking procedural shortcuts.

relationships among members of these informal networks become institutionalized: "unwritten laws" are established, and a fully functioning **informal structure** evolves (Selznick, 1948).

At the same time as the goals of associations have given rise to an informal structure for job performance, they have also spawned an organizational structure that often increases the formality of procedures. This formal organizational structure is called bureaucracy and has an impact on the informal structure.

☐ Bureaucracy

Associations evolved along with literacy and the rise of cities some 5,500 years ago, but **bureaucracy** emerged as the organizational counterpart of the Industrial Revolution only two centuries ago. Although in ordinary usage the term suggests a certain rigidity and red tape, it has a somewhat different meaning to sociologists. Robert K. Merton (1968) defined bureaucracy as "a formal, rationally organized social structure [with] clearly defined patterns of activity in which, ideally, every series of actions is functionally related to the purposes of the organization."

Max Weber, the German sociologist we introduced in Chapter 1, provided the first detailed study of the nature and origins of bureaucracy. Although much has changed in society since he developed his theories, Weber's basic description of bureaucracy remains essentially accurate to this day.

Weber's Model of Bureaucracy: An Ideal Type

Weber viewed bureaucracy as the most efficient—although not necessarily the most desirable—form of social organization for the administration of work. He studied examples of bureaucracy in history and in contemporary times and noted the elements that they had in common. From this work he developed a model of bureaucracy, which is known as an **ideal type.** Weber believed it useful to accentuate or even exaggerate reality in certain situations in order to understand an idea better. An ideal type is just such an exaggeration. When Weber presented his ideal type of bureaucracy, he combined into one those characteristics that could be found in one form or another in a variety of organizations. It is unlikely that we ever would find a bureaucracy that has all the traits presented in Weber's ideal type. However, his presentation can help us understand what is involved in bureaucratic systems. It is also important to recognize that Weber's ideal type is in no way meant to be "ideal" in the sense that it presents a desired state of affairs. In short, an ideal type is an exaggeration of a situation that is used in order to convey a set of ideas. Weber outlined six characteristics of bureaucracies:

1. *A clear-cut division of labor.* The activities of a bureaucracy are broken down into clearly defined, limited tasks, which are attached to formally defined positions (statuses) in the organization. This permits a great deal of specialization and a high degree of expertise. For example, a small-town police department might consist of a chief, a lieutenant, a detective, several sergeants, and a dozen officers. The chief issues orders and assigns tasks; the lieutenant is in charge when the chief is not around; the detective does investigative work; the sergeants handle calls at the desk and do the paperwork required for formal "booking" procedures; and the officers walk or drive through the community, making arrests and responding to emergencies. Each member of the department has a defined status and duty as well as specialized skills appropriate to his or her position.

2. *Hierarchical delegation of power and responsibility.* Each position in the bureaucracy is given sufficient power so that the individual who occupies it can do assigned work adequately and also compel subordinates to follow instructions. Such power must be limited to what is necessary to meet the requirement of the position. For example, a police chief can order an officer to walk a specific beat but cannot insist that the officer join the Lions Club.

3. *Rules and regulations.* The rights and duties attached to various positions are clearly stated in writing and govern the behavior of all individuals who occupy them. That way all members of the organizational structure know

what is expected of them, and each person can be held accountable for his or her behavior. For example, the regulations of a police department might state, "No member of the department shall drink intoxicating liquors while on duty." Such rules make the activities of bureaucracies predictable and stable.

4. *Impartiality.* The organization's written rules and regulations apply equally to all its members. No exceptions are made because of social or psychological differences among individuals. Also, people occupy positions in the bureaucracy only because they are assigned according to formal procedures. These positions "belong to" the organization itself; they cannot become the personal property of those who occupy them. For example, a vice-president of United States Steel Corporation is usually not permitted to pass on that position to his or her children through inheritance.

5. *Employment based on technical qualifications.* People are hired because they have the ability and skills to do the job, not because they have personal contacts within the company. Advancement is based on how well a person does the job. Promotions and job security go to those who are most competent.

6. *Distinction between public and private spheres.* A clear distinction is made between the employees' personal lives and their working lives. It is unusual for employees to be expected to take business calls at home. At the same time their family life has no place in the work setting.

Although many bureaucracies strive at the organizational level to attain the goals that Weber proposed, most do not achieve them on the practical level.

Bureaucracy Today: The Reality

Just as no building is ever identical with its blueprint, no bureaucratic organization fully embodies all the features of Weber's model. Studies of organizations around the world reveal that such elements as degree of hierarchical organization, adherence to rules and regulations, and job specialization vary widely—both between and within organizations (Udy, 1959; Hall, 1963–1964). One thing that most bureaucracies have in common is a structure that separates those whose respon-

sibilities include keeping in mind the overall needs of the entire organization from those whose responsibilities are much more narrow and task oriented. Visualize a modern industrial organization as a pyramid. Management (at the top of the pyramid) plans, organizes, hires, and fires. Workers (in the bottom section) make much smaller decisions limited to carrying out the work assigned to them. A similar division cuts through the hierarchy of the Roman Catholic church. The bishops are at the top, along with archbishops, cardinals, and the pope; the clergy are below. Only bishops can ordain new priests, and they plan the church's worldwide activities. The priests administer parishes, schools, and missions; their tasks are quite narrow and confined. Figure 6.2 illustrates the organizational structure of a large corporation.

How efficient are bureaucracies? On the whole, Weber's model is truly an ideal.

For example, in a small suburb of New York City the 30 employees of the department of public works are required by union contract to work from 8 A.M. to 4 P.M. five days a week. But in reality they work from 8 A.M. to 2 P.M. because of a long-standing practice of letting employees go home as soon as they complete their assigned tasks. This "unwritten rule" was set a number of years ago in an unsuccessful effort to encourage greater productivity, but it soon got out of hand. Employees began to complain when job assignments took more than six hours to complete because they saw the 2 P.M. quitting time as a "right" established by tradition. The superintendent of public works now makes sure that no job will keep an employee past 2 P.M.

Complicated, time-consuming jobs often are stretched out over several days—even when

bureaucracy A formal, rationally organized social structure with clearly defined patterns of activity in which, ideally, every series of actions is fundamentally related to the organization's purpose.

ideal type A simplified, exaggerated model of reality. The ideal type of bureaucracy, as developed by Max Weber, contains six characteristics: (1) a clear-cut division of labor, (2) hierarchical delegation of power and responsibility, (3) rules and regulations, (4) impartiality, (5) employment based on technical qualifications, and (6) a distinction between public and private spheres.

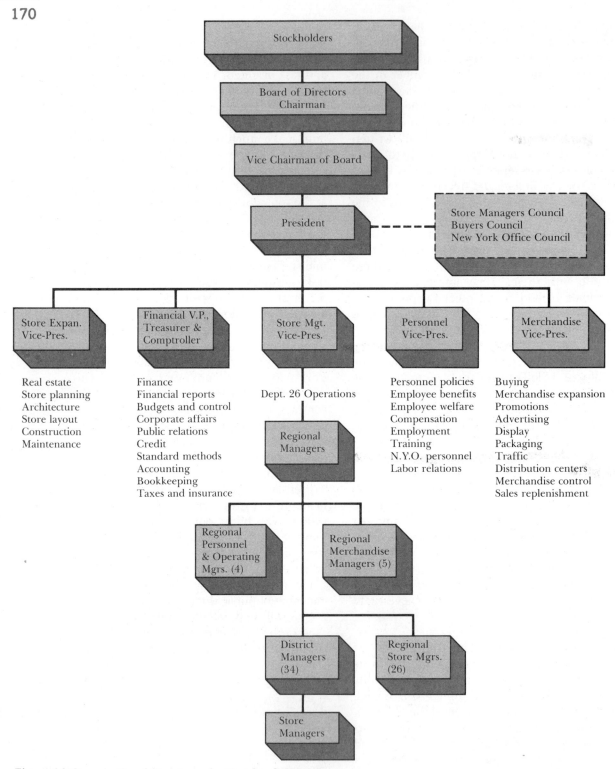

Figure 6.2 Organizational Structure of a Merchandising Company

the work is important to the community's well-being. "The guys want to knock off at two o'clock," the superintendent reports. "If I make them work longer, they're just gonna slow down or do a sloppy job." In their effort to get what they feel is due to them, the employees have lost sight of the purpose of their work: the welfare of the community. They are an in-group; they cover for one another in matters of lateness and incompetence, feeling that they all are in this together, and if they cannot trust one another, whom can they trust?

Although employees enjoy such arrangements and guard them jealously, they may be adversely affected by the system in ways that they do not recognize. Alienation, adherence to unproductive ritual, and acceptance of incompetence are some of the results of a less-than-ideal bureaucracy.

Alienation Job specialization may be efficient, but it also can have negative results. One of these is **alienation,** a term used by Karl Marx to describe the sense of loss and disconnectedness that is supposed to be present among workers in capitalistic societies. This comes about because automation and division of labor eliminate the pride and self-expression that workers would normally derive from the products of their labor (Marx, 1964). As we noted in Weber's model, the same holds for the employees of bureaucracies in general. In addition, their jobs may be so specialized that they have no real idea of how their work contributes to the organization's or society's goals. Indeed, for many employees the goals of the bureaucracy they work for (and its products) are quite unimportant; the security of having a job is all they seek. Such a lack of attachment to the work one does is likely to result in slipshod effort, and the low level of worker morale in many modern businesses seems to bear this out.

Ritualism As Merton (1968) noted, bureaucracies may easily produce overconformity to rules—or what he calls **ritualism.** This results from some of the basic properties of bureaucracy itself. For instance, bureaucracies demand strict adherence to rules in order to en-

sure reliability, but the rules may take on a symbolic meaning far beyond their original rational intent. When failure to follow rules exactly is seen as lack of loyalty to the organization, then rules may become absolute, and following them may become a required ritual. Inflexibility and inefficiency often result. For example, the receptionist who insists that certain forms be filled out before a patient can see the doctor, even though the patient is running a high fever, may have lost sight of the relevance of this procedure to the case at hand.

Incompetence In Weber's model of bureaucracy, workers are hired because they are technically competent, and it is the responsibility of supervisors to retrain, fire, or demote those workers who are incompetent. In reality, however, bureaucracies often are havens for the inept. There are a number of reasons for this, two of which occur quite often.

Laurence J. Peter and Raymond Hull (1969) popularized the notion of incompetence with what they called the "Peter Principle." In bureaucracies, they claimed, employees are promoted until they rise to their "level of incompetence." In other words, because bureaucracies reward good work with advancement, employees keep rising up through the pyramid of authority until finally they reach a job for which they are not qualified. In theory, at least, this means that all positions in a bureaucracy will eventually be filled by individuals who are incompetent to perform what is required of them. This scenario rarely unfolds to its logical extreme, but the fact is that many unqualified persons manage to reach high job levels in bureaucracies, where they often try to hide their incompetence by becoming ritualistic devotees of rules and regulations (Blau and Meyer, 1971).

---

alienation A term used to describe the sense of dissociation that results from feelings of powerlessness and depersonalization, which are supposed to be present among workers in capitalistic societies.

ritualism Overconformity to rules produced by bureaucratic action.

PORTFOLIO III
Socialization and Social Control

From early childhood on we are socialized to be members of our society. This process involves the learning of culturally sanctioned rules for proper behavior. Without a set of commonly accepted rules, behavior would be unpredictable, and we would live in social chaos. Social interaction also involves the learning of subtle rituals and the acceptance of formal positive and negative sanctions.

Starting in the family we begin to see our place in society. We perceive a hierarchy of authority and see how we fit into it. In play groups and in the school we see other types of relationships between friends, between teacher and students, and between adults. At each step we gain greater knowledge of the variety of individual and group interactions. The socialization process continues into adulthood with the workplace becoming a major arena for adult socialization.

All societies and social groups have ways of influencing or molding their members' behavior to conform to group values and norms. Sociologists call these processes mechanisms of social control. Most people become socialized to a range of behavior that is considered acceptable and "normal." Some engage in deviant acts or criminal behavior, defying the norms and mores of society and meeting with negative sanctions. Others step over the boundaries of convention to create works of art, make innovative scientific discoveries, or develop important religious and philosophical ideas.

Family, friends, school, and religion begin the definition of boundaries as early socialization establishes the ground rules for our behavior.

As we grow older our options tend to increase. We can choose to which group we will belong and whose rules we will follow. The overall character of the society in which we live, however, determines what alternatives are available and if there are any rules of order.

Our manner, dress, and values often become defined according to the norms of the workplace.

As adult socialization continues the cycle goes on, some individuals to follow the patterns of order they have learned and some to experience the sanctions for deviation.

At the same time there are more people with college degrees in the current labor market than there are appropriate jobs. The United States Department of Labor has projected that by 1985 there will be 25 percent more people with college degrees in the labor force than will be required. This trend is likely to cause many people to take jobs for which they are educationally overqualified. Interestingly enough, this may cause the opposite of the Peter Principle to come true.

Protectionism Because bureaucracies are concerned about their public images, they often are reluctant to admit to incompetence on the part of their employees. Even when inept employees do considerable damage, supervisors may hesitate to fire them for fear of looking bad themselves or of making their organization look bad to the public. Therefore bureaucracies often will protect incompetent employees in order to protect the bureaucracy from a "black eye." This results in a variety of problems: Many incompetent people are kept on in jobs they cannot handle; some are moved laterally to new jobs equally beyond their skills; and some even are promoted—sometimes with great fanfare—to a job at which they can do less harm (as a figurehead with no authority, for instance).

Bureaucracy and Work in Japan

In recent years it has become common to compare the situation of American and Japanese workers with respect to their positions in the typical work bureaucracy. Our attention has been drawn to the Japanese workplace because of the enormous strides the Japanese have made in the world economy. Currently, the output per hour of work in the United States is about 1 percent higher than it is in Japan and about 10 percent greater than it is in Western Europe (Stoner, 1982). However, our lead in this area has been steadily shrinking, and there has been some concern that we may soon lose out to the Japanese in this area (Capdevielle and Alverez, 1981).

One reason for the Japanese success in the organizational environment stems from apparent differences in the Japanese workplace. Those Japanese working for large corporations operate within the concept of lifetime employment. The Japanese firm will hire a young man with the expectations that he will be employed by the company until his retirement. In effect the Japanese worker is pledging loyalty to the company and in return receives a permanent lifetime job, a far cry from the conflicts between American management and unions and the employment insecurity many American workers face.

In the United States the relationship between employer and employee is seen as a negotiated contract. The Japanese corporation is a miniature welfare state that offers a wide array of benefits and displays a concern for the needs of its workers. This causes the Japanese workers to identify with their employing company rather than with their profession. In contrast, the American workers identify with their profession and feel few qualms about switching from one employer to another in order to achieve personal advancement.

William Ouchi (1981) studied the Japanese organization and devised the "Theory Z" model of management, which many companies have attempted to apply in a modified way to the American workplace. According to Ouchi, Japanese organizations are effective because of (1) lifetime employment; (2) frequent performance reviews, which aid the worker in adjusting to the company's requirements; (3) a very high level of cooperation between management and employees, as well as among the employees themselves; and (4) an interweaving of the workers' social and business lives. In effect the Japanese corporation becomes an integral and continuing part of the workers' lives.

Many people are starting to doubt whether the Japanese system of lifetime employment will continue indefinitely. Should the Japanese economy turn sour for an extended period of time, the current system might be threatened. The Japanese corporation nonetheless offers us an example of how some of the negative aspects of bureaucracy can be avoided.

☐ Formal Organization in the Modern World

Formal organizations helped build modern society, and they dominate its public affairs. Both socialist and capitalist economies (see Chapter 16) are governed by bureaucratic authority systems and formally organized processes of production and distribution. All modern governments are bureaucratized, and for the most part even religious observance is organized by immense formal structures. As we observed earlier, formal organizations are taking over many of the social functions that used to be served by primary groups such as the family. Indeed, modernization and bureaucratization are tightly intertwined developments—each helping to create the conditions that favor the growth of the other. In the midst of these developments stands the individual with a set of needs and goals that may be in conflict with those of the bureaucracy.

Individual versus the Bureaucracy: A Modern Dilemma

Modern society seems caught in a paradoxical dilemma. We need the efficiency of formal organizations and their ability to plan and organize the work of millions of individuals so that people can meet their needs. Personal freedom and fulfillment, however, do not always fit easily into the realities of bureaucratized life. For one thing the nature of bureaucratic structures is such that they tend to result in **oligarchy**—that is, rule by a few individuals who occupy the highest positions in an organization. To the extent that modern society is organized in terms of governmental and private bureaucracies, a danger exists that interlocking networks of oligarchies will run society, subject to little control by the public. Indeed, some scholars believe that this already has come to pass. C. Wright Mills, for example, argued in *The Power Elite* (1956) that in America the oligarchies that rule the nation's corporate, political, and military organizations are strongly interlinked and largely self-perpetuating. Even President Dwight D. Eisenhower, upon retiring from office in 1961, warned of the excessive and unchecked powers of the "military-industrial complex."

Another aspect of the problem of the individual and bureaucracy is how the bureaucratic social environment affects people. In essence, Weber's model tells us that bureaucracy increases in efficiency to the extent that it "depersonalizes" people and their social relationships (Bendix, 1962). Weber himself (1947) was troubled by this issue:

> It is horrible to think that the world could one day be filled with nothing but those little cogs, little men clinging to little jobs and striving towards bigger ones . . . playing an ever-increasing part in the spirit of our present administrative system. . . . This passion for bureaucracy . . . is enough to drive one to despair . . . it is such an evolution we are caught up in, and the great question is therefore not how we can promote and hasten it, but what we can oppose to this machinery in order to keep a portion of mankind free from this parcelling-out of the soul, from this supreme mastery of the bureaucratic way of life.

Robert Michels, a friend of Weber's, also was concerned about the depersonalizing effect of bureaucracy. His views, formulated at the beginning of this century, are still pertinent today.

The Iron Law of Oligarchy

Michels (1911) came to the conclusion that the formal organization of bureaucracies inevitably leads to oligarchy, the condition discussed above, under which organizations that were originally idealistic and democratic eventually come to be dominated by a small self-serving group of people who achieved positions of power and responsibility. This can occur in large organizations because it becomes physically impossible for everyone to get together every time a decision has to be made. Consequently, a small group is given the responsibility of making decisions. Michels believed that the people in this group would become enthralled with their elite positions and more and more inclined to make decisions that protect their power rather than represent the will of the group they are supposed to serve. In effect Michels was saying that bureaucracy and democracy do not mix. Despite any protestations and promises that they would not become like all the rest, those placed in positions of responsibility and power often come to believe that they are indispensable to, and more knowledgeable than, those they serve. As time goes on, they become further removed from the rank and file.

This theory suggests that organizations that wish to avoid oligarchy should take a number of precautionary steps. They should make sure that the rank and file remain active in the organization and that the leaders not be granted absolute control of a centralized administration. As long as there are open lines of communication and shared decision making between the leaders and the rank and file, an oligarchy cannot easily develop.

Clearly, the problems of oligarchy, of the bureaucratic depersonalization described by Weber, and of personal alienation all are interrelated. If individuals are deprived of the power to make decisions that affect their lives in many or even most of the areas that are important to them, withdrawal into narrow ritualism and apathy are likely responses. Such withdrawals seem to constitute a chronic condition in some of the highly centralized socialist countries, especially those of Eastern Europe. However, there are many signs of public apathy in the United States, too. For example, in 1964 about 70 percent of those eligible to vote for president did so. In each of the succeeding national elections this figure has dropped, and in 1980 it was a shade under 53 percent (*Congressional Quarterly,* 1980). Many observers of the contemporary scene have noted a pervasive feeling of helplessness among Americans because of rising costs, high unemployment, and shortages of essential products such as gasoline and heating fuel. Although the government sought to persuade people that the shortages were "real," based on cutbacks in production by the oil-producing nations, a nationwide poll sponsored by *Time* magazine (1979) showed that 63 percent of the people believed that the government was exaggerating the oil and gas shortage. Many believed that the oil "crisis"

was contrived by oil industry leaders. They reasoned that a power structure that can control large, formal organizations can probably also control costs, employment, and production—and might even be able to create a national crisis. If the future is to provide any lessening of such cynicism among the individuals who occupy status in, or depend on, bureaucracies (which includes all of us), then a clear analysis of the shortcomings of the structure must be made.

Bureaucracy and the Future

In addition to the problems with bureaucracies already discussed, there is another difficulty that has implications for the future of bureaucratic organizations—the way that the structure prevents quick decision making. The bureaucratic gap that separates long-range planners of top-level management from short-range decision-making workers is a serious problem. Top-down decision making often becomes less and less workable.

Warren Bennis (1971) expressed this point of view clearly:

> It is my premise that the bureaucratic form of organization is becoming less and less effective; that it is hopelessly out of joint with contemporary realities; that new shapes, patterns, and models are emerging which promise drastic changes in the conduct of . . . managerial practices in general.

Bennis itemized the shortcomings of existing bureaucracies. These include, in somewhat modified form, the following:

1. Bureaucracy, by keeping employees in tightly defined jobs, does not adequately allow for personal growth.
2. It promotes excessive (even ritualistic) conformity and defensive avoidance (groupthink).
3. It does not build into its planned internal functioning the inevitable existence of an informal structure.

oligarchy Rule by a few individuals who occupy the highest positions in an organization.

4. Its systems of control and authority are hopelessly outdated and rigid.
5. Communication is prevented, slowed, or distorted because of hierarchical divisions.
6. Innovative ideas originating from individuals who occupy low-authority positions are ignored.
7. Internal maneuverings for power distract participants in the organization from efficiently pursuing its goals.
8. Because high-level decision makers become entrenched in their positions, they prevent the organization from easily assimilating new technology or individuals with unconventional backgrounds that they do not understand.

The rapid rise of new businesses at the forefront of computer technology seems to support Bennis's views. The most successful appear to be outpacing the older, more established companies by doing away with rigid hierarchical structures. They are also developing new organizational forms featuring interlocking work and planning groups that allow for flexibility in assimilating new information and planning (or changing decisions and rearranging priorities) quickly.

How will bureaucracies change to meet the challenges of the future? Much depends on how the rest of society changes, of course (a topic we shall explore in the final section of this book). However, Bennis (1971) made some interesting predictions about bureaucracies of the future:

> The key word will be "temporary": there will be rapidly changing *temporary systems*. These will be "task forces" organized around problems-to-be-solved. The problems will be solved by groups of relative strangers who represent a set of diverse professional skills. The groups will be arranged on organic rather than mechanical models; they will evolve in response to a problem rather than to programmed role expectations.
> ... *People will be differentiated not vertically, according to rank and role, but flexibly and functionally according to skill and professional training.*

The problem that is far more difficult to solve is the issue of individual freedom in the new organizations. The flexible, creative groupings that Bennis described clearly are for well-educated "professionals." No amount of technological change, however, will alter the fact that in the foreseeable future, minor functionaries performing routine tasks will remain a necessary element in the organization of work. Will these minor functionaries be included in the flexible planning and decision-making groups? Or will the horizontal slash through the organizational pyramid simply have been moved downward a bit, which would allow greater numbers of well-educated managers at the top but cut off and isolate more than ever the minor functionaries on whose shoulders the entire structure ultimately must rest? These are some of the questions that we must face today. Sociologists are still working to find answers. After they come up with some suggested solutions, they will then have to deal with the problem of convincing bureaucrats to try them.

☐ Summary

A social group consists of two or more individuals who interact over a period of time according to some pattern of social organization and who recognize that they constitute a social unit. A social group differs from a statistical category, which consists of people classified together because they share certain characteristics. If people are merely aware of one another, it is not enough to make them a social group.

Sociologists distinguish between primary and secondary groups, in-groups and out-groups, small groups and large groups. All groups must define their boundaries, assign leadership, make decisions, set goals, assign tasks, and control their members' behavior.

A reference group sets and enforces standards of behavior and belief and provides a comparison point against which persons measure themselves and others.

Small groups are social groups such as families, peer groups, and work groups that actually meet together and contain few enough members so that all know one another. The smallest group, called a dyad, contains only two people. Adding a third member to such a group transforms it into a triad. Sociologists study small groups because such groups can have an impact on the course of history, and because they present a microcosm of society and lend themselves to laboratory experiments. One aspect of small groups that is of interest to sociologists is the influence that group members have on one another. The cohesiveness that develops among group members can determine the success of the group as a whole.

In contrast with small groups, associations have clearly defined goals and official ways of doing things. Jobs in associations are broken down into manageable tasks that are assigned to specific individuals.

Associations never operate entirely according to their formal organizational structure. Rather, they contain an informal structure consisting of networks of people who help out one another and take procedural shortcuts.

The most common form of large association in contemporary society is the bureaucracy. A bureaucracy is a social structure that is organized according to rules for actions; all actions are related to the purpose of the organization. Max Weber described an ideal type of bureaucracy in which there would be a clear-cut division of labor, a delegation of power and responsibility based on hierarchy, a written set of rules and regulations, an impartial system of assignment and promotion, a system of advancement based on ability and skills, and a clear distinction between employees' personal and business lives.

Although society needs the efficiency of associations in order to provide goods and services for millions of individuals, the rigidity of bureaucracy often curtails personal freedom and fulfillment. Individuals frequently suffer from alienation, tend to adhere to unproductive ritual in performing their tasks, and often are willing to accept and protect the incompetent. The nature of bureaucratic structures is such that they tend to result in oligarchy—rule by a few individuals who occupy the highest positions in an organization and make decisions without regard for, or communication with, the rank and file. When individuals are deprived of the power to make decisions that affect their lives, they tend to withdraw into ritualism and apathy.

□ For Further Reading

BLAU, PETER, and MARSHALL W. MEYER. *Bureaucracy in Modern Society,* 2d ed. New York: Random House, 1971.   A well-written and comprehensive analysis of the structure, functions, dynamics, and social implications of bureaucracies by two of the field's foremost experts.

DRUCKER, PETER F. *Management.* New York: Harper & Row, 1974.   A landmark study of management within modern bureaucratic institutions. The book looks at management as a social function, examining its tasks, requirements, and functions.

FROMM, ERICH. *The Revolution of Hope.* New York: Harper & Row, 1968.   An argument that we must humanize our technology and bureaucratic structures or run the risk of becoming dehumanized.

HARE, A. PAUL. *Handbook of Small Group Research.* New York: Free Press, 1976.   A major resource book for theories and research on small groups.

JANIS, IRVING L. *Victims of Groupthink.* Boston: Houghton Mifflin, 1973.   An examination of the group processes among decision makers that led to several American foreign policy disasters.

KANTER, ROSABETH MOSS. *Men and Women of the Corporation.* New York: Basic Books, 1977.   An examination of how the corporation's structure affects the behavior of employees. A variety of issues, including gender and working styles, are explored.

KANTER, ROSABETH MOSS, and BARRY A. STEIN, eds. *Life in Organizations.* New York: Basic Books, 1979.   A group of articles about experiences in work organizations.

NAISBITT, JOHN. *Megatrends*. New York: Warner Books, 1984. This book predicts that the coming decade will be a period of great changes and transitions in which the United States will shift from industrial production to providing services and information.

NIXON, HOWARD L., II. *The Small Group*. Englewood Cliffs, N.J.: Prentice-Hall, 1979. A thorough overview of small-group behavior.

OLMSTEAD, MICHAEL S., and A. PAUL HARE. *The Small Group*. 2d ed. New York: Random House, 1978. An examination of interpersonal behavior in small groups.

PERROW, CHARLES. *Complex Organizations: A Critical Essay*. 2d ed. Glenview, Ill.: Scott, Foresman, 1979. A very useful introduction to the study of formal organizations.

WEBER, MAX. *From Max Weber: Essays in Sociology*. Edited and translated by H. H. Gerth and C. Wright Mills. New York: Oxford University Press, 1967. A collection of essays that includes Weber's ideas on power, authority, and leadership within organizations, as well as his classic essay on bureaucracy as an ideal type of social system. Originally published in 1946, the book contains an excellent introduction by the editors that helps make Weber's thoughts more accessible.

WHYTE, WILLIAM. *The Organization Man*. New York: Doubleday, 1956. A modern classic, this book describes the ways in which formal, complex organizations influence the individual and contains observations on their effects on American suburban culture.

7

Communities

If you were asked to define the word **community,** you would probably respond, "That's the place in which a person lives." If you thought about it for a while, however, you would probably come up with a number of other ways in which the term is used. For example, politicians talk about going on fact-finding trips "out into the community." College professors argue about the responsibilities of the "academic community." Environmentalists talk about the "world community."

Even sociologists have difficulty agreeing on a single definition for the word. They may use it to refer to various groups such as prisoners, members of religious organizations, ethnic minority groups, and members of the same profession. They may also use it to refer to a moral or spiritual phenomenon (as in a "search for community," for instance). Or they may even use it to refer to villages, towns, cities, or large metropolitan areas.

Sociologist George Hillery (1955) reviewed the literature and found 94 definitions that had been used by sociologists to describe *community*. Finding a common theme that ran through all of the definitions he encountered, Hillery finally defined *community* as consisting of "persons in social interaction within a geographical area and having one or more additional ties." This definition includes a territorial aspect (geographical area), a sociological aspect (social interaction), and a psychological aspect (common ties). In other words a community consists of people who live close to one another, who interact with one another frequently, and who feel that they have some common traits or values that they share with one another.

Studies of communities and community development have played an important part in helping shape sociological theory. We study communities because they serve as a microcosm of society. By studying a wide variety of communities, we can better understand a complex society. Aspects of social organization that may be difficult to observe and study in the larger society become more easily understood when we focus our attention on a specific community.

☐ Community Functions

Any community must provide some system for supplying its members with those things that are necessary for daily living. Roland Warren (1972) has suggested five such functions:

1. *A system of production, distribution, and consumption.* A community must provide food, clothing, housing, and other goods and services that are needed for basic existence, either by producing them or by importing them from outside.

2. *A system of socialization.* A community must provide mechanisms for transmitting the prevailing knowledge, social values, and dominant behavior patterns to its members. In many American communities the school system is very important in fulfilling this function, as is the family during the early years of a person's life. Sunday schools, 4-H clubs, scout troops, and other community groups oriented toward children also may contribute to this process.

3. *A system of social control.* This requires mechanisms through which conformity to the prevailing group norms are ensured. Formal organizations such as the police, the courts, and the church are important here, as well as less formal groups such as the family and peer groups.

4. *A system of social participation.* Often religious organizations or civic associations perform this function by providing a means for members of the community to interact with one another and to renew their commitments to community values and norms.

5. *A system of mutual support.* When someone is in need because of illness or when a family is in distress because of economic problems, the community must provide ways to help these people. Assistance often comes from relatives, neighborhood groups, social agencies, or religious groups.

Rare, however, is the community that has complete control over, and responsibility for, these functions. Typically they may be performed in conjunction with groups and institutions that are not a part of the community.

For example, although socialization and education may take place in a local neighborhood school, the school system may be organized outside the community structure. The physical boundaries of a school system sometimes go beyond those of a single community, encompassing several communities and outlying areas. In addition, the laws and officials governing a school system often are separate from those of a community.

In order to understand the importance of the functions discussed above to the survival of any community and its members, we shall examine a variety of approaches to the study of communities. In this way we shall illustrate what a community actually is and what it does.

□ Approaches to the Study of Communities

There are several ways of approaching the study of communities. Each approach emphasizes a particular aspect of community life.

The Community as a Territorial Unit

When someone asks you what community you are part of, you will probably answer by referring to a town or a neighborhood: Evanston, the West Side, and so on. We have come to think of the community as the physical place in which peole live. That place has both personal and shared meanings for the inhabitants. This sense of sharing a common area that may have a specific name and a unique identity is the territorial aspect of the community. Guests at a hotel may live together under the same roof for a night, but their identification with the hotel as a place and with one another as guests will remain minimal.

Many communities are located in certain areas because characteristics of that environment have attracted people. For example, natural resources such as coal or timber may lead to the development of a community by people who are looking for a source of income. Think of the communities that sprang up almost overnight in California and Alaska during the gold rush era. Mass transportation and major highways may also affect the location of a community, in that people want to get quickly and easily from their place of residence to jobs and shops. The growth of towns and cities that marked the spread of industrial American society westward followed the major arteries of transportation—rivers and railroads. Thus, although territory in itself may be only one of many factors affecting the formation of a community, it is an important starting point in any analysis of the community.

The Community as a Social Group

Another way to look at a community is to note that it consists of people who are more than an aggregate of isolated individuals and who often interact with one another, have a shared culture, and find their contact with each other to be meaningful (see Chapter 6). Sociologist E. T. Hiller was the first to suggest that the community is one of many social groups. According to Hiller, social groups have several basic properties, including a body of members, one or more tests of membership, a collection of assigned roles, and a set of norms. Because these all seem to be important parts of community structure, it is appropriate in certain instances to look upon the community as a social group.

There are many kinds of communities that meet Hiller's definition of a social group. One example would be the Hutterites, a religious sect living in about 170 small, self-sufficient farming communities in the United States and Canada. Like the Amish, the Hutterites originated in the Protestant Reformation of the sixteenth century. None of their communities, which they call colonies, has survived in Europe, however (Hostetler and Huntington, 1967).

Hutterite colonies consist of a well-defined body of members set off from the surrounding population by their language (a dialect of German), their distinctive dress, and their avoidance of contact with outsiders. Tests

community Consists of people who live close to one another, who interact with one another frequently, and who feel they have some common traits or values they share with one another.

Life in a Hutterite community is fully communal. The members are set off from the surrounding population by language, distinctive dress, and avoidance of contact with outsiders.

of membership include 10 years of intensive education to the Hutterite view of things, including the inherent evil of human nature. Only after this period of indoctrination is the individual baptized as a full member of the community and as a participant in its religion. Hutterites pray both morning and evening to God, whom they worship as the absolute source of all moral authority.

Life in Hutterite colonies is fully communal and highly regulated according to a collection of assigned roles. "By divine order male is over female, husband over wife, older over younger, and parent over child. Women have neither vote nor passive participation in . . . formal decision making" (Hostetler and Huntington, 1967). Finally, the life of the community is governed according to a well-defined and clearly spelled-out set of norms that stresses the subordination of the individual to the life of the group, the inherent value of manual labor, the need to discipline children constantly, and unquestioning submission to the community's brand of Christianity.

Although many communities like the Hutterite colonies fit Hiller's definition of a social group, many do not. Some do not have such clear-cut tests of membership; others lack such an explicit collection of roles. For some, like many urban neighborhoods, even the body of members is difficult to identify. Thus, many sociologists have found it more useful to view the community as a social system rather than as a social group.

The Community as a Social System

In the previous chapter we described several kinds of social groups—primary and secondary, small and large. Most groups are concerned with just a small slice of the whole of their members' lives. The groups themselves are specialized, and their goals are quite narrowly defined. For example, the school, college, or university pertains mainly to the education of individuals and to their preparation for some particular vocation or profession. In the course of a day, members of political parties, bridge clubs, schools, labor unions, and corporations move from one kind of group to another, doing one thing here and another there. Primary groups, like peer groups, mold their members' behavior in many social domains (such as religious beliefs, political practice, career choice, and even the choice of marriage partners). They often do not, however, provide the total social context within which all these activites are pursued. In other words, they usually are not social systems.

The social-systems view looks at the community as a relatively enclosed system of interaction centered on some locality. A collection of small subsystems performs various community functions such as socialization, social control, and mutual support. This approach sees the community as a network of interactions among individuals, groups, and institutions. The community provides a context within which its members can pursue many, if not most, of the activities that occupy them in their daily lives.

The study of a community of Swiss peasants by one of the authors of this text was undertaken from this point of view (Hunter, 1975). Strung out along an alpine ridge was a series of hamlets and isolated farmsteads that comprised a community. It was not set off by a name, nor was it a political entity. In fact, it overlapped the outlying areas of three different townships. The daily life of its members, however, was highly patterned in terms of a social system, especially in the social spheres of emergency mutual aid, reciprocal work arrangements (in which the labor force necessary to complete a task such as threshing typically would exceed the size of each individual family), participation in funerals, patronage of local entrepreneurs such as hog butchers and the baker, formation of local fundamentalist religious sects that met in people's homes rather than in the town churches, organization of formal institutions such as a three-room school, illegal activities such as poaching and moonshining, and last but far from least, the drinking activities of the men of the community who congregated nightly at their reserved table in the back room of the local tavern.

Communities, then, may also be viewed as social arenas in which people cooperate with one another while pursuing—more or less—their social, economic, and political lives.

The Community as a Network of Interaction

As a social system the community encompasses a broad range of interrelated institutions such as families, schools, churches, and polit-

People who live in the same neighborhood may develop a group spirit. Events such as this summer festival help to generate positive feelings among the community members.

ical organizations. Therefore a community offers an ideal setting in which to observe patterns of human interaction in a wide variety of institutional settings. Indeed, these patterns of interaction make up the unique texture of life in each community (Sutton and Kolaja, 1960).

People gain a sense of security when they identify with their community. This identification consists of common values, norms, and goals. George C. Homans uses the term *sentiments* to refer to the positive feelings that develop among community members. Sentiment refers to "an awareness of sharing a way of life that develops among community members as they interact in performing their various activities" (Homans, 1950).

People who live in the same apartment building for many years may not develop a group spirit, whereas entire neighborhoods often do. Residents may have block parties and neighborhood cleanup campaigns. They may donate time and materials to build a vest-pocket park in a tiny vacant lot or rally together to oppose the construction of a highway that will level homes in the area. In many

CASE STUDY
Trauma at Buffalo Creek

The disastrous Buffalo Creek, West Virginia, flood occurred on February 26, 1972. The sudden collapse of a massive dam owned by the Pittston Company (the local coal company and absentee landlord) unleashed 132 million gallons of water and coal waste materials on the unsuspecting people who lived in the hollow along Buffalo Creek. The rampaging water and sludge traveled down the creek in waves between 20 and 30 feet high and at speeds sometimes approaching 30 miles per hour. Buffalo Creek's 16 small towns were devastated by the deluge, over 125 people were killed, and over 4,000 survivors were left homeless. The resulting breakdown of community spirit affected all its members.

This is what Buffalo Creek looked like following the flood that destroyed sixteen small towns. The traumatic effects on the survivors were still evident one and a half years after the flood.

Community on Buffalo Creek can be described as a state of mind that was shared by the people who lived in the hollow; it does not have a name or a cluster of distinguishing attributes. It was a set of unspoken understandings that seemed to be part of the local atmosphere and thus part of the natural order. The key to that network of understandings was a constant readiness to look after one's neighbors and to know without being asked what needed to be done.

The difficulty was that the people who lived along Buffalo Creek invested so much of themselves in that kind of social arrangement that they became absorbed by it, almost captive to it: the community as a whole became an extension of each resident's personality and physical self. This pattern meant not only that each person felt a loss of self after the catastrophe stripped away the greater physical body, their community, but also that these people were no longer able to reclaim as their own the emotional resources each had invested in it. Being neighborly was not a quality the people of Buffalo Creek could carry with them like negotiable emotional currency: the old community was their niche in the classical ecological sense, and their ability to relate to that niche meaningfully was not a skill easily transferred to another setting. This situation was true for those who moved to another community as well as for those who stayed to see a new set of neighbors move in around them.

Science may have gained something when the once-fashionable analogy of comparing human communities to living organisms was abandoned, but it may have lost something too—for a community of the kind being discussed here bears at least a figurative resemblance to an organism. In places like Buffalo Creek the community in general can be described as the locus for activities that are normally regarded as the exclusive property of individuals. It is the community that cushions pain, the community that provides a context for intimacy, the community that represents morality and serves as the repository for old traditions.

Some 615 survivors of the Buffalo Creek flood were examined by psychiatrists one and one-half years after the event, and 570 of them, a grim 93 percent, were found to be suffering from an identifiable emotional disturbance. The nearest expressions in everyday English would be something like confusion, despair, and hopelessness.

Most of the survivors responded to the disaster with a deep sense of loss and a nameless feeling that something had gone grotesquely awry in the order of things, that their minds and spirits had been bruised beyond repair, that they would never again be able to find coherence, and that the world as they knew it had come to an end.

Most of the traumatic symptoms experienced by the Buffalo Creek survivors were a reaction to the loss of community as well as a reaction to the disaster itself; the fear, apathy, and demoralization experienced by the people who lived along the entire length of the hollow were derived as much from the shock of being ripped out of a meaningful community setting as from the shock of meeting that cruel black water. The line between the effects of the two phenomena is difficult to draw. But it seems clear that much of the agony still being felt on Buffalo

Creek is there because the hollow is still too quiet, still showing signs of devastation, with little in the way of nourishing community life.

And the cruel fact is that many survivors, when left on their own, proved to have few inner resources—not because they lacked the heart or the competence certainly, but because they had always used their abilities in the service of the larger society and did not know how to recall them for their own purposes. A good part of their personal strength turned out to be the reflected strength of the collectivity—on loan, as it were, from the communal store—and they discovered to their great discomfort that they had difficulty making decisions, in getting along with others, and in maintaining themselves as separate persons in the absence of a supportive surround.

One result of these problems is that what remains of the community seems to have lost its most significant quality—the power it generated in the people to care for one another in times of need, to console one another in times of distress, to protect one another in times of danger. Looking back, it seems that the general community was stronger than the sum of its parts. When the people of the hollow were sheltered together in the embrace of a secure community, they were capable of extraordinary acts of generosity; when they tried to relate to one another as individuals, as separate entities, they found that they could no longer mobilize whatever resources are required for caring and nurturing.

Behind this inability to care, a wholly new emotional tone can be felt among the people along the creek—a deep distrust even of old neighbors, a fear, in fact, of the very people on whom they once staked their lives. A disaster like the one that came roaring down Buffalo Creek makes everything and everyone in the world seem unreliable, even fellow survivors, and that is a very fragile base on which to build a new community.

Source: Adapted and excerpted from Kai T. Erikson, "Trauma at Buffalo Creek," *Society* (September–October, 1976), pp. 58–64. □

---

so-called ethnic neighborhoods where group spirit is high, residents monitor and mold public behavior simply by sitting at their windows, shouting gossip back and forth, and watching life go by on the streets below (Jacobs, 1961). This group spirit often is a critical element for community members' sense of well-being, and if it breaks down, severe problems may result (see Case Study: "Trauma at Buffalo Creek").

As a focus of interaction, communities—especially small ones with few social institutions and a generally homogeneous culture—have been used by sociologists as natural laboratories in which to test social theories and methods of research. For example, when community conflict emerges, the patterning of splits in the community along social-class lines may be studied.

□ Communities as Units of Observation

Social anthropologists as well as sociologists are interested in the nature and function of the community. In general we can say that social anthropologists and rural sociologists have concentrated on the study of small communities with clearly delineated territories and relatively simple social structures. Urban sociologists usually have directed their attention to problems of specific areas undergoing complex social changes. In either case communities are excellent social units for study.

Folk Societies

The **folk society**—a group of homogeneous, isolated, nonliterate people living in a small community with a high degree of group solidarity (Redfield, 1947)—offers an ideal unit of observation for the student of society. Around the world there remain to this day many isolated settlements, hamlets, villages, and small towns of less than three thousand residents. In such a setting a single researcher or a small research team using the methods of participant observation (see Chapter 2) can get to know almost all the inhabitants and discover much of what is important in their social lives. In addition, such folk societies are ideal for the study of social change because

folk society A group of homogeneous, isolated, nonliterate people living in a small community with a high degree of group solidarity.

individuals, households, and institutions can be traced and monitored over time.

The systematic study of an entire community, however, requires so much observation, record keeping, and analysis that the subjective element of research tends to be a greater problem than in narrower studies. In the late 1920s Robert Redfield (1897–1958), an anthropologist closely associated with Robert Park and other sociologists of the Chicago school, studied a village in Mexico and published what has since become a classic community study entitled *Tepotzlán—A Mexican Village* (1930). To Redfield, Tepotzlán was a relatively well integrated, homogenous village. Social life proceeded smoothly there, and the people, although far from affluent, were quite content. In Redfield's account, the daily forms of cooperation that united the community loomed large.

Seventeen years later Oscar Lewis, another researcher, arrived in Tepotzlán. He went to the village, precisely because Redfield had already studied it, to see the effects of almost two decades of change. Lewis soon found himself not only documenting change but also questioning and criticizing Redfield's original work. In *Life in a Mexican Village: Tepotzlán Restudied* (1951), Lewis tells us that his own studies revealed "the underlying individualism of Tepotzlán institutions and character, the lack of cooperation, the tensions between villages . . . the schisms within the village, and the pervading quality of fear, envy and distrust in interpersonal relations." A far cry from Redfield's view!

Redfield agreed with Lewis's many criticisms of his earlier study. In *The Little Community* (1960), a work that many believe is the best discussion of the nature of communities, Redfield observed that any description of a community must always be incomplete and that the picture it presents inevitably will be determined both by the objective conditions being studied and the researcher's own interests and values. "There are hidden questions behind the two books that have been written about Tepotzlán," Redfield noted. "The hidden question behind my book is, 'What do these people enjoy?' The hidden question behind Lewis's book is, 'What do these people suffer from?' " (1960).

As a unit of observation, then, the community has a great deal to offer. But it also presents certain challenges. One of these is that investigators must be sure to make clear their purposes and any biases that may be hidden within the research (see Chapter 2).

Because anthropologists often study preliterate, relatively simple societies with much less social and cultural heterogeneity than our own, they sometimes claim that the characteristics of one community serve as a valid sample of the life of an entire society. If this held true for all societies, then the job of sociologists would be much easier. Sociologists have found, however, that the study of a community permits insights only into the nature of communities—not into the nature of an entire society. Sociologists are likely to study communities because they wish to find regularities in community functioning—activities, institutions, and problem-solving mechanisms that exist among many different types of communities—in order to discover whether there are similar patterns that indicate how communities in general operate. Such studies have led to an awareness that certain patterns recur as rural communities become urbanized. This has led to an interest in identifying the qualities of community life that characterize different points on the rural-urban continuum.

The Rural-Urban Continuum

Ever since sociologists began writing about communities, they have been concerned with differences between rural and urban societies and with changes from small homogeneous settlements to modern-day urban centers. These changes have been accompanied by a shift in the way people interact and cooperate with one another.

***From* Gemeinschaft *to* Gesellschaft**   In 1887 Ferdinand Tönnies (1865–1936), a German sociologist, published *Gemeinschaft und Gesselschaft*. In this work he examined the changes in social relations attributable to the transition from rural society (organized around small communities) to urban society (organized around large impersonal structures).

In a **Gemeinschaft** ("community"), Tönnies noted, relationships are intimate, cooperative, and personal. The exchange of goods is based on reciprocity and barter, and people look out for the well-being of the group as a whole. In a **Gesellschaft** ("society"), relationships are impersonal and independent—people look out for their own interests, goods are bought and sold, and formal contracts govern economic exchanges. Modern urban society is, in Tönnies's terms, typically a *Gesellschaft,* whereas rural areas retain the more intimate qualities of *Gemeinschaft.*

For example, among the Amish there is such a strong community spirit that should a barn burn down, members of the community will quickly come together to rebuild it. In just a matter of days a new barn will be standing—the work of community members who feel a strong tie and responsibility to another community member who has encountered some misfortune.

In a *Gesellschaft* everyone is seen as an individual who may be in competition with others who happen to share a living space. Tönnies saw *Gesellschaft* as the end product of mid-nineteenth-century social changes that grew out of industrialization in which people no longer automatically want to help one another or to share freely what they have. There is little sense of identification with others in a *Gesellschaft,* in which each individual strives for advantages and regards the accumulation of goods and possessions as more important than the qualities of personal ties.

In small, rural communities and preliterate societies the family provided the context in which people lived, worked, were socialized, were cared for when ill or infirm, and practiced their religion. In contrast, modern urban society has produced many secondary groups in which these needs are met. It also offers far more options and choices than did the society of Tönnies's *Gemeinschaft:* educational options, career options, lifestyle options, choice of marriage partner, choice of whether or not to have children, and choice of where to live. In this sense the person living in today's urban *Gesellschaft* is freer.

Tönnies wrote about what we described in Chapter 6 as an "ideal type," in that no community or city actually could conform to the definitions he presented. However, his descriptions give us a way of beginning our analysis of what certain theorists have postulated as the differences between urban and rural life.

From Mechanical to Organic Solidarity In 1893, barely six years after Tönnies's study, Emile Durkheim (see Chapter 1) published *The Division of Labor in Society,* in which he investigated the reasons for social solidarity. According to Durkheim **social solidarity** emerges from individual commitment and conformity to society and its institutions, which are produced by a **collective conscience**—a society's fundamental values and beliefs. These beliefs also define for its members the characteristics of the "good society," which is one that meets its members' needs—for individuality, for wealth, for superiority over others, for any of a host of other values that could become important to a society's members. Individuals will then fulfill their roles according to the expectations generated by their society's collective conscience.

When a society's collective conscience is pronounced and there is a great commitment to that collective conscience, we have what is known as a **mechanically integrated society.** In this type of society, members have common goals and values and a deep and personal involvement with the community. They

Gemeinschaft A term characterizing rural society, organized around small communities, in which relationships are intimate, cooperative, and personal; the exchange of goods is based on reciprocity and barter; and people look out for the well-being of the group as a whole.

Gesellschaft A term characterizing urban society, organized around large structures, in which relationships are impersonal and independent; goods are bought and sold, and formal contracts govern economic exchanges; and people look out for their own interests.

social solidarity A commitment by individuals to conform to society and its institutions. This commitment is a product of the society's collective conscience.

collective conscience A society's fundamental values and beliefs.

mechanically integrated society A society characterized by a pronounced collective conscience and a strong commitment to that collective conscience. Members of a mechanically integrated society have common goals and values and a deep and personal involvement with the community. They also occupy a limited number of social statuses and engage in similar or even interchangeable roles.

also occupy a limited number of social statuses and therefore engage in similar—or even interchangeable—roles. A modern-day example of such a society is that of the Tasaday, a food-gathering group recently discovered in the Philippines. Theirs is a relatively small, simple society, with little division of labor, no separate social classes, and no permanent leadership or power structure. The Tasaday share more or less equally in their group's activities and goals.

In contrast, in an **organically integrated society,** social solidarity depends on the cooperation of individuals in many different statuses who perform specialized tasks—much like the specialized organs of the human body. The group and the body can survive only if each part fulfills its assigned task: the different elements are interdependent but not interchangeable. With organic integration such as is found in the complex society of the United States, social relationships are more formal and functionally determined than are the close, personal relationships of mechanically integrated groups. The differences between *Gemeinschaft* and *Gesellschaft* as well as between mechanical and organic communities can be identified as we trace the folk-urban continuum.

The Folk-Urban Continuum

Building on the work of Tönnies and Durkheim, Redfield (1934, 1941, 1947) proposed that all communities fall somewhere along a continuum from the most isolated folk communities to the bustling urban communities of modern cities. He defined this continuum in terms of two ideal polar types and suggested that real communities can be arranged into an overlapping sequence that approaches but never actually reaches either pole. One ideal pole is the **folk community,** which (1) is geographically isolated, (2) is culturally simple and socially homogeneous, (3) has its institutions patterned along family and kinship lines, and (4) uses sacred (religious) sanctions to control individuals' behavior. The other ideal pole is the **urban community,** which Redfield never really defined but which he suggested (1) is close to and institutionally interrelated with other communities, (2) is cul-

turally complex and socially heterogeneous, (3) has institutions patterned along formal lines, and (4) uses secular sanctions to control individuals' behavior. Max Weber, in his essay *Die Stadt* (*The City*, 1958a), attempted to define the city, or urban community, in terms of certain recurring features. In his view, an urban community is one in which (1) settlement is dense, with large numbers of people living in tightly packed housing; (2) inhabitants live primarily off trade rather than what they themselves produce; and (3) a relatively independent legal and administrative system is in force (Weber, 1962).

You might think about the place where you grew up and, using Redfield's and Weber's criteria, decide where it "fits" along the folk-urban continuum.

The rural-urban continuum and the folk-urban continuum point to many similar features that mark the transition from simple to complex societies. What factors gave rise to this transition? And what have been its costs and its benefits?

□ The Development of Cities

Cities are so much a part of our experience that it is difficult to imagine a world without them. However, cities are a relatively recent addition to the story of human evolution: the first true cities appeared in the pages of history a scant 5,500 to 6,000 years ago.

The Earliest Cities

Two requirements had to be met in order for cities to emerge. The first was that there had to be a surplus of food and other necessities. Farmers had to be able to produce more food than their immediate families needed to survive. This surplus made it possible for some people to live in places where they could not produce their own food and had to depend on others to supply their needs. These settlements could become relatively large, densely populated, and permanent.

The second requirement was that there had to be some form of social organization that went beyond the family. Even though there might be a surplus of food, there was no guarantee that it would be distributed to

The Temple compound of Nineveh, one of the earliest Sumerian cities on the Tigris River in northern Mesopotamia, housed the priests who ruled the city.

those in need of it. Consequently a form of social organization adapted to these kinds of living environments had to emerge.

The world's first fully developed cities arose in the Middle Eastern area, mostly in what is now Iraq, which was the site of the Sumerian civilization. The land is watered by the giant Tigris and Euphrates rivers, and it yielded an abundant food surplus for the people who farmed there. In addition, this area (called Mesopotamia) lay at the crossroads of the trade networks that already, 6,000 years ago, tied together East and West. Not only material goods but also the knowledge of technological and social innovations traveled along these routes.

Sumerian cities were clustered around temple compounds that were raised high up on brick-sheathed mounds called _ziggurats_. The cities and their surrounding farmlands were believed to belong to the city god, who lived inside the temple and ruled through a class of priests who organized trade caravans and controlled all aspects of the economy. In fact these priests invented the world's first system of writing as well as numerical notation late in the fourth millennium B.C. in order to keep track of their commercial transactions. Because warfare both among cities and against marauders from the deserts was chronic, many of these early cities were walled and fortified,

and they maintained standing armies. In time the generals who were elected to lead these armies were kept permanently in place, and their positions evolved into that of hereditary kingship (Frankfort, 1956).

These early Sumerian cities had populations that ranged between 7,000 and 20,000. However, one Sumerian city, Uruk, extended over 1,100 acres and contained as many as 50,000 people (Gist and Fava, 1974). By today's standards the populations of these early cities seem rather small. They do, however, present a marked contrast with the small nomadic and seminomadic bands of individuals that existed prior to the emergence of these cities.

organically integrated society A society whose social solidarity depends on the cooperation of individuals in many different statuses who perform specialized tasks. With organic integration, social relationships are more formal and functionally determined than are the close personal relationships of mechanically integrated groups.

folk community A type of community characterized by geographic isolation; a simple, homogeneous culture; a structure patterned along family and kinship lines; and the use of religious sanctions to control individuals' behavior.

urban community A type of community characterized by the proximity to and institutional relationship with other communities; a complex, heterogeneous culture; formal institutional patterns; and the use of secular sanctions to control individuals' behavior.

Within the next 1,500 years, cities arose across all of the ancient world. Memphis was built around 3200 B.C. as the capital of Egypt, and between 2500 and 2000 B.C. major cities were built in what is now Pakistan. The two largest, Harappa and Mohenjo-Daro, were the most advanced cities of their day. They were carefully planned in a modern grid pattern with central grain warehouses and elaborate water systems, including wells and underground drainage. The houses of the wealthy were large and multistoried, built of fired brick in neighborhoods that were separated from the humble dried-mud dwellings of the common laborers. Like the Sumerian cities they were supported by a surplus-producing agricultural peasantry and were organized around central temple complexes.

By 2400 B.C. cities were established in Europe, and by 1850 B.C. in China. No fully developed cities were erected in the Americas until some 1,500 years later during the so-called Late Preclassic times (300 B.C. to A.D. 300). In Africa, cities of prosperous traders appeared around A.D. 1000 in Ghana and Zimbabwe (formerly Rhodesia).

Carcassonne, a preindustrial walled city in France, once served as the region's political, commercial, religious, and educational center.

Preindustrial Cities

Gideon Sjoberg (1965) has noted that three things were necessary for the rise of **preindustrial cities**—so named in order to indicate their establishment prior to the Industrial Revolution. First, it was necessary that there be a favorable physical environment. Second, some advanced technology in either agricultural or nonagricultural areas had to have developed in order to provide a means of shaping the physical environment—if only to produce the enormous food surplus necessary to feed city dwellers. Finally, a well-developed system of social structures had to emerge so that the more complex needs of society could be met: an economic system, a system of social control, and a political system were needed.

Preindustrial cities housed only 5 to 10 percent of a country's population. In fact most preindustrial cities had populations of under 10,000. They often were walled for protection and densely packed with residents whose occupations, religion, and social class were clearly evident from symbols of dress, heraldic imagery, and manners. Power typically was shared between the feudal lords and religious leaders.

These cities often served as the seats of political power and as commercial, religious, and educational centers. Their populations were usually stratified into a broad-based pyramid of social classes: A small ruling elite sat at the top; a small middle class of entrepreneurs rested just beneath; and a very large, impoverished class of manual laborers (artisans and peasants) was at the bottom. Religious institutions were strong, well established, and usually tightly interconnected with political institutions, the rule of which they supported and justified in theological terms. Art and education flowered (at least among the upper classes), but these activities were strongly oriented toward expressing or exploring religious ideologies (Sjoberg, 1965).

Industrial Cities

During the European Renaissance a major shift in social values—associated with newly emerging forms of technology, particularly machines—set the stage for industrial cities.

A renewed spirit of inquiry prompted the growth of the sciences (rooted in systematic and empirical investigation of the natural and social environment) and helped people build a more complex society that was based on scientific advances.

Max Weber (see Chapter 1) observed that certain aspects of the Protestant Reformation were particularly instrumental in the expansion of technology. High value was placed on an active life in which work became a moral virtue and a duty. This outlook provided a strong motivation to work and placed a moral value on the material results of a person's labor—changes in thinking that were important in fostering the Industrial Revolution.

We use the term *Industrial Revolution* to refer to the application of scientific methods to production and distribution, wherein machines were used to perform work that had formerly been done by humans or farm animals. Food, clothing, and other necessities could be produced and distributed quickly and efficiently, freeing some people—the social elites—to engage in other activities.

The Industrial Revolution of the nineteenth century forever changed the face of the world. It created new forms of work, new institutions and social classes, and multiplied many times over the speed with which humans could exploit the resources of their environment. In England, where the Industrial Revolution began in about 1750, the introduction of the steam engine was a major stimulus for such changes. This engine required large amounts of coal, which England had, and made it possible for cities to be established in areas other than ports and trade centers through its use for transportation vehicles. Work could take place wherever there were coal deposits; industries grew; and workers streamed in to fill the resulting jobs. Thus, industrial cities arose, cities with populations that were much larger than those of preindustrial times.

Industrial cities are large and expansive, often with no clear physical boundary that separates them from surrounding towns and suburbs. They house a relatively high percentage of the society's population, which works primarily in industrial or service-related jobs. Like the preindustrial cities before them, industrial cities are divided into neighborhoods that reflect differences in social class and ethnicity. (See Table 7.1 for a comparison of the preindustrial and industrial city.)

The industrial cities of today have become centers for banking and manufacturing. Their streets are designed for autos and trucks as well as for pedestrians, and they feature mass transportation systems. They are stratified, but class lines often become blurred. The elite is large and consists of business and financial leaders as well as some professionals and scientists. There is a large middle class consisting of white-collar salaried workers and professionals such as sales personnel, technicians, teachers, and social workers.

Formal political bureaucracies with elected political officeholders at the top govern the industrial city. Religious institutions no longer are tightly intertwined with the political system, and the arts and education are secular with a strong technological orientation. Mass media disseminate news and pattern the consumption of material goods as well as most aesthetic experiences. Subcultures proliferate, and ethnic diversity often is great. As the industrial city grows, it spreads out, creating a phenomenon known as *urbanization*.

☐ Urbanization

The vast majority of the people in the United States live in urban areas. The 1980 census figures, however, reveal an interesting new

preindustrial cities Cities established prior to the Industrial Revolution characterized by a very large impoverished class of manual laborers, a small ruling elite, and a small middle class; strong religious institutions tied to the political system; and a strong commitment to art and education among the upper classes.

industrial cities Cities established during or after the Industrial Revolution, characterized by large populations that work primarily in industrial or service-related jobs, by neighborhoods that reflect differences in social class and ethnicity, a lack of physical boundaries separating the cities from surrounding towns and suburbs, formal political governing bureaucracies, separation of religious and political institutions, secularization of the arts and education, mass media to disseminate information, proliferation of subcultures, and ethnic diversity.

TABLE 7.1   Comparison of the Preindustrial City and the Industrial City

	Preindustrial City	Industrial City
Physical characteristics	A small, walled, fortified, densely populated settlement, containing only a small part of the population in the society	A large, expansive settlement with no clear physical boundaries, containing a large proportion of the population in the society
Transportation	Narrow streets, made for travel by foot or horseback	Wide streets, designed for motorized vehicles
Functions	Seat of political power; commercial, religious, and educational center	Manufacturing and business center of an industrial society
Political structure	Governed by a small, ruling elite, determined by heredity	Governed by a larger elite made up of business and financial leaders and some professionals
Social structure	A rigid class structure	Less rigidly stratified but still containing clear class distinctions
Religious institutions	Strong, well established, tightly connected with political and economic institutions	Weaker, with fewer formal ties to other social institutions
Communication	Primarily oral, with little emphasis on record keeping beyond mercantile data; all records handwritten	Primarily written, with extensive record keeping; use of mechanized print media
Education	Religious and secular education for upper-class males	Secular education for all classes but with differences related to social class

trend: more and more people are moving to small cities and to rural areas in search of open space and "smallness."

We should not confuse urban areas with cities. In fact there are several terms that often are used inappropriately when cities or urban areas are discussed that must be clarified. Thus, when we discuss cities, we are referring to something that has a legal definition. A city is a unit that typically has been incorporated according to the laws of the state within which it is located. Legal and political boundaries may be quite arbitrary, however, and a "city-type," or urban, environment may exist in an area that is not officially known as a city. For example, in New England there are places known as towns—such as Framingham, Massachusetts, with a population of nearly 70,000—that for all practical purposes should be known as cities. Yet they do not adopt the city form of government with a mayor, a city council, and so on because of an attachment to the town council form of government.

Classification of Urban Environments

The legal boundaries of a city seldom encompass all the people and businesses that have an impact on that city. The U.S. Bureau of the Census has realized that for many purposes it is necessary to consider the entire population in and around the city that may be affected by the social and economic aspects of an urban environment. As a result of information collected in the 1980 census, the bureau recognized the need for a new, complex set of terms to describe and classify urban environments; beginning in 1982 the terms applied to urban data are to include urbanized area, urban population, metropolitan statistical area, primary metropolitan statistical area, and consolidated metropolitan statistical area (Federal Committee on Standard Metropolitan Statistical Areas, 1979).

An **urbanized area** contains a central city and the continuously built-up, closely settled surrounding territory that together have a population of 50,000 or more. This term is often confused with **urbanization,** which refers to a process of concentration of population through migration patterns: *urbanized area* refers to a certain place, and *urbanization* refers to a set of events that are taking place.

Urban population refers to the inhabitants of an urbanized area and the inhabitants

In several areas throughout the United States previously separate metropolitan areas form an enormous urban complex known as a megalopolis. The northeast corridor, for example, forms a megalopolis that extends from Washington, D.C., to Boston, with New York City as its hub.

of incorporated or unincorporated areas with a population of 2,500 or more.

A **metropolitan area** is an area that has a large population nucleus, together with the adjacent communities that are economically and socially integrated into that nucleus (U.S. Department of Commerce, 1983). A metropolitan area emerges as an industrial city expands ever outward, incorporating towns and villages into its systems of highways, mass transportation, industry, and government.

A **metropolitan statistical area (MSA)** has either one or more central cities, each with a population of at least 50,000, or a single urbanized area that has at least 50,000 people and that is part of an MSA with a total population of 100,000. Each MSA also contains at least one central county; more than half the population of an MSA resides in these central counties. There also may be outlying counties that are more rural but have close economic and social ties to the central counties, cities, and urbanized areas in the MSA.

An MSA with more than one million people may contain one or more **primary metropolitan statistical areas (PMSAs),** which

urbanized area An area that contains a central city and the continuously built-up and closely settled surrounding territory that together have a population of 50,000 or more.

urbanization A process of concentration of population through migration patterns.

urban population The inhabitants of an urbanized area and the inhabitants of incorporated or unincorporated areas with a population of 2,500 or more.

metropolitan area An area that has a large population nucleus, together with the adjacent communities that are economically and socially integrated into that nucleus.

metropolitan statistical area (MSA) An area that has either one or more central cities, each with a population of at least 50,000, or a single urbanized area that has at least 50,000 people and that is part of an MSA with a total population of 100,000.

primary metropolitan statistical area (PMSA) A large urbanized county or cluster of counties that is part of a metropolitan statistical area with one million people or more.

TABLE 7.2 CMSAs Ranked by 1980 Population and Rate of Population Growth 1980–1990

CMSAs Ranked by 1980 Population		CMSAs Ranked by Rate of Population Growth, 1980–1990	
1. New York-Northern New Jersey-Long Island, NY-NJ-CT*	17,467,300	1. Houston-Galveston-Brazoria, TX	31.8%
2. Los Angeles-Anaheim-Riverside, CA	11,527,000	2. Miami-Fort Lauderdale, FL	19.2
3. Chicago-Gary-Lake County, IL-IN-WI	7,956,400	3. Denver-Boulder, CO	18.6
4. Philadelphia-Wilmington-Trenton, PA-NJ-DE-MD	5,695,200	4. Dallas-Fort Worth, TX	16.6
5. San Francisco-Oakland-San Jose, CA	5,383,400	5. Seattle-Tacoma, WA	14.3
6. Detroit-Ann Arbor, MI	4,763,500	6. Portland-Vancouver, OR-WA	13.9
7. Boston-Lawrence-Salem-Lowell-Brockton, MA-NH*	3,672,100	7. Providence-Pawtucket-Woonsocket, RI*	13.6
8. Houston-Galveston-Brazoria, TX	2,939,400	8. San Francisco-Oakland-San Jose, CA	12.6
9. Dallas-Fort Worth, TX	2,937,900	9. Los Angeles-Anaheim-Riverside, CA	11.8
10. Cleveland-Akron-Lorain, OH	2,840,800	10. Cincinnati-Hamilton, OH-KY-IN	5.9
11. Miami-Fort Lauderdale, FL	2,740,400	11. Kansas City, MO-KS	5.7
12. Pittsburgh-Beaver Valley, PA	2,430,200	12. Chicago-Gary-Lake County, IL-IN-WI	5.6
13. St. Louis-East St. Louis-Alton, MO-IL	2,381,500	13. Detroit-Ann Arbor, MI	5.2
14. Seattle-Tacoma, WA	2,097,400	14. Milwaukee-Racine, WI	4.5
15. Cincinnati-Hamilton, OH-KY-IN	1,664,100	15. Boston-Lawrence-Salem-Lowell-Brockton, MA-NH*	4.5
16. Denver-Boulder, CO	1,621,400	16. Hartford-New Britain-Middletown-Bristol, CT*	4.0
17. Milwaukee-Racine, WI	1,574,400	17. St. Louis-East St. Louis, Alton, MO-IL	3.5
18. Kansas City, MO-KS	1,436,500	18. Philadelphia-Wilmington-Trenton, PA-NJ-DE-MD	3.0
19. Portland-Vancouver, OR-WA	1,300,800	19. New York-Northern New Jersey-Long Island, NY-NJ-CT*	2.6
20. Buffalo-Niagara Falls, NY	1,245,400	20. Cleveland-Akron-Lorain, OH	2.4
21. Hartford-New Britain-Middletown-Bristol, CT*	1,054,200	21. Pittsburgh-Beaver Valley, PA	2.0
22. Providence-Pawtucket-Woonsocket, RI*	867,800	22. Buffalo-Niagara Falls, NY	−0.1

*New England County Metropolitan Areas   *New England County Metropolitan Areas

Source: American Demographics **6**(1) January, 1984.

consist of a large, urbanized county or cluster of counties.

Expanding metropolitan areas draw on surrounding areas for their labor pool and other resources to such an extent that all levels of planning—from the building of airports, sports complexes, and highway and railroad systems to the production of electric power and the zoning of land for industrial use—must increasingly be undertaken with their possible effects on entire regions kept in mind. In America the most dramatic examples of this trend are the Los Angeles metropolitan area, the Dallas–Fort Worth area, and the so-called northeast corridor from Washington, D.C., to Boston, Massachusetts ("Bowash"), which is forming one enormous metropolis—sometimes called a megalopolis—with New York City as its hub. A **megalopolis** is a metropolitan area with a population of one million or more that consists of two or more smaller metropolitan areas. To the federal government these are known as **Consolidated Metropolitan Statistical Areas (CMSAs).**

Despite the much-heralded flow of population to nonmetropolitan areas, more than one-third of all Americans live in the country's 22 megalopolises or CMSAs. New York–Northern New Jersey–Long Island ranks first among the megalopolises/CMSAs in population size, and it will continue to be number one well into the future. However, the Houston–Galveston, Brazoria, Texas, area should experience the most rapid rate of population growth of any CMSA (see Table 7.2 and Focus on Research: "Urban Growth in the Year 2000").

Before a city grows outward to form a metropolitan area or become part of a megalopolis, it has gone through certain internal developments that establish the placement of various types of industrial, commercial, and residential areas.

The Structure of Cities

In the 1920s Robert Park and other members of the Chicago school of sociologists became interested in the internal structure of cities as revealed by what they called the **ecological patterning** (or spatial distribution) of urban groups. In investigating the ways in which cities are patterned by their social and economic systems and by the availability of land, these sociologists proposed a theory based on concentric circles of development.

Concentric Zone Model   The **concentric zone model,** sometimes irreverently called the bull's-eye model, is illustrated in Figure 7.1 (Park, Burgess, and McKenzie, 1925). According to this perspective the typical city has at its center a business district made up of various kinds of office buildings and shops. Radiating out from the business district is a series of adjacent zones: (1) a transitional zone of low-income, crowded but unstable, residential housing with high crime rates, prostitution, gambling, and other vices; (2) a working-class residential zone; (3) a middle-class residential zone; and (4) an upper-class residential zone in what we would now think of as the suburbs. These zones reflect the fact that urban groups are in competition for limited space and that not all space is equally desirable in terms of its location and resources.

The concentric zone model initially was quite influential in that it did reflect the structure of certain cities, especially those like Chicago that rose quite quickly early in the Industrial Revolution before the development

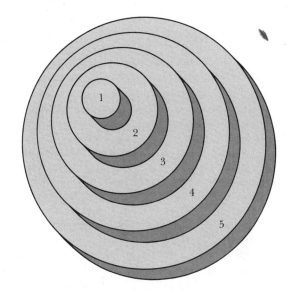

1. Central business district
2. Zone in transition
3. Zone of workingpeople's homes
4. Residential zone
5. Commuter zone

Figure 7.1 Concentric Zone Model

of mass transportation and the automobile introduced the complicating factor of increased mobility. It did not, however, describe many other cities satisfactorily, and other models were needed.

Sector Model   In the 1930s Homer Hoyt (1943) developed a modified version of the concentric zone model that attempted to take

megalopolis Another term for Consolidated Metropolitan Statistical Area. See **CMSA** for definition.

consolidated metropolitan statistical area (CMSA) A metropolitan area with a population of one million or more that consists of two or more smaller metropolitan areas.

ecological patterning A theory proposed by Robert Park and other members of the Chicago school of sociologists to explain the ways in which cities are patterned by their social and economic systems and by the availability of land.

concentric zone model A city model in which the central city is made up of a business district and, radiating from this district, zones of low-income, working-class, middle-class, and upper-class residential units.

FOCUS ON RESEARCH
Urban Growth in the Year 2000

What will metropolitan areas look like in the year 2000? Which cities will grow the most? Which cities will lose the most population? The following discussion attempts to answer some of these questions based on a forecast by the National Planning Association.

One way to make such a forecast would be simply to extend into the future the trends of the 1970s and early 1980s. A forecast of this sort would show only modest growth for the economy, with decreased reliance on manufacturing and increased service and energy-producing activities.

Regionally, such a forecast would indicate that metropolitan areas in the industrial Northeast and Midwest would stagnate. The economic vitality that those cities once had would continue to be drained as population and jobs were lost. The migration pattern of American families in the previous two decades to the rapidly growing cities in the West and South would suggest that the manufacturing centers of the country would no longer lead economic recoveries as they had in the not so distant past.

This forecast, however, would not be entirely accurate. The National Planning Association predicts that the rate of population growth for southern and western metropolitan areas will actually decline. The country's urban population also is expected to decline, as a percentage of the total and manufacturing jobs will still be located predominantly in northern cities in the year 2000.

Why will recent trends in metropolitan areas not continue at the same pace? Metropolitan areas in general have undergone subtle but significant changes in the last decade, reversing trends that have held constant for hundreds of years. Historically, the United States population has become increasingly more urban as people moved from rural areas to find employment in industrial centers.

The growth in the population of urban areas at the expense of population in the surrounding rural areas has long been considered a trademark of advancing societies. However, during the 1970s the percentage of Americans living in metropolitan areas did not grow. Surprisingly, it even declined from 76.0 percent in 1970 to 75.3 percent in 1980. The decline has been more pronounced than these statistics suggest, as rural areas not classified as metropolitan in 1970 were included, because of revised definitions, in the figures in 1980.

The percentage of people living in urban areas is expected to decline in the future. By the year 2000 it is expected to be 74.8 percent. This slowdown in the growth of urban areas relative to the surrounding countryside is new to the United States. The last time that such a slowdown in urban growth occurred was early in the nineteenth century when the country's land area expanded rapidly.

The National Planning Association believes the decline in the urban population is due to employment opportunities. Employment opportunities in all metropolitan areas together are expected to remain stable throughout the end of the century. Approximately 78 percent of all United States jobs will be located in urban areas, though the types of jobs available in the metropolitan areas are changing. By 2000, metropolitan areas are expected to support only 77 percent of all manufacturing jobs.

Manufacturing jobs for the nation as a whole have been growing less rapidly in recent years because of international competition and increased productivity, which reduce the amount of labor required to produce goods. In fact, manufacturing has been supplanted by the service sector as the largest employer of American workers, indicating a major shift in the economy.

Metropolitan trends vary widely according to region. Some metropolitan areas are expected to maintain high growth rates over the next two decades. These are primarily in the West and the South. Houston, Texas, should lead all other metropolitan areas in both new jobs and additional residents over the next 20 years. Indeed, Houston is expected to increase its population by 1.3 million and employment by 1.1 million jobs. By the year 2000, Houston is projected to be the 7th most populous metropolitan area in the country, up from 16th in 1970.

Although many of the cities in the South and West have grown rapidly, constraints to this expansion are appearing. The rate of growth for Houston and other southern and western metropolitan areas should slow, and the same pattern will be seen in most other sunbelt areas.

The cities of the frostbelt can expect some decline in population and employment. The rate and extent of that decline is surprisingly modest, however, and in some cases not a decline at all. Only four metropolitan areas in the entire country are expected to have a net loss of jobs and population over the next 20 years: Elmira, New York; Jersey City, New Jersey; Utica, New York; and New York City.

Although Texas should replace New York State as the second most populous state by the year 2000, the New York metropolitan area will still have the largest population, 9.1 million, and the second largest number of jobs, 4.5 million, of any area in the nation.

One of the most important points in the National Planning Association forecast is that the growth in the South and West will not necessarily come at the expense of the

Northeast and Upper Midwest. These economies appear to be vigorous and capable of supporting their populations and maintain modest growth.

It is true that the greatest growth is likely to occur in the sunbelt areas, but that growth is likely to be new: from new industries and new companies, rather than from massive relocation of firms from the northern cities. In addition, the rate of growth in the sunbelt metropolitan areas is expected to decline over the next 20 years as at least some limits to growth are encountered.

Source: Excerpted from Martin Holdrich, "Prospects for Metropolitan Growth," *American Demographics* **6**(4) (April, 1984), pp. 33–37. □

into account the influence of urban transportation systems. He agreed with the notion that a business center lies at the heart of a city but abandoned the tight geometrical symmetry of the concentric zones. Hoyt suggested that the structure of the city could be better represented by a **sector model,** in which urban groups establish themselves along major transportation arteries (railroad lines, waterways, and highways). Then, as the city becomes more crowded and desirable land is even farther from its heart, each sector remains associated with an identifiable group but extends its boundaries toward the city's edge (see Figure 7.2).

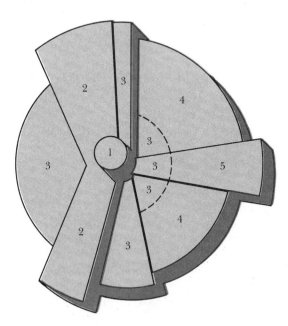

1. Central business district
2. Wholesale, light manufacturing
3. Low-class residential
4. Medium-class residential
5. High-class residential

Figure 7.2 Sector Model

Multiple Nuclei Model   A third ecological model, developed at roughly the same time as the sector model, stresses the impact of land costs, interest-rate schedules, and land-use patterns in determining the structure of cities. This **multiple nuclei model** (Harris and Ullman, 1945) emphasizes the fact that different industries have different land-use and financial requirements, which determine where they establish themselves (see Figure 7.3). Some industries, such as scrap metal yards, need to be near railroad lines. Others, such as plants manufacturing airplanes or automobiles, need a great deal of space. Still others, such as dressmaking factories, can be squeezed into several floors of central business district buildings. Thus similar industries tend to be established near one another, and the immediate neighborhood is strongly shaped by the nature of its typical industry, becoming one of a number of separate nuclei that together constitute the city. In this model, a city's growth is marked by an increase in the number and kinds of nuclei that compose it.

The limitations of the ecological approach to studying urban structure is that it downplays variables that often strongly influence urban residential and land-use patterns.

sector model A modified version of the concentric zone model in which urban groups establish themselves along major transportation arteries around the central business district.

multiple nuclei model An ecological model that emphasizes the fact that different industries have different land-use and financial requirements, which determine where they establish themselves. As similar industries are established close to one another, the immediate neighborhood is strongly shaped by the nature of its typical industry, becoming one of a number of separate nuclei that together constitute the city.

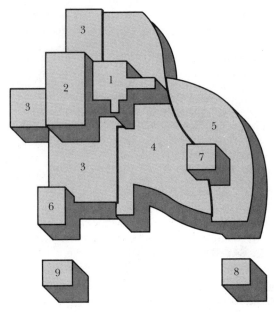

1. Central business district
2. Wholesale, light manufacturing
3. Low-class residential
4. Medium-class residential
5. High-class residential
6. Heavy manufacturing
7. Outlying business district
8. Residential suburb
9. Industrial suburb

Figure 7.3 Multiple Nuclei Model

For instance, the ethnic composition of a city may be a powerful influence on its structure: a city with but one or two resident ethnic groups will look very different from a city with many. Another important variable is the local culture—the history and traditions that attach certain meanings to specific parts of the city. For example, the North End of Boston has become the Italian section of the city. People who normally might leave the city and move to the suburbs have remained in the city neighborhood because of strong ties to the traditions associated with that area. Indeed, cultural factors are important contributors to the continuing trend of urbanization.

Social Interaction in Urban Areas

The anonymity of social relations and the cultural heterogeneity of urban areas give the individual a far greater range of personal choices and opportunities than typically are found in rural communities. People are less likely to inherit their occupations and social positions. Rather, they can pick and choose and even improve their social position through education, career choice, or marriage. Urbanism makes for a complicated and multidimensional society with people involved in many different types of jobs and roles.

Louis Wirth proposed what is now a widely accepted definition of *city* in his classic essay "Urbanism as a Way of Life" (1938). Wirth defined the city as "a relatively large, dense, and permanent settlement of socially heterogeneous individuals." For years urban studies tended to accept Wirth's view of the city as an alienating place where, because of population density, people hurry by one another without personal contact. However, in *The Urban Villagers* (1962) Herbert Gans helped refocus the way sociologists see urban life. Gans showed that urbanities can and do participate in strong and vital community cultures, and a number of subsequent studies have supported this view. For example, researchers in Britain found that people who live in cities actually have a greater number of social relationships than do rural folk (Kasarda and Janowitz, 1974). Other investigators have discovered that the high population density typical of city neighborhoods need not be a deterrent to the formation of friendships; under certain circumstances, city crowding may even enhance the likelihood that such relationships will occur. And Gerald Suttles (1968) showed that in one of the oldest slum areas of Chicago, ethnic communities flourish with their own cultures—with norms and values that are well adapted to the poverty in which these people live.

Of course, increased population size can lead to increased superficiality and impersonality in social relations. People interact with one another because they have practical rather than social goals in mind. For example, adults will patronize neighborhood shops primarily to purchase specific items rather than to chat and share information. As a result, urbanites rarely know a significant number of their neighbors. As Georg Simmel (1955) noted, in rural society people's social relationships are rich because they interact with one another in terms of several role relationships at once (a neighbor may be a fellow farmer, the local baker, and a member of the town council). In urban areas, by contrast, people's relationships tend to be confined to one role set at a time (see Chapter 5).

In urban society the predominance of occupational specialization and job-related interdependency ties together complete strangers into organic (to use Durkheim's term) networks. This was well illustrated by the tugboat workers' strike in New York City during the summer of 1979. It began as a simple labor dispute: the tugboat workers wanted higher wages. Unfortunately for the city, most of the thousands of tons of garbage that are collected by sanitation workers every day are brought to piers, loaded into barges, and hauled out to sea by tugs. The tugboat workers' strike meant that although the garbage could be collected by the city's trucks, there was nothing to do with it—dumps, incinerators, and holding facilities were quickly swamped. Garbage began to pile up on the streets; the mayor declared a health emergency; and the Coast Guard was called in to haul the garbage out to the dumping grounds. However, the Coast Guard balked at the task. Hauling barges is a very difficult job, and even with a direct order to go ahead from then President Carter, the Coast Guard insisted that it would have to make trial runs in order to see how well its sailors could control the enormous barges with their boats (which are smaller and less powerful than the commercial tugs). In the end the strike was settled—but not before the entire city of some seven million inhabitants felt the consequences of the refusal of less than a hundred individuals to continue to perform their jobs.

With increasing numbers of people it also becomes possible for segments or subgroups of the population to establish themselves—each with their own norms, values, and lifestyles—as separate from the rest of the community. Consequently the city becomes culturally heterogeneous and increasingly complex. As people in an urban environment come into contact with so many different types of people, typically they also become more tolerant of diversity than do rural people.

In addition, urban dwellers become dependent on maintaining institutionalized trade relationships with food producers and suppliers of raw materials who live outside the city in what are called the hinterlands. **Hinterlands** are the geographical areas that provide cities with necessary resources. With industrialization, hinterland areas have expanded dramatically to the point that they are gradually growing beyond regional ties and often provide resources to many cities around the world.

Although urban areas may be described as alienating places in which lonely people live in crowded, interdependent, social isolation, there is another side to the coin, one that points to the existence of vital community life in the harshest urban landscapes. Further, urban areas still provide the most fertile soil for the arts in modern society. The close association of large numbers of people, wealth, communications media, and cultural heterogeneity are an ideal context for aesthetic exploration, production, and consumption.

Urban Neighborhoods

People sometimes talk of city neighborhoods as if they were all single, united communities, such as Spanish Harlem or Little Italy in New York City, or Chinatown in San Francisco. These communities do display a strong sense of identity, but to some extent this notion is rooted in a romantic wish for the "good old days" when most people still lived in small towns and villages that were in fact communities and that gave their residents a sense of belonging. Yet, although the sense of community that does develop in urban neighborhoods is not exactly like that in small, closely knit rural communities, it is very much present in many sections throughout a city. Urban dwellers have a mental map of what different parts of their city are like and who lives in them.

Gerald Suttles (1972) found that people living in the city draw arbitrary (in terms of physical location) but socially meaningful boundary lines between local neighborhoods,

---

hinterlands Geographical areas outside cities that offer cities necessary resources, including food and raw materials.

even though these lines do not always reflect ethnic group composition, socioeconomic status, or other demographic variables (see Chapter 20). In Suttle's view, urban neighborhoods attain such symbolic importance in the local culture because they provide a structure according to which city residents organize their expectations and their behavior. For example, in New York City the neighborhood of Harlem (once among the most fashionable places to live) "begins" east of Central Park on the north side of Ninety-sixth Street and is a place that has symbolic significance for all New Yorkers. Whites tend to think of it as a place where they are not welcome and which is inhabited by black and Spanish-speaking people. For many blacks and Hispanics, on the other hand, Harlem represents the "real" New York City and is the place where most of their daily encounters take place.

Even those urban neighborhoods that are well known, that have boundaries clearly drawn by very distinctive landmarks, and that have local and even national meaning are not necessarily homogeneous communities. For ex-

Urban neighborhoods attain symbolic importance in the local culture. Boston's Louisburg Square on Beacon Hill has for many generations been considered the residential area of the upper class.

ample, Boston's Beacon Hill neighborhood is divided into four (or possibly five) subdistricts (Lynch, 1960), and New York's Greenwich Village consists of several communities defined in terms of ethnicity, lifestyle (artists), and subculture (especially homosexual).

On the whole, Jane Jacobs' observations in *The Death and Life of Great American Cities* (1961) generally seem to hold true. She argues that the social control of public behavior and the patterning of social interactions in terms of what might be called community life are to be found on the level of local blocks rather than entire neighborhoods. Once city dwellers venture beyond their own block, they tend to lose their feelings of identification. In fact, one of the typical features of urban life is the degree to which people move through many neighborhoods in their daily comings and goings—rushing here and there without much attention or attachment to their surroundings. Occasionally a city as a whole may have meaning to all or most of its residents

Although urban areas are sometimes described as places that produce alienation, certain urban neighborhoods display a strong sense of identity.

Suburbs are generally thought to be cleaner than cities, less crowded, less noisy, and less crime-ridden. However, many people criticize them for their homogeneity and dependence on the automobile.

and may, for this reason, assume some communitylike qualities. Consider, for example, the community spirit expressed in spontaneous celebrations for homecoming World Series or Super Bowl winners.

Although urban blocks and neighborhoods may offer a rich context for community living, there are some inescapably unpleasant facts about urban America that make many people decide to live elsewhere. Cities and urban areas in general can be crowded, noisy, and polluted; they can be dangerous; and they may have poorer schools than those in the suburbs. Consequently, many families, especially those with children, choose the suburbs as an alternative to urban life. Other city dwellers, such as the elderly living on fixed incomes, may be forced to remain despite their wish to move.

□ Suburban Living

Suburbs consist of those territories that are part of an MSA but outside the central city. According to this definition, 60 million peo-

ple lived in the suburbs in 1960, 74 million in 1970, and 85 million in 1979 (U.S. Department of Commerce, 1979, 1980). In fact, most people now living in metropolitan areas live in suburbs rather than in the central cities (see Popular Sociology: "The Suburbs").

In many respects, at least until recently, suburbs have served as a dramatic contrast to city life. Suburbs generally are cleaner than cities, less crowded, less noisy, and less crime ridden. Often their school systems are newer and better. Many characteristics of urban life, however, have followed people to the suburbs. Like urban neighborhoods, suburban tracts often are quite homogeneous in terms of people's social class. Upper middle-class suburbanites tend to be active in community affairs and to do a lot of socializing. They have less contact with their extended families, (sharing their leisure time instead with friends) than do lower-middle-class suburbanites. The latter focus much more on their homes and

suburbs Those territories that are part of a metropolitan statistical area but outside the central city.

POPULAR SOCIOLOGY
The Suburbs

For generations, farmers mocked the small-scale agriculture beloved by suburban gardeners, and editors of city newspapers derided the lack of suburban cultural facilities. Caught in a sort of cultural cross fire, suburbanites inhabited a no-man's land beyond traditional definition. They still wince when accused of abandoning cities to decay, of living in economically and socially homogeneous settings, and of wasting vast quantities of gasoline in their daily treks between home and workplace. Nevertheless, they are not about to give up their patch of heaven. The following is a review history of suburban development.

More Americans now live in suburbs than in cities and rural areas combined; they love suburban life, if indeed they think about it at all. Today suburbanites accept the sprawling landscape of single-family houses on small lots without questioning its origin. After all, they argue, suburbs have always existed, have they not?

The fact is that suburbs, as we know them, developed relatively recently and largely by accident. In the early nineteenth century, the spread of well-surfaced, reasonably level roads and hundreds of new bridges helped quicken commutes. But it took the steamship to change matters dramatically, at least in the New York City region. Individuals able to pay the fare—and of course, able to buy a farm in the first place—discovered the joys of steaming down the Hudson in the early morning and cruising slowly upstream in early evening. No longer bound by the constraints of owning a horse and carriage, many more people began commuting and enjoying a different lifestyle.

Railroads recast suburban living once again. Unlike the horse and the steamboat, the train ran regardless of the elements, and by the 1860s, railroad commuting had ensnared thousands of upper-class Americans. At first the railroad companies discouraged such short-haul traffic. But gradually, over two decades, Americans came to perceive the wondrous potential of the commuter train. Once the railroad companies understood that convenient, inexpensive trains paid high profits, railroad suburbs sprouted all along routes radiating from the nation's cities.

These new towns became home to thousands of middle-income families who believed that the single-family house on perhaps a quarter-acre of land offered the advantages of both rural and urban living. At the heart of their belief lay half-real, half-fictional memories of the American farm, memories that shaped suburban building and planting.

Even the tiniest house on the smallest lot struck many families as the almost perfect provider of space, sanitation, and security increasingly associated with the farmhouse of the pre-Civil War years. In its design, therefore, the typical suburban house reflected these concerns. Almost always it boasted not only many large closets, but also a large cellar, an attic, a pantry, a back hall—even guest rooms. Part farmhouse, part urban residence, the suburban house was and remains an amalgam of many American values.

The emblem of vast estates, English country homes, and great wealth was the front lawn, and so suburbanites started to yearn for something resembling it. Beginning in the 1880s, suburban families learned an immense amount about lawns, largely through magazine articles. *Scientific American* chronicled the rapid innovation in lawn-mower design; other magazines explained the use of the new machines. By the 1920s almost every suburban family accepted the aesthetic of smoothness, greenness, and shortness; the nation's lawn-mower manufacturers had determined that grass height should be standardized at one and one-half inches, and suburbs everywhere displayed lawns perfect for playing a wide variety of games.

By 1925, 17 million cars roamed American roads and choked city streets. Suburbanites quickly adopted the motorcar as a recreational vehicle; in the evenings and on the weekends they could drive beyond the suburbs into the "real country."

The Great Depression slowed suburban growth of every kind. The subsequent years of war—and particularly gasoline rationing—further stymied suburban development. But throughout the 1930s and 1940s, city dwellers thought about suburbs, dreamed about suburbs, and read about suburbs. And when the GIs came home, they set about moving to the suburbs.

By the mid-1950s, automobile suburbs extended for miles beyond the older railroad suburbs; trolleys had given way to buses; and many single-family houses had been divided into apartments.

Public sentiment was turning against city living. The popular television show "I Love Lucy" shifted its locale from urban apartment to suburban dream house, and the family of "Leave It to Beaver" moved from a small suburban house to a big one on a large lot. Television hammered home the suburban good-life message; each year fewer shows featured urban settings.

Ever-easier financing of homes also changed the suburban landscape. Until the 1920s, house-buying families expected to borrow perhaps 30 to 40 percent of the cost of their property, pay semiannual interest payments based on a rate of 5 or 6 percent, and at the end of three to five years—eight at the most—repay the principal in one lump sum or renegotiate the mortgage. After the 1920s, families borrowed from savings and loan associations and the informal, individual-

The 1950s saw the emergence of the "automobile suburbs." This suburban building boom was also fueled by federally guaranteed mortgages offered to veterans.

lender system began to wither. The massive suburban building boom following World War II resulted from federally guaranteed mortgages offered to veterans. Home-buying ex-GIs needed only the smallest of down payments to acquire their "dream" homes.

Baby-boom children grew up in the open automobile suburbs their parents invented and saw their life depicted in television shows, in magazines, even in grade-school primers. For them such suburbs represented the world, a world of open bicycling and backyard adventure, which was ruled every weekday by women, not men. In a land without public transportation, traveling alone into cities was impossible, indeed unthinkable; everywhere within bicycle range was suburban, and cities meant only the workplaces of fathers. And as continuously increasing traffic slowed the fathers, they looked for jobs in the suburbs. Gradually white-collar employees began deserting the city altogether, and the automobile suburbs entered their present stage.

Today the automobile suburbs no longer appear as they did two decades earlier. A declining birthrate has closed many schools, made large houses unnecessary, and quieted residential streets once thronged with children. Women work outside the home; on weekdays whole streets lie vacant, ripe for burglars, and in the evenings and on weekends there are two automobiles in each driveway. Many commuters no longer fight traffic to and from cities; blue- and white-collar workers now frequently drive to former streetcar suburbs or to adjacent automobile suburbs. Many suburban areas now really are urban areas that have grown horizontally rather than vertically and experience many of the same concerns and problems as large cities do.

Source: Excerpted from John R. Stulgoe, "The Suburbs," *American Heritage* **35**(2) (February-March, 1984), pp. 21–36. □

families and have stronger ties to their extended families—although not so strong as those of rural inhabitants. They socialize much less with friends, are less involved in community affairs, but are the main supporters of churches and service organizations (Gans, 1968). These patterns also hold true for these same groups in the cities.

Suburbs increasingly are suffering from some of the serious problems that used to be thought of as exclusively urban in nature. Perhaps the most dramatic of these is the sharp rise in juvenile alcoholism, drug addiction, and delinquency. At least one reason for this seems to be that suburban areas typically have few resources that address the needs of youth. There is little for teenagers to do, few places for them to go. Consequently they often are bored. Furthermore, as the middle class finds itself suffering more and more from economic strain, suburban populations are less and less willing to spend tax money on social services to address these problems, and even the public buildings and areas of many suburbs are beginning to show signs of "urban" decay.

One characteristic that still separates suburban from city neighborhoods is that sub-

TABLE 7.3   The Declining Population of Large American Cities

City	1950	1980	Population Change since 1950	
			Gain or Loss	Percent
New York	7,891,957	7,015,608	−876,349	−11.1
Chicago	3,620,962	2,969,570	−651,392	−18.0
Philadelphia	2,071,605	1,680,235	−391,370	−18.9
Los Angeles	1,970,358	2,950,010	+979,652	+49.7
Detroit	1,849,568	1,192,222	−657,346	−35.5
Baltimore	949,708	784,554	−165,154	−17.4
Cleveland	914,808	572,532	−342,276	−37.4
St. Louis	856,796	448,640	−408,156	−47.6
Washington, D.C.	802,178	637,651	−164,527	−20.5
Boston	801,444	562,582	−238,862	−29.8
San Francisco	775,357	674,063	−101,294	−13.1
Pittsburgh	676,806	423,962	−252,844	−37.4
Milwaukee	637,392	632,989	−4,403	−0.7
Houston	596,163	1,554,992	+958,829	+160.8
Buffalo	580,132	357,002	−223,130	−38.5

Note: Figures subject to change.

Source: U.S. Department of Commerce, Bureau of the Census and *U.S. News & World Report*, February 16, 1981, p. 59.

urbs tend to be homogeneous with regard to the stage of development of families in their natural life cycle. For example, in the suburbs, retired couples rarely live among young couples who are just starting to have children. Aside from the rather dulling "sameness" of many suburban tracts that results from this, it also creates problems in the planning of public works. For example, a young suburb might well invest money in school buildings, which, some 20 years later, are likely to stand empty when the children have left home.

Gradually the suburban "dream life" is showing signs of strain. Although many wealthy suburbs are still not experiencing these problems, less affluent suburbs—with diminishing resources, obsolete structures resulting from poor planning, and a seeming inability to solve such problems as adolescent boredom and the provision of services for the elderly—appear to be heading for a period of reassessment by those seeking a better life.

☐ The Urban Crisis

If America's suburbs are facing problems, however, its large cities are in crisis. Several years ago New York City teetered at the brink of bankruptcy, and in 1979 the city of Cleveland actually did fall into financial default.

A grim circle of causes and consequences threatens to strangle urban areas. Between 1950 and 1980, 13 of the 15 largest cities in the United States lost population. Only Houston and Los Angeles increased in population (see Table 7.3). Since World War II there has been a migration of both white and black middle-class families out of the cities and into the suburbs. The number of black middle-class families moving to the suburbs increased sharply in the aftermath of the civil rights movement of the 1960s (*New York Times*, 1981). This migration pattern has led to a greater concentration of poor people in the central cities, which is reflected in the loss of revenues that many large cities have experienced. As the more affluent families leave urban areas, so do their tax dollars and the money they spend in local businesses. In fact many businesses have followed the middle-class to the suburbs, taking with them both their tax revenues and the jobs that are crucial to the survival of urban neighborhoods. This has meant a shrinking of the central cities' tax base, while at the same time creating conditions (such as the loss of jobs) that force people to rely on government assistance.

It is not easy to entice suburbanites to move back into cities, even though the U.S. Department of Housing and Urban Development has created several financial incentive programs designed to do so. Because most United States suburbs were created in the last 30 years, their facilities and physical plants (schools and hospitals) are still relatively new, clean, and attractive. So are the shopping centers that continue to mushroom across the country and that offer their suburban patrons local outlets of prestigious "downtown" stores as well as supermarkets, discount warehouses, specialty shops, and even entertainment centers. In the central cities many buildings are old, and apartment dwellers must pay higher rents for accommodations that are inferior to those of their suburban counterparts.

Gans (1977) suggests that if we are to save the central cities, we can do so only by mobilizing resources at the national level and raising central-city residents themselves to middle-class economic status. He believes this is more likely to succeed than trying to convince suburbanites to move back into urban areas. Many people believe, however, that the vicious circle outlined really is a sinking spiral and that some of our cities have already spun downward and out of control. They see no way of resurrecting them and forecast their gradual demise as the population spreads itself out across the country, particularly into the sunbelt of the South and Southwest. But a small countertrend has been started: in the late 1970s many middle-class young adults began to find urban life attractive again. Most of these people were single or were married with no children. This trend has produced an upgrading of previously marginal urban areas and the replacement of some poor residents with middle-class ones, a process known as **gentrification.** Critics contend that gentrification depletes the housing supply for the poor (see Using Sociology: "Gentrification and Homelessness"). Others counter that it improves neighborhoods and increases a city's tax base. So far, however, this trend has been

limited to a handful of cities. If it continues and grows, however, it clearly will have a major impact on the future of urban life and could serve as a convincing argument against doomsday predictions about the city. Sociologists, meanwhile, will have to reconcile themselves to the fact that they did not predict this trend. Real estate speculators did.

☐ Summary

Although sociologists have used many definitions for the word *community,* we have used Hillery's definition, which states that the community consists of persons in social interaction within a geographical area and having one or more additional ties.

Communities must fulfill a number of functions, such as providing (1) a system of production, distribution, and consumption; (2) a system of socialization; (3) a system of social control; (4) a system of social participation; and (5) a system of mutual support.

There are several ways of approaching the study of communities. They can be studied as a territorial unit, as a social group, as a social system, and as a network of interaction. The term *sentiments* is used to refer to the feelings that develop among community members.

Communities serve as useful units of observation for both anthropologists and sociologists. As anthropologists often study relatively isolated, homogeneous communities, they sometimes claim that the characteristics of one community serve as a valid sample of the life of an entire society. Sociologists have found, however, that the study of a community permits insights into the nature of communities—not of a whole society.

The differences between rural and urban communities have been identified by the application of the terms *Gemeinschaft* (community) and *Gesellschaft* (society). In the former, relationships among community members are intimate, cooperative, and personal; in the

gentrification An urban revitalization process that involves the return to marginal urban areas of young, middle-class people, who upgrade the neighborhood and replace some of the poor residents.

USING SOCIOLOGY
Gentrification and Homelessness

In recent years, the downtown sections of many American cities have undergone extensive renovation and revitalization. This "back to the city" or "gentrification" movement has been both hailed as an urban renaissance and condemned for disrupting urban neighborhoods and displacing inner-city residents. The following article discusses how gentrification increases the number of homeless people in urban areas.

As areas of cities become gentrified, rooming house tenants join the homeless population.

As city land becomes more desirable, it has an effect on what is usually considered to be the nation's least desirable housing stock, namely single-room occupancy hotels, rooming houses, and shelters. Although these types of land use have long been seen as the very symbols of urban decay, they serve the vital needs of populations with few resources or alternatives. Gentrification has placed these powerless people in direct competition with relatively powerful and privileged actors for inner-city space. The results may be at least a partial explanation for the growing ranks of the homeless on the streets of many cities.

The movement to the suburbs of post-World War II America emphasized the spatial separation of public and private realms. If "downtown" was the world of public activity, then middle-class people did not live "downtown," but in the private world of the suburb. The suburban ideal of a home is a single-family home, sufficiently large and private to protect the family from scrutiny by the outside community. Downtown, by contrast, is made up of public spaces, where interactions are strictly limited, regulated, and perhaps even ritualized.

If the movement to the suburbs required abandoning the downtown streets at nightfall, there were many people who did not leave the central city. There are, of course, the working-class neighborhoods of the older cities where family life goes on in close proximity to the central business district, under somewhat less private and more crowded conditions than in the suburbs. There are also the marginal people for whom downtown provided alternatives not available elsewhere. Although neighborhoods, urban and suburban, are generally composed of family units, commercial and industrial areas, as well as fringe areas in decaying working-class districts, have tended to provide the single-housing stock vital to poor persons not living in conventional families. Single-room occupancy hotels, rooming houses, and even skid row flophouses all have provided low-cost single accommodations for those who might not be able to come by them elsewhere.

Downtowns in many older cities have also traditionally contained the cities' skid rows and red-light districts, which provided shelter and a degree of tolerance for deviant individuals and activities. Being close to transportation and requiring little initial outlay (often renting by the week), single-room housing has traditionally been utilized by the elderly poor, the seasonally employed, the addicted, and the mentally handicapped.

In recent years, these populations have been supplemented by the growing numbers of deinstitutionalized patients and unemployed young men. These trends, coming at a time when competition for inner-city space has been intensified because of gentrification, have been sharply reflected in shelter populations and on the streets. Men under 21 years old constituted approximately 7 percent of New York City's shelter population in late 1982, whereas there had been virtually none in that age group as late as 1980.

It is therefore important to note recent studies indicating that at least in New York City, the shelter population is becoming younger and blacker, whereas a large minority seems to have had a history of psychiatric problems. Contrary to the traditional image of the shelter population as predominantly aging, white, alcoholic, and almost entirely male, one study showed a female population that was only 40 percent white and predominantly under 40. About 13 percent of these women had come to shelters directly from hospitals. A 1982 survey of homeless men at New York's Keener shelter showed that 33 percent had histories of psychiatric hospitalization.

Clearly, then, the single-room tenant is no longer welcome in the revitalized central city. Certain types of housing stock, which is to say certain types of people, are apparently incompatible with policies of revitalization, particularly policies of partially subsidized "private" sector revitalization. The problem is, then, where should these people go? As former resources have been priced beyond their reach or have simply ceased to exist, many single-room tenants have had to turn to an increasingly reluctant public sector for help. This has served to politicize greatly the simple question of where single-room tenants would be located.

There is a danger in romanticizing rooming houses and shelters. Many of these buildings provided—and still provide—the most squalid conditions of the housing market. Landlords have at times abused tenants with few options, and private shelters have been known to exact penance, prayer, and conversion as the price for the meanest of accommodations. Nevertheless, it is a housing stock that does provide shelter for persons who might otherwise lack shelter. But it is being destroyed and is not being replaced.

Many renovation efforts have been made with sympathy toward the single-room residents. Starting with efforts to bring rooming houses "up to code" in the 1960s, however, these efforts were made without understanding. The only way for many rooming houses to come "up to code," given legal and economic constraints, was for them to cease to exist.

The single-room occupant may be incompatible with gentrification. The deinstitutionalized, the ex-offender, the addicted, the poor, the sick, and the elderly all bring to the central city a "diversity" that the new investors in cultural pluralism want no part of. Yet these people will not go away simply because their housing is eliminated. They remain on our streets and tax the strained resources of the remaining shelters. Unlike the suburb, the newly gentrified inner city cannot close its gates to marginal members of society. It therefore becomes imperative that new alternatives be provided.

Source: Excerpted from Philip Kasinitz, "Gentrification and Homelessness: The Single Room Occupant and the Inner City Revival," *Urban and Social Change Review* **17**(1) (Winter, 1984), pp. 9–14. □

latter, relationships are impersonal and independent. As communities move along the continuum from rural to urban, individuals move toward less personal interaction. The collective conscience of a society determines whether the community will be mechanically or organically integrated.

Preindustrial cities emerged from a favorable physical environment, advanced technology, and a well-developed system of social structures. An economic system, a system of social control, and a political system were necessary. The industrial city was a product of the Industrial Revolution—the application of scientific methods to production and distribution.

The internal structure of cities usually follows a pattern of concentric circles (the concentric zone model), a pattern based on major transportation arteries (the sector model), or a pattern of land-use and financial requirements (the multiple nuclei model).

The U.S. Bureau of the Census has established several categories to define urban areas: the urbanized area, the urban population, the metropolitan statistical area, the primary metropolitan statistical area, and the consolidated metropolitan statistical area. Such categories make possible the study of all the groups and factors that have an impact on an urban population.

The majority of people in the United States live in cities, even though living conditions may be difficult and costs may be high. A migration to the suburbs has been occasioned by the promise of less noise and pollution, a lower crime rate, and better education. In recent years, however, young people who are single or married with no children have been returning to some cities.

Although cities may be viewed as agents of depersonalization and alienation, a spirit of community often exists within blocks or neighborhoods.

☐ For Further Reading

FISCHER, CLAUDE S. *The Urban Experience.* New York: Harcourt Brace Jovanovich, 1976. A well-written introduction to the sociology of the city, including both its urban and subcultural aspects.

JACOBS, JANE. *The Death and Life of Great American Cities.* New York: Random House, 1961. The author criticizes traditional theories of urban planning and tries to explain why urban decay takes place.

NEWMAN, OSCAR. *Community of Interest.* Garden City, N.Y.: Anchor Press/Doubleday, 1980. An interesting book in which the author develops strategies and practical mechanisms for evolving new types of communities and new urban patterns in today's highly mobile society.

REDFIELD, ROBERT. *The Little Community.* Chicago: University of Chicago Press (published in one volume together with *Peasant Society and Culture*), 1960. A short meditation on the "little" community. Redfield looks at it from all possible perspectives: social structure, ecological, holistic, and so forth. This is a classic work—possibly the best single discussion of the nature of community.

ROBERTS, BRYAN. *Cities of Peasants.* Beverly Hills, Calif.: Sage Publications, 1979. An examination of the growth of urban-based industrialism and its impact on the Third World—primarily in Latin America. The book conveys both the flavor of life in the cities of the Third World and the immediacy of their problems.

STEIN, MAURICE R. *The Eclipse of Community.* New York: Harper & Row, 1964. A landmark work in the sociological study of communities. This book brings together materials from several disciplines to cast new light on the nature of the community and its decline in the United States.

SUTTLES, GERALD. *The Social Order of the Slum.* Chicago: University of Chicago Press, 1972. An important study based on the author's experiences living among the blacks, Italians, and Hispanics of Chicago's New West Side slums. The book provides a revealing portrait of the behavior that holds a community together in crisis and conflict.

TOBIN, GARY A. (ed.). *The Changing Structure of the City.* Beverly Hills, Calif.: Sage Publications, 1979. An up-to-date analysis of the urban crisis. Throughout this volume certain themes about the urban crisis recur: poverty; the link among poverty, class, and race; and the need for a mobilization of resources at the national level to combat the decline of the cities.

8

Society

One of sociology's goals is to understand human social behavior. There are two ways in which we can try to do this. First, we can focus on the patterns of interpersonal interactions that characterize our everyday lives—for example, how we as individuals relate to others in face-to-face situations. This is known as the **microsociological** level. Or, second, we can concentrate on the larger aspects of the social structures that affect peoples' lives, such as society, institutions, and communities. This is known as the **macrosociological** level. In this chapter we shall focus on the largest element of all, society.

□ The Nature of Society

Organized and long-lasting societies are rare among most mammals, with the wolf pack, the prairie-dog town, and the baboon troop representing some of the notable exceptions. Society, however, is universal among humans. For this to be so, it must have performed major adaptive functions that have increased the chances of human survival. Society is the social counterpart of those biological adaptive mechanisms that cause one species to survive and another to become extinct. Among certain species of animals, great speed, powerful jaws, or brute strength may be the key adaptive advantage. Among humans, the social organization that results in society has enabled our survival.

Among humans, the members of a particular society are mutually interdependent to an extent unequaled in any nonhuman society. So much so in fact, that often the very survival of each member depends on the behavior of the other members.

Every society is organized in such a way that rules of conduct, customs, and expectations ensure appropriate behavior by its members. The socialization process inculcates these into all members, beginning early in life. Even so, some members may still act in ways threatening to the social fabric of that society. At that point, strong action must be taken to eliminate the threat to the social structure.

The norms, or standards of behavior, are never exactly the same from one society to another. No matter how deviant an act might be in one society, at other times and in other places it may have constituted the norm. Cannibalism, incest, and infanticide all have been normatively proper in one society or another (for an example of how witchcraft serves a normative function among the Ibibio of Nigeria, see Focus on Research: "Witchcraft Among the Ibibio").

Early anthropologists believed that a society's norms determined the behavior of its members. It was believed that people were born into a world in which the society's norms had already been set and that early socialization made these norms an integral part of every member's personality. The way we act often does depend on the norms we have internalized since childhood. Nevertheless, life in a complex society such as ours, often is experienced as negotiable behavior in interaction with other members of the society. That is, in reality we are less likely to be normatively programmed robots who act in a predictable fashion and, instead, act as reasoning individuals who adjust our behaviors to circumstances (Leakey and Lewin, 1977).

Characteristics of Human Societies

The concept of **society** implies a number of characteristics. In a sociological sense, society (1) is a social system, (2) is relatively large, (3) recruits most of its members from within, (4) sustains itself across generations, (5) shares a culture, and (6) occupies a territory.

1. *A society is a social system.* A **social system** is made up of individuals and groups that interact in a relatively stable and patterned manner. A change in one segment of the system will affect all the other parts of the system. For example, in the United States a slowdown in sales in the automobile industry not only threatened the jobs of many thousands of auto workers but also meant great losses for the steel industry, placed enormous burdens on local and state governments where many workers were laid off, threatened the survival of service industries in those areas, and profoundly affected the cost and quality of automobiles for the rest of society.

Much of what sociologists do is to study the ways in which individuals and social groups interact with one another and the ways such interactions affect—and are affected by—both other individual elements of the society and the society as a whole.

2. *A society is relatively large.* A society is the largest and most inclusive social unit that exists. It integrates all the smaller social units of which it is composed—communities and smaller social groups. It follows, then, that a society must be relatively large—"relatively" meaning in comparison with the surrounding population. For example, a small, isolated group like the Stone Age Tasaday of the Philippine rain forest is a complete society, even though it consists of only a few hundred people. At the other extreme, American society is made up of dozens of ethnic groups and millions of people. It is important that a sociologist using the term *society* takes care to indicate whether it is being applied to a community, a nation, or some other social unit.

3. *A society recruits most of its members from within, through reproduction and socialization.* In most instances the members of a society are those who are born into it and who are taught its ways and what is expected of them. The exception to this process is the immigrant, the person who elects to leave one society and join another. Whether a person is born into or joins a society, one requirement holds: Before being accepted as a functioning member of the society, an individual must be socialized into or taught its expectations.

4. *A society sustains itself across generations.* This feature of society is closely related to the fact that societies recruit their members from within (item 3). For a group of people to be a society, they must show an ability to endure and to produce and sustain at least several generations of members. The Ik (pronounced "eek") society in Uganda are on the verge of extinction because they no longer are able to produce and sustain new members. A tribe of nomadic hunters and food-gatherers, they roamed until just before World War II, through parts of what are now Uganda, Kenya, and the Sudan. What was once their major hunting and foraging territory is now a national park, and the Ik have been resettled in seven villages, each containing between 4 and 50 huts. The Ugandan government encourages the Ik to cultivate gardens,

but these often fail because of poor soil and frequent severe droughts. Thus, many old and sick people starve to death, and others barely survive on meager government handouts.

Under these conditions the fabric of Ik social life has been damaged irreparably. Parents no longer bring up their children, but, rather, they expel them from their huts by the age of 3, leaving them to roam, uncared for, in scavenging peer groups. The old and infirm also are ejected and left to die, partly because traditional funeral feasts are beyond people's means, but more importantly because food and medicine are reserved for those who can most benefit from them.

When the climate is good enough for Ik gardens to produce a reasonable yield the people glut themselves and do little to preserve or store their surplus. Storing, they feel, would be a waste of time; they would merely steal from one another as soon as times became hard. Moreover they do not wish to look too prosperous, because then the government would reduce or cut off its aid.

The Ik, according to Colin Turnbull (1972), have lost the most central institution of human society: the family. They have rejected as too costly the binding forces of parent–child love and concern. The constant condition of hunger has destroyed the fiber of their social structure. Deprived of those qualities that we think of as the nobler human characteristics, the Ik continue their wretched existence—an existence in which each person's overriding concern is simply his or her own survival.

---

microsociology The study of the patterns of interpersonal interactions that characterize our everyday lives, such as how individuals relate to one another in face-to-face situations.

macrosociology The study of the larger aspects of the social system whtnin which people conduct their lives. Social structures, such as groups and communities, as well as belief systems, such as communism and religion, are topics of investigation.

society The largest and most inclusive social system that exists. A society recruits most of its members from within, sustains itself across generations, shares a culture, and occupies a territory.

social system Individuals and groups that interact in a relatively stable and patterned manner.

FOCUS ON RESEARCH
Witchcraft among the Ibibio

Different societies have different ways of dealing with social tension and conflict. Totalitarian societies often rely on military or police control to "keep the peace." In democratic societies, elaborate legal systems serve to mediate disputes. Among the Ibibio in Nigeria, a belief in witchcraft serves both as a way of explaining life's misfortunes and as an aid to maintaining the social order.

The period between 1978 and 1979 was not a good one for the Ibibio. There were food shortages, unemployment, and a variety of other social ills. To the Ibibio it seemed clear that evil forces were afoot.

To deal with the problem, Edem Edet Akpan, a young man who claimed to have supernatural powers that enabled him to detect witches, embarked upon a witch-eradication crusade. Edem and his lieutenants traveled about the Ibibio territory identifying witches and vaccinating loyal followers with antiwitchcraft serum to prevent their being bewitched.

Once Edem had detected a witch, the accused's hands and legs were bound, and he was sprinkled with red pepper and black ants and beaten until he confessed. In the process, some people were tortured to death, many seriously injured, and others maimed for life. The crusade was extremely popular. At last, the Ibibio felt, something was being done about their recent bad luck.

Though this scenario may seem strange to those in cultures less mystically inclined, to the Ibibio, blaming unseen spirits for personal or communal misfortune makes perfect sense. In almost any dispute, there is an implied threat by one of the parties to bewitch the other. Thus, to resolve the disagreement, some measure must be taken to see that the threat is not carried out.

The Ibibio have also been experiencing stress because of the rapid social change in Nigeria. Increased urbanization and the development of new types of social relationships have resulted in increased insecurity, anxiety, and tension. These pressures tend to be released in the traditional way, through accusations of witchcraft. There is tension between those who adopt new attitudes and those who still cling tenaciously to traditional practices and ways of life: The returning migrant laborer with some money easily becomes a target of envy.

Belief in witchcraft gives the Ibibio a theory of causation for misfortune, death, and illness. To this extent the belief system represents an attempt to rationalize and comprehend the malevolent forces of nature and the misfortunes of life. Although evils operate only through the medium of human beings, they can also be brought under human control. The parts assigned to the witches presuppose a just world, ordered and coherent, in which evil is not merely outlawed but can also be actively vanquished by human techniques.

A belief in witchcraft also protects many other ideas and beliefs. A farmer blames the failure of his crop on witchcraft and therefore saves himself the embarrassment of admitting that his farming techniques might be antiquated or at fault. If one's illness does not respond to treatment, the next step is to blame it on a witch and thus save oneself from doubting the worth of current medical knowledge and practice.

Belief in witches also serves other useful functions. Suspicion that an elder is a witch makes people fear and respect him, and thieves are less likely to touch his property for fear of retaliatation.

The Ibibios' belief in witchcraft offers them an explanation for what would otherwise be unexplainable and hence potentially disruptive. It also is a means of dealing with misfortunes that otherwise might produce active conflict. Witchcraft affirms group solidarity by defining what is bad, such as all secret and malevolent activities directed against the health, property, and lives of fellow Ibibio. Witchcraft enables the Ibibio to believe that their failure is due not to any fault of their own but to the machinations of others. Thus, despite the generalized anxiety it causes, the operation of witchcraft among the Ibibio serves ingeniously, if not consciously, to maintain the social order.

Source: Adapted from Daniel A. Offiong, "Social Relations and Witch Beliefs Among the Ibibio of Nigeria," *Journal of Anthropological Research* **39**(1) (Spring, 1983), pp. 81–96. □

5. *A society's members share a culture.* Culture, as we explained in Chapter 3, consists largely of systems of symbols, norms, and values shared by members of the society. Sharing a culture gives individuals the vision and sense of purpose to sustain the patterns of interaction that hold together the society. As members of society, each of us acquires a repertory of ways of acting, thinking, and feeling. The French, for example, possess certain standards of achievement and ideas about appropriate behavior for males and females, and

people of various and religious convictions. Although some aspects of French culture may be found in other societies, the entire array of them is exclusively French (for an example of gypsy culture, see Popular Sociology: "Why Gypsies Hate Cats but Love Horses").

More than one culture may be represented in a society, but such subcultures must hold in common certain values and symbols—otherwise the society will splinter apart. The French Canadians in Canada, the Amish in the United States, and the Basques in Spain illustrate the widespread existence of subcultures as well as the mechanisms and problems of integrating them into the greater culture. Most such subcultures keep their own language alive but know and use the language of the larger culture when necessary. They share in the trade and commerce of the larger society and obey its laws. The separatist movements of the Basques and of the French Canadians of Quebec Province and the demonstrations and unrest triggered by these groups, however, are prime examples of what can happen when the people of a subculture

These Vietnamese immigrants are adopting the culture of their new environment of Port Arthur, Texas.

decide they want only their own language, mores, and values—they are no longer content to be part of what they feel is an alien culture. This is a problem that complex societies like our own must struggle with constantly, a theme we shall explore in Chapter 11.

6. *A society occupies a territory.* Many large international organizations sustain themselves across generations and even recruit new members from within. Such organizations include international industrial conglomerates, religious organizations such as the Catholic church, and even secretive clubs, fraternities, and "brotherhoods" such as the Masons or the Elks. However, the term *society*, as we define it here, is restricted to groups whose members mostly live within a specific, clearly defined geographic area. Further, as sociologists use the term, *society* does not refer to task-oriented groups like the Society for the Prevention of Cruelty to Animals. Although such groups use the word *society* in their names, they are associations, not societies. Nor is *society* correctly applied to social classes or subcultural groups, even though we read of "high society" or just "society" in the "society columns" of our nation's newspapers.

The Dissolution of Human Society

There are four conditions that will bring about the dissolution of a society: (1) if its members are killed off; (2) if its members become apathetic, no longer caring whether or not the society continues to exist; (3) if the society falls into a state of chaos from which it cannot free itself; or (4) if the society is absorbed into another society—for example, as a result of conquest (Aberle et al., 1950).

History provides instances of all four of these possibilities. As Americans we must live with the knowledge that our own society thrives amid the shattered ruins of many Native American societies, not a few of which simply were killed off. What happened to the Yana, for example, was not unique; it happened to many similar groups.

In California the Yana were caught in waves of social expansion: first by the Spaniards, then the Mexicans, and finally the Anglo-Americans. The discovery of gold in the

POPULAR SOCIOLOGY
Why Gypsies Hate Cats But Love Horses

People not familiar with the gypsy culture often think that this ethnic group is not interested in cleanliness. In fact, gypsies have a rather elaborate system of taboos regarding hygiene that governs not only their personal cleanliness but also their attitudes toward animals, restaurant food, and public restrooms. The gypsies' rules, however, are often at odds with those of the dominant culture, leading to frequent misunderstandings between the two.

One of the worst insults that nongypsies can hurl at gypsies is to say that they are dirty. Gypsies, in fact, live by a strict code of purity. There sometimes is a difference between, however, the *ritual* purity of the gypsies and the *hygienic* purity laid down in nongypsy laws, and these differences often bring them into conflict.

A gypsy, for example, must never wash dishes in a basin that has been used for any other purpose. This rule is observed as part of his or her identity. A gypsy would never consider washing his hands in the same basin in which he washed his cup. In the gypsies' view, a Gorgio (the gypsies' term for all nongypsies) sink is a dirty thing that has been used for other purposes, like washing the body, food, and dishes. It may even have been used for washing clothes or for draining buckets after floor cleaning. Gorgios will scrub their shoes over sinks or wash their shoes in them. Gypsies consider these practices filthy habits.

Because Gorgios are likely to wash anything in their sinks, eating in public places is considered a hazardous practice. Gypsies who are uncertain about the state of the dishes in a restaurant usually prefer factory-made drinks from bottles to tea from possibly polluted coffee cups. Some even feel it is cleaner to eat with their hands rather than place suspect cutlery in their mouths. Disposable plates, cups, and containers are best because they have never been previously used.

Instead of a sink, gypsies use a collection of bowls for different tasks. The dish-washing bowl is clearly distinguished from the personal-washing bowl. Pride of place is given to the dish-washing bowl—on the formica counter inside the trailer (where the traditional sink has often been boarded up). The personal-washing bowl is often kept outside, and so is the laundry bowl.

If a dish-washing bowl is used for any other purpose, it becomes permanently contaminated. No amount of rinsing or scouring can alter this. One gypsy recounted with horror how a Gorgio public health official had ruined his dish-washing bowl. While the health official was visiting the gypsy camp, she noticed that the gypsy in question had a deep cut in his foot. In her well-meaning way, she grabbed the nice clean bowl she had seen inside his trailer, poured in disinfectant and water, and bathed the man's foot in it. The bowl she had used was the dish-washing bowl. After she left, the gypsies quickly threw it away.

Gypsy cultural practices are based on the strict separation between the inside and outside, not only in the organization of living space, but also in the representation of the body. The inner/outer distinction of the body works as follows: the outer body (or skin) with its discarded scales is accumulated dirt; its by-products of hair and waste both are potentially polluting if recycled through the inner body. Anything taken into the inner body through the mouth must be entirely clean, and so dishes and utensils washed in bowls for washing the outer body are unclean. The gypsies have a word for this special type of uncleanliness—*mochadi,* meaning "ritually unclean." A dusty or grubby living space, which to Gorgios might be disgusting, is seen by the gypsies

as harmless, compared with ritual uncleanliness.

What does this dichotomy represent? The outer body symbolizes the public self, as seen by and presented to the Gorgio. This public self is a protective covering for the inner self, which must be kept pure. The inner body represents the secret ethnic self, which is sustained individually and collectively within the gypsy group.

Once we understand this separation of selves, the gypsy attitude toward animals also begins to make sense. To gypsies, dogs and cats are unclean because they break the rules of cleanliness; they lick their fur, taking their outer bodily dirt into their mouths and inner body. A cat is especially dirty because, as a gypsy explained, "it licks its paws after burying its dirt." The horse, by contrast, is considered absolutely clean. It doesn't lick itself, and it is thought to be especially fastidious because it drinks water by filtering it through closed teeth.

Another animal gypsies value is the hedgehog. Its prickly outer casing makes for a rigid separation between the inner and outer body, and its spines prevent self-grooming. Gypsies attribute to hedgehogs a special ability to counteract pollution; it is seen as an antidote against most plant and animal poisons. Thus eating hedgehog is a way to overcome any uncleanliness within.

Few people outside the gypsy culture know or understand the reasons for gypsy beliefs and practices. Once they are understood, however, they no longer seem quite so strange and bizarre. Instead, they may be seen as the cultural elements of a minority living in a society that does not subscribe to its beliefs.

Source: Based on Judith Okely, "Why Gypsies Hate Cats But Love Horses," *New Society* **63**(1057) February 17, 1983, pp. 251–253.

mid-1800s sealed their fate when the trickle of Anglo-Americans into that region became a flood. They brought with them deadly new diseases such as smallpox, measles, tuberculosis, malaria, typhoid, and pneumonia, which raced through the Native American populations, which lacked immunity to them. These diseases alone wiped out many groups, but the invaders used deliberate means of destruction as well.

Hundreds of Yana died in forced migrations; many others were victims of mass murders and mob violence (see Chapter 18). The Yana fought back ferociously, and eventually the United States Army arrived to contain them. Driven ever more deeply into the wilderness, facing a depletion of wildlife and other sources of food, the Yana were pushed toward starvation. The few remaining bands became scavengers, hiding as long as they could and then raiding isolated homesteads for food. Finally all but one man—Ishi—died or were killed. Ishi was left alone.

Heartbroken, starving, and without further hope, Ishi set out southward, eventually coming on a corral outside Oroville, California, where he was cornered by dogs. When he was brought to the Oroville jail, Ishi thoroughly expected to die. Fortunately, he came to the attention of anthropologists Alfred L. Kroeber and T. T. Waterman, who brought him to Berkeley in 1911, where he was given a place to live at the University of California Museum of Anthropology. There he became something of a celebrity and taught his new friends the history and customs of his extinct people (Kroeber, 1961).

Other societies have been victims of destructive internal forces. Although the Roman civilization fell to the mighty hordes of Vandals, Visigoths, and Huns in the fifth century, its decline actually began as a result of the second and third of the processes we mentioned above: a society's succumbing to internal apathy and chaos. The emperor had been designated divine, and the government had drifted into despotism. Religious strife between pagans and Christians tore apart families and friends. State and church contended for power. Epidemics of pestilence and chronic warfare cut down the empire's population, as did the prevalence of abortion and infanticide. Moral decay spread among the upper classes. The economy sagged, as the Roman Empire imported far more goods than it exported. Taxation and corruption reduced many noble families to bankruptcy and drove large numbers of peasants from their lands, condemning them to serfdom. The hostility between urban and rural folk, which had plagued both the Greek and Roman civilizations throughout their histories, was heightened by these developments. Finally the once unbeatable Roman army was fatally weakened as a succession of adolescent and incompetent emperors lost their hold over it. Increasingly, the army's ranks were filled by slaves, criminals, and foreign mercenaries whose loyalty to Rome was no deeper than their purses. In fact, when the city of Rome itself was sacked by the Visigoths in A.D. 410, many of its inhabitants watched the battles from their rooftops as if they were at the Colosseum. "In this awful drama of a great state breaking into pieces, the internal causes were the unseen protagonists; the invading barbarians merely entered where weakness had opened the door, and where the failure of . . . moral, economic, and political statesmanship had left the stage to chaos, despondency, and decay" (Durant, 1944).

Rome also offers an example of the incorporation of one society by another. The list of its conquests includes most of present-day Europe as well as Syria, Lebanon, Israel, Jordan, Libya, Morocco, Algeria, and parts of Egypt. As Rome's armies conquered the ancient world, its political and economic systems expanded to incorporate the nations it vanquished, and its language left its imprint on the languages spoken there today. In most cases the defeated peoples were made citizens of Rome, and to some degree they were allowed to live according to their own customs. Nevertheless they were expected to support the Roman economy (with taxes) and to obey Roman law. Finally, they were entirely accountable to Roman political authority. These societies thus became subsystems within the complex whole of Roman society.

The Roman Empire attained a high level of complexity and sophistication in its economic systems, literature, methods of warfare, and language that even today have an influence on our customs, thinking, and studies. Not all societies, however, ever become this complex because the structure of a society depends to a great degree on its social organization and technology.

☐ Types of Societies

In this section we shall trace the development of the major types of societies. In tracing this development we shall look at hunting and food-gathering societies, horticultural societies, pastoral societies, agricultural societies, and, finally, industrial societies.

Hunting and Food-Gathering Societies

The members of the earliest human societies—**hunting and food-gathering societies**—survived by foraging for vegetable foods and small game, fishing, collecting shellfish, and hunting larger animals. They did not plant crops or raise animals for future needs; rather, they subsisted from day to day on whatever was at hand. In modern times a few of the world's simplest societies—in Australia, Africa, and South America—still subsist, using these methods and depending to a large degree on tools made of stone, wood, and bone.

If we were to consider the evolutionary cycle during which human beings have been on this earth, we would find that most of it has been spent in hunting and gathering societies. Anthropologists have estimated that humans hunted for at least 1 million years, but it has only been a mere 10 thousand years since the first people began to experiment with the possibilities of organized agriculture. Richard Leakey (Leakey and Lewin, 1977) believes that hunting is the key characteristic in the development of human social organization. Our close primate cousins are primarily vegetarians. Primates are social animals, but a plant-eating existence tends to make the individual members very self-centered and uncooperative. To be a vegetarian is essentially to be solitary. Each member tears a leaf from a branch, or plucks fruit from a tree, and promptly eats it. There is little communal eating or the sharing of food.

Hunting and food-gathering societies still exist today in parts of Australia, Africa, and South America. These Amazon Indians hunt using weapons similar to those of their ancestors.

When our ancestors organized their hunting and gathering, the adoption of sharing opened a behavioral gulf between ourselves and our primate relatives. Sharing was one of a group of traits acquired through hunting and gathering that helped produce an increasingly adaptable way of life. This adaptability enabled the human species to thrive in practically every corner of the globe. We can summarize the package of traits derived from hunting and gathering as follows:

1. *A base camp.* This was a place where infants could be cared for and where meat and plant foods could be brought. This camp became an important social focus.
2. *A division of labor.* Males were the hunters, and females were responsible for child care and for gathering plant foods.
3. *The development of cooperation.* Each person became more dependent on the activities and trust of others in the group. These effects in turn made it possible for a closely knit social group to emerge in which the prolonged socialization of children was possible.

Misconceptions about hunting and gathering societies abound, with Thomas Hobbes's seventeenth-century notion about life in the wild as a prime example: "No arts; no letters; no society; and which is worst of all continual fear and danger of violent death; and the life of man, solitary, poor, nasty, brutish, and short."

Richard Lee (1969a, b) concentrated on discovering the primary elements of the hunting and gathering way of life and studied the !Kung tribe in order to get a picture of life in such a society.

As it turns out, hunting is far from a full-time occupation, and it certainly does not fit Hobbes's description. On the average, the men spend just two and a half days a week hunting. As each workday is approximately 6 hours long, the total amount of time spent hunting may only be 15 hours a week. Meanwhile, the women are not working very hard, either. On every gathering trip they will collect enough food for about three days, leaving the hunter-gatherers with plenty of time for visiting and other leisure activities. We should not really be all that surprised that hunting and gathering is a rather successful existence, for if it were a precarious mode of adaptation, our ancestors would not have survived as well as they did (Leakey, 1981).

There are certain recurring features of economic and social organization that hunters and food-gatherers share—and that set them off as a group from other kinds of societies. Their communities are mobile and small and on the whole the social relationships among individuals tend to be quite egalitarian, in part because there is little private property. There is no social class differentiation, nor are there traditional positions of prestige reserved for favored subgroups. Although men and women perform different functions, both sets of functions are equally valued, and women are the social equals of men. In general, men are primarily responsible for hunting and protecting the group, and the women often hunt smaller game and forage for food (both animal and vegetable). The women typically provide some 60 to 70 percent of the total calories consumed by the group (Lee, 1969b).

Women also take primary responsibility for raising the children. Marriage, in one form or another, is universally present, with monogamy the dominant form. Most social life is organized in terms of peoples' kinship relations—that is, the ways in which people are related to one another through geneology and marriage determine whom they may marry, what kinds of food or material goods they will exchange with one another, whether they observe the same taboos, and so on.

Despite all these similarities, significant differences in social organization do exist among contemporary hunting and food-gathering societies (Martin, 1974). This is hardly surprising because they inhabit environments that vary widely: the jungles of Amazonia, Central Africa, and Malaysia; the frozen wastes of Tierra del Fuego at the southernmost tip of South America and the Arctic shores; and the deserts of Australia and southern Africa. Hunting and food-gathering societies are structured in several different ways: male-centered kinship groups, female-centered kinship groups, and groups organized along kinship lines irrespective of gender. Groups living in harsh climates and with correspondingly low productivity are quite small, often numbering fewer than several hundred individuals. But where nature is bountiful or affords special means of accumulating food surpluses (as on the Northwest Coast of North America, where annual salmon runs provided abundant food that could be stored for year-round consumption), hunting and food-gathering societies could number in the thousands. Similarly, whereas most such groups are seminomadic because of their need to search for food, those who inhabit rich environments have developed sedentary village settlements.

By 200 years ago, hunters and gatherers had dwindled to only about 10 percent of the

hunting and food-gathering societies The earliest human societies whose members survived by foraging for vegetable foods and small game, fishing, collecting shellfish, and hunting larger animals; they did not plant crops or raise animals for future needs but subsisted day to day on whatever was available.

world's population. Now that the world's population is approaching 5 billion, there are fewer than 300,000 hunting people left.

Horticultural Societies

Some 12,000 to 15,000 years ago, coinciding with the retreat of the last glaciers, a drying trend took place in what previously had been rich, subtropical climates, and the giant deserts of Africa, Asia, and the Middle East took shape. Even beyond their constantly expanding borders, new arid conditions made precarious the age-old hunting and food-gathering way of life. Some groups continued to eke out an existence using the old subsistence techniques. Others crowded together in the more abundant regions, harvesting wild grains until population pressures drove them out into less favorable environments. There they attempted to recreate the rich environments they had left. In doing so, they created a new form of subsistence—**horticultural societies**—using human muscle power and hand-held tools (such as digging sticks and hoes) to cultivate gardens and fields (Flannery, 1965, 1968). It is generally agreed that women invented this new and revolutionary form of food production—deliberately planting seeds with the idea of having a sure source of food later on—based on their observations of the relationships between seeds and the growth of plants. This process seems to have repeated itself at least three times in three different places: in the Far East, rice was first domesticated in Thailand about 11,000 years ago (Solheim, 1972); in the Middle East, wheat, barley, and rye were domesticated about 10,000 years ago (Harlan, 1971); and in Mesoamerica, corn was domesticated between 6,000 and 9,000 years ago (Meggars, 1972). From these three centers of origin the cultivation of plants spread outward until it became the most widespread means of subsistence and the economic base on which all civilizations were built.

In contrast with hunting and gathering, farming does not provide a superior diet, a more reliable food supply, or an easier way of obtaining it. In fact, the oposite is true. Farming provides an inferior diet because it is based on a more limited number of foods. It is much less reliable because blights and the vagaries of the weather can produce a famine. Finally, more human effort is expended in farming than in hunting and gathering. The transition from hunting and gathering to farming was made for one main benefit, namely, the fact that more food could be produced from a given acreage. Hunter-gatherers could maintain a superior diet as long as they roamed over a large area and kept their population small enough that the resources would replenish themselves naturally (Farb, 1978).

The movement from hunting and gathering to farming also represented a dramatic social change. Hunters as a people must have faith in the resources of their physical world and in their ability to exploit them. They live in small, intimate, cooperative groups moving from camp to camp as their food supplies dictate. As they roam the land that they may share with other bands, they may encounter confrontations, but they do not search them out.

An agricultural existence produces the exact opposite of this way of life. Because crops must be tended and harvested, farmers are confined to a certain area. A sedentary way of life also offers the possibility of accumulating material possessions. In turn, the land bearing the crops and the farmers' possessions must be defended. A whole new outlook on life thus develops. Agriculture also can support a much greater density of people, therefore giving rise to villages and towns. The possibility of expanding possessions and the ability to have power over others in turn produces the urge to accumulate still more and brings about the necessity of protecting what has already been won. The stage is thus set for conflict and wars.

To hunting and gathering tribes, it made little sense to appropriate the territory of a neighboring band. In contrast, agriculture allowed local populations to grow. If one village decided to take over the crops of another, it would benefit because its own population could then expand with the extra food. In this respect anthropologists would argue that the violence and destruction peculiar to modern times is an outgrowth of the agricultural way of life, and not a biological remnant from our hunting ancestors (Leakey and Lewin, 1977).

There are two distinct approaches to horticulture: **subsistence farming**—producing only enough to feed the group—and **surplus farming**—producing more than can be consumed by the group. Surplus-food-producing societies have very different economic, social, and political systems than subsistence-oriented societies do.

Subsistence Farming Subsistence farmers live in environments that are unfavorable to cultivation. They are most often found in tropical or subtropical jungles where the forest always threatens to overgrow the fields. Because cultivation depletes the land of nutrients, subsistence farmers' settlements must be moved every few years when new fields are cleared. The settlements are small, and competition among neighboring villages typically is high. Indeed, ongoing feuding, raiding, and even prescheduled battles between the forces of nearby villages are not uncommon events. Political organization rarely extends beyond the village, and usually it is organized in terms of positions inherited by males through the kinship system.

When the environment is more benign, the competition and fighting among villages drop remarkably. The political system frequently is organized around related women rather than men, and there are few differences in power and prestige between men and women. In fact, relationships between the sexes approach the egalitarian qualities generally found in hunting and food-gathering societies. Although the production of surplus food is technologically possible, surplus production simply is not a culturally valued norm. Although there is likely to be some degree of role specialization, this, too, is relatively undeveloped—not much greater than among hunting and food gathering groups. With an abundant environment and little in the way of tradeable surpluses, division by social class and designated positions of prestige are minimal (Martin and Voorhies, 1975).

Surplus Farming People who practice surplus farming live in densely populated, per-

manent settlements. They have highly elaborate political institutions that tend to be structured by kinship relations that are male dominated. There is occupational specialization with prestige differences, and social stratification is well established. Because the production of surpluses is a culturally valued norm, such societies are often interested in expansion; consequently, they have an organized military force. Expansion means more land and more captured labor, which in turn establishes an accumulation of greater surpluses that can be used to pay for political support, specialized craftspeople, and conspicuous consumption.

Pastoral Societies

Pastoral societies rely on herding and the domestication and propagation of animals for food and clothing to satisfy the bulk of a group's needs. Animal herds provide milk, dung (for fuel), skin, sheared fur, and even blood (which is drunk as a major source of protein in East Africa).

Pastorial societies appear in many regions that are not suitable for plant domestication, such as semiarid desert regions and the northern tundra plains of Europe and Asia. They are also found in less severe climates, including East African savannas and mountain grasslands. Pastoralism, however, almost never occurs in forest or jungle regions. It is an interesting fact, which scholars have not been able to explain, that no true pastoral societies ever emerged in the Americas before the arrival of the Europeans.

Many pastoral groups rely partly on horticulture to subsist. Most pastoralists are nomads (or seminomads) who follow their herds

horticultural societies The first societies whose members used human muscle power and hand-held tools to cultivate gardens and fields.
subsistence farming An approach to horticulture that involves producing only enough food to feed the group.
surplus farming An approach to horticulture that involves producing more food than can be consumed by the group.
pastoral societies Societies that rely on herding and the domestication and propagation of animals for food and clothing to satisfy the bulk of the group's needs.

Most pastoralists, such as this Masai shepherd in Kenya, are nomads who follow their herds in a never-ending quest for pasture and water.

in a never-ending quest for pasture and water. Hence such societies typically consist of relatively small, mobile communities. The Kazak people from Central Asia, for example, leave some members of their communities behind to plant and harvest grains during the summer, whereas the main body of the group follows the herds of horses and sheep.

Generally, pastoral societies are organized around male-centered kinship groups. When needed resources are predictable, pastoral societies typically are composed of stable groups united under strong political figures. But when resources are unpredictable, they are quick to split apart and compete with one another. Therefore, centralized political leadership does not appear (Salzman, 1967).

There have been times in human history when through bonds of kinship, pastoral societies have organized into enormous sociopolitical entities called **hordes.** The extreme mobility, fierceness, and kinship-based loyalty of these hordes often made them into extraordinary military powers. As such, nomadic pastoralists influenced the course of civilization far more than their numbers alone would suggest. It was to keep out Central Asian hordes that the emperors of the Chou dynasty in China built the Great Wall in the third

and fourth centuries B.C. And it was nomadic pastoralist armies who drove the final nails into the coffin of the Roman Empire in the fourth and fifth centuries A.D. In fact, many of the states of ancient Asia, the Middle East, and Eastern Europe arose partly in protective response to pastoralist raids. But it must be pointed out that pastoralists have influenced civilizations constructively as well, not only destructively. In what is now Hungary, for example, it was nomads themselves who first established some of the oldest politically centralized societies in Europe (Cohen, 1974).

Agricultural Societies

Agricultural societies are distinguished from other groups by their use of the plow in food production. Agriculture is more efficient than horticulture: Plowing turns the topsoil far deeper than does hoeing, allowing for better aerating and fertilizing of the ground and thus improving the yield. Interestingly, early agriculture probably did not yield much more than the food-gatherers were able to harvest in naturally rich environments. However, by about 5500 B.C., farmers in the Middle East were not only using the plow but irrigation (the channeling of water for crops) as well. With irrigation, farming became capable of

Agricultural societies depend on the strength of animals in contrast to the dependence on human muscle power in horticultural societies.

producing huge surpluses—enough to feed large numbers of people who did not produce food themselves.

Reliance on agriculture had dramatic and interrelated consequences for society. Ever-growing populations came together into broad river valleys like those of the Nile in Egypt, the Tigris and Euphrates in the Middle East, the Huang Ho (Yellow River) in China, and the Danube and Rhine in Europe. As we explained in Chapter 7, this rapidly rising and geographically compressed population density gave rise to cities and to new social forms. For the first time society was *not* organized principally in terms of kinship. Rather, occupational diversity and institutional specialization (including differentiated political, economic, and religious institutions) predominated.

As populations grew and cities developed, the need arose for a central organization that could administer the ever-widening and increasingly complex activities that accompanied this growth. Such a central authority could serve the interests of the priest-kings by enabling them to collect taxes; it also provided the means by which a permanent military force with military leaders could be maintained to protect the new centers of pop-

ulation. These developments led to the emergence of the centralized state.

Agriculture also made land that was suitable for farming into a valuable resource. Those who controlled access to arable land and its use soon were rich and powerful because they could command the payment of taxes and political support. By taxing the bulk of agricultural surpluses, political leaders could employ bureaucracies to implement their plans and armies to protect their privileges—both from external enemies and internal rebels. Thus social classes became entrenched, and the state evolved (see Chapter 17).

The tremendous possibilities for social progress that agriculture made available could be seen in Babylon—the cradle of Western civilization—almost 3,000 years ago. Sadly, so were some of the problems that dependence on agriculture created—problems that continue to plague industrial societies of today. These include population crowding (with the associated spread of diseases), overexploita-

hordes Large sociopolitical entities formed by kinship-related pastoral societies.

agricultural societies Societies that use the plow in food production, which enabled large populations to come together and form cities and new social forms.

Although the steam engine was initially mostly a curiosity, it became a critical part of the early Industrial Revolution because it provided the means by which vast quantities of goods could be geographically distributed.

tion of the environment, chronic warfare, and the institutionalization of social inequality.

Industrial Societies

In the last chapter we discussed the industrial city, which emerged in association with the Industrial Revolution. **Industrialism** consists of the use of mechanical means (machines and chemical processes) for the production of goods. The Industrial Revolution at first developed slowly. It had begun in a small way by the mid-eighteenth century and gained momentum by the turn of the nineteenth century. (In 1798, Eli Whitney built the first

American factory for the mass production of guns near New Haven, Connecticut.) By the mid-1800s the Industrial Revolution had swung into high gear with the invention of the steam locomotive and Henry Bessemer's development of large-scale production techniques at his steel works in England in 1858. It is called a revolution because of the enormous changes it brought about in society.

Industrial societies are characterized by more than just the use of mechanical means for production. They constitute an entirely new form of society that requires an immense, mobile, diversely specialized, highly skilled, and well-coordinated labor force. Among other things, to meet the demand for people with specialized and complex skills, many members of the labor force must be educated, at least able to read and write. Hence an educational system open to all is a hallmark of industrial societies—something that was not necessary in preindustrial times. Industrialism also requires the creation of highly organized systems of exchange between the suppliers of raw materials and industrial manufacturers on the one hand, and between the manufacturers and consumers on the other.

Industrial societies are inevitably divided along class lines. The nature of the division varies, depending on whether the society allows private ownership of capital (capitalism) or puts all capital in the hands of the state (socialism). All industrial societies have at least two social classes: (1) a large labor force that produces goods and services but has little or no influence on what is done with them and (2) a much smaller class that determines what shall be produced and how it will be distributed.

Industrialism brought about a tremendous shift of populations. Over the past century and a half, huge numbers of rural peasants and farmers have migrated from the countryside to the cities, transforming themselves into the urban masses. A study of the massive impact of the automobile on American society shows the overwhelming changes wrought by industrialism (see Case Study: "Reaching Toward Autopia").

Kinship, which still played an important role in the organization of preindustrial agricultural societies, now plays a much smaller role in patterning public affairs. Nor do religious institutions (which were very closely tied to political institutions in preindustrial society) dominate the scene: Industrial societies are highly secularized. In general the predominant form of social and political organization in industrial societies is the bureaucracy—that least personal of all formal organizations (see Chapter 6), which itself was inspired by the model of the efficiently functioning machine: the symbol of industrial production and of industrialism as a way of life.

Postindustrial Society

The world has continued to change since the beginning of industrialization. These changes have prompted some sociologists to consider the concept of the **postindustrial society** (Bell, 1973). Whereas industrial societies depend on inventions and advances made by craftspeople, postindustrial societies depend on specialized knowledge to bring about continuing progress in technology. The computer industry, which has experienced such phenomenal growth, is an integral part of postindustrial society. Advances in this field are made by highly trained specialists who work to increase the capabilities of computers. Knowledge and information are the hallmarks of the postindustrial society.

Some people see major problems developing out of movement into the postindustrial age. One such person is French sociologist Jacques Ellul, who wrote an influential book, *The Technological Society* (1964). Industrial technology, Ellul argues, is spreading inexorably around the world, homogenizing social relations among individuals and the interactions between humans and the natural environment. Modern society is caught up in an uncritical dependence on technology to solve all its problems—including the problems (like pollution) that arise from the use of technology itself. We are fully indoctrinated to General Electric's old motto: "Progress is our most important product." And by *progress* we mean technological advance. Nobody, Ellul laments, stops to ask: Why? To what ends?

Perhaps even more important, Ellul observes that it is time somebody asked how we are going to achieve the wonderful society promised us by the technocrats:

service oriented

industrialism The use of mechanical means (machines and chemical processes) for the production of goods.

industrial societies Societies characterized by the use of machines, exchange relationships, division along class lines, secularization, and bureaucracy, and requiring a large, mobile, diversely specialized, highly skilled, and well-coordinated labor force.

postindustrial society A type of society that depends on specialized knowledge to bring about continuing progress in technology; computer technology, the key to advanced knowledge and information, is an integral part of postindustrial society.

CASE STUDY
Reaching Toward Autopia

The automobile is so much a part of our culture that to imagine our lives without it is difficult. Joseph Interrante examined how in the first half of this century the automobile came to be viewed as a basic necessity and how it helped change the character of our communities—urban, suburban, and rural—and, indeed, of our way of life. The automobile promoted the reorganization of American society.

When the first mass-produced automobiles appeared with the introduction of Henry Ford's Model T in 1908, people bought them because they met old transportation needs better than did existing alternatives. They were faster than horse and wagon, and they were not restricted to set routes and schedules, as were trains and streetcars.

As early as the 1920s, people viewed their automobiles as a basic necessity, not just a convenience. A working-class mother of nine living in a medium-sized city told sociologists Robert and Helen Lynd, "We'd rather do without clothes than give up the car." A farm woman, asked by a U.S. Department of Agriculture inspector why her family had purchased a car before equipping their home with indoor plumbing, replied, "Why, you can't go to town in a bathtub!"

The automobile allowed cities to change and expand outward, suburbs to develop, and rural communities to share in some of the advantages once only available to city dwellers. The old cities changed, Major industries kept their corporate headquarters in the city centers but moved their factories out to "industrial satellite cities," such as Gary and East Chicago outside Chicago and East St. Louis and Alton across the Mississippi from St. Louis. Between 1920 and 1930, the proportion of factory employment within the older centers dropped. Every city with a population of at least 100,000

experienced a proportional decline in industrial employment. As manufacturing declined, the proportion of communications, finance, and management, clerical, and professional services increased.

In the 1920s and 1930s, people of all classes moved out of the central cities. Upper-class people moved to rural or semirural areas where they lived on country estates. Middle-class people moved to closer-in suburban "bedroom" communities from which the breadwinners commuted each working day into the cities or to the industrial satellite cities where they held managerial and administrative positions. Members of the working class moved to newly developed communities around the new factory centers. Metropolitan areas no longer expanded along clearly marked rail or streetcar lines but to wherever the private automobile could carry people seeking some open space of their own.

Surprisingly, rural society was affected earlier and more deeply than was urban society by the introduction of the automobile. Farmers bought Tin Lizzies sooner and in greater numbers than did urban residents in the period before World War I. In 1910, 0.17 percent of farm families owned 0.50 percent of the 450,000 registered motor vehicles in the United States. In 1930, slightly more than half of the 23 million automobiles in the United States were owned by rural families.

In urban areas, the introduction of the automobile led to decentralization—the decline of central cities and the growth of the suburbs. In rural areas, the opposite occurred. The smallest crossroads communities stagnated or disappeared. Larger towns grew in importance as shopping, trading, and service centers. Large chain stores, most significantly those operated by mail-order

houses, now found that they could serve their rural customers directly. Doctors, dentists, lawyers, and other professionals could attract sufficient clientele from the surrounding countryside.

Although rural people could travel greater distances with cars than with horse and wagon, studies of automobile travel showed that most trips were made within the local area. Automobile use led not to longer trips but to more frequent trips. Rural families were traveling to towns to purchase a far wider range of goods and services than in the past. Rural families became dependent on these towns for goods and services that they formerly provided for themselves, did without, or ordered by mail. As just one example, by 1930, 66 percent of farm households purchased store-bought bread instead of making their own, as in the past.

Rural families, nearly as much as their urban and suburban counterparts, had become consumers of finished products. They could not survive without frequent trips in their automobiles to nearby towns to purchase these goods. Urban and rural areas became more closely linked, with the once very different cultures ever more similar in their material wants and needs.

Thus, as the automobile satisfied Americans' need for transportation—a need as basic as food, clothing, and shelter—it also changed the social and spatial patterns of American society. Without the automobile, the complexion of American society would, most certainly, be quite different.

Source: Adapted from Joseph Interrante, "The Road to Autopia." In David L. Lewis and Lawrence Goldstein (eds.), *The Automobile and American Culture* (Ann Arbor: University of Michigan Press). Copyright © 1980, 1983 by The University of Michigan. □

USING SOCIOLOGY
Technology and the Changing World of Work

The world of work is currently undergoing a revolution that is as dramatic as the leap from a preindustrial to an industrial society. Most often the computer is at the heart of these changes. Analysts predict that technological innovations are likely to alter the nature of work activities within all economic sectors, affecting the growth and location of employment opportunities and causing significant shifts in the interplay between our jobs and personal lives.

Want to know the scope of the revolution that is currently under way in American business? Consider some statistics. The installation of robots in American industry has been growing by 30 percent per year. In 1970, there were 200 robots busy in American factories, but by 1980, that number had grown to 3,500. Conservative estimates indicate that by 1990 there will be some 35,000 robots toiling away at jobs formerly held by American workers, and by the last decade of the twentieth century, robots will proliferate like rabbits.

Moving out of the factories, the changes are no less dramatic. New technologies will radically alter jobs involving information processing. Typewriters, file cabinets, and mail systems will increasingly be replaced by word processors, computerized data retrieval systems, and video transmissions between computer terminals.

Just as factory workers have been losing jobs to highly skilled, efficient, and obedient robots, so too will file clerks, stenographers, and mail deliverers, and other less-skilled office workers lose their jobs to electronic workhorses.

The dimensions of this dislocation are already clear. National Cash Register, for example, reduced its American work force from 37,000 to 18,000 between 1970 and 1975 because of the increased productivity provided by microelectronic rather than mechanical parts. Robots in the General Motors plant in Lordstown, Ohio, increased productivity by 20 percent, allowing GM to reduce its human force by 10 percent. In Providence, Rhode Island, the *Journal Bulletin* cut its printing staff from 242 workers to 98 as a result of new typesetting technology.

At first glance it may appear that technology, despite its advantages for business, is taking quite a human toll. Most experts believe that in actuality, technological advances generally foster economic and job growth by increasing the quality and quantity of products while lowering the costs. The lower are the costs of products, they reason, the more people there will be who can afford to buy them. The increased demand will then cause producers to employ as many or more workers than before technological innovation.

But although the employment picture in general appears rosy, there is a hitch. As the various applications of technology continue to grow, the number of jobs in traditional industries will decline. Some analysts speculate that over the next 50 years, only about 3 percent of the work force will be employed in manufacturing. A similar decline is forecast for agricultural workers. Workers in these fields have a choice, it seems, of updating their skills or risking being rendered obsolete. General Motors, for example, predicts that 50 percent of its work force in the year 2000 will consist of skilled tradespeople, such as technicians, inspectors, and monitors, compared with 16 percent in 1980. Familiarity with computers will also become essential to all office workers—from managers to secretaries. And jobs in high-tech industries such as communication equipment, instruments, electronic components, and computer services are expected to skyrocket.

The technological revolution also promises to alter the balance between our personal lives and our work lives. After gaining job skills while working full time for a few years, people may increasingly opt to "telecommute" from their homes to their offices via computers. Others, relieved by the computer from the necessity of maintaining a staff of workers, may start small businesses at or near their homes. New businesses opportunities will arise based on servicing the needs of at-home and small business workers.

Just as the hunters and gatherers of antiquity could not have imagined the factory robot or the electronic cottage of the twentieth century, so too is it hard for us to imagine where such technological innovation will lead. Although some social upheaval seems inevitable in such a drastic rethinking of the workplace, there are advantages to be gained both by freeing humans from dangerous and tedious jobs and by the creative possibilities inherent in the new technologies. The challenge will be to maintain a human perspective in an electronic world.

Source: Adapted from Fred Best, "Technology and the Changing World of Work," *The Futurist,* April, 1984, pp. 61–66.   □

Consider, for example, the problems of automation, which will become acute in a very short time. How, socially, politically, morally, and humanly, shall we continue to get there [to technological utopia]? How are the prodigious economic problems, for example, of unemployment, to be solved?

Ellul believes that people will not find satisfactory answers to these questions and the many other practical "hows" that unchecked technological advance will impose on us. Nor is he alone in his pessimism, which is shared by many social scientists, laypersons, and even some politicians.

More recently, theorists like Daniel Bell (1973) have speculated on the characteristics of postindustrial society. The trends they see are based on changes already under way in industrial societies, particularly in the United States. The economies of postindustrial society will be service oriented. Already in the United States more than half of all jobs are in the service sector, and the proportion is expected to increase as computers direct automation in industry and as agriculture becomes more and more mechanized. In fact, some theorists believe that eventually all heavy industry will be located in nonservice-oriented societies. Advanced technology, on which postindustrial society is based, is in turn dependent on well-educated, well-informed scientists, technologists, and social theorists (for a further discussion of this topic, see Using Sociology: "Technology and the Changing World of Work"). Intellectual and technical knowledge and access to the quantities of information made possible by computers are crucial to this kind of society. Government at all levels will play a larger and larger role in society, both as employer and as the seat of policymaking. Residence patterns will change, people moving from the more crowded cities and suburbs in search of space (a trend already substantiated by the 1980 census—see Chapter 7). At the same time, people will be more segregated according to their age and family status.

Despite such evidence that not all the postulated postindustrial trends will continue, it is evident from the impact on society of the computer alone that there will be major and far-reaching changes in industrial society and that these changes are already in evidence. We shall discuss social change in a postindustrial society further in Chapter 20.

☐ Summary

A society is the largest and most inclusive social system that exists. A society recruits most of its members from within, sustains itself across generations, shares a culture, and occupies a territory. Organized and long-lasting societies are rare among most mammals.

When we examine individual social interaction, we are adopting a microsociological view; when we focus on the larger aspects of social systems, we are taking a macrosociological view.

There are four conditions that will bring about the dissolution of a society: (1) if its members are killed off; (2) if its members become apathetic, no longer caring whether or not the society continues to exist; (3) if the society falls into a state of chaos from which it cannot free itself; or (4) if the society is absorbed into another society—for example, as a result of conquest.

Forms of social organization depend on a society's technological development and on the social relationships that arise from it. Hunting and food-gathering groups are subsistence societies that forage for vegetables and game on the basis of what is needed for each day's existence. Horticultural societies are those that plant gardens and fields using only human muscle power and hand-held tools. Such societies are of two types: subsistence farming (producing only enough to feed the group) and surplus farming (producing more than can be consumed by the group).

Pastoral societies rely on the domestication and propagation of animals for existence, whereas agricultural societies cultivate plants with the use of a plow. The introduction of irrigation helped agricultural societies flourish.

Industrial societies arose as a result of the Industrial Revolution. These societies require an immense, mobile, diversely specialized, skilled, and well-coordinated labor force. They have brought about tremendous shifts in population and have led to the establishment of bureaucracy.

Some theorists see drastic changes already in progress that will lead to postindustrial societies, which will be based on technology, information, and knowledge. The computer is the symbol of the postindustrial society. Lifestyles will change: Most people will work in the service, or white-collar, sectors of the economy and live in smaller, less-crowded cities and suburban areas, segregated according to age and family status. Although this view of the future is open to debate—other theorists as well as actual events indicate that many of these trends may change or be reversed—it seems that major changes in modern societies are inevitable.

☐ For Further Reading

DAHRENDORF, RALF. *Class and Conflict in Industrial Society*. Stanford, Calif.: Stanford University Press, 1959.   A conflict approach to the sociological analysis of modern society. It should be read in conjunction with Parsons' *The Social System*.

FARB, PETER. *Humankind*. Boston: Houghton Mifflin, 1978.   A thorough examination of many elements of human behavior.

KROEBER, THEODORA. *Ishi in Two Worlds*. Berkeley and Los Angeles: University of California Press, 1976.   The remarkable story of Ishi, the Yana Indian, who told social scientists what he knew of his people's methods of hunting, their language, myths, and songs. Kroeber recounts Ishi's story with integrity and insight.

LEAKEY, RICHARD. *The Making of Mankind*. New York: Dutton, 1981.   An examination of what our human and prehuman ancestors were like, how they lived, how they evolved, and what they can tell us about ourselves and our future.

LEAKEY, RICHARD E., and ROGER LEWIN. *Origins*. New York: Dutton, 1977.   The authors show that the key to the transformation of an apelike creature into a human being was the ability to share in a complex social structure. This quality of cooperation is the basic feature of humanity.

LEE, RICHARD BORSHAY. *The !Kung San*. Berkeley and Los Angeles: University of California Press, 1980.   An exhaustive study of the !Kung San, one of the world's few surviving hunting and gathering societies. Lee examines the society's group structure, subsistence, technology, nutrition, land use, conflict management, and reaction to social change.

SCHWARTZ, GAIL GARFIELD, and WILLIAM NEIKIRK. *The Work Revolution*. New York: Rawson Associates, 1983.   An examination of the future of work in the postindustrial society.

9 Deviance and Criminal Behavior

If you were asked whether you know right from wrong, you would probably answer "yes." However, if you were asked how you determine what is right and what is wrong, you might have to spend some time thinking about the answer. An immediate response might have to do with the law: What is legal is right; what is illegal is wrong. But what about laws such as those enforcing apartheid in South Africa or unenforceable laws, such as Prohibition, that many people refused to abide by or those acts that are not even mentioned in the law? How do we know that it is right to help a handicapped person cross a busy street? No law compels us to do this. How do we know that it is wrong to gossip about people behind their backs? We could not be arrested for doing so.

The point is that we have certain rules by which most of us live. Some are enforced by law; others are not. This chapter will explore these rules, the reasons for them, the ways in which we learn them, and the causes and effects of their violation.

☐ Cultural Relativism and the Organization of Behavior

In America a man who beats up his wife is doing something wrong and usually illegal. Not so in Kenya, where in August, 1979, a bill regulating marital behavior was voted down by parliament because, among other things, it made wife beating illegal. Kimunai arap Soi, a member of parliament, worried that husbands would no longer be able to teach their wives manners by slapping them. Wafula Wabuge, another (male) member of parliament, worried that the bill would erode the quality of Kenyan married life. Women love their men to slap them, he claimed, "for then the wives call you darling" (*Time,* August 6, 1979).

Defining Normal and Deviant Behavior

What makes wife beating wrong in America but acceptable in Kenya? Why will two men walking hand-in-hand in downtown Minneapolis cause raised eyebrows but pass unnoticed in San Francisco or in Provincetown, Massachusetts? Why do Britons who are waiting to enter a theater stand patiently in line,

whereas people from the Middle East jam together at the turnstile? In other words, what makes a given action—wife beating, men holding hands, cutting into a line—"normal" in one case but "deviant" in another?

The answer is culture—more specifically, the norms and values of each culture (see Chapter 3). Together, norms and values make up the **moral code** of a culture—the symbolic system in terms of which behavior takes on the quality of being "good" or "bad," "right" or "wrong." Therefore, in order to decide whether any specific act is "normal" or "deviant," it is necessary to know more than only *what* a person did. One also must know who the person is (that is, the person's social identity) and the social and cultural context of the act.

For sociologists, then, **normal behavior** is behavior that conforms to the rules or norms of the group in which it occurs. **Deviant behavior** is behavior that fails to conform to the rules or norms of the group (Durkheim, 1960a). Therefore, when we try to assess an act as being normal or deviant, we must identify the group in whose terms the behavior is being judged. Moral codes differ widely from one society to another. For example, there is great variation among societies in their definition of punishable sexual behavior. For that matter, even within a society there exist groups and subcultures whose moral codes differ considerably. Watching television is normal behavior for most Americans, but it would be seen as deviant behavior among the Amish of Pennsylvania. Figure 9.1 indicates people's views of certain acts in the United States, India, and Iran.

Making Moral Judgments

In earlier chapters we stated that sociologists take a culturally relative view of normalcy and deviance. That is, they evaluate behavior ac-

---

moral code The symbolic system, made up of a culture's norms and values, in terms of which behavior takes on the quality of being "good" or "bad," "right" or "wrong."

normal behavior Behavior that conforms to the rules or norms of the group in which it occurs.

deviant behavior Behavior that fails to conform to the rules or norms of the group in which it occurs.

cording to the values of the culture in which it takes place. Ideally, they do not use their own values to judge the behavior of people from other cultures.

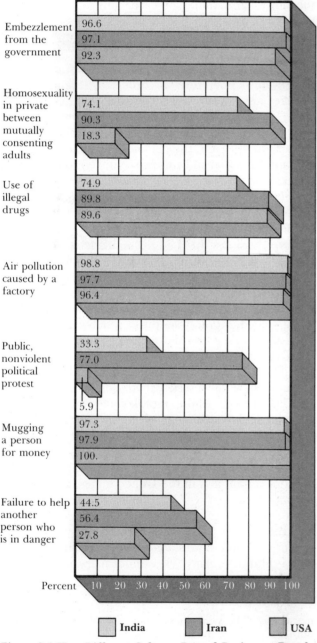

Embezzlement from the government
India 96.6
Iran 97.1
USA 92.3

Homosexuality in private between mutually consenting adults
India 74.1
Iran 90.3
USA 18.3

Use of illegal drugs
India 74.9
Iran 89.8
USA 89.6

Air pollution caused by a factory
India 98.8
Iran 97.7
USA 96.4

Public, nonviolent political protest
India 33.3
Iran 77.0
USA 5.9

Mugging a person for money
India 97.3
Iran 97.9
USA 100.

Failure to help another person who is in danger
India 44.5
Iran 56.4
USA 27.8

Percent 10 20 30 40 50 60 70 80 90 100

India   Iran   USA

Figure 9.1 How Different Cultures Regard Deviance **People in different countries were asked whether certain deviant acts should be punished by law. The percentages of those responding yes in India, Iran, and the United States are compared in the graph above.**

Even though social scientists recognize that there is great variation in normal and deviant behavior and that no science can determine what acts are inherently deviant, there are certain acts that are almost universally accepted as being deviant. For example, parent–child incest is severely disapproved in nearly every society. Genocide, the willful killing of specific groups of people—as occurred in the Nazi extermination camps during World War II—also is considered to be wrong even if it is sanctioned by the government or an entire society. The Nüremberg trials that were conducted after World War II made this point. Even though most of the accused individuals claimed they were merely following orders when they murdered or arranged for the murder of large numbers of people, many were found guilty. The reasoning was that there is a higher moral order under which certain human actions are wrong, regardless of who endorses them. Thus, despite their desire to view events from a culturally relative standpoint, sociologists and others find certain actions wrong, no matter what the context.

☐ Mechanisms of Social Control

In any society or social group, therefore, it is necessary to have means for molding or influencing members' behavior to conform to the group's values and norms. These processes are referred to as **mechanisms of social control,** and sociologists distinguish between internal and external means of control.

Internal Means of Control

As we already observed in Chapters 3 and 5, people are socialized to accept the norms and values of their culture, especially in the context of the smaller and more personally important social groups to which they belong, such as the family. The word *accept* is important here. Individuals conform to moral codes not just by *knowing* what they are but also by *experiencing* discomfort, often in the form of guilt, when they violate those codes. These guilt feelings arise from the anxiety, restlessness, tension, and self-depreciation that are aroused in an individual who engages in behavior that violates internalized norms. In other words, a group's moral code must be internalized and become part of each individual's emotional life as well as his or her thought processes. As this occurs, individuals begin to pass judgment on their own actions: rewards and punishments for conforming to or violating the moral code exist within the person. Hence the moral code of a culture becomes an **internal means of social control**—that is, it operates on the individual even in the absence of reactions by others.

For example, we can see the American moral code at work in the study presented in Table 9.1. This study, known as the National Survey of Crime Severity (NSCS), was conducted in 1977 and described 204 illegal events, from a 16-year-old playing hooky from school, to planting a bomb that killed 20 people in a public building. The survey used a nationwide sample and was the largest measure ever made of how the public ranks the seriousness of specific kinds of offenses.

The researchers found that there is agreement among Americans about the relative seriousness of crimes. What is interesting is that the survey found that many diverse groups of people generally agree about the relative severity of specific crimes. There were some differences, however. For example, the severity scores assigned by blacks and members of other racial groups were generally lower than those assigned by whites, and older people found thefts with large losses to be slightly more severe than did people of other age groups.

External Means of Control: Sanctions

External means of social control are the ways in which others respond to a person's behavior—rewarding or encouraging some kinds, punishing or discouraging others. They are social forces external to the individual that channel his or her behavior into those forms that most closely approximate the culture's norms and values.

Sanctions are rewards and penalties by a group's members that are used to regulate an individual's behavior. Thus all external means of control use sanctions of one kind or another. When the responses encourage the individual to continue acting in a certain way,

they are called **positive sanctions.** When the responses discourage the repetition or continuation of the behavior, they are **negative sanctions.**

Positive and Negative Sanctions Sanctions take many forms, which vary widely from group to group and from society to society. For example, an American audience might clap and whistle enthusiastically to show its appreciation for an excellent artistic or athletic performance, but the same whistling in Europe would be a display of strong disapproval. Or consider the *absence* of a response. In America a professor would not infer public disapproval from the absence of applause at the end of a lecture—such applause by students is the rarest of compliments. In many universities in Europe, however, students are expected to applaud after every lecture (if only in a rhythmic, stylized manner). The absence of such applause would be a horrible blow to the professor, a public criticism of the presentation.

Besides their expression in behavior, most social sanctions have a symbolic side embedded in the systems of meaning of each culture. Such symbolism makes sanctions quite powerful because people's self-esteem and

mechanisms of social control Devices used by all societies and social groups to influence or mold members' behavior to conform to group values and norms.

internal means of social control Psychological mechanisms of social control that operate on individuals even in the absence of reactions by others. Individuals pass judgment on their own actions as reward and punishment for conforming to or violating the moral code existing within the person.

external means of social control The social forces external to the individual that channel his or her behavior into those forms that most closely approximate the culture's norms and values.

sanctions Rewards and penalties used to regulate an individual's behavior. All external means of control use sanctions.

positive sanctions Responses by a group's members to an individual's behavior that encourage the individual to continue acting in a certain way.

negative sanctions Responses by a group's members to an individual's behavior that discourage the repetition or continuation of the behavior.

TABLE 9.1 *American Views on the Severity of Various Offenses*

Severity Score and Offense

72.1—Planting a bomb in a public building. The bomb explodes and 20 people are killed.

52.8—A man forcibly rapes a woman. As a result of physical injuries, she dies.

43.2—Robbing a victim at gunpoint. The victim struggles and is shot to death.

39.2—A man stabs his wife. As a result, she dies.

35.7—Stabbing a victim to death.

33.8—Running a narcotics ring.

27.9—A woman stabs her husband. As a result, he dies.

26.3—An armed person skyjacks an airplane and demands to be flown to another country.

25.9—A man forcibly rapes a woman. No other physical injury occurs.

24.9—Intentionally setting fire to a building causing $100,000 worth of damage.

22.9—A parent beats his young child with his fists. The child requires hospitalization.

21.2—Kidnaping a victim.

20.7—Selling heroin to others for resale.

19.5—Smuggling heroin into the country.

19.5—Killing a victim by recklessly driving an automobile.

17.9—Robbing a victim of $10 at gunpoint. The victim is wounded and requires hospitalization.

16.9—A man drags a woman into an alley, tears her clothes, but flees before she is physically harmed or sexually attacked.

16.4—Attempting to kill a victim with a gun. The gun misfires and the victim escapes unharmed.

15.9—A teenage boy beats his mother with his fists. The mother requires hospitalization.

15.5—Breaking into a bank at night and stealing $100,000.

14.1—A doctor cheats on claims he makes to a Federal health insurance plan for patient services.

13.9—A legislator takes a bribe from a company to vote for a law favoring the company.

13.0—A factory knowingly gets rid of its wastes in a way that pollutes the water supply of a city.

12.2—Paying a witness to give false testimony in a criminal trial.

12.0—A police officer takes a bribe not to interfere with an illegal gambling operation.

11.4—Knowingly lying under oath during a trial.

11.2—A company pays a bribe to a legislator to vote for a law favoring the company.

10.9—Stealing property worth $10,000 from outside a building.

10.5—Smuggling marijuana into the country for resale.

10.3—Operating a store that knowingly sells stolen property.

9.6—Breaking into a home and stealing $1,000.

9.2—Several large companies illegally fix the retail prices of their products.

8.6—Performing an illegal abortion.

8.5—Selling marijuana to others for resale.

8.5—Intentionally injuring a victim. The victim is treated by a doctor but is not hospitalized.

7.9—A teenage boy beats his father with his fists. The father requires hospitalization.

7.5—A person, armed with a lead pipe, robs a victim of $10. No physical harm occurs.

7.4—Illegally getting monthly welfare checks.

7.2—Signing someone else's name to a check and cashing it.

6.5—Using heroin.

6.5—An employer refuses to hire a qualified person because of that person's race.

6.4—Getting customers for a prostitute.

6.3—A person, free on bail for committing a serious crime, purposely fails to appear in court on the day of his trial.

6.2—An employee embezzles $1,000 from his employer.

5.4—Possessing some heroin for personal use.

5.1—A man runs his hands over the body of a female victim, then runs away.

4.9—Snatching a handbag containing $10 from a victim on the street.

4.8—A man exposes himself in public.

4.5—Cheating on Federal income tax return.

4.4—Picking a victim's pocket of $100.

3.8—Turning in a false fire alarm.

2.4—Knowingly carrying an illegal knife.

2.2—Stealing $10 worth of merchandise from the counter of a department store.

2.1—A woman engages in prostitution.

1.9—Making an obscene phone call.

1.6—Being a customer in a house of prostitution.

1.6—A male, over 16 years of age, has sexual relations with a willing female under 16.

1.4—Smoking marijuana.

1.3—Two persons willingly engage in a homosexual act.

1.1—Disturbing the neighborhood with loud, noisy behavior.

1.1—Taking bets on the numbers.

0.9—A youngster under 16 years old runs away from home.

0.8—Being drunk in public.

0.2—A youngster under 16 years old plays hooky from school.

Source: Center for Studies in Criminology and Criminal Law. University of Pennsylvania, Philadelphia, *The Seriousness of Crime: Results of a National Survey,* as reported in U.S. Department of Justice, *Report to the Nation on Crime and Justice* (Washington, D.C.: U.S. Government Printing Office, October, 1983), pp. 4–5.

sense of identity are strongly affected by the symbols inherent in society's reactions. Imagine the positive feelings experienced by Olympics gold medalists or those elected to Phi Beta Kappa, the national society honoring excellence in undergraduate study. Or consider the negative experience of being given the "silent treatment" such as that imposed on cadets who violate the honor code at the military academy at West Point. (To some this is so painful that they drop out.)

Sanctions often have important material qualities as well as symbolic meanings. Nobel Prize winners receive not only public acclaim but also a hefty check (now close to $200,000). The threat of loss of employment may accompany public disgrace when an individual's deviant behavior becomes known. In isolated, preliterate societies, social ostracism can be the equivalent of a death sentence.

Both positive and negative sanctions work only to the degree that people can be reasonably sure that they will be applied as a consequence of a given act. In other words, they work on people's expectations. Whenever such expectations are not met, sanctions lose their ability to mold social conformity.

On the other hand, it is important to recognize a crucial difference between positive and negative sanctions. When society applies a positive sanction, it is a sign that social controls are successful: The desired behavior has occurred and is being rewarded. When a negative sanction is applied, it is as a result of the failure of social controls: The undesired behavior has not been prevented. Therefore, a society that frequently must punish people is failing in its attempts to promote conformity. A school that must expel large groups of students or a government that must frequently call out troops to quell protests and

When Mary Lou Retton won the Olympics gold medal for women's gymnastics, the symbolic meaning of the formal positive sanction was far more important than the material value of the medal.

riots should begin to look for the weaknesses in its own system of internal means of social control to promote conformity.

Formal and Informal Sanctions   Some sanctions are applied in a public ritual, as in the awarding of a prize or an announcement of expulsion. Such responses to actions are called **formal sanctions** and usually are under the direct or indirect leadership of social authorities. Not all sanctions are formal, however. Many social responses to a person's behavior involve actions by group members that arise spontaneously with little or no formal lead-

formal sanctions Sanctions that are applied in a public ritual, usually under the direct or indirect leadership of social authorities. Examples: the award of a prize or the announcement of an expulsion.

ership. These responses are called **informal sanctions.** Gossip is an informal sanction that is used universally. Congratulations are offered to people whose behavior is being encouraged. In teenage peer groups, ridicule is a powerful, informal, negative sanction. In contemporary American society, informal sanctions influence us while we are in our own groups. The anonymity and impersonality of urban living, however, decreases the influence of these controls when we are outside the surveillance of members of our friendship and kinship groups. We usually are not under continuous observation by those on whom we are dependent for survival.

A Typology of Sanctions   Figure 9.2 shows the four main types of social sanctions, defined by combining the two sets of sanctions we have just discussed: informal and formal, positive, and negative. Although formal sanctions might appear to bc stronger influences on behavior, it is actually the informal sanctions that have a greater impact on people's self-images and future behavior. This is because informal sanctions usually occur more frequently and come from close, respected associates.

1. **Informal positive sanctions** are smiles, pats on the back, handshakes, congratulations, hugs, and all other actions through which

Informal positive sanctions include all actions through which individuals spontaneously express their approval of another's behavior.

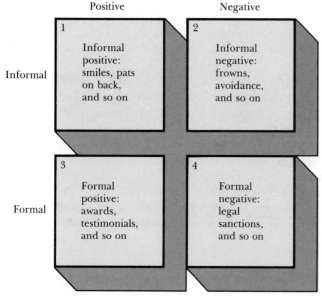

	Positive	Negative
Informal	1 Informal positive: smiles, pats on back, and so on	2 Informal negative: frowns, avoidance, and so on
Formal	3 Formal positive: awards, testimonials, and so on	4 Formal negative: legal sanctions, and so on

Figure 9.2 Types of Social Sanctions

individuals spontaneously express their approval of another's behavior.

2. **Informal negative sanctions** are spontaneous displays of disapproval or displeasure, such as frowns, damaging gossip, or impolite treatment directed toward the violator of a group norm.

3. **Formal positive sanctions** are public affairs, rituals, or ceremonies that express social approval of a person's behavior. These occasions are planned and organized. In our society they include such events as tickertape parades for national heroes, the presentation of awards or degrees, and public declarations of respect or appreciation (sports banquets, for example).

4. **Formal negative sanctions** are actions that express institutionalized disapproval of a person's behavior. They usually are applied within the context of a society's formal or-

ganizations—schools, corporations, the legal system, for example—and include expulsion, dismissal, fines, and imprisonment. They flow directly from decisions made by a person or agency of authority, and frequently there are specialized agencies or personnel (such as a board of directors, a government agency, or a police force) to enforce them.

All societies as well as formal organizations have ways of punishing and preventing deviant behavior. As you will see, however, sociologists must deal with the paradox that deviant behavior is a "normal" and necessary part of society.

□ The "Normality" of Deviant Behavior

Social life without the means of molding individuals' behavior and attitudes to conform to group values and norms is not imaginable. Indeed, all societies succeed in producing this conformity to a remarkable degree. It is astounding, really—especially in the enormous industrialized societies of the modern world—that so many millions of individuals manage to cooperate with one another and meet one another's expectations sufficiently to keep the society together and working. Nonetheless, as Emile Durkheim observed in *The Rules of Sociological Method*, deviant behavior is "an integral part of all healthy societies" (1958). Why is this? The answer, Durkheim suggested, is that in the presence of deviant behavior, a social group becomes united in its response. In other words, deviant behavior creates opportunities for groups to experience and enact their unity, a process that is necessary to promote the cooperation essential to the survival of any group. Durkheim described the response to a scandal in a small town, for example:

> [People] stop each other on the street, they visit each other, they seek to come together to talk of the event and to wax indignant in common. From all the similar impressions which are exchanged, from all the temper that gets itself expressed, there emerges a unique temper . . . which is everybody's without being anybody's in particular. That is the public temper. (1958)

When life is uneventful, people begin to take for granted one another and the meaning of their social interdependency. A deviant act, however, can reawaken group sentiment. Because it represents a threat to the moral order, a deviant act focuses people's attention on their value of the group; the process of responding to this threat heightens each person's sense of being a group member. It appears, as Kai T. Erikson (1966) found, that "unless the rhythm of group life is punctuated by occasional moments of deviant behavior . . . social organization . . . [is] impossible." For example, when a group of youngsters in New Haven, Connecticut, vandalized a monument to Holocaust victims, members of the Jewish community were drawn together by their condemnation of the act and worked together to see that repairs were made. Deviant behavior, then, performs important social functions in promoting group unity and reinforcing group structure and organization.

Deviance also offers society's members an opportunity to rededicate themselves to their social controls. Think of the consequences of the Watergate scandal in promoting rededication to democratic political ideals and a strong, comforting sense that despite its obvious flaws, the American political system really does work. In some cases, deviant behavior actually helps teach society's rules by provid-

informal sanctions Responses by a group's members to an individual's behavior that arise spontaneously with little or no formal leadership.

informal positive sanctions Spontaneous actions such as smiles, pats on the back, handshakes, congratulations, and hugs, through which individuals express their approval of another's behavior.

informal negative sanctions Spontaneous displays of disapproval of a person's behavior. Impolite treatment is directed toward the violator of a group norm.

formal positive sanctions Actions, such as public affairs, rituals, or ceremonies, that express social approval of a person's behavior.

formal negative sanctions Actions, such as expulsion, dismissal, or imprisonment, that express institutionalized disapproval of a person's behavior and are usually applied within the context of a society's formal organizations, including schools, corporations, and the legal system.

ing illustrations of violation. Knowing what is wrong is a step toward understanding what is right.

Deviance, then, may be functional to a group in that it (1) causes the group's members to close ranks, (2) prompts the group to organize in order to limit future deviant acts, (3) helps clarify for the group what it really does believe in, and (4) teaches normal behavior by providing examples of rule violation. Finally, in some situations, tolerance of deviant behavior acts as a safety valve and actually prevents more serious instances of nonconformity. For example, most public schools have eliminated dress codes, realizing that allowing teenagers to express feelings of rebellion through wearing nonestablishment clothing is preferable to a confrontation that could result in a major battle of wills.

Even though deviant behavior is seen as a "normal" ingredient in the makeup of society, scholars nevertheless inquire into its causes.

☐ Theories of Deviance

Because deviant behavior is so troublesome and because it is found everywhere, much effort has been devoted to understanding its roots. Three approaches to this problem have emerged: biological, psychological, and sociological.

Biological Explanations

Biological explanations of deviance generally are quite pessimistic. They trace deviant behavior primarily to inherited factors and downplay the importance of environmental influences. From this point of view, deviant individuals are born, not made.

Cesare Lombroso (1835–1901) was an Italian doctor who believed that too much emphasis was being put on "free will" as an explanation for deviant behavior. He spent much of his life studying and dissecting dead prisoners in Italy's jails and concluded that their criminality was associated with an animal-like body type that revealed an inherited "primitiveness" (Lombroso-Ferrero, 1972). He also believed that certain criminal types could be identified by their head size, facial char-

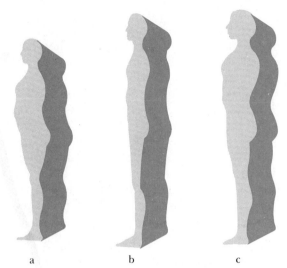

a   b   c

Figure 9.3 Sheldon's Body Types **William Sheldon identified three basic body types. (a) Endomorph: soft, round, and fat. (b) Ectomorph: skinny, fragile, and with a sensitive nervous system. (c) Mesomorph: muscular, agile, and physically strong. Sheldon believed mesomorphs were more inclined toward criminal behavior than the other two types, but subsequent research has cast considerable doubt on this conclusion.**

acteristics (size and shape of the nose, for instance), and even hair color. His writings were met with heated criticism from scholars who pointed out that perfectly normal-looking people have committed violent acts. (Modern social scientists would add that by confining his research to the study of prison inmates, Lombroso used a biased sample, thereby limiting the validity of his investigations.)

In this century William H. Sheldon, and his coworkers carried out body measurements of thousands of subjects to determine whether personality traits are associated with particular body types. They found that human shapes could be classified as three particular types (see Figure 9.3): *endomorphic* (round and soft), *ectomorphic* (thin and linear), and *mesomorphic* (ruggedly muscular) (Sheldon and Tucker, 1940). They also claimed that certain psychological orientations are associated with body type. They saw endomorphs as being relaxed creatures of comfort; ectomorphs as being inhibited, secretive, and restrained; and mesomorphs as being assertive, action oriented, and uncaring of others' feelings (Sheldon and Stevens, 1942).

Sheldon did not take a firm position on whether temperamental dispositions are inherited or are the outcome of society's responses to individuals based on their body types. For example, Americans expect heavy people to be good-natured and cheerful, skinny people to be timid, and strongly muscled people to be physically active and inclined toward aggressiveness. Anticipating such behaviors, people often encourage them. In a study of delinquent boys, Sheldon and his colleagues (1949) found that mesomorphs were more likely to become delinquents than were boys with other body types. Their explanation of this finding emphasized inherited factors, although they acknowledged social variables. The mesomorph is quick to anger and lacks the ectomorph's restraint, they claimed. Therefore, in situations of stress, the mesomorph is more likely to get into trouble, especially if the individual is both poor and not very smart. Sheldon's bias toward a mainly biological explanation of delinquency was strong enough for him to have proposed a eugenic program of selective breeding to weed out those types predisposed toward criminal behavior.

The biological basis for deviant behavior is still being investigated today. According to one of the latest theories, in some men the tendency for criminal behavior is genetically determined (McConnell, 1977; Reid, 1979). Other investigations, however, have yielded conflicting data and conclusions so that the question of biologically, or at least genetically, determined deviant behavior is still far from being resolved.

Psychological Explanations

Psychological explanations of deviance downplay biological factors and emphasize instead the role of parents and early childhood experiences in producing deviant behavior. Although such explanations stress environmental influences, there is a significant distinction between psychological and sociological explanations of deviance. Psychological orientations assume that the seeds of deviance are planted in childhood and that adult behavior is a manifestation of early experiences rather than an expression of ongoing social or cultural factors. The deviant individual therefore is viewed as a psychologically "sick" person who has experienced emotional deprivation or damage during childhood.

Psychoanalytic Theory Psychoanalytic explanations of deviance are based on the work of Sigmund Freud and his followers. Psychoanalytic theorists believe that the **unconscious**, the part of us consisting of irrational thoughts and feelings of which we are not aware, causes us to commit deviant acts.

According to Freud, our personality has three parts: the id, our irrational drives and instincts; the superego, our conscience and guide as internalized from our parents and other authority figures; and the ego, the balance among the impulsiveness of the id, the restrictions and demands of the superego, and the requirements of society. Because of the id, all of us have deviant tendencies, though through the socialization process we learn to control our behavior, and many of these tendencies are driven into the unconscious. In this way most of us are able to function effectively according to our society's norms and values. For some, however, the socialization process is not what it should be, and their internal equilibrium is not very resilient. As a result, the individual's behavior is not adequately controlled by either the ego or superego, and the wishes of the id take over. Consider, for example, a situation in which a man has been driving around congested city streets looking for a parking space. Finally he spots a car that is leaving and pulls up to wait for the space. Just as he is ready to park his car, another car whips in and takes the space. Most of us would react to the situation with anger. We might even roll down the car window and direct some angry gestures and strong language at the offending driver. There have been cases, however, in which the angry driver has pulled out a gun and shot the offender. Instead of sim-

unconscious The part of us that consists of irrational thoughts and feelings of which we are unaware and which causes us to commit deviant acts.

ply saying, "I'm so mad I could kill that guy," the offended party acted out the threat. Psychoanalytic theorists might hypothesize that in this case, the id's aggressive drive took over, because of an inadequately developed conscience.

Psychoanalytic approaches to deviance have been strongly criticized because the concepts are very abstract and cannot easily be tested. For one thing, the unconscious can be neither seen directly nor measured. Also there is an overemphasis on innate drives at the same time that there is an underemphasis on social and cultural factors that bring about deviant behavior.

◀ *Behavioral Theories* According to the behavioral view, people adjust and modify their behavior in response to the rewards and punishments their actions elicit. If we do something that leads to a favorable outcome, we are likely to repeat that action. If our behavior leads to unfavorable consequences, we are not eager to do the same thing again (Bandura, 1969). Those of us who live in a fairly traditional environment are likely to be rewarded for engaging in conformist behavior, such as working hard, dressing in a certain manner, or treating our friends in a certain way. We would receive negative sanctions if our friends found out that we had robbed a liquor store. For some people, however, the situation is reversed. That is, deviant behavior may elicit positive rewards. A 13-year-old who associates with a delinquent gang and is rewarded with praise for shoplifting, stealing, or vandalizing a school is being indoctrinated into a deviant lifestyle. The group may look with contempt at the "straight" kids who study hard, do not go out during the week, and make career plans. According to this approach, deviant behavior is learned by a series of trials and errors. One learns to be a thief in the same way that one learns to be a sociologist.

Sociological Explanations

Sociologists have been interested in the issue of deviant behavior since the pioneering efforts of Emile Durkheim in the late nineteenth century. Indeed, one of the major sociological approaches to understanding this problem derives directly from his work. It is called anomie theory.

Anomie Theory Durkheim published *The Division of Labor in Society* in 1893. In it he argues that deviant behavior can be understood only in relation to the specific moral code it violates: "We must not say that an action shocks the common conscience because it is criminal, but rather that it is criminal because it shocks the common conscience" (1960a).

Durkheim recognized that the common conscience, or moral code, has an extremely strong hold on the individual in small, isolated societies in which there are few social distinctions among people and everybody more or less performs the same tasks. Such mechanically integrated societies, he believed, are organized in terms of shared norms and values: All members are equally committed to the moral code (see Chapter 7). Therefore, deviant behavior that violates the code is felt by all members of the society to be a personal threat. As society becomes more complex—that is, as work is divided into more numerous and increasingly specialized tasks—social organization is maintained by the interdependence of individuals. In other words, as the division of labor becomes more specialized and differentiated, society becomes more organically integrated. It is held together less by moral consensus than by economic interdependence. A shared moral code continues to exist, of course, but it tends to be broader and less powerful in determining individual behavior. For example, political leaders among the Cheyenne Indians led their people by persuasion and by setting a moral example (Hoebel, 1960). In contrast with the Cheyenne, few modern Americans actually expect exemplary moral behavior from their leaders, despite the public rhetoric calling for it. Rather, political leadership is exercised through formal, institutionalized channels.

In highly complex, rapidly changing societies such as our own, some individuals come to feel that the moral consensus has weakened. Some persons lose their sense of belongingness, the feeling of participating in a meaningful social whole. For them values and norms have little impact: The culture no longer provides adequate guides for behavior. Such individuals feel disoriented, frightened, and alone. Durkheim used the term **anomie** to refer to this condition of "normlessness." He found that it was a major cause of suicide, as we discussed in Chapter 1. Robert Merton built on this concept and developed a general theory of deviance in American society.

Merton (1938, 1968) believes that American society pushes individuals toward deviance by overemphasizing the importance of monetary success while failing to emphasize the importance of using legitimate means to achieve that success. Those individuals who occupy favorable positions in the social-class structure have many legitimate means at their disposal to achieve success. However, those who occupy unfavorable positions lack such means. Thus the goal of financial success combined with the unequal access to important environmental resources creates deviance.

As you can see in Figure 9.4, Merton identified four types of deviance that emerge from this strain. Each type represents a mode of adaptation on the part of the deviant individual. That is, the form of deviance a person engages in depends greatly on the position she or he occupies in the social structure. Specifically, it depends on the availability to the individual of legitimate, institutionalized means for achieving success. Thus some individuals accept the culturally validated goal of success but find deviant ways of going about reaching it. Merton calls them **innovators.** Con artists, embezzlers, bank robbers, fraudulent advertisers, drug dealers, corporate criminals, crooked politicians, cops on the take—each is trying to "get ahead" using whatever means are available.

Ritualists are deviant in a very different way. Once they realize that they will never achieve a higher level of success, they deemphasize or reject the importance of making a lot of money. However, because they have a stable job with a predictable income, they remain within the labor force but refuse to take risks that might jeopardize their occupational security. Many ritualists are often tucked away in large institutions such as government bu-

Mode of adaption		Culture's goals	Institutionalized means
Conformists		Accept	Accept
Deviants	Innovators	Accept	Reject
	Ritualists	Reject	Accept
	Retreatists	Reject	Reject
	Rebels	Reject/Accept	Reject/Accept

Figure 9.4 Merton's Typology of Individual Modes of Adaptation: Conforming and Deviant Conformists accept both (a) the goals of the culture and (b) the institutionalized means of achieving them. Deviants reject either or both. Rebels are deviants who may reject the goals or the institutions of the current social order and seek to replace them with new ones that they would then embrace.

reaucracies. Here they "cross each *t*" and "dot each *i*," following and enforcing rules more precisely (and mindlessly) than ever was intended. Their deviance is in giving up the belief in being able to move beyond their present level of attainment.

Another group of people also lacks the means to attain success but does not have the institutional security of the ritualists. These **retreatists** pull back from society altogether. They are the drug and alcohol addicts who can no longer function—the hobos, panhandlers, and so-called street people who live on the fringes of society and who have ceased to pursue culturally legitimate goals.

anomie The feeling of some individuals that their culture no longer provides adequate guidelines for behavior; a condition of "normlessness" in which values and norms have little impact.

innovators Individuals who accept the culturally validated goal of success but find deviant ways of reaching it.

ritualists Individuals who deemphasize or reject the importance of success once they realize they will never achieve a higher level of monetary success.

retreatists Individuals such as drug addicts, alcoholics, hobos, and panhandlers who have pulled back from society altogether and who do not pursue culturally legitimate goals through the culturally legitimate means of society's institutions.

TABLE 9.2   Sutherland's Principles of Differential Association

1. Deviant behavior is learned.
2. Deviant behavior is learned in interaction with other persons in a process of communication.
3. The principal part of the learning of criminal behavior occurs within intimate personal groups.
4. When deviant behavior is learned, the learning includes (a) techniques of committing the act, which are sometimes very complicated or sometimes very simple, and (b) the specific direction of motives, drives, rationalizations, and attitudes.
5. The specific direction of motives and drives is learned from definitions of the legal codes as favorable or unfavorable. That is, a person learns reasons for both obeying and violating rules.
6. A person becomes deviant because of an excess of definitions favorable to violating the law over definitions unfavorable to violating the law.
7. Differential associations may vary in frequency, duration, priority, and intensity.
8. The process of learning criminal behavior by association with criminal and anticriminal patterns involves all the mechanisms used in any other learning.
9. Although criminal behavior is an expression of general needs and values, it is not explained by those general needs and values, because noncriminal behavior is an expression of the same needs and values.

Source: Adapted from Edwin H. Sutherland and Donald R. Cressey. *Criminology,* 10th ed. (Philadelphia: Lippincott, 1978), pp. 80–82.

Finally, there are the **rebels.** They reject both the goals of what to them is an unfair social order and the institutionalized means of achieving them. Rebels seek to tear down the old social order and build a new one with goals and institutions that they can support.

Merton's theory has become quite influential among sociologists. It is useful because it emphasizes external causes of deviant behavior that are within the power of society to correct. The theory's weakness is its inability to account for the presence of certain kinds of deviance that occur among all social strata and within almost all social groups in American society: for example, juvenile alcoholism and drug dependence and family violence (spouse beating and child abuse). Another approach, called cultural transmission theory, has provided some insight into such behavior.

Cultural Transmission Theory   This theory relies strongly on the concept of learning, growing out of the work of Clifford Shaw and Henry McKay, who received their training at the University of Chicago. They became interested in the patterning of delinquent behavior in that city, when they observed that Chicago's high-crime areas remained the same over the decades—even though the ethnic groups living in those areas changed. Further, they found that as members of an ethnic group moved out of the high-crime areas, the rate of juvenile delinquency in that group fell; at the same time the delinquency rate for the newly arriving ethnic group rose. Shaw and McKay (1931, 1942) discovered that delinquent behavior was taught to newcomers in the context of juvenile peer groups. And because such behavior occurred, on the whole, only in the context of peer-group activities, youngsters gave up their deviant ways when their families left the high-crime areas.

Edwin H. Sutherland and his student Donald R. Cressey (1978) built a more general theory of juvenile delinquency on the foundation laid by Shaw and McKay. It is called the **theory of differential association,** and its central notion is that criminal behavior is learned in the context of intimate groups (see Table 9.2). When criminal behavior is learned, it includes two components: (1) criminal techniques (such as how to break into houses) and (2) criminal attitudes (that is, rationalizations that justify criminal behavior). In this context, people who become criminals are thought to do so when they associate with the rationalizations for breaking the law more than with the arguments for obeying the law. They acquire these attitudes through long-standing interactions with others who hold these views. Thus, in the gang culture of inner-city neighborhoods, status is often based on criminal activity. Even arrests and imprisonment are events worthy of respect. A youngster exposed to and immersed in such a value system will associate with it, if only in order to survive.

In many respects, differential association theory is quite similar to the behavioral theory we discussed earlier. Both emphasize the learning or socialization aspect of deviance. Both also point out that deviant behavior emerges in the same way that conformist behavior emerges; it is merely the result of different experiences and different associations.

Labeling Theory **Labeling theory** shifts the focus of attention from the deviant individual to the social process by which a person comes to be labeled as deviant and the consequences of such labeling for the individual. This view emerged in the 1950s from the writings of Edwin Lemert (1972). Since then many other sociologists have elaborated on the labeling approach.

Labeling theorists note that although we all break rules from time to time, we do not necessarily think of ourselves as deviant—nor are we so labeled by others. However, some individuals, through a series of circumstances, do come to be defined as deviant by others in society. Paradoxically, this labeling process actually helps bring about more of the deviant behavior.

Being caught and branded as deviant has important consequences for one's further social participation and self-image. The most important consequence is a drastic change in the individual's public identity. Committing an improper act and being publicly caught at it places the individual in a new status, and he or she may be revealed to be a different kind of person than they formerly were thought to be. Such people may be labeled as thieves, drug addicts, lunatics, or embezzlers and treated accordingly.

To be labeled as a criminal, one need commit only a single criminal offense, and that is all the term refers to. Yet the word carries a number of connotations of other traits characteristic of anyone bearing the label. A man who has been convicted of breaking into a house and thereby labeled as a criminal is presumed to be a person likely to break into other houses. Police operate on this premise and round up known offenders for investigation after a crime has been committed. In addition, it is assumed that such an individual is likely to commit other kinds of crimes as well, because he or she has been shown to be a person without "respect for the law." Therefore, apprehension for one deviant act increases the likelihood that that person will be regarded as deviant or undesirable in other respects.

Even if no one else discovers the deviance or enforces the rules against it, the individual wh has committed it acts as an enforcer. Such individuals may brand themselves as deviant because of what they did and punish themselves in one way or another for the behavior (Becker, 1963).

There appear to be at least three factors that determine whether a person's behavior will set in motion the process by which he or she will be labeled as deviant: (1) the importance of the norms that are violated, (2) the social identity of the individual who violates them, and (3) the social context of the behavior in question. Let us examine these more closely.

1. *The importance of the violated norms.* As we noted in Chapter 3, not all norms are equally important to the people who hold them. The most strongly held norms are mores, and their violation is likely to cause, in short order, the culprit to be labeled deviant. The physical assault of elderly persons is an example. For less strongly held norms, however, much more nonconformity is tolerated, even if the behavior is illegal. For example, running red lights is both illegal and

rebels Individuals who reject both the goals of what to them is an unfair social order and the institutionalized means of achieving them and who propose alternative societal goals and institutions.

theory of differential association A theory of juvenile delinquency based on the position that criminal behavior is learned in the context of intimate groups. People who become criminals do so as a result of associating with the values of others who engage in criminal activities.

labeling theory A theory of deviance based on the position that the social process by which individuals come to be labeled as deviant contributes to causing more of the deviant behavior.

potentially very dangerous, but in some American cities it has become so commonplace that even the police are likely to "look the other way" rather than pursue violators.

2. *The social identity of the individual.* A rich person or an entertainment "personality" caught shoplifting or even using narcotics has a fair chance of being treated indulgently as an "eccentric" and let off with a lecture by the local chief of police. A poor person or a member of a racial or ethnic minority group is much more likely to feel the heavy hand of the law and face criminal charges. In all societies there are those whose wealth or power (or even force of personality) enable them to ward off being labeled deviant despite behavior that violates local values and norms. Such individuals are buffered against public judgment and even legal sanction. Conversely, there are those marginal or powerless individuals and groups, such as welfare recipients or the chronically unemployed, toward whom society has a "hair-trigger" response, with little tolerance for nonconformity. Such people quickly are labeled deviant when an opportunity presents itself.

3. *The social context.* The social context within which an action takes place also is important. In a certain situation an action might be considered deviant, whereas in another context it will not. Notice that we say social context, not physical location. The nature of the social context can change even when the physical location remains the same. For example, for most of the year the New Orleans police manage to control open displays of sexual behavior, even in the famous French Quarter. However, during the week of Mardi Gras, throngs of people freely engage in what at other times of the year would be called lewd and indecent behavior. During Mardi Gras the social context invokes norms for evaluating behavior that do not so quickly lead to the assignment of a deviant label.

Labeling theory has led sociologists to distinguish between primary and secondary deviance. **Primary deviance** is the original behavior that leads to the application of the label to an individual. **Secondary deviance** is the behavior that people develop as a result of having been labeled as deviant (Lemert, 1972).

For example, a teenager who has experimented with illegal drugs for the first time and is arrested for it may be labeled as a drug addict and face ostracism by peers, family, and school authorities. Such negative treatment may cause this person to turn more frequently to using illegal drugs and to associating with other drug users and pushers, resorting to robberies and muggings to get enough money to buy the drugs. Thus the primary deviant behavior and the labeling resulting from it lead the teenager to slip into an even more deviant lifestyle. This new lifestyle would be an example of secondary deviance.

Labeling theory has proved to be quite useful. It explains why society will label certain individuals deviant but not others, even when their behavior is similar. There are, however, several drawbacks to labeling theory. For one thing, it really does not explain primary deviance. That is, even though we may understand how labeling may produce future, or secondary, acts of deviance, we do not know why the original, or primary, act of deviance took place. In this respect, labeling theory explains only part of the deviance process. Another problem is that labeling theory ignores the instances when the labeling process may deter a person from engaging in future acts of deviance. It looks at the deviant as a misunderstood individual who really would like to be an accepted, law-abiding citizen. Clearly, this is an overly optimistic view.

It would be unrealistic to expect any single approach to explain deviant behavior fully. In all likelihood some combination of the various theories discussed is necessary to gain a fuller understanding of the emergence and continuation of deviant behavior.

☐ Crime and Punishment in America

Crime is behavior that violates a society's criminal code. In the United States what is criminal is specified in written law, primarily state statutes. Federal, state, and local jurisdictions often vary in their definitions of crimes, though they seldom disagree in their definitions of serious crimes. (See Table 9.3

FOCUS ON RESEARCH
Protecting Yourself During a Violent Crime

Most violent victimizations do not result in serious injury. Yet certain types of responses seem to be more often associated with serious injury than others do. The following discussion looks at the relationship between the type of crime, the kind of response by the victim, and the likelihood of serious injury.

Robbery victims are the least likely to try to talk themselves out of being victimized, and the most likely to do nothing when compared to victims of a variety of violent crimes. On the other hand rape victims are more likely to use force, try a verbal response, or attract attention, and less likely to do nothing than victims of other violent crimes.

Information gathered from the 1973 and 1979 National Crime Survey noted that using physical force, trying to attract attention, and doing nothing to protect oneself, resulted in the highest proportions of seriously injured victims (16%, 14%, and 12% respectively). On the other hand, those who tried to talk themselves out of their predicament, or took nonviolent evasive action were less likely to incur serious injury (both 6%).

The National Crime Survey provided no information on the sequence of events in a crime incident. Thus, the relatively high relationship between no self-protective response with injury may reflect either passive victims presenting no obstacles to injury, or victims who are injured at the start of an incident and who are reluctant to risk further harm by acting in any other way. Consequently, the data do not always indicate the probability of subsequent injury resulting from various self-protective strategies, but they do suggest that some actions may be more dangerous than others.

The pattern of serious injury associated with a variety of self-protective measures was consistent for all NCS-measured violent crimes except robbery and simple assault. Victims of these crimes were less likely than victims of other violent crimes to be injured seriously if they did nothing to protect themselves. This finding is important, since each type of violent crime tends to provoke different responses by victims. For example, rape victims are particularly likely to use physical force to repel rapists. This may be an automatic reaction to being grabbed, or it may be a deliberate act intended to be self-protective. In either case, the NCS data indicate that a victim who uses physical force against an offender runs a relatively high risk of injury.

These results further suggest that normal responses to different types of violent crimes may not be helpful in avoiding injury. Rape victims took those actions more likely to be tied to injury more frequently than did assault victims. In fact, violent crime victims as a group tended to take the self-defensive actions that were more, rather than less, closely related to serious injury.

Each incident of violent crime has unique features that may affect how victims are able to protect themselves, but the NCS data suggest that the responses of physical force, attracting attention, or deliberate inaction are related to a higher likelihood of injury. Nonviolent evasive action or trying to talk yourself out of the predicament appears to be the safest response to a violent crime.

Source: U.S. Department of Justice, *Report to the Nation on Crime and Justice* (Washington, D.C.: U.S. Government Printing Office, October 1983), p. 23. □

for the characteristics of the most common serious crimes.)

A distinction is often made between violent crimes and property crimes. A violent crime is an unlawful event such as homicide, rape, and assault that may result in injury to a person. Robbery is also a violent crime because it involves the use or threat of force against the person (see Focus on Research: "Protecting Yourself During a Violent Crime").

A property crime is an unlawful act that is committed with the intent of gaining property but that does not involve the use or threat of force against an individual. Larceny, burglary, and motor vehicle theft are examples of property crimes.

Criminal offenses are also classified according to how they are handled by the criminal justice system. In this respect most jurisdictions recognize two classes of offenses:

primary deviance A term used in labeling theory to describe the original behavior that leads to an individual being labeled as deviant.

secondary deviance A term used in labeling theory to describe the behavior that people develop as a result of having been labeled as deviant.

crime Behavior that violates society's criminal laws.

TABLE 9.3 Characteristics of the Most Common Serious Crimes

Crime	Definition	Facts
Homicide	Causing the death of another person without legal justification or excuse.	Homicide is the least frequent violent crime. 93% of the victims were slain in single-victim situations. At least 55% of the murderers were relatives or acquaintances of the victim. 24% of all murders occurred or were suspected to have occurred as the result of some felonious activity.
Rape	Unlawful sexual intercourse with a person, by force or without legal or factual consent.	Most rapes involved a lone offender and a lone victim. About 36% of the rapes were committed in the victim's home. 58% of the rapes occurred at night, between 6 p.m. and 6 a.m.
Robbery	Unlawful taking or attempted taking of property that is in the immediate possession of another, by force or threat of force.	Robbery is the violent crime that typically involves more than one offender (in about half of all cases). Slightly less than half of all robberies involved the use of a weapon. Less than 2% of the robberies reported to the police were bank robberies.
Assault	Unlawful intentional inflicting, or attempted inflicting, of injury upon the person of another. *Aggravated assault* is the unlawful intentional inflicting of serious bodily injury or unlawful threat or attempt to inflict bodily injury or death by means of a deadly or dangerous weapon with or without actual infliction of injury. *Simple assault* is the unlawful intentional inflicting of less than serious bodily injury without a deadly or dangerous weapon or an attempt or threat to inflict bodily injury without a deadly or dangerous weapon.	Simple assault occurs more frequently than aggravated assault. Assault is the most common type of violent crime.
Burglary	Unlawful entry of any fixed structure, vehicle, or vessel used for regular residence, industry, or business, with or without force, with the intent to commit a felony or larceny.	42% of all household burglaries occurred without *forced* entry. In the burglary of more than 3 million American households, the offenders entered through an unlocked window or door or used a key (for example, a key "hidden" under a doormat). About 34% of the no-force household burglaries were known to have occurred between 6 a.m. and 6 p.m. Residential property was targeted in 67% of reported burglaries, nonresidential property accounted for the remaining 33%. Three-quarters of the nonresidential burglaries for which the time of occurrence was known took place at night.
Larceny (theft)	Unlawful taking or attempted taking of property other than a motor vehicle from the possession of another, by stealth, without force and without deceit, with intent to permanently deprive the owner of the property.	Pocket picking and purse snatching most frequently occur inside nonresidential buildings or on street locations. Unlike most other crimes, pocket picking and purse snatching affect the elderly as much as other age groups. Most personal larcenies with contact occur during the daytime, but most household larcenies occur at night

TABLE 9.3 *(continued)*

Crime	Definition	Facts
Motor vehicle theft	Unlawful taking or attempted taking of a self-propelled road vehicle owned by another, with the intent of depriving the owner of it permanently or temporarily.	Motor vehicle theft is relatively well reported to the police because reporting is required for insurance claims and vehicles are more likely than other stolen property to be recovered. About three-fifths of all motor vehicle thefts occurred at night.
Arson	Intentional damaging or destruction or attempted damaging or destruction by means of fire or explosion of the property without the consent of the owner, or of one's own property or that of another by fire or explosives with or without the intent to defraud.	Single family residences were the most frequent targets of arson. More than 17% of all structures where arson occurred were not in use.

Source: Bureau of Justice Statistics, *Dictionary of Criminal Justice Data Terminology, 1981; FBI Uniform Crime Reports, 1981;* Bureau of Justice Statistics, *National Crime Survey, 1981;* as reported in *Report to the Nation on Crime and Justice* (Washington, D.C.: Government Printing Office, 1983).

felonies and misdemeanors. Felonies are not distinguished from misdemeanors in the same way in all areas, but most states define felonies as offenses punishable by a year or more in a state prison. Although the same act may be classified as a felony in one jurisdiction and as a misdemeanor in another, the most serious crimes are never misdemeanors, and the most minor offenses are never felonies.

It is important not to confuse a society's moral code with its legal code. Some legal theorists have argued that the legal code is an expression of the moral code, but this is not necessarily the case. For example, most American towns have laws against jaywalking, but it is not an offense against morals. Conversely, it is possible to violate American "moral" sensibilities without breaking the law.

What, then, is the legal code? The **legal code** consists of the formal rules, called **laws,** adopted by a society's political authority. The code is enforced through the use of formal negative sanctions when rules are broken. Ideally, laws are passed to promote conformity to those rules of conduct that the authority believes are necessary for the society to function and that will not be followed if left solely to people's internal controls or the use of informal sanctions. Occasionally, laws are passed to benefit or protect specific interest groups with political power, rather than society at large (Quinney, 1974).

Uniform Crime Reports

It is very difficult to know with any certainty how many crimes are committed in America each year. In its yearly *Uniform Crime Reports* the FBI compiles statistics turned in by police departments from across the nation. But sociologists and critics in other fields note that for a variety of reasons, these statistics are not always reliable. For example, each police department compiles its own figures, and so definitions of the same crime vary from place to place.

Not all criminal activity can be analyzed, because the FBI's national statistics exist only for certain categories of crime. For example, not included are federal offenses—political corruption, tax evasion, bribery, and violation of environmental-protection laws, for example—or organized crime. Also, although some so-called white-collar crimes (those generally committed by more affluent citizens, such as embezzlement by a banker) are included in the *UCR*, they are not part of the list of serious crimes or the Crime Index and ordinarily are not used in computing overall crime trends and statistics. These crimes are far from

legal code The formal body of rules adopted by a society's political authority.

laws Formal rules adopted by a society's political authority.

trivial, however. The United States Justice Department investigated the major American oil companies for relabeling "old" oil long in storage as "new" oil produced after price deregulation. The relabeling process—clearly illegal—may well have cost American customers more than $1 billion as of 1980.

Other factors affect the accuracy of the crime figures and rates published in the *Reports*—for example, a law-enforcement agency or a local government may change its method of reporting crimes, so that the new statistics reflect a false increase or decrease in the occurrence of certain crimes. These changes may even be deliberate: the government or agency may want to stress its achievements or gain some other benefit (Reid, 1979).

National Crime Survey

In order to learn more about crimes and the victims of crime, in 1973 the *National Crime Survey* began to measure crimes not reported to the police as well as those that are reported. Except for homicide (which is well reported in police statistics) and arson (which is difficult to measure using survey techniques), the *National Crime Survey* measures the same crimes as does the *Uniform Crime Reports*. However, the method of gathering the data is different. Whereas the *Uniform Crime Reports* depends on police departments' records of reported crimes, the *National Crime Survey* periodically attempts to assess the total number of crimes committed. This is done by asking a national sample of 60,000 households, representing 135,000 people over the age of 12, about their experiences as victims of crime during a specified period of time. The 1981 survey noted that personal crimes of theft were less likely to be reported than were violent crimes (27 percent versus 47 percent); that males are less likely to report violent crimes than are females (44 percent versus 52 percent); and that younger victims are less likely to report crimes than are older victims. For an example of the reporting rates for a variety of crimes, see Table 9.4.

The *Uniform Crime Reports* and the *National Crime Survey* produce different results because they serve different purposes and are based on different sources of information. The

TABLE 9.4   Percentages of Selected Crimes Reported to the Police

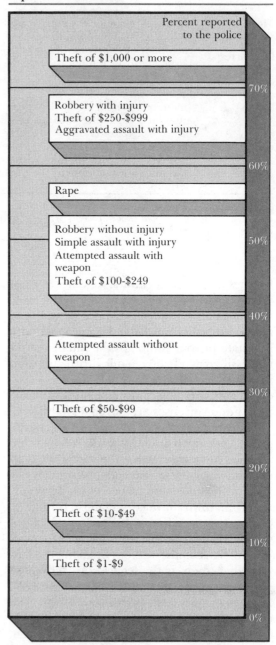

Source: Bureau of Justice Statistics, *National Crime Survey, 1984* (Washington, D.C.: Government Printing Office, 1985).

UCR counts only crimes coming to the attention of the police, whereas the NCS obtains information on both reported and unreported crimes. The UCR counts crimes committed against individuals, businesses, and

TABLE 9.5 Arrests for Serious Crimes by Age, 1982

			Percent					
Charge	Total all ages	Male	Under 18	18–24	25–44	45–54	55–64	65+
Total arrests	10,287,000	83.4	16.8	34.1	39.9	5.5	2.7	.9
Serious crimes	2,151,000	79.9	30.4	32.6	30.9	3.4	1.8	.9
Murder and nonnegligent manslaughter	18,000	86.7	7.4	34.0	48.1	6.3	2.9	1.3
Forcible rape	30,000	99.0	14.5	35.1	44.2	4.0	1.7	.5
Robbery	134,000	92.6	26.3	41.7	30.1	1.4	.4	.1
Aggravated Assault	261,000	86.5	12.9	31.9	46.0	5.7	2.5	.9
Burglary	416,000	93.2	14.3	38.3	22.9	1.2	.4	.1
Larceny-theft	1,169,000	70.	32.3	29.8	30.3	4.0	2.3	1.3
Motor vehicle theft	106,000	91.1	34.6	37.4	25.5	1.8	.6	.2
Arson	17,000	87.8	37.5	24.4	31.3	4.4	1.7	.5

Source: U.S. Department of Commerce, Bureau of the Census, Statistical Abstract of the United States, 1985 (Washington, D.C.: Government Printing Office, 1984), p. 173.

government agencies as well as any other victims. The *NCS* counts only crimes committed against persons over 12 within a household. The two surveys may also, in some instances, count crimes differently. For example, a situation in which a criminal robs a victim and steals someone else's car for the getaway will be recorded in the *UCR* as a robbery, the more serious crime, but it may be recorded in the *NCS* as two crimes.

Each survey is subject to the kinds of errors and problems typical to its method of data collection. Despite their respective drawbacks, they both are valuable sources of data on nationwide crime.

Kinds of Crime in America
It should be obvious that the crime committed can vary considerably in terms of the impact it has on the victim and on the self-definition of the perpetrator of the crime. White-collar crime is as different from street crime as organized crime is from juvenile crime. In the next section we shall examine these differences.

Juvenile Crime **Juvenile crime** refers to the breaking of criminal laws by individuals under the age of 18. Regardless of the specific statistics' reliability, one thing is clear: Serious crime among our nation's youth is a matter of great concern. The arrest records for 1981

show that youths under age 18 were more likely to be picked up for property crimes than were older persons (36 percent versus 14 percent). Arrests, however, are only a general indicator of criminal activity. The greater number of arrests among young people may be due partly to their lack of experience in committing crimes and partly to their involvement in the types of crimes for which apprehension is more likely, for example, purse snatching versus fraud. In addition, because youths often commit crimes in groups, the resolution of a single crime may lead to several arrests. (See Table 9.5 for arrest rates by age.)

Indeed, the major differences between juvenile and adult offenders are the importance of gang membership and the tendency of youths to engage in group criminal activities. Gang members are more likely than are other young criminals to engage in violent crimes, particularly robbery, rape, assault, and weapons violations.

Serious juvenile offenders are predominantly male, are disproportionately minority group members—compared with their proportion in the population—and are typically disadvantaged economically. They are likely

juvenile crime The breaking of criminal laws by individuals under the age of 18.

USING SOCIOLOGY
The Best-Laid Schemes: Diversion— the Concept and the Reality

Ten years after he had proposed the use of diversion in juvenile justice, Edwin M. Lemert looked back with dismay at what had happened to his original concept. What had looked good in theory had become distorted in application.

Diversion is a process in which individuals who have been involved in delinquent acts and would normally be dealt with by police or court action are instead handled by other community agencies. In the area of juvenile justice, diversion would achieve several ends; it would avoid the labeling of young people as juvenile delinquents, help overcome the clogging of juvenile courts with a backlog of minor cases, keep young people in the community and out of detention, and encourage community involvement in and responsibility for dealing with youthful offenders. The goals that Professor Lemert wished to attain through the use of diversion are more than justified when these four situations are considered in depth.

Once labeled a youthful offender, a young person may have difficulty living down this "record." The community may view and react to a youth so labeled only as a juvenile delinquent. With diversion, a youth can be helped without being branded with a negative label.

At least half the cases finally brought before juvenile courts are dismissed. Many others result in only minor charges and the release of the offender. Diversion would keep many of these cases out of the courts, allowing the courts to concentrate on the more serious cases.

A third justification for diversion is that any period of detention for a young person can mean valuable time out of school, time that may be lost forever, forcing the youth to drop back a year in school or even

to drop out. This sacrifice is especially painful when it results from a prehearing detention. Charges may be dropped by the court, but the youth's life has already been disrupted. Diversion avoids this problem by keeping the youth in the community.

And finally, by encouraging the community to be actively involved in helping youthful offenders, diversion compels the community to recognize its responsibilities for conditions leading to youthful revolt and to recognize that much youthful revolt is not deviance but normal behavior, a "storm and stress" stage that youths pass through on the way to maturing into reasonably law-abiding citizens.

All too quickly, Lemert's concept of diversion went wide of its mark in application. Police and probation departments saw diversion as their responsibility. In many areas, police set up their own in-house diversion programs and hired their own personnel. Instead of responsibility shifting to the community, it only shifted from the courts to the police, keeping the handling of youthful offenders within a law-enforcement framework. Even where cases were referred to community agencies, the police retained, or even increased, their control. These supposedly independent agencies were dependent on the police for their referrals and hence for the justification of their programs and their funding.

The result was more, not fewer, youths under police control. Many youths, especially younger ones, who otherwise would have been released because of lack of evidence or because the act was a status offense— one that would not be considered a crime if committed by an adult— were now instead referred to police-

controlled diversion programs. Such referrals, at least in appearance, labeled them as youthful offenders— the opposite of what Lemert had hoped would result from this interpretation of diversion.

In many communities, youths referred to diversion programs by the police had to express "contrition"—they had to show they were sorry—under the stern warning that otherwise they would be referred to the courts. They had to report weekly and keep records of all their activities—very much as if they were under official probation, which can only come after a court hearing. Under such diversion programs, the rights of young people were more readily abused than could occur under normal court action.

According to Lemert, not only have the purposes of diversion been perverted, but police power has been extended over youths and types of behavior not previously subjected to control. The police never should have become involved in diversion. Police should be concerned with social control, not rehabilitation for which they are neither trained nor professionally inclined. The way to make diversion work is to take it out of the hands of the police and the juvenile court system. Lay boards must be set up to screen youthful offenders either for police and court action where the offense merits such attention or for truly independent community help agencies that are able to deal with offenders more in need of community guidance than of social control.

Source: Edwin M. Lemert, "Diversion in Juvenile Justice: What Hath Been Wrought," *Journal of Research in Crime and Delinquency* **18** (1) (January, 1981), pp. 34–46. □

to exhibit interpersonal difficulties and behavioral problems both in school and on the job. They are also likely to come from one-parent families or families with a high degree of conflict, instability, and inadequate supervision.

There is conflicting evidence on whether juveniles tend to progress from less to more serious crimes. The evidence suggests that violent adult offenders began their careers with violent juvenile crimes; thus they began as and remained serious offenders. However, minor offenses of youths are often dealt with informally and may not be recorded in crime statistics (U.S. Dept. of Justice, 1983).

The juvenile courts—traditionally meant to treat, not punish—have had limited success in coping with such juvenile offenders (Reid, 1979). Defenders of the juvenile courts contend, nonetheless, that there would be even more juvenile crime without them. Others, arguing from learning and labeling perspectives, charge that the system has such a negative impact on children that it actually encourages **recidivism,** that is, repeated criminal behavior after punishment (Paulsen, 1967). All who are concerned with this issue agree

that the juvenile courts are less than efficient. One reason for this is that perhaps two-thirds of juvenile court time is devoted to processing children guilty of what are called **status offenses,** behavior that is criminal only because the person involved is a minor (examples are truancy and running away from home). Recognizing that status offenders clog the courts and add greatly to the terrible overcrowding of juvenile detention homes, the Connecticut General Assembly passed a bill in 1979 to deinstitutionalize status offenders. It created instead a new legal category called "family with service needs" and thereby routed such children away from the justice system and into the social service network. This example of **diversion**—steering youthful offenders away from the juvenile justice system to nonofficial social agencies—may help overcome the pessimism of those who developed the concept, notably Edwin M. Lemert. In Using Sociology: "The Best Laid Schemes: Diversion—the Concept and the Reality," Lemert explains how his ideas of the goals of diversion have been distorted and misused in actual practice, particularly by police systems.

Street Crime   **Street crime** consists of crimes committed in public. It includes crimes against persons and against property. Although the incidence of street crime is high, the bulk of such crime is committed by a relatively small number of chronic offenders. For example, Marvin Wolfgang and his colleagues (1972) followed the activities of 10,000 boys in Philadelphia over a period of years. Of this group, 35 percent were arrested before their eighteenth birthday. But of these, 56 percent accounted for 84 percent of all offenses; 46 percent committed only one offense, and of these 75 percent were status offenses. Only 10 of the 1,613 boys who committed just one offense were guilty of a serious crime.

Shoplifting by an individual under 18 is considered a juvenile crime and is dealt with differently than if it is committed by someone over 18.

recidivism Repeated criminal behavior after punishment.

status offenses Behaviors, such as truancy and running away from home, that are criminal only because the individuals involved are minors.

diversion Steering youthful offenders away from the juvenile justice system to nonofficial social agencies.

street crime Crimes committed in public.

The bulk of urban street crime is committed by a relatively small number of chronic offenders.

Street criminals tend to be young and male. Of those arrested for serious street crimes reported by the FBI in 1982, almost 31 percent were 18 or under, and 80 percent were males (see Table 9.5).

Whereas by far the majority of violent crimes used to occur among people who knew one another—in families, among relatives and social acquaintances—violence committed against strangers has risen in the last few years. This has added greatly to a growing "terror of the night," because people feel that violence may strike them anonymously and unpredictably.

American cities are by far the most dangerous anywhere. For example, there are more murders in any one of the cities of New York, Detroit, Los Angeles, or Chicago each year than in all of England and Wales combined. In 1960 there were 390 murders in New York City; in 1970 there were 1,117; and in 1980 there were 1,787. The increase becomes even more dramatic when we realize that the population of that city declined by one million people between 1970 and 1980 (U.S. Dept. of Commerce, 1984).

White-Collar Crime The term **white-collar crime** was coined by Edwin H. Sutherland (1940) to refer to individuals who, while occupying positions of social responsibility or high prestige, break the law in the course of their work, for the purpose of illegal personal or organizational gain. Another term often used to refer to what typically are nonviolent crimes by "respectable" individuals is *upper-world crime*. White-collar crimes include such illegalities as embezzlement, bribery, fraud, theft of services, kickback schemes, and others in which the violator's position of trust, power, or influence has provided the opportunity to use lawful institutions for unlawful purposes. White-collar offenses frequently involve deception.

It is difficult to know the extent of white-collar crime because so much of it goes unreported. White-collar criminals often have the social "clout" to minimize their chances of being punished and labeled.

The annual cost of white-collar crime in America alone is staggering. The federal government pegs it at $40 billion, but other estimates run as high as $100 billion. Estimates for specific categories of white-collar crime include bribery, $3 billion; insurance fraud, $10 billion; consumer embezzlement, $3 billion; and fraud, $20 billion (Bequai, 1977). In all probability, white-collar crime costs Americans more than do all other crimes put together (Sutherland, 1961).

White-collar crime, although not as visible as street crime, is nevertheless a problem of major proportions. Not only is it very expensive, it is a threat to the fabric of society. Sutherland (1961) has argued that because white-collar crimes involve a violation of public trust, they contribute to a disintegration of social morale and threaten the social structure. This problem is compounded by the fact that in the few cases in which white-collar criminals actually are prosecuted and convicted, punishment usually is relatively light (Reid, 1979).

New forms of white-collar crime involving political and corporate institutions have emerged in the past decade. For example, the dramatic growth in high technology has brought with it sensational accounts of computerized "heists" by sophisticated criminals seated safely behind computer terminals. The possibility of electronic crime has spurred widespread interest in computer security, by business and government alike.

Organized Crime **Organized crime** refers to structured associations of individuals or groups who come together for the purpose of obtaining gain mostly from illegal activities. Organized crime groups possess some of the following characteristics:

They conduct their activities in a methodical, systematic, or highly disciplined and secret fashion.

In at least some of their activities they commit or threaten to commit acts of violence or other acts that are likely to intimidate.

They insulate their leadership from direct involvement in illegal activities by their intricate organizational structure.

They attempt to gain influence in government, politics, and commerce through corruption, graft, and legitimate means (U.S. Dept. of Justice, 1983).

Organized crime has its roots in the decaying neighborhood of ethnic minorities. It is organized nationally through a "governing structure of 24 "families" or "syndicates' dominated by men of Sicilian descent (Cressey, 1969). Figure 9.5 shows the organizational structure of a typical organized crime family.

Organized crime makes most of its money through providing illegal goods and services. It was Prohibition that gave it the ability to organize nationwide, because for the first time there was a uniform national demand for illegal goods: alcoholic beverages. Today organized crime profits from illegal activities that include illegal gambling, the smuggling and sale of illicit drugs, the production and distribution of pornography, prostitution, and loan sharking. In order to be able to account for and spend their wealth, the families of organized crime have bought controlling interests in innumerable "legitimate" businesses

in which their funds can be "laundered" and additional, legitimate profits can be made (Wickman, Whitten, and Levey, 1980). For example, profits from an illegal gambling operation can show up on the books of a legitimate, cash-oriented business such as a restaurant or vending-machine enterprise.

Virtually all major figures in organized crime insist they are nothing but business people. Al Capone, the head of Chicago's organized crime syndicate in the 1920s, protested vigorously when newspapers called him a racketeer. "I call myself a businessman," he explained. "I make my money by supplying a public demand. If I break the law, my customers, who number hundreds of the best people in Chicago, are as guilty as I am. The only difference is that I sell and they buy" (Silberman, 1978). Although Capone's logic clearly was self-serving, his observation is accurate: Organized crime exists only because it is supported actively and tolerated passively by most Americans. Without customers, organized crime would die.

Victims of Crime

We have been discussing crime statistics, the types of crimes committed, and who commits them. But what about the victims of crime? Is there a pattern? Are some people more apt to become crime victims than others are? It seems that this is true; victims of crime are not spread evenly across society. Although as we have seen, the available crime data are not always reliable, a pattern of victimization can be seen in the reported statistics. A person's race, sex, age, and socioeconomic status have a great deal to do with whether that individual will become a victim of a serious crime.

Statistics show that overall, males are much more likely to be victims of serious crimes than females are. When we look at crimes of violence and theft separately, however, a more complex picture emerges. Victims of crime are

white-collar crime Crimes committed by individuals who, while occupying positions of social responsibility or high prestige, break the law in the course of their work.

organized crime Structured associations of individuals or groups who come together for the purpose of obtaining gain mostly from illegal activities.

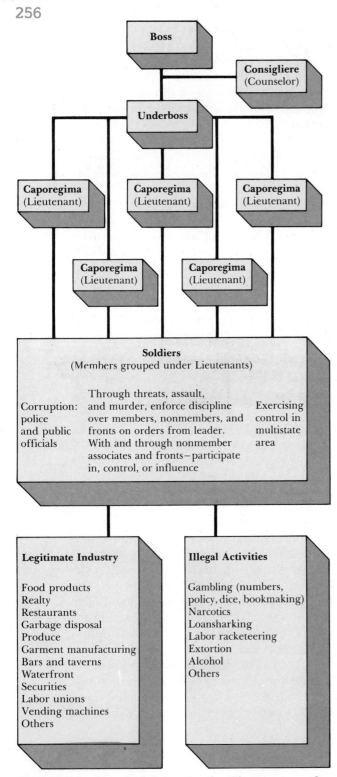

Figure 9.5 An Organized Crime Family   The structure of a "successful" crime syndicate is often that of an efficient business hierarchy.

more often men than women. Younger people are much more likely than the elderly are to be victims of crime. Blacks are more likely to be victims of violent crime than are whites or members of other racial groups. People with low incomes have the highest violent-crime victimization rates. Theft rates are the highest for people with low incomes (less than $3,000 per year) and for those with high incomes (more than $25,000 per year). Students and the unemployed are more likely than are housewives, retirees, or the employed to be victims of crime. Rural residents are less often crime victims than are people living in cities (U.S. Dept. of Justice, 1983).

Despite the growing and well-founded concern about crimes against the elderly, figures show that it is young people between the ages of 16 and 24 who are most likely to be victims of serious crimes and that this rate decreases steadily with age.

As if to underscore that official figures and trends are not the final word on the subject of crime, a marketing and communications professor conducted a study that showed that some people, regardless of their race, sex, age, or socioeconomic status, unconsciously project nonverbal cues that invite criminal assault (see Popular Sociology: "Don't Walk Like a Victim"). The study dealt with people's responses, not just statistics, and the data were collected from "crime experts"—convicted muggers.

Victimless Crime

Usually we think of crimes as involving culprits and victims—that is, individuals who suffer some loss or injury as a result of a criminal act. But there are a number of crimes that do not produce victims in any obvious way, and so some scholars have coined the term *victimless crime* to refer to them.

Basically, **victimless crimes** are acts that violate those laws meant to enforce the moral code. Usually they involve the use of narcotics, illegal gambling, public drunkenness, the sale of sexual services, or status offenses by minors. If heroin addicts can support their illegal addiction legitimately, then who is the victim? If prostitutes provide sexual gratification for a fee, who is the victim? If a person

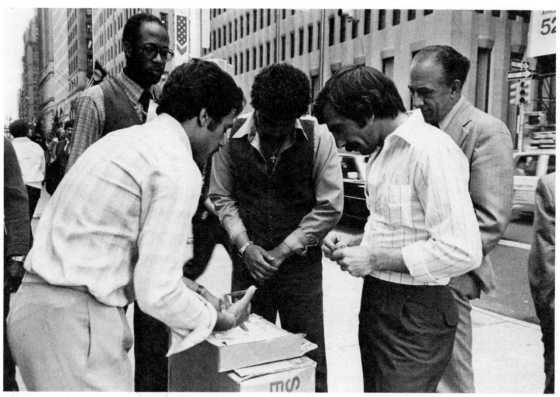

Illegal gambling is often referred to as a victimless crime. That is, it violates laws meant to enforce the moral code. In this photo we have an example of a con game—three card monte—as well as illegal gambling.

bets $10 or $20 per week with the local bookmaker, who is the victim? If someone staggers drunk through the streets, who is the victim? If a teenager runs away from home because conditions there are intolerable, who is the victim?

Some legal scholars argue that the perpetrators themselves are victims: Their behavior damages their own lives. This is, of course, a value judgment, but then the concept of deviance depends on the existence of values and norms (Schur and Bedau, 1974). Others note that such offenses against the public order do in fact contribute to the creation of victims, if only indirectly: Heroin addicts rarely can hold jobs and eventually are forced to steal to support themselves; prostitutes are used to blackmail people and to rob them; chronic gamblers impoverish themselves and bring ruin on their families; drunks drive and get into accidents and may be violent at home; and so on.

Clearly the problems raised by the existence of victimless crimes are complex. In recent years American society has begun to recognize that at least some crimes truly are victimless and that they should therefore be decriminalized. Two major activities that have been decriminalized in many states and municipalities are the smoking of marijuana (though not its sale) and sex between unmarried, consenting adults of the same gender.

Criminal Justice in America
Every society that has established a legal code has also set up a **criminal justice system—**

victimless crimes Acts that violate those laws meant to enforce the moral code, usually involving narcotics, illegal gambling, public drunkenness, the sale of sexual services, or status offenses by minors.

criminal justice system Personnel and procedures for arrest, trial, and punishment to deal with violations of the law.

POPULAR SOCIOLOGY
Don't Walk Like a Victim

Sometimes a large city newspaper will pick up and report at some length a study that relates to the citizens of the city, as was the case with the following excerpt from a feature article in the Boston Globe *on victims of muggings.*

It's not your age.

It's not your sex.

It's not even the mere fact of walking alone in a high-crime area that appears to make some people more "muggable" than others. It's the way you walk that sends out easy-to-assault cues to potential assailants.

Hofstra University marketing and communications professor Betty Grayson became intrigued with the fact the some police officers and many imprisoned criminals seemed able to tell at a glance which potential victims would offer the least resistance to attack. Were the cops and muggers just using some kind of intuition? Or were there specific behavioral cues—which no one seemed able to specify—to which they were responding?

Grayson began her study by using a fixed, hidden videotape camera to take frontal shots as people walked along the street. She kept the camera on each subject for about 7 seconds, the length of time, she figured, that it would take for a mugger to size up a victim.

She and three assistants sorted the subjects into four categories of 20 people each: young women (under 35), young men (under 35), older women (over 45), and older men (over 45). Armed with videotapes, Grayson then set about finding imprisoned criminals who could help her create a scale of "muggability"—or as she puts it, likelihood of assault.

Grayson first showed the tapes to about 60 inmates who were told to say whatever they felt in response to each subject. She audiotaped their responses and listed the main reactions on the blackboard. She then asked the inmates to rank their responses in order, which turned out to be

1. Most assaultable, a very easy rip-off.
2. An easy dude to con.
3. You could take that one out.
4. Looks like a fairly easy hit.
5. You could stand a problem.
6. Could give you a little static.
7. Would be a problem, could give you a hard time.
8. A hard dude to knock off, wouldn't mess with him.
9. Would be heavy, would give you a hard time.
10. Would avoid it, too big a situation, too heavy.

With this 1-to-10 "muggability" scale, Grayson then asked a second group of 53 prisoners—all convicted of violent assaults on strangers—to rate the 60 videotaped subjects on their potential "muggability."

Whenever more than half the prisoners agreed that a potential victim fell into the first three, most-easy-to-mug categories, Grayson put that videotape into a special category, which ultimately contained 20 people, male and female, young and old.

With the help of Jody Zacharias, executive director and on the staff of the Laban Institute of Movement Studies, Grayson analyzed the way these 20 people walked, searching for cues that could account for the prisoners' assessment of them as "easy marks."

The researchers used a movement-analysis technique created by an Austro-Hungarian dancer-choreographer, Rudolf Laban, born in 1879. In recent years many dancers, physical therapists, and behavioral scientists have been using Laban's notation system as a precise, nonverbal way of writing down symbols to represent tiny fragments of movement.

Upon analysis, the 20 most muggable people turned out to have a number of distinctive movements, five of which, Grayson says, were apparently crucial in signaling vulnerability. Although Grayson says she does not like to place value judgments on the muggable people's style of walking—even to say that perhaps the sum of their body signals indicates they may appear to walk off balance—she says that the nonverbal ways in which a person presents himself or herself to the world are crucial.

Specifically, the most muggable people tended to take strides that were of unusual length, either too short or too long. Instead of walking heel to toe, they walk flatfooted. Instead of swinging their left arm while striding with their right foot, they moved their left arm and left foot, then right arm and right foot together. Instead of the usual figure 8-like sway of upper body and lower body, the most muggable people seemed to move their torsos at cross purposes to the bottom half of their bodies.

And instead of moving "posturally" (letting the movement start from within the body core), potential victims seemed to move "gesturally" (moving one part of the body, an arm for instance, as though the movement started outside the body). Indeed, the most muggable people seemed to walk as though they were less in touch with their bodies.

"These movements were highly significant," says Grayson. "They overrode (the variables of) sex and age. I would like to replicate this study on a bigger scale because it appears that nonverbal communication, body language, and other ways you communicate without words, are probably more important than anything else you do. It's not age or sex which communicates something, it's the way you handle your age, or your sex. It's how you present yourself to the world."

Grayson believes that the "muggability" cues are probably both sent by potential victims and received by potential assailants partly or totally unconsciously. Nevertheless, she says, by isolating the movements that seem to trigger "muggability," people, especially victims of multiple assaults, may be taught to move without signaling vulnerability.

Source: Adapted from Judy Foreman, "How to Tell If You Are 'Muggable,'" *Boston Globe* (January 20, 1981). □

---

personnel and procedures for arrest, trial, and punishment—to deal with violations of the law. The relative effectiveness of such a system has a major impact on the incidence of deviant behavior, and especially crime, in a society.

Many scholars agree that the American system of criminal justice is in serious trouble. Crime rates continue to rise; jails are crowded to the roofbeams; and convicts who return to the streets quickly revert to their criminal ways.

The "Funnel" Effect   One complaint voiced by many of those concerned with our criminal justice system is that although many crimes are committed, few people ever seem to be punished. The **funnel effect** begins with the fact that of all the crimes committed, only about 50 percent are reported to the police, and only about 26 percent lead to an arrest. Next, false arrests, lack of evidence, and plea bargaining (negotiations in which individuals arrested for a crime are allowed to plead guilty to a lesser charge of the crime, thereby saving the criminal justice system the time and money spent in a trial) reduce the number of complaints that actually are brought to trial to 6 percent. In the end, only about 1 percent is sent to prison (Humphrey and Milakovich, 1981).

Ernest van den Haag and others contend from such figures that crime goes unchecked because street-wise criminals know that their chance of being caught and punished is very small indeed; therefore punishment has lost its force as a negative sanction.

[In New York City] police and city officials have tacitly agreed to allow certain kinds of criminal behavior to go on without harassment or punishment. The authorities have enlarged the scope of unchallenged criminal behavior to include not only quality-of-life offenses such as aggressive panhandling, smoking in the subway, drunkenness, brawling, urinating on sidewalks and in the subways, but also certain muggings, burglaries, narcotics transactions, purse snatchings, car thefts, and larcenies.

There is neither the manpower nor the courtroom space available for police to make the kinds of disorderly-conduct arrests they routinely made in the past. If outraged citizens complain strenuously enough, a patrolman will try to move the violators along or issue a summons. These summonses are not really supposed to be a deterrent to the offender so much as a pacifier for the angry citizen. [In 1980] transit cops issued 100,000 summonses for smoking on trains, urinating on platforms, beating the fare, loud radio playing, drunkenness, brawling, and other antisocial acts. Eight out of ten of those violators who were served never even bothered to show up in court—nor were they pursued by the police. (Pileggi, 1981)

To be fair, the situation is not quite as bad as it appears. In regard to serious crimes, the number of arrests is considerably more than it is for crimes in general. For example, of the following crimes reported to the police, the percentages that were cleared by an arrest were (U.S. Dept. of Justice, 1983):

Murder	72%
Aggravated assault	58%
Forcible rape	48%
Robbery	24%

funnel effect The condition in our criminal justice system in which few people are punished for the crimes they commit: Of all the serious crimes reported, only 26 percent lead to arrest; only 6 percent of arrested individuals actually come to trial; and only about 1 percent serves time in prison.

CASE STUDY
Women in Prison

Separate women's prisons did not exist until late in the nineteenth century. Before that, men, women, and children occupied the same dungeons, almshouses, and jails. The following describes the evolution of separate facilities for men and women.

In recent years the number of women in prison has increased dramatically. This situation is a reflection of changing women's roles as well as changes in the courts' attitude toward sending women to prison.

As prison reform began in this country, the practice was to segregate women into sections of the existing institutions. There were few women inmates, a fact that was used to "justify" not providing them with a matron. Vocational training and educational programs were not even considered. In 1873 the first separate prison for women, the Indiana Women's Prison, was opened, with its emphasis on rehabilitation, obedience, and religious education. Other institutions followed thereafter. Separate institutions for women continued to be the usual pattern of incarceration for women until the first modern coed prison was established in this country in 1971. Gradually other states built facilities for women, but even today only slightly over one-half of the states have separate facilities. Some states contract with other states to incarcerate their female offenders; others have sections set aside in men's prisons.

Most women's prisons were originally located in rural areas or small towns. In some cases, towns have grown up around them so that many are now at least fairly close to additional facilities and resources. Still, many women offenders are in prisons quite a distance removed from family and friends and are not accessible by public transportation.

In contrast with institutions for adult males, institutions for adult women are generally more aesthetic and less secure. Women inmates are usually not considered high security risks, nor have they proved to be as violent as male inmates are. There are some exceptions, but on the whole women's institutions are built and

maintained with the view that their occupants are not great risks to themselves or to others.

Women inmates also usually have more privacy than men do while incarcerated, and they usually have individual rooms. With the relatively smaller number of women in prison, there is a greater opportunity for the inmates to have contact with the staff, and there is also a greater chance for innovation in programming.

Correctional institutions for women traditionally, and to a great extent even today, reflect the expected role that women will play in society. In the late nineteenth century, when reformers advocated separate institutions for women, the emphasis was on reformatories, not prisons, and in those institutions women were to learn the behaviors appropriate to their role in society. They lived in cottages that were like "homes," not in large institutional-type structures characteristic of prisons for men.

Female, as compared with male,

inmates appear to have greater difficulty adjusting to the absence of their families, especially to the absence of their children. According to one study, the majority of female offenders have dependent children living at home at the time of their incarceration. In those cases, only 10 percent had husbands who made arrangements for child care. For 85 percent of the women, their families took care of the children. The average number of children per inmate mother was 2.48. It was estimated that in 1979 there were 21,000 children in this country who had mothers in prison.

Some provisions have been made to increase female offenders' contacts with their children. The Bedford Hills Correctional Facilities in New York actually provides a nursery for inmate mothers, who are allowed to keep their babies for up to one year. In California and Mississippi, women inmates are allowed family visits overnight; New York allows women to stay with their families up to 30 hours during private visits, which take place in trailers.

In 1981 there was a 15-percent increase in the number of women in state and federal prisons, an increase greater than that for males. Between 1970 and 1981 the number of females in prison rose by more than 150 percent, whereas that for men increased by 78 percent. Yet because the number of women in prison is so much smaller than the number of men, the women's share of the prison population remained at 4 percent.

Men commit more crimes and are arrested for more serious crimes than women are. Women are more likely to commit property crimes such as larceny, forgery, fraud, and embezzlement, and drug offenses. They are less likely to be involved in robbery or burglary.

Source: Adapted from Sue Titus Reid, *The Correctional System* (New York: Holt, Rinehart and Winston, 1981), pp. 289–297; and U.S. Department of Justice, *Report to the Nation on Crime and Justice* (Washington, D.C.: Government Printing Office, 1983), p. 35. □

Larceny-theft	19%
Burglary	14%
Motor Vehicle theft	14%

But what about punishment? Those who criticize the system in terms of its "funnel" effect seem to regard only a term in prison as an effective punishment. Yet the usual practice is to send to prison only those criminals whose terms of confinement are set at over one year. The number of American prisoners, after declining through the 1960s, rose sharply through the 1970s (see Figure 9.6). Many thousands of other criminals receive shorter sentences and serve them in municipal and county jails (see Case Study: "Women in Prison"). Thus, if the number of people sent to local jails as well as to prison are counted, the funnel effect is less severe than it often is portrayed. The question then becomes one of philosophy: Is a jail term of less than one year an adequate measure for the deterrence of crime? Or should all convicted criminals have to serve longer sentences in federal or state prisons, with jails used primarily for pretrial detention? We do not propose to answer that question here, but sociologists are concerned with the study of prisons in regard to their intended goals as well as their latent functions.

Prisons **Prisons** are institutions run by federal or state governments for detaining convicted criminals. They are intended to accomplish at least four goals: (1) separation of criminals from society, (2) punishment of criminal behavior, (3) deterrence of criminal behavior, and (4) rehabilitation of criminals.

1. *Separation of criminals from society.* Prisons accomplish this purpose once convicted felons reach the prison gates. Inasmuch as it is important to protect society from individuals who seem bent on repeating destructive behavior, prisons are one logical choice among several others, such as exile and capital punishment (execution). The American criminal justice system relies principally on prisons to segregate convicts from society, and in this regard they are quite efficient.

2. *Punishment of criminal behavior.* There can be no doubt that prisons are extremely unpleasant places in which to spend time. They are crowded, degrading, boring, and dangerous. Not infrequently prisoners are victims of one another's violence. Inmates also are constantly supervised, sometimes harassed by guards, and deprived of normal means of social, emotional, intellectual, and sexual expression. Prison undoubtedly is a severe form of punishment.

3. *Deterrence of criminal behavior.* The rising crime figures cited earlier suggest that prisons have failed to achieve the goal of deterring criminal behavior. There are some good reasons for this. First, by their very nature, prisons are closed to the public. Few people know much about prison life, nor do they often think about it. Inmates who return to society frequently brag to their peers about their prison experiences in order to recover their self-esteem. To use the prison experience as a deterrent, the very unpleasant as-

prisons Institutions run by federal or state governments for detaining convicted criminals.

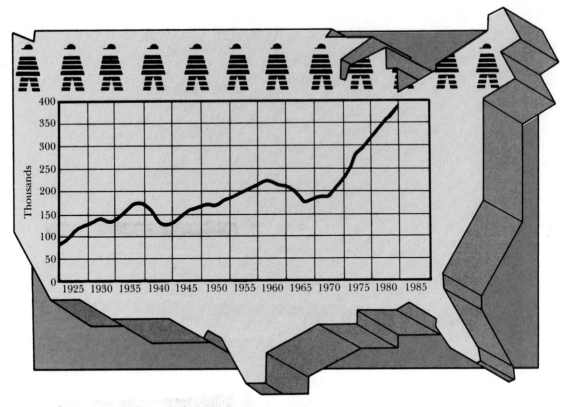

Figure 9.6 Total Population of State and Federal Prisons in the United States, 1925–1982

pects of prison life would have to be constantly brought to the attention of the population at large. To promote this approach, some prisons have allowed inmates to develop programs introducing high school students to the horrors of prison life. From the scanty evidence available to date, it is unclear whether such programs really deter people from committing crimes. Another reason that prisons fail to deter crime is the funnel effect we described earlier. No punishment can deter undesired behavior if the likelihood of being punished is minimal. Thus the argument regarding the relative merit of different types of punishment is pointless until there is a high probability that whatever forms are used will be applied to all (or most) offenders.

4. *Rehabilitation of criminals.* Many Americans believe that **rehabilitation**—the resocialization of criminals to conform to society's values and norms and the teaching of usable

work habits and skills—should be prisons' most important goal. It is also the stated goal of almost all corrections officials. Yet there can be no doubt that prisons do not come close to achieving this aim. According to the FBI, about 70 percent of all inmates released from prison are arrested again for criminal behavior (Reid, 1979).

Sociological theory provides ample explanations for this fact. For example, Sutherland's ideas on cultural transmission and differential association point to the fact that inside prisons, the society of inmates has a culture of its own, in which obeying the law is not highly valued. New inmates are quickly socialized to this peer culture and adopt its negative attitudes toward the law. Further, labeling theory tells us that once somebody has been designated as deviant, his or her subsequent behavior often conforms to that label. Prison inmates who are released find it difficult to be accepted in the society at large

Prisons often deprive individuals of normal social contact. Here two inmates have found a way to interact within the confines of a penal environment.

and to find legitimate work. Hence former inmates quickly take up with their old acquaintances, many of whom are active criminals. It thus becomes only a matter of time before they are once more engaged in criminal activities.

This does not mean that prisons should be torn down and all prisoners set free. As we have indicated, prisons do accomplish important goals, though certain changes are needed. Certainly it is clear that the entire criminal justice system needs to be made more efficient and that prison terms as well as other forms of punishment must follow predictably the commission of a crime. Another idea, which gained some approval in the late 1960s but seems of late to have declined in popularity, is to create "halfway" houses and other institutions in which the inmate population is not so completely locked away from society. This way, they are less likely to be socialized to the prison's criminal subculture. Labeling theory suggests that if the process of delabeling former prisoners were made open, for-

mal, and explicit, released inmates might find it easier to win reentry into society. Finally, just as new prisoners are quickly socialized into a prison's inmate culture, released prisoners must be resocialized into society's culture. This can be accomplished only if means are found to bring ex-inmates into frequent, supportive, and structured contact with stable members of the wider society (again, perhaps, through halfway houses). The simple separation of prisoners from society undermines this goal.

To date, no society has been able to come up with an ideal way of confronting, accommodating, or preventing deviant behavior. Although much attention has been focused on the causes of and remedies for deviant behavior, no theory, law, or social-control mechanism has yet provided a fully satisfying solution to the problem.

rehabilitation The resocialization of criminals to conform to society's values and norms and the teaching of **usable work habits and skills.**

□ Summary

A culture's norms and values make up its moral code. Thus normal behavior is that conforming to the rules or norms of the group in which it occurs. Deviant behavior, on the other hand, is that failing to conform to those rules or norms.

The processes through which societies and groups influence their members' behavior are called mechanisms of social control. Internal and external means of control, positive and negative sanctions, and formal and informal sanctions are the specific means through which social control operates.

Emile Durkheim maintained that deviant behavior is a necessary part of a healthy society. This is so because deviance can cause a group's members to close ranks, prompt a group to organize to prevent future deviant acts, help the group clarify its goals, and teach normal behavior by providing examples of violation.

A number of scholars have proposed theories to account for the occurrence of deviant behavior in society. Biological theories are based on the relationship of body type or genetic factors to deviance. Psychological theories include a psychoanalytic approach and a behavioral approach. Sociological explanations of deviance include the anomie theory of Durkheim and Merton, cultural transmission theory, and labeling theory.

Crime is behavior that violates a society's criminal code. In its yearly *Uniform Crime Reports,* the FBI compiles statistics on the amount of crime in the United States, based on police reports. In order to learn more about crime and the victims of crime, the *National Crime Survey* measures both reported and unreported crimes.

Crime takes a variety of different forms. Juvenile crime refers to the breaking of criminal laws by individuals under the age of 18. Street crime consists of crimes committed in public. White-collar crime is committed by people who while occupying positions of social responsibility or high prestige break the law in the course of their work, for illegal personal or organizational gain. Organized crime refers to structured associations of individuals or groups who come together for the purpose of obtaining gain, mostly from illegal activities.

The characteristics of crime victims, who are often neglected in statistics and reports, show a definite pattern regarding age, sex, race, and socioeconomic status. Some states have recognized that victimless crimes such as smoking marijuana and consenting homosexuality should be decriminalized.

The American criminal justice system is seen as having created a funnel effect in which few people seem to be punished. Prisons, too, are viewed as having failed to attain all their goals. They succeed in the separation of criminals from society and the punishment of criminal behavior, but they fail in the deterrence of criminal behavior and the rehabilitation of criminals.

□ For Further Reading

BECKER, HOWARD S. *Outsiders: Studies in the Sociology of Deviance.* New York: Free Press, 1963. A simply and clearly written introduction to the labeling theory of deviance. The extensive use of case materials makes for entertaining as well as informative reading.

ERIKSON, KAI T. *Wayward Puritans: A Study in the Sociology of Deviance.* New York: John Wiley, 1966. An elegant study of three "crime waves" that washed over seventeenth-century Puritan society, analyzed from the point of view of labeling theory. An engagingly written, interesting, and thoughtful work.

FERRELL, RONALD A., and VICTORIA L. SWIGERT. *Deviance and Social Control.* Glenview, Ill.: Scott, Foresman, 1982. An examination of classical and contemporary approaches to deviance and social control.

GOFFMAN, ERVING. *Asylums.* Garden City, N.Y.: Doubleday, 1961. A classic study of the social situation of mental patients and other inmates of total institutions. It is clearly written, provocative, and challenging. The author views institutions from the "inside" and looks out at the "normal" society that builds them.

LOWNEY, JEREMIAH, ROBERT W. WINSLOW, and VIRGINIA WINSLOW. *Deviant Reality: Alternative World Views.* 2d ed. Boston: Allyn & Bacon, 1981. A series of readings in which firsthand accounts are given of deviant behavior.

POLSKY, NED. *Hustlers, Beats, and Others.* Chicago: Aldine, 1967. A collection of lively essays describing the author's fieldwork among the marginal citizens of our society. Although the book is primarily descriptive, it uses sociological theory with clarity and rigor.

RUBINGTON, EARL, and MARTIN S. WEINBERG. *Deviance: The Interactionist Perspective.* 4th ed. New York: Macmillan, 1981. A collection of readings that examines deviance from the interactionist perspective.

SILBERMAN, CHARLES E. *Criminal Violence, Criminal Justice.* New York: Random House, 1978. An extended meditation on our system of criminal justice: the police, the courts, and prisons. A wealth of information is presented with freshness of thought. The book raises many difficult questions and provides many reasonable answers.

TRAUB, SCOTT H., and CRAIG B. LITTLE (eds.). *Theories of Deviance.* 2d ed. Itasca, Ill.: F. E. Peacock, 1980. This book studies the major theoretical perspectives on deviance, including functionalism, social disorganization, cultural conflict, anomie, differential association, and labeling theories.

Social Inequality

■　　■　　■　　■　　■　　■　　■　　■

Part Four

10

Social Stratification

The subject of class in the United States is a touchy one, indeed. As Americans, we like to think we live in a classless society. After all, we do not have inherited ranks, titles, or honors. We do not have coats of arms or rigid caste rankings. Besides, equality among men—and women—is an ideal guaranteed by our Constitution and summoned forth regularly in speeches from podiums and lecterns across the land.

But are we all really equal, or are some people "more equal than others"? In his book *Inequality in an Age of Decline* (1980), Paul Blumberg went so far as to call the idea of class "America's forbidden thought." Although many people are reluctant to talk about it, there are class distinctions in America based on race, education, family name, career choice, or wealth. These remain despite legislation, free public education, and political idealism.

Up to this point we have been looking at social interaction—how people function in social units. In this chapter we shall examine how, after people come together, differences among them begin to appear. This is the phenomenon of social stratification. Our emphasis is on the occurrence and impact of social stratification on the social organization of the United States. We shall not pass judgment, but we shall explore a variety of theories and criticisms in order to provide a basis for judgment for the reader.

☐ The Nature of Social Stratification

Before we try to analyze social stratification, we should first find out what it includes. Social differentiation, evaluation, and inequality are the major ingredients of stratification.

Social Differentiation and Social Evaluation

The concept of **social differentiation** is fairly universal. It consists of shared perceptions of variation among individuals, social positions, or groups (Vanfossen, 1979). This observation of differences is not always accompanied by qualitative judgment, however. For example, a 5-year-old child is seen as being different from an infant but is not necessarily viewed as being superior because of the age difference.

When qualitative judgments are made on the basis of individual characteristics or behaviors, the process is referred to as **social evaluation.** Although a society may not value a 5-year-old more highly than an infant, it might place a value on old people. Compare, for example, the attitude of respect for the elderly in Japan with the attitude toward senior citizens in the United States. Values placed on physical characteristics and personality habits also vary from one society to another. For example, among Europeans and Americans, body hair on adult males is considered to be "manly" and acceptable, but it is seen by the Japanese as "ugly." Americans promote competitiveness and individualism; the !Kung San of the Kalahari Desert in southern Africa value cooperativeness and modesty (Lee, 1980). Individuals who have characteristics favored by their culture have an advantage over those who do not. It is easier for them to win respect and prestige, to make friends, to find a mate, and to achieve positions of leadership. In all societies there are some people who are favored, who have more pres-

The elderly receive greater respect in Japanese society than in North American society. This is an example of social evaluation in which qualitative judgments are made about selected groups of people.

Apartheid in South Africa results in social inequality. These individuals are boarding a segregated vehicle in Johannesburg.

tige, and who are admired; and there are others who are avoided and looked down on. In addition all groups—even hunters and food gatherers, the most equal-minded of societies—make distinctions on the basis of age and sex (see Chapter 8).

Social Inequality

The outcome of social evaluation is **social inequality,** which is the uneven distribution of privileges, material rewards, opportunities, power, prestige, and influence among individuals or groups. When social inequality becomes part of the social structure and is transmitted from one generation to the next, **social stratification** exists.

Dividing a society into ranks, grades, or positions, social stratification is perpetuated by the major institutions of society such as the economy, the family, religion, and education. For example, consider the situation in South Africa. The whites, numbering only 4.3 million, rule a country that has some 18 million blacks and a little over 3 million people of mixed ancestry and Asian origins. The whites have ruled South Africa for over three hundred years, and they own almost all of its land and industry. Though white South Africans enjoy one of the highest standards of

living in the world, most blacks there live in poverty. This situation is brought about and perpetuated by a government policy known as *apartheid,* which refers to the biological, territorial, social, educational, economic, and political separation of the various racial groups that make up the country. Yet even here in America, where no such formal policy exists, we have stratification based on wealth. The wealthy have greater access to better education, medical care, and jobs, and these advantages perpetuate their privileged position in our society.

social differentiation The shared perceptions of variation among individuals, social positions, or groups, which is not always accompanied by qualitative judgments.

social evaluation The process of making qualitative judgments of individuals, social positions, or groups on the basis of individual characteristics or behaviors.

social inequality The uneven distribution, as a result of social evaluation, of privileges, material rewards, opportunities, power, prestige, and influence among individuals or groups.

social stratification A condition that exists when social inequality becomes part of the social structure and is transmitted from one generation to the next. Social stratification divides a society into ranks, grades, or positions and is perpetuated by society's major institutions.

Social Mobility

Social mobility is the movement of an individual or a group within a stratification system that changes the individual's or group's status in society. The degree of social mobility in different societies varies. An **open society** attempts to provide equal opportunity to everyone to compete for the role and status desired, regardless of race, religion, gender, or family history. In a **closed society** the various aspects of people's lives are determined at birth and then remain fixed. There are no purely open or completely closed societies. Even the most democratic societies make a practice of assigning some roles and statuses, and even the most closed societies have a certain amount of mobility. For example, in the United States, an open society, blacks and women continue to struggle against job discrimination. On the other hand, even in a closed society, such as the estate system of medieval Europe, a wealthy merchant whose social position was low could buy his way into the nobility and consolidate his family's new social status by marrying his children off to landed aristocracy.

Mobility may come about because of changing one's occupation, marrying into a certain family, and so on. Movement that involves a change in status (see Chapter 5) with no corresponding change in social class is known as **horizontal mobility.** A lawyer who decides to become a physician has moved horizontally in the social hierarchy—the change in career involves little or no change in prestige, power, or wealth, hence no change in class.

When the movement is up or down in the hierarchy, resulting in a change in social class, **vertical mobility** has occurred. A bank president who makes poor investments may be fired, losing both personal wealth and prestige and becoming downwardly mobile. Not only individuals but also statuses themselves move up and down in the American social hierarchy.

Vertical mobility can operate intragenerationally—social changes during the lifetime of one individual—or intergenerationally—changes in the social level of a family through two or more generations. The example of the bank president represents downward **intragenerational mobility,** whereas a family in which the parents are laborers who manage to send their children through college to become professionals—editors, stockbrokers, engineers, or the like—has accomplished upward **intergenerational mobility.**

Usually a person's social rank in the stratification hierarchy is consistent and comparatively easy to identify. However, many people do not fit neatly into one social category—their situations are examples of **status inconsistency.** A person whose great wealth is known or suspected to have been acquired illegally will not be accepted into a high social rank. In the United States a black physician, despite the high prestige of the profession, may also be denied a higher social position because of race.

Factors Affecting Social Mobility In the United States many people believe that if individuals work hard enough they can become upwardly mobile—that is, they will become part of the next higher social class. In fact there are several other factors that affect social mobility. For example, there may be social structural factors that may either help or hinder social mobility. During periods of economic expansion the number of professional and technical jobs increases. These white-collar jobs can often be filled by upwardly mobile members of other classes. When the supply of jobs increases, one group can no longer determine who will get all the jobs. Consequently people from lower social classes who have the necessary talent and skills are able to fill some of the positions without having any inside connections. During periods of economic contraction, however, the opposite is true. Getting a job depends on factors that go beyond talent or experience, such as family ties or personal friendships.

Societies also differ in terms of how much they encourage social mobility. The values and norms of American society encourage upward mobility. In fact, Americans are expected to try to succeed and better their status in life. We often look with contempt at those

India's caste system is an example of a rigid form of stratification based on religious beliefs.

who have no desire to move up the social-class ladder or, worse yet, are downwardly mobile.

What is it that produces mobility? Level of education appears to be an extremely important factor. As would be expected, the greater is the level of education attained by the children, the stronger will be the probability of their upward movement. It can even be claimed that the impact of education on occupational status is greater than that of father's occupational status. It is difficult to separate these two factors, however, because the father's occupation often has an impact on the amount of education received by his children.

The degree of social mobility in a society thus depends in great measure on the type of stratification system that exists.

☐ Stratification Systems

There are two major ways in which stratification can come about: (1) People can be assigned to societal roles, using as a basis for the assignment an ascribed status—some easily identifiable characteristic, such as sex, age, family name, or skin color, over which they have no control. This will produce the caste and estate systems of stratification. (2) People's positions in the social hierarchy can be based to some degree on their achieved statuses (see Chapter 5), gained through their individual, direct efforts. This is known as the class system.

social mobility The movement of an individual or a group within a stratification system that changes the individual's or group's status in society.

open society An ideal-type society that provides equal opportunity to everyone to compete for the role and status desired, regardless of race, religion, gender, or family history.

closed society A society in which the various aspects of people's lives are determined at birth and remain fixed.

horizontal mobility Movement that involves a change in status with no corresponding change in social class.

vertical mobility Movement up or down in the social hierarchy that results in a change in social class.

intragenerational mobility Social changes during the lifetime of one individual.

intergenerational mobility Changes in the social level of a family through two or more generations.

status inconsistency Situations in which people rank differently (higher or lower) on certain stratification characteristics than on others.

The Caste System

In a **caste system** there is a rigid form of stratification based on ascribed characteristics such as skin color or family identity. People are born into, and spend their entire lives within, a caste, with little chance of leaving it.

Contact between castes is minimal and governed by a set of rules or laws. If interaction must take place, it is impersonal, and there is ample display of the participants' superior-inferior status. Access to valued resources is extremely unequal. A set of religious beliefs often justifies a caste system. The caste system as it existed for centuries in India before the 1950s is a prime example of how this kind of inflexible stratification works.

The Hindu caste system, in its traditional form in India, consisted of four *varnas* ("grades of being"), each of which corresponded to a body part of the mythical Purusa, whose dismemberment gave rise to the human species. Purusa's mouth issued forth priests (Brahmans), and his arms gave rise to warriors (Kshatriyas). His thighs produced artisans and merchants (Vaishyas), and his feet brought forth menial laborers (Shudras). Hindu scripture holds that each person's *varna* is inherited directly from his or her parents and cannot change during the person's life (Gould, 1971).

Each *varna* had clearly defined rights and duties attached to it. Hindus believed in reincarnation of the soul *(karma)* and that to the extent that an individual followed the norms of behavior of his or her *varna,* the state of the soul increased in purity, and the individual could expect to be born to a higher *varna* in a subsequent life. (The opposite was also true, in that failure to act appropriately according to the *varna* resulted in a person's being born to a lower *varna* in the next life.)

This picture of India's caste system is complicated by the presence of thousands of subcastes, or *jatis.* Each of these *jatis* corresponds in name to a particular occupation (leather worker, shoemaker, cattle herder, barber, potter, and so on). Only a minority within each *jati* actually perform the work of that subcaste; the rest find employment when and where they can.

It is important to note that the Hindus have never placidly accepted the caste system.

Scholars have frequently noted continuous changes during the centuries of the caste system's development. Even today, changes in the caste system are taking place. *Varnas* are all but nonexistent, and officially the Indian caste system is outlawed, although it still exists informally.

The Estate System

The **estate system** is a closed system of stratification in which a person's social position is based on ownership of land, birth, or military strength. An **estate** is a segment of a society that has legally established rights and duties. Because the estate system is a closed system involving ascribed statuses, it is similar to a caste system, although not as extreme. Some mobility is present, but by no means as much as exists in a class system.

The estate system of medieval Europe is a good example of how this type of stratification system works. The three major estates in Europe during the Middle Ages were the nobility, the clergy, and, at the bottom of the hierarchy, the peasants. A royal landholding family at the top had authority over a group of priests and the secular nobility, who were quite powerful in their own right. The nobility were the warriors; they were expected to be brave and give military protection to the other two estates. The clergy not only ministered to the spiritual needs of all the people but were often powerful landowners as well. The peasants were legally tied to the land, which they worked in order to provide the nobles with food and a source of wealth. In return, the nobles were supposed to provide social order, not only with their military strength, but also as the legal authorities who held court and acted as judges in disputes concerning the peasants who belonged to their land. The peasants had little freedom or economic standing, low social status, and almost no power. Just above the peasants was a small but growing group, the merchants and craftsmen. They operated somewhat outside the estate system in that although they might achieve great wealth and political influence, they had little chance of moving into the estate of the nobility or warriors. It is worth noting that it was this marginal group, which was less constricted by norms governing the

The highest ranking on scales measuring occupational prestige is held by Justices of the United States Supreme Court.

behavior of the estates, that had the flexibility to gain power when the Industrial Revolution undermined the estate system, starting in the eighteenth century.

Individuals were born into one of the estates and remained there throughout their lives. Under unusual circumstances people could change their estate, as for example when peasants—using produce or livestock saved from their own meager supply or a promise to turn over a bit of land that by some rare fortune belonged to them outright—could buy a position in the church for a son or daughter. For most, however, social mobility was difficult and extremely limited because wealth was permanently concentrated among the landowners. The only solace for the poor was the promise of a better life in the hereafter (Vanfossen, 1979).

The Class System

Several social classes are present in a society that has a **class system** of stratification. A **social class** consists of a category of people who share similar opportunities, similar economic and vocational positions, similar lifestyles, and similar attitudes and behavior. Class boundaries are maintained by limitation on social interaction, intermarriage, and mobility into that class. Because a class system usually results from industrialization and is present in all industrial societies, both capitalist and communist, mobility in a class system is greater than that in a caste or an estate system. This

mobility is often the result of an occupational structure that supposedly opens up higher-level jobs to anyone with the education and experience required. A class society encourages striving and achievement. Here in the United States we should find this concept familiar, for ours is basically a class society.

There is little agreement among sociologists as to how many social classes exist in the United States and what their characteristics may be. However, at least two researchers agree that there are five social classes in the United States: upper class, upper-middle class, lower-middle class, working class, and lower class (Rossides, 1976; Kahl, 1960). Table 10.1 presents stratification data for each of these classes.

caste system A rigid form of social stratification based on ascribed characteristics such as skin color or heredity. People are born into and spend their entire lives within a caste with little chance of leaving it.

estate system A closed system of stratification in which social position is based on ownership of land, birth, and military strength. The estate system is based on ascribed statuses that allow only limited mobility.

estate A segment of a society that has legally established rights and duties.

class system A system of social stratification that contains several social classes and in which greater social mobility is permitted than in a caste or estate system.

social class A category of people who share similar opportunities, similar economic positions, similar lifestyles, and similar attitudes and behavior.

POPULAR SOCIOLOGY
Society's Most Prestigious Phone Book

One of the upper class's quaintest institutions is a little-known address and telephone book called the Social Register. *It lists the names and various addresses of about 65,000 families and single adults, as well as information concerning each person's membership in clubs and ancestral societies, colleges and universities attended, and year of graduation. It is one of the best sources of information on the upper class that is available to social scientists.*

The black and orange volumes of the *Social Register* were created in 1887 by an upper-class socialite as a business venture. Although the publication once covered socially prominent people in 24 cities across the country, after 1920 it was restricted to only 13 of the largest cities in the nation. With the exception of San Francisco, they all are east of the Mississippi: New York, Boston, Philadelphia, Baltimore, Washington, Chicago, St. Louis, Buffalo, Pittsburgh, Cleveland, and Cincinnati-Dayton.

Although the *Social Register* may serve as a status symbol for some of its listees, it seems likely that most of the people who fill out the biographical information blanks and buy a copy do so because of the useful information it contains, including addresses, telephone numbers, and lists of marriages and deaths for each year. As an additional feature, there is a section in the back entitled "Married Maidens." It lists all the women in the register alphabetically by their maiden names, with the married names adjacent, thereby making it possible to locate old friends.

Although the emphasis is on useful information, there is a place in the *Social Register* for social-status information, as well. Following each adult or couple's name, there may appear a set of capital letters, abbreviations, and numbers that reveal membership in clubs and ancestral societies, colleges and universities attended, and year of graduation. A family's *Social Register* listing might read as follows:

Smith Jr. and   989-8034
Mrs. Jas W.   45 June Lane
(Helen L.
Jones)
Sm., Bhm.,
Chi., Ncd.,
H'54 SL'55

Smith Mr.   Easton, Mass.
Kenneth F.—   02193
at Cornell

Juniors Mr.
Wm. C.—at
St. Paul's

By checking the lengthy list of abbreviations and symbols at the beginning of the book, it can be determined that Mr. Smith graduated from Harvard in 1954 and is a member of the Somerset Club in Boston and the Bohemian Club in San Francisco and that Mrs. Smith graduated from Sarah Lawrence in 1955 and is a member of the Chilton Club in Boston and the National Society of Colonial Dames. As for the children, it is readily apparent that one is at Cornell and the other at St. Paul's, a boarding school.

New people are added to the *Social Register* through recommendations by those who already are listed. Some accounts suggest applicants are screened by committees, but there is no solid evidence for this claim. The belief that there is a vigilant screening committee is based on the fact that some people seem to be dropped each year for reasons of divorce, unacceptable marriages, or involvement in distasteful activities. Society-page writers study each new edition to determine who has been deleted and then speculate on the reasons. No pattern seems to emerge. Some divorcees are deleted, but some are not. Some people who marry entertainers or other non-Social Registerites are missing the next year, though others are not.

It must be emphasized that the *Social Register* association does not decide who is and who is not a member of the upper class. Rather, its *Social Register* is merely a telephone book with perhaps a certain snob appeal. On the other hand, the very fact that the venture has persisted since 1887 and receives biography forms yearly from tens of thousands of families is no small testament in and of itself to the existence of a great many self-conscious members of the upper class in America.

Source: Excerpted from G. William Domhoff, *Who Rules America Now?* (Englewood Cliffs, N.J.: Prentice-Hall, 1983), pp. 20–24. □

---

1. *The upper class.* Members of the upper class have great wealth, often going back for many generations. They recognize one another and are recognized by others by reputation and lifestyle. They usually have high prestige and a lifestyle that excludes those from other classes. Members of this class often have an influence on the society's basic economic and political structure. The upper class usually isolates itself from the rest of society by residential segregation, private clubs, and private schools. (For a discussion of how the up-

per class records information about its members, see Popular Sociology: "Society's Most Prestigious Phone Book.") It is estimated that in the United States, the upper class consists of from 1 to 3 percent of the population.

2. *The upper-middle class.* The upper-middle class is made up of successful business and professional people and their families. They are usually just below the top in an organizational hierarchy but still command a reasonably high income. Many aspects of their lives are dominated by their careers, and continued success in this area is a long-term consideration. These people often have a college education, own property, and have a savings reserve. They live in comfortable homes in the more exclusive areas of a community, are active in civic groups, and carefully plan for the future. (For a discussion of how this segment of society will increase in size over the next decade, see Focus on Research: "The Age of Rising Affluence.")

3. *The lower-middle class.* The lower-middle class shares many characteristics with the upper-middle class, but they have not been able to achieve the same kind of lifestyle because of economic or educational shortcomings. Usually high school graduates with modest incomes, they are the lesser professionals, clerical and sales workers, and upper-level manual laborers. They emphasize respectability and security, have some savings, and are politically and economically conservative.

4. *The working class.* The working class is made up of factory employees and other blue-collar workers. These are the people who keep the country's machinery going. They are assembly-line workers, auto mechanics, and repair personnel. They live adequately but with little left over for luxuries. Although they have little time to be involved in civic organizations, they are very much involved with their extended families. Many of them have not finished high school.

TABLE 10.1 *Social Stratification in the United States by Occupation*

Class	Percent of Labor Force	Occupation	Education	Children's Education
Upper class	—*	Corporate ownership; upper-echelon politics; honorific positions in government and the arts	Liberal arts education at elite schools	College and postcollege
Upper-middle class	27.3	Professional and technical fields; managers; officials; proprietors	College and graduate training	College and graduate
Lower-middle class	24.9	Clerical and sales positions; small business owners; semiprofessionals; farmers	High school; some college	Option of college
Working class	31.7	Skilled and semiskilled manual labor; craftspeople; foremen; nonfarm workers	Grade school; some or all of high school	High school; vocational school
Lower class	16.1	Unskilled labor and service work; private household work and farm labor	Grade school; semi-illiterate	Little interest in education; high school dropouts

*Included in percent for upper-middle class. Probably 1–3 percent.

Source: Adapted from U.S. Department of Commerce, Bureau of the Census, *Statistical Abstract of the United States, 1981* (Washington, D.C.: Government Printing Office, 1981).

FOCUS ON RESEARCH
The Age of Rising Affluence

The traditional diagram of income distribution is a triangle, with most people in the middle or at the bottom and the wealthy elite few at the top. But the income triangle is starting to resemble a rectangle in the United States. New income projections for 1995 show that many more households will become affluent in the years ahead. The implications of this income shift will be felt in a variety of areas.

In 1995 the number of households in the United States with incomes under $25,000* will be about the same as in 1980. But for the first time, the number of households with incomes above $25,000 may well be equally as large. This new affluence will not be limited to professionals, nor to those in a few chosen careers, nor even to households in specific age or educational brackets. Rather, it will be an affluence that cuts across many types of households. It is further predicted that in the next decade, the number of households earning $35,000 or more will grow faster than will those in any other income category.

Traditional husband–wife households will represent the lion's share of the superaffluent, defined as those

*All income data are adjusted to 1980 dollars.

earning $50,000 and over in 1980 dollars. The number of households in this category is expected to triple.

In fact, it is predicted that all the growth in the number of married couples will be in the top income class. Although this luxury income bracket was the smallest segment in 1980, it will be one of the largest by 1995—reaching 11 million, or almost 20 percent of all husband–wife households. This income level will reflect, in part, further increases in the number of working wives—a rate of increase that is fastest in the upper-income brackets.

This growth in household affluence will be accompanied by an aging of households. As the members of the baby boom who were born in the late 1940s, 1950s, and early 1960s grow older, middle-aged households will outnumber the "young marrieds" households that grew rapidly in the 1970s and depressed household income averages.

As the numbers of people in these upper-income categories grow, their needs and wants will have a ripple effect throughout many areas of society. There will be a greater demand for quality housing, for example. Products and services that are designed to enhance the physical self (especially those promising restored

youthfulness), such as cosmetic surgery, health spas, exercise facilities, and diet programs, will increase in popularity. This group will also be interested in programs that support the psychological self: counseling, education, stress-management training, and self-improvement courses. They can also be expected to cultivate those activities and interests that have traditionally been favored by people in upper-income brackets—art, ballet, opera, symphony concerts, and world travel.

There are two groups that will not share equally in the trend toward rising affluence. They include people aged 55 to 64 and those over 65. Many older households will remain below the poverty level, and those households headed by people over 65 will be the poorest of all.

Will the increase in the number of affluent cause there to be a greater concern for the poor, or will the poor be pushed out of the spotlight by the changing economic climate? We can only speculate at this time on what effect this trend will have on social responsibility.

Source: Adapted from William Lazer, "How Rising Affluence Will Reshape Markets," *American Demographics* **6**(2) (February, 1984), pp. 17–21. □

---

5. *The lower class.* These are the people at the bottom of the economic ladder. They have little in the way of education or occupational skills and are consequently either unemployed or underemployed. Lower-class families often have many problems, including broken homes, illegitimacy, criminal involvement, and alcoholism. Members of the lower class have little knowledge of world events, are not involved with their communities, and do not usually identify with other poor people. Because of a variety of personal and economic problems, they often have no way of improving their lot in life. For them, life is a matter of surviving from one day to the next.

Money, power, and prestige are unequally distributed among these classes. However, an achievement ideology is shared by members of all five classes, which makes them believe that the system is just and that upward mobility is open to all (Vanfossen, 1979).

☐ The Dimensions of Social Stratification

Scholars who study social stratification recognize three dimensions along which societies are stratified: economics, power, and prestige.

Economics

The total economic assets of an individual or a family are known as wealth. For people in the United States, wealth includes income, monetary assets, and various holdings that can be converted into money. These holdings include stocks, bonds, real estate, automobiles, precious metals and jewelry, and trusts (Jeffries and Ransford, 1980).

Information on income and wealth in the United States (see Tables 10.2 and 10.3) shows that there continues to be a high concentration of wealth in the hands of a relatively small number of people. This point is highlighted by the fact that the richest 1 percent of the American population owns about 20 percent of the nation's wealth. This figure was as high as 36 percent in 1929 and illustrates dramatically the extent to which the nation's wealth is controlled by a very few (U.S. Dept. of Commerce, 1984).

Poverty In a general sense, poverty refers to a condition in which people do not have enough money to maintain a standard of living that includes the basic necessities of life. The federal government defines poverty by setting up specific income levels, below which

TABLE 10.2 *Percentage of Families in Each Income Group in 1983*

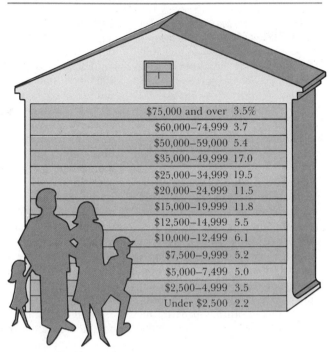

$75,000 and over	3.5%
$60,000–74,999	3.7
$50,000–59,000	5.4
$35,000–49,999	17.0
$25,000–34,999	19.5
$20,000–24,999	11.5
$15,000–19,999	11.8
$12,500–14,999	5.5
$10,000–12,499	6.1
$7,500–9,999	5.2
$5,000–7,499	5.0
$2,500–4,999	3.5
Under $2,500	2.2

Source: U.S. Department of Commerce, Bureau of the Census.

people are considered to be living in poverty. In 1982, this minimum income level was $9,862 for a nonfarm family of four (see Table 10.4). The poverty-level income figures do not include income received in the form of noncash benefits, such as food stamps, medical care, and subsidized housing. (For a further discussion of how the poverty levels are determined, see Using Sociology: "When Are You Truly Poor and Needy?")

TABLE 10.3 *Percentage of Total Income* Received by U.S. Families at Various Income Levels, 1950–1983*

Income Rank of Families	1950	1955	1960	1965	1970	1975	1978	1983
Lowest fifth	4.5	4.8	4.8	5.2	4.1	4.3	4.3	4.7
Second fifth	12.0	12.3	12.2	12.2	10.8	10.4	10.3	11.1
Middle fifth	17.4	17.8	17.8	17.8	17.4	17.1	16.9	17.1
Fourth fifth	23.4	23.7	24.0	23.9	24.5	24.7	24.7	24.4
Highest fifth	42.7	41.3	41.3	40.9	43.3	43.4	43.9	42.7
Highest 5 percent	17.3	16.4	15.9	15.5	16.8	16.3	16.6	15.8

*Does not reflect income received in the form of noncash benefits, such as food stamps, medical care, and subsidized housing.

Source: Adapted from U.S. Department of Commerce, Bureau of the Census, *Current Population Reports*, Series P-60, no. 145 (1978), and no. 126 (1981), p. 23, and *Statistical Abstract of the United States, 1985* (Washington, D.C.: Government Printing Office, 1984), p. 448.

USING SOCIOLOGY
When Are You Truly Poor and Needy?

The above question may seem somewhat strange. We could say that although we may have trouble precisely defining poverty, we all would know it when we experience it. The federal government, however, has been trying to answer this question and, as you will see in the following excerpt, has had a good deal of trouble coming up with a satisfactory answer.

Depending on which official or quasi-official approach one uses, it is possible to document that anywhere from 14 million to 45 million Americans are living in poverty. The actual fact is we do not really have an unequivocal way of determining how many poor people there are in the United States. Despite what the public and public officials believe, the "poverty index" was not originally intended to certify that any individual or family was "in need." In fact the government has specifically warned against using the index for administrative use in any specific program.

The poverty index has become less and less meaningful over the years. However, its continued use and misuse has given it somewhat of a sacred character. In addition, few people who cite it know how it is calculated and choose to assume it is a fair measure for determining the number of poor in the country.

The poverty index was first used in 1965, and designated the official statistic for documenting the poor in 1969. It was calculated in the following way. First, it estimated the national average dollar-cost of a frugal but adequate diet. Then because a 1955 study had shown that food accounted for an average of one-third of basic budgets for United States families of three or more people, food costs were multiplied by three to estimate how much total cash income was needed to cover food and other necessities.

It was never a sufficiently precise indicator of need to make it an indisputable test of which individuals and families were poor and which were not. Regional differences in cost of living were enough to throw it off. As time went on other factors skewed it further.

Food typically accounts for a considerably smaller proportion of family expenses now than it did previously. A poverty index developed today would probably have to multiply minimal food costs by a factor of five instead of three. There are also now about 8 million households who receive food stamps, valued at 10 billion dollars, which is not considered "income" under existing poverty-index rules. Complicating the issue further, the market value of in-kind benefits, such as housing subsidies, school lunch programs, and health care services among others, has jumped from $2.2 billion to more than $72.5 billion. In-kind transfers intended for the low-income populations now ex-

ceed cash public assistance by more than two-to-one. These facts lead to the inescapable conclusion that

1. Some of the people below the present "poverty line" are not among the truly needy.
2. Some of those above that line are.

When you come right down to it, why do we need a measurement of poverty? What does it mean on the flesh and blood level to be below the poverty line? As we shall see, the concept of the "truly needy" may be more significant than the poverty index.

The truly needy have been defined as "unfortunate persons who, through no fault of their own have nothing but public funds to turn to in order to secure a minimal standard of living."

There are poor people in the United States today—millions of them, by any socially responsible standard. There are millions of Americans who need help from the more fortunate members of the society in which they live, and there are many who are not getting it for one reason or another. The main goal at this point should be to identify these people and provide them with the assistance they need.

Source: Joseph M. Dukert, "Who Is Poor? Who Is Truly Needy?" *Public Welfare* **41** (1) (Winter, 1983), pp. 17–22. □

Poverty seems to be present among certain groups much more than among others. In 1983, 15.2 percent of all Americans lived below the poverty level. Only 12.1 percent of all whites, however, were living in poverty, whereas 35.7 percent of all blacks and 28.4 percent of all those of Spanish origin were below the poverty level (see Figure 10.1). People living in the Appalachian region of the United States had a considerably higher chance of living in poverty than did those living elsewhere. In states such as Kentucky, the percentage of people below the poverty level was 26 percent, and in Mississippi, it was 22.1 percent (U.S. Dept. of Commerce, 1984).

Different types of families also have different poverty levels. In 1981, only 6.8 percent of families with both a husband and wife

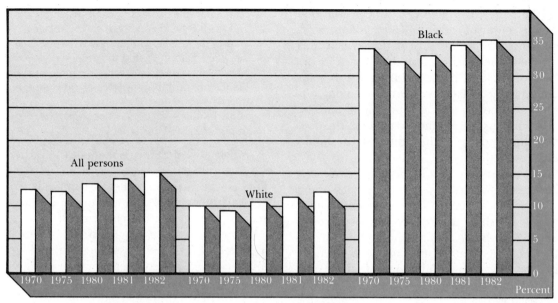

Figure 10.1 Percent of Persons Below Poverty Level: 1970–1982

Source: U.S. Department of Commerce, Bureau of the Census, *Statistical Abstract of the United States, 1984* (Washington, D.C.: Government Printing Office, 1983), p. 444.

present lived in poverty. For male-headed families, the figure was 10.3 percent, though for female-headed families, the figure increased dramatically to 34.6 percent (U.S. Bureau of Census, 1982). This has caused some sociologists to refer to the "feminization of poverty," a phrase referring to the dispro-

portionate concentration of poverty among women.

Power

One of the most widely used definitions of power in sociology is a variation of one suggested by Max Weber. **Power** is the ability to attain goals, control events, and maintain influence over others—even in the face of opposition.

In the United States, ideas about power often have their origins in the struggle for independence. It is a cliché of every Fourth of July speech that the colonists fought the Revolutionary War because of a desire to have a voice in how they were governed, and particularly in how they were taxed. The colonists were also making revolutionary political demands on their own political leaders as well, by insisting that special conventions be elected to frame constitutions and that the constitutions be ratified by a vote of all free white males without regard to property ownership.

TABLE 10.4   Poverty Levels Based on Income*
for Families and Unrelated Individuals: 1983

Size of Unit	Income
1 person	$5,061
Under 65	5,180
Over 65	4,775
2 persons	6,483
Under 65	6,697
Over 65	6,023
3 persons	7,938
4 persons	10,178
5 persons	12,049
6 persons	13,630
7 persons	15,500
8 persons	17,170
9 or more persons	20,310

*Does not reflect income received in the form of noncash benefits.

Source: U.S. Department of Commerce, Bureau of the Census, *Statistical Abstract of the United States, 1985* (Washington, D.C.: Government Printing Office, 1984), p. 429.

power The ability to attain goals, control events, and maintain influence over others—even in the face of opposition.

In the past, governments had been founded on the power of religious leaders, kings, self-appointed conventions, or parliaments. It was the middle classes' resolve for a voice in the decision-making process during the revolutionary period that succeeded in changing our thinking about political representation. The revolutionary period helped develop the doctrine that "power" in the United States should belong to "the people."

Every society has highly valued experiences and material objects. It can be assumed that most people in society would like to have as great a share as possible of these experiences and objects. Those who end up having the most of what people want are then, by inference, the powerful (Domhoff, 1983).

In almost all societies the distribution of power is institutionalized so that some groups consistently have more power than others do. In 1956 C. Wright Mills, in his book *The Power Elite*, attacked the view that American democracy meant that simply by voting all citizens could exercise power over the major decisions that affected their lives. Mills claimed that most Americans in fact are quite powerless and that power in America is held by a relatively small segment of society from whose ranks the leaders of government, industry, and the military usually come. He further argued that it is the leaders of these three interrelated hierarchies who shape the course of events in America.

Mills took great pains to explain that America does not have a single ruling class, an aristocracy of noble families who inherit great power. But that does not mean that membership in the class called the **power elite**—the group of people who control policymaking and the setting of priorities in America—is open to all:

> The bulk of the very rich, the corporate executives, the political outsiders [those high-ranking planners and bureaucrats who survive in power even as different administrators come and go], the high military, derive from, at least, the upper third of the income and occupational pyramids. Their fathers were at least of the professional and business strata, and very frequently higher than that. They are native-born Americans of native parents, primarily from urban areas, and, with the exceptions of the politicians among them, overwhelmingly from the East They are mainly Protestants, especially Episcopalian or Presbyterian. In general, the higher the position, the greater the proportion of men within it who have derived from and who maintain connections with the upper classes. (Mills, 1956)

Mills showed that members of the power elite typically are graduates from a small number of prestigious colleges, belong to certain exclusive social and country clubs, and frequently marry within elite circles.

Some sociologists disagree with Mills' view of power in America, observing that a large number of groups compete for power. Each group is out for itself, and cooperation between them is minimal. Hence there can be no "power elite." A major proponent of this position, Arnold Rose, presented his ideas in *The Power Structure* (1967). He believes that there are power structures within every organized area of society. Within each of these power structures there is a small elite that has unusual influence. However, there are so many power structures and so many elites that it is wrong to assume that they ordinarily have any power beyond their specific spheres. Their power, moreover, is institutionally limited. At times, however, the power of one elite segment may expand (for instance, as a result of changing political regimes, the military may gain or lose influence over government spending for defense and policy decisions).

Most likely, however, the truth is somewhere in the middle. For example, in both the military and the arts there is a small elite that exerts great influence in its particular group. However, whereas the military elite's decisions and its ability to control events virtually affect the lives and futures of all Americans, the same cannot be said of the arts. The influence of the art elite is felt primarily in its own sphere and in fact can be overridden by other power elites—the government, for instance, which can withhold financial support for different areas of the arts, thus affecting the kinds, number, and quality of artistic presentations. Rose seems to have ignored the fact that often there is cooperation between different power structures—the political elite and large corporations, for example. In addition, G. William Domhoff found that what he called a "governing class" in America, defined in terms of economic (wealth and income) and social (education, club membership) variables. This governing class numbers about 0.5 percent of the total U.S. population. Although it is less tightly organized than is the power elite suggested by Mills, its members are, nevertheless, very rich, do intermarry, spend their time in the same clubs, attend the same schools, and are extremely powerful. Despite their political party registration, the members of this governing class agree on the value of free enterprise, the profit motive, and the private ownership of property.

Domhoff suggests that even with the turmoil of the 1960s and 1970s,

> There continues to be a small upper class that owns 20 to 25 percent of all privately held wealth and 45 to 50 percent of all privately held corporate stock, sits in seats of formal power from the corporate community to the federal government, and wins much more often than it loses on issues ranging from the nature of the tax structure to the stifling of reform in such vital areas as consumer protection, environmental protection, and labor law. (Domhoff, 1983)

Prestige

Prestige consists of the approval and respect an individual or group receives from other members of society. There are two types of prestige. To avoid confusion we can call the first type *esteem*, which is potentially open to all. It consists of the appreciation and respect a person wins in his or her daily interpersonal relationships. Thus, for example, among your friends there are some who are looked up to for their outgoing personalities, athletic abilities, reliability in times of need, and so on.

The second form of prestige is much more difficult for many people to achieve. This is the honor that is associated with specific statuses (social positions) in a society. Regardless of personality, athletic ability, or willingness to help others, individuals such as Supreme Court justices, state governors, physicians,

physicists, and foreign service diplomats acquire prestige simply because they occupy these statuses. Access to prestigious statuses usually is difficult: generally speaking, the greater the prestige a status has, the more difficult it is to gain it. For example, few positions carry as much prestige as that of president of the United States—and few positions are as hard to attain.

Occupations are perhaps the most visible statuses to which prestige is attached in industrial society. Figure 10.2 shows the prestige ranking of selected occupations in the United States. These rankings, first undertaken in the 1940s by the National Opinion Research Center, have remained quite stable since then (Hodge et al., 1966; Treiman, 1977). In general, they appear to conform to the broad categories discussed under occupation and wealth.

There are, of course, times and places when stratification according to prestige groups and social classes is not fully parallel. For example, in the American South many of the existing aristocratic families were financially ruined after the Civil War, and their fall in economic position was matched by a fall from political power. Although Northern industrialists and politicians subsequently replaced them in the hierarchies of wealth and politics, the Northerners never achieved the social prominence, the local esteem, and the respect that were accorded the Southern aristocrats simply by virtue of their birth into "prominent" families.

☐ Theories of Stratification

Social philosophers have long tried to explain the presence of social inequality—that situation in which the very wealthy and powerful coexist with the poverty-stricken and socially ineffectual. In this section we shall discuss the theories that try to explain this phenomenon.

power elite The group of people who control policymaking and the setting of priorities in America.

prestige The approval and respect an individual or group receives from other members of society.

Figure 10.2 Prestige Ratings of Various Occupations

Occupation	Rating	Occupation	Rating	Occupation	Rating
U.S. Supreme Court Justice	94	Owner of a factory that employs about 100 people	80	Railroad conductor	66
Physician	93			Plumber	65
Nuclear physicist	92	Artist who paints pictures that are exhibited in galleries	78	Automobile repairman	64
Scientist	92			Playground director	63
Government scientist	91			Barber	63
State governor	91	Musician in a symphony orchestra	78	Machine operator in a factory	63
Cabinet member in federal government	90	Author of novels	78	Owner-operator of a lunch stand	63
College professor	90	Economist	78	Corporal in the regular army	62
U.S. representative in Congress	90	Official of an international labor union	77	Garage mechanic	62
Chemist	89	Railroad engineer	76	Truck driver	59
Lawyer	89	Electrician	76	Fisherman who owns his own boat	58
Diplomat in the U.S. Foreign Service	89	County agricultural agent	76	Clerk in a store	56
Dentist	88	Owner-operator of a printing shop	75	Milk route man	56
Architect	88	Trained machinist	75	Streetcar motorman	56
County judge	88	Farm owner and operator	74	Lumberjack	55
Psychologist	87	Undertaker	74	Restaurant cook	55
Minister	87	Welfare worker for a city government	74	Singer in a nightclub	54
Member of the board of directors of a large corporation	87	Newspaper columnist	73	Filling station attendant	51
Mayor of a large city	87	Policeman	72	Dockworker	50
Priest	86	Reporter on a daily newspaper	71	Railroad section hand	50
Head of a department in a state government	86	Radio announcer	70	Night watchman	50
Civil engineer	86	Bookkeeper	70	Coal miner	50
Airline pilot	86	Tenant farmer—one who owns livestock and machinery and manages the farm	69	Restaurant waiter	49
Banker	85	Insurance agent	69	Taxi driver	49
Biologist	85	Carpenter	68	Farmhand	48
Sociologist	83	Manager of a small store in a city	67	Janitor	48
Instructor in public schools	82	A local official of a labor union	67	Bartender	48
Captain in the regular army	82	Mail carrier	66	Clothes presser in a laundry	45
Accountant for a large business	81	Traveling salesman for a wholesale concern	66	Soda fountain clerk	44
Public school teacher	81			Sharecropper—one who owns no livestock or equipment and does not manage farm	42
Building contractor	80			Garbage collector	39
				Street sweeper	36
				Shoe shiner	34

This chart shows how Americans have ranked the prestige of various occupations. Generally, the most prestigious jobs are those that require the greatest number of years of formal education and those that pay the highest income.

Source: Donald J. Treiman, *Occupational Prestige in Comparative Perspective* (New York: Academic Press, 1977), pp. 318–329.

The Functionalist Theory

Functionalism is based on the assumption that the major social structures contribute to the maintenance of the social system (see Chapter 1). The existence of a specific pattern in society is explained in terms of the benefits that society receives because of that situation. In this sense the function of the family is the socialization of the young, and the function of marriage is to provide a stable family structure.

The functionalist theory of stratification as presented by Kingsley Davis and Wilber Moore (1945) holds that social stratification is a social necessity. Every society must select individual members to fill a wide variety of social positions (or statuses) and then motivate those people to do what is expected of them in these positions, that is, fulfill their role expectations. For example, our society needs teachers, engineers, janitors, police officers, managers, farmers, crop dusters, assembly-line workers, firefighters, textbook writers, construction workers, sanitation workers, chemists, inventors, artists, bank tellers, athletes, pilots, secretaries, and so on. In order to attract the most talented individuals to each occupation, society must set up a system of differential rewards based on the skills needed for each position.

> If the duties associated with the various positions were all equally pleasant . . . all equally important to social survival, and all equally in need of the same ability or talent, it would make no difference who got into which positions. . . . But actually it does make a great deal of difference who gets into which positions, not only because some positions are inherently more agreeable than others, but also because some require special talents or training and some are functionally more important than others. Also, it is essential that the duties of the positions be performed with the diligence that their importance requires. Inevitably, then, a society must have, first, some kind of rewards that it can use as inducements, and, second, some way of distributing these rewards differentially according to positions. The rewards and their distribution become part of the social order, and thus give rise to stratification. (Davis and Moore, 1945)

According to Davis and Moore, (1) different positions in society make different levels of contributions to the well-being and preservation of society; (2) filling the more complex and important positions in society often requires talent that is scarce and has a long period of training; and (3) providing unequal rewards ensures that the most talented and best-trained individuals will fill the roles of greatest importance. In effect, Davis and Moore mean that those people who are rich and powerful are at the top because they are the best qualified and are making the most significant contributions to the preservation of society (Zeitlin, 1981).

Many scholars, however, disagree with Davis and Moore (Tumin, 1953), and their arguments generally take two forms. The first is philosophical and questions the morality of stratification. The second is scientific and questions its functional usefulness. Both criticisms share the belief that social stratification does more harm than good, that is, it is dysfunctional.

According to functionalist theory, the people at the top of the stratification ladder—such as the Prince and Princess of Wales—are there because of their significant contributions to the preservation of society.

The Immorality of Social Stratification On what grounds, one might ask, is it morally justifiable to give widely different rewards to different occupations, when all occupations contribute to society's ongoing functioning? How can we decide which occupations contribute "more"? After all, without assembly-line workers, mail carriers, janitors, seamstresses, auto mechanics, nurses' aides, construction laborers, truck drivers, secretaries, shelf stockers, sanitation workers, and so on, our society would grind to a halt. How can the $500,000-a-year incomes of a select few be justified when the earnings of over 12 percent of the American population fall below the poverty level determined by the federal government and many others have trouble making ends meet? Why are the enormous resources of our society not more evenly distributed?

Many people find the moral arguments against social stratification convincing enough. But there are other grounds on which stratification has been attacked, namely, that it is destructive for individuals and the society as a whole.

The Neglect of Merit and Talent Regardless of whether social stratification is morally "right" or "wrong," many critics contend that it undermines the very functions that its defenders claim it promotes. A society divided into social classes (with limited mobility between them) is deprived of the potential contributions of many talented individuals born into the lower classes. From this point of view it is not necessary to do away with differences in rewards for different occupations. Rather, it is crucial to put aside all the obstacles to achievement that currently handicap the children of the poor.

Barriers to Free Competition It can also be claimed that access to important positions in society is not really open. That is, those members of society who occupy privileged positions allow only a small number of people to enter their circle. Thereby, shortages are created artificially. This, in turn, increases the perceived worth of those who are in the important positions. For example, the American

Medical Association (AMA) is a wealthy and powerful group that exercises great control over the quality and quantity of physicians available to the American public. Historically the AMA has had a direct influence on the number of doctors that are produced each year, effectively creating a scarcity of physicians. Though in recent years this policy has been softened, a direct result of this influence is that medical care costs and physicians' salaries have increased more rapidly than has the pace of inflation.

Functionally Important Jobs When we examine the functional importance of various jobs, we become aware that the rewards attached to jobs do not necessarily reflect the essential nature of the functions. Why should a Hollywood movie star receive an enormous salary for starring in a film and a child-protection worker receive barely a living wage? It is difficult to prove empirically which positions are most important to society or what rewards are necessary to persuade people to want to fill certain positions.

Modern Conflict Theory

As we saw, the functionalist theory of stratification assumes society to be a relatively stable system of interdependent parts in which conflict and change are abnormal. Functionalists maintain that stratification is necessary for the smooth functioning of society. Conflict theorists, on the other hand, see stratification as the outcome of a struggle for dominance. Basically, conflict theory assumes that people act in their own self-interest in a material world in which exploitation and power struggles are prevalent. Those who attain power exploit those who have little, by creating an ideology and value system that is designed to legitimize their dominance and privilege. There are five aspects of modern conflict theory:

1. Social inequality emerges through the domination of one or more groups by other groups. Stratification is the outgrowth of a struggle for dominance in which people compete for scarce goods and services. Those who control these items gain power and prestige.

Dominance can also result from the control of property, as others become dependent on the landowners.

2. Those who are dominated have the potential to express resistance and hostility toward those in power. While the potential for resistance is there, it sometimes lies dormant. Opposition may not be organized because the subordinated groups may not be aware of their mutual interests. They may also be divided because of racial, religious, or ethnic differences.

3. Conflict will most often center on the distribution of property and political power. The ruling classes will be extremely resistant to any attempts to share their advantage in these areas. Economic and political power are the most important advantages in maintaining a position of dominance.

4. What are thought to be the common values of society are really the values of the dominant groups. The dominant groups establish a value system that justifies their position. They control the systems of socialization, such as education, and impose their values on the general population. In this way the subordinate groups come to accept a negative evaluation of themselves and believe those in power have a right to that position.

5. Because those in power are engaged in exploitative relationships, they must find mechanisms of social control to keep the masses in line. The most common mechanism of social control is the threat or the actual use of force, which can include physical punishment or the deprivation of certain rights. However, more subtle approaches are preferred. By holding out the possibility of a small amount of social mobility for those who are deprived, the power elite will try to induce them to accept the system's basic assumptions. Thus the subordinate masses will come to believe that by behaving according to the rules, they will gain a better life (Vanfossen, 1979).

Historical Foundations of Conflict Theory

Current views of the conflict theory of stratification are based on the writings of Karl Marx. In turn, Max Weber developed many of his ideas in response to Marx's teaching.

Marx saw the stratification that emerged from the power struggles for scarce resources as the key factor in understanding society.

> The history of all hitherto existing society is the history of class struggles. [There always has been conflict between] freeman and slave, patrician and plebian, lord and serf, guild-master and journeyman, in a word, oppressor and oppressed. . . . (Marx and Engels, 1961)

Those who have achieved power are determined to maintain their advantage. They do this by setting up a political structure and a value system that become the dominant ones for society and that support their position. In this way the legal system, the schools, and the churches are shaped in ways that benefit those in power. As Marx and Engels put it, "The ruling ideas of each age have always been the ideas of its ruling class" (1961). Thus the pharaohs of ancient Egypt ruled because they claimed to be gods. And in the first third of this century, America's capitalist class justified its position by misusing Darwin's theory of evolution: they adhered to the view—called Social Darwinism (see Chapter 1)—that those who rule do so because they are the most "fit" to rule, having won the evolutionary struggles that promote the "survival of the fittest."

Marx was most interested in the social impact of the capitalist mode of production, whereby those who control capital control society. These capitalists, whom Marx called the **bourgeoisie**, use capital, labor, technology, and natural resources to make a profit. The mass of people in society, called the **proletariat**, have no resources other than their labor, which they sell to the capitalists. The capitalists exploit the workers, gain control of production, and accumulate more capital through the sale of the products.

As capitalism develops, two conflicting trends emerge. On the one hand, the capi-

bourgeoisie The label used by Karl Marx to describe the capitalists in society who use capital, labor, technology, and natural resources to make a profit.

proletariat The label used by Karl Marx to describe the mass of people in society who have no resources other than their labor, which they sell to the capitalists.

talists try to maintain and strengthen their powerful position. On the other hand, class conflict develops because the workers are being exploited. This is so because their labor enables the capitalists to make a profit. That is, in Marxist terms, they are not really being paid what their labor is worth. The workers become increasingly angry about their relationship with the capitalists and eventually organize to further their common interests and struggle against their common opponent. This class conflict will inevitably lead to a revolution by the workers and the overthrow of the capitalists. The workers subsequently become the rulers of society and abolish the capitalist system of private ownership of the means of production. Ideally, in Marx's view, they will then bring about a classless society in which everyone is a worker and exploitation is eliminated.

Marx was basically a materialist. He believed that people's lives are centered on how they deal with the material world. The key issue is how wealth is distributed among the people. There are at least four ways by which wealth can be distributed:

1. *To each according to need.* In this kind of system, the basic economic needs of all the people are satisfied. These needs include food, housing, medical care, and education. Extravagant material possessions are not basic needs and have no place in this system.

2. *To each according to want.* Here wealth will be distributed according to what people desire and request. Material possessions beyond the basic needs are now included.

3. *To each according to what is earned.* People who live according to this system become themselves the source of their own wealth. If they earn a great deal of money, they can lavish extravagant possessions upon themselves. If they earn little, they must do without.

4. *To each according to what can be taken— by whatever means.* Under this system everyone ruthlessly attempts to acquire as much wealth as possible without regard for the hardships that might be brought on others because of these actions. Those who are best at exploiting others become wealthy and powerful, and the others become the exploited and poor (Cuzzort and King, 1980).

In Marxist terms, the first of these four possibilities is what would happen in a socialist society. Although many readers will believe that the third possibility describes our society (according to what is earned), Marxists would say that a capitalist society is characterized by the last choice—you take whatever you can get in any possible way. In this sense, the Marxist theory of stratification is clearly tied to a political ideology, based on a specific interpretation of what a capitalist society is like and how a socialist society could bring about the perfect situation. Max Weber agreed with Marx on many issues related to stratification:

1. People are motivated by self-interest.
2. Group conflict is a basic ingredient of society.
3. Those who do not have property can defend their interests less well than can those who have property.
4. Economic institutions are of fundamental importance in shaping the rest of society.
5. Those in power promote ideas and values that help them maintain their dominance.
6. Only when exploitation becomes extremely obvious will the powerless object.

From those areas of agreement Weber went on to add to and modify many of Marx's basic premises. Weber was not interested in society as a whole but in the groups formed by self-interested individuals who compete with one another for power and privilege.

Weber rejected the notion that the control of production is the key to a broad-ranging theory of the history of society. He believed there were three sources of stratification: economic class, social status, and political power. Economic classes arise out of the unequal distribution of economic power, a point on which both Marx and Weber agreed. Weber went further, however, maintaining that social status is based on prestige or esteem— that is, status groups are shaped by lifestyle, which is in turn affected by income, value system, and education. People recognize others who share a similar lifestyle and develop social bonds with those who are most like themselves. From this inclination comes an attitude of exclusivity: Others are defined as being not as good as those who are a part of the status group. Weber recognized that there is a relationship between economic stratification and social-status stratification. Typically, those who have a high social status also have great economic power.

Inequality in political power exists when groups are able to influence events in their favor. For example, representatives from large industries lobby at the state and federal levels of government for legislation favorable to their interests and against laws that are unfavorable. Thus the petroleum industry has pushed for lifting restrictions on gasoline prices; the auto industry lobbied for quotas on imported cars. In exchange for "correct" votes, a politician is often promised substantial campaign contributions from wealthy corporate leaders or endorsement and funding by a large labor union whose members' jobs will be affected by the government's decisions. The individual consumer who will pay the price for such political arrangements is powerless to exert any influence over these decisions.

Class, status, and power, though related, are not the same. One can exist without the others. To Weber they are not always connected in some predictable fashion, nor are they always tied into the economic mode of production. As we mentioned earlier, a southern "aristocratic" family may be in a state that is often labeled "genteel poverty," but the family name still elicits respect in the comunity. This kind of status is sometimes denied to the rich, powerful labor leader whose family connections and school ties are not acceptable to the social elite. In addition, status and power are often accorded to those who have no relationship to the mode of production. Henry Kissinger, for example, controlled no industry, nor did he have any great personal wealth; yet his influence was felt by the heads of state the world over.

Criticisms of Conflict Theory   Conflict theories of stratification can be criticized on a number of grounds:

1. It is difficult to prove or test conflict theory. How can dominance or exploitation be measured and empirically related to events in society?
2. Conflict theory lends itself to an attitude of conspiracy. In fact, dominance usually arises out of an unorganized and unconscious process.
3. Societies are more than mere reflections of their economic interests. Many other events shape society and, for that matter, bring about inequality.

Marx's predictions about the future of capitalism have not been accurate. He predicted that workers would become worse off as capitalism progressed. In this sense he did not anticipate the emergence of labor unions or the influence of government agencies. Under capitalism, workers have achieved victories and obtained benefits that Marx never anticipated. A system of ever-increasing exploitation and a continuing worsening of conditions has not materialized. In fact, it is in the underdeveloped and recently industrialized countries that worker discontent is most pronounced. It can also be claimed that the idea of a classless society is unrealistic, as any complex society requires some central institutions to coordinate its functioning.

The Need for Synthesis

Any empirical investigation will show that neither the functionalist nor the conflict theory of stratification is entirely accurate. This does not mean that both are useless in understanding how stratification operates in society. Rolf Dahrendorf (1959) suggests that the two theories are really complementary rather than opposed to each other. (Table 10.5 compares the two.) We do not need to choose between the two but instead should see how each is qualified to explain specific situations. For example, functionalism may help explain why differential rewards are needed to serve as an incentive for a person to spend many years training to become a lawyer. Conflict theory would help explain why the AMA acts to limit the number of practicing physicians: By creating a shortage of doctors, the medical profession ensures itself of a privileged posi-

TABLE 10.5 *Functionalist and Conflict Views of Social Stratification: A Comparison*

The Functionalist View	*The Conflict View*
1. Stratification is universal, necessary, and inevitable.	1. Stratification may be universal without being necessary or inevitable.
2. Social organization (the social system) shapes the stratification system.	2. The stratification system shapes social organizations (the social system).
3. Stratification arises from the societal need for integration, coordination, and cohesion.	3. Stratification arises from group conquest, competition, and conflict.
4. Stratification facilitates the optimal functioning of society and the individual.	4. Stratification impedes the optimal functioning of society and the individual.
5. Stratification is an expression of commonly shared social values.	5. Stratification is an expression of the values of powerful groups.
6. Power is usually legitimately distributed in society.	6. Power is usually illegitimately distributed in society.
7. Tasks and rewards are equitably allocated.	7. Tasks and rewards are inequitably allocated.
8. The economic dimension is subordinate to other dimensions of society.	8. The economic dimension is paramount in society.
9. Stratification systems generally change through evolutionary processes.	9. Stratification systems often change through revolutionary processes.

Source: Arthur L. Stinchcombe, "Some Empirical Consequences of the Davis-Moore Theory of Stratification," in Jack L. Roach, Llewellyn Gross, and Orville R. Gursslin (eds.), *Social Stratification in the United States* (Englewood Cliffs, N.J.: Prentice-Hall, 1969), p. 55.

tion and a high income, at the expense of the general population.

In addition to explaining why social stratification exists, sociologists want to know how prevalent it is and so have developed certain methods for studying and measuring the existence of social stratification in a society.

☐ Studying Social Stratification

A common way of measuring social stratification in a society is to divide people into a specified number of social classes: We have already discussed five social classes in the United States. Social classes differ in many different characteristics, and there is some disagreement among sociologists as to what is most important in determining social class. For example, if we were to define social class solely in terms of income, a number of problems would immediately become obvious. In many large cities a sanitation worker may receive a higher starting pay than does a public school teacher. Thus if income were our sole criterion for determining social class, we would have to admit that the trash collector belongs to a higher social class than does the public school teacher. By the same token we would have to assign upper-class status to organized-crime figures who "earn" hundreds of thou-

sands of dollars a year. Obviously, we must find a system of measurement that will avoid some of these problems. Sociologists have devised three approaches to measuring social class: the objective approach, the reputational approach, and the subjective approach.

Objective Approach

When using the **objective approach** to the measurement of social stratification, the researcher must decide in advance that a certain number of social classes will be used and then determine what criteria will be used for assigning people to each of the classes. This method was first instituted by August Hollingshead (1949) in his study of the people of New Haven, Connecticut. Hollingshead used occupation, amount of education, and place of residence to put the people in that community into one of five categories that are similar to the social classes discussed earlier. The objective method does not rely on subjective feelings or the attitudes of others in assessing social class. It gives the impression of being precise and can be used for large populations. The problem with this method is that the sociologist arbitrarily decides how many social classes there will be and what characteristics will put a person into one of the categories. There naturally will often be a difference of opinion among sociologists on these items, and therefore the approach is not really as objective as its label implies.

Reputational Approach

With the **reputational approach,** social class is determined by the opinions other members in the community have about an individual. This approach was first used by W. Lloyd Warner and Paul Lunt (1941) in their study of a town in Massachusetts. Through personal contact with many of a community's members, researchers using this approach come to understand how the community members divide one another into various social categories. Some people may be defined as "high society," some as "trash," and others as "good old boys." From these judgments the researchers come up with a number of categories and then proceed to classify the community's members. The problem with this method is that it requires subjective judgments by both the researcher and the local people. In addition, it can be used only in a small community in which most people either know or know of one another.

Subjective Approach

In the **subjective approach** to measuring stratification, the people being studied are asked to put themselves into one of several categories. There may be only a few categories, such as upper, middle, and lower class, or as many as 10. No matter how many categories people are given to choose from, the middle category is the one most often selected—a tendency that reduces the method's accuracy and usefulness. People's judgments will be influenced greatly by the wording of the questions that the researcher asks as well as by the researcher's attitude. People also tend to play down the fact that there are social classes or that they are important. Consequently, they often do not treat the issue very seriously.

☐ Consequences of Social Stratification

Studies of stratification in the United States have shown that social class affects many factors in a person's life. Striking differences in health and life expectancy are apparent among the social classes, especially between the lower-class poor and the other social groups. As might be expected, lower-class people are sick more frequently than are others. In one series of studies, 24 percent of inner-city blacks and Hispanics, who make up most of the urban poor, reported a member of their family currently ill. For whites living in the impoverished region of Appalachia, the number was 31 percent. Among affluent families, however, only 7 percent reported someone currently sick (Enos and Sultan, 1977).

Closely related to health are diet and living conditions—here, too, the upper classes have a distinct advantage over the lower class, as they have access to better and more sanitary housing and can afford more balanced and nutritious food.

A direct consequence of social stratification, associated with health and living conditions, is seen in each social class's life-expectancy pattern. Not surprisingly, lower-class people do not live as long as do those in the upper classes. The children of unskilled working-class parents have a mortality rate that is 50 percent higher than that of children of the middle and upper classes (Kotelchuck, 1976). And white males born in 1982 have a life expectancy almost five years longer than that for black and other minority males, many of whom are concentrated in the lower-income brackets (U.S. Dept. of Commerce, 1984).

Family, childbearing, and child-rearing patterns also vary according to social class. Women in the higher-income groups who have more education tend to have fewer children than do lower-class women with less schooling. Women more often head the family in

objective approach The approach to measuring social stratification in which researchers decide in advance that a certain number of social classes will be used and then determine what criteria will be used for assigning people to each of the classes.

reputational approach The approach to measuring social stratification in which social class is determined by the opinions of other community members about an individual.

subjective approach The approach to measuring social stratification in which the people being studied are asked to put themselves into one of several categories.

CASE STUDY
Prisons Are for the Poor

Jeffrey H. Reimann of the School of Justice of American University, Washington, D.C., has made a detailed review of studies on the relationship between a person's social class and the possibility of his or her arrest, conviction, and sentencing if accused of a crime. His disturbing but not unexpected conclusions: "For the same criminal behavior the poor are more likely to be arrested; if arrested, they are more likely to be charged; if charged, more likely to be convicted; if convicted, more likely to be sentenced to prison; and if sentenced, more likely to be given longer prison terms than members of the middle and upper classes." How can such inequality of justice exist in a country that prides itself on fairness and "equality before the law"? Can such an indictment of our criminal justice system be substantiated? Reimann offers overwhelming evidence to support his arguments.

The poor are singled out for harsher treatment at the very beginning of the criminal justice system. Although many surveys show that almost all people admit to having committed a crime for which they could be imprisoned, the police are prone to arrest a poor person and release, with no formal charges, a higher-class person for the same offense. A well-to-do teenager who has been accused of a criminal offense is frequently just held by the police at the station house until the youngster can be released to the custody of the parents; poorer teenagers who have committed the same kind of crime more often are automatically charged and referred to juvenile court. For example, among juvenile offenders in California in 1966, statewide 46.5 percent were arrested and referred to juvenile court. But in the upper-middle-class community of Lafayette, only 17.9 percent were so handled. Far more were released to their families, the assumption being that middle- and upper-class families provide an environment that discourages criminal activity.

Employee theft occurs at all levels within corporations, but the executive caught stealing is far less apt to be prosecuted than, say, a custodian so caught. A 1967 study revealed that for the same amount stolen, 73 percent of low-status employees (cleaners, stock and service workers) caught were prosecuted, whereas only 50 percent of high-status employees (executives, salespersons, white-collar workers) were prosecuted.

The poor tend to commit violent crimes and crimes against property—they have little opportunity to commit such white-collar crimes as embezzlement, fraud, or large-scale tax evasion—and they are much more severely punished for their crimes than upper-class criminals are for theirs. Yet white-collar crimes are far more damaging and costly to the public than poor-people crimes are. It has been estimated by the government that white-collar crimes cost over $40 billion a year—more than 10 times the total amount of all reported thefts and over 250 times the amount taken in all bank robberies!

Even the language used to describe the same crime committed by an upper-class criminal and a poor one reflects the disparity in the treatment they receive. The poor thief who takes $2,000 is accused of stealing and usually receives a stiff prison sentence. The corporate executive who embezzles $200,000 merely has "misappropriated" the funds and is given a token punishment, such as a suspended sentence or even no arrest at all on the promise to make restitution. A corporation often can avoid criminal prosecution by signing a "consent decree," which is in essence a statement that it has done nothing wrong and promises never to do it again. Were this ploy available to ordinary burglars, the police would have no need to arrest them; a burglar would merely need to sign a statement promising never to burgle again and file it with the court.

Once charged, the poor are usually dependent on court-appointed lawyers or public defenders to handle their cases. The better off rely on private lawyers who have more time, resources, and personal interests for defending their cases. One study showed that private lawyers were able to obtain dismissal or acquittal of charges in two-thirds of their cases. The success rate among court-appointed lawyers and public defenders was only one in four.

The type of crime committed also affects the conviction rate. In a six-month study of convictions in the Southern District Court of New York in 1974, the conviction rates were found to be 80 percent for violent crimes, 53 percent for nonviolent crimes other than white-collar crimes, and only 36 percent for white-collar crimes.

If convicted of the same kind of crime as a well-to-do offender is, the poor criminal is more likely to be sentenced and will generally receive a longer prison term. A study of individuals with no prior records convicted in federal courts showed that 84 percent of the nonpoor were recommended for probation, whereas only 73 percent of the poor were so recommended. Only 15 percent of the nonpoor received prison sentences; 23 percent of the poor were imprisoned. Although the percentage differences may not seem very great, by this stage there are far fewer of the nonpoor originally accused of crimes—most have been sifted out of the criminal justice system. They managed to avoid arrest, indictment, or conviction. At each stage of the criminal justice system, the proportion of poor involved increases. As for prison terms, the sentence for burglary, a crime of the poor, is generally over twice as long as that for fraud, whereas a robber will draw an average sentence more than six times longer than that of an embezzler.

The end result is a prison system heavily populated by the poor. For example, in 1972 the national median income was $9,255. That is, 50 percent of the total population earned more than this amount. But only about 10 percent of the inmates in local jails were at or above this income level before entering prison. The majority had incomes below the poverty level. What·is being punished? Crime or poverty?

Source: Adapted from Jeffrey H. Reimann, "The Rich Get Richer and the Poor Get Prison," In *Ideology, Class, and Criminal Justice* (New York: John Wiley, 1979), pp. 95–128. ☐

the lower class, compared with women in the other groups. Middle-class women discipline their children differently than do working-class mothers. The former will punish boys and girls alike for the same infraction, whereas the latter often have different standards for sons and daughters. Also, middle-class mothers will judge the misbehaving child's intention, whereas working-class women are more concerned with the effects of the child's action.

A serious consequence of social stratification is the connection between social class and crime involvement on the one hand and mental illness on the other. The possibility of conviction for criminal activity and the seriousness of the sentence in·the event of conviction show definite patterns related to the social class of the offender (see Case Study: "Prisons Are for the Poor"). In the same way, the types of mental illness·suffered seem to be correlated with social class, as is the likelihood of spending time in a mental hospital (Hollingshead and Redlich, 1958; Bottomore, 1966; Jencks et al., 1972).

Although we have discussed social stratification in abstract terms, you should be aware that it has very real and immediate consequences for individuals. In fact, no other single variable affects people's lives to the degree that social class membership does.

☐ Summary

The main ingredients of social stratification are social differentiation, social evaluation, and social inequality. The concept of social differentiation consists of the perception of variations among individuals, social positions, or groups. When qualitative judgments are made on the basis of these perceptions, the process is labeled as social evaluation. The outcome of social evaluation is social inequality—the uneven distribution of privileges, rewards, opportunities, power, prestige, and influence. The process through which people try to overcome social inequality is known as social mobility—the movement of an individual or a group within a stratification system that changes the individual's or group's status in society. Social mobility is greater in an open society than in a closed society. Mobility may be horizontal or vertical, intragenerational or intergenerational.

Social stratification can be determined by assignment to roles, which results in the caste and estate systems. Or it can come about through the direct actions of individuals, a situation that forms a class system. The caste system stratifies society on the basis of ascribed characteristics such as skin color or heredity. The estate system, based on ownership of land, birth, and military strength, has legally established rights and duties ascribed to each segment. A social class consists of a group of people who share similar opportunities, economic position, and lifestyle. At least two researchers agree that there are five social classes in the United States: the upper class, the upper-middle class, the lower-middle class, the working class, and the lower class. Social mobility is the movement of an individual or a group within a stratification hierarchy.

The federal government defines poverty by setting up specific income levels below which people are considered to be living in poverty. Poverty appears to be present among certain groups much more so than among others.

Power is the ability to attain goals, control events, and maintain influence over others—

even in the face of opposition. The group of people who control policy making in a society has been referred to as the power elite.

The two major theories of stratification are functionalist and conflict. Functionalist theory is based on the assumption that the major social structures contribute to the maintenance of the social system. Criticisms of this theory include questions about the morality of stratification and about the scientific usefulness of functionalism. Conflict theory sees social stratification as the expression of the struggle for wealth and power. Karl Marx and Max Weber were its chief proponents.

Social stratification can be studied by using three approaches: (1) the objective ap-proach, in which the researcher decides in advance that a certain number of social classes will be used and then determines the criteria for assigning people to each class; (2) the reputational approach, in which social class is determined by the opinions members of the community have about an individual; and (3) the subjective approach, in which the people being studied are asked to put themselves into one of several classes.

Several factors in a person's life can be affected by social class: such widely different consequences as life expectancy, child-rearing practices, and mental illness can be influenced by an individual's social class designation.

☐ For Further Reading

AULETTA, KEN. *The Underclass.* New York: Random House, 1982. A detailed look at street criminals, hustlers, and transients and efforts carried out to improve their station in society.

BLUMBERG, PAUL. *The Future of Inequality in an Age of Decline.* New York: Oxford University Press, 1980. An important work that examines some of the social consequences of the new era of limited resources and declining expectations.

DOMHOFF, G. WILLIAM. *Who Rules America Now?* Englewood Cliffs, N.J.: Prentice-Hall, 1983. The author demonstrates that there exists an upper class that comprises only 0.5 percent of the population and yet dominates key positions within this upper class and the corporate community.

HUTTON, J. H. *Caste in India: Its Nature, Functions and Origins.* New York: Oxford University Press, 1963. The authoritative analysis of India's caste system. Hutton recounts the history of the system and explains how it is supported by the Hindu religion.

JENCKS, CHRISTOPHER, et al. *Who Gets Ahead? The Economic Determinants of Success in America.* New York: Basic Books, 1979. A landmark contribution to sociological analysis and theory. This book expands on Jencks' earlier work, *Inequality* (1972), and Gintis and Bowles, *Schooling in Capitalist America* (1975). Unfortunately, it is difficult reading and is almost incomprehensible to those without a strong background in statistics. In addition, the authors do not discuss the social-policy implications of their conclusions.

LARSON, MAGALI S. *The Rise of Professionalism.* Berkeley and Los Angeles: University of California Press, 1979. An authoritative analysis of the professional-technical stratum in American society.

LENSKI, GERHARD. *Power and Privilege: A Theory of Social Stratification.* New York: McGraw-Hill, 1966. A discussion of stratification as a result of the ways in which power is exercised in a society. A major work in the theory of social stratification, this book is particularly interesting because it analyzes social stratification in all types of societies—from the most simple to the modern industrial states.

LIPSET, SEYMOUR MARTIN, and REINHARD BENDIX. *Social Mobility in Industrial Society.* Berkeley and Los Angeles: University of California Press, 1966. A classic study of social mobility in several industrial societies, including the

United States. The authors argue that there are only small differences in upward mobility among the industrial societies they studied and that the existence of such mobility has been exaggerated in the case of the United States.

MILLS, C. WRIGHT. *The Power Elite.* New York: Oxford University Press, 1956. A provocative and absorbing account of America's wealthiest, most prestigious, and most powerful individuals who, Mills argues, actually run the country. Although Mills gathers an impressive array of data to support his argument, his conclusions still are considered to be controversial.

ROSSIDES, DANIEL W. *The American Class System.* Boston: Houghton Mifflin, 1976. A sophisticated, in-depth analysis of classes in American society.

SILK, LEONARD, and MARK SILK. *The American Establishment.* New York: Basic Books, 1980. An analysis of those who have great power and influence in American society.

VANFOSSEN, BETH E. *The Structure of Social Inequality.* Boston: Little, Brown, 1979. An extremely well written and thorough text using empirical and theoretical research to examine social stratification.

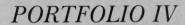

PORTFOLIO IV
Mexican-American Farm Laborers

When qualitative judgments are made on the basis of individual characteristics or behaviors, the process is referred to as social evaluation. *The outcome of social evaluation is* social inequality, *which is the unequal distribution of privileges, material rewards, opportunities, power, prestige, and influence among individuals or groups. When social inequality becomes part of the social structure and is transmitted from one generation to the next,* social stratification *exists.*

Mexican-American farm laborers occupy positions on the lower rungs of our stratification system, often earning less than the minimum wage set by the United States Government. Nevertheless, even this wage is more than they could earn in Mexico. Growers argue that without a cheap supply of labor parts of our agricultural industry would collapse.

Many of the seven million Mexican-Americans, or Chicanos, in the United States are farm laborers. They are the backbone of much of our fruit and produce industry. Their low wages—one-third of all Mexican-Americans live below the poverty level—determine retail food costs and industry profits.

Several Mexican-American farmers formed a cooperative in Salinas, California. Their goal was to buy their own land so that they would not have to be dependent on doing day labor. Shares of the land were divided according to the number of children in each family. Families worked their own land, with a percentage of their profits going to pay off loans, water, and insecticide and fertilizer costs. A successful strawberry harvest earned enough to pay off the bank, and this cooperative now has full title to its property.

11 Racial and Ethnic Minorities

. . . an African daisy and an English daisy are both flowers, but totally different kinds. (Alice Walker, *The Color Purple*)

Which is better—a tulip or a hyacinth? An aster or a chrysanthemum? Most people would find preposterous the idea of rating flowers on some sort of value scale. Certainly, a person may prefer daffodils to gladiolas, but few people would go so far as to say that one is intrinsically *better* than another. Why then, we might ask, does it make any better sense to judge human beings on the basis of color, hair texture, or country of origin?

Even though reason tells us that such externals should make no difference in a person's worth, the history of human relations is rife with cases in which superficial differences were the basis for unimaginable cruelty and injustice.

In this chapter we shall explore the issues and situations that arise when groups of people of different races and ethnic origins are confronted with the necessity of living together.

☐ The Concept of Race

The term *race* has been a highly controversial concept for a long time, and the origin of the word is not known. Many authorities suspect that it is of Semitic origin, coming from a word that some translations of the Bible render as "race," as in the "race of Abraham" but that is otherwise translated as "seed" or "generation." Other scholars trace the origin to the Czech word *raz*, meaning "artery" or "blood"; others to the Latin *generatio* or the Basque *arraca* or *arraze*, referring to a male stud animal. Some trace it to the Spanish *ras*, itself of Arabic derivation, meaning "head" or "origin." In all these possible sources, the word has a biological significance that implies descent, blood, or relationship.

We shall use the term **race** to refer to a category of people who are defined as similar because of a number of physical characteristics. Often it is based on an arbitrary set of features chosen to suit the labeler's purposes and convenience. As long ago as 1781, German physiologist Johann Blumenbach realized that racial categories did not reflect the actual divisions among human groups. As he put it, "When the matter is thoroughly considered, you see that all [human groups] do so run into one another, and that one variety of mankind does so sensibly pass into the other, that you cannot mark out the limits between them" (Montagu, 1964). Blumenbach believed racial differences were superficial and changeable, and modern scientific evidence seems to support this view.

Throughout history, races have been defined along genetic, legal and social lines, each presenting its own set of problems.

Genetic Definitions

Geneticists define race by noting differences in gene frequencies among selected groups. The number of distinct races that can be defined by this method depends on the particular genetic trait under investigation. Differences in traits, such as hair and nose type, have proved to be of no value in making biological classifications of human beings. In fact, the physiological and mental similarities among groups of people appear to be far greater than any superficial differences in skin color and physical characteristics. Also, the various so-called racial criteria appear to be independent of one another. For example, any form of hair may occur with any skin color—a narrow nose gives no clue to an individual's skin pigmentation or hair texture. Thus, Australian aborigines have dark skins, broad noses, and an abundance of curly-to-wavy hair; Asiatic Indians also have dark skins but have narrow noses and straight hair. Likewise, if head form is selected as the major criterion for sorting, an equally diverse collection of physical types will appear in each category thus defined. If people are sorted on the basis of skin color, therefore, all kinds of noses, hair, and head forms will appear in each category.

Legal Definitions

By and large, legal definitions of race have not been devised to determine who was black or of another race, but who was *not white*. The laws were to be used in instances in which separation and different treatments were to be applied to members of certain groups. Segregation laws are an excellent example. If railroad conductors had to assign someone to either the black or white cars, they needed fairly precise guidelines for knowing whom to seat where. Most legal definitions of race were devices to prevent blacks from attending white schools, serving on juries, holding certain jobs, or patronizing certain public places. The official guidelines could then be applied to individual cases. The common assumption that "anyone not white was colored," although imperfect, did minimize ambiguity.

There has been, however, very little consistency among the various legal definitions of race that have been devised. The state of Missouri, for example, made "one-eighth or more Negro blood" the criterion for nonwhite status. Georgia was even more rigid in its definition and noted:

> The term "white person" shall include only persons of the white or Caucasian race, who have no ascertainable trace of either Negro, African, West Indian, Asiatic Indian, Mongolian, Japanese, or Chinese blood in their veins. No person, any of whose ancestors [was] . . . a colored person or person of color, shall be deemed to be a white person.

Virginia had a similar law but made exceptions for individuals with one-fourth or more Indian "blood" and less than one-sixteenth "Negro blood." These Virginians were regarded as Indians as long as they remained on an Indian reservation, but if they moved, they were regarded as blacks (Novit-Evans and Welch, 1983; Berry and Tischler, 1978).

Most of these laws are artifacts of the segregation era. However, if people think that all vestiges of them have disappeared, they are wrong. As recently as 1982 a dispute arose over Louisiana's law requiring anyone of more than one-thirty-second African descent to be classified as black. Louisiana's one-thirty-second law is actually of recent vintage, having come into being in 1971. Before this law, racial classification depended on what was referred to as "common repute." The 1971 law was intended to eliminate racial classifications by gossip and inference. In September, 1982, Mrs. Susie Guillory Phipps, having noticed that her birth certificate classified her as "colored,"

filed to have her classification changed to white. The state objected and produced an eleven-generation family tree tracing Mrs. Phipps's ancestry back to an early eighteenth-century black slave and a white plantation owner (Novit-Evans and Welch, 1983).

Social Definitions

The social definition of race, which is the decisive one in most interactions, pays little attention to an individual's hereditary physical features or to whether his or her percentage of "Negro blood" is one-fourth, one-eighth, or one-sixteenth. According to social definitions of race, if a person presents himself or herself as a member of a certain race and others respond to that person as a member of that race, then it makes little sense to say that he or she is not a member of that race. (See Popular Sociology: "Can a Man Change His Race?")

In Latin American countries, having black ancestry or black features does not automatically define an individual as black. For example, in Brazil many individuals are listed in the census as, and are considered to be, white by their friends and associates even if they had a grandmother who was of pure African descent. It is much the same in Puerto Rico, where anyone who is not obviously black is classified as either mulatto or white. In the Republic of South Africa, a sharp distinction is drawn between the natives and the Cape coloured, who have mixed black white ancestry. The latter, at least until recently, were accorded privileges denied to blacks, and they held a social position intermediate between that of the dominant whites and the subordinate blacks.

The U.S. Census relies on a self-definition system of racial classification and does not apply any legal or genetic rules. In the 1980 census the term *race* did not appear, though respondents were asked an open-ended question about their ancestry, with 15 possi-

---

race A group of people who are defined as similar because of a number of physical characteristics. Often it is based on an arbitrary set of features chosen to suit the labeler's purposes and convenience. Racial categories do not reflect actual divisions among groups.

POPULAR SOCIOLOGY
Can a Man Change His Race?

How do we tell who is black and who is white? By skin color? By hair texture? Or by how a person defines himself? This question rocked the City Council in Stockton, California, when an apparently white man ran for a seat representing a minority district claiming he was, in fact, black.

In 1983 Ralph Lee White, a black man, lost his seat on the Stockton City Council to Mark Linton Stebbins, a pale-skinned, blue-eyed man with kinky reddish-brown hair. White claims Stebbins would not represent the minority district because he is white and misrepresented his race to the community. Stebbins says he is black.

Birth records show Stebbins' parents and grandparents are white. He has five sisters and one brother, all of whom are white. Yet, when asked to declare his race he notes: "First, I'm a human being, but I'm black."

Stebbins points out that he was raised as a white person and did not come to regard himself as black until he moved to Stockton. "As far as a birth certificate goes, then I'm white, but I am black. There is no question about that."

Ralph Lee White is still unconvinced, especially with his former Council seat having gone to Stebbins. "Mark committed fraud," he said. "He won the election because

he told Blacks he was Black. The district's Whites, he told them he was White. I don't mind defeats, but I can't take cheating. Now, his mama's White and his daddy's White, so how can he be Black? If the mama's an elephant and the daddy's an elephant, the baby can't be a lion. He's just a White boy with a permanent."

Stebbins said the issue of race is tied to identifying with a community in terms of beliefs, aspirations, and concerns. He believes much more than birth records go into determining a person's racial identity.

Stebbins thinks that relying on birth records to determine his race is a meaningless exercise that oversimplifies a complex issue. He believes there are no "objective" criteria for determining race.

Stebbins now belongs to a black Baptist church and to the NAACP. Most of his friends are black. He has been married three times, first to a white woman, and then to two black women. He has three children from the first two marriages; two are being raised as whites, the third as black. He considers himself black—"culturally, socially, genetically."

Stebbins says he is still unraveling the threads of his heritage. They are threads, he says, he could easily disclose, "ending all this insanity." But Stebbins explains he chooses not to do so because the issue involves

Mark Stebbins and his wife Jennet.

other people.

Stebbins' earliest impressions about race were formed during childhood when he was taunted by other children for his "nigger hair."

He summarizes his feelings by quoting a poem by black poet Paul Lawrence Dunbar, who recalled a childhood visit to Baltimore when he was approached by a white child who called him "nigger": "I saw all of Baltimore from May to December,/But of all I saw that's all that I remember."

Source: Based on David Judson and David Olson, "Birth Records Say Stebbins Kin Whites," *Stockton Record,* January 17, 1984, pp. 1, 4; and "Uproar Over Stebbins' Roots Echoes Far from District 9," *Stockton Record,* April 1, 1984, pp. 1, 4.

ble groups listed. If a person of mixed racial parentage could not provide a single response to the question, the race of the person's mother was used. If a single response could not be provided for the mother, then the first race listed was used.

☐ The Concept of Ethnic Group

An **ethnic group** has a distinct cultural tradition with which its own members identify and which may or may not be recognized by others (Glazer and Moynihan, 1975). An ethnic group need not necessarily be a numerical minority within a nation (although the term sometimes is used that way).

Many ethnic groups form subcultures (see Chapter 3): they usually possess a high degree of internal loyalty and adherence to basic customs, making for similarity in family patterns, religion, and cultural values. They often possess distinctive folkways and mores; customs of dress, art, and ornamentation; moral codes and value systems; and patterns of recreation. There is usually something to which the whole group is devoted, such as a monarch, a religion, a language, or a territory. Above all there is a feeling of association. The group's members are aware of a relationship because of a shared loyalty to a cultural tradition. The folkways may change, the institutions may become radically altered, and the object of allegiance may shift from one trait to another, but loyalty to the group and the consciousness of belonging remain as long as the group exists. An ethnic group may or may not have its own separate political unit; it may have had one in the past, it may aspire to have one in the future, or its members may be scattered through existing countries. Political unification is not an essential feature of this classification. Accordingly, despite the unique cultural features that set them apart as subcultures, many ethnic groups—Arabs, French Canadians, Flemish, Scots, Jews, and Pennsylvania Dutch, for example—are part of larger political units. The Soviet Union is composed of more than a hundred ethnic groups, including Polish Kazak, German, Armenian, Georgian, Tartar, and Ukrainian.

☐ The Concept of Minorities

Whenever race and ethnicity are discussed, it is usually assumed that the object of the discussion is a minority group. Technically this is not always true, as we shall see shortly. A minority is often thought of as being small in number. The concept of minority, rather than implying a small number, should be thought of as implying differential treatment and exclusion from full social participation by the dominant group in a society. In this sense we shall use Louis Wirth's definition of a **minority** as "a group of people who, because of physical or cultural characteristics, are singled out from others in the society in which they live for differential and unequal treatment, and who therefore regard themselves as objects of collective discrimination" (Linton, 1945).

In his definition, Wirth speaks of "physical and cultural characteristics" and not of gender, age, disability, or undesirable behav-

ioral patterns. It is obvious that he is referring to racial and ethnic groups in his definition of minorities. Some writers have suggested, however, that many other groups are in the same position as those more commonly thought of as minorities and endure the same sociological and psychological problems. In this light, women, homosexuals, adolescents, the aged, the deformed, the radical right or left, and intellectuals can be thought of as minority groups.

☐ Problems in Race and Ethnic Relations

As different kinds of people have come together, there have been difficulties between and among the various groups. People's suspicions and fears are often aroused by those whom they feel to be "different."

Prejudice

There are many definitions of prejudice. Prejudice, one popular way of putting it states, is being down on something you are not up on, the implication being that prejudice results from a lack of knowledge of or familiarity with the subject. People, particularly those with a strong sense of identity, often have feelings of prejudice toward others who are not like themselves. Literally, *prejudice* means a "prejudgment." According to Louis Wirth (1944), prejudice is "an attitude with an emotional bias." But there is a problem with this definition. All of us, through the process of socialization, acquire attitudes, which may not be in response only to racial and ethnic groups but also to many things in our environment. We come to have attitudes toward cats, roses, blue eyes, chocolate cheesecake, television programs, and even ourselves. These attitudes run the gamut from love to hate, from esteem to contempt, from loyalty to indiffer-

---

ethnic group A group that has a distinct cultural tradition with which its own members identify and which may or may not be recognized by others.

minority A group of people who, because of physical or cultural characteristics, are singled out from others in the society in which they live for different and unequal treatment and who therefore regard themselves as objects of collective discrimination.

ence. How have we developed these attitudes? Has it been through the scientific evaluation of information, or by other, less logical means?

For our purposes we shall define **prejudice** as an irrationally based negative, or occasionally positive, attitude toward certain groups and their members.

What is the cause of prejudice? Although pursuing that question is beyond the scope of this book, we can list some of the uses to which prejudice is put and the social functions it serves. First, a prejudice, simply because it is shared, helps draw together those who hold it. It promotes a feeling of "we-ness," of being part of an in-group—and it helps define such group boundaries. Especially in a complex world, belonging to an in-group and consequently feeling "special" or "superior" can be an important social identity for many people.

Second, when two or more groups are competing against one another for access to scarce resources (jobs, for example), it makes it easier if one can write off his or her competitors as somehow "less than human" or inherently unworthy. Nations at war consistently characterize each other negatively, using terms that seem to deprive the enemy of any humanity whatsoever.

Third, psychologists suggest that prejudice allows us to "project" onto others those parts of ourselves that we do not like and therefore try to avoid facing. For example, most of us feel stupid at one time or another. How comforting it is to know that we belong to a group that is inherently more intelligent than another group! Who does not feel lazy sometimes? But how good it is that we do not belong to that group—the one everybody knows is lazy!

Of course, prejudice also has many negative consequences, or *dysfunctions*, to use the sociological term. For one thing, it limits our vision of the world around us, reducing social complexities and richness to a sterile and empty caricature. But aside from this effect on us as individuals, prejudice also has negative consequences for the whole of society. Most notably, it is the necessary ingredient of discrimination, a problem found in many societies–including own own.

Discrimination

Prejudice is a subjective feeling, whereas discrimination is an overt action. **Discrimination** simply means differential treatment, usually unequal and injurious, accorded to individuals who are assumed to belong to a particular category or group. For example, in many societies, old people are subject to considerable mistreatment, abuse, and indifference, whereas in other societies they are accorded privileges and respect. Women, too, have often been denied certain rights and privileges and have been the objects of discrimination in economic, religious, political, and social affairs. At some time or another, most of our minorities have been subjected to differential treatment.

Prejudice does not always result in discrimination. Although our attitudes and our overt behavior are closely related, they are neither identical nor dependent on each other. We may have feelings of antipathy without expressing them overtly or even giving the slightest indication of their presence. This simple fact—namely, that attitudes and overt behavior vary independently—has been applied by Robert Merton to the classification of racial prejudice and discrimination. There are,

"Do you know what I like about you, Rachel? You're old, like me."

Drawing by Weber; © 1974 The New Yorker Magazine, Inc.

he believes, the following four types of people.

Unprejudiced Nondiscriminators These people are neither prejudiced against the members of other racial and ethnic groups nor do they practice discrimination. They believe implicitly in the American ideals of justice, freedom, equality of opportunity, and dignity of the individual. Merton recognizes that people of this type are properly motivated to spread the ideals and values of the creed and to fight against those forms of discrimination that make a mockery of them. At the same time, unprejudiced nondiscriminators have their shortcomings. They enjoy talking to one another, engaging in mutual exhortation and thereby giving psychological support to one another. They believe their own spiritual house is in order, thus they do not feel pangs of guilt and accordingly shrink from any collective effort to set things right.

Unprejudiced Discriminators This type includes those who constantly think of expediency. Though they themselves are free from racial prejudice, they will keep silent when bigots speak out. They will not condemn acts of discrimination but will make concessions to the intolerant and will accept discriminatory practices for fear that to do otherwise would hurt their own position.

Prejudiced Nondiscriminators This category is for the timid bigots who do not accept the tenets of equality for all but conform to it and give it lip service when the slightest pressure is applied. Here belong those who hesitate to express their prejudice when in the presence of those who are more tolerant. Among them are the employers who hate certain minorities but hire them rather than run afoul of affirmative-action laws and the labor leaders who suppress their personal racial bias when the majority of their followers demand an end to discrimination.

Prejudiced Discriminators These are the bigots, pure and unashamed. They do not believe in equality, nor do they hesitate to give free expression to their intolerance both in

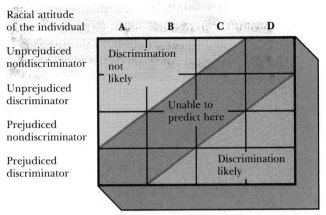

Situation A: strong social pressure not to discriminate
Situation B: weak social pressure not to discriminate
Situation C: weak social pressure to discriminate
Situation D: strong social pressure to discriminate

Figure 11.1 The Influence of Situational Factors on Racial Behavior As this diagram shows, the degree of social pressure being exerted can cause individuals of inherently dissimilar attitudes to exhibit relatively similar behaviors in a given situation.

their speech and in their actions. For them there is no conflict between attitudes and behavior. They practice discrimination, believing that it is not only proper but in fact their duty to do so (Berry and Tischler, 1978).

Knowing a person's attitudes does not mean that that person's behavior always can be predicted. Attitudes and behavior are frequently inconsistent because of such factors as the nature and magnitude of the social pressures in a particular situation. The influence of situational factors on behavior can be traced in Figure 11.1

Institutionalized Prejudice and Discrimination

Sociologists also tend to distinguish between individual and institutional prejudice and discrimination. When individuals display prejudicial attitudes and discriminatory behavior, it is often based on the assumption of the out-

prejudice An irrationally based negative, or occasionally positive, attitude toward certain groups and their members.

discrimination Differential treatment, usually unequal and injurious, accorded to individuals who are assumed to belong to a particular category or group.

group's genetic inferiority. By contrast, when there is **institutionalized prejudice and discrimination,** we are referring to complex societal arrangements that restrict the life chances and choices of a specifically defined group, in comparison with those of the dominant group. In this way, benefits are given to one group and withheld from another. Society is structured in such a way that people's values and experiences are shaped by a prejudiced social order. Discrimination is seen as a by-product of a purposive attempt to maintain social, political, and economic advantage (Davis, 1979).

An argument can be made that institutionalized prejudice and discrimination are responsible for the substandard education that many blacks receive in the United States. Schools that are predominantly black tend to be inferior at every level to schools that are predominantly white. The facilities for blacks are usually of poorer quality than are those for whites. Many blacks also attend unaccredited black colleges where the teachers are less likely to hold advanced degrees and are poorly paid. The poorer education that blacks receive is one of the reasons they generally are in lower occupational categories than whites

Schools that are predominantly black tend to be inferior at every level to schools that are predominantly white. It is argued that institutionalized discrimination is responsible for this situation.

are. In this way, institutionalized prejudice and discrimination combine to maintain blacks in a disadvantaged social and economic position (Duberman, 1976).

Institutionalized prejudice and discrimination are very much factors in race relations in South Africa. In 1948, the government formally institutionalized total segregation, and *apartheid* ("separateness") has become a national policy. It extends into every aspect of life, from education to job and marriage restrictions, all the way down to separate doorways for the different "races" in public buildings. Although some *apartheid* restrictions have been relaxed recently as a result of intense international pressures, the basic policy is unlikely to be abolished in the near future.

Under the *apartheid* system, the population of South Africa is divided into four groups, rigidly defined in "racial" terms. At the top are the whites—descendants of the original Dutch (called Afrikaners) and British colonists. Below the whites are the Asians, descendants of Malaysian slaves and recent immigrants from the East. Below the Asians are the coloreds, descendants of unions among the three other groups (although official Afrikaner policy outlawed such "race mixing" until the law was changed in 1985). Finally, at the very bottom of the hierarchy, are the blacks, descendants of the original native populations and the Bantu-speaking peoples who fought the Dutch settlers for the territory. Laws have been enacted to keep these four "races," or castes, separate from one another—but most especially to ensure that economic and political power remained in the hands of the whites, who today number some 4.9 million people, out of a total population of 31 million (22.5 million of whom are blacks).

Apartheid serves the economic and political interests of the ruling white caste, and it is built into almost all the institutions of South African society—especially those controlled by Afrikaners. Since 1857 the Dutch Reformed church, the largest religious denomination in South Africa, has endorsed segregation and declared that the only salvation of the people's existence lies in the separation of the races (Carstens, 1978). Carstens points out that about 70 percent of all Christians in South

Africa are black, suggesting that the Reformed church's concern clearly is to preserve the "racial" caste system—not Christianity.

South Africa's educational system also embodies *apartheid*. Not only are its schools fully segregated and centrally controlled, but *apartheid* also is taught as a valued norm. Support of separation of the races is instilled in every student.

The dangers of pollution through sexual contact between "racial" castes are driven home in many textbooks; the emphasis is on the plight of the children of mixed racial parentage who, it is claimed, are rejected by blacks and whites alike.

The current policy of the South African government is to "resolve" the racial problem by relocating all 20 million blacks to 10 Bantustans that are in the process of being given token "independence" and that occupy 13.7 percent of South Africa's land area. But the Bantustans are located in the least desirable regions and clearly cannot be self-supporting. Thus most black males must continue to live and work in white South Africa, but are deprived of all rights as South African citizens, because they are citizens of the politically "independent" Bantustan nations. This "solution" perpetuates the presence in South Africa of cheap and easily exploited black workers at the same time it attempts to defuse the accusations of racism that are leveled at the South African government.

□ Patterns in Racial and Ethnic Relations

Relations among racial and ethnic groups seem to include an infinite variety of human experiences. They run the gamut of emotions and appear to be utterly unpredictable, capricious, and irrational. They range from curiosity and hospitality, at the one extreme, to bitter hostility at the other. In this section we shall show that there is a limited number of outcomes when racial and ethnic groups come into contact. These include assimilation, pluralism, subjugation, segregation, expulsion, and annihilation. In some cases, these categories overlap—for instance, segregation

can be considered a form of subjugation—but each has distinct traits that make it worth examining separately.

Assimilation

Assimilation is the process whereby groups with different cultures come to have a common culture. It refers to more than just dress or language and includes less tangible items such as values, sentiments, and attitudes. We are really referring to the fusion of cultural heritages.

Assimilation is the integration of new elements with old ones. The transferring of one culture from one group to another is a highly complex process, often involving the rejection of ancient ideologies, habits, customs, language, and attitudes. It includes, also, the elusive problem of selection. Of the many possibilities presented by the other culture, which ones will be adopted? Why did the American Indians, for example, when they were confronted with the white civilization, take avidly to guns, horses, rum, knives, and glass beads, while showing no interest in certain other features to which whites themselves attached the highest value?

In the process of assimilation, one society sets the pattern, for the give and take of culture seems never to operate on a fifty-fifty basis. Invariably one group has a much larger role in the process than the other does, and various factors interact to make them so. Usually one of the societies enjoys greater prestige than the other, giving it an advantage in the assimilation process; or one is better suited for the environment than the other; or one has greater numerical strength than the other. Thus the pattern for the United States was set by the British colonists, and to that pattern the other groups have been asked to adapt.

institutionalized prejudice and discrimination Complex societal arrangements in which one or more institutions within a society are structured in such a way as to give benefits to one group and withhold them from another. The values and experiences of people within the society are shaped by a prejudiced social order.

assimilation The process whereby a minority gradually gives up its own cultural patterns and acquires those of the dominant group.

11.1

The Roots of Pluralism

The person principally responsible for the development of the theory of cultural pluralism was Horace Kallen, born in the area of Germany known as Silesia. He came to Boston at the age of 5 and was raised in an orthodox Jewish home. As he progressed through the Boston public schools, he underwent a common second-generation phenomenon. He started to reject his home environment and religion and developed an uncritical enthusiasm for the United States. As he put it, "It seemed to me that the identity of every human being with every other was the important thing, and that the term 'American' should nullify the meaning of every other term in one's personal makeup. . . ."

While Kallen was a student at Harvard, he experienced a number of shocks. Working in a nearby social settlement, he came in contact with liberal and socialist ideas and observed people expressing numerous ethnic goals and aspirations. This exposure caused him to question his definition of what it meant to be an American.

This quandary was compounded by his experiences in the American literature class of Professor Barrett Wendell, who believed that Puritan traits and ideals were at the core of the American value structure. The Puritans, in turn, had modeled themselves after the Old Testament prophets. Wendell even suggested that the early Puritans were largely of Jewish descent. These ideas led Kallen to believe that he could be an unassimilated Jew and still belong to the core of the American value system.

After discovering that he could be totally Jewish and still be American, he came to realize that the application could be made to other ethnic groups as well. All ethnic groups, he felt, should preserve their own separate culture without shame or guilt. As he put it, "Democracy involves not the elimination of differences, but the perfection and conservation of differences."

Pluralism is a philosophy that not only assumes that minorities have rights but also considers the lifestyle of a minority group to be a legitimate and even desirable way of participating in society. □

This process has often been referred to as **Anglo conformity**—the renunciation of the ancestral cultures in favor of Anglo-American behavior and values (Gordon, 1964, Berry and Tischler, 1978).

Sometimes assimilation is a major goal of a country, as it was in the Soviet Union immediately after the 1917 revolution. The leaders of the new socialist state believed that regional and ethnic "nationalism" was a holdover from feudal times and could be exploited by enemies of the new regime to divide and conquer the Soviet Union. During the 1930s and 1940s an intensive program of "Russification" was carried out through the school system, with the intention of making Russian the one true national language. Nonetheless, regional ethnic identification in the Soviet Union remains very strong both in people's sense of their own individual identity and as a form of protest against the continued political dominance by the Great Russians, who (as of the 1970 census) made up 53.5 percent of the entire population. Even though Russian is the official language of the entire nation, some 96 to 98 percent of the major ethnic minorities in the Soviet Union continue to use their own languages in daily life (Pipes, 1975).

Although assimilation frequently has been a professed political goal in the United States, it has seldom been fully achieved. For example, consider the case of the Native Americans (Indians). In 1924 they were granted full United States citizenship. Nevertheless, the federal government's policies regarding the integration of Native Americans into American society wavered back and forth until the Hoover Commission Report of 1946 became the guideline for all subsequent administrations. The report stated that

> A program for the Indian peoples must include progressive measures for their complete integration into the mass of the population as full, tax-paying [members of the larger society]. . . . Young employable Indians and the better cultured [sic] families should be encouraged and assisted to leave

According to the theory of pluralism, the differences between various ethnic groups within a society should be preserved and celebrated.

the reservations and set themselves up on the land or in business. (Shepardson, 1963)

However, to this day Native American groups remain largely unassimilated into the mainstream of American life. About 55 percent live on or near reservations, and most of the rest live in impoverished urban "ghettos."

Other groups, whether or not by choice, also have not been assimilated. The Amish, for instance, have steadfastly maintained their subculture in the face of Anglo conformity pressures from the larger American society.

China provides an interesting example of what might be called "reverse" assimilation. Usually it is the defeated minority groups who are assimilated into the culture of the politically dominant group. In the seventeenth century, however, Mongol invaders conquered China and installed themselves as rulers. The Mongols were nomadic pastoralists (see Chapter 8). They were so impressed with the advanced achievements of the Chinese civilization that they gave up their own ways and took on the trappings of Chinese culture: language, manners, dress, and philosophy. During their rule the Mongols fully assimilated the Chinese culture.

Pluralism

Pluralism, or the development and coexistence of separate racial and ethnic group identities within a society, is a philosophical viewpoint that attempts to produce what is considered to be a desirable social situation. When people use the term *pluralism* today, they believe they are describing a condition that seems to be developing in contemporary American society. They often ignore the ideological foundation of pluralism (see Box 11.1: "The Roots of Pluralism").

Pluralism is a reaction against assimilationism and the melting-pot idea. It is a philosophy that not only assumes that minorities have rights but also considers the lifestyle of the minority group to be a legitimate, and even desirable, way of participating in society. The theory of pluralism celebrates the differences among groups of people. The theory also implies a hostility to existing inequalities in the status and treatment of minority groups. Pluralism has provided a means for minorities to resist the pull of assimilation, by allowing them to claim that they constitute the very structure of the social order. From the assim-

Anglo conformity A form of assimilation that occurs in the United States. Anglo conformity refers to the renunciation of the ancestral culture in favor of Anglo-American behavior and values.

pluralism The development and coexistence of separate racial and ethnic group identities in a society in which no single subgroup dominates.

ilationist point of view, the minority is seen as a subordinate group that should give up its identity as quickly as possible. Pluralism, on the other hand, assumes that the minority is a primary unit of society and that the unity of the whole depends on the harmony of the various parts.

Switzerland provides an example of balanced pluralism that so far has worked out exceptionally well (Kohn, 1956). After a short civil war between the Catholics and the Protestants in 1847, a new constitution—drafted in 1848—established a confederation of cantons (states), and church–state relations were left up to the individual cantons. The three major languages—German, French, and Italian—were declared official languages for the whole nation, and their respective speakers were acknowledged as political equals (Petersen, 1975).

Switzerland's linguistic regions are culturally quite distinctive. Italian-speaking Switzerland has a Mediterranean flavor; in French-speaking Switzerland one senses the culture of France; and German-speaking Switzerland is distinctly Germanic. However, all three linguistic groups are fiercely pro-Swiss, and the German-Swiss especially have strong anti-German sentiments.

Subjugation

One of the consequences of the interaction of racial and ethnic groups has been subjugation—the subordination of one group and the assumption of a position of authority, power, and domination by the other. The members of the subordinate group may for a time accept their lower status and even devise ingenious rationalizations for it.

In theory we could assume that two groups may come together and develop an egalitarian relationship. However, there are few cases in which racial and ethnic groups have established such a relationship. For the most part this is so because there are few instances in which group contact has been based on the complete equality of power. Differences in power will invariably lead to a situation of superior and inferior position. The greater is the discrepancy in the power of the groups

involved, the greater the extent and scope of the subjugation will be.

Why should different levels of power between two groups lead to the domination of one by the other? Gerhard Lenski (1966) proposed that it is because people have a desire to control goods and services. No matter how much they have, they are never satisfied. In addition, high status is often associated with the consumption of goods and services. Therefore demand will exceed supply, and as Lenski claims, a struggle for rewards will be present in every human society. The outcome of this struggle thus will lead to the subjugation of one group by the other.

According to Lenski's argument, in many cases the efforts of one group to dominate another group are motivated by a desire to control goods and services. When a racial or ethnic group is placed in an inferior position, its people are often eliminated as competitors. In addition, their subordinate position may increase the supply of goods and services available to the dominant group.

Segregation

Segregation is actually a form of subjugation. It refers to the act, process, or state of being set apart. It is a situation that places limits and restrictions on the contact, communication, and social relations among groups. Many people think of segregation as a negative phenomenon—a form of ostracism imposed on a minority by a dominant group—and this is most often the case. However, for some groups such as the Amish or Chinese who wish to retain their ethnicity, segregation is voluntary.

The practice of segregating people is as old as the human race itself. There are examples of it in the Bible and in preliterate cultures. American blacks were originally segregated by the institution of slavery and later by both formal sanction and informal discrimination. Although some blacks formed groups that preached total segregation from whites as an aid to black cultural development, for most it is an involuntary and degrading experience. The word ghetto is derived from the segregated quarter of a city where the Jews in Europe were often forced to live. Native American tribes were often forced to choose segregation on a reservation in preference to annihilation or assimilation. Segregation has operated in a wide range of circumstances.

Expulsion

Expulsion is the process of forcing a group to leave the territory in which it resides. This can be accomplished indirectly by making life increasingly unpleasant for a group, as the Germans did for Jews after Adolf Hitler was appointed chancellor in 1933. Over the following six years, Jews were stripped of their citizenship, made ineligible to hold public office, removed from the professions, and forced out of the artistic and intellectual circles to which they had belonged. In 1938 Jewish children were barred from the public schools. At the same time the government encouraged acts of violence and vandalism against Jewish communities. These actions culminated in *Kristallnacht*, November 9, 1938, when the windows in synagogues and Jewish homes and businesses across Germany were shattered and individuals were beaten up. Under these conditions, Jews left Germany by the thousands. In 1933 there were some 500,000 Jews in Germany; by 1940—before Hitler began his "final solution"—only 220,000 remained (Robinson, 1976).

Expulsion can also be accomplished through direct means—that is, forced migration. Some estimates of the number of blacks transported from Africa to the Americas during the slave trade years range as high as 30 million. For Brazil alone, the estimates range from 3 to 18 million.

Forced migration also was a major aspect of the United States government's policies toward Native American groups in the nineteenth century. For example, when the army needed to protect its lines of communication to the West Coast, Colonel "Kit" Carson was ordered to move the Navajos of Arizona and New Mexico out of the way. He was instructed to kill all the men who resisted and to take everybody else captive. He accomplished this in 1864 by destroying their cornfields and slaughtering their herds of sheep,

A Jewish family with their furniture and possessions passing before a jeering crowd during their expulsion from Memel, Germany, in 1939.

thereby confronting the Navajos with starvation. After a last showdown in Canyon de Chelly, some eight thousand Navajos were rounded up in Fort Defiance. They then were marched on foot three hundred miles to Fort Sumner, where they were to be taught the ways of "civilization" (Spicer, 1962).

subjugation The subordination of one group and the assumption of a position of authority, power, and domination by the other.

segregation A form of subjugation, segregation refers to the act, process, or state of being set apart. It places limits and restrictions on contact, communication, and social relations among groups.

ghetto A term derived from the segregated quarter of a city where the Jews in Europe were often forced to live. It is now used to classify a segregated housing area occupied by members of a (usually) poor minority, such as black, Hispanic, Asian, and so on.

expulsion The process of forcing a group to leave the territory in which it resides.

forced migration The process of actually moving people from one location to another.

Will the United States Finally Sign the Genocide Convention?

Enemies of the United States have criticized this country for its failure to ratify the Genocide Convention. They claim that this failure indicates that the United States condones or even practices genocide. But as the following analysis points out, most of the objections to the convention in the United States rest on legal considerations, many of which are intertwined with sociological considerations including the fundamental question, "What constitutes a group?"

The sheer magnitude and horror of the Nazi attempt to exterminate the Jews provoked outrage and attempts by the nations of the world to prevent such circumstances from arising again. On December 11, 1946, the General Assembly of the United Nations passed by unanimous vote a resolution affirming that genocide was a crime under international law that the civilized world condemned and for the commission of which both principals and accomplices alike would be held accountable and would be punished. The assembly called for the preparation of a convention on genocide that would define the offense more precisely and provide enforcement procedures for its repression and punishment.

After two years of study and debate, the draft of the convention on genocide was presented to the General Assembly, and it was adopted. Article II of the convention defines genocide as

. . . any of the following acts committed with intent to destroy, in whole or in part, a national, ethnical, racial or religious group as such:

(a) Killing members of the group;
(b) Causing serious bodily or mental harm to members of the group;
(c) Deliberately inflicting on the group conditions of life calculated to bring about its physical destruction in whole or part;

(d) Imposing measures intended to prevent births within the group;
(e) Forcibly transferring children of the group to another group.

The convention furthermore provided that any of the contracting parties could call on the United Nations to take action under its charter for the "prevention and suppression" of acts of genocide. In addition, any of the contracting parties could bring charges before the International Court of Justice.

Here in the United States, President Harry Truman submitted the resolution to the Senate on June 16, 1949, for ratification. However, the Senate did not act on the measure, and the United States did not sign the document. In 1984 President Ronald Reagan again requested the Senate to hold hearings on the convention so that it could be signed. But again, Senate approval was not forthcoming. The reasons for not signing the convention in 1949 and the objections that were raised again in the 1980s reflect an attempt to prevent the limitation of the constitutional rights of United States citizens, rather than an endorsement of genocide. Some of the objections raised over the years have centered on a number of issues.

What constitutes a group? Most of the objections noted that the various articles were too vague. To begin with, in Article II(a), a question was raised about what actually constitutes a "national, ethnical, racial, or religious group as such." It was pointed out that there are all kinds of groups, such as groups that get together for bargaining on a labor contract, protest groups, and groups that go on trips together. Could actions against these groups be considered as genocide?

Questions were also raised about how many people are needed to make up a group. Is a group made

up of two, or three, or millions? A police officer who wantonly shot two Black Muslims would be charged with homicide. However, if it could be claimed that the individuals were shot because they were members of a particular group, the crime would no longer be homicide alone but genocide as well, and the accused could be brought before an international tribunal.

What constitutes mental harm? Article II(b) states that genocide involves "causing serious mental harm to members of the group." Here again the wording was considered to be too vague. Mental harm was assumed to mean permanent injury or impairment to the mental faculties. However, some would claim that segregation of schoolchildren could constitute genocide, based on the U.S. Supreme Court ruling in the *Brown* v. *Board of Education of Topeka, Kansas* case of 1954, which stated that segregating black schoolchildren from whites caused feelings of inferiority and damaged blacks' personalities and learning capabilities in ways that could not be undone.

What constitutes physical destruction? This question was raised about Article II(c), which states that genocide also includes "inflicting on the group conditions of life calculated to bring about its physical destruction in whole or in part." It was argued that this could be interpreted to mean that a city could be charged with genocide for causing its minority populations to live in a ghetto or slum.

What constitutes the prevention of birth? In Article II(d), genocide is meant to include "imposing measures intended to prevent births within the group." Here questions were raised about whether compulsory sterilization of mental defectives or encouragement of the use of contraceptives among the poor could be construed as genocide. The opponents pointed to instances in which birth control clinics and individuals dispensing birth control information to minority groups had been accused of genocide.

What constitutes forcible transfer of children? According to Article II(e), genocide also includes "forcibly transferring children of the group to another group." The opponents asked whether the compulsory busing of black children to white schools and vice versa could be construed as genocide.

The senators were also con-cerned about the fact that certain actions protected under the free-speech amendment of the American Constitution would be outlawed under the United Nations Genocide Convention. For example, racial slurs or stronger statements such as "kill Whitey" or "shoot cops" could be considered as "incitement to commit genocide" under Article II of the convention.

Questions were also raised about how genocide differs from modern warfare in which hundreds of thousands of people could be killed with one bomb. And many other objections to the convention have been raised on technical matters such as extradition treaties and due process under the law. But of greatest concern to Americans have been the sociolegal questions discussed in this article. One final point to note is that in the nearly 40 years of its existence, the Genocide Convention has never been used to bring charges of genocide against a country. Numerous examples of genocide have occurred during that period.

Source: Adapted from Brewton Berry and Henry L. Tischler, *Race and Ethnic Relations* (Boston: Houghton Mifflin, 1978), pp. 362–366. □

Although expulsion is an extreme attempt to eliminate a certain minority from an area, annihilation is the most extreme action one group can take against another.

Annihilation

Annihilation refers to the deliberate practice of trying to exterminate a racial or ethnic group. In recent years it has also been referred to as *genocide*, a word coined to describe the crimes committed by the Nazis during World War II—crimes that induced the United Nations to draw up a convention on genocide. (See Using Sociology: "Will the United States Finally Sign the Genocide Convention?") Annihilation is the denial of the right to live of an entire group of people, in the same way that homicide is the denial of the right to live of one person.

Sometimes annihilation occurs as an unintended result of new contact between two groups. For example, when the Europeans arrived in the Americas, they brought with them a disease, smallpox, new to the people they encountered. Native American groups, the Blackfeet, the Aztecs, and the Incas, among many others, who had no immunity at all against this disease, were nearly wiped out (McNeill, 1976). In most cases, however, the extermination of one group by another has been the result of deliberate action. Thus the native population of Tasmania, a large island off the coast of Australia, was exterminated by Europeans in the 250 years after its discovery in 1642.

The largest, most systematic program of ethnic extermination was the murder of close to 6 million Jews by the Nazis before and during World War II. In each country occupied by the Germans, the majority of the Jewish population was killed. Thus, in the mid-1930s, before the war, there were about 3.3 million Jews in Poland, but at the end of the war in 1945 there were only 73,955 Polish Jews left (Baron, 1976). Among them, not a single known family remained intact.

Although there have been recent attempts to portray this mass murder of Jews as a secret undertaking of the Nazi elite that was not widely supported by the German people, the historical evidence suggests otherwise. For example, during a wave of anti-Semitism (anti-Jewish prejudice, accompanied by violence and repression) in Germany in the 1880s—long before the Nazi regime—only 75 German scholars and other distinguished citizens protested publicly. During the 1930s the majority of German Protestant churches endorsed the "racial" principles that were used by the Nazis to justify first the disenfranchisement of Jews, then

annihilation The deliberate practice of trying to exterminate a racial or ethnic group; also known as genocide.

311

their forced deportation, and finally their extermination. (Jews were blamed for a bewildering combination of "crimes," including "polluting the purity of the Aryan race," and causing the rise of communism while at the same time manipulating capitalist economies through their "secret control" of banks.)

It would seem, then, that the majority of Germans supported the Nazi racial policies or at best were apathetic (Robinson, 1976). Although in 1943 both the Catholic church and the anti-Nazi Confessing church finally condemned the "murder of innocent people" and pointedly stated that "race" was no justification for murder, it is fair to say that even this opposition was "mild, vague, and belated" (Robinson, 1976). But the fact that such objections were raised points out that the Nazis' plan to exterminate all Jews was not a well-kept military secret. The measure of its success is that some 60 percent of all Jews in

Europe—36 percent of all Jews in the world—were slaughtered (computed from figures in Baron, 1976).

Another "race" also slated for extermination by the Nazis were the Gypsies, a people made up of small wandering groups who appear to be the descendants of the Aryan invaders of India, the Central Eurasian nomads mentioned in Chapter 10. For the last thousand years or so, Gypsy bands have ". . . spread throughout the continents, . . . rejected, subjected but unassimilated . . ." (Ulc, 1975). In Europe they are widely disliked and constantly accused of small thefts and other criminal behavior.

Many different racial and ethnic groups are found throughout the United States. Below we shall examine their settlement patterns, current distribution, and treatment by other Americans.

☐ Racial and Ethnic Groups in American Society

Around the time of its War of Independence, America's population was mostly English and Protestant (60.9 percent). It also included smaller numbers of people from other northwestern European countries as well as sprinklings from other nations such as Poland and Switzerland. Catholics were few in number, and Jews were fewer yet. Blacks, at slightly over 500,000, made up about 20 percent of the total population (U.S. Bureau of the Census, 1976). Records on Native Americans are incomplete. But in any event they were not seen as part of the new nation: generally they were treated with hostility and contempt, and force was used to drive them inland, away from the Atlantic coastline where the 13 colonies were being established (Gordon, 1975).

What is America's racial and ethnic composition today? The United States is perhaps the most racially and ethnically diverse country in the world. (Table 11.1 shows the major groups and their populations.) And unlike many other countries, it has no ethnic group that makes up a numerical majority of the population. In the following discussion, we shall examine the major groups in American society.

TABLE 11.1 Population of Major Racial and Ethnic Groups in the United States

Race or Ethnic Origin	Population	Percent of Total Population
Blacks	26,896,000	11.7
German	15,234,000	6.9
British (WASPs)	10,892,000	4.9
Irish	8,357,000	3.8
Mexican	7,700,000	3.2
Italian	6,778,000	3.1
Jewish	5,861,000	2.6
Polish	3,459,000	1.6
Spanish (includes people from Central or South America, Cuba, Spain, and other Spanish origin except Mexican and Puerto Rican)	3,072,000	1.4
French	2,914,000	1.3
Puerto Rican	1,400,000	0.8
Russian	1,475,000	0.7
Native Americans (Indians)	1,420,000	0.6
Chinese	806,027	0.4
Filipinos	774,640	0.3
Japanese	701,000	0.3
Other	117,011,000	—

Source: Adapted from U.S. Department of Commerce, Bureau of the Census, *Statistical Abstract of the United States 1984*, and *1980 Census of Population*, Supplementary Reports, no. PC80-S1-3, p. 6; and Morris Fine et al. (eds.), *American Jewish Yearbook* (Philadelphia: Jewish Publication Society, 1980), p. 9.

11.2
The New Colossus

Emma Lazarus, herself a young Jewish immigrant, described the hope that America represented—and still represents to many people throughout the world—in this poem, which is inscribed on the base of the Statue of Liberty.

Not like the brazen giant of Greek fame,
   With conquering limbs astride from land to
      land;
   Here at our sea-washed, sunset gates shall stand
A mighty woman with a torch, whose flame
Is the imprisoned lightning, and her name
   Mother of Exiles. From her beacon-hand
   Glows world-wide welcome; her mild eyes
      command
The air-bridged harbor that twin cities frame.
"Keep ancient lands, your storied pomp!" cries she
   With silent lips. "Give me your tired, your poor,
Your huddled masses yearning to breathe free;
   The wretched refuse of your teeming shore.
Send these, the homeless, tempest-tost to me,
   I lift my lamp beside the golden door!"

White Anglo-Saxon Protestants

Of 227,350,000 Americans in 1980, 61,312,000 claimed some English, Scottish, or Welsh origin. These Americans of British origin are often grouped together as white Anglo-Saxon Protestants (WASPs). Although in numbers they are a minority within the total American population, they have been in America the longest (aside from the Native Americans, a marginal group but growing rapidly in number) and, as a group, have always had the greatest economic and political power in the country (Mills, 1963). As a result, white Anglo-Saxon Protestants often have acted as if they were the ethnic majority in America, influencing other ethnic groups to assimilate or acculturate to their way of life, the ideal of Anglo conformity (Cole and Cole, 1954). Interestingly, although white Anglo-Saxon Protestants are the economically dominant ethnic group in America, they do not have the highest per-family income. White Anglo-Saxon families have an average income only slightly higher than that of the average American family (U.S. Dept. of Commerce, 1983).

The Americanization of immigrant groups has been the desired goal of the dominant white Anglo-Saxon Protestants during many periods in American history. Contrary to the romantic sentiments expressed on the base of the Statue of Liberty (see Box 11.2), immigrant groups who came to America after the British Protestants had become established met with considerable hostility and suspicion.

The 1830s and 1840s saw the rise of the "native" American (WASPs) movement, directed against recent immigrant groups (and especially Catholics). In 1841 the American Protestant Union was founded in New York City to oppose the "subjugation of our country to control of the Pope of Rome, and his adherents" (Leonard and Parmet, 1971). On the East Coast it was the Irish Catholics who were feared, and in the Midwest it was the German "freethinkers." Protestant religious organizations across America joined forces and urged "native" Americans to organize in order to offset "foreign" voting blocs. They also conducted intimidation campaigns against "foreigners" and attempted to persuade Catholics to renounce their religion for Protestanism (Leonard and Parmet, 1971).

As the twentieth century dawned, American sentiments against immigrants from

Southern and Eastern Europe were running high. In Boston the Immigration Restriction League was formed, which directed its efforts toward keeping out "racially inferior" groups—who were depicted as inherently criminal, mentally defective, and marginally educable. The league achieved its goals in 1924 when the government adopted a new immigration policy that set quotas on the numbers of immigrants to be admitted from various nations. Because the quotas were designed to reflect (and reestablish) the ethnic composition of America in the 1890s, they heavily favored the admission of immigrants from Britain, Ireland, Germany, Holland, and Scandinavia. This new policy was celebrated as a victory for the "Nordic" race (Krause, 1966).

Another expression of Anglo conformity pressure was the Americanization Movement, which gained strength from the nationalistic passions brought on by World War I. Its stated purpose was to promote the very rapid acculturation of new immigrants. Thus "federal agencies, state government, municipalities, and a host of private organizations joined in the effort to persuade the immigrant to learn English, take out naturalization papers, buy war bonds, forget his former origins and culture, and give himself over to patriotic hysteria" (Gordon, 1975).

From World War II until the early 1960s, Anglo conformity was pretty much an established ideal of the American way of life. In the last decades, there has been a strong organized reaction among other ethnic groups against Anglo conformity. Strong social-political movements, organized along ethnic group lines, have formed. Blacks led the way in the later 1960s with the Black Power Movement, and they were joined by Italian Americans, Mexican Americans (Chicanos), Puerto Ricans, Native Americans, and others. America once again is focusing on its ethnic diversity, and the assumptions of Anglo conformity are being questioned.

Other "White Ethnic" Groups

Sociologists often refer to the descendants of immigrants from Southern and Eastern Europe as "white ethnics" (Novak, 1972). Currently the term is used to refer to any whites who are not of Northern European origin or Protestant. As a group, white ethnics are the largest ethnic minority in America, though the separate ethnic groups do not appear to have accepted their shared sociological label. Many of these immigrants have not been ready to discard their distinctive native cultures and embrace American ways. People from these groups often have come to the United States to better themselves economically, not to adopt a new lifestyle. Their goals have often been to earn enough money to send to relatives back home and eventually to return there themselves. Immigrants from the same country have tended to form their own communities—the Little Italies and the Germantowns, for instance—following their own customs and speaking their native languages. Each group has sought to preserve its own ethnic identity, and therefore explicit political cooperation among these groups has not materialized (Levine and Herman, 1974). (For a discussion of how one of these groups, Italian Americans, has been portrayed in the media, see Case Study: "How the Media Portray Italian Americans.")

Jews

There is no satisfactory answer to the question "What makes the Jews a people?" other than to say, "The fact that they see themselves—and are seen by others—as one." Judaism is a religion, of course, but many Jews are nonreligious. Some think of Jews as a "race," but their physical diversity makes this notion absurd. For more than two thousand years, Jews have been dispersed around the world. Reflecting this geographic separation, three major Jewish groups have evolved, each with its own distinctive culture: the *Ashkenazim*—the Jews of Eastern and Western Europe (excluding Spain); the *Sephardim*—the Jews of Turkey, Spain, and western North Africa; and the "Oriental" Jews of Egypt, Ethiopia, the Middle East, and Central Asia. Nor are Jews united linguistically. In addition to speaking the language of whatever nation they are living in, many Jews speak one or more of three Jewish languages: Hebrew, the language of ancient and modern Israel; Yiddish, a Germanic language spoken by Ashkenazi

CASE STUDY
How the Media Portray Italian Americans

Since the massive immigration of Italians to the United States during the latter part of the nineteenth century and the early years of the twentieth century, the media have persistently used a pattern of stereotypes to portray Italian Americans. This widespread perspective has had certain effects on how Italian Americans view themselves as individuals and as members of a multiethnic society and on how the general public views them.

Judging by popular films, books, and television programs, to be Italian American in our society is to be either a criminal or an undereducated, working-class tough. These two stereotypes have been so consistently advanced by the popular media that Italian Americans themselves have come to believe their validity.

Although the working-class image is more recent, the association of Italians with criminal activity dates from before the turn of the century. Following the murder of a police superintendent in October, the magazine *Popular Science Monthly* of December 1890 featured an article entitled "What Shall We Do with the Dago?" In it, Italian immigrants were described as a serious threat to society. A "Dago" was viewed as a small, swarthy, stiletto-wielding, and plotting type.

By 1908, New York City was in the grip of a "Black Hand" mania. The influence of the Black Hand was believed to be so great that many journalists were convinced that all murders and tenement fires in Italian-American neighborhoods were the work of this sinister Italian-dominated organization. The *New York Times* at that time editorialized that Italian criminals in America were "sufficiently alike to constitute a separate class."

Hollywood of the 1930s thrived on gangster movies. Italian-American characters were portrayed in numerous films, beginning with

John Travolta plays Italian Tony Manero in the film "Saturday Night Fever."

Edward G. Robinson's role as Rico in *Little Caesar* in 1930 and continuing into the 1970s and early 1980s with such films as *The Godfather*, Parts I and II, *Gloria*, and *Prince of the City*. In between there have been countless movies, including a number made especially for television, in which Italian and Italian-American characters have been depicted as criminals, whether loosely organized as a mob or structured on the basis of real and fictive kinship ties.

The gangster image of the Italian American has been so pervasive and convincing that Alistair Cooke, while hosting an American heritage television program during the bicentennial celebration year, selected Al Capone as a famous Italian American.

Hollywood got a great deal of mileage from portraying Al Capone as a brutal gangster who led a group of coconspirators called the "Mob." But by the 1970s, a new variety of Italian-American criminal came to be seen as the norm. Although ruthless to those who would harm his relatives or betray him, Don Corleone, the "Godfather," was nonetheless depicted as a generous, loyal family man. Hence, in less than a century, the perception of an Italian-American criminal association has varied from a secret band of co-conspirators to loosely organized mobs and finally to the image of a crime "family."

In recent years another Italian-American stereotype has come to be pervasive in the media, that of the blue-collar, working-class character who is frequently good-hearted but often not too bright. Laverne of "Laverne and Shirley," Fonzi of "Happy Days," Tony Manero of "Saturday Night Fever," and "Rocky" and "Rocky II", are typical examples of this stereotype.

Laverne, for example, is portrayed as the archetypal Italian-American female: tough, dumb, coarse, big-hearted, and in a perpetual state of sexual arousal. Fonzi typifies the Italian-American working-class male: undereducated, crude, sexually irresistible, and given to solving problems with threats of violence or, if necessary, with his fists.

What has been the effect of these consistently portrayed stereotypes on the public perception of Italian Americans and on the members of the ethnic group itself?

Scholars generally acknowledge that at the very least, the media reinforce prevalent attitudes, values, perceptions, and behaviors as they constantly interact with what Walter Lippman so aptly characterized as the "pictures in our heads." And in the absence of other, contradictory data, the media may well shape those same attitudes, perceptions, and behaviors.

The image of the Italian American as criminal has been constantly represented over the past 90 years. Although the working-class image is more recent, it too has become a persistent stereotype.

Impressionable Italian Americans and those with little or no non-media information with which to make a more accurate assessment of the caricatures are probably most affected by the media representation. Not only do many Italian Americans view themselves as a lower-class ethnic group, but many non-Italian Americans probably have a similar "picture in their heads."

Surveys conducted by students in a seminar on media portrayals suggest that substantial numbers of people representing a variety of ethnic groups accepted as relatively accurate the media depictions of Italian Americans. The greatest number felt that the Mafia image was an authentic portrayal.

It is difficult to say how these popular images affect Italian Americans in the marketplace for jobs, in political contests, or in a court of law. But in a highly competitive society, individuals are often the ones to pay for such negative perceptions of an entire ethnic group.

Source: Adapted from Anthony L. LaRuffa, "Media Portrayals of Italian-Americans," *Ethnic Groups* **4** (1982), pp. 191–206. □

A large number of Eastern Europeans immigrated to America between the 1880s and the 1920s to escape anti-Semitism.

Jews; and Ladino, an ancient Romance language spoken by the Sephardim.

The first Jews came to America from Brazil in 1654, but it was not until the mid-1800s that large numbers of Jews began to arrive. These were mostly German Jews, refugees from European anti-Semitism. Then, with especially violent anti-Semitism erupting in Eastern Europe in the 1880s, there was a massive increase in Jewish immigration to America. It came in two "waves": in the last two decades of the nineteenth century and in the first two decades of the twentieth.

Jewish immigration was similar to that of other groups, in that it consisted overwhelmingly of young people, though the Jewish immigration also had some unique features. First, it was much more a migration of families than was that of other European immigrants, who were mostly single males. Second, Jewish immigrants were much more committed to staying here: two-thirds of all immigrants to the United States between 1908 and 1924 remained, but 94.8 percent of the Jewish immigrants settled here permanently. Third, the Jewish immigrant groups contained a higher percentage of skilled and urban workers than did other groups. And fourth, especially after the turn of the century, there were many scholars and intellectuals among Jewish immigrants, which was not true of other immigrant groups (Howe, 1976).

These differences account for the fact that even though Jews encountered at least as much hostility from white Anglo-Saxon Protestants as did other immigrant groups (and also were subject to intense prejudice from Catholics), they have had relatively more success in pulling themselves up the socioeconomic ladder. Of the approximately six million Jews in America today, 53 percent of those working are in the professions and business (versus 25 percent for the nation as an average).

Blacks

Blacks are the second largest racial group in the country. The 1980 census figures showed 26,896,000 blacks living in the United States, about 12 percent of the total population of 227,375,000 (U.S. Dept. of Commerce, 1983). Of these, roughly three-quarters live in urban areas, and about 47 percent live in the North (Herbers, 1981; U.S. Bureau of the Census, 1981). This is a significant shift from the 1940s, when roughly 80 percent of American blacks lived in the South and worked in agriculture. (For a discussion of how the black population is changing, see Focus on Research: "Emerging Black Ethnics.")

In 1619, when the first 20 blacks were unloaded from a Dutch man-of-war at Jamestown, Virginia, they were given the status of indentured servants. The blacks did not enjoy this status very long, however, and they began to be treated with more severity than were the white European indentured servants. By the end of the seventeenth century, the status of blacks had changed to one of slavery. The underlying factor was the demand for a labor supply. Black slaves were preferable to white indentured servants for several reasons: (1) their skin color and facial features made them easy to identify should they escape; (2) because they were only slaves, the women could be put to work in the fields, contrary to the custom for indentured women; (3) as slaves,

the services of blacks were available for life, whereas those of indentured servants were available only for a few years; and (4) their children, unlike servants' children, were also valuable property. Black slaves, therefore, eventually displaced white indentured servants in the cotton and tobacco colonies.

For years most whites and blacks in the United States interacted only as owner and slave. There were, to be sure, free blacks, whose number rose to nearly half a million by 1860. Most of them had been set free by their owners for reasons of sentiment or ideals or because of some meritorious service performed while in slavery. Others were the descendants of free mothers (white or black) or of unions between Native Americans (Indians) and blacks; and some, through their own thrift, had earned enough to buy their freedom.

Although the Civil War marked the end of slavery, it did not signal the beginning of equality for blacks. Southern states enacted laws, known as Black Codes, which placed limitations on blacks' ownership and rental of property, possession of firearms, testimony in court, freedom of speech and movement, choice of occupation, and voting privileges. Heavy penalties were levied for vagrancy and breach of contract, creating what amounted to a system of forced labor. After several decades, a new pattern emerged—white Southerners called it "white supremacy," and blacks referred to it as "second-class citizenship." Its features are well known. Blacks were virtually deprived of their rights of citizenship. Their economic opportunities were severely limited, with many occupations closed to them and a "job ceiling" established in those areas in which they were allowed to work. The educational facilities provided for them were inferior to those provided for whites. They were barred from most hotels, restaurants, theaters, barber shops, auditoriums, parks, and playgrounds; the accommodations offered to them on trains, streetcars, and buses were separate but seldom equal. They were restricted and exploited as home owners or tenants. The medical facilities available to them were limited, with the result that they suffered high mortality rates. In courts and at the hands of the law, they did not enjoy the same treatment accorded to whites.

FOCUS ON RESEARCH
Emerging Black Ethnics

Americans typically view whites as members of ethnic groups—German, Irish, Mexican, and so on. But they see blacks simply as black. Now, says an observer, they may have to start viewing blacks differently.

As black immigration has increased during the past two decades, black immigrants and their offspring are accounting for a greater share of all blacks in the United States, according to Population Reference Bureau demographer Leon Bouvier.

The proportion of black immigrants in the total black population is now greater than the proportion of nonblack immigrants in the total nonblack population. "In some cities," Bouvier notes, "black immigrants are becoming an increasingly visible segment of the black population. Washington, D.C., now has six Ethiopian restaurants."

By analyzing unpublished data from the Immigration and Naturalization Service, Bouvier was able to estimate the number of blacks who immigrated to the United States, by counting arrivals from countries that have predominantly black populations, such as Belize in Central America, Guyana in South America, and the islands of the West Indies, excluding Cuba. He counted all countries in Africa except those of North Africa, which are predominantly Arab, and South Africa. Even so, says Bouvier, this procedure probably still underestimates the number of black immigrants.

By these calculations, the number of black immigrants rose from under 49,000 in 1969 to over 73,000 in 1979, an almost 50-percent increase. Stated even more dramatically, there were fewer than 4,000 black immigrants to the United States in 1954. In the 1980s, it is estimated that the tide has swelled to about 80,000 per year.

Currently, there are only about 819,000 blacks born abroad living in the United States, plus their descendants, compared with a native-born black population of 26 million. Assuming an annual immigration of about 72,000 per year, there would be 2.5 million black immigrants and their descendants in the United States by the year 2000, in a total black population of 33 million. By 2030, their numbers should nearly double to 4.8 million, whereas native-born blacks and their descendants would increase only to 37 million.

"The black population may be entering a new era," Bouvier observed. "The white population went through turmoil at the turn of the century when the foreign influx was heavy. It caused problems among different white ethnic groups. A similar problem may emerge among blacks."

Source: Adapted from "Emerging Black Ethnics," *American Demographics*, **6** (2) (February, 1984), p. 11. □

During World War I, blacks began to break the barriers of the system as they slowly started to gain power. Their horizons expanded as some 400,000 of them moved from the rural South to the urban North to fill the employment vacuum created by the curtailment of immigration from Europe. Nearly 350,000 entered the armed services, and 100,000 served overseas. Blacks from different parts of the country were brought together, giving them the opportunity to share new insights and goals. They began to demand their rights as citizens, with the result that during and immediately after World War I, whites reacted by initiating race riots in scores of cities and towns throughout the country. Blacks not only made demands but were prepared to fight for them. The United States Supreme Court, which had long sanctioned the white supremacy and separate-but-equal philosophies, began to render verdicts favorable to the black cause.

World War II saw an acceleration of the movement toward equality. The number of black officers in the armed services grew. President Franklin D. Roosevelt issued an executive order that forbade racial discrimination in defense industries and created the Fair Employment Practices Committee. The Supreme Court continued to hand down decisions favorable to blacks.

Changes have continued since World War II. President Harry Truman in 1947 established the Committee on Civil Rights, and the following year saw the publication of its significant report, *To Secure These Rights*. The armed services were integrated. Many states adopted fair employment practices laws. In 1954 the Supreme Court handed down its historic decisions regarding the inequality of separate educational facilities.

The changing status of blacks could be seen by their prominence on Olympic teams and in radio, television, and the movies. Black novelists, poets, and artists were winning international acclaim, and black scholars began to receive appointments in leading universities. Their political power began to be used effectively, and the major parties vied for their vote. Big business became aware of their economic importance and began to compete for their patronage.

The black demands for equality grew more insistent than ever in the 1960s and 1970s. They grew impatient with the slow pace of school integration and became disillusioned when they observed how the rulings of the courts and the acts of Congress were ignored or evaded. "Freedom Rides," demonstrations, marches, sit-ins, boycotts, and numerous other forms of protest became daily occurrences throughout the country. Blacks had finally become powerful enough to fight against their second-class status.

Today, however, despite decades of intensive political struggle as well as significant progress, social and economic equality still evades blacks; for example, the income of black families still averages only 59 percent that of whites and only 62 percent of the national average—just 2 percent above Indians, who have the lowest average income (U.S. Bureau of the Census, 1981). Most sociologists believe that this is the result of enduring prejudice directed against blacks.

Mexican Americans

Concentrated in the Southwest, the 7.7 million Mexican Americans are the fourth largest ethnic group in the country. Often called Chicanos or incorporated under the larger category of Hispanics, they are predominantly Catholic and Spanish-speaking. The term *Chicano* is somewhat controversial. It has long been used as a slang word in Mexico to refer to people of low social class. In Texas it came to be used for Mexicans who illegally crossed over the border in search of work. Recently, however, many Mexican Americans have taken to using the term themselves to suggest a tough breed of individuals of Mexican ancestry who are committed to achieving success in this country and are willing to fight for it (Madsen, 1973).

In his study of Mexican Americans in Texas, William Madsen (1973) notes that among them, three "levels of acculturation" may be distinguished. Although American technology is appreciated by most Mexican Americans, one group has retained its Mexican peasant culture, at least in regard to values. Another group consists of persons torn between the traditional culture of their parents and grandparents on the one hand and Anglo-American culture (learned in American schools) on the other. Many individuals in this group suffer crises of personal and ethnic identity. Finally there are those Mexican Americans who have acculturated fully and achieved success in Anglo-American society. Some remain proud of and committed to their ethnic origins, but others would just as soon forget them and assimilate fully into the Anglo-American world.

Mexican Americans have been exploited for many years as a source of cheap agricultural labor. Their average family income is 76 percent of the national average (Urban Institute, 1978). Also, because of their poverty, they have long been willing to do the "stoop labor" (literally bending over and working close to the ground, or menial labor in general) that most Anglo Americans refuse. For almost two decades the United Farm Workers Union, under the leadership of Cesar Chavez, has been attempting to organize Mexican-American farm workers. This has been more than just a labor movement, however. Union pickets march under banners urging ethnic solidarity among the people of La Raza ("the race").

In recent years the issue of illegal Mexican immigration into the United States has received a great deal of attention. This is an outgrowth of a change in the immigration law that took effect on January 1, 1977, limiting to 20,000 the number of people that could come from any one country. This law, coupled with the economic conditions in Mexico and the possibility of obtaining employment in the United States, has produced a marked increase in the number of illegal immigrants from Mexico. Estimates of the total number of illegal Mexican immigrants in the United States at any given time range from 4 to 12 million (Fogel, 1979).

Like blacks, Mexican Americans have yet to be allowed to achieve true equality in the United States.

Puerto Ricans

In 1898 the United States fought a brief war with Spain and as a result took over the former Spanish colonies in the Pacific (the Philippines and Guam) and the Caribbean (Cuba and Puerto Rico). Puerto Ricans were made full citizens of the United States in 1917. Although government programs improved their education and dramatically lowered the death rate, rapid population growth helped keep the Puerto Rican people poor. American business took advantage of the large supply of cheap, nonunion Puerto Rican labor and built plants there under very favorable tax laws.

A large number of Puerto Ricans have migrated to the American mainland seeking better economic opportunities. Currently there are some 1.4 million Puerto Ricans here, with the majority living in the New York City area. Many make frequent return trips to the island. Despite language barriers (Puerto Ricans are Spanish-speaking), cultural differences, and "racial" prejudice (Puerto Ricans range in skin color from light to dark), Puerto Ricans have managed to pull slightly ahead of blacks in family income, at 63 percent of the national average (Urban Institute, 1978). However, as of 1979, 38.8 percent of Puerto Ricans living on the mainland still were below the poverty level (U.S. Dept. of Commerce, 1980).

Asian Americans

The first Asians to settle in America in significant numbers were the Chinese. Some 300,000 of them migrated here between 1850 and 1880 in order to escape the famine and warfare that plagued their homeland. Initially they settled on the West Coast, where they took back-breaking jobs mining and building railroads. However, they were far from welcome and were subjected to a great amount of harassment. In 1882 the government limited further Chinese immigration for 10 years. This limitation was extended in 1892 and again in 1904, finally being repealed in 1943. The state of California set special taxes on Chinese miners, and labor unions (except the Industrial Workers of the World) fought to keep them out of the mines because they took jobs from white workers. In the late 1800s and early 1900s, numerous riots and strikes were directed against the Chinese, who drew back into their "Chinatowns" for protection. The harassment proved successful. In 1880 there were 105,465 Chinese in the United States. By 1900 the figure had dropped to 89,863 and by 1920, to 61,729. The Chinese population in the United States began to rise again only after the 1950s (U.S. Bureau of the Census, 1976). Figures from the 1980 census show 806,027 ethnic Chinese in the United States (U.S. Bureau of the Census, 1981), making them the largest group of Asian origin.

Japanese immigrants began arriving in the United States shortly after the Chinese—and quickly joined them as victims of prejudice and discrimination. Feelings against the Japanese ran especially high in California, where one political movement attempted to have them expelled from the United States. In 1906 the San Francisco Board of Education decreed that all Asian children in that city had to attend a single, segregated school. The Japanese government protested, and after negotiations, the United States and Japan reached what became known as a "gentlemen's agreement." The Japanese agreed to discourage emigration, and President Theodore Roosevelt agreed to prevent the passage of laws discriminating against Japanese in the United States.

Initially, Japanese immigrants were minuscule in number: in 1870 there were only 55 Japanese in America and in 1880 a mere 148. By 1900 there were 24,326, and subsequently their numbers have grown steadily. By 1970 they had surpassed the Chinese (U.S. Bureau of the Census, 1976), but figures from the 1980 census showed that despite a sharp increase since 1970, the number of ethnic Japanese—701,000—was far fewer than the number of Chinese (U.S. Bureau of the Census, 1981).

Japanese Americans were subjected to especially vicious mistreatment during World War II. Fearing espionage and sabotage from among the ethnic minorities with whose home countries the United States was at war, President Franklin D. Roosevelt signed Executive Order 9066 empowering the military to "remove any and all persons" from certain regions of the country. Although before the United States entered World War II, many German Americans actively demonstrated on behalf of Germany, no general action was taken against them as a group. Nor was any general action taken against Italian Americans. Nonetheless, General John L. DeWitt ordered that *all* individuals of Japanese descent be evacuated from three West Coast states and moved inland to "relocation" camps for the duration of the war. In 1942, 110,000 Japanese, including some 70,000 who were American citizens, were moved and imprisoned solely because of their national origin— even though not a single act of espionage or sabotage against the United States ever was attributed to one of their number (Simpson and Yinger, 1972). Many lost their homes and possessions in the process.

The education, occupations, and income attainments of both Japanese and Chinese Americans have been far above the national average. In 1960, 19 percent of Chinese men and 18 percent of Japanese men had completed a four-year college education, compared with only 10 percent of white males. In 1970, 26.5 percent of all Chinese and 19 percent of all Japanese were employed in professional or technical positions. For the general population this figure was 14.9 percent. The average income of Japanese-American families is 32 percent above the national average, and for Chinese-Americans it is 12 percent above the national average (U.S. Dept. of Commerce, 1983).

Native Americans (Indians)

Early European colonists encountered Native American societies that in many ways were as advanced as their own. Especially impressive were their political institutions. For example, the League of the Iroquois, a confederacy that ensured peace among its five member nations and was remarkably successful in warfare against hostile neighbors, was the model that Benjamin Franklin drew on when he was

This Japanese store in Los Angeles was closed at the beginning of World War II by order of the United States Treasury Department. Most Japanese Americans lost their homes and businesses when they were moved to relocation camps in 1942.

planning the Federation of States (Kennedy, 1961).

However, the colonists and their descendants never really questioned the view that the land of the New World was theirs. They took land as they needed it—for agriculture, for mining, and later for industry—and drove off the native groups. Some land was purchased, some acquired through political agreements, some through trickery and deceit, and some through violence. In the end, hundreds of thousands of Native Americans were exterminated by disease, starvation, and deliberate massacre. By 1900 only some 250,000 Indians remained (perhaps one-eighth of their number in pre-Colonial times) (McNeill, 1976). In recent years, however, their numbers have grown dramatically.

According to the 1980 United States census figures there were 1,420,000 Indians in the country (up from 791,839 in 1970) (U.S. Dept. of Commerce, 1983), about 55 percent of whom live on or near reservations administered fully or partly by the federal govern-

Many American Indians live on segregated reservations. This is a particularly poor Navajo reservation in Arizona.

ment's Bureau of Indian Affairs (BIA). Many of the rest are living in Indian enclaves in urban areas where since 1952, 100,000 have been relocated by the BIA (Snyder, 1971).

Interestingly enough, nearly seven million Americans claimed American Indian ancestry on the 1980 census ancestry question. Yet only somewhat more than one million identified themselves as American Indians. Most people who claimed American Indian ancestry did so in combination with another ancestry group such as the English or Irish.

On the whole, Native Americans are at the bottom of the American socioeconomic ladder. Their family income is only 60 percent that of whites, and their life expectancy two-thirds of the national average. One-third of all adults are illiterate; 74 percent use contaminated water; and most live in overcrowded conditions (averaging 5.4 occupants in two rooms, against the national average of 2.4 people in four rooms) (U.S. Dept. of Commerce, 1983).

Prospects for the Future

As is evident by now, the many racial and ethnic groups in the United States present a complex and constantly changing picture. Some trends in intergroup relations can be discerned and are likely to continue—new ones may emerge as new groups gain prominence. New ethnic associations are likely to develop as a result of refugee movements in recent years—Vietnamese and mainland Chinese immigrants are examples, as are the 125,000 Cubans who recently were shipped to the United States by the Castro regime. The resurgence of ethnic-identity movements will probably spread and may be coupled with more collective protest movements among disaffected ethnic and racial minorities, who are demanding that they be given equal access to the opportunities and benefits of American society.

It is important to realize that the old concept of the United States as a "melting pot" is both simplistic and idealistic. Many groups have entered the United States. Most encountered prejudice, some severe discrimination, and others the pressures of Anglo conformity. Contemporary American society is the outcome of all these diverse groups coming together and trying to adjust. Indeed, if these groups are able to interact on the basis of mutual respect, this diversity may offer America strengths and flexibility not available in a homogeneous society.

☐ Summary

All societies are stratified, and people's places in the social hierarchy are often determined on the basis of their racial or ethnic identity. Problems arise when people with different racial and cultural traits must live together.

The term *race* refers to a category of people who are defined as similar because of a number of physical characteristics. Often it is based on an arbitrary set of features chosen to serve the labeler's purposes and convenience.

An ethnic group has a distinct cultural tradition with which it identifies and may or may not be identified by others. Members of the group are aware of their relationship because of shared loyalty, to an outside object and to one another.

The concept of minority implies a group that receives differential treatment and is excluded from full social participation by the dominant group in a society.

Prejudice is an irrationally based negative, or occasionally positive, attitude toward certain groups and their members. Although prejudice is a feeling, discrimination is an action, meaning that differential treatment is accorded to individuals who are assumed to belong to a particular category or group. In some societies, institutions are structured in such a way as to discriminate, giving benefits to one group and denying them to another. The system of *apartheid*, practiced in South Africa, is an example of such institutionalized discrimination.

When racial and ethnic groups come together, any one of several patterns can emerge: assimilation, pluralism, subjugation, segregation, expulsion, or annihilation.

Assimilation is the process whereby groups with different cultures come to have a common culture. Pluralism refers to the coexistence of separate racial and ethnic groups within a society. Subjugation is the subordination of one group by another. A form of subjugation, segregation, is the act, process, or state of being set apart. Most often, but not always, it is a negative phenomenon imposed on a minority by a dominant group. Expulsion is the process of forcing a group to leave the territory in which it resides, and annihilation, or genocide, is the deliberate attempt to exterminate a racial or ethnic group.

Two hundred years ago America's population was mostly English and Protestant. Today, white Anglo-Saxon Protestants (WASPs) make up only about 5 percent of the population. Other "white ethnic" groups—whites who are not of Northern European origin or Protestant—can be thought of as the largest ethnic minority in the United States, though these groups often do not share a common identification.

The first Jews arrived in the United States in 1654, but they did not begin to settle here in large numbers until the mid-1800s. Today there are approximately six million Jews in America.

In 1619 the first 20 blacks were brought to North America. Originally given the status of indentured servants, blacks were soon reduced to the status of slaves. Although slavery officially ended with the Civil War, the struggle against prejudice and institutionalized discrimination has continued to the present day. The United States' 26.9 million blacks are the nation's second largest racial group.

The 7.7 million Mexican Americans are the fourth largest ethnic group in this country. Puerto Ricans, who were made United States citizens in 1917, have migrated in large numbers to the mainland. Currently there are some 1.4 million Puerto Ricans here. As of the 1980 census there were 806,027 ethnic Chinese and 701,000 Japanese in the United States.

Driven from their territory and exterminated by disease, starvation, and deliberate massacre, by 1900 Native Americans (Indians) had been reduced in population to

250,000, about one-eighth of their original number. By 1980 their population had increased to over 1.4 million.

Some future trends in intergroup relations can be discerned. New ethnic associations, resurgence of ethnic identity movements, and collective protests among disaffected ethnic and racial minorities may grow, even though there seems to be less prejudice and discrimination. In the future, American society will be pluralistic, gaining strength and flexibility from its diverse racial and ethnic subgroups.

☐ For Further Reading

ALLPORT, GORDON W. *The Nature of Prejudice.* Reading, Mass.: Addison-Wesley, 1954. The classic work on the social psychology of prejudice. Allport describes his concept of the authoritarian personality and offers a comprehensive and detailed account of prejudice—its roots in individual psychology and social structure, its expressions in interpersonal relations and society, and its impact on the individual and the community.

BERRY, BREWTON, and HENRY L. TISCHLER. *Race and Ethnic Relations.* 4th ed. Boston: Houghton Mifflin, 1978. A description and analysis of the phenomena that arise when groups of people who differ racially or culturally come into contact with one another. This book offers unique contributions to ideas about race and ethnic relations.

GLAZER, NATHAN, and DANIEL P. MOYNIHAN (eds.). *Ethnicity: Theory and Experience.* Cambridge, Mass.: Harvard University Press, 1975. A wide-ranging collection of articles by leading scholars dealing with both theoretical issues of ethnicity and case studies, such as minorities in China, nationality problems in the Soviet Union, subnations of Western Europe, ethnic pluralism in Canada, and the reemergence of ethnicity as a force in American political institutions.

MONTAGU, ASHLEY (ed.). *The Concept of Race.* New York: Collier Books, 1964. A collection of scholarly articles by social scientists and biologists, attacking the concept of race as a biologically unsound and invalid method of classifying human beings.

MYRDAL, GUNNAR. *An American Dilemma.* New York: Harper & Row, 1962 (orig. 1944). A revised edition of the author's classic study of blacks in American society.

ROSALDO, RENATO, and R. A. CALVERT. *Chicanos: The Evolution of a People.* Rev. ed. Huntington, N.Y.: Krieger, 1981. This collection of readings explores the history of the Chicano population, their problems, and current important issues.

SCHERMERHORN, RICHARD A. *Comparative Ethnic Relations: A Framework for Theory and Research.* Chicago: University of Chicago Press, 1978. An examination of racial and ethnic relations using both the functionalist and conflict perspectives.

SOWELL, THOMAS. *Essays and Data on American Ethnic Groups.* Washington, D.C.: Urban Institute, 1978. A brilliant analysis of ethnic groups in the United States by a leading black social scientist.

STEINBERG, STEPHEN. *The Ethnic Myth: Race, Ethnicity and Class in America.* New York: Atheneum, 1981. Steinberg argues that class, rather than race or ethnicity, is the most useful variable for explaining differences in intergroup mobility.

WILSON, WILLIAM. *The Declining Significance of Race.* Chicago: University of Chicago Press, 1978. An argument that class is now more important than race in determining economic success among American blacks. This book, not surprisingly, has provoked a major debate among black scholars. Harvard sociologist Charles V. Willie skillfully rebuts Wilson's thesis in *The Caste and Class Controversy* (Bayside, N.Y.: General Hall, 1980).

12 Gender Roles

The third-century Chinese scholar Fu Hsüan penned these lines about the status of women in his era:

Bitter indeed it is to be born a woman,
It is difficult to imagine anything so low!
Boys can stand openly at the front gate,
They are treated like gods as soon as they
  are born . . .
But a girl is reared without joy or love,
And no one in her family really cares for
  her,
Grown up, she has to hide in the inner
  rooms,
Cover her head, be afraid to look others in
  the face,
And no one sheds a tear when she is mar-
  ried off . . .

(Quoted in Bullough, 1973)

In nineteenth-century Europe, attitudes toward women had not improved apprecia-bly. The father of modern sociology, Auguste Comte (1851), in constructing his views of the perfect society also dealt with questions about women's proper role in society. Comte saw women as the mental and physical inferiors of men. "In all kinds of force, whether phys-ical, intellectual or practical, it is certain that man surpasses women in accordance with the general law prevailing throughout the animal kingdom." Comte did grant women a slight superiority in the realms of emotion, love, and morality.

Comte believed women should not be al-lowed to work outside the home, to own property, or to exercise political power. Their gentle nature required that they remain in the home as mothers tending to their chil-dren and as wives tending to their husbands' emotional, domestic, and sexual needs. Comte viewed equality as a social and moral danger to women. He felt progress would result only from making the female's "life more and more domestic; to diminish as far as possible the burden of out-door la-bour." Women in short, were to be "the pam-pered slaves of men."

Comte and Fu Hsüan refer to both sex and gender characteristics in their descrip-tions. Sociology makes an important distinc-tion between sex and gender. **Sex** refers to the biological distinctions between men and women. At birth the biologically determined differences are most evident in the male and female genitalia. In general, sex differences are made evident by physical distinctions in anatomical, chromosomal, hormonal, and physiological characteristics.

Gender refers to the social, psychological, and cultural attributes of masculinity and femininity that are based on the above bio-logical distinctions. Gender pertains to the so-cially learned patterns of behavior and the psychological or emotional expressions of at-titudes that distinguish males from females. Ideas about masculinity and femininity are culturally derived and pattern the ways in which males and females are treated from birth onward. Gender is an important factor in shaping people's self-images and social iden-tities. Whereas sex refers to an ascribed sta-tus, in that a person is born either a male or female, gender is learned through the social-ization process and thus is an achieved status.

Are gender-role differences innate? The dominant view in many societies is that gen-der identities are expressions of what is "nat-ural." People tend to assume that acting mas-culine or feminine is the result of an innate, *inborn* biologically determined process rather than the result of socialization and social-learning experiences. In order to support the view that gender-role differences are innate, people have sought evidence from religion, the biological sciences, and the social sciences to support their respective positions. Whereas most re-ligions tend to support the biological view, both biology and the social sciences provide evidence that suggests that what is "natural" about sex roles expresses both innate and learned characteristics.

☐ Religious Views

Many religions have overtly acknowledged that men are superior to women. For example, the Judeo-Christian story of creation presents a God-ordained sex-role hierarchy, with man created in the image of God and woman a subsequent and secondary act of creation. This account has been used as the theological jus-tification that man is superior to woman, who was created to assist and help man and bear

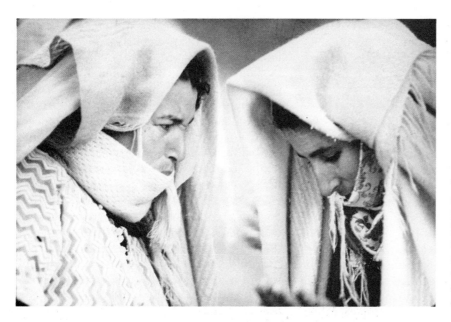

The status of women is often determined by religious views. In Morocco women are prevented from owning property and do not enjoy many of the privileges of men.

his children. This kind of legitimation of male superiority is called a **patriarchal ideology.**

> For a man indeed ought not to have his head veiled, forasmuch as he is the image and glory of God: but the woman is the glory of the man: for neither was the man created for the woman but the woman for the man: for this house ought the woman to have a sign of authority on her head. (I Cor. 11:3–10)

In traditional India, the Hindu religion conceived of women as strongly erotic and thus a threat to male asceticism and spirituality. Women were cut off physically from the outside world. They wore veils and voluminous garments and were never seen by men who were not members of the family. Only men were allowed access to and involvement with the outside world.

Womens' precarious and inferior position in traditional India is illustrated further by the ancient Manu code, which was drawn up between 200 B.C. and A.D. 200. The code states that if a wife had no children after 8 years of marriage, she would be banished; if all her children were dead after 10 years, she could be dismissed; and if she had produced only girls after 11 years, she could be repudiated.

Stemming from the Hindu patriarchal ideology was the practice of prohibiting women from owning and disposing of property. The prevalent practice in traditional Hindu India was that property acquired by the wife belonged to the husband. Similar restrictions on the ownership of property by women also prevailed in ancient Greece, Rome, and Israel, China, and Japan. Such restrictions are still followed by fundamentalist Muslim states like Saudi Arabia and Iran.

☐ Biological Views

Supporters of the belief that the basic differences between males and females are biologically determined have sought evidence from two sources: studies of other animal species, including nonhuman primates—monkeys and apes—and of the physiological differences between men and women. We shall examine each in turn.

Ethology is the scientific study of animal behavior. Ethologists have observed that there

sex The biological differences between men and women that are made evident by physical distinctions in anatomical, chromosomal, hormonal, and physiological characteristics.

gender The social, psychological, and cultural attributes of masculinity and feminity that are based on biological distinctions.

patriarchal ideology The belief that men are superior to women and should control all important aspects of society.

ethology The scientific study of animal behavior.

are sexual differences in behavior throughout much of the nonhuman animal world. Evidence indicates that these differences are biologically determined—that in a given species, members of the same sex behave in much the same way and perform the same tasks and activities. Popularized versions of these ideas, such as those of Desmond Morris in *The Human Zoo* (1970) or Lionel Tiger and Robin Fox in *The Imperial Animal* (1971), generalize from the behavior of nonhuman primates to that of humans. They maintain that in all primate species, including *Homo sapiens*, there are fundamental differences between males and females. They try to explain human male dominance and the traditional sexual division of labor in all human societies on the basis of inherent male or female capacities. They even have extended their analysis to explain other human phenomena such as war and territoriality through evolutionary comparisons with other species. A more sophisticated treatment of this same theme is found in the field of sociobiology, (see Chapter 1), the study of the genetic basis for social behavior (Wilson, 1975, 1978).

Sociobiologists believe that much of human social behavior has a genetic basis. Patterns of social organization such as family systems, organized aggression, male dominance, defense of territory, fear of strangers, the incest taboo, and even religion are seen to be rooted in the genetic structure of our species. The emphasis in sociobiology is on the inborn structure of social traits.

Opponents of this view use two types of arguments to criticize it. First, they note that sociobiologists have overlooked recent studies showing the important role learning plays among nonhuman primates in their acquisition of social and sexual behavior patterns (Montagu, 1973). Second, critics of sociobiology observe that those who generalize from animal behavior to human behavior fail to take into account fundamental differences between human and nonhuman primates, such as the human use of a complex language system. Even though they freely acknowledge the biological basis for sex differences, these critics claim that among humans, social and cultural factors overwhelmingly account for the

variety in the roles and attitudes of the two sexes. Human expressions of maleness and femaleness, they argue, although influenced by biology, are not determined by it; rather, gender identities acquired through social learning provide the guidelines for appropriate gender-role behavior and expression.

Though not denying the impact of social and cultural influences on gender roles and sex-linked behavior, some investigators maintain that the genetic and physiological differences between the sexes also influence (but do not predetermine) what types of things members of each sex can do and learn and the ease with which they do so (Rossi, 1977). According to this view, the study of sex roles should take into account well-established biological and physiological differences between the sexes in such traits as size and muscle development (both usually greater in males); physiological and mental development (males ahead in some areas, females in others); longevity (females live longer than men do and have a lower death rate at all ages); and susceptibility to disease and physical disorders (generally greater in males). For instance, some diseases that primarily affect males have a genetic basis and are related directly to the male sex chromosomes (the XY chromosomes), which differ from the female sex chromosomes (XX). Among these sex-linked ailments are color-vision defects, blood-clotting disorders (hemophilia), deficiencies in immunity, and baldness.

Women's gender role in our society also has been affected greatly by the sharp decline in infant mortality and maternal deaths in childbirth and by the widespread availability and use of contraceptives—women now have greater freedom and can spend more of their lives pursuing nontraditional activities.

Although many differences between males and females have a biological basis, other physical conditions may be tied to cultural influences and variations in environment and activity. Men react differently to psychological stress than women do: each sex develops severe but dissimilar symptoms. Changing cultural standards and patterns of social behavior have had a pronounced effect on other traits that formerly were thought to be sex linked. For example, the rising incidence of lung cancer among women—a disease historically associated primarily with men—can be traced directly to changes in social behavior and custom, not biology: Women now smoke as freely as men do.

In sum, differing learned behaviors do contribute to the relative prevalence of certain diseases and disorders in each sex. But as has been pointed out, not all male-female differences in disease and susceptibility can be attributed to these factors. In addition to genetically linked defects, differences in some basic physiological processes such as metabolic rates and adult secretion of gonadal hormones may make males more vulnerable than females to certain physical problems.

Most sociologists believe the way people are socialized has a greater effect on their gender identities than do biological factors. Cross-cultural and historical research offers support for this view, revealing that different societies allocate different tasks and duties to men and women and that males and females have culturally patterned conceptions of themselves and of one another.

☐ Sociological Views: Cross-Cultural Evidence

Until the pioneering work of anthropologist Margaret Mead (1901–1978) was published in the 1930s, it was widely believed that gender identity (what then was called sex temperament) was a matter of biology alone. It never occurred to Westerners to question their culture's definitions of "male" and "female" temperament and behavior, nor did most people doubt that these were innate properties. In 1935 Mead published a refutation of this assumption in *Sex and Temperament*, which has become a classic. While doing research among isolated tribal groups on the island of New Guinea, she found three societies with widely differing expectations of male and female behavior. The Arapesh were characterized as gentle and home loving, with a belief that men and women were of equivalent temperament. Both adult men and women subordinated their needs to those of the younger or weaker members of the society. The Mundugamor, by contrast, assumed a natural hostility between members of the same sex and only slightly less hostility between the sexes. Both sexes were expected to be tough, aggressive, and competitive. The third society, the Tchambuli, believed that the sexes were temperamentally different, but the gender roles were reversed relative to the Western pattern.

> I found . . . in one, both men and women act as we expect women to act—in a mild parental responsive way; in the second, both act as we expect men to act—in a fierce initiative fashion; and in the third, the men act according to our stereotype for women—are catty, wear curls and go shopping, while the women are energetic, managerial, unadorned partners. (Mead, 1935)

Table 12.1 summarizes the characteristics of these three societies.

TABLE 12.1 Summary of the Characteristics of Three Societies in New Guinea Studied by Margaret Mead

Group	Gender Behavior	How It Is Displayed
Mundugamor	Behavior similar to that of stereotypical male in United States	Men and women are equally fierce, arrogant, aggressive, possessive, violent, competitive, and jealous.
Arapesh	Behavior similar to that of stereotypical female in United States	Both men and women are gentle, cooperative, responsive, and attentive to the needs of others.
Tchambuli	Reversal of stereotypical male and female behavior in United States	Women are practical and dependable, work well together, and do all the fishing. Men are flighty, dependent on women and catty and tend to gossip. Most men are skilled in several arts—dancing, carving, painting, weaving, and the like.

Source: Adapted from Margaret Mead, *Sex and Temperament* (New York: Morrow, 1963 [orig. 1936]).

Mead states her conclusion simply and powerfully:

> The material suggests that we may say that many, if not all, of the personality traits which we have called masculine or feminine are as lightly linked to sex as are the clothing, the manners, and the form of head-dress that a society at a given period assigns to either sex. (Mead, 1935)

Subsequent research has, on the whole, justified Mead's conclusion. Three elements contribute to the development of an individual's gender identity: (1) genetic factors, (2) efforts by other members of the society to mold the child into whatever the culture considers to be appropriately male or female, and (3) spontaneous imitative learning by the child (imitating the behavior of adults who themselves have been molded to their culture's norms by their socialization).

Although Mead's findings are interesting and suggestive, anthropologists have cautioned against overinterpreting them. They point out that Mead's research was limited to a matter of months and that her then husband and collaborator Reo Fortune rejected her view that the Arapesh did not distinguish between male and female temperaments. Furthermore, recent research (Maccoby and Jacklin, 1975) points out four areas of difference between the sexes—in girls and boys, at least:

1. Girls have greater verbal ability than boys do.
2. Boys excel in visual-spatial ability.
3. Boys excel in mathematical ability.
4. Boys are more aggressive than girls are.

Most sociologists tend to agree that even in preliterate societies, culture is central to the patterning of gender roles. Nevertheless, biological factors may play a more prominent part in structuring gender roles in societies less technologically developed than our own. Anthropologist Clellan S. Ford (1970) believes that for preindustrial peoples, "the single most important biological fact in determining how men and women live is the differential part they play in reproduction." The woman's life is characterized by a continuing cycle of preg-

nancy, childbearing, and nursing for periods up to three years. By the time the child is weaned, the mother is likely to be pregnant again. Not until menopause, which frequently coincides with the end of the woman's life itself, is her reproductive role over. In these circumstances it is not surprising that such activities as hunting, fighting, and forest clearing usually are defined as male tasks; gathering and preparing small game, grains, and vegetables; tending gardens; and building shelters are typically female activities, as is caring for the young.

In an early study George Murdock (1937) provided data on the division of labor by sex in 224 preliterate societies. Such activities as metalworking, making weapons, woodworking and stoneworking, hunting and trapping, building houses and boats, and clearing the land for agriculture were tasks performed by men. Women's activities included grinding grain; gathering and cooking herbs, roots, seeds, fruits, and nuts; weaving baskets; making pottery; and making and repairing clothing. In a review of the cross-cultural literature (D'Andrade, 1966), it was concluded that the division of labor by sex occurs in all societies. Generally, male tasks require vigorous physical activity or travel, whereas female tasks are less physically strenuous and more sedentary.

Nevertheless, one should not overestimate the importance of biological factors in sex-role relationships. As noted earlier, even though physiological factors tend to play an influential part in gender-role differences, biology does not determine these differences. Rather, people acquire much of their ability to fulfill their gender roles through socialization.

☐ What Produces Gender Inequality?

Sociologists have devoted much thought and research to answering this question. They have also tried to explain why in most societies, males dominate. There have been two theoretical approaches used to explain male dominance and gender inequality: functionalism and conflict theory.

The Functionalist Viewpoint

From Chapter 1 you may recall that functionalists (or structural functionalists, to be more precise) believe that society consists of a system of interrelated parts that all work together to maintain the smooth operation of society. Functionalists argue that it was quite useful in preindustrial societies to have men and women fulfill different roles. The society was more efficient when tasks and responsibilities were allocated to particular people who were socialized to fulfill specific roles.

The fact that the human infant is helpless for such a long time has made it necessary that someone look after the child. It is also logical that the mother who gives birth to the child and nurses it is also the one to take care of it. Because women spent their time near the home, they also then took on the duties of preparing the food, cleaning clothes, and attending to the other necessities of daily living. To the male fell the duties of hunting, defending the family, and herding. He also became the one to make economic and other decisions important to the family's survival.

This division of labor led to a situation in which the female was largely dependent on the male for protection and food, and so he became the dominant partner in the relationship. This dominance, in turn, caused his activities to be more highly regarded and rewarded. Over time, this pattern came to be seen as natural and was thought to be tied to biological sex differences.

Talcott Parsons and Robert Bales (1955) have been responsible for applying functionalist theory to the modern family. They argue that the division of labor and role differentiation by sex are universal principles of family organization and are functional to the modern family also. They believe the family functions best when the father assumes the *instrumental role*, which focuses on relationships between the family and the outside world. It mainly involves supporting and protecting the family. The mother concentrates her energies on the *expressive role*, which focuses on relationships within the family and requires the mother to provide the love and support needed to sustain the family. The male is required to be dominant and competent, and the female should be passive and nurturant.

As can be imagined, there has been much criticism of the functionalist position. The view that gender roles and gender stratification are inevitable does not fit with cross-cultural evidence and the changing situation in American society (Crano and Aronoff, 1978). Critics contend that industrial society can be quite flexible in assigning tasks to males and females. Furthermore, the functionalist model was developed during the 1950s, an era of very traditional family patterns, and rather than being predictive of family arrangements, it is merely representative of the era during which it became popular.

The Conflict Theory Viewpoint

The functionalist theory viewpoint may explain why gender-role differences emerged, but it does not explain why they have persisted. According to the conflict theory position, males dominate females because of their superior power and control over key resources. A major consequence of this domination is the exploitation of women by men. The subordinate position of women benefits men, who thereby obtain greater economic, political, and social power. According to conflict theory, as long as the dominant group benefits from the existing relationship, it has little incentive to change it. The resulting inequalities are therefore perpetuated long after they may have served any functional purpose. In this way, gender inequalities resemble race and class inequalities.

Conflict theorists believe the main source of gender inequality is the economic inequality between men and women. Economic advantage leads to power and prestige. If men have an economic advantage in society, it will produce a superior social position in both society and the family.

Friedrich Engels (1942) linked gender inequalities to capitalism, contending that primitive, noncapitalistic hunting and gathering societies without private property were egalitarian. As these societies developed capitalistic institutions of private property, power came to be concentrated in the hands of a minority of men who used their power to subordinate women and to create political institutions designed to maintain their power. Engels also believed that to free women from subordination and exploitation, society must abolish private property and other capitalistic institutions. Engels believed that socialism was the only solution to gender inequality.

Today many conflict theorists accept the view that gender inequalities may have evolved because they were initially functional. Many functionalists also agree that gender inequalities are becoming more and more dysfunctional. They agree that the origins for gender inequalities are more social than they are biological.

Gender-Role Socialization

Gender-role socialization is a lifelong process whereby people learn the values, attitudes, motivations, and behavior considered appropriate to each sex by their culture. In our society, as in all others, males and females are socialized differently. In addition, each culture defines gender roles differently. This process is not limited to childhood but continues through adolescence, adulthood, and into old age.

Childhood Socialization Even before a baby is born, its sex is a subject of speculation, and the different gender-role relationships it will form from birth on already are being decided.

> A scene from the early musical "Carousel" epitomizes (in somewhat caricatured form) some of the feelings that parents have about bringing up sons as opposed to daughters. A young man discovers he is to be a father. He rhapsodizes about what kind of son he expects to have. The boy will be tall and tough as a tree, and no one will dare to boss him around; it will be all right for his mother to teach him manners but she mustn't make a sissy out of him. He'll be good at wrestling and will be able to herd cattle, run a riverboat, drive spikes, etc. Then the prospective father realizes, with a start, that the child may be a girl. The music changes to a gentle theme. She will have ribbons in her hair; she will be sweet and petite (just like her mother) and suitors will flock around her. There's a slightly discordant note, introduced for comic relief from sentimentality, when the expectant father brags that she'll be half again as

> bright as girls are meant to be; but then he returns to the main theme: she must be protected, and he must find enough money to raise her in a setting where she will meet the right kind of man to marry. (Maccoby and Jacklin, 1975)

Parents carry in their minds images of what girls and boys are like, how they should behave, and what they should be in later life. Parents respond differently to girls and boys right from the beginning. After studying the behavior of parents and their infants, Michael Lewis (1972) reported that there are significant differences in the very early socialization of males and females. Thus, girls are caressed more than boys, but boys are jostled and roughhoused more. Mothers talk more to their daughters, and fathers interact more with their sons.

A variety of research studies (Lynn, 1969; Maccoby and Jacklin, 1975) reveals that there are persistent differences in the parental gender-role socialization of children. These differences are reinforced by other socializing agents—siblings, peers, educational systems, and the mass media (see Case Study: "Gender-Role Stereotyping in Picture Books for Preschool Children"). Indeed, R. J. Stoller (1967), director of the UCLA Gender Research Clinic, states that by the first two or three years of life, core gender identity—the sense of maleness or femaleness—is established as a "result of the parents' conviction that their infant's assignment at birth to either the male or female sex is correct."

The pervasive manner in which the individual is socialized into the appropriate gender role can be best illustrated by cases in which an erroneous gender assignment was made at birth. For example, consider the case of Frankie, who, mistakenly classified as a male at birth, was socialized as a male. At the age of 5, "he" was brought to the hospital for examination and was diagnosed then as a female whose clitoris had been mistaken for a small penis. Lindesmith and Strauss (1956), in a report based on an unpublished document made available to them by one of the nurses assigned to the case, state that Frankie showed a decided preference for the company of little boys in the children's ward and

Parents respond differently to girls and boys. Boys receive roughhousing while girls are hugged or caressed.

a disdain for little girls and their "sissy" activities. After the child's real sex had been determined, the nurses were required to treat Frankie as a little girl. One of the nurses observed that this was not easy:

> This didn't sound too difficult—until we tried it. Frankie simply didn't give the right cues. It is amazing how much your response to a child depends on that child's behavior toward you. It was extremely difficult to keep from responding to Frankie's typically little boy behavior in the same way that I responded to other boys in the ward. And to treat Frankie as a girl was jarringly out of key. It was something we all had to continually remind ourselves to do. Yet the doing of it left all of us feeling vaguely uneasy as if we had committed an error. . . . About the same time Frankie became increasingly aware of the change in our attitude toward her. She seemed to realize that behavior which had always before brought forth approval was no longer approved. It must have been far more confusing to her than it was to us and certainly it was bad enough for us. Her reaction was strong and violent. She became

extremely belligerent and even less willing to accept crayons, color books and games which she simply called "sissy" and threw on the floor. (Lindesmith and Strauss, 1956)

Adolescent Socialization Most societies have different expectations for adolescent girls and boys. Erik Erikson (1968) believes the most important task in adolescence is the establishment of a sense of identity. He believes that during the adolescent stage, both boys and girls undergo severe emotional crises centered on questions of who they are and what they will be. If the adolescent crisis is satisfactorily resolved, a sense of identity will be developed; if not, role confusion will persist. According to Erikson, adolescent boys in our society generally are enouraged to pursue role paths that will prepare them for some occupational commitment, whereas girls generally are encouraged to develop behavior patterns designed to attract a suitable mate. Erikson

gender-role socialization The lifelong process whereby people learn the values, attitudes, and behavior considered appropriate to each sex by their culture.

CASE STUDY
Gender-Role Stereotyping in Picture Books for Preschool Children

An important factor in the socialization process is the books children read or look at, particularly picture books for preschool children. Therefore, the literature available to children contributes heavily to their view of the roles played by men and women. The following study reveals that considerable sex typing and stereotyping existed in children's literature.

Picture books play an important part in socializing children to gender roles in American society. Through books, children learn what boys and girls their own age do, say, and feel; what is right and wrong; and what is expected of them. Books provide children with role models of what they can and should be like when they grow up. Children's books reflect cultural values and are instrumental in getting children to accept them.

This study, conducted by sociologists Lenore J. Weitzman, Debra Eitler, Elizabeth Hokada, and Catherine Ross, examined the treatment of gender roles in what were generally considered the best-illustrated children's books—the winners of the Caldecott Medal, which until very recently was awarded by the American Library Association for distinguished illustration. Winning titles were ordered by almost all children's libraries in the United States.

The researchers did a statistical analysis of all Caldecott winners from the inception of the award in 1938 until 1970. In addition, to avoid bias they also examined Newbery Award winners (the American Library Association's prize for the best book each year for school-age children) and Little Golden Books that had sold over three million copies (inexpensive books that reach a more broadly based audience than do the more expensive Caldecott winners) as well as children's etiquette books and others that prescribe behavior.

Findings from these three supplementary samples strongly paralleled those from the Caldecott sample.

The first point noted was that in children's books, females were mainly invisible. Most children's books were about boys, men, and male animals, and most dealt exclusively with male adventures. When women did appear, they often played insignificant roles, remaining inconspicuous and nameless. Since the Caldecott award's inception through 1970, the ratio of titles featuring males to those featuring females was 8:3. Children exposed to the list of titles of what were designated as the very best children's books were bound to receive the impression that girls are not as important because few people have bothered to write books about them. The content of the books did little to dispel this impression.

In the world of picture books, boys were active, and girls were passive. Boys are presented in exciting and adventuresome roles, and they engaged in varied pursuits that demanded independence. The more riotous activities were reserved for boys. Archie and Peter race, climb, and hide in the story of *Goggles*. Obadiah travels to the wharf in the cold of Massachusetts winter, and Sylvester searches for rocks in the woods.

In contrast, most of the girls were passive and immobile. Some of them were restricted by their clothing, as skirts and dresses are easily soiled and prohibit more venturesome activities. In *The Fool of the World and the Flying Ship*, the hero is dressed in a sensible manner, which does not inhibit his movements. The princess, however, for whom all the exploits are waged, remains no more than her long gown allows her to be: a prize—a passive creature symbolizing the reward for the adventurous male.

While girls serve, boys lead. Lupin, the Indian boy in *The Angry Moon*, directs the escape from the moon god. He leads Lapowinsa, a girl exactly his size and age, every step of the way. Even at the end of the story, after the danger is past, Lupin goes down the ladder first "so that he could catch Lapowinsa if she should slip."

For boys, camaraderie is developed through shared adventures. *The Fool of the World* depends on the help and talents of his male companions. In *Goggles*, two male companions together outwit a gang of older boys. In contrast, girls are rarely shown working or playing together. Although in reality, women spend much of their time with other women, picture books suggest that women cannot exist without men. A girl's role is defined primarily in relation to the boys and men in her life. Sam turns to a boy, not a girl, to accomplish her fantasies; her dreams would have no reality without Thomas.

It is easy to understand why many little girls might have preferred to identify with the male role, but the girl who did find the male role more attractive was faced with a dilemma. Girls who wanted to be more than placid and pretty were left without an acceptable role alternative. They had to choose between alienation from their own sex and alienation from their behavioral and temperamental preferences.

The rigidity of gender-role stereotypes was harmful to little boys as well. They often felt equally constrained by the necessity to be fearless and clever at all times. Although girls were allowed a great deal of emotional expression, a boy who cried or expressed fear was unacceptable. Just as the only little girls who were heroines in picture books had boys' names or were foreign princesses, the only boys who cried in picture books were animals—frogs, toads, and donkeys.

The image of the adult woman in children's books was also stereotyped and limited. In most of the stories, the sole adult woman was identified only as a mother or a wife. Sylvester's mother is shown sweeping, packing a lunch, knitting, and crying. And Noah's wife, who had an important part in the biblical story of the flood, is completely omitted from the children's book version.

In the Caldecott sample, not one woman had a job or profession. In a country where so many women are in the labor force and work outside the home, it is absurd to find that women in picture books were only mothers and wives. Moreover, the way motherhood was presented in children's books was unrealistic. Real mothers drive cars, read books, vote, take children on trips, balance checkbooks, engage in volunteer activities, work in the garden, fix things in the house, are active in local politics, and belong to various organizations. The picturebook mother was almost always confined to the house, although she was usually shown as too well dressed for housework. Her duties were not portrayed as challenging or difficult. Nor did these picture books provide a realistic image of fathers and husbands. Fathers never helped in the mundane duties of child care, dishwashing, cooking, cleaning, or shopping.

From their work, the researchers concluded that preschool children were being exposed to an extremely gender-stereotyped view of the world through picture books at a time when they were forming their self-images and future expectations. The girls and women depicted were a dull and traditional lot. Little girls received attention and praise for their attractiveness, whereas little boys were admired for their achievements and cleverness. Most of the women had status by virtue of their relationships to specific men—they were the wives of kings, judges, adventurers, and explorers, but they themselves were not the rulers, judges, adventurers, or explorers. The world of picture books never told little girls that as women they could find fulfillment outside the home or through intellectual pursuits. Women were excluded from the world of sports, politics, and science. Ironically, many of the books were written by prize-winning female authors whose own lives were probably unlike those they advertised.

A basic flaw in this study was its focus on Caldecott winners. Because at the time the award was given primarily for illustration, certain types of books were more likely to win than others. These usually included fairy tales, Bible stories, and stories from other cultures and other periods. These stories lend themselves particularly well to elaborate illustration but are also more likely to contain the types of stereotypes elaborated on above than contemporary children's stories. For example the 1974 Caldecott medal went to *Duffy and the Devil*, which begins: "Squire Lovel of Trove had no wife. His housekeeper, Old Jone, did the cooking and cleaning for him." The gender-role bias here is quite obvious. However, this was a popular play in Cornwall, England, in the nineteenth century. The retelling of stories from another era will more often than not include the gender-role biases of that period.

On some occasions the Caldecott winner is a new story. When this happens, the gender-role bias problems are usually not present. For example, the 1982 medal went to *Jumanji*, which is about a brother and sister, Peter and Judy, who find a jungle adventure game. There are no instances of gender-role bias in this story. Judy beats Peter in a race home, and she is the one who reads the directions for the game and tells Peter how to play. And Peter is the one who is about to cry at one point in the game.

Contemporary children's book authors, the majority of whom are women, are well aware of the problems of gender-role stereotyping in books. In the years that have passed since this study was completed, both authors and publishers have made a determined effort to eliminate the kinds of problems noted here.

Source: Abridged and adapted from Lenore J. Weitzman, Debra Eitler, Elizabeth Hokada, and Catherine Ross, "Sex-Role Socialization in Picture Books for Pre-school Children," *American Journal of Sociology* **77** (May, 1972), pp. 1125–1150. □

---

observes that it is more difficult for girls than for boys to achieve a positive identity in Western society. This is because women are encouraged to be more passive and less achievement oriented than men are and to stress the development of interpersonal skills—traits that are not highly valued in our society. Males, on the other hand, are encouraged to be competitive, to strive for achievement, and to assert autonomy and independence—characteristics that are held in high esteem in our competitive society.

The result of the adolescent gender-role socialization process becomes evident during

FOCUS ON RESEARCH
Men Who Cry

In our culture, crying is an acceptable expression of sadness. But acceptable for whom? Women are expected to cry when they are sad, but many men have been taught since they were small that such behavior is inappropriate. As changes take place in society's view of appropriate gender-role behavior, we might expect men to feel more comfortable in expressing their sadness through tears. The following discussion examines this possibility.

"Big boys don't cry" has long been a staple of American child-rearing. In traditional households, boys are taught that crying as an expression of sadness is a sign of weakness, sensitivity, emotionalism, and other feminine traits.

Thus, we may say that little boys are not *by nature* less expressive of their emotions than little girls are, but that they have *learned* not to cry, just as they have learned to share toys or drink from a cup.

But what happens in families whose views of appropriate gender-role behavior are less traditional? Will these little boys feel freer to cry as adults? A recent study investigated the correlation between gender roles and crying and found some interesting patterns.

The study was based on a random sample of 680 husbands and wives who answered questions regarding gender-role orientation, income, education, general level of sadness, and frequency of crying. The study found that indeed, women are more likely to cry than men are. In the data, 19 percent of the women reported crying in the past week, whereas only 3 percent of the men had.

When the data on frequency of crying, however, were correlated with gender-role orientation, some differences began to emerge. Women, it seems, felt free to cry, regardless of whether they held traditional or nontraditional attitudes toward gender-role behavior. It was found, however, that very traditional men—those who believed that men by nature are strong, competitive, and ambitious, whereas women are nurturant, unambitious, and happiest at home—were less likely to cry than were men who did not hold such traditional beliefs.

The study also found that socioeconomic status had an effect on crying. Those men with higher incomes and more education were more likely to have less traditional beliefs about gender roles, and thus they might be expected to feel free to cry more often. It was found, however, that greater education and income lowered the general level of sadness, and so these men had fewer occasions to cry than their less fortunate peers did.

Men in lower socioeconomic positions are more likely to be sad, but because they usually hold traditional views of gender-role behavior, they are less inclined to cry when sad. As a result, crying tends not to be common for men at all socioeconomic levels, but for different reasons.

We might also say that men who do cry express not only their sadness but also their acceptance of the similarity in men's and women's emotional responses.

Source: Based on Catherine E. Ross and John Mirowsky, "Men Who Cry," *Social Psychology Quarterly* **47** (2) (1984), pp. 138–146. □

---

young adulthood (ages 18 to 21). This is a period of transition from the earlier economic and psychological dependence on one's parents to the beginning of independent living. Research shows that during this period, young men experience more stress and less satisfaction with their lives than do young women (Frieze et al., 1978). Men at this age seem more burdened and concerned by the expectations and demands of their socialization process. Much of this anxiety arises from the pressure that young men face in choosing an occupation, a decision that they feel will be the prime determinant of their adult lives—affecting their future economic resources, social expectations, and friendship networks as well as defining their future work activities. (For a discussion of how another aspect of gender-role socialization affects men, see Focus on Research: "Men Who Cry.")

Traditionally, the pressure to choose a lifelong occupation has not been as severe for women at this age because their socialization emphasized marriage as their central adult role. Outside employment was seen as a temporary occupation subordinate to, and contingent on, marriage and future familial roles. The choice of a husband, not a job, was women's primary concern.

The predominant personality characteristics of young women during this period include a strong dependency on others for support, approval, and direction. Their sense of self is less clearly defined than that of men, and there is a tentativeness in their quest for personal identity. Many of these personality characteristics are associated with their marriage goals.

Nonetheless, female gender roles are changing rapidly, although much of this attitude toward careers and marriage undoubtedly still remains part of the thinking of many people in our society. Girls are being encouraged not to limit themselves to these stereotyped roles and attitudes. More and more young women expect to pursue careers before and during marriage and child rearing. Marriage is no longer considered the only desirable goal for a woman, nor is it any longer even considered necessary to a woman's success and happiness.

Adult Socialization Gender-role socialization continues into adulthood. Three personality characteristics associated with adult sex differences are gender identity, self-esteem, and achievement motivation (Mandle, 1979). Because of cultural socialization, women are less likely to have an independent sexual identity than are men. That is, they tend to see their female identity as largely defined by, and dependent on, the characteristics of their husbands and children.

Low self-esteem is, according to Mandle, the second personality trait characteristic of adult women, associated with psychological feelings of inadequacy and even self-hatred. One manifestation of this is that both men and women consistently devalue the attributes of women. In one study (Goldberg, 1968), a psychologist asked female college students to read a number of professional articles from each of six fields and to rate them for persuasive impact, profundity, writing style, professional competency, and overall value. Half the women received articles purportedly written by a male author (for example, John T. McKay), and half got the identical articles supposedly written by a woman (for example, Joan T. McKay). The woman gave consistently lower ratings to the identical articles when they were attributed to a female author than when they were attributed to a male author.

The third personality characteristic believed to be typical of women is low achievement motivation. Women are socialized to deemphasize qualities that are highly regarded in our society—competition, independence, intellectual achievement, and leadership. (Of course, these personality traits, like most others, are not intrinsically "good" or "bad"—the value placed on each is culturally determined.) Judith Bardwick and Elizabeth Douvan (1971) point out that the result of these factors is that "very few women have succeeded in traditionally masculine roles, not only because of disparagement and prejudice, but largely because women have not been fundamentally equipped and determined to succeed."

The job fields that women dominate are those that utilize skills of nurturance and empathy and that deemphasize such traits as aggressiveness and competitiveness or treat them as largely dysfunctional. These jobs include teaching, nursing, and secretarial work. It should be noted that all these occupations pay poorly compared with many male-dominated positions. (For a discussion of how women approach interpersonal issues differently than men do, see Using Sociology: "Women Think Differently Than Men Do.")

Gender-role socialization also is fostered by a society's concepts of proper public behavior—its rules of etiquette, or good man-

Gender-role socialization traditionally de-emphasized aggressiveness and competitiveness for women. A profession such as law, which requires these traits, has seen a large influx of women in recent years as gender roles have been re-examined.

USING SOCIOLOGY
Women Think Differently Than Men

Little girls often say they do not like to play games in which people win and lose, get their feelings hurt, or are made to feel sad. In a society in which such slogans as "looking out for Number One" and "may the best man win" express the accepted values, this perspective seems weak and ineffectual. Instead of dismissing the little girls' viewpoint as irrelevant and unimportant, Carol Gilligan, a professor at the Harvard Graduate School of Education, challenged this predominantly male bias. Why not, she asked, listen to what the little girls are saying and see their perspective as a strength?

Men often think that the highest praise they can bestow on a woman is to compliment her for "thinking like a man." That usually means that the woman has been decisive, rational, firm, and clear. To "think like a woman" in our society has always had negative overtones, being characterized as fuzzy, indecisive, unpredictable, tentative, and softheaded.

Carol Gilligan recently published a book challenging the value judgments made about male, versus female, styles of reasoning, especially in the area of moral decision making. In her book, *In a Different Voice*, she argues that a woman's perspective on things is not inferior to a man's; it is just different.

To illustrate what she means, Gilligan describes the different responses that 11-year-old boys and girls made to an example used by Lawrence Kohlberg and discussed more fully in Chapter 4. In the example, Heinz, a fictional character, is caught up in a complex moral question. Heinz's wife is dying of cancer. The local pharmacist has discovered a drug that might cure her, but it is very expensive. Heinz has done all he can to raise the money necessary to buy it but can come up with only half the amount, and the druggist demands the full price. The question is: Should Heinz steal the drug?

Boys and girls differ significantly on how they answer this question. Boys often see the problem as the man's individual moral choice, stating that Heinz should steal the drug, as the right to life supersedes the right to property. Case closed.

The girls Gilligan questioned always seemed to get bogged down in peripheral issues. No, they maintained, Heinz should not steal the drug, because stealing is wrong. Heinz should have a long talk with the pharmacist and try to persuade him to do what is right. Besides, they point out, if Heinz steals the drug, he might be caught and go to jail. Then what would happen to his wife? What if there were children?

Instead of labeling this tentativeness as a typical example of women's inability to make firm decisions, Gilligan sees it as an attempt to deal with the consequences of actions rather than simply with what is "right." For women, moral dilemmas involving people have a greater complexity and therefore a greater ambiguity.

If your morality stresses the importance of not hurting others, as seems to be the case with most women, you will often face failure. As one of the men Gilligan interviewed said, making a moral decision is often a matter of "choosing the victim." There is "violence inherent in choice," Gilligan writes, "and the injunction not to hurt can paralyze women."

If you base your decision on an absolute principle (for example, abortion is murder; therefore it is wrong), you may then act with the decisiveness so admired by both men and women. If you base your decision on what you imagine is likely to happen (for example, if this child would be born with no father; if the fetus is likely to be seriously defective; if the mother's life would be endangered by the birth; and so on), you will often face uncertainty. Women, whose value systems are more focused on people than on principles, consequently find themselves wrestling with the problems that might result from their decisions.

Gilligan hopes that by ceasing to label a man's perspective as right and a woman's wrong, we can begin to understand that each may be valuable, though different. For this to happen, according to Gilligan, girls and women must gain confidence in their own ethical perspectives. Indeed, Gilligan feels, if society finally accepted a women's moral view of the interconnectedness of actions and relationships, it could have enormous consequences for everything from scholarship to politics to international relations.

Based on Carol Gilligan, *In a Different Voice* (Cambridge: Harvard University Press, 1982); interviews by Amy Gross, "Thinking like a Woman," *Vogue*, May, 1982, pp. 268–269, 333–335); and Lindy Van Gelder, "Carol Gilligan: Leader for a Different Kind of Future," *Ms*, January, 1984, pp. 37–40, 101. □

ners. In traditional social behavior between the sexes in public places and in everyday life—the rules by which men are expected to open doors for women, walk on the outside of pavements (possibly to protect women from being splashed or pelted by garbage), and ask women for permission to smoke in their presence—the recurrent pattern is for men to defer to women. Underlying these deferential patterns is an imputation of women's helplessness, weakness, and frailty. Supporters of traditional rules of etiquette fail to see that these deferential patterns are in reality forms of social control that perpetuate and reinforce the power of men.

☐ Gender Inequality and Work

Women's numerical superiority over men has not enabled them as yet to avoid discrimination in many spheres of American society. In this discussion we shall focus on economic and job-related discrimination, because these data are easily quantified and serve well to highlight the problem. It should be remembered, though, that discrimination against women in America actually is expressed in a far wider range of social contexts and institutions (Davidson and Gordon, 1979).

Job Discrimination

Working women as a group consistently earn less than working men do. In 1982 the median weekly income for men was $371, and for women it was $241 (U.S. Dept. of Commerce, 1984). Job discrimination against women is a pervasive and complicated phenomenon. One study of business firms identified three ways in which women experience discrimination in the business world: (1) during the hiring process, when women are given jobs with lower occupational prestige than are men with equivalent qualifications; (2) through unequal wage policies, by which women receive less pay than men do for equivalent work; and (3) in awarding promotions—women find it more difficult than men to advance up the career ladder (Staires, Quin, and Shepard, 1976).

Discrimination against women in the economic sector is often quite subtle. Women are more or less channeled away from participation in occupations that are socially defined as appropriate to men. For example, it cannot really be argued that women bank presidents are paid less than men are; instead, there are almost no women bank presidents. Women and men often do not perform equal work; therefore the phrase "equal pay for equal work" has little relevance. In some instances, similar work is performed by men and women, but there may be two job titles and two pay scales, for example, administrative assistant and executive secretary. The first may be a male or female; the second is usually a female and is likely to be paid less (Davidson and Gordon, 1979).

Some scholars have attempted to explain these facts by claiming that women—or at least American women—have a "fear of success" that keeps them from getting ahead in the business world. This hypothesis was advanced by a female researcher, Matina S. Horner (1972), in a much-quoted article, but no subsequent experiments have replicated her original findings. And Horner's initial research has been severely criticized for its methodology because, among other things, the coders who rated the degree to which subjects showed "fear of success" already knew which subjects were male or female. Thus it is likely that research bias contaminated the study (Levine and Crumrine 1975). (For an examination of some of the subtle factors in women's advancement in the work world, see Popular Sociology: "Women in Male-Dominated Professions: The Unfinished Revolution.")

Actually, this "explanation" of why women find it difficult to earn as much money as men do is an example of what William Ryan (1971) called "blaming the victim" in a classic book of that title. This practice, which often is directed against minority groups, consists of finding the reason for discrimination against a group in some characteristic that is supposed to typify the group's members. Thus, for example, in the mid-1970s a male judge in Wisconsin refused to sentence a man convicted of rape to a term in jail because he believed that women dress so provocatively that it is unreasonable to expect men to keep themselves under control (Davidson and Gordon, 1979). In fact, rape is virtually the only crime in America in which the victim's personality and life story may be used to get a defendant declared "not guilty."

Work and Family Roles

The almost universal classification of women to secondary status has had a profound effect on their work and family roles. Anthropologist Sherry Ortner (1974) observed that "everywhere, in every known culture, women

POPULAR SOCIOLOGY
Women in Male-Dominated Professions: The Unfinished Revolution

In recent years women have succeeded in record numbers in entering formerly male-dominated professions. Although significant numbers of women are now achieving positions of responsibility in such fields as banking, law, and architecture, many are finding themselves ill equipped to deal with the latent resistance to women that they are encountering from their male colleagues.

"Being ignored is like feeling you're a gnat; you ask a question and you get brushed off."

A 35-year-old lawyer

"I get a lot of visibility. But I'm used. I'm like the department hooker. Whenever there's a show, I go on. I become visible, but I don't get a lot of rewards for it."

A vice-president for marketing at a California bank

"Until you're initiated into the signals, you're going to be speaking English among a group of people speaking French."

A manager of in-house publications for a bank

Why in modern America do women feel like gnats, hookers, and foreigners? These are not voices from the ghetto or sweatshop. These are the voices of bankers, lawyers, and architects—women with ambition, talent, and determination who have achieved recognition and responsibility in their chosen fields. Why, after approximately five years of professional life, do many of them feel stressed and anxious? Why, after the considerable struggle it took to arrive at this point, do these women look around and ask, "Is that all there is?"

These questions and others regarding what it *felt* like to be a young professional woman in America today intrigued psychologist and management consultant Beth Milwid. She felt the statistics regarding numbers of women in the work force, and salary differentials gave little information about how these women on the cutting edge of a social revolution were experiencing their jobs on a day-to-day basis. Using the oral-history research approach, Milwid interviewed 30 California women, all in their late twenties to early thirties and all working in the male-dominated fields of banking, law, and architecture. Although the sample she studied is small and regional, Milwid believes the experiences of these women are typical of a larger cross-section of women working in male-dominated professions.

The women Milwid interviewed were swept up by the optimism of the 1970s and encouraged to think of entering professions that had previously excluded them or limited their numbers. As far as their professional training was concerned, the revolution seemed to have been won. In business school, law school, and graduate school, gender was no longer assumed to be a limitation, and few women anticipated that it would be a factor in their professional lives. All believed that hard work and merit would carry them along, though this rather astonishing innocence quickly dissipated.

During their initial "testing" period, nearly all these women felt pressure not merely to be good at their jobs but also to be perfect. They grew worried and tense if anything went wrong, and they reprimanded themselves severely for oversights. The men, they noticed, did not seem to be as harsh on themselves. As one architected noted, "If the men don't know the answers, it just rolls off their backs."

Once the testing period was over, the women came face to face with an even more formidable obstacle—the male-dominated company culture. The impenetrability of the old boys' network, they found, was real. Although relationships with male peers were generally comfortable, those with older men, the men with the real power, were not. Decisions were being made in ways to which the women had no access.

In addition to the social barriers the women experienced, many found that the psychological baggage that they brought to an essentially masculine culture prevented them from feeling comfortable in their new roles. From early childhood on, women in our culture are taught to be "nice," to be liked, and to value relationships over everything else. In male-dominated professions, those values can cause women serious conflict. Bankers, for example, said they needed to learn to be more assertive in order to move up in their profession. Architects said they had to learn to be firmer in their opinions and more confident about presenting their work. Lawyers had the greatest difficulty in this area, as many grew anxious when they had to argue and felt that raising objections in court would not be "polite." Whatever their specific problems, all the interviewees felt the behavioral expectations of their jobs were in conflict with the way they were raised.

Despite the difficulties they had experienced on a personal level, most of the women interviewed felt that their presence in the professions had had some positive effects on the workplace. They believed that their natural tendencies toward idealistic striving and participative management had made the office, courtroom, or design table a "better place to be in the morning."

Nonetheless, the study points out that we can no longer expect that the large numbers of women in the male-dominated professions will necessarily cause those institutions to change. As Milwid notes, "Rigidly structured male-dominated professions can accommodate women without having to change their normative behavior." If that "normative behavior" results in women feeling like gnats and hookers, then it is clear that mere access to a profession is only the first step in a much larger accommodation process.

Source: Adapted from Louise Bernikow, "We're Dancing as Fast as We Can," *Savvy* **5** (4) (April, 1984), pp. 40–44. ☐

---

are considered in some degree inferior to men." One important result of this attitude is the exclusion of women from participation in, or contact with, those areas of the particular society believed to be most powerful, whether they be religious or secular.

Another anthropologist, Michelle Rosaldo (1974), believes "women's status will be lowest in those societies where there is a firm differentiation between domestic and public spheres of activity and where women are isolated from one another and placed under a single man's authority in the home." She believes that the time-consuming and emotionally compelling involvement of a mother with her child is unmatched by any single involvement and commitment by a man. The result is that men are free to form broader associations in the outside world through their involvement in work, politics, and religion. The relative absence of women from these public spheres results in their lack of authority and power. Men's involvements and activities are viewed as important, and the cultural systems accord authority and value to men's activities and roles. In turn, women's work, especially when it is confined to domestic roles and activities, tends to be oppressive and lacking in value and status. Women are seen to gain power and a sense of value only when they are able to transcend the domestic sphere of activities. This differentiation is most acute in those societies that practice sexual discrimination. Societies in which men value and participate in domestic activities tend to be more egalitarian.

According to Rosaldo, contemporary America, though giving perfunctory lip service to the idea of sexual equality, still is organized in such a way as to heighten the dichotomy between private and public, domestic and social, and female and male spheres of activity. Further, because of the demands of family life, women tend to be relegated to the domestic sphere. Yet, when the society assesses the relative value of different kinds of work, the tendency is to place greater value and higher priority on the public work associated with men than on the domestic work associated with women. This attitude is symbolized by the phrase "only a housewife." This splitting off of female from male work and the consequent devaluation of women's work are encouraged by social pressures for women to give up outside employment so they can devote themselves almost exclusively to the care of small children and to sacrifice their career aspirations for the demands of the family. These normative structures perpetuate the assignment of women to the domestic, private sphere, whereas men are almost exclusively involved in the higher-valued and higher-status activities of the public sphere. As we pointed out earlier, however, progress is being made toward sexual equality. Female gender-roles are changing, and women now find it possible to combine the domestic and public spheres or to abandon the former entirely. For an interesting example of the subtle socialization that continues to produce gender-role differences among "liberated" men and women, see Box 12.1: "Men and Women—Complementary but Equal?"

For men and women to have roles of equal value, they must be equally involved in all activities, including work, both in the outside world and in the home.

☐ Gender Inequality and Social Status

Some scholars have observed that gender roles in America in some ways resemble a two-level caste system in which women occupy a lower caste and men the upper (Myrdal, 1944). As you may remember, a caste is a layer within

12.1

Men and Women—Complementary But Equal?

Daryl and Sandra Bem, a husband-and-wife team of psychologists, have devised two passages that expose the accepted ideological rationalization that women and men have complementary but equal positions in our society.

> Both my wife and I earned Ph.D. degrees in our respective disciplines. I turned down a superior academic post in Oregon and accepted a slightly less desirable position in New York where my wife could obtain a part-time teaching job and do research at one of the several other colleges in the area. Although I would have preferred to live in a suburb, we purchased a home near my wife's college so that she could have an office at home where she would be when the children returned from school. Because my wife earns a good salary, she can easily afford to pay a maid to do her major household chores. My wife and I share all other tasks around the house equally. For example, she cooks the meals, but I do the laundry for her and help her with many of her other household tasks. (Bem and Bem, 1976)

At first glance, the man speaking in this passage seems to express an egalitarian gender-role relationship that rejects traditional sexist ideology. But Bem and Bem point out that such a marriage may not be an instance of interpersonal equality at all. There may be hidden assumptions about the "natural" role of women that are based on traditional ideology. These unconscious assumptions become clear in the comparison passage in which the roles of the husband and wife are reversed:

> Both my husband and I earned Ph.D. degrees in our respective disciplines. I turned down a superior academic post in Oregon and accepted a slightly less desirable position in New York where my husband could obtain a part-time teaching job and do research at one of the several other colleges in the area. Although I would have preferred to live in a suburb, we purchased a home near my husband's college so that he could have an office at home where he would be when the children returned from school. Because my husband earns a good salary, he can easily afford to pay a maid to do his major household chores. My husband and I share all other tasks around the house equally. For example, he cooks the meals, but I do the laundry for him and help him with many of his other household tasks. (Bem and Bem, 1976)

This reversal of characters vividly illustrates that the first passage, rather than representing an egalitarian ideology, in fact perpetuates a sexist one. Why is it "her" maid, "her" laundry, "her" household tasks, and so forth? The first passage is an example of the subtlety of a nonconscious ideology. On the other hand, the second passage sounds absurd because it goes counter to the same nonconscious sexist ideology. As Sandra and Daryl Bem (1976) put it, "A truly equalitarian marriage would permit both partners to pursue careers or outside commitments which carry equal weight when all important decisions are to be made." □

---

a system of social stratification in which movement up or down is very difficult. Generally, people are born into a particular caste and remain there all their lives. Although women are part of every social class in America, within each class they are a distinct subgroup, discriminated against both socially and economically. Thus, even if a woman moves up the socioeconomic ladder to a higher social class, she still will be deprived of equal access to all the rewards enjoyed by the men of that social and economic class. For example, even professional women may still find it more difficult than men to get credit from banks (although discrimination because of sex technically is illegal).

For the last century and a half, American women have been searching for means to combat their inferior social status. In 1848 this country's first women's rights conference was held in Seneca Falls, New York. The first two decades of this century saw the emergence of strong women's organizations, and in 1920 the Nineteenth Amendment to the U.S. Constitution gave women the right to vote. The civil rights movement of the 1960s gave rise to the contemporary women's movement, which has stressed organizing politically to combat discrimination. The women's movement also has searched for means to undo and counteract some of the effects of traditional female socialization in our society: the tendency for women to be passive and dependent on males, to put the careers of husbands ahead of their own, and so forth.

The first two decades of this century saw the emergence of strong women's organizations leading the fight for women's suffrage.

☐ Future Trends

Earlier in this chapter we alluded to certain conditions in contemporary society that have had great significance and impact on gender roles and family relations. Demographic changes, lengthened life spans, the decline in infant and child mortality and in maternal deaths during childbirth, lower birthrates, the dissociation of reproduction from sexual activities, and the shorter period of time devoted to maternity in relation to women's total life expectancy—all have contributed to changes in attitudes and behavior in the family.

Throughout the twentieth century, women have been gaining in legal equality. Changes in women's legal status include the right of suffrage, rights of separation and divorce, and rights of equal employment and opportunity. Although equality has not been fully realized, there has been marked improvement in the power and status of women compared with their position during the nineteenth century. The result has been the growth of female independence.

Observing these changes in England, two researchers (Young and Willmott, 1973) have concluded that a new family form has emerged, one that embraces the ideals of the nuclear family with some notable differences; they call this new form the *symmetrical family*. The **symmetrical family** is one in which the continued differences in the work opportunities and ways of life of husbands and wives are recognized and accepted but in which there is marked egalitarianism between the sexes.

Couples, and particularly husbands, no longer feel they must devote as much time to earning a living and providing for the family as in the past. They are now able to spend more time with their families in home-centered and leisure activities. The new egalitarianism is realized in the assumption of joint responsibility in planning for children and in greater involvement of the husband in the rearing of the children. This enlightened attitude toward women's and men's roles is expressed in the symmetrical family by the belief that neither husband nor wife should have any monopoly in any sphere of activity. Women, then, have the same right and responsibility as men to become involved in work outside the home as well as in it. The result has been a movement of women back to the labor force, the usual pattern being for the

symmetrical family A family in which the continued differences in the work opportunities and ways of life of husbands and wives are recognized and accepted but in which there is marked egalitarianism between the sexes.

wife to stay at home during the early years of child rearing and then to take a part-time job before accepting full-time employment as the children grow older.

However, in spite of this new concept of family roles, Michael Young and Peter Willmott (1973) believe that the traditional pattern of the husband as the primary wage earner will continue. They observe that there is a growing tendency for wives to become responsible both for their outside work as well as for all domestic tasks—hardly the ideal situation implicit in the concept of the symmetrical family. In the real world, in contrast with the egalitarian ideal, women have had to assume extra duties to justify working outside the home, whereas men's roles and duties have remained more or less the same. This "dual role" or "double burden" of women is practiced among the London families interviewed by Young and Willmott.

Despite this unbalanced situation, Young and Willmott believe that men's and women's worlds eventually will merge. The result will be a true sharing of tasks by men and women in both domestic and outside work. They recognize the problems that will have to be resolved: determining who will care for the children and arranging schedules of work and leisure so that the family can spend time together are just two. Generally, these two investigators are optimistic about the future: they believe both family wants and men's and women's individual needs can be fulfilled.

This hopeful portrait of future family life is not shared by all contemporary sociologists (Hutter, 1981). They see changes in gender-role relationships necessitating dramatic redefinitions of husband–wife and parent–child relationships. Some of the difficulties in reworking gender roles are most apparent in marriages that fail and end in divorce.

We now shall consider the impact of gender-role changes in marriage and the family on American legal processes regarding divorce and child custody. The current legal picture illustrates these changes.

Divorce Laws

In an analysis of the implications of recent changes in divorce laws, Lenore Weitzman and Ruth Dixon (1980) emphasize that the laws governing divorce reflect society's definition of marriage, provide guidelines for appropriate marriage behavior, and spell out the reciprocal rights and obligations of marriage partners. Divorce laws also define the continued obligations that the formerly married couple have to each other after they divorce. As Weitzman and Dixon explain,

> One can generally examine the way a society defines marriage by examining its provisions for divorce, for it is at the point of divorce that a society has the opportunity to reward the marital behavior it approves of, and to punish spouses who have violated its norms.

Given this viewpoint, the authors assert that a study of changing divorce laws will reveal changes in family and gender-role patterns. For this reason they chose to examine no-fault divorce laws to demonstrate how "this new legislation seeks to alter the definition of marriage, the relationship between husbands and wives, and the economic and social obligations of former spouses to each other and to their children after divorce."

No-fault divorce refers to a new body of law that allows couples to dissolve their marital bonds without either partner's having to assume blame for the failure of the marriage. Weitzman and Dixon (1980) argue that no-fault divorce reflects changes in the traditional view of legal marriage. By eliminating the fault-based grounds for divorce and the adversary process, the new law recognizes the more contemporary view that frequently both parties are responsible for the breakdown of the marriage. Further, the law recognizes that previously the divorce procedure often worsened the situation by forcing potentially "amicable" individuals to become antagonists.

No-fault divorce laws advocate that the financial aspects of marital dissolution are to be based on equity, equality, and economic need rather than on fault- or gender-based role assignments. Alimony also is to be based on the respective spouses' economic circumstances and on the principle of social equality, not on the basis of guilt or innocence. No longer is alimony automatically awarded to the "injured party," regardless of that person's financial needs—no-fault divorce does not recognize an "injured party." The new laws seek to reflect the changing circumstances of women and their increased participation in the labor force. By so doing, they encourage women in their efforts to become self-supporting. Under no-fault divorce law, husbands are not automatically expected to continue to support their ex-wives throughout their lives.

Weitzman and Dixon see the overall impact of no-fault legislation as the redefinition of the traditional marital responsibilities of men and women by the institution of a new norm of equality between the sexes. Husbands are no longer automatically designated as the head of the household solely responsible for support, nor are wives alone expected to assume the responsibility of domestic household activities and child rearing. Sex-neutral obligations that fall equally upon the husband and wife have been institutionalized by these new divorce laws. These changes are reflected most clearly in the new considerations for alimony allocation. In addition, property is to be divided on an equal basis. Finally, child-support expectations and the standards for child custody also reflect the new egalitarian criteria of no-fault divorce legislation. Under these new laws, both father and mother are expected to be equally responsible for the financial support of their children after divorce. Mothers are no longer to receive custody of the child automatically; rather, a sex-neutral standard instructs judges to award custody in the "best interests of the child."

In conclusion, though praising the changes in divorce legislation, Weitzman and Dixon raise one important point of caution. No-fault divorce laws are based on an idealized picture of women's social, occupational, and economic gains in achieving an equality that in fact may not reflect their actual conditions and circumstances. This discrepancy between reality and the ideal can have extremely detrimental effects on women's ability to become self-sufficient after divorce:

> Thus, while the aims of the no-fault laws, i.e., equality and sex-neutrality, are laudable, the laws may be instituting equality in a society in which women are not fully prepared (and/or permitted) to assume equal responsibility for their own and their children's support after divorce. Public

No-fault divorce has emerged as a means for couples to dissolve a marriage without either partner having to assume blame for wrongdoing.

> policy then becomes a choice between temporary protection and safeguards for the transitional woman (and for the older housewife in the traditional generation) to minimize the hardships incurred by the new expectations, versus current enforcement of the new equality, with the hope of speeding the transition, despite the hardships this may cause for current divorces. (Weitzman and Dixon, 1980)

Child-Custody Laws

Child custody is one of the areas of divorce law in which the gap between the ideal and the reality still is apparent. Although the new no-fault legislation approaches the question of child custoday in a sex-neutral way, mothers still are awarded legal custody of children in about 90 percent of American divorce cases (Weiss, 1979b). Until recently, divorce laws generally discriminated against fathers in custody cases. Fathers often were advised by legal counsel of the futility of contesting custody, and the burden of proof was on the father to document the unfitness of the mother

---

no-fault divorce A new body of law that allows couples to dissolve their marital bonds without either partner having to assume blame for the marriage's failure.

or to affirm his ability to be a better parent than the mother.

However, there has been an increased recognition of fathers' rights regarding custody, reflecting the changing role of American fathers and the reevaluation of the judicial practice of automatically awarding custody to the mother. In addition to giving more fathers custody of their children, the courts are now beginning to view joint custody as another legal option. Let us look at some of the factors that have inspired the changes already under way in divorce and child-custody laws.

Impetus for Change

The 1980s are seeing a change in the economic expectations of Americans, for whom the luxuries of the past are seen as the necessities of today. This change has increased the economic necessity for women to work. The transition of women into the labor force has been made smoother as a result of the women's movement, which has persuaded most men and women of the legitimacy of women's work. This acceptance of women in the work force has led to the growth of dual-income families, with more and more households composed of working parents who share domestic tasks and child care. Kelin E. Gersick (1979) expressed these changes this way:

> In recent years . . . the role of the American father has been enjoying a resurgence. Several factors may be involved: a decrease in the average man's working hours and resulting increase in leisure time; the woman's dissatisfaction with her role limitations and movement toward greater economic and social flexibility; and the spreading disenchantment with material acquisition as the exclusive measure of the good life, along with the espousal of close relationships as a principal measure of happiness. Whatever the reasons, there appears to be a recent upswing in father's involvement in their families.

Criticism of the legal presumption that the mother always should gain custody of the child began to appear in the 1960s, and by the early 1970s some state statutes requiring that mothers be preferred had been repealed (Weiss, 1979a).

☐ Summary

Sociology distinguishes between sex—the biological differences between women and men—and gender—the social and cultural definitions of femininity and masculinity.

Two views of the nature of gender-role behavior have been proposed: either it is innate and biologically determined or it is acquired through socialization and social learning experiences.

Many religions manifest a patriarchal ideology—the belief that men are superior to women and should control all the important aspects of a society. This ideology has been used to legitimate discrimination against women, denying them rights, power, and freedom of action.

Ethologists and sociobiologists are convinced that human social and gender-role behavior, like that of other animals, is biologically and genetically determined. Critics of sociobiology maintain that social learning is the important factor.

There is evidence for both views. Many differences between men and women have a physiological or genetic basis. At the same time, other differences between males and females may be linked to cultural influences and variations in environment and activities.

Cross-cultural and historical research offers support for the belief of most sociologists that socialization has a greater effect on gender-role behavior than biology does. Studies indicate that every culture exhibits different, culturally patterned gender-role behavior and gender identities. Other studies show that in all preindustrial societies there generally is a division of labor and activities by sex. Most scholars agree that in all societies, biology may influence but does not determine differences in gender roles.

Socialization is the process by which people learn the values, attitudes, and behavior appropriate to their culture. In all cultures, males and females are socialized differently. In our society, gender identity is established by the age of 2 or 3.

Different societies have different role expectations for adolescent girls and boys. In our society, boys' roles prepare them for an occupation, and girls' roles are designed to enable them to attract a suitable mate. Boys win approval for behavior that is competitive, aggressive, and oriented toward independence and achievement (highly valued traits in our society), whereas girls are encouraged to be passive and dependent.

The three personality traits associated with adult gender roles are gender identity, self-esteem, and achievement motivation. Because women are encouraged to develop traits that are not valued highly by our society, they tend to have weaker gender identities and lower self-esteem than men do.

Women experience discrimination in almost all spheres of American life, and nowhere is it more apparent than on the job. Men often are paid more and/or hold higher job titles than women do for equivalent work and qualifications. Women also find it more difficult to climb the career ladder.

Traditionally, men participate more in public spheres of activity, which in our society carry esteem and power, whereas women generally fulfill roles in the domestic sphere, which lacks status and value. True equality between the sexes will be achieved only when both sexes take part equally in all spheres of activity, domestic and public.

Women tend to occupy a lower social status than men do in every social class. The women's rights movement has helped improve this situation. Women have gained many legal rights, and their status, independence, and power have increased. A new family form has emerged—the symmetrical family—in which husbands and wives ideally share roles and responsibilities. However, the reality often falls short of this ideal.

The new no-fault divorce laws recognize the more equal roles of wives and husbands. Also, child-custody laws now recognize that fathers have custody rights and may be better parents than mothers are.

Gender roles in our society are changing, and traditional distinctions are blurring. Although strong family bonds are expected to continue, the roles of both sexes eventually should approach true equality.

☐ For Further Reading

BARUCH, GRACE, ROSALIND BARNETT, and CARYL RIVERS. *LifePrints*. New York: McGraw-Hill, 1983. The authors note that for women at midlife, autonomy, self-esteem, control, and intimacy are equally important; that there are many possible patterns that achieve this mix; and that a good job is more important to a woman's mental health than was ever before thought.

DEGLER, CARL N. *At Odds: Women and the Family in America from the Revolution to the Present*. New York: Oxford University Press, 1980. Degler draws on diaries and letters to give a sense of what it was like to be a woman in the last century.

GERZON, MARK. *A Choice of Heroes*. Boston: Houghton Mifflin, 1982. Gerzon examines five traditional archetypes of the American male: the Frontiersman, the Soldier, the Breadwinner, the Expert, and the Lord. These images, he believes, influence the character and behavior of all white middle-class American men.

ILLICH, IVAN. *Gender*. New York, Pantheon, 1982. Illich examines what we believe to be progress in gender relations and shows that many of the changes that have taken place in the last two centuries have not had the results we anticipated.

KANTER, ROSABETH MOSS. *Men and Women of the Corporation*. New York: Basic Books, 1977. An interesting and widely recognized study of the career and interaction patterns of men and women in a large corporate setting.

NEWLAND, KATHLEEN. *The Sisterhood of Man*. New York: Norton, 1979. Newland gives an overview of changes that women have experienced under the law, in education, the family, work, and so on.

WEITZ, SHIRLEY. *Sex Roles: Biological, Psychological, and Social Foundations*. New York: Oxford University Press, 1977. This book attempts to give an integrated view of the various influences on sex roles.

Institutions

■　■　■　■　■　■　■　■

Part Five

13 Marriage, Family, and Alternative Lifestyles

☐ **Defining the Family**
   ☐ Functions of the Family
      ☐ *Regulating Sexual Behavior*
      ☐ *Patterning Reproduction*
      ☐ *Organizing Production and Consumption*
      ☐ *Socializing Children*
      ☐ *Providing Care and Protection*
      ☐ *Providing Social Status*
   ☐ Family Structures
☐ **Defining Marriage**
   ☐ Romantic Love
   ☐ Marriage Rules
   ☐ Marital Residence
   ☐ Mate Selection
      ☐ *Age*
      ☐ *Race*
      ☐ *Religion*
      ☐ *Social Status*
☐ **Industrialism and the Family**
   ☐ Modern Trends
      ☐ *Changes in Household Size*
      ☐ *Premarital Sex*
      ☐ *Working Women*
      ☐ *Family Violence*
      ☐ *Divorce*
☐ **Alternatives to Marriage**
   ☐ The Growing Single Population
   ☐ Single-Parent Families
   ☐ Cohabitation
   ☐ Homosexual and Lesbian Couples
☐ **The Future: Bright or Dismal?**
☐ **Summary**

351

The American family has undergone more change in the last 25 years than in the last 250. Although information about family life during the earliest days of our country is not very precise, it does appear quite clear, beginning with the 1790 census, that the American family was quite stable. Divorce and family breakup were not common. If a marriage ended because of desertion, death, or divorce, it was seen as a personal and community tragedy.

The American family has always been quite small. There has never been a strong tradition here of the extended family, where relatives and several generations lived within the same dwelling. Even in the 1700s, the American family consisted of a husband, wife, and approximately three children. This private, inviolate enclave made it possible for the family to endure severe circumstances and to help build the American frontier.

By the 1960s, radical changes were becoming evident. The marriage rate began to fall, and the divorce rate, which had been fairly level, began its accelerating upward trend. By the late sixties and early seventies, fertility began to decline, reaching 16.0 live births per 1,000 people in the population in 1982, compared with 23.8 per 1,000 in 1960 (U.S. Dept. of Commerce, 1984).

The situation in the 1980s shows that this trend is continuing. In 1982 there were nearly 2.5 million marriages, though there were also 1.25 million divorces. This information is even more striking when we realize that divorce statistics do not include desertion or other forms of marital breakup, such as annulment or legal separation.

There also are other signs of change and family instability. The cohabitation rate has been climbing, with 1.8 million unmarried couples living together in 1983 (Spanier, 1983). The number of children born out of wedlock (especially among teenagers) also has been rising sharply. Out of 3,612,000 children born in 1980, 665,700, or 18.5 percent, were born to single women. Among blacks, the percentage of children born out of wedlock was 55.2 percent (U.S. Dept. of Commerce, 1984).

The inescapable conclusion that can be drawn from all this is that the American family is in a state of transition. But transition to what? In this chapter we shall study the institution of the family and look more closely at the current trends and what they forecast for the future.

☐ Defining the Family

For a long time, social scientists defined the family in a way that reflected "common knowledge." For example, in his classic study of social organization and the family, George P. Murdock (1949) defined the family as

> a social group characterized by common residence, economic cooperation, and reproduction. It includes adults of both sexes, at least two of whom maintain a socially approved sexual relationship, and one or more children, own or adopted, of the sexually cohabiting adults.

This definition has proved to be too limited. For one thing, it excludes many kinds of social groups that seem, on the basis of the functions they serve, to deserve the label of family. For example, in America single-parent families are widely recognized. If we expand our perspective to include other societies, we find that quite a few seem to lack the kind of group described by Murdock. For example, in 1954, Melford Spiro, an anthropologist, as was Murdock, studied Israeli *kibbutzim* (pronounced kee-boots-eem)—agricultural communities with communal living, collective ownership of all property, and the communal rearing of children. In some *kibbutzim*, the children sleep apart from their parents in "children's houses" and are cared for in peer groups by child care workers assigned by the *kibbutz*. Spiro's studies at first seemed to indicate that the institution of the family did not exist within the *kibbutz*, that the psychological and social functions of the family were provided by the *kibbutz* as a whole. However, as Spiro himself later pointed out (1960), many features typical of the family exist in the *kibbutz*: couples marry and plan for children; parents call only their own children "son" and "daughter"; and parents and children together form identifiable subgroups within the *kibbutz*, even though the children

In the Israeli *kibbutz* children are cared for in peer groups by childcare workers. The children spend approximately two hours with their parents each day.

live in the children's houses. Furthermore, one of the most valued times of day is the late afternoon when children of all ages return to their parents' rooms for several hours of uninterrupted socializing. So even in the *kibbutz*, the family exists as a significant social group.

Despite Murdock's restricted definition of the family, it was his 1949 study of kinship and family in 250 societies, which showed the institution of the family to be present in every one of them, that led social scientists to believe that some form of the family is found in every known human society.

Perhaps a better understanding of the concept of the family may be gained by examining the various functions it performs in society.

Functions of the Family

Social scientists often assign to the fundamental family unit—married parents and their offspring—a number of the basic functions that it serves in most, if not all, societies. Although in many societies the basic family unit serves some of these functions, in no society does it serve all of them completely or exclusively. For example, among the Nayar of India, a child's biological father is socially irrelevent. Generally another man takes on the social responsibility of parenthood (Gough,

1952). Or consider the Trobrianders, a people living on a small string of islands north of New Guinea. There, as reported by anthropologist Bronislaw Malinowski (1922), the father's role in parenthood was not recognized, and the responsibility for raising children fell to the family of their mother's brother.

Nor is the basic family always the fundamental unit of economic cooperation. Among artisans in preindustrial Europe, the essential economic unit was not the family but rather the household, typically consisting of the artisan's family plus assorted apprentices and even servants (Laslett, 1965). In some societies, members of the basic family group need not necessarily even live in the same household. Among the Ashanti of western Africa, for example, husbands and wives each live with their own mother's relatives (Fortes et al., 1947). In America a small but growing number of two-career families is finding it necessary to set up separate households in different communities—sometimes hundreds of miles apart. Husband and wife travel back and forth between these households to be with each other and the children on weekends and during vacations.

In all societies, however, the family does serve the basic social functions discussed below.

Regulating Sexual Behavior No society permits random sexual behavior. All societies have an **incest taboo**, which forbids sexual intercourse among closely related individuals—although *who* is considered to be closely related varies widely. Almost universally, incest rules prohibit sex between parents and their children and between brothers and sisters. But there are exceptions: The royal families of ancient Egypt, the Inca nation, and Hawaii did allow sex and marriage between brothers and sisters. In America, marriage between parents and children, brothers and sisters, grandparents and grandchildren, aunts and nephews, and uncles and nieces is defined as incest and is forbidden. In addition, approximately 30 states prohibit marriage between first cousins. The incest taboo usually applies to members of one's family (however the family is defined culturally) and thus it promotes marriage—and consequently social ties—among members of different families.

Patterning Reproduction Every society must replace its members. By regulating where and with whom individuals may enter into sexual relationships, society also patterns sexual reproduction. By permitting or forbidding certain forms of marriage (multiple wives or multiple husbands, for example) a society can encourage or discourage reproduction.

Organizing Production and Consumption In preindustrial societies the economic system often depended on each family's producing much of what it consumed. In almost all societies, the family consumes food and other necessities as a social unit. Therefore, a society's economic system and family structures often are closely correlated.

Socializing Children Not only must a society reproduce itself biologically by producing children, it also must ensure that its children are encouraged to accept the lifestyle it favors, to master the skills it values, and to perform the work it requires. In other words, a society must provide predictable social contexts within which its children are to be socialized (see Chapter 4). The family provides such a context almost universally, at least dur-

ing the period when the infant is dependent on the constant attention of others. The family is ideally suited to this task because its members know the child from birth and are aware of its special abilities and needs.

Providing Care and Protection Every human being needs food and shelter. In addition, we all need to be among people who care for us emotionally, help us with the problems that arise in daily life, and back us up when we come into conflict with others. Although many kinds of social groups are capable of meeting one or more of these needs, the family often is the one group in a society that meets them all.

Providing Social Status Simply by being born into a family, each individual inherits both material goods and a socially recognized position defined by ascribed statuses (see Chapter 5). These statuses include social class or caste membership and ethnic identity. Our inherited social position, or "family background," probably is the single most important social factor affecting the predictable course of our lives.

Thus we see that Murdock's definition of the family, based primarily on structure, is indeed too restrictive. A much more productive way of defining the family would be to view it as a universal institution that generally serves the functions discussed above, although the way it does so may vary greatly from one society to another. The different ways in which various social functions are fulfilled by the institution of the family depend, in some instances, on the form the family takes.

Family Structures

The most basic family form is the **nuclear family**, that is, a married couple and their children. The nuclear family is found in all societies, and it is from this form that all other (composite) family forms are derived.

There are two major composite family forms: polygamous and extended families (see Figure 13.1). **Polygamous families** are nuclear families linked together by multiple marriage bonds, with one central individual married to several spouses. When the central

The nuclear family consists of a married couple and their children.

person is male and the multiple spouses are female, the family is **polygynous**. When the central figure is female and the multiple spouses are male, the family is **polyandrous**. Polyandry is known to exist only in a very few societies.

Extended families include other relations and generations in addition to the nuclear family, so that along with married parents and their offspring there may be the parents' parents, siblings of the parents, the siblings' spouses and children, and in-laws. All the members of the extended family live in one house or in homes close to one another, forming one cooperative unit.

Families, whether nuclear or extended, trace their relationships through the generations in several different ways. Under the **patrilineal system**, the generations are tied to-

incest taboo Societal prohibition that forbids sexual intercourse among closely related individuals.

nuclear family The most basic family form, made up of parents and their children, biological or adopted.

polygamous families Nuclear families linked together by multiple marriage bonds, with one central individual married to several spouses.

polygynous family A polygamous family unit in which the central person is male and the multiple spouses are female.

polyandrous family A polygamous family unit in which the central figure is female and the multiple spouses are male.

extended families Families that include, in addition to nuclear family members, other relatives such as the parents' parents, the parents' siblings, and in-laws.

patrilineal system A system that traces the relationship of family generations through the males of the family: all members trace their kinship through the father's line.

In a polygynous marriage a man has two or more wives. Here we see an Iranian Bakhtiari chief with his wives and children.

Nuclear form

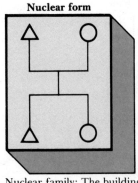

Nuclear family: The building
block of all family forms

Key:
△ Male
○ Female
⌐⌐ Marriage
⌐⌐ Sibling tie
| Descent

Composite forms

I Polygamy

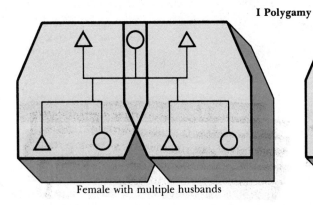

Female with multiple husbands

(a) Polyandry

Male with multiple wives

(b) Polygyny

II Extended Families

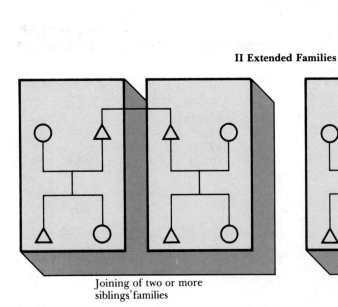

Joining of two or more
siblings'families

(a) Horizontal

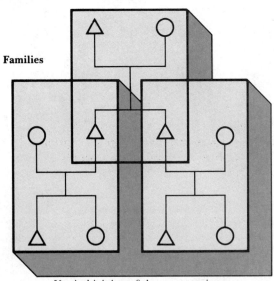

Vertical joining of three generations:
Parents and the families
of some of their children

(b) Vertical

Figure 13.1 Forms of the Family   The diagram
above shows the variations that the two major
composite family forms—polygamous and
extended—can assume. The basic unit within
all variations, however, is the nuclear family.

gether through the males of a family; all members trace their kinship through the father's line. Under the **matrilineal system**, just the opposite is the case: The generations are tied together through the females of a family. Under the **bilateral system**, descent passes through both females and males of a family. Although in American society, descent is bilateral, the majority of the world's societies are either patrilineal or matrilineal (Murdock, 1949).

In patrilineal societies, social, economic, and political affairs usually are organized around the kinship relationships among men, and men tend to dominate the public affairs. Polygyny often is permitted, and men also tend to dominate family affairs. When men dominate their families in these ways, sociologists use the term **patriarchal** to describe the family. The **matriarchal family**, in which most family affairs are dominated by women, is relatively uncommon but does exist nonetheless. Typically it emerges in matrilineal societies. The matriarchal family is becoming increasingly more common in American society, however, with the rise of single-parent families (most often headed by mothers).

Whatever form the family takes and whatever functions it serves, it generally requires a marriage in order to exist. Like the family, marriage varies from society to society in its forms.

☐ Defining Marriage

Marriage is an institution found in all societies. It is the socially recognized, legitimized, and supported union of individuals of opposite sexes. It differs from other unions (such as friendships) in that (1) it takes place in a public (and usually formal) manner; (2) it includes sexual intercourse as an explicit element of the relationship; (3) it provides the essential condition for legitimizing offspring (that is, it provides newborns with socially accepted statuses); and (4) it is intended to be a stable and enduring relationship. Thus, although almost all societies allow for divorce—that is, the breakup of marriage—no society endorses it as an ideal norm.

Romantic Love

Our culture is relatively unique in believing that there is a compatibility between romantic love and the institution of marriage. Not only do we believe they are compatible, but we also generally expect that they coexist. Our culture implies that without the prospect of marriage, romance is immoral and that without romance, marriage is empty. This view underlies most romantic fiction and other media presentations.

Romantic love can be defined in terms of five dimensions: (1) idealization of the loved one, (2) the notion of a one and only, (3) love at first sight, (4) love winning out over all, and (5) an indulgence of personal emotions (Lantz, 1982).

Throughout most of the world's other societies, romantic love is unknown or seen as a strange maladjustment. It may exist, but it has nothing to do with marriage. Marriage in these societies is seen as an institution that organizes or patterns the establishment of economic, social, and even political relationships among families. Three families ultimately are involved: the two families that produced the two spouses—their respective **families of origin** or **families of orientation**—and the family created by the spouses' union—their **family of procreation**. Differing rules for marriage and for residence after marriage result in the creation of very different household and family forms.

matrilineal system A system that traces the relationship of family generations through the females of the family; all members trace their kinship through the mother's line.

bilateral descent system A system that traces the relationship of family generations through both female and male family members. This system applies in American society.

patriarchal family A family in which most family affairs are dominated by men.

matriarchal family A family in which most family affairs are dominated by women.

marriage The socially recognized, legitimized, and supported union of individuals of opposite sexes.

family of orientation The nuclear family in which one is an offspring, the family in which one is raised. Also family of origin.

family of procreation The family that is created by the spouses' union to produce offspring.

Modern culture is rare in believing that romantic love and marriage go together.

Marriage Rules

In every society, marriage is the binding link that makes possible the existence of the family. All societies have norms or rules governing who may marry whom and where the newlywed couples should live. These rules vary, but there are certain typical arrangements that occur in many societies around the world.

Almost all societies have two kinds of marriage norms or rules: rules of **endogamy** limit the social categories from within which one can choose a marriage partner. For example, many Americans still attempt to instill in their children the idea that one should "marry one's own kind," that is, someone within the ethnic, religious, or economic group of one's family of origin.

Rules of **exogamy**, on the other hand, require an individual to marry someone outside his or her culturally defined group. For example, in many tribal groups, members must marry outside their lineage. In the United States there are laws forbidding the marriage of close relatives, although the rules are variable.

These norms vary widely across cultures, but everywhere they serve basic social functions. Rules of exogamy determine the ties and boundaries between social groups, linking them through the institution of marriage and whatever social, economic, and political obligations go along with it. Rules of endogamy, by requiring people to marry within specific groups, reinforce group boundaries, and perpetuate them from one generation to the next.

Marriage rules also determine how many spouses a person may have at one time. Among many groups—Europeans and Americans, for example—marriage is **monogamous**—that is, each person is allowed only one spouse at a time. However, many societies allow **multiple marriages**, in which an individual may have more than one spouse (polygamy). Polygyny, the most common form of polygamy, is found among such diverse peoples as the Swazi of Africa, the Tiwi of Australia, and, formerly, the Blackfeet Indians of the United States. Polyandry is extremely rare. Murdock (1949) lists only 3 societies that practice polyandry, from among his sample of 250: the Toda of India, the Sherpa of Nepal, and the Marquesan Islanders of the South Pacific.

As Marvin Harris (1975) notes, "Some form of polygamy occurs in 90 percent of the world's cultures." But within each such society only a minority of people actually can afford it. In addition, the Industrial Revolution favored monogamy for reasons we shall discuss shortly. Therefore, monogamy is the most common and widespread form of marriage in the world today.

Marital Residence

Once two people are married, they must set up housekeeping. In most societies there are strongly held norms that govern where a couple settles down. Sociologists call these norms **marital residence rules. Patrilocal residence** calls for the new couple to settle down near or within the husband's father's household—as among Greek villagers and the Swazi of Africa. **Matrilocal residence** calls for the new couple to settle down near or within the wife's mother's household—as among the Hopi Indians of the American Southwest.

The Blackfeet Indians allowed new couples to choose whether to live with the husband's or wife's family of origin; this system is called **bilocal residence**. In modern industrial society, newlyweds typically have even more freedom, and **neolocal residence** is common. With this type of residence, the couple may choose to live virtually anywhere, even thousands of miles from their families of origin. In practice, however, it is not unusual for American newlyweds to set up housekeeping near one of their respective families.

Marital residence rules play a major role in determining the compositions of households. With patrilocal residence, groups of men remain in the familiar context of their father's home, and their sisters leave to join their husbands. In other words, after marriage the women leave home to live as "strangers" among their husband's kinfolk. With matrilocal residence just the opposite is true: Women and their children remain at home, and husbands are the "outsiders." In many matrilocal societies, this situation often leads to considerable marital stress, with husbands going home to their own mothers' families when domestic conflict becomes intolerable.

Bilocal residence and neolocal residence allow greater flexibility and a wider range of household forms because young couples may move to places in which the social, economic, and political advantages may be greatest. One disadvantage of neolocal residence is that a young couple cannot count on the immediate presence of kinfolk to help out in times of need or with demanding household chores (including the raising of children). In the United States today, a new phenomenon, the surrogate, nonkin "family," made up of neighbors, friends, and colleagues at work, may help fill this void (Wolfe, 1981). In other societies, polygynous neolocal families help overcome such difficulties, with a number of wives cooperating in the division of household work.

Mate Selection

Like our patterns of family life, America's rules for marriage, which are expressed through mate selection, spring from those of our society's European forebears. Because we have been nourished, through songs and cinema, by the notions of "love at first sight," "love is blind," and "love conquers all," most of us probably are under the impression that in the United States there are no rules for mate selection. Research shows, however, that this is not necessarily true.

If we think statistically about mate selection, we must admit that in no way is it random. Consider for a moment what would happen if it were: Given the population distribution of the United States, blacks would be more likely to marry whites than members of their race; upper-class individuals would have a greater chance of marrying a lower-class person; and various culturally unlikely but statistically probable combinations of age, education, and religion would take place. In actual fact, **homogamy**—the tendency of like to marry like—is much more the rule.

There are numerous ways in which homogamy can be achieved. One way is to let

endogamy Societal norms that limit the social categories from within which one can choose a marriage partner.

exogamy Societal norms that require an individual to marry someone outside his or her culturally defined group. The incest taboo is an example of exogamy.

monogamous marriage The form of marriage in which each person is allowed only one spouse at a time.

multiple marriage A form of marriage in which an individual may have more than one spouse (polygamy).

marital residence rules The rules that govern where a newly married couple settles down and lives.

patrilocal residence Marital residence rules that require a newly married couple to settle down near or within the husband's father's household.

matrilocal residence Marital residence rules that require a newly married couple to settle down near or within the wife's mother's household.

bilocal residence Marital residence rules that allow a newly married couple to live with either the husband's or wife's family of origin.

neolocal residence Marital residence rules of modern industrial society in which newly married couples may choose to live virtually anywhere, even thousands of miles from their families of origin.

homogamy The tendency of an individual to choose a spouse with a similar racial, religious, ethnic, educational, age, and socioeconomic background.

Old Glory

Symbols are collective representations; they are shared by a group and have meanings which are understood by members of that group. Symbols, such as a nation's flag, are an aspect of a group's identity and often a point of pride recognized by insiders and outsiders alike. The importance of the symbols lies in the meanings that are shared and communicated through their use.

All communication involves the use of symbols. A symbol is a word, gesture, or object that stands for something else. Shaking hands is a symbolic act, as is shaking one's fist. All around us are symbols that stand for beliefs and values. The American flag is rich in symbolism, and in this photo essay you will see its symbolic significance for our society. The flag has been used in family, religious, educational, economic, and political contexts to portray American values. The presence of the flag, whether hanging from someone's porch, waved at a rally, or flown in battle, evokes the meanings and emotions of patriotism and national solidarity.

Political parties as well as nation states are well aware of the symbolic nature of the flag. During the Democratic and Republican National Conventions thousands of flags decorate convention halls. They are also an important presence at the Olympics. The flag is seen as a symbol of democracy itself.

The flag is always present in our culture. To a politician it may symbolize democracy. To a clergyman it may symbolize a sense of common humanity that is the root of democracy. To a family of new immigrants it may symbolize freedom.

someone older and wiser, such as a parent or matchmaker, pair up appropriately suited individuals. Throughout the history of the world, this has been one of the most common ways by which marriages have taken place. The role of the couple in question can range from having no say about the matter whatsoever to having some sort of veto power. In the United States, most people who get married do not use the services of a matchmaker, though the end result in terms of similarity of background is so highly patterned that it could seem as if a very conscious homogamous matchmaking effort were involved.

Age In American society, people generally marry within their own age range. There are comparatively few marriages in which there is a wide gap between the ages of the two partners. In addition, only 15 percent of American women marry men who are younger than themselves. On the average, men marry women who are 2.5 years younger than they are. This is, however, related to age at the time of marriage. For example, 20-year-old men marry women with a median age of 19—only a one-year difference. Twenty-five-year-old men marry women with a median age of 22. For 30-year-old men, the median age for wives is 25; for 60-year-old men, the median age for wives is 50.

The age at the time of first marriage is fairly young. The median age at the time of first marriage has fluctuated since the turn of the century. In 1890, the median age for men was 26.1 and 22.0 for women. By 1960 it had dropped to 22.8 and 20.3 respectively. Since that time it has risen again, so that in 1980 it was 23.6 for men and 21.8 for women (U.S. Dept. of Commerce, 1984).

Age homogamy appears to hold for all groups within the population. Studies show that it is true for blacks as well as whites and for professionals as well as laborers. Clearly, the norms of our society are very effective in causing people of similar age to marry each other (Leslie, 1979; Hollingshead, 1951; Glick and Landau, 1950).

Race Homogamy is most obvious in the area of race. As late as 1966, 19 states sought to stop interracial marriage through legislation. The laws varied widely, and there was great confusion because of various court interpretations. In Arizona before 1967, it was illegal for a white person to marry a black, Hindu, Malay, or Asian. The same thing was true in Wyoming, and residents of that state were also prohibited from marrying mulattos.

Since that time, the number of interracial marriages has risen from 0.7 percent of all marriages in 1968 to 1.6 percent in 1980, based on a sample of 31 states that kept marital records by race in both years. We are barely at the point today at which 2 in 100 marriages are racially mixed.

The most common type of interracial marriage—between a white bride and a black groom—has increased the most. Such marriages rose from 0.2 to 0.5 percent of all marriages in that time period. Marriages uniting black brides and white grooms were not nearly so common, but they increased too, from 0.1 to 0.2 percent of all marriages.

Marriages between a white spouse and a spouse of a race other than black doubled between 1968 and 1980, but marriages uniting a black spouse with a spouse of a race other than white remain rare—less than 0.1 percent of all marriages in both years (for a more extensive discussion of this issue, see Using Sociology: "The Interracial Melting Pot").

Religion Religious homogamy is not nearly as widespread as is racial homogamy, though most marriages still do involve people of the same religion. Attitudes toward religious intermarriage vary somewhat from one religious group to another, with Jews and Catholics more opposed to it than Protestants are. Attitudes toward religious intermarriage have also changed over time. For example, in 1970 the Catholic church dropped it requirement that the non-Catholic partner in an intermarriage promise to raise the children as Catholics. The church also allowed local bishops the option of granting dispensation from the requirement that all marriages be performed by a priest. An important consideration that will produce variations in the religious intermarriage rate is the proportion of a particular religious group in the population.

USING SOCIOLOGY
The Interracial Melting Pot

In 1967 the Supreme Court ruled that states could no longer prohibit marriages between people of different races. Since that time, the number of interracial marriages in America has doubled. These racially mixed marriages exhibit some interesting differences from marriages between members of the same race.

In 1966 the state of Virginia's Supreme Court of Appeals had to decide on the legality of a marriage that had taken place in Washington, D.C., in 1958 between Richard P. Loving, a white man, and his part-Indian and part-black wife, Mildred Loving. The court unanimously upheld the state's ban on interracial marriages. The couple appealed the case to the United States Supreme Court, which agreed to decide whether state laws prohibiting racial intermarriage were constitutional. Previously, all courts had ruled that the laws were not discriminatory because they applied to both whites and nonwhites. However, on June 12, 1967, the Supreme Court ruled that states could not outlaw racial intermarriage.

Compared with marriages between people of the same race, interracial marriages are more likely to take place in a state other than the one in which the bride or groom was born. Research shows that among white couples, 60 percent of the brides and 57 percent of the grooms marry in the state in which they were born. But in interracial marriages, only 45 percent of white brides and 37 percent of white grooms marry in their state of birth.

In comparison with marriages between spouses of the same race, interracial marriages more frequently involve at least one partner who has been married before. In addition, brides and grooms who married interracially tended to be older than the national average. In 1980, the ages at first marriage for

While the total numbers are small, racially mixed marriages have become increasingly frequent in America's melting pot.

brides and grooms, regardless of race, were 21.8 and 23.6, respectively. But, for example, white brides were found to be 23.4 when marrying a black groom and 22.4 when marrying a groom of another race. Black brides who married black grooms were, on the average, 23.1 years old, but 23.8 when marrying a white groom and 23.6 when marrying a groom of another race.

The degree of education of the participants also differs in interracial marriages. White grooms who marry interracially are more likely to have completed college than are those who marry white brides. In all-white couples, 18 percent of the grooms hold college degrees. In a marriage involving a white groom and a black bride, 24 percent of the men finished college. In contrast, only 5 percent of black grooms paired with brides of other races had completed college, whereas 13 percent of black grooms of white brides, and 9 percent of black grooms whose spouses were also black held college degrees.

Although the rate of interracial

marriage is growing, the proportions vary widely by state. The state with both the highest number and the greatest proportion of interracial marriages is Hawaii. Nearly one-fourth of all marriages there are interracial, the majority of which are Asian-Caucasian unions. Florida runs a distant second, and in Illinois, the 1,173 interracial marriages include 665 white brides marrying black grooms—the highest number of marriages of that combination in any state. The record for the reverse combination—black brides marrying white grooms—is held by New Jersey. Alaska comes closest to Hawaii in the proportion of interracial marriages recorded: 13 percent of the state's marriages are interracial. None of the other states even approach this figure.

Even though their total numbers are still small, racially mixed marriages have become increasingly common in America's melting pot.

Source: Sections adapted from Barbara Foley Wilson, "Marriage's Melting Pot," *American Demographics* **6** (7) (July, 1984), pp. 34–37, 45. ☐

Religious leaders are often concerned about religious intermarriage for a variety of reasons. Some claim that one or both intermarrying parties are lost to the religion, and others believe that the potential for marital success is decreased greatly in an intermarriage. Studies have shown that there are several complex factors in intermarriage and that simplistic and unequivocal predictions are not warranted. For example, a study in Iowa of Catholic-Protestant marriages concluded that though there was a slightly higher divorce rate among intermarried couples, the results did not justify predictions of marital problems. Moreover, the study also showed that Presbyterians, Methodists, and Baptists who married persons of other Protestant denominations had higher marital survival rates than did those who married within their denomination (Burchinal and Chancellor, 1963). Most marriages still do involve those of the same religion marrying each other. There is, however, a clear trend of more religious intermarriages in the United States today.

Social Status Level of education and type of occupation are two measures of social status. In these areas there is usually a great deal of similarity between people who marry each other. Men tend to marry women who are slightly below them in education and social status, though these differences are within a narrow range. Wide-ranging differences between the two people often contain an element of exploitation. One partner may either be trying to make a major leap on the social class ladder or be looking for an easy way of taking advantage of the other partner because of unequal power.

The typical high school environment often plays a major role in maintaining social status homogamy, as it is in high school that students have to start making plans about their future careers. Some may go to college, and others may plan on going to work directly after graduation. This process causes the students to be divided into two groups: the college-bound and the work force–bound. Although the lines separating these two groups are by no means impenetrable, in many high schools these two groups maintain separate social activities. In this way barriers against dating and future marriage between those of unlike social status are set up. After graduation, those who attend a college are more likely to associate with other college students and choose their mates from that pool. Those who have joined the work force are more likely to choose their mates from that environment. In this way, similarities in education between marriage partners really are not accidental.

As with several of the items we have discussed already, education, social class, and occupation produce a similarity of experience and values among people. Just as growing up in an Italian family may make one feel comfortable with Italian customs and traits, going to college may make one feel comfortable with those who have experienced that environment. Similarities in social status, then, are as much a result of socialization and culture as conscious choice. We most likely will marry a person we feel comfortable with—a person who has had experiences similar to our own.

☐ Industrialism and the Family

Most scholars agree that the Industrial Revolution had a strong impact on the family. In his influential study of family patterns around the world, William J. Goode (1963) showed that the modern, relatively isolated nuclear family with weak ties to an extensive kinship network is well adapted to the pressures of industrialism.

First, industrialism demands that workers be geographically mobile so that a work force is available wherever new industries are built. The modern nuclear family, by having cut many of its ties to extended family networks, is freer to move. And it was among laborers' families that extended kinship ties first were weakened. Only in the last few decades have middle- and upper-class families become similarly isolated.

Second, industrialism requires a certain degree of social mobility (see Chapter 10). This is so that talented workers may be recruited to positions of greater responsibility (with greater material rewards and increased prestige). A family that is too closely tied to other families in its kinship network will find it difficult to "break free" and climb into a higher social class. On the other hand, if families in the higher social classes are too tightly linked by kinship ties, newly "arriving" families will find it very difficult to "fit into" their new social environment. Hence the isolated nuclear family is well suited to the needed social mobility in an industrial society.

A third point is that the modern nuclear family allows for inheritance and descent through both sides of the family. Further, material resources and social opportunities are not inherited mainly by the oldest males (or females), as in some societies. This means that all children in a family will have a chance to develop their skills, which in turn means that industry will have a larger, more talented, and flexible labor force from which to hire workers.

By the early twentieth century, then, the nuclear family had evolved fully among the working classes of industrial society. It rested on (1) the child-centered family; (2) **companionate marriage** (that is, marriage based on romantic love); (3) increased equality for women; (4) decreased links with extended families or kinship networks; (5) neolocal residence and increased geographical mobility; (6) increased social mobility; and (7) the clear separation between work and leisure. There was also boring and alienating work and an associated expectation that the nuclear family would fulfill the function of providing emotional support for its members.

Modern Trends

There has been another historical period that has had a profound effect on the American family. World War II accelerated a process that had already been under way during the Depression years. The war made it necessary for hundreds of thousands of women to work outside the home in order to support their families. They often had to take jobs, vital to the American economy, that had been vacated when their husbands went to fight overseas. After the war, an effort was made to "defeminize" the work force. Nevertheless, many women remained on the job, and those who left now knew what it was like to work for compensation outside the home. Things

were never the same again for the American family, and family life began to change.

The initial changes were not all that apparent. On the contrary, by the 1950s the United States had entered the most family-oriented period in its history. This was the era of the baby boom, and couples were marrying at the youngest ages in recorded American history. During the 1950s, 96 percent of those people in the child-bearing years married (Blumstein and Schwartz, 1983). The war years' experiences also paved the way for secondary groups and formal organization (see Chapter 6) gradually to take over many of the family's traditional activities and functions. As social historian Christopher Lasch (1977) points out, this trend was supported by public policymakers who came to see the family as an obstacle to social progress. Because the family preserved separatist cultural and religious traditions and other "old-fashioned" ideas that stood in the way of "progress," social reformers sought to diminish the family's hold over its children. Thus the prime task of socializing the young was shifted from the family to centrally administered schools. Social workers intruded into the home, offering constantly expanding welfare services to families by outside agencies. The juvenile court system expanded in the belief that deficiencies in families of youthful offenders caused crime among children.

Thus, the modern period has seen what sociologists refer to as the *transfer of functions* from the family to other, outside institutions. This transfer has had a great effect on the family and underlies the trends that currently are troubling many people.

There are several problems in trying to assess the prevailing state of the family. Some feel that the family is deteriorating, and they cite appropriate examples of divorce rates and single-parent families to support their view. Others think of the family as an institution that is in transition but just as stable as ever. Was the family of the past a stable extended family unit with everyone working for the betterment of the whole? Or has the family structure changed throughout history in response to the economic and political changes within society? In this section we shall explore these views and attempt to clarify the current direction of family life. (For an idea of what today's students think about marriage and family, see Focus on Research: "Attitudes Toward Marriage and Family Life Among College Students.")

Changes in Household Size Although changes in household size may be neither a positive nor a negative change, some social scientists use this point to support a negative view of the future of the family. The American household of 1790 had an average of 5.8 members. By 1982 the average number had dropped to less than half that—2.73 (Glick, 1984). The same trend also has been evident in other parts of the world. The average rural household in Japan in 1660 often had 20 or more members, but by the 1960s the rural Japanese household averaged only 4.5 members.

It has been suggested that one reason for the reduction in size of the American household is that today it is very unlikely for us to house unrelated people (Cohen, 1981). Until the 1940s, for a variety of reasons, it was common for people to have nonkin living with them, either as laborers in the fields or as boarders who helped with the rent payment.

The reduction in the number of nonrelatives living with the family explains only part of the continuing reduction in the average household size. Another reason that has often been cited is a rapid decrease in the number of aging parents living with grown children and their families. Some point to this as evidence of the fragmentation and loss of intimacy present in the contemporary family. At the turn of the century over 60 percent of those 65 or older lived with one or more of their children, but in 1970 this figure was down to 18 percent.

How can we account for so many more old people living apart from their families? We might be tempted to say that the family has become so self-centered and so unable to fulfill the needs of its members that the elderly have become the first and most obvious castoffs. However, this trend of the elderly living away from their children can also be seen as a result of the increasing wealth of

the population, including the elderly. The percentage of the total population living in poverty dropped from 12.6 percent to 11.6 percent between 1970 and 1979. For the elderly, the drop was from 24.5 percent to 15.1 percent, indicating that their position relative to that of the general population has improved greatly (U.S. Bureau of the Census, 1981).

This change in the elderly's economic position is more likely to be responsible for their living apart from their children than is any supposed deterioration in family life—older people themselves are choosing to live independently. As gerontologist Gary R. Lee (1981) notes:

> While we have good evidence that the elderly *did* frequently live with their children around the turn of the century, we have no evidence that they *wanted* to do so, then or now. In our culture, unlike some others such as the Japanese, dependence on children in one's old age is no virtue, and most older people seem to prefer to avoid dependence and the appearance of dependence if they have the necessary resources. They have been increasingly likely to have these resources. Because of this, they have been increasingly able to stay in their own homes, or in homes of their own choosing, and have less often been forced to rely on the largesse of children. They are not being ignored, they are being independent.

Another reason for the change in the size of the households is the increasing divorce rate. As more families separate legally and move apart physically, the numbers of people living under one roof have fallen.

A further explanation for the smaller families of today is the tendency of young people to postpone marriage and the increase in the number of working women. On the average, today's newlyweds are 1.5 years older than were their counterparts in 1960. As people marry later, they have fewer children. Many couples also are deciding to have no children; as more and more women become involved in work and careers, they tend to

companionate marriage Marriage based on romantic love.

FOCUS ON RESEARCH
Attitudes Toward Marriage and Family Life Among College Students

In the last few decades, marriage and family life in America have undergone a tremendous upheaval, and young adults have experienced many of these changes firsthand. They have often seen their families split by divorce and have lived as part of single-parent families. These young adults are now developing and defining the concept of marriage and family life of the future as they assume the roles of spouses and parents. A recent study showed how they view such topics as cohabitation, premarital sexual relations, child rearing, marriage, and divorce.

Many researchers would agree that today's college students hold very different attitudes about marriage and family life than did their predecessors. However no comprehensive study had been done which documented those changes. Recently a study was undertaken at four Southwestern universities which explored the beliefs held by contemporary students toward marriage and the family.

The subjects of the study were 5,237 students from universities in Arkansas, Louisiana, Oklahoma, and Texas. These universities were sampled since they were likely to enroll students from varied socioeconomic and living environments. Fifty-seven percent of the subjects studied were women, and 43 percent were men. Their mean age was 20 years.

Subjects were asked to complete *The Marriage and Family Life Attitude Survey*, a well-known test for measuring perceptions about marriage and family life.

The results may be summarized as follows:

1. *Cohabitation and Premarital Sexual Relations.* Respondents were divided as to whether it is wrong to engage in sexual intercourse before marriage. Nearly 55 percent said they have or would engage in sexual intercourse before marriage, while 31.8 percent stated they hadn't or wouldn't. Seventy-two percent indicated that it is not acceptable to experience sexual intercourse without love of one's partner. Sixty-four percent believed they would not cohabit before marriage; if they did, the majority would tell their parents.

2. *Marriage and Divorce.* Seventy-five percent of the respondents viewed their parents' marriage as happy. Over 90 percent saw marriage as a lifelong commitment. The majority of respondents did not believe divorce was acceptable with or without children. While close to 80 percent believed they had the skills necessary for a good marriage, the respondents were evenly divided as to whether or not they were prepared for marriage.

3. *Childhood and Child Rearing.* Eighty-eight percent view childhood as a happy experience. The majority of respondents would leave their children with a relative or in a daycare center if both spouses worked. Respondents were divided as to whether a parent should stay home to rear children, but strongly believed the responsibility of child-rearing should be equally divided between both parents. Fully 54 percent felt that children were not necessary in a marriage, but approximately 76 percent felt that having two or more children was desirable for a marriage.

4. *Division of Household Labor and Professional Employment.* The majority of respondents felt that household chores should be divided equally, but felt there are certain chores that are better suited for men, and others for women. Results indicated that equal careers were agreeable, but it was not necessary that both spouses work. Approximately 64 percent would move with spouse because of a job offer in a different locality.

5. *Marital and Extramarital Sexual Relations.* The vast majority agreed that sexual relations were important in a marriage, and that sexual advances should be initiated by either partner. Extramarital sex was not acceptable under any conditions.

6. *Parental Relationships.* Approximately 75 percent of the respondents indicated that they would marry someone regardless of the partner's parental disapproval. If a spouse's parents were disliked, a majority would still visit them. They also felt that each spouse's parents should be seen an equal amount of time. However, 60 percent indicated that parents were not to intervene in matters pertaining to the couple's marriage. Seventy-five percent designated that their parents wanted them to get married.

The results from this study do not seem to indicate any great radical change taking place in the attitudes of America's college students. If anything, they seem to display a certain level of idealism about marriage and family life. Present divorce statistics indicate a discrepancy between these attitudes and the reality of what is occurring in American society. It is likely that many of these people will have their views challenged, if they follow along the paths of previous generations.

Source: Don Martin and Maggie Martin, "Selected Attitudes Toward Marriage and Family Life among College Students," *Family Relations* **33** (2) (April, 1984), pp. 293–299. ☐

defer marriage and limit the number of children they bear.

All these factors point to what, according to 1980 census data, are the most significant causes of the sharp decline in the average size of the American household: the decrease in the number of children per family and the increase in the number of people living alone (Herbers, 1981). These facts will ultimately have some important consequences for the entire structure of society.

Premarital Sex The 1970s and 1980s have seen widespread changes in attitudes toward premarital sex and the corresponding increase in the number of people who routinely have sex before marriage. The revolution in attitudes toward premarital sex was triggered by the social upheavals of the 1960s and 1970s, the accompanying changes in the gender roles, and, of course, the development and accessibility of effective contraceptives. Studies by the National Opinion Research Center (NORC) (1977) reflect this radical change in attitudes. In 1963, 80 percent of the people surveyed felt that premarital sex was wrong, compared with only 30 percent in 1975. Other research indicates the enormous change in female sexual experience in that period—there was a far greater increase in premarital sex among teenage girls and women than among men (Zelnik and Kantner, 1972, 1979).

Coming to terms with the constraints on our marriage choices can be a sobering experience: What we thought to be freedom of choice in selecting a mate is revealed instead by various studies to be governed by rules and patterns. Such studies are also helpful in predicting the future of American family life.

Working Women Although further progress is still necessary, a woman's economic potential in the work place is significantly greater than in the past. Between 1947 and 1984, the proportion of married women who were working more than doubled, rising from 21.4 percent to 52.8 percent. Contrary to popular belief, this shift was not the result of economic necessity alone. Many more women are working because of a desire for the rewards and self-satisfaction that go along with a job. A 1980 Roper poll showed that 57 percent of women between 18 and 29 preferred jobs over the traditional housewife role. As more women go to college or become trained in a particular area, they may be reluctant to follow a life of domesticity that leaves their other skills and training unused.

A 1979 nationwide survey by the Newspaper Advertising Bureau found that a majority of those questioned believed that working women (that is, those with paying jobs) have a more stimulating, rich, and full life than do housewives whose work is limited to maintaining their home and family. The majority also believed that women with paying jobs have a higher sense of self-worth, of meaningful personal identity than do housewives. Furthermore, housewives themselves share that view: Fewer than half said they had a "full" life at home, and most of the 1,041 working women interviewed said that they would continue to work even if it were no longer financially necessary. American women apparently are less and less satisfied with their traditional role as housewife and homemaker. Accordingly, changing gender roles can be a source of serious strain on many marriages today. (For a discussion of the problems accompanying women's career and family de-

In 1984 nearly 53 percent of all married women worked outside the home.

CASE STUDY
Women, and the Fifty-nine-cent Dollar

The average woman earns 59 percent of what a man earns. Many reasons have been cited for this wage gap, among them the difference in pay between jobs traditionally defined as male and those defined as female, the downward pull on the average exerted by families headed by women with no husband present, and salary discrimination based on sex. Researcher Barbara E. Bryant, however, thinks there is another factor that contributes to perpetuating this gap, the lifestyle choices made by women themselves.

Supermom—that paragon of energy and talent who can simultaneously juggle baby, career, household, and social responsibilities without missing a deadline or a birthday card—has become a recurrent figure in the popular media. But despite the glamour associated with such tales, for a majority of American women, returning to work as soon as possible after their baby is born does not represent the ideal. Rather, a full 46 percent of women polled in 1982 said that if given the choice, they would stay at home while their children were young and then combine jobs with homemaking throughout the rest of their careers. What is more, the number of women expressing a preference for this combination of roles has dropped only 3 percentage points since 1975.

In 1982, 12 percent of women believed the ideal lifestyle was to be mainly a job holder or a career woman, up from 5 percent in 1975. Twenty percent would choose to be mainly a homemaker, down just 2 percentage points from 1975. Twenty-two percent would combine a job or career with homemaking, using day care if they had children—down from 24 percent in 1975.

But a preference for staying home with preschool children cut across all subgroups. There was no difference of opinion on this point between homemakers and those who were employed. The 46 percent who chose staying at home with young children as the ideal lifestyle included 49 percent of those who were currently employed—an even higher share than the 41 percent of the nonemployed who expressed this preference!

Despite this stated preference, the number of women who in fact stay home has been dropping steadily. The percentage of women employed outside the home rose from 42 percent in 1975 to 54 percent in 1982. That figure includes 54 percent of all married women with children at home.

The working mothers included those who took jobs because of economic necessity but would rather have been at home full time, as well as those who took a maternity leave and returned to work quickly.

The kind of women who expressed the strongest preferences for staying home while their children were young were those who regarded homemaking as a creative activity. They found life at home more interesting and varied than the jobs they had held in offices and retail stores. For some in this group, a part-time job was the compromise between what they wanted to do and what they had to do to afford the middle-class life they wanted for their families.

Although the gap in median income between women and men narrowed by three percentage points between 1979 and 1982—reflecting in large measure the career-oriented outlook of younger women—it is not discrimination alone that keeps the income gap so large, as some people charge.

It is also women's lifestyle preferences. Whatever the benefits of an at-home mother for mother or child, women who make this choice must assess realistically the trade-off they are making between their lifestyle desires and opportunities for career advancement. Unless a woman finds a way to return to the work force better prepared than when she left, she will be at a disadvantage compared with the men and the other women who have kept working. She will have less experience, less seniority, and a shorter salary history.

Some women who return to work after rearing a child have updated their skills and reenter the work force even better able to cope with the new technologies and management approaches than are men who have worked continuously. Most, however, return to be forever frustrated by earning less than do the men their age. Is job discrimination the cause of their frustration, or is it a consequence of socialization and lifestyle choices? As with all social issues, it is most likely a complex combination of several of these factors.

Nearly half of American women say they want to move in and out of the labor force, finding it ideal to stay at home with their small children and combining work with family life later on. Men have not been free to make this choice. The price of this choice for women, however, may be an earnings gap that they can never subsequently succeed in closing.

Source: Based on Barbara E. Bryant, "Women, and the Fifty-nine-cent Dollar," *American Demographics* Aug. 1983, pp. 28–31. □

cisions, see Case Study: "Women's Lifestyle Choices Linked to Wage Gap.")

Family Violence According to a recent nationwide survey (Straus, Gelles, and Steinmetz, 1980), every year some 8 million Americans are assaulted by members of their own families. Spouses attack each other, parents attack children, and even children attack and hurt both their parents and one another: every year, 16 percent of all couples come to blows with each other, and more than a third of the time these violent confrontations include severe punching, kicking, and even biting: 3 percent of all children are punched, kicked, or bitten by parents; and over a third of all siblings assault one another severely.

In general, research has shown the incidence of family violence to be highest among urban lower-class families. It is high among families with more than four children and in those in which the husband is unemployed. Families in which child abuse occurs tend to be socially isolated, living in crowded and otherwise inadequate housing. Research on family violence has tended to focus on lower socioeconomic groups, but scattered data from school counselors and mental health agencies suggest that family violence also is a serious problem among America's more affluent households. In fact, in a recent study, two sociologists found that the highest incidence of violence was in families in which both husband and wife were high school graduates. A related finding was that the children most likely to act violently toward their siblings were those whose parents had had some college education (Kenney, 1980). Other research indicates that violence often begins when couples are dating. It is apparent from these observations that more research focused on family violence in the middle and upper classes is called for (Parke and Collmer, 1975).

Sociologists have not yet been able to answer the following questions: Is family violence on the rise in American society? Or is it simply being reported and recorded more accurately than it used to be? Certainly some researchers feel that family violence is an accepted, pervasive attribute of American life (Kenney, 1980). Is family violence more prevalent in the United States than in other industrial societies or in nonindustrial societies? What are the causes of family violence? These questions must be studied before it is possible to assess what can be done to help prevent the occurrence of this disturbing aspect of family life in America.

Of all the changes apparent in modern American family life, the increasing incidence of divorce is one of the most prominent. Even though the statistics are indisputable, the impact of a high divorce rate on the family, its structure, and even its existence is hotly debated.

Divorce Although the marriage rate has remained almost constant, the rate of divorce in America has risen fivefold since 1910. In 1970, of all American males, 2.5 percent were divorced. These figures more than doubled, to 5.9 percent, in 1982. The figures for women are higher, though roughly proportional, being 2.9 percent and 7.8 percent for 1970 and 1982, respectively. For certain age groups, the figures are considerably higher. For example, among 35- to 44-year-old males and females, the percentage divorced is 10.3 and 13.4, respectively (U.S. Dept. of Commerce, 1984).

The likelihood of divorce varies considerably with several factors. For example, education levels seem to have a strong effect on divorce rates (see Figure 13.2). The likelihood of a first marriage ending in divorce is nearly 60 percent for those people with some college education but no bachelor's degree. Those people who have a college degree but no graduate school training have nearly a 40 percent chance of divorce and are the least divorce-prone. We could argue that those people with the personality traits and family background that lead them to achieve a college degree are also those most likely to achieve marital stability.

Women who have gone on to graduate school have a greater likelihood of divorce than do less-educated women: Approximately 53 percent of them will divorce. The problem for these women is the difficulty of combining career, marriage, and child rearing without

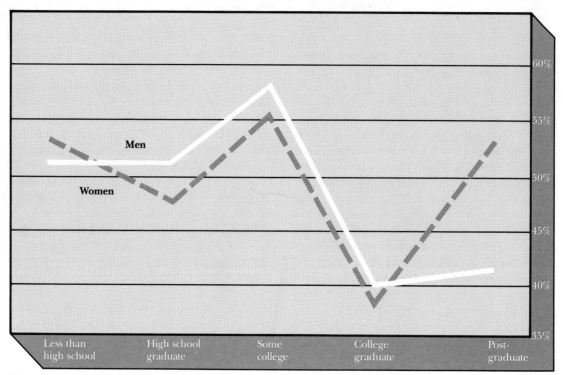

Figure 13.2 Divorce and Education: Ages 25–34

Source: Paul C. Glick, "How American Families Are Changing," *American Demographics* **6**(1) (January, 1984), p. 24.

the necessary societal supports for these often competing roles. As more and more women earn graduate degrees and as some of the barriers impeding women in combining professional and personal lives are removed, the higher rate of divorce for these women may also decline.

Divorced men are more likely to remarry than are divorced women. Divorced men usually marry women who are at least five years younger than they are. In this way divorced men end up having a larger pool of potential partners than do divorced women, for whom the pool of potential partners decreases as they age.

For divorced women in their thirties, the likelihood of remarriage declines with increasing levels of education. Those women with no college education remarry rather quickly, whereas those with more education wait longer or remain unmarried (Glick, 1984).

Even though the rate of increase in divorce rates may be leveling off, there is little evidence to suggest that the rate will decline. Current divorce rates imply that half of all marriages will end in divorce. Many argue that society cannot tolerate such a high rate of

marital disruptions, although 30 years ago, few would have believed society could tolerate even one-third of all married couples divorcing, but that level has already been reached by some marriage cohorts.

The large number of divorces is itself a force that keeps the divorce rate high. These divorced people join the pool of available marriage partners, and a large majority remarry. These remarriages then have a higher overall risk of divorce and thus an impact on the overall divorce rate.

Even though divorce rates were lower in 1910, 1930, and 1950 than they are today, can we assume that family life then was happier or more stable? Divorce during those periods was expensive, legally difficult, and socially stigmatized. Many who would have otherwise considered divorce remained married because of these factors. Is it thus accurate to say that it was better for the children and society for the partners to maintain these marriages?

It should be pointed out that the higher incidence of divorce in no way implies a general disillusionment with the institution of marriage. About 75 percent of divorced women and 85 percent of divorced men remarry (Reiss, 1980). Nor are children an impediment to remarriage—55 percent of divorces involve children, and most investigators feel that divorce need not cause lasting emotional damage in children (Longfellow, 1979).

The high divorce rates of today can be traced to many factors. First, a number of legal changes have taken place to make divorce a more realistic possibility for those couples who are experiencing difficulties. Many states have instituted "no-fault" divorce laws, and many others have liberalized the grounds for divorce to include mental cruelty and incompatibility. These are rather vague terms and can be applied to many problem marriages. Even changes by the American Bar Association, which now allow lawyers to advertise, contribute to the increased divorce rate. Advertisements that state that an uncomplicated divorce will cost only $150 put this option within the reach of many couples. (For an example of another trend in divorce laws, see Popular Sociology: "The Trend Toward Joint Custody.")

These legal changes are but a reflection of society's attitudinal changes toward divorce. We are a far cry from a generation ago when divorce was to be avoided at all costs, and when it did occur, it became a major source of embarrassment for the entire extended family. When the divorced status of a president of the United States such as Ronald Reagan is of little concern to the general public, we can be sure that the role of peer-group and public opinion in preventing divorce has been greatly diminished.

As divorce becomes more common, it also becomes more visible, and such visibility can actually produce more divorces. Others become a model of how difficult marriages are handled. The model of people suffering in an unhappy marriage is being replaced by one in which people start new lives after dissolving a marriage.

Divorce also may be encouraged by the increasing tendency, mentioned earlier, for outside social institutions to assume traditional family functions that once helped hold the family together. Then again, divorce has become a viable option because people can look forward to living longer today, and they may be less willing to endure a bad marriage if they feel there is time to look for a better way of life.

Another reason for today's high divorce rate is that we have come to expect a great deal from marriage. It is no longer enough, as it might have been at the turn of the century, for the husband to be a good provider and the wife to be a good mother and family caretaker. We now look to marriage as a source of emotional support in which each spouse complements the other in a variety of social, occupational, and psychological endeavors.

Divorce rates have also increased because the possibilities for women in the work force have improved. During earlier eras, divorced women had great problems contending with the financial realities of survival, and many were discouraged from seeking a divorce because they could not envision a realistic way of supporting themselves. With their greater economic independence, many women can now consider divorce as an option.

In view of the sharp rise in the divorce rate and the other changes apparent in the American family, it is not surprising to find that many people are choosing different forms of family life as alternatives to marriage.

☐ Alternatives to Marriage

A number of options are increasingly available to people who, for various reasons, find the traditional form of marriage impractical or incompatible with their lifestyles. More young people are selecting cohabitation as a permanent alternative to marriage (although many more consider it more as a prelude to marriage). In addition, some older men and women are opting to live together in a permanent relationship without getting married. These people choose cohabitation primarily for economic reasons—many would lose sources of income or control of their assets if they entered into a legal marriage. Several other options are discussed below.

The Growing Single Population

Americans have traditionally been the marrying kind. In 1980, about 95 percent of the U.S. population aged 45 and older had been married. Younger people, however, may be

POPULAR SOCIOLOGY
The Trend Toward Joint Custody

In 1979 only six states had statutes with express joint custody provisions. Today more than thirty states have replaced traditional sole-custody laws with joint custody statutes, and legislation is pending in many other jurisdictions. Is joint custody of children after divorce an idea whose time has come, or is it still in need of careful evaluation before it gains widespread acceptance?

In a legal sense, joint custody means that parental decision-making authority has been given equally to both parents after a divorce. It implies that neither parent's rights will be considered paramount. Both parents will have an equal voice in the children's education, upbringing, and general welfare.

Joint legal custody is not a determinant of physical custody or postdivorce living arrangements. It is, however, often confused with complicated situations in which parents share responsibility for the physical day-to-day care of the children. Such arrangements usually require children to alternate between the respective parent's residences every few days, weeks, or months.

While alternating living environments may accompany joint custody decisions, in most instances they do not. In 90 to 95 percent of joint custody awards the living arrangements are exactly the same as those under sole-custody orders, namely, the child physically resides with only one parent. However, both parents make decisions regarding the welfare of the child.

Those who believe joint legal custody is a good idea cite a variety of reasons. They note that sole-custody arrangements, which almost always involve the child living with the mother, weaken father-child relationships. They create enormous burdens for the mothers and tend to exacerbate hostilities between the custodial parent and the "visiting" parent. They continue to perpetuate outmoded sex-role stereotyping. Studies also show that sole-custody arrangements are associated with poverty, antisocial behavior in boys, depression in children, lower academic performance, and juvenile delinquency.

Advocates of joint custody note other benefits as well. One psychologist writes: "A child raised with both parents has both sexes *available* as role models. . . . If a child needs and loves both parents and is denied equal access to them, the child is, in effect, denied his or her own appropriate sense of self."

Such arguments assume that by giving fathers the opportunity to be "available" as nurturers, to be accessible, they will begin to participate more in the lives of their children—furthermore, that such participation will have beneficial effects on children.

Before we too quickly assume that joint custody alleviates problems and produces benefits, we should note that it is far from being a panacea. If couples had trouble communicating and agreeing on things before the divorce, there is no reason to assume that they will have an easier time of its afterwards. Most joint-custody orders are vague and do not decide at what point the joint custodial parent's rights end and those of the parent with the day-to-day care of the child begin. What sorts of responsibilities can one parent require of the other parent? Issues such as these can easily erupt into disputes, particularly when a history of disagreement and distrust has preceded the joint-custody arrangement.

Joint custody does not give either parent the right to prevail over the other. In order to solve serious disputes the parents must return to court. In court they must engage in litigation to prove that one or the other is "unfit"—the very process that the original decision of joint custody was to have avoided.

As the number of marriages ending in divorce continues to increase, and laws change in favor of joint custody, this arrangement will become more prevalent. Joint custody appears to work best with those parents who have the capacity, desire, and energy to make it work—and for the children whose characteristics and desires allow them to expend the effort necessary to make it work and to thrive under it.

Source: Adapted from Susan Brown, "Changes in Laws Governing Divorce: An Evaluation of Joint Custody Presumptions", in *Journal of Family Issues* **5** (2) (June, 1984), pp. 200–223. ☐

---

rejecting this tradition. In 1970, only 11 percent of the women and 19 percent of the men between the ages of 25 and 29 had never been married. In 1981, 22 percent of the women and 34 percent of the men of that age had never been married.

This trend may mean only that more young people are postponing marriage, but on the other hand, it could mean that a growing proportion of adults are staying single permanently. Households that contain only one person are projected to increase at twice the rate for all households. Currently 40 percent of one-person households are maintained by persons aged 65 or older, and women make up fully 61 percent of the single-person

TABLE 13.1 *Marital Status of Population by Sex and Age, 1983*

| Age | Percent Distribution | | | | | | | |
| | Single | | Married | | Widowed | | Divorced | |
	M	F	M	F	M	F	M	F
18–19 years	96.2	87.0	3.7	12.5	—	—	.2	.6
20–24 years	73.2	55.5	25.3	40.6	.1	.2	1.5	3.7
25–29 years	38.2	24.8	55.7	66.2	.1	.5	6.0	8.6
30–34 years	19.6	13.0	71.7	75.3	—	.7	8.7	11.0
35–44 years	8.6	6.3	81.8	78.5	.3	2.1	9.2	13.0
45–54 years	6.0	4.5	84.5	78.6	1.4	6.3	8.2	10.6
55–64 years	4.2	4.4	87.5	70.6	3.2	17.7	5.1	7.3
65–74 years	5.6	5.1	81.8	50.6	9.0	39.2	3.7	5.2
75 years and over	3.1	6.0	72.5	24.9	21.8	66.6	2.6	2.6

Source: U.S. Department of Commerce, Bureau of the Census, *Current Population Reports*, Series P-20, no. 389; *Statistical Abstract of the United States, 1985* (Washington, D.C.: Government Printing Office, 1984), p. 37.

households. More than 6 million women aged 65 or older live alone, but fewer than 1.5 million men do so. By far the fastest rate of growth in single-person households has occurred among persons under 35 years of age, and this pattern seems likely to continue (Glick, 1984). (See Table 13.1 for the percentage of single people in various age categories.)

Single-Parent Families

There has been a significant increase in the number of single-parent families in the United States. One-fifth of all American children do not live with both parents. Most single-parent families are the result of divorce or separation and less frequently the death of a spouse. The increase in the divorce rate is a major reason for the increase in single-parent families. Most divorced parents now set up new households, whereas in earlier times many of them would have returned to their own parents' household.

Some single-parent families arise from illegitimate births, when the mother decides against putting her child up for adoption. It is estimated that one out of every seven births today involves an unmarried woman. In the United States, only 80.8 percent of all white children under 18 are living with both parents, and only 42.4 percent of black children are doing so. (U.S. Dept. of Commerce, 1984).

Single parents initially do not intend to change the remaining family relationship radically upon entering their new status, though they soon discover that things cannot be done as before. Single parents do not have the same resources, time, or money that once was available to the family. The children eventually become junior partners in the family and end up having to be much more responsible and independent than before. Outsiders looking at a single-parent family often interpret the behavior that accompanies this status as the result of excessive permissiveness by the single parent.

The parent–child relationship in a single-parent family is often closer than in the traditional nuclear family. A second parent is not available to establish a close relationship with the children. To the single parent, the children are what is left of the previous family.

The increase in the divorce rate has produced a rise in the number of single-parent families.

Sample Cohabitation Agreement

THIS AGREEMENT, is made this day, the _____ day of the month of _____ 19 _____ , between JOHN DOE and AGNES DULLY in the city of _____ state of _____ .

Both persons mutually agree as follows:

1. We are both over the majority age of 21 as of this date; we are both high school (college) graduates, and we hereby acknowledge that we both worked out and drew up this agreement together and freely, and have read, considered, understood and agreed completely to the contents and provisions of this agreement.

2. We are not now married to each other (or to anyone else); and we have been living together since the month of _____ 19 _____ and plan to do so indefinitely.

3. All property or assets which were acquired by either John or Agnes before their living together, (including their debts or other obligations) as listed below, shall remain the sole property of that person. The property or assets for John are: _____

_____

The property or assets for Agnes are: _____

_____

4. While we are living together, all income earned or property accumulated by either John or Agnes, belongs to both of us in equal shares, and should we ever separate, or should one or both of us meet with death, all such accumulated property or income shall be liquidated and divided equally by or for both sides; or, upon mutual agreement, one of us may buy out the other.

5. Should either John or Agnes win, inherit or be given property or assets in the future, such property or assets shall belong only to the person who wins it or to whom it is given.

6. Notwithstanding any of the provisions of this agreement, each of us reserves the right, however, to freely assign or give any part or the whole of our respective belongings or entitlements, by will, written instrument, or otherwise, to anyone that one or the other wishes, including assigning or giving same to each other herein.

7. We shall share the living expenses for maintaining ourselves and our household as follows:

8. Any extraordinary bills, debts, or other obligations incurred by either one of us without the expressed written consent and authorization of the other shall be the separate debt or obligation of the one incurring it; but any debts and obligations which both of us co-signed for or otherwise incurred together shall be the joint obligation of both for which we shall both be jointly responsible.

9. If we shall ever separate, neither of us (or our heirs, executors or legal representatives) shall have any written claim for property or support from the other except as set forth in this agreement.

10. If a disagreement should arise over the interpretation or fulfillment of any of the clauses in this agreement, the matter shall be submitted to arbitration to be resolved, and for this we hereby appoint the following person(s) or institutions to act as the arbitrators in such matters: _____

_____

Any decisions made on the disputed issues by such arbitrators shall be final for both of us. The costs and expenses incurred for arbitration, or otherwise incurred for enforcing or litigating the disputed matters in a court of law, shall be borne solely by the party who is found to be at fault.

SIGNED: _____ _____
John Doe Date

_____ _____
Agnes Dully Date

Source: Benji O. Anosike, *How To Draw Up Your Own Couples' Agreement Without Lawyers* (New York: Do It Yourself Legal Publishers, 1982), pp. 33–34.

The children become extremely important emotionally to the single parent. Taking care of and raising the children properly often become the most important aim. In single-parent families consisting of a mother and daughter, it is common to hear their relationship described as similar to that existing between two sisters.

This close parent–child relationship can have some negative effects as well. For example, a single parent may become extremely dependent on the relationship. As the child matures, it may be difficult to continue the relationship at its previous level of intensity. Often the parent may begin to feel isolated, while the grown child ends up feeling guilty. However, children usually adjust reasonably well to single-parent situations, and it would be wrong to assume that they are at a marked disadvantage compared with children in two-parent families (Weiss, 1979a).

Cohabitation

The increasing incidence of couples living together out of wedlock—called *cohabitation*— is a phenomenon that may well have an impact on the American family. Although we have a great deal of information on marriages, we have very little on cohabitation in the United States within the last 15 years, and almost no information about it before that time.

All of our information on cohabitation is quite recent. Graham Spanier (1983), using data from a 1981 population survey, estimated that there were 1.8 million unmarried couples of the opposite sex living together in the United States. This represents almost 4 percent of all couples, a 14-percent increase in the practice over 1980 and a 300-percent increase over 1970. It is possible that the increase in cohabitation figures represents better data collection as much as it represents an increase in couples living together. However, all signs point to a striking increase in cohabitation. (See Box 13.1 for a sample agreement designed to clarify certain legal rights during cohabitation.)

Even though the percentage of cohabiting couples in the total population is relatively small, the proportion of such couples in certain age groups is quite striking. If we look at couples in which the man is under 25,

the percentage of cohabitors is 7.4. Although this figure is still considerably lower than that in some countries, such as Sweden where the cohabitation rate is about 12 percent, it may be indicative of a trend (Cherlin, 1981).

Clayton and Voss (1977) found that 18 percent of American men had at one time lived with a woman for six months or more without being married, though only 5 percent of those men were living with a woman when they were interviewed. Cohabitation was more common among black men than among white and more prevalent among urban residents than among rural. The majority of cohabiting men had been married.

It is unlikely that the increase in cohabitation will continue indefinitely. If it did, cohabitation would start to become more common than marriage. However, now that cohabitation does not produce as much disapproval as it once did, it is likely it will become more common and more visible.

Cohabitation should not be seen as a rejection of traditional marriage. There are a number of characteristics regarding cohabiting couples that are quite different from those of traditionally married couples. First of all, cohabitation is primarily a *childless* lifestyle. Seventy-two percent of cohabiting couples in 1981 did not have any children living with them. When cohabitors consider adding children to their unit, they are very reluctant to do so without marriage.

All signs also point to the fact that for most couples, cohabitation is not a lifetime commitment. Most of the men in the Clayton and Voss study did *not* plan to marry their present partners and in fact did not do so (Blumstein and Schwartz, 1983).

Homosexual and Lesbian Couples

A phenomenon that is not new but one that has become more and more visible is the household consisting of a homosexual or lesbian couple. Before 1970 almost all gay people wished to avoid the risks that would come with a disclosure of their sexual preference.

Traditionally, researchers and the media have concentrated on ways in which gays and lesbians are different from heterosexuals. There has been little attention paid to the fact that gay men and lesbian women form long-

Little attention has been paid to the fact that gay men and lesbian women who form long-term relationships face similar issues as traditional couples.

term relationships and have problems similar to those of heterosexual couples.

It appears evident that there have been a number of historical changes in how same-sex couples have interacted. Blumstein and Schwartz (1983) believe that homosexual couples followed the family patterns that were typical of each era. During the fifties when the traditional gender roles in marriage went unchallenged (husband as provider, wife as homemaker and nurturer), same-sex couples fell into a similar pattern of role playing. The terms *butch* and *femme*, which were part of lesbian terminology, reflected a stringent division between masculine and feminine roles. A *butch* woman was expected to perform male tasks and to be more involved in the couple's financial support, and the *femme* was expected to act along more traditionally feminine lines. Although gay men did not use the same terms, there was also an expectation that one partner would be more masculine and the other more feminine.

Traditional role playing is no longer common in same-sex couples. The women's movement and the reevaluation of gender roles in our society have affected lesbian women and gay men just as much as they have af-

fected heterosexuals. Consequently, the same aspects of challenge and change that heterosexual couples have had to deal with have also had to be confronted by same-sex couples.

The desire to form a relationship with another person appears to be quite strong among gays and lesbians. A Kinsey study in the late 1960s found that 71 percent of their sample of gay men between the ages of 36 and 45 were living with a partner. In the 1970s, Bell and Weinberg found that one-fourth of the lesbians in their study stated that being in a permanent relationship was the "most important thing in life," and another 35 percent believed that it was very important. Eighty-two percent of the women they interviewed were living with someone. By and large, gay men and lesbian women who were not in a relationship reported that they had been in one previously and believed that they would be in one again in the future. There is no doubt that "couplehood," as either a reality or an aspiration, is as strong among gay men and lesbian women as it is among heterosexuals (Blumstein and Schwartz, 1983).

☐ The Future: Bright or Dismal?

Given all these changes in the American family, should we be concerned that marriage and family life as we know it will one day disappear? Probably not. The divorce rate is high and will continue to be high during the 1980s. It is important, however, to keep things in perspective. Divorce is just as much a social universal as is marriage. In fact, throughout human history only one society is known that did not allow for divorce—the ancient Incas of South America.

In addition, even though the divorce rate is high, the remarriage rate is also very high. The vast majority—about 80 percent—of people who divorce remarry—usually within a short period of time after they divorce. The rising divorce rate does not necessarily mean that people are giving up on marriage. It just means there is a growing belief that marriage can be better. The high remarriage rate indicates that people are willing to continue trying until they reach their expectations. Obtaining a divorce does not mean that the person believes that the idea of marriage is a mistake—only that a particular marriage was a mistake.

The institutions of marriage and the family have proved to be both extremely flexible and durable and have flourished in all human societies under almost every imaginable condition. As we have seen, these institutions take on different forms in differing social and economic contexts, and there is no reason to suspect that they will not continue to do so. Therefore, to make predictions about the future of the American family is equivalent to making predictions about the future of American society in particular and industrial society in general. This is extremely difficult to do, given the social, economic, political, and ecological problems facing us. However, for the foreseeable future, it seems reasonable to assume that the forces of industrialism and public policy that helped shape the current nuclear family in its one-parent and two-parent forms will persist. And therefore the contemporary nuclear family will continue to provide the basic context within which American society will reproduce itself for several generations to come.

☐ Summary

Although there may be some argument about the definition of the family, most sociologists agree that some form of family is found in all societies and that it serves several basic functions: regulating sexual behavior, patterning reproduction, organizing production and consumption, socializing children, offering care and protection, and providing social status.

The basic family form is the nuclear family: a married couple and their children. There are two major composite family forms: polygamous and extended. Polygamous families are nuclear families linked together by multiple marriage bonds, with one central individual married to several spouses. Polygamous families can be polygynous or polyandrous.

Extended families are nuclear families linked by descent, by sibling ties, or by both.

Marriage is an institution found in all societies. It takes place in a public manner; it includes sexual intercourse as an explicit element of the relationship; it provides the essential condition for legitimizing offspring; and it is intended to be a stable and enduring relationship. In many societies marriage has less to do with romantic love than with the establishment of social, economic, and political relationships among families.

Marriage rules vary from society to society. Almost all societies have two kinds of marriage rules: rules of endogamy, which limit the social categories within which one should marry; and rules of exogamy, the requirement that an individual marry outside his or her culturally defined group. Marriage rules also determine how many spouses a person may have at one time.

Most societies also have norms governing marital residence; these rules play a large role in determining the composition of households.

The modern American family assumed its current form during the Industrial Revolution, and modern American practices of mate selection reflect this new kind of family life. Although we might like to think of marriage and mate selection as being dependent on nothing other than falling in love, in reality it is tied to a variety of less-than-romantic factors: age, race, religion, and social status.

The American family has been undergoing a number of changes. Sociologists have observed a transfer of functions from the family to other, outside institutions. Other trends include changes in household size, the growing number of working women, a growth in family violence, and an increase in the divorce rate.

Sociologists have also marked the emergence of alternatives to marriage. The single population has been growing rapidly as marriage is becoming less universal. The number of single-parent families has also increased because of high divorce rates and the many children born out of wedlock. The incidence of cohabitation has grown, as has the number of homosexual and lesbian couples.

The institution of the family has proved to be flexible and durable and has flourished in all human societies under almost every imaginable condition. There is no reason, therefore, to think that the family will not continue to provide the basic context within which American society will carry on.

☐ For Further Reading

BLUMSTEIN, PHILIP, and PEPPER SCHWARTZ. *American Couples*. New York: Morrow, 1983. An excellent study of a variety of couple arrangements.

CAPLOW, THEODORE, HOWARD M. BAHR, BRUCE A. CHADWICK, REUBEN HILL, and MARGARET HOLMES WILLIAMSON. *Middletown Families: Fifty Years of Change and Conformity*. Minneapolis: University of Minnesota Press, 1982. A team of social scientists returned to the midwestern community immortalized in the Lynds' classic studies. They duplicated the original studies and concluded that continuity, not change, was the dominant characteristic.

GELLES, RICHARD, and MURRAY A. STRAUS. *Behind Closed Doors*. New York: Anchor Press, 1980. Probably the best and most up-to-date sociological analysis of the phenomenon of child abuse. Other excellent books on the broader subject of family violence include Gelles, *Family Violence* (Sage Publications, 1979); and Suzanne K. Steinmetz and Murray Straus (eds.), *Violence in the Family* (Dodd, Mead, 1974).

GORDON, CHAD, and GAYLE JOHNSON (eds.). *Readings in Human Sexuality: Contemporary Perspectives*. 2d ed. New York: Harper & Row, 1981. Many of the superb articles in this collection deal with issues of sexual relations both inside and outside the marital relationship. The book's historical and cross-cultural perspectives illuminate present-day behaviors.

HUNT, MORTON. *The Natural History of Love*. New York: Funk and Wagnalls, 1959. A lively and amusing history of the concept of romantic love.

Journal of Marriage and the Family. Published by the National Council on Family Relations, Minneapolis, Minnesota. Probably the best academic journal published on the subject of marriage and the family. Articles come from a variety of academic disciplines and often are quite well written. Other journals in this area include *Children Today, The Family Coordinator*, and the *Journal of Marriage and Family Counseling*.

LASCH, CHRISTOPHER. *Haven in a Heartless World: The Family Besieged*. New York: Basic Books, 1977. Lasch argues that the more the modern family has come to be needed as a haven of decency and love in a cruel world, the less capable it has become of providing these comforts.

LASLETT, PETER. *Family Life and Illicit Love in Earlier Generations: Essays in Historical Sociology*. New York: Cambridge University Press, 1977. A monumental work by a distinguished British sociologist on the nature of the family and sexual relations in Western society.

SPIRO, MELFORD E. "Is the Family Universal?" *American Anthropologist*, **56** (October, 1954), pp. 839–846. Spiro's classic article on the nature of the family and family life in the Israeli *kibbutz*. His reevaluation of the central thesis in this article is contained in his "Addendum," in Normal W. Bell and Ezra F. Vogels (eds.), *A Modern Introduction to the Family*, New York: Free Press, 1960.

STEIN, PETER J. *Single Life: Unmarried Adults in Social Context*. New York: St. Martin's Press, 1981. An interesting examination of an alternative to the traditional nuclear family arrangement.

WIERSMA, G. E. *Cohabitation: An Alternative to Marriage?* The Hague: Netherlands Interuniversity Demographic Institute, 1983. Distributed by Kluwer, Boston. The author studied cohabiting couples in the Netherlands and the United States and then compared them on several background and relationship variables.

14

Religion

Tears come to her eyes. . . . She screams, falls on the floor. . . . She rises and stands rigid. . . . Then she closes her eyes and dances away. She jerks her hips . . . and her breasts. "Hallelujah!" she screams out. "I love you—love, love, love you!"

She stops moving and sits down with a happy look on her face.

Thus does Sara Harris describe this woman's religious experience in her book *Father Divine* (Harris, 1971). Such extreme religious fervor may be difficult to comprehend by those who have never experienced it, but it can be studied and understood in relation to the many other ways people experience and practice religion. The important thing to realize is that although religion assumes many different forms, it is a universal human institution. To appreciate the many possible kinds of religious experiences, from the extremely emotional scene described by Harris to the quiet meditation of a Buddhist monk, requires an understanding of the nature and functions of religion in human life and society.

Certain symbols, such as the cross, have been given a sacred meaning by the religion which has adopted them as part of its belief system.

☐ The Nature of Religion

Religion is recognized as one of society's important institutions. It is a system of beliefs and practices shared by a group of people that helps them explain and function in the present world using the concepts of the supernatural and the sacred.

In his classic study *The Elementary Forms of the Religious Life*, first published in 1915, Emile Durkheim observed that all religions divide the universe into two mutually exclusive categories: the profane and the sacred. He wrote, "In all the history of human thought there exists no other example of two categories of things so profoundly differentiated or so radically opposed to one another." By **profane** Durkheim meant all empirically observable things, that is, things that are knowable through common, everyday experiences. In contrast, the **sacred** consists of all things kept separate or apart from everyday experience, things that are awe inspiring and knowable only through extraordinary experience.

The sacred may consist of almost anything: objects fashioned just for that purpose (like a cross); a geographical location (Mount Sinai); a place constructed for religious observance (a temple); a word or phrase ("Our Father, who art in heaven . . ."); or even an animal (the cow to Hindus, for example). To devout Muslims the sabbath, which falls on Friday, is a sacred day of the week. To Hindus the cow is holy, not to be killed or eaten. These are not ideas to be debated—they simply exist as unchallengeable truths. Similarly, to Christians, Jesus of Nazareth was the Messiah; to Muslims, Jesus was a prophet; but to sociologists, the person of Jesus is a religious symbol. Religious symbols acquire their particular sacred meanings through the religious belief system of which they are a part.

Durkheim believed every society must distinguish between the sacred and the profane. This distinction is essentially between the social and nonsocial. What is considered sacred has the capacity to represent shared values, sentiments, power, or beliefs. The profane is not supported in this manner; it may have utility to one or more individuals, but it has little public relevance.

We may look at Babe Ruth's bat as an example of the transformation of the profane to the sacred. At first it was merely a profane object that had little social value in itself. Today, however, one of Babe Ruth's bats is enshrined in baseball's Hall of Fame. It is no longer used in a profane way but instead is seen as an object that represents the values, sentiments, power, and beliefs of the baseball community. The bat has gained some of the qualities of a sacred object, thus changing from a private object to a public object.

In addition to sacred symbols and a system of belief, religion also includes specific **rituals**. These include patterns of behavior or practices that are related to the sacred. For example, the Christian ritual of Holy Communion is much more than the eating of wafers and drinking of wine. To many participants these objects are the body and blood of Jesus Christ. Similarly, the Sun Dance of the Plains Indians was more than merely a group of braves dancing around a pole to which they were attached by leather thongs that pierced their skin and chest muscles. It was a religious ritual in which the participants were seeking a personal communion.

The Elements of Religion

All of the world's religions contain certain shared elements, including ritual and prayer, emotion, belief, and organization.

Ritual and Prayer All religions have formalized social rituals, but many also feature private rituals such as prayer. Of course, the particular events that make up rituals vary widely from culture to culture and from religion to religion.

All religions include a belief in the existence of beings or forces that are beyond the ability of human beings to experience. In other words, all religions include a belief in the supernatural. Hence, they also provide means for individuals to address or communicate with supernatural beings or forces, typically by speaking aloud while holding the body in a conventionalized posture or making stylized movements or gestures—what in our culture is called **prayer.**

In some societies, magic serves some of

All religions include a belief in the supernatural. Prayer is the traditional means of communication that is used.

religion A system of beliefs and practices shared by a group of people that helps them explain and function in the present world, using the concepts of the supernatural and the sacred.

profane The profane consists of all empirically observable things that are knowable through ordinary everyday experiences.

sacred The sacred consists of all things kept separate or apart from everyday experiences, things that are awe inspiring and knowable only through extraordinary experience.

rituals Patterns of behavior or practices related to the sacred.

prayer A religious ritual that enables individuals to communicate with supernatural beings or forces, typically by speaking aloud while holding the body in a conventional posture or making stylized movements or gestures.

POPULAR SOCIOLOGY
Baseball Magic

Ex-professional baseball player, George Gmelch, applies Bronislaw Malinowski's principles of the use of magic to America's summer pastime.

> We find magic wherever the elements of chance and accident, and the emotional play between hope and fear have a wide and extensive range. We do not find magic wherever the pursuit is certain, reliable, and well under the control of rational methods.
>
> Bronislaw Malinowski

Professional baseball is a nearly perfect arena in which to test Malinowski's hypothesis about magic. The great anthropologist was not, of course, talking about sleight of hand but of rituals, taboos and fetishes that men resort to when they want to ensure that things go their own way. Baseball is rife with this sort of magic, but, as we shall see, the players use it in some aspects of the game far more than in others.

Everyone knows that there are three essentials of baseball—hitting, pitching and fielding. The point is, however, that the first two, hitting and pitching, involve a high degree of chance. The pitcher is the player least able to control the outcome of his own efforts. His best pitch may be hit for a bloop single while his worst pitch may be hit directly to one of his fielders for an out. He may limit the opposition to a single hit and lose, or he may give up a dozen hits and win. It is not uncommon for pitchers to perform well and lose, and vice versa; . . .

Hitting, too, is a chancy affair. Obviously, skill is required in hitting the ball hard and on a line. Once the ball is hit, however, chance plays a large role in determining where it will go, into a waiting glove or whistling past a falling stab.

With respect to fielding, the player has almost complete control over the outcome. . . . Next to the pitcher or hitter, the fielder has little to worry about when he knows that better than 9.7 times in ten he will execute his task flawlessly.

If Malinowski's hypothesis is correct, we should find magic associated with hitting and pitching, but none with fielding. Let us take the evidence by category—ritual, taboo and fetish.

Ritual After each pitch, ex-major leaguer Lou Skeins used to reach into his back pocket to touch a crucifix, straighten his cap and clutch his genitals. Detroit Tiger infielder Tim Maring wore the same clothes and put them on exactly in the same order each day during a batting streak. Baseball rituals are almost infinitely various. After all, the ballplayer can ritualize any activity he considers necessary for a successful performance, from the type of cereal he eats in the morning to the streets he drives home on.

Usually, rituals grow out of exceptionally good performances. When the player does well he cannot really attribute his success to skill alone. He plays with the same amount of skill one night when he gets four hits as the next night when he goes hitless. Through magic, such as ritual, the player seeks greater control over his performance, actually control over the elements of chance. The player, knowing that his ability is fairly constant, attributes the inconsistencies in his performance to some form of behavior or a particular food that he ate. When a player gets four hits in a game, especially "cheap" hits, he often believes that there must have been something he did, in addition to his ability, that shifted luck to his side. If he can attribute his good fortune to the glass of iced tea he drank before the game or the new shirt he wore to the ballpark, then by repeating the same behavior the following day he can hope to achieve similar results. (One expression of this belief is the myth that eating certain foods will give the ball "eyes," that is, a ball that seeks the gaps between fielders.) In hopes of maintaining a batting streak, I once ate fried chicken every day at 4:00 P.M., kept my eyes closed during the national anthem and changed sweat shirts at the end of the fourth inning each night for seven consecutive nights until the streak ended. . . .

Rituals associated with hitting vary considerably in complexity from one player to the next, but they have several components in common. One of the most popular is tagging a particular base when leaving and returning to the dugout each inning. . . . It is not uncommon for a hitter who is playing poorly to try different combinations of tagging and not tagging particular bases in an attempt to find a successful combination. Other components of a hitter's ritual may include tapping the plate with his bat a precise number of times or taking a precise number of warm-up swings with the leaded bat. . . .

Because pitchers only play once every four days, the rituals they practice are often more complex than the hitters', and most of it, such as tugging the cap between pitches, touching the rosin bag after each bad pitch or smoothing the dirt on the mound before each new batter, takes place on the field. Many baseball fans have observed this behavior never realizing that it may be as important to the pitcher as throwing the ball. . . .

Taboo Mentioning that a no-hitter is in progress and crossing baseball bats are the two most widely observed taboos. It is believed that if the pitcher hears the words "no-hitter" his spell will be broken and the no-hitter lost. As for the crossing of bats, that is sure to bring bad luck; batters are therefore extremely careful not to drop their bats on top of another. Some players elaborate this taboo even further. On one occasion a teammate became quite upset when another player tossed a bat from the batting cage and it came to rest on top of his. Later he explained that the top bat would steal hits from the lower one. For him, then, bats contain a finite number of hits, a kind of baseball "image of limited good." Honus Wagner, a member of baseball's Hall of Fame, believed that each bat was good for only 100 hits and no more. Regardless of the quality of the bat he would discard it after its 100th hit. . . .

Taboos are . . . of many kinds. One athlete was careful never to step on the chalk foul lines or the chalk lines of the batter's box. Another would never put on his cap until the game started and would not wear it at all on the days he did not pitch. Another had a movie taboo in which he refused to watch a movie the day of a game. Often certain uniform numbers become taboo. If a player has a poor spring training or a bad year, he may refuse to wear the same uniform number again. I would not wear double numbers, especially 44 and 22. On several occasions, teammates who were playing poorly requested a change of uniform during the middle of the season. Some players consider it so important that they will wear the wrong size uniform just to avoid a certain number or to obtain a good number. . . .

Fetishes These are standard equipment for many baseball players. They include a wide assortment of objects: horsehide covers of old baseballs, coins, bobby pins, protective cups, crucifixes and old bats. Ordinary objects are given this power in a fashion similar to the formation of taboos and rituals. The player during an exceptionally hot batting or pitching streak, especially one in which he has "gotten all the breaks," credits some unusual object, often a new possession, for his good fortune. For example, a player in a slump might find a coin or an odd stone just before he begins a hitting streak. Attributing the improvement in his performance to the new object, it becomes a fetish, embodied with supernatural power. While playing for Spokane, Dodger pitcher Alan Foster forgot his baseball shoes on a road trip and borrowed a pair from a teammate to pitch. That night he pitched a no-hitter and later, needless to say, bought the shoes from his teammate. They became his most prized possession. . . .

The use of fetishes follows the same pattern as ritual and taboo in that they are connected only with hitting or pitching. In nearly all cases the player expressed a specific purpose for carrying a fetish, but never did a player perceive his fetish as having any effect on his fielding.

I have said enough, I think, to show that many of the beliefs and practices of professional baseball players are magical. Any empirical connection between the ritual, taboo and fetishes and the desired event is quite absent. Indeed, in several instances the relationship between the cause and effect, such as eating tuna fish sandwiches to win a ball game, is even more remote than is characteristic of primitive magic. Note, however, that unlike many forms of primitive magic, baseball magic is usually performed to achieve one's own end and not to block someone else's. Hitters do not tap their bats on the plate to hex the pitcher, but to improve their own performance.

Finally, it should be plain that nearly all the magical practices that I participated in, observed or elicited, support Malinowski's hypothesis that magic appears in situations of chance and uncertainty. The large amount of uncertainty in pitching and hitting best explains the elaborate magical practices used for these activities. Conversely, the high success rate in fielding, .975, involving much less uncertainty, offers the best explanation for the absence of magic in this realm.

Source: George Gmelch, "Baseball Magic," *Trans-Action* 8 (8) (June, 1971), pp. 39–54. □

---

the functions of religion, though there are some essential differences between the two. **Magic** is a type of interaction with the supernatural. It differs from other types of religious beliefs in that there is no worship of a god or gods; instead there is an active attempt to coerce spirits or to control supernatural forces. Magic is used to manipulate and control matters that seem to be beyond human control and that may involve danger and uncertainty. It is usually a means to an end, whereas religion is usually an end in itself, although prayer may be seen as utilitarian

when a believer asks for some personal benefit. In most instances, religion serves to unify a group of believers, whereas magic is designed to help the individual who uses it (Malinowski, 1954). (For an interesting discussion of the use of magic in contemporary society, see Popular Sociology: "Baseball Magic.")

magic Interaction with the supernatural; no worship of a god or gods, but, rather, an attempt to coerce spirits or control supernatural forces.

Emotion   One of the functions of ritual and prayer is to produce an appropriate emotional state. This may be done in many ways. In some religions, participants in rituals deliberately attempt to alter their state of consciousness through the use of drugs, fasting, sleep deprivation, and induction of physical pain. Thus Scandinavian groups ate mushrooms that caused euphoria, as did many native Siberian tribes. Various American Indian religions feature the use of peyote, a button-like mushroom that contains a hallucinogenic drug. And for a while in the late 1960s, a number of countercultural groups in America relied on LSD and other drugs to induce religious experiences.

Although not every religion attempts to induce altered states of consciousness in believers, all religions do recognize that such states may happen and believe that they may be the result of divine or sacred intervention in human affairs. Prophets, of course, receive divine inspiration. Religions differ in the degree of importance they attach to such happenings.

All religions demand some public shared participation. This place of worship is a Bahai temple.

Belief   All religions endorse a belief system that usually includes a supernatural order and also often a set of values to be applied to daily life.

Belief systems can vary widely. Some religions believe that a valuable quality can flow from a sacred object—animate or inanimate, part or whole—to a lesser object. Numerous Christian sects, for instance, practice the "laying on of hands," whereby a healer channels "divine energy" into afflicted people and thus heals them. Some Christians also believe in the power of "relics" to work miracles simply because these objects once were associated physically with Jesus or one of the saints. Such beliefs are quite common among the world's religions: native Australians have their sacred stones, and shamans from among African, Asian, and North American societies heal through sympathetic touching. In some religions the source of the valued quality is a personalized deity. In others it is a reservoir of supernatural force that is tapped.

Organization   Many religions have an organizational structure through which specialists can be recruited and trained, religious meetings conducted, and interaction facilitated between society and the members of the religion.

The organization also will promote interaction among the members of the religion in order to foster a sense of unity and group solidarity. Rituals may be performed in the presence of other members. They may be limited to certain locations such as temples, or they may be processions from one place to another. Although some religious behavior may be carried out by individuals in private, all religions demand some public, shared participation.

Major Types of Religion

The earliest available evidence for religious practice comes from the Middle East. In Shanidar Cave in Iraq, archaeologist Ralph Solecki (1971) found remains of burials of Neanderthals—early members of our own species, *Homo sapiens*, once believed to be brutish but now recognized as fully human—dating between 60,000 and 45,000 years ago (see

Chapter 3). Bodies were tied into a fetal position, buried on their sides, provided with morsels of food placed at their heads, and covered with red powder and sometimes with flower petals. These practices—the food and the ritual care with which the dead were buried—point to a belief in some kind of existence after death.

Using studies of present-day cultures as well as historical records, sociologists have devised a number of ways of classifying religions. One of the simplest and most broadly inclusive schemes recognizes four types of religion: supernaturalism, animism, theism, and abstract ideals.

Supernaturalism **Supernaturalism** is a belief system that postulates the existence of supernatural forces that can and often do influence human events. These forces are thought to inhabit animate and inanimate objects alike—people, trees, rocks, places, even spirits or ghosts—and can come and go at will. The Melanesian/Polynesian concept of *mana* is a good example of the belief of an impersonal supernatural power.

Mana is a diffuse, nonpersonalized force that acts through anything that lives or moves, although inanimate objects such as an unusually shaped rock also may possess mana. The proof that a person or thing possesses mana lies in its observable effects. A great chief, merely by virtue of his position of power, must possess mana, as does the oddly shaped stone placed in a garden plot that then unexpectedly yields huge crops. Although it is considered dangerous because of its power, mana is neither harmful nor beneficial in itself, but it sometimes may be used by its possessors for either good or evil purposes. An analogy in our culture might be the scientific phenomenon of nuclear power, which is a natural force that intrinsically is neither good nor evil but can be turned to either end by its possessors. We must not carry the analogy too far, however, because we are able to account for nuclear power according to natural, scientific principles and can predict its effects reliably without resorting to supernatural explanations. A narrower, less comprehensive, but more appropriate analogy in Western society

is our idea of "luck," which can be good or bad and over which we feel we have very little control.

Although on the one hand certain objects possess mana, taboos may exist in relation to other situations. A **taboo** is a sacred prohibition against touching, mentioning, or looking at certain objects, acts, or people, and violating a taboo results in some form of pollution. Taboos may exist in reference to foods not to be eaten, places not to be entered, objects and people not to be touched, and so on. Even a person who becomes a victim of some misfortune may be accused of having violated a taboo and may also become stigmatized.

Taboos exist in a wide variety of religions. Polynesian peoples believed that their chiefs and noble families were imbued with powerful mana that could be deadly to commoners. Hence, elaborate precautions were taken to prevent physical contact between commoners and nobles. The families of the nobility intermarried (a chief often would marry his own sister), and chiefs actually were carried everywhere to prevent them from touching the ground and thereby killing the crops. Many religions forbid the eating of selected foods. Jews and Muslims have taboos against eating pork at any time, and until fairly recently, Catholics were forbidden to eat meat on Fridays. Most cultures forbid sexual relations between parents and children and between siblings (the incest taboo).

Supernatural beings fall into two broad categories: those of nonhuman origin, such as gods and spirits, and those of human origin, such as ghosts and ancestral spirits. Chief among those of nonhuman origin are the gods who are believed to have created themselves and may have created or given birth to other gods. Although gods may create, not all peoples attribute the creation of the world to them.

supernaturalism A belief system that postulates the existence of impersonal supernatural forces that can, and often do, influence human events.

mana A Melanesian/Polynesian concept of the supernatural that refers to a diffuse, nonpersonalized force that acts through anything that lives or moves.

taboo A sacred prohibition against touching, mentioning, or looking at certain objects, acts, or people.

Many of those gods thought to have participated in creation have retired, so to speak. Having set the world in motion, they no longer take part in day-to-day activities. Other creator gods remain involved in ordinary human activities. Whether or not a society has creator gods, many other affairs are left to lesser gods. For example, the Maori of New Zealand have three important gods, a god of the sea, a god of the forest, and a god of agriculture. They call upon each god for help in the appropriate area.

Below the gods in prestige but often closer to the people, are the unnamed spirits. Some of these can offer constructive assistance, and others take pleasure in deliberately working evil for people.

Ghosts and ancestor spirits represent the supernatural beings of human origin. Many cultures believe that everyone has a soul, or several souls, which survive after death. Some of these souls remain nearby the living and continue to be interested in the welfare of their kin (Ember and Ember, 1981).

Animism **Animism** is the belief in animate, personalized spirits or ghosts of ancestors that take an interest in and actively work to influence human affairs. Spirits may inhabit the bodies of people and animals as well as inanimate phenomena such as winds, rivers, or mountains. They are discrete beings with feelings, motives, and a will of their own. Unlike mana, spirits may be intrinsically good or evil. Although they are powerful, they are not worshiped as gods, and because of their humanlike qualities, they can be manipulated—wheedled, frightened away, or appeased—by

TABLE 14.1 *Membership of the World's Major Religions* Chapter 22

Religions	North America[1]	South America	Europe[2]	Asia[3]	Africa	Oceania[4]	World
Total Christian	252,458,670	196,599,780	337,678,150	104,098,695	147,076,000	18,781,550	1,056,692,845
Roman Catholic	138,875,530	185,251,200	178,032,590	57,265,290	56,999,270	5,215,440	621,639,320
Eastern Orthodox	5,648,620	355,250	47,069,040	2,762,810	9,401,840[5]	407,650	65,645,210
Protestant[6]	107,934,520	10,993,330	112,576,520	44,070,595	80,674,890[7]	13,158,460	369,408,315
Jewish	7,611,940	749,580	4,643,810	4,008,850	231,980	73,980	17,320,140
Muslim[8]	1,580,980	406,190	20,190,500	380,068,940	152,943,570	87,000	555,277,180
Zoroastrian	2,750	2,600	14,000	224,370	900	1,000	245,620
Shinto[9]	50,000	—	—	33,000,000	—	—	33,050,000
Taoist	33,250	12,975	13,500	20,500,000	850	2,900	20,563,475
Confucian	99,750	58,925	450,500	162,500,000	2,550	18,390	163,130,115
Buddhist[10]	336,290	241,090	238,300	250,097,200	15,000	23,700	250,951,580
Hindu[11]	309,100	637,400	442,890	459,708,450	1,165,600	326,470	462,589,910
Totals	262,482,730	198,708,540	363,671,650	1,414,206,505	301,436,450	19,314,990	2,559,820,865
Population[12]	389,914,000	259,644,000	761,195,000	2,771,419,000	516,037,000	23,677,000	4,721,886,000

[1]Includes Central America and the West Indies.

[2]Includes the U.S.S.R. and other countries with established Marxist ideology where continuing religious adherence is difficult to estimate.

[3]Includes areas in which persons have traditionally enrolled in several religions, as well as mainland China with a Marxist establishment.

[4]Includes Australia and New Zealand as well as islands of the South Pacific.

[5]Includes Coptic Christians, of restricted status in Egypt and precariously situated under the military junta in Ethiopia.

[6]Protestant statistics vary widely in style of reckoning affiliation. See *World Church Membership.*

[7]Including a great proliferation of new churches, sects, and cults among African Christians.

[8]The chief base of Islam is still ethnic, although missionary work is now carried on in Europe and America. In countries where Islam is established, minority religions are frequently persecuted and accurate statistics are rare.

[9]A Japanese ethnic religion, Shinto declined rapidly after the Japanese emperor surrendered his claim to divinity (1947); a revival of cultic participation in the homeland had chiefly literary significance. Shinto does not survive well outside Japan.

[10]Buddhism has produced several renewal movements in the last century that have gained adherents in Europe and America. Although persecuted in Tibet and sometimes elsewhere in Asia, it has shown greater staying power than other religions of the East. It also transplants better.

[11]Hinduism's strength in India has been enhanced by its connection with the national movement, a phenomenon also observable in the world of Islam. Modern Hinduism has developed several renewal movements that have won adherents in Europe and America.

[12]U.S. Department of Commerce, Bureau of the Census, *World Population: 1983.*

Source: The *1984 Britannica Book of the Year.* (Chicago: Encyclopaedia Britannica, Inc., 1983), p. 601.

using the proper magic rituals. For example, among many Native American and South American Indian societies (as well as many other cultures in the world), sickness is thought to be caused by evil spirits. Shamans, or medicine men or women, are able to effect cures because of their special relationships with these spirits and their knowledge of magic rituals. If the shamans are good at their jobs, they are able to persuade or force the evil spirit to leave the sick person or to discontinue exerting its harmful influence. In our own culture, there are people who consult mediums, spiritualists, and Ouija boards in an effort to contact the spirits and ghosts of departed loved ones.

Theism   People who practice **theism** believe in divine beings—gods and goddesses—who shape human affairs. Gods are powerful beings worthy of being worshiped. Most theistic societies practice **polytheism**, the belief in a number of gods. Each god or goddess usually has particular spheres of influence such as childbirth, rain, or war, and there is generally one who is more powerful than the rest and oversees the others' activities. In the ancient religions of Mexico, Egypt, and Greece, for instance, we find a host of gods and goddesses, sometimes called a **pantheon**.

Monotheism is the belief in the existence of only one god. Only three religions are known to be monotheistic: Judaism and its two offshoots, Christianity and Islam. Yet these three religions have the greatest number of believers worldwide (see Table 14.1). Even these faiths are not purely monotheistic, however, for they include in their tenets a belief in such divine or semidivine beings as angels, a devil, saints, and the Virgin Mary. Nevertheless, because in all three religions there is such a strong belief in the supremacy of one all-powerful being, they are considered to be monotheistic.

Abstract Ideals   This type of religion focuses not on a belief in supernatural forces, spirits, or beings but on the **abstract ideals** of correct ways of thinking and behaving. The goal is not to acquire supernatural power, manipulate spirits, or worship gods but to achieve

Meditation, as practiced by Eastern religions, is a response to the basic human need to understand the purpose of life.

personal awareness, a higher state of being and consciousness, through religious rituals and practices and adherence to moral codes of behavior. Buddhism is an example of a religion based on abstract ideals. The Buddhist's ideal is to become "one with the uni-

animism The belief in animate, personalized spirits or ghosts of ancestors that take an interest in, and actively work to influence, human affairs.

theism A belief in divine beings—gods and goddesses— who shape human affairs.

polytheism The belief in a number of gods.

pantheon The hierarchy of deities in a religious belief system. Examples include the deities of ancient Mexico, Egypt, and Greece.

monotheism The belief in the existence of only one god.

abstract ideals A type of religion that focuses on correct ways of thinking and behaving rather than on a belief in supernatural forces, spirits, or beings. Buddhism is an example of a religion based on abstract ideals.

verse," not through worship or magic, but by meditation and correct behavior.

Despite the profound differences in their basic assumptions, each of these types of human belief systems is recognized as religion because they all share certain basic attributes.

□ A Sociological Approach to Religion

When sociologists approach the study of religion, they focus on the relationship between religion and society. The functionalist sociologists have examined the functions religion plays in social life. Conflict theorists, on the other hand, have viewed religion as a means for justifying the political status quo. In the following section we will examine each of these two approaches in detail.

The Functions of Religion

Since at least as early as 60,000 years ago, as indicated by the Neanderthal burials at Shanidar Cave, religion has played a role in all known human societies. The question that interests us here is, what universal functions does religion have? Sociologists have identified four categories of religious function: satisfying individual needs, promoting social cohesion, providing a world view, and acting as a form of social control.

Satisfying Individual Needs   Religion offers individuals ways to reduce anxiety and to promote emotional integration.

Although Sigmund Freud (1918, 1928) thought religion to be irrational, he saw it as helpful to the individual in coming to terms with impulses that induce guilt and anxiety. Freud argued that a belief in lawgiving, powerful deities can help people reduce their anxieties by providing strong, socially reinforced inducements for controlling dangerous or "immoral" impulses.

Further, in times of stress, individuals can calm themselves by appealing to deities for guidance or even for outright help, or they can calm their fears by "trusting in God." In the face of so many things that are beyond human control and yet may drastically affect human fortunes (such as droughts, floods, or other natural disasters), life can be terrifying. It is comforting to "know" the supernatural causes of both good fortune and bad. Thus, each year in the state of Orissa in India, people walk barefoot through a trench filled with glowing coals. This tests their faith in the power of Kali (the mother goddess) to protect them, and their success in accomplishing this feat unharmed proves the active and protective role played by Kali in the villagers' daily lives (Freeman, 1974).

Some people attempt to control supernatural forces through magical ritual practices. Such attempts at magic should not be compared with rational thought or empirical investigation. Rather, they are two separate spheres of human thought and expression.

Social Cohesion   Emile Durkheim, one of the earliest functional theorists, noted the ability of religion to bring about group unity and cohesion. According to Durkheim, all societies have a continuing need to reaffirm and uphold their basic sentiments and values. This is accomplished when people come together and communally proclaim their acceptance of the dominant belief system. In this way people are bound to one another, and as a result, the stability of the society is strengthened.

Not only does religion in itself bring about social cohesion, but often the hostility and prejudice directed at its members by outsiders helps strengthen their bonds. For example, during the 1820s, Joseph Smith, a young farmer from Vermont, claimed that he had received visits from heavenly beings that enabled him to produce a six-hundred-page history of the ancient inhabitants of the Americas, known as the Book of Mormon. Shortly after the establishment of the Mormon church, Smith had a revelation that "Zion," the place where the Mormons would prepare for the millennium, was to be established in Jackson County, Missouri. Within two years, 1,200 Mormons had bought land and settled in Jackson County. The other residents in this area became concerned about the influx and in 1833 published their grievances in a document that became known as the "manifesto," or secret constitution. They charged the Mormons with a variety of transgressions and pledged to remove them from Jackson County. Several episodes of conflict followed that eventually forced the Mormons to move into an adjoining county. These encounters with a hostile environment produced a sense of collective identity at a time when it was desperately needed. Their church was less than two years old and included individuals from diverse religious backgrounds. There was a great deal of internal discord, and if it had not been for the unity that resulted from the conflict with the townspeople, the group might have disappeared altogether (MacMurray and Cunningham, 1973).

Durkheim's interest in the role of religion in society was aroused by his observation that religion, like the family, seemed to be a universal human institution. This universality meant that religion must serve a vital function in maintaining the social order. Durkheim felt that he could best understand the social role of religion by studying one of the simplest kinds—the totemism of the aboriginal Australian. A **totem** is an ordinary object such as a plant or animal that has become a sacred symbol to and of a particular group or clan, such as the aborigines, who not only revere the totem but also identify with it. Thus, reasoned Durkheim, religious symbols such as totems, as well as religion itself, arose from society itself, not outside it. When people recognize or worship supernatural entities, they are really worshiping their own society. They do not realize their religious feelings are actually the result (a crowd reaction) of the intense emotions aroused when people gather together at a clan meeting, for example. They look for an outside source of this emotional excitement and may settle on a nearby, familiar object as the symbol of both their religion and their society. Thus society—the clan—is the origin of the clan members' shared religious beliefs, which in turn help cement together their society.

Durkheim sees religious ritual as an important part of this "social cement." Religion, through its rituals, fulfills a number of social functions: it brings people together physically, promoting social cohesion; it reaffirms the group's beliefs and values; it helps maintain norms, mores, and prohibitions so that

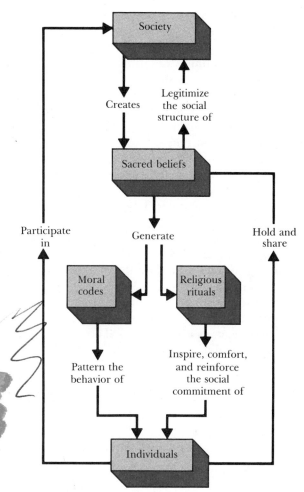

Figure 14.1 Society, Religion, and the Individual: A Functionalist View

violation of a secular law—murder or incest, for instance—is also a violation of the religious code and may warrant ritual punishment or purification; it transmits a group's cultural heritage from one generation to the next; and it offers emotional support to individuals during times of stress and at important stages in their life cycle, such as puberty, marriage, and death (see Figure 14.1).

In Durkheim's view, these functions are so important that even a society that lacks the

totem An ordinary object, such as a plant or animal, that has become a sacred symbol to and of a particular group or clan which not only reveres the totem but identifies with it.

idea of the sacred must substitute some system of shared beliefs and rituals. Indeed, some theorists see communism as such a system. Soviet communism has its texts and prophets (Marx, Engels), its shrines (Lenin's tomb), its rituals (May Day parade), and its unique moral code. Durkheim thought that much of the social upheaval of his day could be attributed to the fact that religion and ritual no longer played an important part in people's lives, and without a shared belief system, the social order was breaking down.

Although many sociologists today take issue with Durkheim's explanation of the origins of religion based on totemism, they nevertheless recognize the value of his functional approach in understanding the vital role of religion in society.

Secular society depends on external rewards and pressures for results, whereas religion depends on the internal acceptance of a moral value structure. Durkheim believed that because religion is effective in bringing about adherence to social norms, society usually presents these as an expression of a divine order. For example, in ancient China, as

Marxists believe religion plays a major role in justifying the political status quo.

in France until the late eighteenth century, political authority—the right to rule absolutely—rested securely on the notion that emperors and kings ruled because it was divine will that they do so—"the divine right of kings." In Egypt the political authority of pharaohs was unquestioned because they were more than just kings; they were believed to be gods in human form.

But religion serves to legitimize more than just political authority. Although many forms of institutionalized inequality do not operate to the advantage of the subgroups or individuals affected by them, they help perpetuate the larger social order and often are justified by an appeal to sacred authority. In such situations, although religion serves as a legitimator of social inequality, it does function to sustain societal stability. Thus the Afrikaners of South Africa justify their policy of *apartheid* on religious grounds (see Chapter 11); the Jews in Europe were kept from owning land and were otherwise persecuted "because" they had "killed Christ" (Trachtenberg, 1961); and even slavery has been defended on religious grounds. In 1700 Judge John Saffin of Boston wrote of

the Order that God hath set in the world, who hath Ordained different degrees and orders of men, some to the High and Honorable, some to be Low and Despicable . . . yea, some to be born slaves, and so to remain during their lives, as hath been proved. (Montagu, 1964a)

It must be pointed out that religions do not *always* legitimize secular authority. In feudal Europe the church had its own political structure, and there often was tension between church and state. Indeed, just as the church often legitimized monarchs, it also excommunicated those who failed to take its wishes into account. However, the fact remains that religious institutions usually do dovetail quite neatly with other social institutions, legitimizing and helping sustain them. For example, though church and state in medieval Europe were separate structures and often conflicted, the church nonetheless played an important role in supporting the entire feudal system.

Establishing World Views According to Max Weber in his classic book *The Protestant Ethic and the Spirit of Capitalism*, religion responds to the basic human need to understand the purpose of life. In doing so, religion must give meaning to the social world within which life takes place. This means creating a world view that can have social, political, and economic consequences. For instance, there is the issue of whether salvation can be achieved through active mastery (hard work, for example) or through passive contemplation (meditation). The first can be seen in Calvinism, and the second approach is evident in several of the Eastern religions. Another major issue in creating a world view is whether salvation means concentrating on a supernatural world, this world, or an inner world.

Using these ideas, Weber theorized that Calvinism fostered the Protestant ethic of hard work and asceticism and that Protestantism was an important influence on the development of capitalism. Calvinism is rooted in the concept of predestination, which holds that before they are born, certain people are selected for heaven and others for hell. Nothing anyone does in this world can change this. The Calvinists consequently were anxious to find out whether they were among those chosen for salvation. Worldly success, especially the financial success that grew out of strict discipline, hard work, and self-control, was seen as proof that a person was among the select few. Money was accumulated not to be spent but to be displayed as proof of one's chosenness. Capitalist virtues became Calvinist virtues. It was Weber's view that even though capitalism existed before Calvinist influence, it really blossomed only with the advent of Calvinism.

Weber's analysis has been criticized from many standpoints. Calvinist doctrines were not so uniform as Weber pictured them, nor was the work ethic confined to the Protestant value system. Rather, it seems to have been characteristic of the times, promoted by Catholics as well as Protestants. Finally, one could just as well argue the reverse, that the social and economic changes leading to the rise of industrialism and capitalism stimulated the emergence of the new Protestantism—a po-sition that Marxist analysts have taken. Today it is generally agreed that although religious beliefs did indeed affect economic behavior, the tenets of Protestantism and capitalism tended to support each other. However, the lasting value of Weber's work is his demonstration of how religion creates and legitimizes world views and how important these views are to human social and political life.

Adaptations to Society Religion can also be seen as having adaptive consequences for the society in which its exists. For example, many would view the Hindu belief in the sacred cow, which may not be slaughtered, as a strange and not particularly adaptive belief. The cows are permitted to wander around freely and defecate along public paths.

Marvin Harris (1966) has suggested that there may be some beneficial economic consequences in India from not slaughtering cattle. The cows and their offspring provide a number of resources that could not easily be provided in other ways. For example, a team of oxen is essential to India's many small farms. Oxen could be produced with fewer cows, but in order to do so, food production would have to be devoted to feeding those cows. With the huge supply of sacred cows, although they are not well fed, the oxen are produced at no cost to the economy.

Cow dung is also necessary in India for cooking and as a fertilizer. It is estimated that dung equivalent to 45 million tons of coal is burned annually. Alternative sources of fuel, such as wood or oil, are scarce and/or costly.

Although the Hindus do not eat beef, those cattle that die naturally or are slaughtered by non-Hindus are eaten by the lower castes. Without the Hindu taboo against eating beef, these other members of the Indian hierarchy would not have access to this food supply. Therefore, because the sacred cows do not compete with people for limited resources and because they provide a cheap source of labor, fuel, and fertilizer, the taboo against slaughtering cattle may be quite adaptive.

When societies are under great stress or attack, their members sometimes fall into a state of despair analagous, perhaps, to a person who becomes depressed. Institutions lose their meaning for people, and the society is threatened with what Durkheim called *anomie*, or "normlessness." If this continues, the social structure may break down, and the society may be absorbed by another society, unless the culture can regenerate itself. Under these conditions there sometimes emerge powerful religious movements that stress the need to return to "the good old values" of the previous, "uncorrupted" tradition. Sociologists call such developments religious **revitalization movements**, and many of them can be found in the pages of history and even are in existence today.

In the 1880s, the once free and proud Plains Indians lived in misery, crowded onto barren reservations by soldiers of the United States government. Cheated out of the pitiful rations that had been promised them, they lived in hunger—and with memories of the past. Then a Paiute by the name of Wovoka had a vision, and he traveled from tribe to tribe to spread the word and demonstrate his Ghost Dance. Give up fighting he told the people. Give up all things of the white man. Give up guns, give up European clothing, give up alcohol, give up all trade goods. Return to the simple life of the ancestors. Live simply—and dance! Once the Indian people are pure again, the Great Spirit will come, all Indian ancestors will return, and all the game will return. A big flood will come, and after it is gone, only Indians will be left in this "good time."

Wovoka's Ghost Dance spread among the defeated tribes. From the Great Plains to California, Indian communities took up the slow, trancelike dance. Some believed that the return of the ancestors would lead to the slaughter of all whites. For others, the dance just rekindled pride in their heritage. But for whatever reasons, the Ghost Dance could not be contained, despite the government soldiers' attempts to ban it.

On December 28, 1890, the people of a Sioux village camped under federal guard at Wounded Knee, South Dakota, and began to dance. They ignored orders to stop and continued to dance until suddenly someone fired a shot. The soldiers opened fire, and soon over 200 of the original 350 men, women, and children were killed. The soldiers' losses were 29 dead and 33 wounded, mostly from their own bullets and shrapnel. This slaughter was the last battle between the Indians of the Plains and the soldiers of the dominant Anglo society (Brown, 1971).

The Conflict Theory View

Karl Marx argued that "the ruling ideas of each age have always been the ideas of the ruling class" (Marx and Engels, 1961), and from this it was a small step to his claim that the dominant religion of a society is that of the dominant class, an observation that has been borne out by historical evidence. Marxist scholars emphasize religion's role in justifying the political status quo, by cloaking political authority with sacred legitimacy and thereby making opposition to it seem immoral.

The concept of alienation is an important part of Marx's thinking, especially in his ideas of the origin and functions of religion. **Alienation** is the process by which people lose control over the social institutions they themselves have invented; they then begin to believe that these institutions are separate from themselves, a part of the outside world that they are powerless to change. People begin to feel like strangers—aliens—in their own world. Marx further believed that religion is one of the most alienating influences in human society, affecting all other social institutions and contributing to a totally alienated world.

According to Marx, "Man makes religion, religion does not make man" (Marx, 1967). The function of God thus was invented to serve as the model of an ideal human being. People soon lost sight of this fact, however, and began to worship and fear the ideal they had created as if it were a separate, powerful supernatural entity. Thus religion, because of the fear people feel for the nonexistent god they themselves have created, serves to alienate people from the real world.

Marx saw religion as the tool that the upper classes used to maintain control of society and to dominate the lower classes. In fact, he referred to it as "the opiate of the masses," believing that through religion, the masses were kept from actions that might change their relationship with those in power. The lower classes were distracted from taking steps for social change by the promise of happiness through religion—if they followed the rules established by religion, they would receive their reward in heaven, and so they had no reason to try to change or improve their condition in this world. These religious beliefs made it easy for the ruling classes to continue to exploit the lower classes: religion served to legitimize upper-class power and authority. Although modern political and social thinkers do not accept all of Marx's ideas, they recognize his contribution to the understanding of the social functions of religion.

Although as we have seen, religion performs a number of vital functions in society—helping maintain social cohesion and control while satisfying the individual's need for emotional comfort, reassurance, and a world view—it also has negative, or dysfunctional, aspects.

Karl Marx would be quick to point out a major dysfunction of religion: through its ability to make it seem that the existing social order is the only conceivable and acceptable way of life, it obscures the fact that people construct society and therefore can change society. Religion, by imposing the acceptance of supernatural causes of conditions and events, tends to conceal the natural and human causes of social problems in the world. In fact, in its role of justifying, or legitimating the status quo, religion may very well hinder much-needed changes in the social structure. By diverting attention from injustices in the existing social order, religion discourages the individual from taking steps to correct these conditions.

An even more basic and subtle dysfunction of religion is its insistence that only one body of knowledge and only one way of thinking are sacred and correct, thereby limiting independent thinking and the search for further knowledge.

☐ Organization of Religious Life

Several forms or types of organization of religious groups are found in society.

The Universal Church

A **universal church** includes all the members of a society within one united moral community (Yinger, 1970). It is fully a part of the social, political, and economic status quo and therefore accepts and supports (more or less) the secular culture. In preliterate society, in which religion is not really a differentiated institution but rather permeates the entire fabric of social life, a person belongs to the church simply by being a member of the society. In more complex societies, this religious form cuts across divisions of the social structure, such as social classes and ethnic groups, binding all believers into one moral community. A universal church, however, does not seek to change any conditions of social inequality created by the secular society and culture, and indeed, it may even legitimize them. (An example is the Hindu religion of India, which perpetuates a rigid caste system.)

The Ecclesia

Like the universal church, an **ecclesia** extends itself to all members of a society. However, it has so completely adjusted its ethical system to the political structure of the secular society that it has come to represent and promote the interests of the ruling classes. In this process the ecclesia loses adherents among the lower social classes, who increasingly reject it for membership in sects, be these sacred or "civil" (Yinger, 1970). The Russian Orthodox church, for example, must be seen as an ecclesia. With the rise of political and religious turmoil in Russia early in this century, the church tied itself firmly to the interests of the

revitalization movements Powerful religious movements that stress a return to the religious values of the past. These movements spring up when a society is under great stress or attack.

alienation The process by which people lose control over the social institutions they themselves have invented.

universal church A church that includes all the members of a society within one united moral community.

ecclesia A church that shares the same ethical system as the secular society and that has come to represent and promote the interests of the ruling classes. Example: the Russian Orthodox church.

czar and the aristocracy. Along with them it was crushed and dispersed by the 1917 Bolshevik revolution.

The Denomination

A **denomination** tends to limit its membership to a particular class, ethnic group, or regional group, or at least to have its leadership positions dominated by members of such a group. It has no official or unofficial connection with the state, and any political involvement is purely a matter of choice by the denomination's leaders, who may either support or oppose any or all of the state's actions and political positions. Denominations do not withdraw themselves from the secular society. Rather, they participate actively in secular affairs and also tend to cooperate with other religious groups. These two characteristics distinguish them from sects, which are separatist and unlikely to be tolerant of other religious persuasions (Yinger, 1970). (For that matter, universal churches, by their very nature, also typically dismiss other religions.) In America, Lutheranism, Methodism, other Protestant groups, Catholicism, and Judaism embody the characteristics of a denomination.

The Sect

A **sect** is a rather small group that adheres quite strictly to religious doctrine that often includes unconventional beliefs or forms of worship. Sects generally represent a withdrawal from secular society and an active *rejection* of secular culture (Yinger, 1970). For example, the Dead Sea Scrolls show clearly that the beliefs of both early Christian and Jewish sects such as the Essenes were rooted in a disgust with society's self-indulgent pursuit of worldly pleasures and in a rejection of the corruption perceived in the prevailing religious hierarchy (Wilson, 1969).

Early in their development, sects often are so harsh in their rejection of society that they invite persecution. Some actually thrive on martyrdom, which causes members to intensify their fervent commitment to the faith. (Consider, for example, the Christian martyrs in Rome before the conversion to Christianity of the Emperor Constantine.)

Millenarian Movements

Throughout human history in times of stress, religious leaders have emerged, foretelling the end of the world, the destruction of all evil people and their works, and the saving of the just, who must stop whatever they are doing to follow the bearers of the Message. Because these teachings prophesy the end of an era—often represented by the symbolic number of one thousand years—sociologists call such religious phenomena **millenarian movements**.

In the early 1950s, in the midwestern town of Lake City (a fictitious name), several people formed a group around a middle-aged woman named Mrs. Keech. This woman, who had the remarkable ability to "tune in" to communication from extraterrestrial beings, had recently received an urgent message: on December 21, 1955, the earth would be destroyed, and only the "elect" would be taken aboard a spacecraft and saved.

Mrs. Keech and her followers were told that the earth had actually been populated by refugees from the planet Car, which had been blown to pieces when "scientists" under the leadership of Lucifer ineptly lost control of the atomic weapons they had built to fight the "people who followed the light" in the service of God under the leadership of Jesus Christ. After that cosmic disaster, Lucifer led his legions to earth, and the "forces of light" rebuilt their civilization on other planets. Human beings, because they had lost their "cosmic knowledge," were intent on following the scientists and Lucifer—and hence were doomed to destruction.

On the night of December 21, the faithful gathered around Mrs. Keech, took off all their jewelry, ripped zippers from pants and hooks from bras (metal could not be worn on space journeys), and waited for their saviors. When the ships failed to come, Mrs. Keech received a message setting a new date for the Reckoning. But most of the followers became disheartened, and the group slowly drifted apart (Festinger, Rieken, and Schachter, 1956).

How can we understand Mrs. Keech's group? Although on television, it is much in style to portray the 1950s as "happy days," this was hardly the case. Less than a decade earlier, America had dropped two atomic bombs on cities in Japan—and from then on, the world lived with the real possibility of the extermination of all human life through nuclear warfare. The 1950s brought their own age of anxiety: the Berlin blockade, the Soviet development of their own atomic bomb, and the Korean War.

The Cult

Although a sect often develops in response to a rejection of certain religious doctrine or ritual within the larger religious organization, a cult usually introduces totally new religious ideas and principles. Cults generally have charismatic leaders who expect total commitment. Members of cults, who are usually motivated by an intense sense of mission, often must give up individual autonomy and decision making. Many cults require resocialization practices so strong as to make the member seem unrecognizable in personality and behavior to former friends and relatives.

Because the activities and excesses of some cults have taken over the headlines in recent years, we may tend to forget or even dismiss the fact that many major religions began as cults and sects.

☐ Aspects of American Religion

The Pilgrims of 1620 sought to build a sanctuary where they would be free from religious persecution, and the Puritans who followed 10 years later intended to build a community embodying all the virtues of "pure" Protestantism, a community that would serve as a moral guide to others. Thus religion pervaded the social and political goals of the early English-speaking settlers and played a major role in shaping the nature of colonial society. Today the three main themes that characterize religion in America are widespread belief, secularism, and ecumenism.

Widespread Belief

Americans generally take religion for granted. Although they differ widely in religious affiliation and degree of church attendance, almost all Americans claim to believe in God. In a 1968 Gallup poll, 98 percent of Americans responded affirmatively when asked whether they believed in God. In 1976, almost a decade later, in another Gallup survey, 94 percent answered yes to the same question. Nine out of every 10 Americans have a religious preference, even if they maintain no formal church affiliation, and 4 out of every 10 American adults attended either church or synagogue each week during 1981 (Gallup, 1982).

Evidence as to whether America is experiencing a "religious revival," as some have claimed, is contradictory. Attendance at religious services began to rise slightly in the late 1970s, after falling for decades. In 1960, 47 percent of the people questioned said they had attended a church or synagogue during the week before they were polled; although this figure dropped to 40 percent in 1971, it showed a slight but sustained increase to a little more than 41 percent between 1976 and 1978. On the other hand, the number of people who said that religion was very important in their lives dropped by 18 percent, from 71 to 53 percent, between 1965 and 1978 (*Public Opinion*, 1980). Complicating matters still further, the percentage of Americans who feel religion is increasing its influence on American life was almost the same in 1978 (39 percent) as it was in 1965 (36 percent)—although there were wide swings in public attitudes in the intervening years, ranging from a low of 15 percent in 1969 to a high of 45 percent in 1976 (*Public Opinion*, 1980). By and large, and despite dire warnings of the erosion of reli-

denomination A religious group that tends to limit its membership to a particular class, ethnic group, or religious group, or at least to have its leadership positions dominated by members of such a group.

sect A small religious group that adheres strictly to religious doctrine involving unconventional beliefs or forms of worship.

millenarian movements Religious movements that prophesy the end of the world, the destruction of all evil people and their works, and the saving of the just. Like revitalization movements, these movements usually develop in times of stress.

cult A religious movement that usually introduces totally new religious ideas and principles. Cults usually have charismatic leaders who expect a total commitment from the cult members, who are usually motivated by an intense sense of mission.

TABLE 14.2   Membership in Religious Groups in the United States 1982

Religious Group	Number of Members
Protestant	76,754,000
Roman Catholic	52,089,000
Jewish	5,725,000
Eastern Orthodox (Christian)	3,860,000
Other Catholic churches	925,000
Buddhist	100,000
Miscellaneous	151,000
Total	139,603,000

Source: U.S. Department of Commerce, Bureau of the Census, *Statistical Abstract of the United States, 1985* (Washington, D.C.: Government Printing Office, 1984), p. 51.

giosity because of new ways of thinking and innovative lifestyles, most Americans still seem to believe in and practice various forms of religion.

More than half of all religiously affiliated individuals belong to a Protestant denomination, clearly reflecting America's colonial history (see Table 14.2). But other denominations are also well represented, especially Catholicism and Judaism. There are well over 200 formally chartered religious organizations in America today. Such pluralism is not typical of other societies and has resulted primarily from the waves of European immigrants who began to arrive in the postcolonial era. Americans' traditional tolerance of religious diversity can be seen also as a reflection of the constitutional separation of church and state, so that no one religion is recognized officially as better or more acceptable than any other.

Secularism

Many scholars have noted that modern society is becoming increasingly **secularized**, which means that religious institutions are being confined to ever-narrowing spheres of social influence, while people turn to secular sources for moral guidance in their everyday lives (Berger, 1967). This shift is reflected in the reactions of Americans who, for the most part, are notoriously indifferent to, and ignorant of, the basic doctrines of their faiths. Stark and Glock (1968) report that a poll of Americans found that 67 percent of Protestants and

40 percent of Catholics could not correctly identify Father, Son, and Holy Spirit as constituting the Holy Trinity; 79 percent of Protestants and 86 percent of Catholics could not correctly identify a single prophet from the Old Testament; and finally, 41 percent of Protestants and 81 percent of Catholics could not identify the first book of the Bible.

Of course, social and political leaders still rely on religious symbolism to influence secular behavior. The American Pledge of Allegiance tells us that we are "one nation, under God, indivisible . . ." and our currency tells us that "In God We Trust." Since the turn of the century, however, modern society has turned increasingly to science, rather than religion, to point the way. Secular political movements have emerged that attempt to provide most if not all of the functions for their followers that traditionally have been fulfilled by religion. For example, communism prescribes a belief system and an organization that rival those of any religion. Like religions, communism offers a general conception of the nature of all things and provides symbols that, for its adherents, establish powerful feelings and attitudes and supply motivation toward action. Thus, some political movements lack only a sacred or supernatural component to qualify as religions. But in this increasingly secular modern world, sacred legitimacy appears not to be necessary for establishing meaning and value in life.

Ecumenism

Partially as a response to secularism, a tendency toward **ecumenism** has been evident among many of the religions in the United States. This refers to the trend among many religions to draw together and project a sense of unity and common direction.

Unlike religious groups in Europe, where issues of doctrine have fostered sectlike hardline separatism among denominations, in America most religious groups have focused on ethics, that is, how to live the good and right life. There is less likelihood of disagreement over ethics than over doctrine. Hence, American Protestant denominations typically have had rather loose boundaries, with members of congregations switching denominations rather easily and churches featuring guest appearances from ministers of other denominations. In this context, ecumenism has flourished in the United States far more than in Europe.

This overview of the current status of religion in the United States makes it possible to understand how closely religion is tied to other components of American society.

☐ Major Religions in the United States

Between the 1960s and 1980s, some religious groups became involved in secular affairs such as the civil rights, antiwar, and nuclear freeze movements. Today the major denominations are struggling with questions of doctrine and practice in response to dissatisfaction among their members. Although some practices have been liberalized, doctrine has often been reaffirmed more strictly.

Protestantism

Because American Protestantism is fragmented into so many groups, many sociologists simply have classified all non-Catholic Christian denominations in the general category of "Protestant." It should be kept in mind, however, that there are differences—of greater or lesser significance—among the various denominations (see Table 14.3).

Approximately 56 percent of the people in the United States who are affiliated with a religious group are Protestant (see Table 14.2), with Baptists accounting for about one-third of that figure. (See Table 14.3 for other statistics regarding the major religious faiths in the United States.) Episcopalians represent the wealthiest and best-educated segment of the Protestant population, but at the same time they are the smallest of the Protestant denominations (*Public Opinion*, 1978).

The Protestant denominations often represent opposite poles on a continuum. On the one hand, many Protestant groups are rather liberal in their views. At the same time, there has been a major growth in numbers and impact among the fundamentalists and other evangelicals. About one-third (at least 13 million) of the members of Protestant churches

In recent years female ministers have emerged within the Protestant Church.

that belong to the National Council of Churches (NCC) are evangelicals and fundamentalists; 33.5 million more belong to Protestant groups that are not affiliated with the NCC. Evangelicals are diverse in their beliefs and practices—for example, fundamentalists are the most politically conservative and believe in the most literal interpretation of the Bible. The Pentacostalists "speak in tongues" and believe in miraculous cures wrought by faith and prayer. Members of evangelical groups come from many denominations of Christianity, Episcopalian to Roman Catholic. They share a number of beliefs and practices: the absolute authority of the Bible, the born-again experience (which is seen as a conscious, intensely personal spiritual commitment to Christ), and the necessity of spreading their message to as many people as possible (nowadays by making full use of mass media such as television and radio to reach potential audiences of 20 million or more—

secularization The process by which religious institutions are confined to ever-narrowing spheres of social influence, while people turn to secular sources for moral guidance in their everyday lives.

ecumenism The trend among many religions to draw together and project a sense of unity and common direction.

TABLE 14.3 Profiles of Major Religious Faiths in the United States (1979)

	Population Distribution	Protestants	Roman Catholics	Jews	Eastern Orthodox	No Religious Preference
National	100%	100%	100%	100%	100%	100%
Sex						
Male	48	45	47	49	54	64
Female	52	55	53	51	46	36
Race						
White	88	84	96	99	99	87
Non-white	12	16	4	1	1	13
Education						
College	30	28	27	56	37	40
High school	55	55	58	35	44	51
Grade school	15	17	15	9	19	9
Region						
East	27	19	41	60	44	24
Midwest	27	29	27	6	32	23
South	28	36	16	16	7	20
West	18	16	16	18	17	33
Age						
18 years	3	2	4	1	2	3
19 years	2	2	3	2	2	3
20 years	3	2	3	2	2	4
21–24 years	10	9	11	8	10	19
25–29 years	11	10	11	10	7	18
30–34 years	10	9	10	9	9	14
35–39 years	9	8	9	8	8	9
40–44 years	7	7	8	8	9	6
45–49 years	8	8	8	9	11	6
50–59 years	15	17	15	15	17	8
60–69 years	12	14	11	14	12	6
70 years and older	10	12	7	14	11	4
Income						
$20,000 and over	32	31	34	49	37	31
12,000–19,999	28	28	30	19	24	27
10,000–11,999	8	9	8	6	9	9
6,000–9,999	14	14	13	10	13	14
4,000–5,999	8	8	7	7	6	8
Under 4,000	8	9	7	7	8	8
Politics						
Republican	21	26	15	9	12	11
Democrat	44	42	49	58	43	33
Independent	32	30	31	29	42	50
City size						
1,000,000 and over	20	13	30	57	34	25
500,000–999,999	13	11	15	14	22	17
50,000–499,999	26	26	26	20	26	28
2,500–49,999	16	18	12	4	5	14
Under 2,500, Rural	25	32	17	5	13	16
Marital status						
Married	66	69	65	61	69	50
Single	17	14	21	23	21	37
Widowed	9	10	8	10	6	3
Separated	2	2	2	1	*	3
Divorced	5	5	4	5	3	7

*Less than 1 percent

Note: Figures sometimes do not add to 100% due to an "undesignated" category.

Source: "Religion in America 1981," Gallup Opinion Index, Report No. 184, p. 19.

see Using Sociology: "Impact of Religious TV Programs").

Since the 1960s there has been a 10-percent drop in the membership of the United Methodists and United Presbyterians, and the Episcopalians have seen a 15-percent decline. At the same time, the more conservative denominations have increased dramatically. In the same period of time there has been an 18-percent increase in the number of Baptists, a 37-percent increase among the Assemblies of God, and a 34-percent increase among Seventh-Day Adventists (U.S. Dept. of Commerce, 1983).

At the present time the fundamentalists and evangelical Christians have become an extremely visible and vocal segment of the Protestant population, and their presence has been felt through the media and through their support of political candidates. Why are the fundamentalist and evangelical churches gaining such popularity? Some of their appeal may lie in the sense of belonging and the comfort they offer through their belief in a well-defined and self-assured religious doctrine—no ambiguities and hence few moral choices to be made.

The growth of these churches reflects religion's role as a social institution, changing over time and from place to place, partly in response to concurrent social and cultural changes and partly itself acting as an agent of social change.

Catholicism

One of the most important developments in the recent history of Catholicism was the ecumenical council (Vatican II) called by Pope John XXIII, which met from 1962 to 1965 and thoroughly reexamined Catholic doctrine. This ecumenical council led to many changes, often referred to as "liberalization" and including the substitution of common language for Latin in the Mass. One unintended consequence (or latent function) of Vatican II was that the centralized authority structure of the Catholic church was called into question. Laypersons and priests felt free to dispute the doctrinal pronouncements of bishops and even of the pope himself. This trend became especially apparent after the

pope's 1968 ban on the use of contraception. Andrew Greeley, a sociologist who also is a Catholic priest, believes that this ban helped undermine the pope's credibility. He found that between 1963 and 1976, the percentage of Catholics who believed that "Jesus invested the church's leadership in the Pope" dropped from 70 percent to 42 percent (Greeley, McCready, and McCourt, 1975). During the same period, the percentage of Catholics using some form of birth control rose from under 60 percent to 75 percent (Westoff and Jones, 1977).

More recently, Pope John Paul II attempted to revitalize Catholicism by traveling abroad and pursuing ecumenical reunification with Protestant and Eastern Orthodox denominations. Toward the end of 1979, he attended a mass celebrated by Patriarch Dimitrios I of the Eastern Orthodox church, thereby cutting through over 500 years of icy relations between the two denominations. In 1982 he became the first pope to visit England.

At the same time, however, the Vatican launched a campaign to crack down on dissent within the Catholic church. In 1979, it interrogated Edward Schillebeeck, an internationally famous liberal Catholic theologian from the Netherlands, and it formally de-

A Catholic priest celebrating Mass.

USING SOCIOLOGY
Impact of Religious TV Programs

The Princeton Religion Research Center, an interfaith, nondenominational research organization, in conjunction with Gallup International, in 1981 conducted a national survey of various aspects of religion in the United States. One area on which they focused was the effect of religious programming over the electronic media on church involvement in the United States.

There are 1,400 religious radio stations, 35 religious TV stations and 4 religious TV networks currently in operation.

The survey was undertaken because of the amount of controversy surrounding the so-called electronic church, particularly those religious programs using television and radio evangelists. Much controversy has surrounded the so-called electronic church, particularly those religious programs using TV and radio evangelists.

The electronic church has proved to be one of the most remarkable developments in American religion, with an estimated 1,400 religious radio stations, 35 religious TV stations, and 4 religious TV networks currently in operation.

Some pastors have expressed concern that the electronic church will cause their members to decrease their involvement in local churches and will keep prospective members from joining a church.

Others worry about the effects of the electronic media on the quality of Christian life and feel that such programs can make religion too easy and comfortable, encourage individualized religion and undermine religious commitment. Still others object to what they consider the "show business" aspects of certain religious programs on radio and television.

But defenders of the electronic church point out that religious programs on radio and television reach a vast number of people who might not be reached otherwise and, in fact, are the only way to contact many of the elderly, the infirm, and the handicapped.

Other supporters of the use of the media to convey a religious message feel that such efforts raise the level of awareness of the unchurched and make them more likely to become involved in the community of active believers. Some evangelists, including Drs. Billy Graham and Robert Schuller, actively encourage their listeners to participate in the life of local churches.

In seeking to determine who watches religious television programs, interviewers asked the question, "Have you watched any religious TV programs in the last 12 months?" Fifty percent responded that they had, a high proportion of which were Protestants (particularly members of Baptist churches), older

Effect of TV Programs on Local Church Involvement (Based on Viewers of Religious TV Programs)

	Increased	Lessened	No Difference	Don't Know
National	27%	7%	65%	1%
Protestants	30	6	63	1
Catholics	22	7	70	1
Under 30 years	25	10	64	1
18–24	25	13	60	2
25–29	24	5	71	*
30–49	26	6	67	1
50 and over	29	7	63	1
Church attenders	34	2	63	1
Nonattenders	20	12	66	2
Church members	29	6	64	1
Nonmembers	20	10	68	2
Religion is				
Very important to life	32	5	62	1
Fairly important	17	9	72	2
Not at all important	2	25	72	1

*Less than 1 percent

people, women, nonwhites, and people living in the South. The table indicates the percentage of people in various categories who responded "yes" to the question.

In seeking to discover the impact of watching religious programs on church involvement, the same people who responded "yes" to the first question were asked, "Would you say that religious television programs have increased your involvement in your local church and its activities over the last years?"

As may be seen from the table, the findings show that as many as one-third of those who watch reli-

gious television programs said that these programs have had an effect of one kind or another on their involvement in their local church and its activities over the last three years. Among these people, opinion is heavily on the side that religious television programs have *increased* rather than decreased their involvement. These results should allay some of the fears expressed by clergy mentioned earlier.

In assessing the findings today, readers should bear in mind that survey respondents are referring to television religious programs of a wide variety, including not only

programs that feature evangelicals preaching but also telecasts of religious services, crusades, religious talk shows, documentaries, and dramatizations based on the Bible.

The survey does not attempt to assess the impact of the electronic church on religious beliefs, attitudes and practices, which calls for additional careful and detailed research.

Source: Adapted from "Religion in America: The Gallup Opinion Index, 1981," The Gallup Organization, Inc., and The Princeton Religion Research Center, Inc., Report No. 184 (January, 1981), pp. 65–66, 75. □

---

clared that Germany's Hans Kung had "departed from the integral truth of Roman Catholic faith, and therefore he can no longer be considered a Catholic theologian or function as such in a teaching role" (*Time*, 1979). Among other things, Kung's writings attacked the doctrine of the pope's infallibility in pronouncements on matters of faith. The pope also let it be known that homosexuality was not compatible with Catholic doctrine, and he set back the hopes of many by proclaiming that women could not expect to be admitted eventually to priesthood within the church. In addition, members of the clergy were banned from participating in politics as elected officials.

From a sociological perspective it appears that as the Catholic church pursues ecumenism, its leadership is experiencing a need to define its boundaries more clearly. To accomplish this, it is hardening its doctrinal lines and setting stricter limits on religious practice, by formally designating deviants.

Judaism

There is a strong identification among Jews on both a cultural and a religious level, and many feel that they have common ties because of their religion. This sense of connectedness is an important aspect in understanding current trends within the religion.

Jews can be divided into three groups, based on the manner in which they approach traditional religious precepts. Orthodox Jews observe traditional religious laws very closely. They maintain strict dietary laws and do not work, drive, or engage in other everyday practices on the Sabbath. Reform Jews, on the other hand, allow for major reinterpretations of religious practices and customs, which are often in response to changes in society. For example, a Reform congregation in Sudbury, Massachusetts, published a nonsexist prayerbook that received worldwide attention. Conservative Jews represent a compromise between the two extremes. They are less traditional than the Orthodox Jews are but not as willing to make major modifications in religious observance, as the Reform Jews are apt to do. In addition, there is a large secularized segment of the Jewish population that still identifies itself as Jewish but refrains from formal synagogue affiliation.

Like the situation among Protestants, there are social-class differences among the various Jewish groups. Reform Jews are the best educated and have the highest incomes. For Orthodox Jews, religious, not secular, education is the goal. They have the lowest incomes and the least amount of secular education. As might be expected, Conservative Jews are located between these two poles.

CASE STUDY
Converts to Judaism

According to the Bible, God told the Jewish people to be fruitful and multiply. In the United States, it seems the group is doing neither. Recent surveys estimate there are 5.3 million Jews in the United States, 13 percent fewer than in 1972. Demographers predict the population will further decline by 5 to 17 percent by the end of the century. The American Jewish community is thus facing a crisis, and each branch, if not each member, of the religious community has a differing opinion on how to respond. The following discussion presents some of the views.

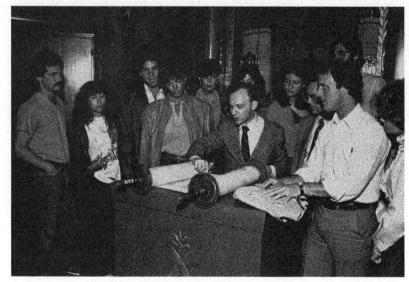

A rabbi with a conversion class in a Reformed congregation. Most people attend the class with a Jewish partner, usually a spouse or future spouse.

The reasons for the decline are varied. For one thing, Jews in the U.S. aren't bearing enough children to replace themselves: the Jewish fertility rate has been estimated at between 1.3 to 1.7 per lifetime—well below the replacement rate of 2.1. For another, the Jewish population is aging: about 40 percent of America's Jews will reach the end of their life expectancy within the next generation. Jewish immigration from the Soviet Union, which helped maintain population levels in the 1970s, has slowed to a trickle. And immigration from Israel, although believed to be large, doesn't appear to result in many permanent U.S. citizens. Finally, more young Jews are choosing to marry outside the faith, fanning ancient fears among their elders of assimilation and loss of Jewish identity.

How to stem this population erosion is evolving into an urgent—and divisive—issue for American Jewry, one that has heightened underlying friction between traditionalists and liberals. Amid a gathering storm of controversy, Jewish religious and lay groups are attempting to expand the definition of who is a Jew, offer incentives to increase family size, and—in a radical break with tradition—seek converts to Judaism.

Jewish groups fear that a further decline in the number of American Jews would lessen their political influence, and their ability to defend their interests. Liberal Jewish leaders warn of major domestic political consequences, because Jews have tended to support and vote for Democrats. Others see a potential cultural loss for a nation in which Jewish scientists, artists and performers have flourished. While Jews account for roughly 2 percent of the U.S. population, for example, they have given America 20 percent of its Nobel laureates.

While many of the reasons for the shrinking of the population are demographic in nature, the issue of how to stem the tide has been the cause of some major rifts between the various branches of the religion. Recent statistics, for example, put the rate of Jewish intermarriage at one in four. Strictly observant Jews blame their more liberal co-religionists for this high percentage. The liberal Reform movement has become far more tolerant of mixed marriages in recent years. In sharp contrast to even 10 years ago, interfaith couples have little difficulty today finding rabbis willing to marry them.

Jewish leaders concede that in an open society like the United States, the taboo against intermarriage was perhaps destined to break down. "The biggest problem we have is the problem of freedom," says Rabbi Alexander Schindler, the president of the Union of American Hebrew Congregations, the central organization of the Reform movement. "In Europe, historically, there were two choices: Stay Jewish and live apart from everyone else, or convert and be more or less accepted. In America, there is no outward compulsion to keep us in."

A subject that has provoked even more controversy is the Reform movement's break with the tradition of matrilineal, or motherly descent. In 1983, Reform leaders declared that Judaism could be passed on to children by their fathers as well as by their mothers. Up to that time, the child of a Jewish man and a Gentile woman wasn't recognized as a Jew.

The resolution evoked the wrath of Orthodox and ultra-Orthodox Jews. In a full-page advertisement in the *New York Times*, one group likened patrilineal descent to "treating the epidemic by declaring it to be the symptom of good health."

The tactic only makes the assimilation problem worse, according to Gilbert Klaperman, the president of the Rabbinical Council of America, which represents the main body of the Orthodox sector of the faith. He explains that it eliminates one of the main deterrents to intermarriage: the knowledge that children born of such a union won't be considered Jewish.

American Jews are also split over the Reform movement's attempts to seek converts to Judaism. This so-called Outreach program represents a break with centuries of Jewish tradition in which proselytizing has been disdained.

The Outreach program, which has been tested for the past few years, is deliberately low-key. It forgoes the flashy advertising and airwave sermonizing typical of many Christian evangelical movements. Rather, Outreach sessions resemble college comparative religion seminars. In the Boston area, the site of one of the nation's strongest Outreach programs, synagogues offer year-round introductory classes in Judaism for interfaith couples, as well as monthly follow-up gatherings for converts.

But to many Jews, the Outreach conversions make a mockery of Jewish teachings. "This is a sign of the Reform movement's desperation," says Rabbi Klaperman. He and other traditionalists argue that the means to combat assimilation lies not in new converts but in shoring up traditional values among existing Jews.

"It's a moral and spiritual absurdity to argue about the survival of the Jewish people as an end in itself," says Rabbi Cohen of the Jewish Theological Seminary, the academic and religious center for Conservative Judaism in the U.S. "If you're concerned about the survival of Judaism as a bearer of certain values, then I understand. Five hundred thousand committed co-religionists are a far more powerful force than 50 million with a nominal attachment."

Source: Gary Putka, "As Jewish Population Falls in U.S., Leaders Seek to Reverse Trend," *Wall Street Journal*, April 13, 1984, p. 1, 10. □

The state of Israel has played a major role in shaping current Jewish thinking. For many Jews, identification with Israel has come to be a secular replacement for religiosity. Support for the country is tied to many deep psychological and emotional responses. To many, Israel and its continued existence represent a way of guaranteeing that never again will millions of Jews perish in a Nazi Holocaust. The country is seen as a homeland that can help defend world Jewry from the unwarranted attacks that have occurred against Jews throughout history. For many Jews, identification with, and support for, the state of Israel is important to the development of their cultural and/or religious ties.

Recently the Jewish community has had to deal with the issue of ordination of women rabbis. Reform Jews have moved in this direction without a great deal of difficulty, and today women are the leaders of a few Reform congregations around the country. But the issue of women rabbis produced a bitter fight among Conservative Jews. At this time, the first group of Conservative women rabbis is being trained. Orthodox Jews have not had to address the issue, as for them the existence of a woman rabbi would represent too radical a departure from tradition to be contemplated. (For an examination of another issue affecting the Jewish community, see Case Study: "Converts to Judaism.")

All religions and denominations are affected by the current mood of the country. A heightened social consciousness results in demands for reform, whereas stressful times often produce a movement toward the personalization of religion. In any event, while traditional forms and practices of religion may be changing in the United States, religion itself is likely to continue to function as a basic social institution.

Social Correlates of Religious Affiliation

Religious affiliation seems to be correlated strongly with many other important aspects of people's lives: direct relationships can be traced between membership in a particular religious group and a person's politics, professional and economic standing, and ed-

FOCUS ON RESEARCH
America's Religious Mosaic

Nowhere is the diversity of the American people more evident than in their religious denominations. There are more than one thousand different religious groups in the United States, which vary widely in religious practices, moral views, class structure, family values, and attitudes. A recent survey found surprisingly large and persistent differences among even the major religious groups.

The national census is prohibited from asking about religion, so the U.S. Government generally has little to say on the matter. But since 1972, the General Social Surveys conducted by the National Opinion Research Center have been following Americans' religious attitudes and practices. This group has correlated information on a variety of issues with religious affiliation. Some of its findings are summarized below.

It is useful to think of American Protestant religious denominations as ranked on a scale as to their degree of traditionalism. At the conservative end are the fundamentalists (Pentecostals, Jehovah's Witnesses, etc.), Southern Baptists, and other Baptists. Next come the middle moderates (Lutherans, Methodists, and inter- or non-denominationalists), and finally the liberal elite (Unitarians, Congregationalists, Presbyterians, and Episcopalians.) This distinction among Protestants is important because the various branches often differ so markedly in their attitudes, especially toward social issues, that they resemble other religions more than the various denominations of their own.

For example, nearly 90 percent of the fundamentalists and Baptists believe in an afterlife. Among the moderate middle and liberal elite, belief slips to about 80 percent. Similarly, 75 percent of American Catholics say they believe in an afterlife, while only 25 percent of Jews

do. Forty-six percent of people with no religious affiliation believe in an afterlife.

Church attendance and strength of religious faith also vary widely. Among fundamentalists, 51 percent say they attend church weekly, and 58 percent say their faith is strong. Only about 22 to 24 percent of Lutherans and Methodists say they attend weekly, and the proportion with strong religious faith is in the 33- to 40-percent range. A slim 18 percent of Episcopalians attend church weekly, and 31 percent report strong faith.

Catholics are distinguished by their regular church attendance: 42 percent go to church every week, and 41 percent say their faith is strong. Jews, on the other hand, rarely go to religious services (8 percent each week), but report a comparatively high sense of attachment to their faith, with 42 percent saying their faith is strong. It may be that many Jews identify themselves as ethnically Jewish even though they do not actively follow ritual and attend services.

Fundamentalists and Baptists believe in a strict and traditional sense of sin. They are most likely to condemn homosexual, extramarital, and premarital sex, and to favor outlawing pornography. Sexual permissiveness increases among the middle moderates and is highest among the liberal elite. Catholics tend to resemble the Protestant center, while Jews are even more liberal than the Protestant liberals.

Similar differences in morality appear in attitudes toward drugs and alcohol. Fundamentalists and Baptists are the least likely to smoke, drink, go to bars, or favor the legalization of marijuana. At the other end of the scale on these issues are the people with no religious affiliation. For example, 88 percent of

fundamentalists oppose the legalization of marijuana, as do 80 percent of the middle moderates, 76 percent of Presbyterians, 70 percent of Episcopalians, 75 percent of Catholics, 59 percent of Jews, and 41 percent of people with no religious affiliation.

The major Protestant denominations also differ sharply in their class and social standing. Non-black fundamentalists and Southern Baptists have an average annual household income less than $15,000. Income averages $16,300 for Lutherans, $17,000 for Methodists, $20,500 for Presbyterians, $21,700 for Episcopalians, $17,400 for Catholics, $23,300 for Jews, and $17,600 for people with no religious affiliation. Similar differences occur for occupational prestige and for education, where Jews and Episcopalians average three more years of schooling than fundamentalists and Baptists.

Given the wide differences in values and attitudes among religious groups, the relative proportion of the population that belongs to each group helps determine the shape of society. Protestants make up about 64 percent of the adult population, according to data from the General Social Survey. Among the five major Protestant families, the largest are the Baptists, who account for 21 percent of the adult population. Second are the Methodists with 12 percent, and next are the Lutherans with 8 percent. Roman Catholics, representing about one-quarter of the adult population, are the largest single religious denomination. Jews are 2 to 3 percent, followed by a host of religions such as Eastern Orthodox, Muslim, Hindu, Sufi, and Baha'i, which add up to a little over 1 percent.

These percentages are in a constant state of flux, however, since demographic factors such as birthrates and migration patterns may influence the numbers of people in any given religion. Religious conversion can also affect percentages. Fundamentalism, for example, is gaining among the young and winning converts.

Despite trends toward ecumenicalism, it seems that the magnitude of religious differences, the persistence of established faiths, and the continual development of new faiths will ensure that this pattern of religious diversity will continue.

Source: Tom Smith, "America's Religious Mosaic," *American Demographics* **6** (7) (June, 1984), pp. 19–23. ☐

---

ucational level, family life, social mobility, and attitudes toward controversial social issues. Some of these correlates are shown in Table 14.3.

For example, Jews, who in the 1980 census represented only 2.9 percent of the total population, are proportionally the best-educated group; they also have higher incomes than Christians in general; and a greater proportion are represented in business and the professions. Despite their high socioeconomic and educational levels, however, Jews, like Catholics, occupy relatively few of the highest positions of power in the corporate world and politics: these fields generally are dominated by white Anglo-Saxon Protestants. Among Christian groups, there appears the same correlation among denomination, social and professional prestige, and income level. For example, Episcopalians, the smallest Protestant denomination, consistently rank highest in social prestige and income.

Other studies show equally interesting relationships between politics and religious affiliation. A Gallup profile (1982) of major religious faiths in the United States in 1979 revealed that 58 percent of Jews were Democrats and only 9 percent were Republicans. A lower proportion of Catholics, but still almost 50 percent, were Democrats, and 15 percent were Republicans. Protestants showed the lowest proportion of Democrats (42 percent) and the highest proportion (26 percent) of Republicans.

The positions of people on controversial social questions also seem to be correlated, to some extent, with their religious affiliations. The fundamentalist and evangelical Protestant sects generally are more conservative on key issues than are the major Protestant sects. According to the Gallup Opinion Index (1982), however, the pollings of dissimilar groups are sometimes not as divergent as might be expected. On issues such as the ERA proposal, for instance, evangelicals and nonevangelicals polled 53 percent and 66 percent in favor, respectively. On the other hand, for issues of deeply personal morality (abortion, for example) and religion (such as the Supreme Court interdiction against prayer in public schools), the differences were very sharp indeed.

Although it is clear that religious associations show definite correlations with people's political, social, and economic lives, we must be careful not to ascribe a cause-and-effect relationship to such data, which at most can be considered an indicator of an individual's attitudes and social standing.

The social and political correlates of religious affiliation have had a significant impact on the directions of the various religious denominations and sects in the United States. (For a further discussion of the variety of religious attitudes and values, see Focus on Research: "America's Religious Mosaic.")

☐ Summary

Religion is a system of beliefs and practices shared by a group of people that helps them to explain and function in the present world through the concept of the supernatural and the sacred. The sacred consists of all things kept separate from everyday experience, things that are knowable only through extraordinary experiences. Religion also includes rituals, patterns of behavior that are related to the sacred.

All the world's religions include ritual and prayer, emotion, belief, and organization. A simple, inclusive scheme of classifying religions recognizes four major types: supernaturalism, animism, theism, and abstract ideals.

In addition, they perform functions on both an individual and a social level, satisfying individual needs, promoting social cohesion, establishing world views, and providing social control. Religion also has its dysfunctional aspects. It tends to conceal the human causes of conditions and events and may hinder much-needed social changes as well as independent thinking and the search for new knowledge.

There is a clear relationship between religion and other social institutions during times of social change. In times of stress, three religious phenomena typically appear: revitalization movements, millenarian movements, and sectarian splitting.

Several forms or types of organization of religious groups are found in society, including the universal church, the ecclesia, the denomination, the sect, and the cult.

Today the three main themes that characterize religion in America are widespread belief, secularism, and ecumenism. Americans are more churchgoing than Europeans, with more than half of all religiously affiliated individuals belonging to a Protestant denomination.

Currently, the major religions and denominations in the United States are struggling with questions of doctrine and practice in response to dissatisfaction among their members. Although some practices have been liberalized, such as the language of the Catholic Mass and the acceptance of female clergy among Protestants, doctrine has often been reaffirmed more strictly. In Protestantism, fundamentalist and evangelical churches have been gaining popularity and have become both visible and vocal on the national scene.

Judaism also is undergoing changes. An important factor is the influence of the identification of many American Jews with the state of Israel. In addition, two of the three groups, Conservatism and Reform, are dealing with the issue of women being ordained as rabbis. And Judaism, like other religions in America, has experienced secularization.

☐ For Further Reading

BELLAH, ROBERT N., and PHILLIP E. HAMMOND. *Varieties of Civil Religion*. San Francisco: Harper & Row, 1980.   An enlightening historical examination of civil religion.

BROMLEY, DAVID G., and ANSON D. SHUPE, JR. *"Moonies" in America: Cult, Church, and Crusade*. Beverly Hills, Calif.: Sage Publications, 1979.   An examination of Sun Myung Moon's Unification Church. This book analyzes the process of the construction of social motives by the movement and its anticult opponents.

BUTLER, E. M. *Ritual Magic*. New York: Cambridge University Press, 1979 (orig. 1949).   A classic study of ritual magic texts and practices. The book examines the careers of noted magicians and considers several myths regarding the devil.

COX, HARVEY. *Turning East*. New York: Simon & Schuster, 1977.   One of the best and most insightful accounts of the new "Eastern" religions in America; a sympathetic analysis of the reasons that so many young Americans have "turned East."

DURKHEIM, EMILE. *The Elementary Forms of Religious Life*. New York: Collier Books, 1961 (orig. 1915).   Durkheim's theory of the origin of religion. He viewed religion as a product of the collective consciousness of society.

GELLNER, ERNEST. *Legitimization of Belief*. New York: Cambridge University Press, 1975.   An examination of various prescientific belief systems within which science could, and did, emerge and develop.

GLOCK, CHARLES Y., and ROBERT N. BELLAH (eds.). *The New Religious Consciousness*. Berkeley and Los Angeles: University of California Press, 1976.   An attempt to shed some light on the phenomenal upsurge in religious fervor, particularly among the young, since the late 1960s.

GREELEY, ANDREW M. *The American Catholic: A Social Portrait.* New York: Basic Books, 1977. One of the best in-depth studies of Catholics in American society.

HADDEN, JEFFREY K., and CHARLES E. SWANN. *Prime Time Preachers: The Rising Power of Televangelism.* Reading, Mass.: Addison-Wesley, 1981. An interesting examination of religious programming on American television.

MCGUIRE, MEREDITH B. *Religion: The Social Context.* Belmont, Calif.: Wadsworth, 1981. An excellent introduction to the sociology of religion, examining the impact of social change and secularization on religious institutions.

WEBER, MAX. *The Protestant Ethic and the Spirit of Capitalism* (Talcott Parsons, trans.). New York: Scribner's, 1958 (orig. 1904–1906). Weber's classic work on the relation of the acceptance of Protestant values and the rise of the capitalist economic system in Europe.

WILLIAMS, PETER. *Popular Religion in America.* Englewood Cliffs, N.J.: Prentice-Hall, 1980. The author looks at the variety of religions practiced in the United States.

15

Education

In the broadest sense, all societies must have an educational system. That is, they must have a way of teaching the young the tasks that are likely to be expected of them as they develop and mature into adulthood. If we accept this definition of an educational system, then we must believe that there really is no difference between education and socialization. And as Margaret Mead (1943) observed, in many preliterate societies, no such distinction is made. Children learn most things informally, almost incidentally, simply by being included in adult activities.

☐ Goals and Functions of Education

One of the few points on which all scholars agree is that education in America today is in a state of uncertainty. Across the country there is little concurrence among school board members, principals, teachers, parents, students, and educational theorists concerning these basic questions: What should be the *functions* of schools? What *curricula* should be taught? What are the best teaching *techniques*? *Who* should determine what is taught (parents, school boards, teachers, students, or state departments of education)?

If we consider that schools are one of the major means of cultural transmission—both "vertically" (between generations) and "horizontally" (in disseminating knowledge to adults)—this lack of consensus concerning every important aspect of schooling points to something beyond the educational system itself, to a crisis in the whole of American culture. It is important to understand something of the nature of this cultural crisis before we turn to a narrower discussion of the functions of education in America today. Our pluralistic American society contains many important cultural differences among its various ethnic groups and social classes. Nevertheless, for a society to hold together, there must be certain "core" values and goals—some common traits of culture—that its constituent social elements share to a greater or lesser degree (see Chapter 4). In America, it seems that this "core culture" itself is in a period of rapid change.

As early as 1955, George Spindler (1955) saw a new set of values emerging (see Table 15.1), values prominently featuring a *relativistic approach to morality* (whatever one's own group advocates is right) and a *hedonistic, present-time orientation* (the future is uncertain, therefore enjoy the present). And in 1979, social historian Christopher Lasch (1979) diagnosed what he believed had become the dominant culture principle: America, he proclaimed, had succumbed to the "cult of narcissism," that is, to an infantile preoccupation with one's own comfort and desires. It is in the context of these exaggeratedly divisive problems of social pluralism, then, that the current state of education in America must be examined.

Manifest Functions

What social needs does our educational system meet? What are its tasks and goals? Education has several **intended** (manifest, or predetermined) **functions** and some **unintended** (latent) **functions**.

Socialization In modern industrialized societies, a distinction is made between education and socialization. In ordinary speech, we differentiate between socialization and education by talking of "bringing up" and educating children as two separate tasks. As Rhoda Metraux (1955) found, in modern society these two aspects of socialization are quite compartmentalized: whereas rearing children is an informal activity, education or schooling is formal. The role prescriptions that determine interactions between students and teachers are clearly defined, and the curriculum to be taught is explicit. Obviously, the educational process goes far beyond just formalized instruction. In addition, children also learn things in their families and among their peers. But in school their master status (see Chapter 5) is that of student, and their primary task is to learn what is taught.

intended functions The manifest or predetermined functions of education. Example: the transmission of knowledge.

unintended functions The latent functions of education. Example: child care.

Schools, as differentiated, formal institutions of education, emerged as part of the evolution of civilization. Until about two hundred years ago, however, education, because it basically did not help people become more productive in practical ways, was a luxury that very few could afford. This changed dramatically with the industrialization of Western culture. New production techniques required workers with specialized skills, and a professional and well-trained managerial class was needed to oversee factory planning and production. When the Industrial Revolution moved workers out of their homes and into factories, the labor force initially consisted not only of adults but also of children in abundance. The subsequent prohibition of child labor created the necessity for places other than the home where children could be cared for, and today the school system in its various forms stands at the center of all industrial societies.

Cultural Transmission The most obvious goal of education is to transmit major portions of a society's knowledge from one generation to the next. Sociologists call this manifest function **cultural transmission.** In relatively small, homogeneous societies, in which almost all members share in the culture's norms, values, and perspectives, cultural transmission is a matter of consensus and needs few specialized institutions. But in a complex, pluralistic society like ours, with competition among ethnic and other minority groups for economic and political power, the decision as to what aspects of the culture will be transmitted is the outgrowth of a complicated process.

A school's curriculum often reflects the ability of organized groups of concerned citizens to impose their views on an educational system, whether local, statewide, or nationwide. Thus it was a political process that caused black history to be introduced into elementary, high school, and college curricula dur-

---

TABLE 15.1   *The Emergence of New American Values*

Traditional Values	*Emergent Values*
Puritan morality (Respectability, thrift, self-denial, sexual constraint; a puritan is someone who can have anything he wants, as long as he doesn't enjoy it!)	*Sociability* (One should like people and get along well with them. Suspicion of solitary activities is characteristic.)
Work-success ethic (Successful people worked hard to become so. Anyone can get to the top if he tries hard enough. So people who are not successful are lazy, or stupid, or both. People must work desperately and continuously to convince themselves of their worth.)	*Relativistic moral attitude* (Absolutes in right and wrong are questionable. Morality is what the group thinks is right. Shame rather than guilt is appropriate.)
Individualism (The individual is sacred, and always more important than the group. In one extreme form, the value sanctions egocentricity, expediency, and disregard for other people's rights. In its healthier form the value sanctions independence and originality.)	*Consideration for others* (Everything one does should be done with regard for others and their feelings. The individual has a built-in radar that alerts him to others' feelings. Tolerance for the other person's point of view and behaviors is regarded as desirable, so long as the harmony of the group is not disrupted.)
Achievement orientation (Success is a constant goal. There is no resting on past glories. If one makes $9,000 this year he must make $10,000 next year. Coupled with the work-success ethic, this value keeps people moving, and tense.)	*Hedonistic, present-time orientation* (No one can tell what the future will hold, therefore one should enjoy the present—but within the limits of the well-rounded, balanced personality and group.)
Future-time orientation (The future, not the past, or even the present, is most important. Time is valuable, and cannot be wasted. Present needs must be denied for satisfactions to be gained in the future.)	*Conformity to the group* (Implied in the other emergent values. Everything is relative to the group. Group harmony is the ultimate goal. Leadership consists of group-machinery lubrication.)

Source: George D. Spindler, "Education in a Transforming American Culture," *Harvard Educational Review* **25** (Summer, 1955), p. 149. Copyright © 1955 by the President and Fellows of Harvard College.

One task of educational institutions is to teach basic skills and to transmit society's knowledge.

ing the 1960s. Similarly, it was political activism that caused the creation of women's studies majors in many colleges. And even though the concept of evolution is a cornerstone of modern scientific knowledge, it is political pressure (from Christian fundamentalists) that causes textbooks to refer to it as the "theory" of evolution, prevents its being taught outright in certain states, and in other states has led to government insistence that teachers give "equal time" to "other points of view."

Many people would agree that citizen input into school curricula is important because it ensures that what is taught reflects the cultural values. In keeping with this viewpoint, during the 1960s under President Lyndon B. Johnson, the federal government began to finance the creation of community boards to give poor people some control over local school curricula and the hiring and firing of teachers. State and local courts and legislatures followed this lead and in many cities mandated community-based school boards and advisory groups with significant political power. But a study commissioned by the National Institute of Education (1979) cast doubt on the usefulness of this approach. Investigating the impact of community boards on schools in Boston, Atlanta, and Los Angeles, the institute found that their actual impact had been minor. The research found that these groups typically are recruited from among the poor,

who themselves were inadequately educated and hence lack many of the skills necessary to effect substantial changes. Also, community groups typically are controlled by city governments, and educational bureaucracies have found ways to limit their influence. Perhaps for these reasons, such community groups have tended to focus on narrow and minor issues rather than on major school policies. Nor have they produced any major educational leaders who could introduce wide-ranging reforms. In fact, given the overall lack of effectiveness of community boards, the (NIE) study recommended eliminating federal and state program policies requiring them.

Academic Skills   For students not going to college, high school graduation is an extremely important juncture, as it is the point of entry into the job market, calling for the practical application of certain basic and important academic skills. Yet a study by the Carnegie Foundation (1979) found that 20 percent of all high school graduates nationwide had failed to master the "basic work skills." Other surveys of high school seniors have found that large numbers cannot balance a

cultural transmission The transmission of major portions of a society's knowledge, norms, values, and perspectives from one generation to the next. Cultural transmission is an intended function of education.

POPULAR SOCIOLOGY
How Can Professors Produce
Creative Thinking?

Harvard professor C. Roland Christensen believes that in some college and university classrooms, students are so stifled by their instructors that they display "all the active involvement of robots in heat." To be truly effective, a teacher must not only have mastered the subject matter but also has to be a strong "discussion leader." A professor should be someone who is acutely sensitive to individual students' needs, to the dynamics of learning, and who can take command of the instructional process. The following is a discussion of how this is done through the use of questions.

Asking questions is a key skill needed for "discussion teaching."

The most important skills an instructor can bring to the classroom are techniques for "questioning, listening, and responding," says David A. Garvin of the Harvard Business School. "Questioning really is the key skill requirement—it's the way the instructor manages and directs the group. We generally assume that answers are the critical thing," and that it's the instructors' role to provide them or to correct their students, he observes, but "a body of knowledge consists of questions as well as it does of answers."

In focusing on questioning as the teacher's primary tool, Mr. Garvin offers the following "typology of questions" through which teachers can guide their students in analyzing case studies and other learning material:

*Broad diagnostic questions that provide a springboard for opening up a discussion, such as "What's your interpretation [of a given situation]"? and "What's the problem?"
*Specific questions of "action or decision," calling on students to suggest, for example, what someone in a given situation should do.
*Questions of extension and synthesis, such as "How does that com-

ment tie in [with another student's comment]?" and "What are the implications [of a student's observation] for the issues we've been discussing?"
*Questions of priority or ranking: "What's the most important issue?"
*Questions that challenge and test: "Do you really believe that?" "What's the evidence to support your view?"
*Simple questions of clarification: "What do you mean by that?"
*Factual, "fill in the blank" questions, which Mr. Garvin says many teachers use too often.
*Hypothetical questions: "Suppose that instead of being the smallest company, the firm were the largest—would you change your recommendations in any way?"
*Summary questions: "What themes or lessons have emerged from this discussion?"

The main point for discussion leaders is knowing when and how to use one or another type of question. To Professor Christensen, questions are "beautiful," and he particularly likes

questions that diagnose and explore relationships.

At the same time, a teacher's ability to listen to what the students are saying forms a vital link between the teacher's questions and his or her response to the answers. Mr. Garvin gives these examples of things to listen for in a classroom:

*Particulars, content, logic, consistency, and substance.
*Nuance and tone, a raised voice, a tremor in the voice.
*The speaker's point of view and the degree of authority or doubt with which something is said.
*The speaker's degree of emotional involvement and commitment.
*How a comment relates to the overall discussion or to other comments.
*Opportunities for moving a discussion forward.
*What the class as a whole is communicating.
*What is being left unsaid.

The professor must carefully consider his or her response to students' comments. In some instances it may be best to say nothing at all, or perhaps the teacher should rephrase or highlight something a student has said. On other occasions, the teacher may want to request further comment on a point.

Questioning, listening, and responding are "very hard skills to master, but they are crucial." As Professor Hildebidle of Massachusetts Institute of Technology noted, "I would wish to be remembered less for what I knew or said than for what others figured out, in my presence, how to do. An effective teacher is one who, to an unusual degree, seems just to happen to be nearby when the dawn comes."

Source: Adapted from "College Teaching by the 'Case Method': Actively Involving Students Is the Aim," and "Asking Questions Is the Key Skill Needed for 'Discussion Teaching'," by Robert L. Jacobson, *Chronicle of Higher Education* **28** (22) (July 25, 1984), pp. 17, 20. □

checkbook, figure simple interest, name the last five presidents of the United States, or even fill out a job application form correctly. Indeed, for at least the past five years, it has been a matter of national recognition and concern that many high school graduates can barely read.

As a result of such revelations, a new "back-to-basics" movement has made great headway in recent years, despite opposition from teachers' organizations. This movement stresses the importance of basic skills such as the "three Rs," and the elimination of "frivolous electives." Widespread dissatisfaction with education at the local level and a corresponding public consensus in favor of standardized competency have led to Minimum Competency Testing (MCT), which requires that a student demonstrate mastery of basic skills on a standardized test in order to receive a high school diploma. By 1980 MCT had become law in many states, including New York, Massachusetts, and Florida, with many others seriously considering the concept.

✷Innovation   The primary task of educational institutions is to transmit society's knowledge, and part of that knowledge consists of the means by which new knowledge is to be sought.

Learning how to think independently and creatively is probably one of the most valuable tools the educational institution can transmit (see Popular Sociology: "How Can Professors Produce Creative Thinking?"). This is especially true in the scientific fields in institutions of higher education. Until well into this century, scientific research was undertaken more as a hobby than as a vocation. This was because science was not seen as a socially useful pursuit. Gregor Mendel (1822–1884), who discovered, by breeding peas, the principles of genetic inheritance, worked alone in the gardens of the monastery where he lived. And Albert Einstein supported himself between 1905 and 1907 as a patent office employee while making several trail-blazing discoveries in physics, the most widely known of which is the "special theory of relativity."

Today, science obviously is no longer the province of part timers. Modern scientific research typically is undertaken by highly trained professionals, many of whom frequently work as teams; and the technology needed for exploration of this type has become so expensive that most research is possible only under the aegis of extensive government or corporate funding. It was estimated that in 1983, $8.65 billion in federal funding would be spent

CR/© 1974 United Features Syndicate, Inc.

for research (U.S. Dept. of Commerce, 1983). In research and development, the areas of national defense, space exploration, and health research receive by far the greatest amount of support. In research alone, the leading three areas are life sciences (biological sciences and agriculture), engineering, and the physical sciences.

The achievements of government and industrial research and development notwithstanding, the importance of the contributions to science by higher academic institutions cannot be overestimated. First, there could be no scientific innovations—no breakthroughs—without the training provided by these schools. In the United States alone, 7,888 doctorates were awarded in 1981 in the biological and physical sciences and engineering, and during 1980 the combined fields of science employed 364,000 scientists in institutions of higher education (U.S. Dept. of Commerce, 1983). Second, the universities of the highest caliber continue to serve as the point of origin for some of the most significant research currently undertaken in both the biological and the physical sciences.

Latent Functions

In addition to their manifest or intended functions, the schools in America have come to fulfill a number of functions that they were not originally designed to serve.

Child Care   One latent function of many public schools is to provide child care outside the nuclear family. This has become increasingly important since World War II, when women began to enter the labor force in large numbers. As of 1982, 63.2 percent of married females with school-age children (ages 6 to 17) were in the labor force; also, 74.9 percent of divorced women work (U.S. Dept. of Commerce, 1983).

A related service of schools is to provide children with at least one nutritious meal a day. In 1975 the number of public school pupils in the United States participating in federally funded school lunch programs was 25,289,000, at a cost of $1.28 billion. By 1982 the number of pupils in the school lunch program had dropped to 23,100,000, at a cost of

$2.2 billion (U.S. Dept. of Commerce, 1983). Recent across-the-board federal reductions have established new and stringent criteria of eligibility for the program and in addition have appreciably reduced the monetary amount of government subsidization.

Postponing Job Hunting   More and more young American adults are choosing to continue their education after graduating from high school. In 1982, 34.5 percent of male and 31.6 percent of female high school graduates were enrolled in college (U.S. Dept. of Commerce, 1983). Even though some of these individuals also work at part-time and even full-time jobs, an important latent function of the American educational system is to slow down the entry of young adults into the labor market. This helps keep down unemployment, as well as competition for low-paying unskilled jobs.

Two factors point to the possibility that college enrollments may not continue at their present volume. A report by the Carnegie Council on Policy Studies in Higher Education (1979) predicts that by 1997 there will be fewer college students in American colleges and universities simply because there will be 23 percent fewer 18-to-20-year-old individuals in the national population. A more immediate and more alarming cause of decreased enrollments may be the rigor that is now being applied to the government subsidization of student loans. Strict new criteria for loan eligibility are being enforced, and in addition, higher interest rates and shorter repayment periods may mean that thousands fewer students from all socioeconomic levels will be able to afford a college education or graduate studies.

The Conflict Theory View

To the conflict theorist, society is an arena for conflict, not cooperation. In any society, certain groups come to dominate others, and social institutions become the instruments by which those in power are able to control the less powerful. The conflict theorist thus sees the educational system as a means for maintaining the status quo, and it is able to carry out this task in a variety of ways.

Social Control   In the United States, schools have been assigned the function of developing personal control and social skills in children. Although the explicit, formally defined school curriculum emphasizes basic skills such as reading and writing, much of what is taught is in fact oriented away from practical concerns. Many critics point out that much of the curriculum (other than in special professional training programs) has little direct, practical application to everyday life. This has led conflict theorists and others to conclude that the most important lessons learned in school are not those listed in the formal curriculum but, rather, are the social *attitudes and values* that schools drum into children explicitly and implicitly. This **"hidden" curriculum** is what prepares children to accept the requirements of adult life and to "fit into" the social, political, and economic statuses the society provides.

The educator John Holt (1972) lists seven lessons in "discipline" the American schoolchild typically learns—lessons that never appear in a formal lesson plan. Among these are the following:

1. Do what you're told without questioning or resisting, whenever I or any other authority tell you to do something.
2. Go on doing what you're told for as long as you're told. Never mind how dull, disagreeable, or pointless the task may seem. It's not for you to decide.
3. Do whatever we want you to do, *willingly.* Do what you're *expected* to do.
4. If you don't do these things, you will be punished and will deserve to be.

In order to succeed in school, a student must learn both the official (academic) curriculum and the hidden (social) curriculum. The hidden curriculum is often an outgrowth of the structure within which the student is asked to learn. Within the framework of mass education, it would be impossible to provide instruction on a one-to-one basis or even in very small groups. Consequently, students are usually grouped into relatively larger classes. Because this system obviously demands a great deal of social conformity by the children, those

who divert attention and make it difficult for the teacher to proceed are punished. In many respects the hidden curriculum is a lesson in being docile. For example, an article in *Today's Education*, the journal of the National Education Association, gives an experienced teacher's advice to new teachers: "During the first week or two of teaching in an inner-city school, I concentrate on establishing simple routines, such as the procedure for walking downstairs. I line up the children, and . . . have them practice walking up and down the stairs. Each time the group is allowed to move only when quiet and orderly."

Social skills are highly valued in American society, and a mastery of them is widely accepted as an indication of a child's maturity. The school is a "miniature society," and many individuals fail in school because they are either unable or unwilling to learn or use the values, attitudes, and skills contained in the hidden curriculum. We do a great disservice to these students when we make them feel that they have failed in education, when they have in fact only failed to conform to the school's socialization standards.

Screening and Allocation: Tracking   It is hardly surprising that a society's schools tend to mirror—and reproduce—its system of social stratification (see Chapter 10). In Europe, many school systems soon branch apart into parallel but unequal **tracks**—academic and social levels—typically followed by the children of different social classes. In Switzerland, for example, after attending four grades of *Primarschule*, children are separated into three groups based on academic achievement. The lowest performers finish out their compulsory education in *Primarschule* and then usually take up apprenticeships for entry into the manual trades. The middle group advances into *Sekundarschule* and from there usually into private schools for advanced

"hidden" curriculum The social attitudes and values learned in school that prepare children to accept the requirements of adult life and to "fit into" the social, political, and economic statuses of adult life.

tracks The academic and social levels typically assigned to and followed by the children of different social classes.

USING SOCIOLOGY
The Best "Jewish Mother" in the World

What factors produce scholastic success? Native ability? Effort? A superior school system? Or are there other, less obvious, reasons why some children do well while their peers perform less capably? Scholars studying cross-cultural scholastic effectiveness recently isolated a key factor they feel contributes to the widely recognized Japanese educational advantage. Their findings may surprise you, but Jewish mothers the world over will no doubt say, "I told you so."

The ten-year-old boy is not doing well in school. Despite his family's high expectations, he is about to flunk out. His mother, who is particularly upset with his scholastic performance, falls ill. The child blames himself for his mother's sickness and redoubles his efforts at school. His grades improve, and his mother's illness suddenly disappears.

The son in another family does no chores. "Why?" asks a researcher. "Because," his mother replies, "it would break my heart to take him away from his studies."

Typical Jewish mother stories, right? Wrong. In each case, the "Jewish mother" was actually Japanese. The Japanese mother is, according to researchers in the vanguard of cross-cultural studies of scholastic effectiveness, a key factor in the Japanese educational advantage. Says George De Vos, a University of California—Berkeley anthropologist who has been studying Japanese culture for 25 years, "She is the best 'Jewish mother' in the world."

Harvard University psychologist Jerome Kagan concurs. "Until her child goes to school," Kagan says, "the Japanese mother devotes herself to the rearing of the child. In verbal and nonverbal ways, she reminds the child of her deep, deep, warm feelings and that the child is the most important thing in the world to her. Then she says, 'After all I've done for you, don't disappoint me.'

The relationships between Japanese mothers and their children tend to be more intense than is the case in Western cultures.

She's like the Jewish mother who says, 'What do you mean you're not hungry—after I've slaved all day over a hot stove for you.'"

The decline of education in the United States has been well-documented. While politicians and educators all search for ways to remedy the situation, some researchers are looking to the Orient for answers. The Japanese, in particular, seem to be vastly outperforming their American counterparts. For example, in one study comparing fifth-graders in an American Midwestern city to those in Tokyo, not one of the 20 American classrooms did as well in math as any of the Japanese classes. In other words, the average score of the highest-achieving American class was below the worst-performing Japanese class. Only one of the 100 top-scoring fifth-grade math students was American.

While researchers cite many reasons for this learning gap, most agree that the values instilled in the children at home are crucial. "The Japanese mother is a very important influence on the education of her children," says De Vos. "She takes it upon herself to be the responsible agent, reinforcing the educational process instituted in the schools."

The most single-minded Japanese "Jewish" mother is known as *kyoiku-mama*, which translates roughly as "education-mama." She approaches the responsibility for her children's education with unrelenting fervor. She pushes her children to excel academically and sends them to after-school classes, known as *juku*, or to private tutors to assure good grades. Mothers are also so highly vocal in the influential Japanese PTA's that some Japanese half-jokingly suggest that the organization be renamed the MTA.

The relationship between Japanese mothers and their children tends to be more intense than is

416

found in Western cultures. As one researcher wrote, a Japanese mother "views her baby much more than do Western mothers as an extension of herself, and psychological boundaries between the two of them are blurred."

In his culture, says one Japanese professor, "the training of children is not simply a technical matter, but one that involves the deepest mutual and reciprocal relationships between parent and child."

As De Vos points out, "The Japanese are extremely conscious in their child-rearing of a need to satisfy the feeling of dependency developed within an intense mother–child relationship in order to maintain compliance and obedi-

ence. Goodwill must be maintained so that the child willingly undertakes the increasingly heavy requirements and obligations placed upon him in school and at home."

If the Japanese mother–child relationship could be summarized in a word, that word would be *amae*. While *amae* resists precise English translation, it can be characterized as love combined with a strong sense of reciprocal obligation and dependence.

Amae is at the foundation of Japanese teaching. It is the bond between mother and child, and later, child and teacher, that makes the child, according to one University of Tokyo professor, "more attentive to what others say, think and feel;

more willing to accept the intrusion of significant others into his or her learning, thinking and feeling; more likely to model after them; better ready to work together; more responsive to recognition from them; and more willing to strive for a common goal."

If Japanese math and science scores are any indication, then Japanese mothers seem to be on to something. So take a lesson from the Japanese. Don't close this book when you finish this paragraph. Make your mother happy and proud. Keep studying!

Source: Perry Garfinkel, "The Best 'Jewish' Mother in the World," *Psychology Today*, September, 1983, pp. 56–60. □

---

training in business and management. The most academically gifted students attend *Progymnasium* for five years, then usually advance to *Gymnasium* for four more. The very best of these students go on to attend universities or technical institutes in preparation for careers in academia, in the professions, or in the upper echelons of industry and government.

The Swiss approach might seem ideal in that it fits pupils' capabilities to the differing requirements of jobs, but the "catch" is that in most cases children follow educational paths that cause them to wind up in jobs or careers that are socially equivalent to those of their parents. In this way, then, Switzerland's educational system both reflects and perpetuates the social system of the wider society.

From its beginning, the American school system *in principle* has been opposed to tracking. Legislators saw in compulsory public education a way to allow each individual to rise to what was believed to be the level of his or her "innate" ability. This approach had several goals. First, it was intended to diminish the grip of inherited social stratification by providing the means for individuals to rise as high as their achieved skills would allow. In the words of Horace Mann, an influential American educator of the late nineteenth

century, public education was to be "the great equalizer of the conditions of men." The second goal of mass education, closely related to the first, was the desired "Anglo-conformity" of the crowds of immigrants whose ethnic and cultural diversity was seen by many as a dangerous source of potential social chaos (see Chapter 11). The third aim of universal public education was to give workers a wide range of skills to match the requirements of an increasingly complex industrial economy.

Despite the principles on which it is based, the American educational system utilizes **tracking**—the stratifying of students by ability, social class, and various other categories—in ways less formal but no less real than the Swiss system. Although tracking in American education is not as formally structured or as irreversible as in most other industrial societies, it is influenced by many factors, including socioeconomic status, ethnicity, and place of residence. It is also consistently expressed in the differences between public and private schools as well as in the difference among public schools. (In New York City, for example, there are highly competitive math and

tracking The stratification of students by ability, social class, and various other categories.

science–oriented and arts-oriented high schools, neighborhood high schools, and vocational high schools.) And of course, tracking occurs in higher education in the selection of students by private colleges and universities, state colleges, and junior colleges.

Tracking begins with stratifying students into "fast," "average," and "slow" groups, from first grade through high school. It can be difficult for a student to break out of an assigned category because teachers come to expect a certain level of performance from that individual. In turn, the student, sensing this expectation, will often give the level of performance that is expected. In this way, tracking becomes a self-fulfilling prophecy.

In one study of this phenomenon, Rosenthal and Jacobson (1966) gave IQ tests to 650 lower-class elementary school pupils. Their teachers were told that the test would predict which of the students were the "bloomers" or "spurters." In other words, the tests would identify the superior students in the class. This approach was in fact not the one employed. Twenty percent of the students were randomly selected to be designated as "superior," even though there was no measured differ-

ence between them and the other 80 percent of the school population. The point of the study was to determine whether the teacher's expectations would have any effect on the "superior" students. At the end of the first year, all the students were tested again. There was a significant difference in the gain in IQ scores between the "superior" group and the control group. This gain was most pronounced among those students in the first and second grades. Yet the following year, when these students were promoted to another class and assigned to teachers who had not been told that they were "superior," they no longer made the sorts of gains they had evidenced during the previous year. Nonetheless, the "superior" students in the upper grades did continue to gain during their second year, showing that there had been long-term advantages from positive teacher expectations for them. Apparently the younger students needed continuous input to benefit from the teacher's expectations, whereas the older students needed less. (For a further discussion of how adult input can affect children's educational achievements, see Using Sociology: "The Best 'Jewish Mother' in the World.")

Private schools often deliver a better quality of education than public schools. They also serve as tracks into elite colleges.

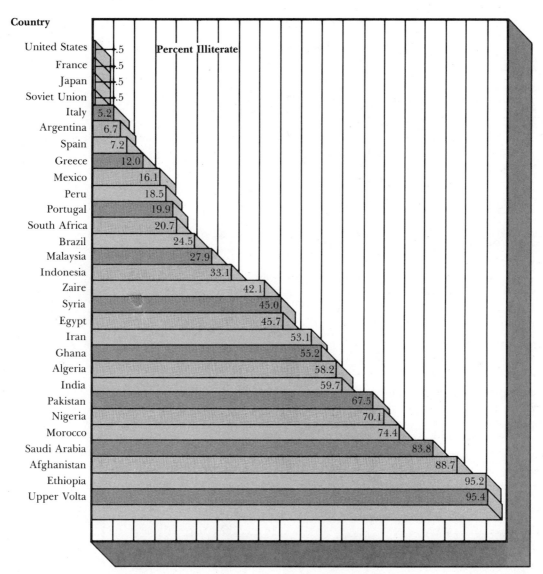

Country   **Percent Illiterate**

United States .5
France .5
Japan .5
Soviet Union .5
Italy 5.2
Argentina 6.7
Spain 7.2
Greece 12.0
Mexico 16.1
Peru 18.5
Portugal 19.9
South Africa 20.7
Brazil 24.5
Malaysia 27.9
Indonesia 33.1
Zaire 42.1
Syria 45.0
Egypt 45.7
Iran 53.1
Ghana 55.2
Algeria 58.2
India 59.7
Pakistan 67.5
Nigeria 70.1
Morocco 74.4
Saudi Arabia 83.8
Afghanistan 88.7
Ethiopia 95.2
Upper Volta 95.4

Figure 15.1 Illiteracy Rates by Country for People 15 Years Old and Over—1980

Source: U.S. Department of Commerce, Bureau of the Census, *Statistical Abstract of the United States. 1984* (Washington, D.C.: Government Printing Office, 1983), pp. 863–864.

☐ Issues in American Education

How well have American schools done in educating the population? The answer to this question depends on the standards one applies. As a nation, America has one of the lowest illiteracy rates in the world (see Figure 15.1). In 1979, illiterates constituted only 0.5 percent of the population (U.S. Dept. of Commerce, 1984), and unquestionably the general literacy of Americans is rapidly increasing. Whereas in 1960 only 41.1 percent of all Americans aged 25 and older had finished high school, by 1982 this figure had risen to 71.0 percent (U.S. Dept. of Commerce, 1984). (See also Figure 15.2.) Literacy, however, is by no means evenly distributed. In 1979, 0.4 percent of all whites age 14 and over were illiterate, whereas 1.6 percent of all blacks 14 and over were illiterate (see Table 15.2).

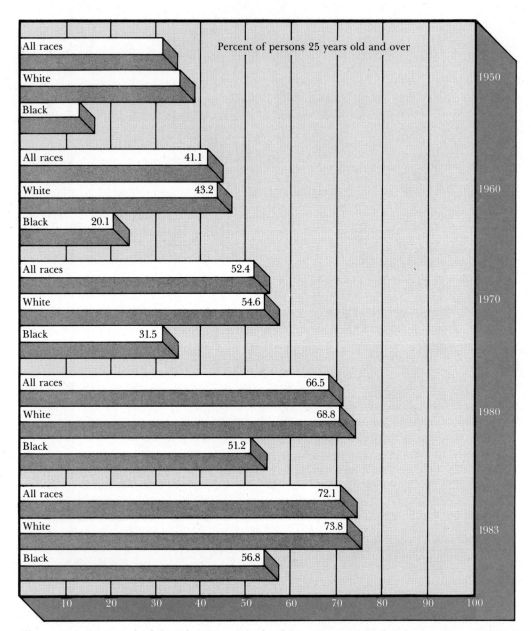

Figure 15.2 Percent of Adults Who Have Completed Four Years of High School or More: 1950–1983

Source: U.S. Department of Commerce, Bureau of the Census, Statistical Abstract of the United States, 1984 and Statistical Abstract of the United States, 1985 (Washington, D.C.: Government Printing Office, 1983 and 1984), pp. 134 and 135, respectively.

Unequal Access to Education

As a result of the Civil Rights Act of 1954, the federal government attempted to document the degree to which equality of education among all groups had been achieved. It financed a cross-sectional study of 645,000 children in grades 1, 3, 6, 9, and 12 attending some four thousand different schools across the country. The results, appearing in James S. Coleman's now-famous report *Equality of Educational Opportunity* (1966), supported unequivocally the conclusion that "American education remains largely unequal in most parts of the country, including those where Negroes form any significant proportion of the population." Coleman noted further that

TABLE 15.2   American Illiteracy—1959 to 1979

| | Percent Illiterate of the Population | | | | | | | | |
| | Total | | | White | | | Black | | |
Age	1959	1969	1979	1959	1969	1979	1959	1969	1979
Total 14 years and over	2.2	1.0	0.5	1.6	0.7	0.4	7.5	3.6	1.6
14–24 years	0.6	0.3	0.2	0.5	0.2	0.2	1.2	0.5	0.2
24–44 years	1.2	0.5	0.3	0.8	0.4	0.2	5.1	1.3	0.5
45–64 years	2.6	1.1	0.7	1.8	0.7	0.5	11.3	5.5	2.6
65 years and over	6.5	3.5	1.4	5.1	2.3	0.8	25.5	16.7	6.8

Source: U.S. Department of Commerce, Bureau of the Census, *Current Population Reports*, Series P-20, nos. 99 and 217; and *Statistical Abstract of the United States, 1984* (Washington, D.C.: Government Printing Office, 1983), p. 146.

on all tests measuring pupils' skills in areas critical to job performance and career advancement, not only did Native Americans, Mexican Americans, Puerto Ricans, and blacks score significantly below whites but also that the gaps widened in the higher grades. Now for a subtle but extremely important point: although there are acknowledged wide inequalities of educational opportunity throughout the United States, the discrepancies between the skills of minorities and those of their white counterparts could not be accounted for in terms of how much money was spent on education per pupil, quality of school buildings, number of labs or libraries, or even class sizes. In spite of good intentions, a school presumably cannot usually outweigh the influence of the family backgrounds of its individual students and of the family background of its student population as a whole. The Coleman study thus provided evidence that schools per se do not play as important a role in student achievement as was once thought. It appears that the home environment, the quality of the neighborhood, and the types of friends and associates one has are much more influential in school *achievement* than is the quality of the school facilities or the skills of teachers. In effect, then, the areas that schools have least control over—the areas of social influence and development—are the ones that are the most important to determining how well an individual will do in school.

School Integration

Another finding of the Coleman report was that lower-class nonwhite students showed better school achievement when they went to school with middle-class whites. Racial segregation, however, has made this a rare possibility. There are two types of segregation. The first, **de jure segregation**, is an outgrowth of local laws that prohibit one racial group from attending school with another. In 1954 the Supreme Court declared this form of segregation illegal. The second type, **de facto segregation**, is the much more common today. De facto segregation results from residential patterns in which minority groups often live in areas of a city where there are few whites or none at all. Consequently, when children attend neighborhood schools, they are usually taught in an environment that is racially segregated. (For a discussion of some of the unanticipated consequences of school desegregation, see Case Study: "The Quiet Death of Black Colleges.")

A direct outgrowth of the influence of the Coleman report in pointing to the harm of de facto segregation has been the busing of children from one neighborhood to another in order to achieve racial integration in the schools. The fundamental assumption underlying school busing was that it would bring about improved academic achievement among

de jure segregation Segregation that is an outgrowth of local laws that prohibit one racial group from attending school with another.

de facto segregation Segregation of community or neighborhood schools that results from residential patterns in which minority groups often live in areas of a city where there are few whites or none at all.

CASE STUDY
The Quiet Death of Black Colleges

Sometimes what seems to be progressive legislation can have dramatically different consequences than what was intended. In the 1960s and early 1970s, in an attempt to promote desegregation, a number of historically black colleges were forced, by Title IV of the 1964 Civil Rights Act, to merge with neighboring all-white schools. At the same time, formerly all-white schools began to recruit blacks, causing black colleges to lose some of their best prospective students. By the early 1980s, many black educators were claiming that desegregation had, in fact, destroyed the ethnic identity of these institutions and had actually reduced the educational opportunities available to many blacks.

In the years before desegregation went into effect, black students often enrolled—by their own choice or because of the limited options open to them—in all-black colleges and universities. Particularly in the South, a number of privately supported black colleges flourished, providing a quality education for blacks. Other state-supported educational institutions for blacks coexisted with similar facilities for white students.

Following the passage of the Civil Rights Act of 1964, it was no longer legal to segregate these institutions on the basis of race. Consequently, many formerly all-black institutions merged with white colleges and universities in the same system. All-black Maryland State College, for example, became the University of Maryland—Eastern Shore. Similarly, the University of Arkansas incorporated all-black Arkansas A & M.

By the 1980s, however, a strange thing had begun to happen. Formerly black schools like Lincoln University in Missouri, West Virginia State, and the University of

Maryland—Eastern Shore all had predominantly white student bodies. Delaware State and Maryland's Bowie State were over one-third white, and Kentucky State's student body was 49 percent white.

Private black colleges and universities, such as Fisk University in Nashville, Atlanta University, Tuskegee Institute of Alabama, and Howard University of Washington, D.C., were facing other problems as well. Black students with good scholastic records were being recruited away from black institutions. The best of the black faculty was also lured away by promises of higher salaries, smaller teaching loads, and better working conditions. Black middle-class families began sending their children to Yale, Oberlin, and Stanford, instead of to the schools from which they themselves had graduated.

As operating costs increased in the 1970s, many black private schools were forced to dip repeatedly into endowment funds to cover day-to-day operating expenses. Then, in 1982, the Reagan administration dealt black colleges another serious blow. At that time, the secretary of education ordered the end of all further student loans to institutions whose defaults in repaying National Direct Student Loans totaled 25 percent or more. Predictably, this decision primarily affected schools with large numbers of students from working-class backgrounds or from minority communities. From the vantage point of black campuses, the judgment had a major impact, as it came at a time when black unemployment was at a postwar high.

The effect of this and other

budget cuts was immediate. The director of student financial aid at Tougaloo College said that many prospective students had been forced into "military service as a way to get college money."

But the problems of black institutions transcend mere dollars and cents. The National Center for Education Statistics, a research division of the U.S. Department of Education, notes that "the number of degrees at the bachelor's level or above awarded to black students slipped 1.6 percent from 1976 to 1981, to 82,000 from 83,400. At the master's level, the number of degrees awarded fell 16 percent for blacks and only 4 percent for whites." Between 1976 and 1981, the only major gain in black college enrollment was in vocational and occupational programs.

Black leaders insist that the battle to maintain a Fisk University or an Atlanta University as an all-black center for scholarship is in no way contradictary to the demand for a desegregated, pluralistic society. The effort to maintain black colleges is, they say, the attempt to guarantee blacks access to higher education.

W. E. B. DuBois observed at the 71st anniversary commencement of Knoxville College in Tennessee in 1946: "Are [black] institutions worth saving? . . . I am convinced that there is a place and a continuing function for the small Negro College. [They] have an unusual opportunity to fill a great need and to do a work which no other agency can do so well."

Source: Based on Manning Marable, "The Quiet Death of Black Colleges," *Southern Exposure* **12** (2) (March-April, 1984), pp. 31–39. □

minority groups. Nationwide, many parents, both black and white, responded negatively to the idea that their school-age children must leave their home neighborhoods. Reactions have taken varied forms, ranging from hostile pickets who defy local and national militia to community organizations and parents' committees who persistently lobby for constitutional antibusing legislation. Busing is being continued today, but in a decreasing number of communities and often only on a voluntary basis.

One factor that has increased the difficulty of integrating public schools is so-called **white flight**, the continuing exodus of white Americans by the hundreds of thousands from the cities to the suburbs. White flight has been prompted partly by the migration of blacks from the South to the inner cities of the North and Midwest during the past two decades, but some authorities strongly maintain that it is also closely related to school-desegregation efforts in the large cities.

In a later view of desegregation attempts (1977), James Coleman vastly revised his position in his 1966 report, stating that urban desegregation has in some instances had the self-defeating effect of emptying the cities of white pupils. Some authorities (Pettigrew and Green, 1975), however, took exception to the Coleman thesis, and others believe that what may appear to be flight is more directly related to the characteristic tendency of the American middle class to be "upwardly mobile" and constantly to seek a better lifestyle. Even though there is some evidence of a countertrend in which middle-class whites are beginning to "regentrify" inner cities, there seems to be no abating of this migration. Nor have most established communities relinquished the ideal of self-determination as embodied in the right to maintain "neighborhood" schools.

The Gifted

The very term *gifted* is emotionally loaded. The word may evoke feelings that range from admiration to resentment and hostility. Throughout history, people have displayed a marked ambivalence toward the gifted. It was not unusual to view giftedness as either di-

vinely or diabolically inspired. Genius was often seen as one aspect of insanity. Aristotle's observation "There was never a great genius without a tincture of madness" continues to be believed as common folklore.

People also tend to believe that intellectualism and practicality are incompatible. It is expressed in such sayings as "He (or she) is too smart for his (her) own good" or "It's not smart to be too smart." High intelligence is often assumed to be incompatible with happiness.

There is little agreement on what constitutes giftedness. The most common measure is performance on a standardized test. All those who score above a certain level are defined as gifted, though there are serious problems when this criterion alone is used. Arbitrary approaches to measuring giftedness tend to ignore the likelihood that active intervention could increase the number of candidates among females, the disabled, and selected minorities, groups that are often underrepresented among the gifted.

Females tend to be underrepresented among the gifted because popular culture deems that high intelligence is incompatible with femininity; thus some girls quickly learn to deny, disguise, or repress their abilities. Minorities are hindered by the fact that commonly used assessment tools discriminate against ethnic groups whose members have had different cultural experiences or use English as a second language. The intellectual ability of disabled youngsters is often overlooked. Their physical handicaps may mask or divert attention away from their mental potential, particularly when communication is impaired, as this is a key factor in assessment procedures.

Teachers often confuse intelligence with unrelated school behaviors. Children who are neat, clean, and well mannered, have good handwriting, or manifest other desirable but

white flight The exodus of large numbers of white Americans from the cities to the suburbs, partially in reaction to the migration of blacks from the South to the inner cities of the North and Midwest. White flight has increased the difficulty of integrating inner-city public schools.

FOCUS ON RESEARCH
The Mystery of Child Prodigies

As in Mozart's day, the world continues to be fascinated by the phenomenon of child prodigies. But until recently, little was known about what makes these children tick or why there seem to be many at some points in history and not in others. Researchers are now investigating the phenomenon and finding that for a child to become a prodigy, certain factors must come together at just the right time and place.

Currently about 50 percent of the chess prodigies in the United States live in San Francisco, Los Angeles, and New York. In the 18th and 19th centuries, a disproportionate number of musical prodigies came out of Vienna, Austria. Why is it that some eras and areas seem to nurture a flowering of genius—even among children—while others produce little?

Recent research into the phenomenon of child prodigies has shed some light on a subject that, for all its fascination, has seen a remarkable deficit of scientific investigation. David Henry Feldman, a psychologist at Tufts University, is one of the leading practitioners in the relatively new field of prodigy research.

One of the first problems Feldman encountered in his research was defining what is meant by the term "child prodigy." Webster's dictionary says a prodigy is "a highly gifted or academically talented child." Feldman thought that definition too vague considering the many variables in the lives and traits of superbright children. He prefers to define a child prodigy as "a person who performs at or near the level of a professional at a very early age."

This definition is interesting since it speaks of "the level of a professional" instead of using the more frequently cited measures of verbal and mathematical abilities. Harvard University psychologist Howard Gardner would seem to agree with Feldman that conventional IQ tests are often not useful in identifying many brilliant and talented youngsters because they focus on only two skills, language and math.

Gardner asserts that the human mind is not a single entity, but a constellation of seven specific intelligences, each controlled by different parts of the brain. These intelligences include musical ability, bodily talent, spatial perception and personal sensitivity, as well as linguistic and mathematical skills. They develop according to their own timetables, and they operate independently, but they can function cooperatively, as well. One or more intelligences can outshine the rest, Gardner says, and musical talent is usually the first intelligence to emerge—conceivably because musical ability does not seem to require as much experience in the real world as other skills.

Feldman's research seems to corroborate Gardner's theory of multiple intelligences. In fact, he divides prodigies into at least two groups. Omnibus prodigies, he says, are those who excel in two or more fields of endeavor, whereas single-purpose prodigies, like Mozart, have one supreme gift. Single-purpose prodigies far outnumber their more versatile counterparts.

But how does any single child come to have the qualities that make for brilliance? Gardner speculates that while a youngster's potential for brilliance is transmitted by his parents, the people in his immediate family may not show any special gifts themselves. Often, however, research into the couple's family background will reveal talented relatives on either or both sides.

But good genes alone are not enough, Gardner maintains. "The potential has to be triggered by something in the environment, and it must be nourished."

Feldman concurs with Gardner's emphasis on the importance of nurture as well as nature. In fact, Feldman is the originator of the "coincidence" theory of child prodigies, which holds that, for genius to occur, "all of the things that go into it must coincide at exactly the right time, in exactly the right place, under exactly the right conditions. There has to be a cultural preparation and an appreciative audience."

Hence, we come back to the chess prodigies in New York and Los Angeles. Feldman would explain their disproportionate numbers by pointing out that the children's homes are in population centers where there are chess clubs—where interest in the game runs high. Seven-year-old chess whizzes in these cities can test themselves against other gifted or experienced players. They have been born in a period of history which believes in encouraging chess prod-

Wolfgang Amadeus Mozart was considered to be extremely gifted. In 1762 he traveled throughout Europe, where he was hailed as "the greatest prodigy that Europe or that human nature has to boast of."

igies. So too with musically talented children in 18th century Vienna, or youngsters with literary ability in Elizabethan England.

There is some evidence that the nation's population of gifted children—and possibly, prodigies—is growing. Researchers who test large numbers of children have detected a startling proportion in the 170- to 180-IQ range.

But while psychologists would agree that early exceptional ability should be nurtured in order to thrive, they do not necessarily think that the current movement to produce "superbabies" by forcefeeding a diet of mathematics and vocabulary to infants is a good idea. Pediatricians have begun seeing children with backlash symptoms—headaches, tummy-aches, hair-tearing, anxiety, depression—as a result of this pressure to perform.

History has shown that being an authentic child prodigy creates problems enough of its own. The fine line between nurturing genius, and trying to force a bright, but not brilliant child to be something he is not, is clearly one that must be walked with care.

Source: Roderick MacLeish, "Gifted by Nature, Prodigies Are Still Mysteries to Man," *Smithsonian* **14** (12) (March, 1984), pp. 71–79. □

---

irrelevant classroom traits may often be thought to be very bright.

Teachers often associate giftedness with children who come from prominent families, have traveled widely, and have had extensive cultural advantages. Teachers are likely to discount high intelligence when it might be present in combination with poor grammar, truancy, aggressiveness, or learning disabilities.

The first attempt to deal with the gifted in public education took place in the St. Louis schools in 1868. The program involved a system of flexible promotions enabling high-achieving students not to have to remain in any grade for a fixed amount of time. By the early 1900s, special schools for the gifted began to appear.

There has never been a consistent, cohesive national policy or consensus on how to educate the gifted. Those special programs that have been instituted have reached only a small fraction of those who conceivably could benefit from them. A serious problem with the education of the gifted arises from philosophical considerations. Many teachers are reluctant to single out the gifted for special treatment, as they feel that the children are already naturally privileged. Sometimes, attention given to gifted children is seen as anti-democratic.

No matter how inadequate it may seem, the effort to provide for the educational needs of learning-disabled children has far exceeded that expended for the gifted. Similarly, the time and money spent on research for educating the slower children far outstrip that set aside for research on materials, methodology for teaching, and so on, for the gifted.

When schools do have enrichment programs, they are rarely monitored as to their effectiveness. Enrichment programs are often provided by teachers totally untrained in dealing with the gifted, for it is assumed that anyone qualified to teach is presumably capable of teaching the gifted. Yet most basic teacher certification programs do not require even one hour's exposure to information on the theory, identification, or methodology of teaching such children in the classroom. Most administrators do not have the theoretical background or practical experience necessary to establish and promote successful programs for the gifted.

It appears that there are more than 2.5 million schoolchildren in the United States that can be described as gifted, or about 3 percent of the school population. Giftedness is essentially *potential*. Whether these children will achieve their potential intellectual growth will depend on many factors, not the least of which is the level of educational instruction they receive. We must question why we continue to show such ambivalence toward the gifted and why we are willing to tolerate incompetence and waste in regard to such a valuable resource (Baskin and Harris, 1980). (For a further discussion of this issue, see Focus on Research: "The Mystery of Child Prodigies.")

Adolescent Alienation

Although all educators and sociologists agree that American education in general is in a

426

state of uncertainty, some maintain that with the problems of adolescent alienation and classroom crime, we have moved beyond mere uncertainty toward crisis. A study by the Carnegie Council on Policy Studies in Higher Education (1979) found that boredom and alienation among high school students were major problems. In fact, one survey found that nearly one-half of high school graduates, when looking back on their high school experience 11 years later, did *not* consider that experience to have been "valuable" or even "fairly useful." Interestingly, almost half of today's high school students do not consider their schoolwork demanding enough. There is a feeling among these students that they are "doing time"—not unlike prisoners. The Carnegie Council found that high schools typically encourage student passivity and dependency and often fail to address their students' real social and economic needs and concerns.

In many urban schools vandalism and security problems stifle the educational goals.

Associated with alienation, alcoholism, and drug abuse, violence has become a common element of daily life in America's high schools. In 1978, the National Institute of Education reported to Congress that in a typical month, America's schools have 280,000 assaults on students and 5,200 assaults on teachers. In addition, there are 2.4 million thefts and 42,000 incidents of vandalism (Sullivan, 1979). In 1978, in the schools of New York City alone there were 1,856 assaults, 1,097 robberies, 68 cases of sexual abuse, and 317 "incidents" involving weapons (Kleiman, 1979). Classroom crime is not limited to inner-city schools; it haunts suburban classrooms, too.

Public awareness of misconduct and crime in our schools is evident throughout the United States, and the news media have left to the imagination few aspects of these problems. The combined results of surveys made over the past few years show that 84 percent of Americans consider the disciplinary system in our schools inadequate. Currently, discipline in many high schools has had to be increased to the point of constant and strictly enforced regimentation, with security guards patroling hallways and stationed on campuses, and rest rooms locked whenever not in use. Educators question these suppressive measures as a lasting solution to school crime, but as in society itself, the methods that prevail are the ones that guarantee the most safety to the greatest number of people. Young people today are being socialized to live with agents of authoritarian control constantly among them. Will this result in a generation inured to suppression and passive (although perhaps grudging) acceptance of authority? Or, alternatively, will this and successive generations learn contempt for a society that must resort to crude force to promote a modicum of public safety? Neither outcome is heartening.

Standardized Testing

In American schools, the standardized test is the most frequently used means of evaluating students' aptitudes and abilities. Every year more than 100 million standardized tests are administered, ranking the mental talents of individuals from nursery school to graduate school.

Children encounter standardized tests almost from the first day they come to school. Usually their first experience with testing takes the form of an intelligence test. These are given to more than two million youngsters each year. Students are also required to take a number of achievement tests, beginning in elementary school. High school and college seniors take college admissions tests that decide whether they will be accepted at universities and graduate schools.

Much criticism has been leveled against standardized tests. The testing services claim their tests merely try to chart, scientifically and objectively, different levels of mental achievement and aptitude. The critics charge that the tests are academically invalid and biased against minorities.

The Educational Testing Service's Scholastic Aptitude test (SAT) is the best-known college admissions test and is required by about 1,200 colleges and universities. Another 2,800 American colleges require or recommend the American College Test (ACT). Students wishing to go to graduate school are required to take other exams which are tailored to measure the ability and skills used in the field that they wish to enter.

The ETS claims to be meticulous in its test construction. The ETS hires college students, teachers, and professors to assist its staff in writing questions. Each of the approximately three thousand questions that are created each year are reviewed by about 15 people for style, content, or racial bias.

The criticism of standardized tests, however, continues to grow. Many claim that all standardized tests are biased against minorities. The average black or Hispanic youngster encounters references and vocabulary on a test that is likely to be more familiar to white middle-class students. Many others oppose the secrecy surrounding the test companies. Groups have pushed for "truth in testing," meaning that the test makers must divulge all exam questions and answers shortly after the tests are given. This would enable people to evaluate the tests more closely for cultural bias and possible scoring errors. The testing industry is opposed to such measures, as they would force it to create totally new tests for each administration, without the possibility of reusing valid and reliable questions.

No one would claim that standardized tests are perfect measuring instruments. At best they can provide an objective measure to be used in conjunction with teachers' grades and opinions. At worst, they may discriminate against minorities or not validly measure potential ability. Yet college admissions officers insist that results from standardized college admissions tests give them a significant tool to use in evaluating students from a variety of backgrounds and many different parts of the country.

☐ Summary

In its broadest sense, education has the function of teaching us what is both expected and required of us by the culture in which we live. As we grow from childhood into adulthood, we acquire the knowledge and skills that will prepare us to fulfill our own needs and those of society. Much of a child's learning occurs through socialization (being reared or "brought up"), and much also results from schooling (education). So-called primitive cultures tend not to compartmentalize socialization and education, whereas in modern Western societies socialization is distinguished as an informal activity and education as a formal one.

Every year over 100 million standardized tests are administered at all grade levels.

In America, from the late nineteenth century onward, public education has been heralded as "the great equalizer of the conditions of men," offering every individual the opportunity for intellectual, social, and material advancement to the limits of his or her innate abilities. Although many modern educators concur as to the educational system's overall responsibilities, the conflicting values of our pluralistic society have produced a lack of consensus regarding which curricula should be taught, which teaching techniques are best, and who should determine what students will be expected to learn.

The functions that the educational system serves can be divided into manifest (intended) ones and latent (incidental, or unintended) ones. The manifest functions include socialization and cultural transmission, the passing on to successive generations the norms and values of the society or group to which one belongs. Teaching academic and social skills and innovation are other manifest functions. Latent functions include child care and the postponement of job hunting by young adults.

Conflict theorists view the educational system as a means for maintaining the status quo, which has caused them to conclude that the most important lessons learned in school are the social values and attitudes that schools teach children explicitly and implicitly. This is sometimes known as the hidden curriculum. Conflict theorists also see the schools as maintaining the status quo through screening and tracking.

The United States has one of the lowest illiteracy rates in the world, though American education still has a number of problems, including unequal access to education. Although the U.S. Supreme Court in 1954 outlawed racial segregation in the schools, the ethnic makeup of thousands of American communities, particularly in the inner cities, sustains existing patterns of all-white and all-minority schools. Court-ordered busing, initiated as a means of desegregating schools and thereby promoting better academic performance among minorities, has generally been resisted by white and black parents and in some instances has caused large numbers of whites to migrate from the cities to the suburbs.

Two other current and related problems in American education are adolescent alienation and school crime. Almost half of today's high school students find school boring and lacking in intellectual challenge. It is now obvious to professionals and parents that deficiencies in school curricula and poor teaching methods have led to many of the disciplinary problems in city and suburban schools alike. These problems include violence, theft, and alcohol and drug abuse in both elementary and high schools. Although many schools have been forced to adopt "police tactics" to maintain order and safety, these measures alarmingly contradict the motives and ideals of education.

Teaching the gifted and the continued importance of standardized testing to our society are major concerns today.

Our schools reflect society as a whole. If education is in a state of upheaval because of crime, social inequality, and racial unrest, it is because these problems also confront the rest of our culture. Society produces the schools, and the schools produce the individuals who will make up society. In this way, cultural values—currently in flux throughout the United States—directly influence education, and vice versa.

☐ For Further Reading

CLARK, BURTON R. *The Higher Education System: Academic Organization in Cross-National Perspective.* Berkeley and Los Angeles: University of California Press, 1983. Clark presents a conceptual framework for the analysis of differences among systems of higher education, refines and specifies many of the concepts used in the literature, and provides a wealth of information on many substantive issues.

CLARK, REGINALD M. *Family Life and School Achievement: Why Poor Black Children Succeed or Fail.* Chicago: University of Chicago Press, 1983. Clark identifies several variables that will determine whether a child will succeed or fail in school. Success depends on whether the family has been able to teach the child social survival skills and knowledge compatible with what is required in school.

COPPERMAN, PAUL. *The Literacy Hoax: The Decline of Reading, Writing, and Learning in the Public Schools and What We Can Do About It.* New York: Morrow, 1979. An influential argument for the back-to-basics and minimum competency testing movements. Copperman argues that the decline in American children's academic skills can be traced to such causes as open education, electives in high school, and lack of authority among teachers and principals. Critics charge him with misusing and misinterpreting data.

CREMIN, LAWRENCE, A. *Traditions of American Education.* New York: Basic Books, 1977. Cremin traces the shifting patterns of educational institutions over time and shows how they have interacted with other social institutions.

FITZGERALD, FRANCIS. *America Revised: History Schoolbooks in the Twentieth Century.* Boston: Little, Brown, 1979. A fascinating look at what goes into American history textbooks and why. They are, FitzGerald writes, consensus documents—the creations of school boards, state legislatures, and special-interest groups—and are written "to tell children what their elders want them to know . . . not necessarily what anyone considers the truth of things."

JENCKS, CHRISTOPHER, et al. *Who Gets Ahead? The Economic Determinants of Success in America.* New York: Basic Books, 1979. A follow-up to Jencks's influential *Inequality* (1972) and an expansion on his theme that the schools do very little to serve their goal of equalizing opportunity.

PARKER, GAIL THAIN, *The Writing on the Wall: Inside Higher Education in America.* New York: Simon & Schuster, 1979. A witty and biting critique of higher education in general and college professors in particular. Parker suggests that both tenure and the bachelor's degree be eliminated. She hopes for a return to education in the pure sense, with no promise of a job or a degree.

SIZER, THEODORE R. *Horace's Compromise.* Boston: Houghton Mifflin, 1984. A creative weaving together of observations about life in high schools.

WALLACE, NANCY. *Better Than School.* New York: Larson Publications, 1983. The story of a family that withdrew their son from school to experiment with home-based education.

16

The Economy

It is difficult for us to look objectively at our own economic system. After all, we have grown up as a part of it and interacted with it every day. We tend to take it for granted that whenever we want to buy something such as a book, soap, or a car, we will be able to do so, without considering that a complicated economic system is required to get these items to us. The economy affects more than our pocketbooks. Our sense of well-being, social interactions, and political decisions are inextricably linked to the economy.

☐ Economic Systems

In its simplest terms, the function of the **economy** is to organize land, labor, capital, and technology for the production, distribution, and consumption of goods and services. Through the production function, we build homes, grow food, make clothing, and engage in all economic activities. We also provide such necessary human services as transportation and health care. To be useful, all these goods and services must be distributed throughout the society. We depend on impersonal distribution systems to bring us such essential items as food, water, housing, clothing, health care, transportation, and communication, all of which we consume according to our ability to pay for them.

These functions are performed in different ways by the capitalistic and socialistic economic systems. We shall study each of these systems in its relationship to the modern American economy.

Capitalism

In its classic form, **capitalism** is an economic system based on private ownership of the means of production and in which resource allocation depends largely on market forces. The government plays only a minor role in the marketplace, which works out its own problems through the forces of supply and demand.

Adam Smith is regarded as the father of modern capitalism. He set forth his ideas in his book *The Wealth of Nations* (1776), which is still used today as a yardstick for analyzing economic systems in the Western world. According to Smith, capitalism has four features: private property, freedom of choice, freedom of competition, and freedom from government interference.

Private Property Smith believed that the ability to own private property acted as an incentive for people to be thrifty and industrious. These motivations, although selfish, will benefit society, because those who own property will respect the property rights of others.

Freedom of Choice Along with the right to own property is the right to do with it what one pleases as long as it does not harm society. Consequently, people are free to sell, rent, trade, give away, or retain whatever they possess.

Freedom of Competition Smith believed society would benefit most from a free market in which there is unregulated competition for profits. Supply and demand would be the main factors determining the course of the economy.

Freedom from Government Interference Smith believed government should promote competition and free trade and keep order in society. It should not regulate business or commerce. The best thing the government can do for business is leave it alone. This view that government should stay out of business is often referred to as *laissez-faire capitalism*. (The French words *laissez-faire* are translated as "allow to act.") (For an example of the conflicts between laissez-faire capitalism and government interference, see Case Study: Profits versus Public Health: "The Cigarette Dilemma.")

In the United States the government does play a vital role in the economy. Therefore,

economy An institution whose primary function is to organize land, labor, capital, and technology for the production of goods and services.

capitalism An economic system in which private individuals and corporations determine investment decisions, own the means of production, and use the forces of the marketplace to determine prices, production, and profits.

CASE STUDY
Profits versus Public Health: The Cigarette Dilemma

Why is it that Americans can be so outspoken about the possible hazards of saccharin, hair dyes, coffee, and Red Dye #2 and so reluctant to face the confirmed hazards of cigarette smoking? The answers are complex, but one critic suggests that the economic clout of the tobacco industry is so enormous and far-reaching that few institutions (including the federal government) are willing to risk the financial consequences of alienating it.

Each year some 400,000 Americans die prematurely from diseases associated with cigarette smoke. Regular smokers increase their risk of death from lung cancer by over 700 percent, cancer of the larynx by 500 percent, esophagus 400 percent, and mouth 300 percent. The risk of emphysema for smokers increases 1,300 percent and of coronary heart disease, 100 percent. Moreover, repeated studies indicate that tobacco is more addictive than heroin is, producing very strong physical dependence.

It goes without saying that if the cigarette were being considered for introduction today, there is no way it would meet the safety criteria of either the Food and Drug Administration or the Consumer Product Safety Commission. With some 35,000 medical citations in the literature indicting tobacco use for a vast array of human diseases, why is so little being done to cope with what is inarguably the most far-reaching public health threat of this century?

One reason, suggests Elizabeth Whelan, executive director of the American Council on Science and Health, is money. Tobacco, particularly in the form of cigarettes, is Big Business in the United States. With 640 billion cigarettes smoked in 1982 at a cost to smokers of over $21 billion, the economic stakes are very high. Tobacco is grown in 22 American states and is our sixth

largest cash crop. It also supports a huge and complex supply network which extends the chain of economic dependence on tobacco to include a full spectrum of industries, including manufacturers of farm supplies and equipment, transportation, advertising, and, in turn, those who depend on these suppliers. Thus, the economic ripple effect extends from the tobacco manufacturers, to Madison Avenue ad agencies, and finally to newspapers and magazines, which derive over $1 billion annually in revenues from cigarette ads. In addition, any list of "cigarette dependents" must include federal, state, and local governments, which receive more than $6 billion in cigarette sales and excise taxes each year.

According to Whelan, there are four ways that tobacco interests flex their economic muscle when they perceive any threat to their most important product—cigarettes. First, they rely on the corporate clout of their family companies. For example, R. J. Reynolds, manufacturer of Camels, also owns Del Monte canneries and Kentucky Fried Chicken. Similarly, Philip Morris is the parent company for Miller Beer and Seven-Up. When the company's tobacco-producing divisions are feeling pressure (for example, from Congress), they rally the "sibling" companies around the cigarette flag.

Second, tobacco executives know that businesses need clients and that the tobacco empire is a very valuable client. Thus, a major chemical company that produces agricultural chemicals is part of the tobacco "family" too, because, if it spoke out on the dangers of cigarettes, it might lose those affluent customers.

Third, by teaming up with the manufacturers of other products that might be the subject of bad press or increased government regulation,

the cigarette manufacturers are constantly seeking potential allies who will stand by them in the name of Big Business and free enterprise.

Fourth, the cigarette manufacturers demonstrate their economic clout through the use of some of the most elaborate and extravagant advertising and promotional budgets in American history. Although they deny publicly that cigarettes are devastating to health, there is no possibility that the decision makers at the big five tobacco companies are unaware of the risk associated with their product. Thus, they have made a conscious decision that their own economic well-being is far more important than the health of Americans. Advertising is their primary mechanism for neutralizing the medical fears among smokers and keeping the "pleasures" of smoking in the public's mind. Though smokers today are understandably very nervous and unsure of the legitimacy of their smoking behavior, cigarette advertising reinforces them by giving them reassurance when they need it and communicating that lots of good-looking and healthy young people smoke.

Although the cost to the nation in lost taxes and other economic benefits gleaned from the tobacco industry would be very high should cigarettes be banned or otherwise regulated, the cost to society of allowing the tobacco industry to continue its present course is also very high. Smoking costs the nation each year about $11 billion in direct medical expenses and $36 billion in lost productivity due to illness and premature death. American non-smokers also pay enormous amounts of money each year for the smokers' "right" to light up.

Instead of ignoring the problem, as the tobacco industry hopes the nation will continue to do, Whelan suggests there are several ways to fight back, short of outlawing cigarettes. One way is to let those who wish to smoke do so but also to let the smokers and companies that market cigarettes assume the costs of extensive medical care, lost workdays, fire damage, and increased life insurance costs that the habit entails.

Second, both voluntary and government agencies should escalate their attempts to strengthen the warning label on the cigarette pack—and to vary it occasionally to refer to specific diseases caused by ciga-rettes. This idea appears to have been accepted.

Third, by prohibiting advertisements associating cigarette smoking with glamour, youth, and good clean fun or even eliminating them entirely except at the point of purchase, the editorial hesitancy to cover the topic of cigarettes in popular magazines might be overcome.

Finally, research on a substance that could help smokers break their addiction—a type of methadone for cigarettes—should be encouraged.

The complexity of the cigarette's ongoing devastation to public health in America sometimes appears overwhelming, as it intermeshes human frailty with a powerful industry committed to promoting that frailty at any cost. However, the costs of ignoring the problem are even more enormous—both economically and in the untold human suffering that cigarette smoking causes.

Source: Based on Elizabeth M. Whelan, "Big Business versus Public Health: The Cigarette Dilemma," *USA Today,* May, 1984, pp. 61–66.

---

the U.S. system cannot be seen as an example of pure laissez-faire capitalism. Rather, many have referred to our system as modified capitalism, also known as a mixed economy. (Rachman and Mescon, 1982) A **mixed economy** combines free-enterprise capitalism with governmental regulation of business, industry, and social-welfare programs. Although private property rights are protected, the forces of supply and demand are not allowed to operate with total freedom. The distribution of resources takes place through a combination of market and governmental forces. Because there are few nationalized industries in this country (the Tennessee Valley Authority and Amtrak are two exceptions), the government uses its regulatory power to guard against private-industry abuse. Our government is also involved in such areas as antitrust violations, the environment, and minority employment. Ironically, this involvement may be even greater than it is in some of the more socialistic European countries.

The Marxist Response to Capitalism

Karl Marx was quite critical of nineteenth-century capitalism, believing that it contains several contradictions that are the seeds of its own destruction. The main problem with capitalism, he contended, is that profits will decline as production expands. This in turn will force the industralist to exploit the laborers and pay them less in order to continue to make a profit. As the workers are paid less or are fired, they are less able to buy the goods being produced. This then causes profits to fall even farther, leading to bankruptcies, greater unemployment, and even a full-scale depression. After an increasingly severe series of depressions, the workers will rise up and take control of the state. They then will create a socialist form of government in which private property is abolished and turned over to the state. The workers now will control the means of production and the exploitation of workers will end.

The reality of capitalism has not matched Marxist expectations. The level of impoverishment that Marx predicted for the workers has not taken place, as labor unions have been able to obtain higher wages and better working conditions for the labor force. Marx thought these changes could only come about through revolution. Labor-saving machinery has also led to higher profits without the predicted unemployment, and the production of goods to meet consumer demands has increased accordingly.

Marxists have offered a number of explanations for capitalism's continued success. Some have suggested that capitalism has been able to survive because Western societies have been able to sell their excess goods to devel-

mixed economy An economy that combines free-enterprise capitalism with government regulation of business, industry, and social welfare programs. Example: the U.S. economy.

oping countries and that these sales have enabled the capitalists to maintain high prices and profits. However, Marxists see this as only a temporary solution to the inevitable decline of capitalism. Eventually the whole world will be industralized, and the contradictions in capitalism will be revealed. They believe the movement toward socialism has not been avoided, but only postponed.

Socialism

Socialism is often presented as an alternative to capitalism. **Socialism** is an economic system in which the government owns the sources of production, including factories, raw materials, and transportation and communication systems. Centralized planning, which is oriented toward output rather than profit, ensures that key industries run smoothly and that the "public good" is met. Individuals are heavily taxed in order to support a range of social-welfare programs that benefit every member of the society. Many socialist countries are described as having a "cradle-to-grave" welfare system.

Instead of the market's determining prices, under socialism, prices for major goods and services are set by government agencies. Socialists believe that major economic, social, and political decisions should be made by elected representatives of the people in conjunction with the broader plans of the state. The aim is to influence the economic system so that wealth and income are distributed as equally as possible. The belief is that everyone should have such essentials as food, housing, medical care, and education before some people can have luxury items, such as cars and jewelry. Accordingly, in socialist societies, consumer items are very expensive, whereas the basic necessities are inexpensive by Western standards.

The Capitalist View of Socialism

Capitalists view the centrally planned economies of the socialist societies as concentrating power in the hands of one group whose authority is based on party position. Any worker's disagreement with the policies of this group is seen as disloyalty to the state. The workers thus are controlled both economically and politically.

Capitalists also question the fact that if essential goods and services are subsidized by the state and the consumers do not pay their full cost, what will prevent them from using more than they are entitled to and taking advantage of the system? If the producers of goods and services are immune from competition and have few incentives, what will encourage them to produce high-quality products?

The critics of socialism believe the workers actually have very little freedom and that the centrally planned economy is ineffective, compared with a system based on market forces and individual incentives.

Democratic Socialism

In Western Europe, democratic socialism has evolved as an alternative to revolution and state ownership of the means of production. European social democratic parties have chosen to work within the democratic system. Under the parliamentary system, these parties have been able to use the electoral process to win representation in the government. They have been able to enact their economic programs by being elected to office, as opposed to the violence and expropriation of property that Marx endorsed.

In Sweden and Great Britain, some industries are privately owned, and others are state owned. For the most part, the industries that are state owned are those that are most vital to the country's well-being. The government also provides for essential needs as prescribed under socialism. Taxation in these countries is quite high in order to pay for the various programs and to prevent a few from becoming very wealthy.

Social democrats support an economy that contains both publicly and privately owned businesses. Certain enterprises can remain in private hands as long as government policies can ensure that they are responsive to the nation's common welfare. The social democrats have also attempted to appeal to middle-class workers and highly trained technicians, as well as to industrial workers.

The democratic socialism movement is an example of the convergence of the capitalist and socialist economic theories, a trend that has been evident for some time now. Capi-

Corporate directors gain control of a corporation by owning a majority of the corporation's stock.

talist systems have seen an ever-greater introduction of state planning and government programs, and socialist systems have seen the introduction of market forces and the profit motive. The growing economic interdependence of the world's nations will help continue this trend toward convergence.

☐ The United States Economy

Although considered a mixed economy, our economic system is still based on the concept of private ownership of the means of production and distribution. To understand who owns the bulk of America's private production and distribution systems, we must look at the private corporation.

Private Corporations

The most important form of business ownership in the United States, the **corporation** is considered a legal entity with rights similar to those of an individual. A corporation has the major advantage of protecting its owners from personal responsibility for business lia-

bilities. As of 1980, the most recent year in which information is available, there were more than 2.7 million privately owned corporations in America, with combined receipts of $6,361 billion (U.S. Dept. of Commerce, 1983). The power of today's corporations has evolved over the years, and one of the most important stimuli to its growth was the separation of corporate ownership and control.

Separation of Corporate Ownership and Control Big business, as we know it today, is a twentieth-century phenomenon. Before the

socialism An economic system in which the government owns the sources of production, uses centralized planning to set production and distribution goals, and heavily taxes the rich and middle class to support a wide range of social-welfare programs.

corporation The most important form of business ownership in the United States, the corporation is considered a legal entity with all the rights of an actual person. A corporation has the major advantage of protecting its owners from personal responsibility for business liabilities.

turn of the century, the country's largest companies, including DuPont, Swift, Armour, and Ford were family owned and family controlled. Men like John D. Rockefeller, Andrew Carnegie, and J. P. Morgan built industrial empires on a scale never to be duplicated. Their companies grew at such speed that by the early 1900s, family ownership and control became impractical. It was at this time that the control of the principal American corporations passed from their owners to salaried managers who decided production, marketing, and pricing policies. In addition, legal ownership was placed in the hands of thousands and sometimes millions of anonymous stockholders. By 1963 not one of the nation's 200 largest corporations was privately owned, and in nearly 85 percent of the cases no single stockholder or even group of stockholders owned even 10 percent of a corporation (Samuelson, 1976).

It would thus appear that present-day corporate ownership and control are firmly divided between company stockholders and managers, respectively. However, some financial analysts maintain that this separation is illusory; they point out that although the small group of directors of a corporation together may own as little as 5 percent of the stock, such an amount is sufficient to ensure control of the company, as the rest of the stock often is spread among so many stockholders that none owns even a fraction of that percent. As a result, the control of the typical large corporation effectively resides in one small group of top managers and directors.

•Oligopoly

Expansion and growth are key elements of American business. It is the goal of all corporations to capture increasingly larger shares of the market and thus to diminish the effectiveness of their competition. The end result of corporate expansion is corporate **oligopoly**, the domination of industries and markets by a handful of monolithic corporations.

The automobile industry is a good example of how oligopoly works. In 1904, when the auto industry was still in its infancy, 35 separate manufactureres competed with one another in the marketplace. This began to change in 1908 when General Motors was founded. By the late 1940s, General Motors and Ford had acquired most of their smaller competitors, with the result that today only four major auto makers remain in the American market. In a more current example, the Nabisco company increased its sales by 126.5 percent by merging with Standard Brands to become Nabisco Brands. As a result of this move, Nabisco soared 92 places on *Fortune* magazine's list of the 500 largest U.S. industrial corporations, from number 152 in sales to number 60 (*Fortune*, 1982).

The power of America's largest companies is expressed in the performances of "the *Fortune* 500." In 1981 the sales of these 500 companies totaled $1,773.4 billion, which was 61 percent of the nation's **gross national product (GNP)**, or the total dollar value of all goods and services produced in a given year in the United States. All together they earned $84.2 billion in profits and employed 15.6 million workers, which represented 15 percent of the nation's entire labor force (*Fortune*, 1982).

Critics of corporate oligopoly charge that corporate power of this magnitude undermines the capitalistic principle of free competition among many manufacturers. With only a few firms controlling the market, corporations no longer need to strive to provide consumers with the best products at the lowest prices. Furthermore, they can engage in such practices as parallel pricing, in which similar products from various conglomerates all are priced at approximately the same level and are essentially indistinguishable in quality from one another.

•Conglomerates

A **conglomerate** is formed when firms that produce goods in greatly diversified fields come together under one corporate head. International Telephone and Telegraph (ITT), one of the nation's largest conglomerates, includes such unrelated firms as a hotel chain, a rental car company, a bakery products manufacturer, an insurance company, a publisher, a glass company, and many others. In total, ITT operates more than 150 affiliated companies.

Conglomerate mergers first became popular during the late 1960s when approximately $14 billion in assets were acquired by companies by purchasing (merging with) other companies. Conglomerate activity declined during the early 1970s but picked up again as the 1980s approached, and in 1979 nearly $16 billion in assets changed hands through merger transactions (Louis, 1982). Unchecked, conglomerate mergers can pose serious problems to businesses and consumers alike. A sales leader can gain even more power at the expense of its competitors after becoming part of a powerful conglomerate. Mergers can also create a favorable environment for corporate secrecy and monopolization.

Multinationals

Companies that do business in more than one country are considered **multinational corporations**. Most of these companies are based in the United States and export their products abroad, but increasingly, the United States is becoming a prime market for foreign multinationals seeking to tap the vast American market. In 1980 four of the five leading U.S. multinationals, including Exxon, Mobil, Texaco, and Standard Oil of California, were oil companies (*Forbes*, 1980).

Corporations expand their activities abroad for a number of reasons. Often, they find cheaper sources of labor and raw materials, a ready market for their goods, less stringent regulations, and effective tax credits for business done abroad. Unfortunately, when unchecked by government regulations, multinational corporations have abused their power in foreign markets, by taking unfair profit margins and using exploitative employment, investment, and marketing practices. In one of the most extreme cases of this abuse, ITT worked with the United States Central Intelligence Agency to overthrow Salvadore Allende, the democratically elected president of Chile, who had begun to nationalize the commercial holdings of ITT as well as those of other U.S. corporations. (For an example of how one man has had an effect on multinations doing business in South Africa, see Focus on Research: "Big Business's South African Report Card.")

Coca-Cola has become a multinational corporation by expanding its market to every corner of the globe. This photo was taken in Greece.

Corporate Bureaucracy

Huge corporations control people as well as money. Formally organized **corporate bureaucracies** have an explicit hierarchy, definite procedural rules, and a well-maintained division of labor, employing millions of workers who are viewed as members of the or-

oligopoly The domination of industries and markets by a handful of monolithic corporations.

gross national product (GNP) The total dollar value of all goods and services produced in a given year in the United States.

conglomerate A corporation that controls many other firms in greatly diversified fields.

multinational corporation A corporation that does business in more than one nation.

corporate bureaucracy A formally structured business organization with an explicit hierarchy, definite procedural rules, and a well-maintained division of labor.

FOCUS ON RESEARCH
Big Business's South African Report Card

American business's involvement in South Africa has been a hot political issue on campuses and Capitol Hill for more than a decade. Many critics feel that American business has no place in a country whose government endorses the racist policy known as apartheid. Major corporations who are reluctant to withdraw completely from the country have sought a way to make their presence more palatable to investors and political activists back home. One solution has been to submit to a code of conduct that rates their progress toward desegregation.

Students are not the only ones worried about making passing grades. Such prestigious corporate names as Exxon, Mobil, IBM, Citicorp, and Merck submit to a yearly final exam that questions everything from their efforts to promote equality, to spending on social programs at their facilities in South Africa. Their responses are then graded—on a curve—and each year a third or more of the companies flunk. Although failure carries no tangible penalty, *F* students running South African subsidiaries risk getting a royal roasting from their corporate superiors.

This strange system was developed by Leon H. Sullivan, a black Baptist minister from Philadelphia. In 1977 he drew up a voluntary code of conduct for American companies doing business under the stifling system called *apartheid*. This code, called the Sullivan Principles, states that companies should provide desegregated eating, comfort, locker-room, and work facilities; equal and fair employment practices for all employees; equal pay for all employees doing equal or comparable work; and improved housing, transportation, schooling, recreation, and health facilities for employees, among other goals.

Companies who sign this pledge must pay as much as $7,000 per year to support the administrative struc-

Congress has considered legislation that would require all U.S. companies operating in South Africa to adhere to a set of standards contrary to apartheid restrictions.

ture that oversees compliance with the code. They also must agree to observe minimum-wage rules that do not apply to competitors outside the Sullivan club, and they must acknowledge the right of black unions to organize their workers. Another big expense is the charitable effort called for by the code. The companies have laid out $78 million over the years on schools, housing, and other social programs. In addition, some companies spend $100,000 a year on paperwork and administrative matters required for compliance.

But simply subscribing to the code and paying the required dues will not guarantee a company a passing grade at the end of the year. The real test is a company's responses on an annual questionnaire, that in 1983 covered 55 pages with 116 questions calling for both data and brief essays. The scorekeeper of compliance with Sullivan's principles is D. Reid Weedon, a senior vice-president of Arthur D. Little, the Cambridge, Massachusetts, consulting firm. Companies can

get two passing grades on their reports: "making good progress" or the less-desirable "making progress." They can also flunk. The trick is that Weedon keeps his grading system a secret and does not tell respondents which questions really count. Many answers are not graded at all. The scores, however, are published.

In 1983, 62 reporting companies passed—Ford, Coca-Cola, and Monsanto among them. Failing marks went to Carnation, Firestone, W. R. Grace, and 34 other companies. Companies fail if they do not meet the tests for the principles relating to workplace equality. But even those that do well on basic principles can fail by not spending enough on good causes.

Though the participating companies often protest that the system is riddled with inequities and misguided incentives, it does seem to be having a positive effect. The workplaces of virtually all Sullivan companies are now desegregated, and last year employers provided education or job training for some 50,000 workers. However, the glue holding together the Sullivan system is not these commendable results but, rather, the growing political opposition in the United States to South African investments.

Congress has considered legislation, supported by Sullivan, prohibiting new investments in South Africa. If passed, the law would require all U.S. companies operating in South Africa to adhere to principles similar to Sullivan's. Companies with failing grades would be subject to million-dollar fines.

Although progress has been made by the companies who subscribe to his code, Leon Sullivan is not yet satisfied. During a trip to South Africa in 1980, Sullivan spoke before some 250 executives of signatory companies. "They expected a pat on the back," he says, "but I blasted them. I *had been* to Soweto, [the bleak, segregated township in which blacks are forced to live]. I *had seen apartheid*. The gauntlet *had* to be laid. I told them that on a scale from 1 to 100 they were an 8, which was an improvement because they were a zero before."

Sullivan has spent only six days in South Africa, but insists he is kept well informed by advisers. He is content, he says, to push for reform from the United States. In meetings with companies that have subscribed to his principles, Sullivan berates them for "using the principles as camouflage" and urges them to do "more, more, more." Says a participant, "I just can't believe the way Sullivan pushes those executives around. All anybody ever says to him is, "Yes, sir. No, sir. Yes, sir."

Sullivan shrugs off the criticism of his methods. Says he, "I am not the solution to South Africa. I am only one man with moral perspectives. People may question my methods but not my intent. Nobody but my wife or God can tell me what to do." Plenty of business people bound by Sullivan's principles wish they could say the same.

Source: Based on Stratford P. Sherman, "Scoring Corporate Conduct in South Africa," and H. John Steinbreder, "The Man Behind the Sullivan Principles," *Fortune*, July 9, 1984, pp. 168–172. □

---

ganization rather than as individuals. The result, critics charge, is a dehumanized working environment in which individuals lose their sense of self-worth and pride in a job well done.

Although corporate bureaucracies have serious flaws, they are also necessary to the smooth functioning of industrial production. Without clear lines of authority, an explicit division of labor, and a formal system of rules and regulations, corporations would not be able to achieve their production goals or earn profits for their shareholders. A major reason for this is the sheer size of today's corporations. (With 741,000 employees, General Motors could not operate without a highly structured bureaucracy.)

Although recognized by our legal system as an entity separate and apart from the individuals who run them, a corporation is nothing more than a collection of people—a labor force—who have come together to produce goods and services.

□ The U.S. Labor Force

In recent years the American labor force has undergone many changes as a result of improved agricultural technology, and increases in the number of white-collar and service employees.

More Food, Fewer Farmers

American technology has changed the American farm and the American farmer. With fewer than 3 percent of the labor force employed as farm workers, America's farm machine provides more food than does any other agricultural system on earth, with a great deal to spare. Each of the nation's 2.4 million farm workers gives each American more than 2,500 pounds of grain and 256 pounds of beef each year, far more than the 1,500 pounds of grain and 126 pounds of beef produced by Soviet farmers, who make up 24 percent of the Soviet labor force. Moreover, farming capacity in the United States has increased remarkably over the years. In 1940 each U.S. farm worker was producing enough food to feed 10.7 people, but by 1982 each farmer was feeding 60 Americans (U.S. Dept. of Commerce, 1983).

Although we may take this constant food supply for granted today, only within the last two hundred years have farmers been able to feed more than their immediate families. This important aspect of industrialization has freed 97 percent of Americans to work in nonagricultural jobs.

TABLE 16.1 *Changing Job Patterns in the United States, 1958–1982*

| | Total Employed | | Percentage Change |
	1958	1982	
White-collar workers	26,827,000	53,470,000	Up 99
Professionals, technicians	6,961,000	16,952,000	Up 144
Managers, administrators	6,785,000	11,493,000	Up 69
Sales workers	3,977,000	6,580,000	Up 65
Clerical workers	9,104,000	18,446,000	Up 103
Blue-collar workers	23,356,000	29,597,000	Up 27
Craft, and other skilled workers	8,469,000	12,272,000	Up 45
Operatives	11,393,000	12,806,000	Up 12
Nonfarm laborers	3,495,000	4,518,000	Up 30
Service workers	7,515,000	13,736,000	Up 83
Farm workers	5,338,000	2,723,000	Down 50

Source: U.S. Department of Commerce, Bureau of the Census, *Statistical Abstract of the United States 1984* (Washington, D.C.: Government Printing Office, 1983), p. 417.

The White-Collar Society

There is another trend that is currently transforming the American work force. Blue-collar jobs—long the mainstay of our economy—are growing at a slower rate than are white-collar jobs. **Blue-collar occupations** require either specific skills or physical effort to produce goods and services. **White-collar occupations** include professionals, managerial, sales, and clerical jobs. In 1970, white-collar workers represented 48.3 percent of the labor force, and blue-collar workers represented 35.3 percent of the labor force. In 1982, white-collar workers had increased their share of the labor force to 53.7, and blue-collar workers represented only 29.7 percent of the labor force (U.S. Dept. of Commerce, 1983). Table 16.1 shows the degree to which this shift to a white-collar society is taking place.

To a large extent, this change is due to the explosion of technology that has transformed the workplace in recent years. Job opportunities in many old-line manufacturing industries have all but disappeared, while the same innovations have created high-technology, white-collar jobs. Despite these changes, blue-collar occupations still account for nearly 30 million jobs, and according to the Bureau of Labor Statistics, sluggish growth or not, 5 million new blue-collar job openings will swell the work force during the 1980s.

In addition to traditional white- and blue-collar jobs, service occupations are filled by nearly another 14 million workers. **Service occupations** encompass a range of jobs that center on providing a service rather than on producing a tangible product. (Hotel and restaurant workers, nurses, police officers, barbers, government workers, and flight attendants are examples of people in service positions.) Between 1958 and 1982 the number of people in service jobs went up 83 percent.

According to Irving F. Leveson, director of economic studies at the Hudson Institute in New York, the service-occupation sector is a stabilizing force in the U.S. economy. Although goods-producing industries are sensitive to economic change, service industries tend to fluctuate less than do others in employment, wages, and production (Arenson, 1982). Part of the reason for this is the nature of service commodities. When times are difficult economically, people continue using the same automobiles, stoves, cameras, and other goods that they purchased years before. In contrast, although they may cut down on some service purchases such as travel and dining out, most people continue to use essentially the same level of services in periods of economic stress. In addition, the movement of women in the labor force has resulted in an increased demand for such services as child care, restaurant meals, and cleaning (Arenson, 1982).

Along with the move to a white-collar society has come greater affluence, more leisure, better health, and longer lifespans.

Affluence, Leisure, and Health Along with the move to white-collar society has come greater affluence, more leisure, and better health. More people are employed and own homes and cars than at any previous time. In 1982, over 113 million workers were in the civilian labor force. The median family income, expressed in constant 1982 dollars, jumped from $13,308 in 1950 to $23,433 in 1982. Whereas 55 percent of all housing units were owner occupied in 1950, this percentage increased to 65.3 in 1981. The proportion of households owning a car jumped from 60 to 84 percent between 1951 and 1981. (For a discussion of a group that has been receiving attention because of its affluence, see Using Sociology: "The Homosexual Economy.")

In addition, we now are better educated than ever before. In 1981, the average individual aged 25 or older had completed 12.6 years of school—compared with 9.3 years in 1950. Americans now also have more time to enjoy their money. In 1981 the average workweek lasted for 35.2 hours, which represents a significant decrease from the 42.2 hour workweek of 1951. (See Figure 16.1 for a breakdown of median weekly salaries for various jobs.)

Americans are also living longer and healthier lives than ever before. A female born in 1982 can expect to live for 78.2 years, and a male can expect to live 70.8 years. This compares with an average life expectancy in 1920 of 53.6 years for males and 54.6 years for females (U.S. Dept. of Commerce, 1983).

In addition, the death rate per 1,000 people has been significantly reduced. In 1960, 9.5 people per 1,000 died, but by 1982, the latest year for which information is available, the death rate had dropped to 8.6. Significant progress has been made in the treatment of such medical problems as heart disease, influenza, pneumonia, tuberculosis, diseases of early infancy, congenital anomalies, and peptic ulcer, and more sophisticated treatment usually means fewer deaths (U.S. Dept. of Commerce, 1981).

blue-collar occupations Occupations that require either specific skills or physical effort to produce goods and services.

white-collar occupations Occupations that include professional, managerial, sales, and clerical jobs.

service occupations Occupations that center on providing services rather than producing tangible products.

USING SOCIOLOGY
The Homosexual Economy

Far from being spurned by the heterosexual society, the homosexual community has recently become the focus of commercial interests that recognize that courting the gay customer may be very good for business.

If the novelists Ernest Hemingway and Scott Fitzgerald were alive today, they might rephrase their legendary exchange thus: Scott, "Homosexuals are different from you and me." Ernest, "Yes, they have more money."

The affluence of the average adult male homosexual is easily explained. With neither wife nor children to support and generally without a heavy mortgage or a big insurance policy, he has a comparatively large discretionary income. If he shares his home with another bachelor, there are two unfettered salaries to pour into what has become known as the "gay lifestyle."

With the removal of criminal penalties for homosexual behavior and the accompanying decline of the need to keep homosexual preferences secret, the homosexual has come out of the closet and into the marketplace. National advertisers and retailers thus are now treating homosexuals as important consumers.

As well as having great buying power, homosexuals are proving to be trend setters in fashion. Doubt it? Think of "male" cosmetics, blow-dried hair, and ruffled shirts—all once identified with homosexuals but now sported by heterosexuals as well. To become the center of commercial attention is a rapid turnaround for a group that, scarcely a decade ago, was next to invisible.

Now that these groups of free-spending city dwellers have been identified, advertisers are beating a path to their doors. Newspapers aimed at a homosexual readership are attracting advertisements from a growing number of "straight" companies that would have regarded them as taboo a few years ago. The papers range from *The Advocate*, a San Francisco–area publication that claims a readership of 350,000, to *Gay Alaska*, with a circulation of about 1,000.

Readership surveys by *The Advocate* and other gay papers have confirmed the comparatively large disposable income of the homosexual community. One survey found that 36 percent of the readers of *The Advocate* earned over $35,000 in 1980; 40 percent owned two or more cars; and 87 percent had full-time jobs. A survey by the British publication *Gay News* showed that English homosexuals share their American counterparts' interest in leisure and luxury products. A typical reader of *Gay News* eats more meals in restaurants than does the average householder, buys more books, goes to the theater more often, and is far more likely to buy such products as video recorders and home computers. British homosexuals buy more wine and spirits than heterosexuals do and take more vacations abroad. But they buy far fewer tickets to sports events.

Real estate agents are especially happy to do business with the gay community. A study by the Kinsey Institute in the San Francisco Bay Area showed that homosexuals were generally welcome as tenants, as landlords expected them to use their income and recognized decorating skills to improve the property.

The homosexual property owner has also been a key factor in the gentrification of decaying sections of inner cities. In Washington, D.C., areas such as Foggy Bottom, Capitol Hill, and Shaw, where families with children feared to tread, gay buyers have bought and restored decaying town houses to a semblance of their former grandeur.

In today's more tolerant climate, homosexuals are openly engaged in commerce far outside the stereotypical trades of hairdressing, interior decoration, and nursing. Some 17 homosexual business associations have been set up in the United States, headed by the National Association of Business Councils.

Homosexuals can now conduct from other homosexuals almost every transaction in their lives. Business directories list homosexual real estate agents, doctors, lawyers, tax accountants, and psychotherapists. The Spartacus International Gay Guide lists homosexually oriented hotels, bars, and saunas around the world from Afghanistan to Zambia, with a special member's club card to businesses offering discounts to members. Like other minorities, some homosexuals prefer to do business only with one another. As one printer in Boston said, "I hire only gay people. A lot of gay young people have to move away from home, and they have trouble finding a niche in a big city. Giving them jobs is what I can do to help."

Although accurate statistics on the size of the gay population are hard to come by, the homosexual community is becoming increasingly visible because of its spending patterns. And these show them to be an attractive market target: unmarried, childless, concerned with career and self-enhancement, and with the income to indulge their taste and style.

Source: Based on "The Homosexual Economy," *The Economist*, January 23, 1982, pp. 71–72. ☐

Women in the Labor Force

In just 22 years, the number of women holding jobs outside the home has more than doubled, from less than 22 million in 1960 to nearly 48 million in 1982. With 63.1 percent of all women over the age of 15 working, women now constitute 42.7 percent of the labor force. (See Table 16.2 for a comparison of these labor force participation rates in selected countries around the world.) This rise reflects such factors as a change in attitude toward the role of women in society, high divorce rates, women's search for professional satisfaction, the later average age of marriage, and the need for two incomes instead of one.

It seems that there has been a massive influx of women into the labor force. A significant proportion of this growth is primarily due to a drop in the exit rate of women from the work force. In the past women would work for a certain period of time and then devote themselves to family matters. Now more women tend to remain in their jobs for the reasons stated above. For a discussion of an idea whereby women would be reimbursed for their homemaking efforts, see Popular Sociology: "Paid Homemaking: An Idea Whose Time Has Come?"

Unfortunately, despite their numbers, women have shown little success in equalizing entrenched discriminatory pay patterns. Women's pay scales continue to be considerably lower than those for men. Part of the reason for this is the concentration of women in low-paying clerical and service jobs. But women must also contend with the discriminatory practices that pay them less than they do men, even when they have the same educational and work experience.

◆Comparable Worth

You have probably noticed that there are wide discrepancies in pay for jobs that seem to require similar levels of skill and training, a fact that has caused some people to call for a system of comparable worth. The idea of comparable worth, or pay equity, as it is sometimes called, rests on three propositions. First, that it is possible to compare jobs, even if they are totally dissimilar, and establish some ap-

Characteristic	Wage
All Workers	$309
Male	371
16–24 years old	231
25 years and over	403
Female	241
16–24 years old	194
25 years and over	257
White	317
Male	382
Female	244
Black	247
Male	281
Female	223
Hispanic origin	242
Male	272
Female	207

Occupation	
Professional and technical	410
Managers, administrators	430
Salesworkers	317
Clerical workers	248
Craft and kindred workers	375
Operatives, except transport	252
Transport equipment operatives	323
Nonfarm laborers	243
Service workers	203
Farmworkers	190

Figure 16.1 Median Weekly Earnings of Full-Time Wage and Salary Workers—1982

Source: U.S. Bureau of Labor Statistics, Bulletin 2096, and *Employment and Earnings,* monthly, as reported in U.S. Department of Commerce, Bureau of the Census, *Statistical Abstract of the United States, 1984* (Washington, D.C.: Government Printing Office, 1983), p. 434.

propriate pay relationship between them. Second, pay relationships that have been established by supply and demand are frequently inequitable and discriminatory, particularly with respect to women's pay. Third, the government must intervene in order to ensure that pay relationships are correct. The

443

TABLE 16.2   Labor Force Participation Rates of Females in Selected Countries—1982–1983

Country	Labor Force Participation Rate (%) 1982	Females as Percent of Total Labor Force 1983
United States	61.4	43.0
Canada	58.9	41.5
France	52.9	39.3
Germany, F.R.	49.8	38.4
Italy	40.3	34.2
Japan	55.9	39.5
Sweden	75.9	46.6
United Kingdom	57.7	39.6

Source: U.S. Department of Commerce, Bureau of the Census, *Statistical Abstract of the United States 1985* (Washington, D.C.: Government Printing Office, 1984), p. 852.

comparable worth idea is an extension of the federal Equal Pay Act of 1963, which required employers to pay men and women equally when they do the same job. Proponents of the comparable worth idea wish to extend this proposition to dissimilar jobs that are nevertheless deemed to be comparable in value.

In order to establish which jobs are comparable, the employer would hire one of the many consulting firms that specialize in job evaluation studies. The consultant would rank the jobs according to a variety of criteria, such as knowledge and skill required to do the work, the accountability of the person doing the job, and any hazards or unpleasantness associated with the work.

These aspects would then lead to a total point score for each job, and the points would determine the range for the job's base pay. If after the evaluation, jobs thought to be comparable had different pay scales, it would be assumed that an inequity existed. For example, if jobs predominantly held by men paid more than comparable jobs held by women, it could be an example of sex discrimination.

Studies have shown that women's work has been underpaid. When a comparison was made between job categories that were either predominantly (70 percent or more) male or predominantly female, it was found that male jobs paid about 20 percent more on the average after adjustment for point scores. By and large there has been no overall gain for women's pay, relative to men's.

Among the problems with the comparable worth system is the inherent subjectivity in the job evaluations. Job evaluation consultants inevitably differ among themselves on what factors to measure and what weights to assign to the different factors. Another problem with the job evaluation scores is that they do not take into account labor market issues. What if two jobs turned out to be of comparable worth, but one was hard to fill and the other had an endless supply of applicants? For example, a San Jose, California, study

Studies have shown that traditionally female job categories have had low salaries.

POPULAR SOCIOLOGY
Paid Homemaking: An Idea Whose Time Has Come?

Feminists have long decried the fact that work that earns no pay earns no respect and no power. No work demonstrates this truism better than homemaking does, a labor that is unremitting but financially unrewarded in our society. In an age when many families are being forced to take a hard look at the social and economic costs of the two-career household, it may be time to consider whether we should not have a national policy that would reward a parent for staying home to care for his or her child.

Americans love their children. In fact, everyone from politicians to greeting card manufacturers likes to refer to them as our "most precious national resource" or rhapsodize about how they immeasurably improve the quality of a couple's life.

But parents in the United States have no economic incentive to care for their children at home. If that strikes no one as strange, it is only because our nation takes it for granted that economic incentives belong in the marketplace and that other motives explain behavior at home. So, full-time care for a "price-less" child by that child's natural parent in a supportive home environment is unrewarded economically.

Much has been written about the advent of the two-career family and the problems that face working parents in finding suitable day care for their children. Often, it has been found, women would like to stay at home with their small children, but family finances preclude that option. Hence, presence (or absence, depending on your point of view) is the coin in which the parent–child relationship pays the price for two-paycheck marriages, or for one-parent households in which the parent is employed outside the home.

Some people have begun to question whether this arrangement is really advantageous to children, to

parents, or even to society as a whole. They suggest that instead of forcing the child's best care provider—his or her parents—out of the home to earn money, some arrangement might be made whereby the care provider is compensated for his or her labor at home. Think of it as a G.I. Bill for parents.

One such plan was proposed by Neil Gilbert in his book *Capitalism and the Welfare State* (Yale University Press, 1983). Gilbert proposes that the full-time homemaker receive a "social credit" for each year spent at home with children who are under 17 years of age. According to this plan, the accumulated credits would either pay for higher education or entitle the homemaker to preferred hiring status in the Civil Service once the children were raised and the parent was ready to enter or reenter the labor market. Gilbert specifies the federal government as the provider of this benefit that, like a veteran's benefit, would compensate the homemaker for time spent out of the work force but in service to the nation.

In Gilbert's scheme, each unit of social credit (one child per year of full-time care) could be exchanged for "(a) tuition for four units of undergraduate academic training, (b) tuition for three units of technical school training, (c) tuition for two units of graduate education, or (d) an award of one-fourth of a preference point on federal civil service examinations." In this scenario, the parent is the beneficiary of the tuition credits. The policy might be even more attractive if the homemaker's child could be the one to receive the credits when he or she was ready for college.

The social-credit idea bars no parent, male or female, from opting for paid employment outside the home. It does not even discourage

outside work. It simply provides an incentive to parents who might prefer homemaking to labor market activity. It also answers the need of those parents who bring home the second paycheck just "to put the kids through college." Under this plan, they would stay home, accumulate the social credits, and eventually redeem them in tuition payments.

The program would be more flexible, and thus more practical and attractive, if parents could alternate on the full-time homemaker responsibility. In effect, the parents would commit themselves as a couple to the provision of one full-time homemaker's services each year, from the birth of a child until his or her 17th birthday. Such a shared responsibility for earning social credits through homemaking could promote cooperation over career competition between spouses in the modern marriage.

Critics of the policy might well suggest that it is a middle-class program that neglects the needs of the working poor who, credits or not, cannot afford not to work. Such criticism is quite fair. It also demonstrates the need for a national family policy that would encourage flexible work schedules, make day care facilities more widely available, and make child care expenses more readily deductible.

The proposal is clearly intended to reinforce the nuclear family unit by rewarding a parent for remaining at home. As a policy idea, it will go nowhere unless there is widespread conviction that society needs the services of full-time homemakers.

Source: Based on William J. Byron, S.J., "Paid Homemaking: An Idea in Search of a Policy," *USA Today* **113** (2740) (July 1984), pp. 84–86. □

The problem of unemployment is particularly acute for teenagers. In 1983 the unemployment rate for males aged 16 to 19 averaged over 22 percent.

showed that librarians and electricians had comparable worth and therefore were entitled to the same pay, about $3,000.00 a month. However, this salary is about $300.00 a month more than it needs to be to hire and retain first-rate librarians. Meanwhile it is too low to hire electricians, since they are in big demand in Silicon Valley, a short distance away. The solution was to pay the librarians even more than the $3,000.00 a month in order to reach a level that would also attract the electricians. A third problem with the comparable worth proposal is that in order to be completely fair, it should attempt to adjust the pay levels in all jobs; that is, there should also be reductions in pay for certain kinds of jobs. At the moment, proponents of this plan are mostly concerned with raising the pay level of jobs held by women.

It appears unlikely that a comprehensive system of comparable worth will be instituted in the near future, but it is likely that we shall see special "equity" raises for certain kinds of jobs that have been traditionally held by women (Seligman, 1984).

Youth in the Labor Force

There are two distinctly different faces of youth in the American work force today. The first, born at the end of the "baby boom" of the late 1950s and 1960s and now attending college, graduate school, or already in the work force, is better educated than any previous generation our country has known. The second, consisting of teenagers who have dropped out of high school, is unemployed and largely unemployable. These two groups have little else in common except youth.

A positive picture of youth in the work force emerges if we analyze adults in the population bulge between 25 and 44 years of age. In 1960, the median years of school completed by whites over 25 years of age was 10.9 and by blacks, 8.0. By 1982 the number of years of schooling completed by each group had jumped to 12.6 and 12.2, respectively. Today, most Americans finish or nearly finish high school, a trend that has unquestionably affected youth of every socioeconomic class. With more years of better education behind them, young people are expecting to get more satisfying, higher paying jobs than their parents have. (However, as will be seen later in this chapter, they often are disappointed.)

The problem of unemployment is particularly acute for teenagers. In 1983, the unemployment rate for males 16 to 19 averaged 22.4 percent. The situation was far worse for black males than for whites: The rate of unemployment among black teenage males was 48.5 percent—twice that for all teenagers (U.S. Dept. of Commerce, 1984).

This picture is likely to continue in the years ahead, as the demand for unskilled labor in manufacturing industries continues to decline and as increasing numbers of teenagers leave school functionally illiterate and with no employable skills.

There are more than 174,000 unions in the United States representing a wide variety of workers.

Labor Unions

As the size and power of corporations in the United States grew, workers needed a means to protect themselves against the sometimes unfair, unequal, and inhuman treatment they received at the hands of their employers. Realizing that power was possible only if they united, the workers formed **labor unions** in order to bargain collectively for higher wages, better working conditions, job security, fringe benefits, and grievance procedures.

There are more than 174,000 separate collective bargaining unions in the United States, representing 21,784,000 workers throughout the country. Unions represent approximately 19 percent of the 113.6 million workers in the labor force, with the greatest concentration of union membership and power held by the nation's eight largest unions (U.S. Dept. of Commerce, 1984).

Contract negotiations between unions and corporate management are a give-and-take process. Neither side gets—or expects—exactly what is asked for when the talks begin, but most often settlements are reached, and labor-management peace is assured for the term of the contract. When talks break down, unions have the ultimate weapon of a strike, or work cessation, at their disposal. Used as a last resort to pressure management to come to terms, strikes can cause extreme difficulties on both sides. Companies can no longer produce the goods and services that keep them in business, and workers are left with no means of earning a living.

Although its impact in the economy remains substantial, the union movement has fallen upon hard times in recent years. During the past two decades, unions have experienced either no growth or a loss of growth, and they now represent the smallest share of the U.S. labor force since World War II. Blue-collar unions, such as the United Steel Workers of America, have sustained the harshest effects. Plant closings in the auto, steel, rubber, and trucking industries, for example, have caused widespread unemployment, with a decline in union membership. Moreover, as such plants reopen and as other plants modernize, automation will take a further toll on blue-collar union membership. Experts predict that within the next 15 years, approximately 25,000 blue-collar workers will lose their jobs to robots. Although twice as many jobs will be created in the robot industry itself, unfortunately, many of these jobs will be for skilled technological workers rather than unskilled workers (*Money*, 1982).

labor union An organization of workers who have united in order to bargain collectively for higher wages, better working conditions, job security, fringe benefits, and grievance procedures.

Many of the growth industries in the white-collar, technological fields of computers and electronics have long been outside organized labor's domain. As these industries continue to expand, unions will have an increasingly difficult time maintaining their slice of the work-force pie. Their only ray of hope lies in the expansion of such service industry unions as the American Federation of State, County, and Municipal Employees (AFSCME), whose membership more than tripled between 1968 and 1980 (U.S. Dept. of Commerce, 1984).

These trends have caused unions to rethink many of their long-held goals. Instead of pushing for the big wage and benefit "packages" common in the 1960s and 1970s, unions are now focusing on job security as their key bargaining element. Unions such as the United Auto Workers and the Teamsters have actually given back some of their earlier gains in order to keep plants open and jobs secure. AFL-CIO President Lane Kirkland summed up the current plight of the union movement when he said in an address in 1982: "We are here to struggle for the elevation of the condition of working people, and nobody ever told us it would be easy. . . . One of the poorest services a union can do for its members is to negotiate a beautiful agreement with marvelous conditions and no jobs."

Professional Organizations Most professionals in the U.S. work force are not unionized. Rather, they form such **professional organizations** as the American Medical Association, the American Bar Association, and the National Education Association, in order to further their common interests. Such organizations may endorse political candidates who share their views and may lobby for or against legislation that affects their membership.

☐ The Role of Government in the Economy

Workers and corporations alike must contend with the enormous power of government to regulate economic activity and bring about desired economic goals. Like it or not, government is an essential ingredient in our cap-italistic economy. By issuing money and credit it makes economic activity possible; by settling cases in its judicial system it makes contracts binding and private property inviolate; by regulating business activity it protects businesses, workers, and consumers from illegal competitive practices; by buying products it employs workers throughout the economy and stimulates economic growth; and by taxing or not taxing profits it influences nearly every aspect of economic activity. As we examine some of the ways in which government makes its presence felt in the economy, our focus turns to a pivotal question: How much government is enough?

Regulation and Control of Industry and Trade

Federal intervention in the economy began during the 1800s when at the initiation of business, government began to build roads, railroads, and canals to facilitate the transport of goods and workers throughout the country and also began regulating banks, credit, and the circulation of money to establish security in the economic system. It was at this time, too, that Americans began to feel the need for governmental protection against unscrupulous business leaders. Left unchecked, many of these large firms expanded and formed oligopolies, practiced discriminatory employment, exploited workers, wasted valuable natural resources, and bribed and pressured high government officials in order to attain their goals. As a result, the first protective regulations regarding industry and trade were passed. (As early as 1906, government regulations protected consumers from contaminated foods and dangerous drugs.)

Today, governmental regulations extend into nearly every aspect of our nation's economic life. Fifty-four regulatory agencies set rules in such diverse areas as radio and television station licensing, fuel efficiency and safety standards for cars and trucks, licensing and control of nuclear power plants, and the protection of employees against on-the-job accidents in some 3.5 million work situations. The economy spends billions each year on government rules and regulations, a cost that usually must be passed along to the consumer. When, for example, General Motors spends billions of dollars to improve the crash resistance of its car bumpers, that cost is transmitted to consumers in the form of higher automobile prices. And the money spent by industries to meeting government clean air requirements is quickly translated into higher utility bills, more expensive washing machines, and so on.

Control of Money Flow

The ebb and flow of economic activity that causes recession or boom does not simply happen but is manipulated in certain important ways by the government's monetary and fiscal policies.

Monetary Policy   Early in the century, when bank failures were rampant and the resulting personal and business bankruptcies ruinous, the federal government passed the Federal Reserve Act to control the availability and flow of money in the economy. As a result of this act, the Federal Reserve System was established to regulate the U.S. banking system and control the country's supply of money and credit to ensure economic growth and a stable dollar. The Federal Reserve, which is also known as the "Fed," attempts to control economic cycles through three distinct **monetary policies.**

Through its **reserve requirements**, the Federal Reserve determines the amount in a bank's checking and saving accounts needed to be retained as security for the deposits it accepts from customers. By increasing the reserve requirement, the Fed decreases the amount banks have available for consumer and business loans. By decreasing this requirement, it makes money more available.

The Fed also uses an **open-market operation**, which buys and sells government securities to control the money supply. When it buys U.S. Treasury obligations on the open market, it increases the money supply available to banks, thereby making consumer and business loans more readily available. When it sells U.S. Treasury securities, it decreases the money supply.

Finally, the Fed manipulates the national money supply through its **discount rate**—the rate of interest charged to banks making loans. When the Fed's member banks need money, they come to the Fed, which acts as their central source of funds. When faced with a high discount rate, which makes the money they borrow more expensive, banks are discouraged from issuing new consumer and business loans. A low rate, on the other hand, makes the cost of money cheaper and encourages greater loan activity.

Fiscal Policy   Government **fiscal policy** attempts to influence economic activity by raising and lowering levels of government spending, borrowing, and taxing. The government can stimulate the economy by spending more money than it collects. The extra money the government puts into the economy increases consumer and business demands for products and services. To slow economic activity, the government takes the opposite tack, tightening its budget purse strings and increasing taxes.

Our system of progressive income taxes, which levies higher taxes on higher incomes, also influences economic activity. In prosperous times, when business activity and consumer spending are higher, federal taxes take a large share of earned income, which helps dampen inflationary pressures. When, on the other hand, business and consumer activity are slow, less tax money is collected, which in

professional organization A formal organization that attempts to further the interests of its members, who are professionals. Example: the American Medical Association.

monetary policy The controls set forth by the Federal Reserve System to control the supply of money and credit in the economy.

reserve requirements One of the three primary monetary policies of the Federal Reserve, reserve requirements determine the amount in a bank's checking and savings accounts that must be kept as security for deposits.

open-market operation One of the three primary monetary policies of the Federal Reserve, the open-market operation buys and sells government securities.

discount rate One of the three primary monetary policies of the Federal Reserve, the discount rate is the interest charged by the Fed to banks making loans.

fiscal policy Government policy that attempts to influence economic activity by raising and lowering levels of government spending, borrowing, and taxation.

turn encourages consumer and business spending. This result can also be achieved by lowering the tax rate.

Special-Interest Groups

The government does not make its spending and policy decisions in a vacuum. It is subject to interest-group pressure from major corporations, labor unions, professional organizations, and civil rights organizations, among others, all of which try to maintain or increase programs that are favorable to them. The American Council of Life Insurance, for example, attempts to influence government leaders on behalf of the country's life insurance companies. The AFL-CIO works on behalf of the millions of union members. And the American Bar Association attempts to enhance the interest of lawyers.

Much of the pressure that interest groups exert on government occurs during political campaigns. Interest groups such as the American Medical Association and the AFL-CIO contribute millions of dollars to congressional candidates whom they feel will champion their interests once they are in office. These contributions are intended to create a feeling of indebtedness in government leaders who believe—rightly or wrongly—that they could not have been elected without interest-group support.

The monetary and fiscal policies chosen by a president to improve the nation's economy benefit some groups more than others. These policies, which are a reflection of the president's political philosophy, may favor business, the working class, or the poor in need of government assistance, for example. Critics of the Reagan administration charge that current governmental policies are slanted to promote corporate interests and to diminish social welfare programs. Instead of helping those in need, the Reagan administration has shifted the country's economic focus back to the military-industrial establishment.

The Military-Industrial Complex

The military and industrial segments of the economy are inextricably linked through Defense Department contracts that invest billions of dollars each year in private industry and local economies. Between 1982 and 1987 the Pentagon is expected to spend $1.3 trillion dollars, a great part of which will go directly into the coffers of private industry (*U.S. News & World Report*, 1982).

It is an established economic fact that such "defense dollars" are the lifeblood of many states. In California alone, defense spending accounted for $16.7 billion of corporate income during 1981, which translates into thousands of jobs, billions in employment income, and millions in tax revenues. Experts estimate that the Pentagon's projected defense spending in 1982 alone will create 330,000 jobs nationwide and that many more jobs will be spawned as an indirect result of this activity. At the Lockheed plant at Marietta, Georgia, for example, a Pentagon contract to build 50 C-5 transport planes promises to pump $5 billion and 7,000 new jobs into the economy. And at California's Rockwell International Corporation, a $2.2 billion contract for the B-1 long-range bomber created more than 4,100 jobs (*U.S. News & World Report*, 1982).

The comingling of military and industrial power raises questions about whether it is possible to make military decisions independently without being influenced by the related economic consequences. That is, when millions of people have a vested interest in building fighter bombers, guns, and aircraft carriers, it becomes difficult for politicians to support reduced military spending.

☐ Specialization and Economic Interdependence

The operation of world economics is comparable in many ways to the practice of modern medicine. We exist in an era of specialization that makes our economy unable to operate without considerable help from many other countries.

The peak of U.S. self-sufficiency occurred immediately after World War II when most of the world's manufacturing facilities, advanced technology, and capital were located in this country. Since then, we have come to realize that such economic self-sufficiency may not be in our nation's best interest. We

Japan can manufacture automobiles far more cheaply than the United States because of significantly lower labor costs. Here we see workers in a Toyota factory.

may not always have the raw materials, cheap or skilled labor supply, or climate to produce goods in the most efficient way. Although we are the world's undisputed agricultural leader, for example, we are no longer competitive with Japan and other Far Eastern countries that can manufacture automobiles, apparel, and other products far more efficiently than we can. In fact, some critics have suggested that the United States try to emulate the Japanese system.

The result of this specialization is world economic interdependence that makes the United States the trading partner of almost every other country. This usually works to our advantage—we generally receive the raw materials and finished products we want when needed and at the prices desired—but interdependence also has its negative side. For example, the 1973 OPEC oil embargo, which caused the price of oil to jump more than 300 percent, also produced severe inflation and recession in the United States and other countries.

We repeat the same pattern of specialization and economic interdependence within our own country among individuals and businesses. The work we do in producing specialized goods and services enables us to earn money to buy the food, clothing, housing, and other products and services produced by other workers. When we lose our jobs and stop buying, we send shock waves throughout the entire economy.

☐ Summary

The function of the economy is to organize land, labor, capital, and technology for the production, distribution, and consumption of goods and services. These functions are performed in different ways by the capitalist and socialist economic systems. In its classic form, capitalism is an economic system based on private ownership of the means of production and in which resource allocation depends largely on market forces. The government plays only a minor role in the marketplace, which works out its own problems through the forces of supply and demand. Adam Smith is regarded as the father of modern capitalism.

Many have referred to the system of capitalism that exists in the United States as a mixed economy, which combines free-enterprise capitalism with governmental regulation of business, industry, and social welfare programs.

Socialism is an economic system in which the government owns the sources of production, including factories, raw materials, and transportation and communication systems. Socialists believe major economic, social, and political decisions should be made by elected representatives of the people in conjunction with the broader plans of the state.

In Western Europe, democratic socialism has evolved as an alternative to socialism. European social democratic parties have chosen to work within the democratic system. They have been able to enact their economic programs by getting elected to office, as opposed to the violence and expropriation of property that Marx endorsed.

The most important form of business ownership in the United States, the corporation is considered a legal entity with rights similar to those of an individual. If corporations expand too far, the end result is oligopoly, the domination of industries and markets by a handful of monolithic corporations.

A conglomerate is formed when firms that produce goods in greatly diversified fields come together under one corporate head. Companies that do business in more than one country are considered to be multinational corporations.

In recent years, the American labor force has changed as a result of improved agricultural technology and increases in the number of white-collar and service employees. The American people now have more affluence and leisure, and better health.

In just 22 years, the number of women holding jobs outside the home has more than doubled. The idea of comparable worth has been presented, based on the fact that pay relationships established by supply and demand are frequently inequitable and discriminatory, particularly with respect to women's pay.

Labor unions exist in order to bargain collectively for higher wages, better working conditions, and job security. Most professionals are not unionized; rather, they form professional organizations.

The government exerts enormous power over the economic activities of corporations and individual workers, regulating nearly every aspect of the nation's economic life and also controlling the nation's flow of money through federal monetary and fiscal policies. The Federal Reserve attempts to maintain a healthy economy through its reserve requirements, open-market operation, and discount rate. The government's fiscal policy attempts to influence economic activity by raising and lowering taxes and the level of government spending and borrowing. Government spending decisions are subject to interest-group pressure from a variety of sources. This pressure is especially powerful from the military-industrial complex.

☐ For Further Reading

BECKER, GARY S. *The Economic Approach to Human Behavior*. Chicago: University of Chicago Press, 1977. Becker presents fascinating economic models to account for complex forms of social behavior.

DURKHEIM, EMILE. *The Division of Labor in Society*. New York: Free Press, 1933. A classic sociological work that presents a theory of capitalist development. This book is interesting because of its historical significance.

FRIEDMAN, MILTON. *Free to Choose*. New York: Harcourt Brace Jovanovich, 1979. A favorable presentation of the merits and benefits of capitalism and the free-market system. Friedman argues that the "invisible hand" of the marketplace can correct many social ills.

FUCHS, VICTOR R. *How We Live: An Economic Perspective on Americans from Birth to Death*. Cambridge, Mass.: Harvard University Press, 1983. Fuchs offers an economic explanation of individual choices that have brought about societal changes in work, family, education, and health.

GALBRAITH, JOHN KENNETH. *Economics and the Public Purpose*. Boston: Houghton

Mifflin, 1973. A synthesis of Galbraith's research and thinking on advanced industrial capitalism.

GINSBURG, HELEN. *Full Employment and Public Policy: The United States and Sweden.* Lexington, Mass.: Lexington Books, 1983. Ginsburg explores labor market theory and labor market behavior and tries to answer the question: Why have attempts to enforce a full-employment policy in the United States failed, whereas Swedish policies have been successful?

KERR, CLARK, and JEROME ROSCOW (eds.). *Work in America: The Decade Ahead.* New York: Van Nostrand Reinhold, 1979. A series of articles that examine the current and future issues in work.

SMELSER, NEIL J. *The Sociology of Economic Life.* 2d ed. Englewood Cliffs, N.J.: Prentice Hall, 1975. A review of the history of economic sociology and an examination of the influence of social factors on institutions, economic behavior, and economic development.

TERKEL, STUDS. *Working.* New York: Random House, 1974. A collection of interviews with workers across the United States, who talk about the work they do and how they feel about their jobs.

17

The Political System

It has been said that politics, like baseball, is the great American pastime. Every two years we elect members of Congress, every four years a president. We elect municipal and state officials, delegates to conventions, judges, sheriffs, dogcatchers, and members of sewer commissions. Candidates ring our doorbells, shake our hands, stuff our mailboxes, and exhort us through our television sets. They make promises they often cannot keep. This is politics, American style. This chapter will help clarify what is unique about our two-party system and where the American political system fits into the whole spectrum of political institutions.

□ Politics, Power, and Authority

What *is* politics? Lately the word has been used in a wide range of contexts that tend to obscure its meaning. Some authors speak of the "politics of sex," others of the "politics of the family," and a well-known psychiatrist has written on the "politics of experience" (Laing, 1967).

Politics, from the sociological perspective, is the institutionalized process through which decisions that affect a community, a municipality, a state, or a society as a whole are made and enforced. Politics includes the process by which people acquire and use power through the instrument of the state. Hence, running for president of the United States is a political activity. So is enacting legislation. So is taxing town property owners to subsidize the digging of sewers. So is going to war. But contrary to the currently popular usage mentioned above, rape is not a political activity, nor is family violence. However, the passage and enforcement of laws and policies regarding rape and family violence are indeed political actions.

Politics and Power

Max Weber (1958a) referred to **power** as the ability to carry out one person's or group's will, even in the presence of resistance or opposition from others. In this sense, power is the capability of making others comply with one's decisions, often exacting compliance through the threat or actual use of sanctions, penalties, or force.

The implication is that one person or group exercises power over another. Hence, power is an element of many types of relationships, a complex phenomenon that covers a broad spectrum of interactions. At one pole is **authority**—power that is regarded as legitimate by those over whom it is exercised, who also accept the authority's legitimacy in imposing sanctions or even in using force if necessary. For example, here in the United States few people are eager to pay income taxes; yet most do so regularly. Most taxpayers accept the authority of the government not only to demand payment but also to impose penalties for nonpayment.

At the other extreme is **coercion**—power that the people or groups over whom it is exerted regard as illegitimate. Their compliance is based on fear of reprisals that are not recognized as falling within the range of accepted norms.

A robber who holds up a liquor store owner at gunpoint is exercising illegitimate power, or coercion. At the same time, a fire inspector who extorts a bribe by threatening to harass the storekeeper with unwarranted inspections and fines also is using coercion. From these examples it becomes evident that coercive power can be employed by people either in or out of positions of authority.

In some relationships the division of power is spelled out clearly and defined formally. Employers have specific powers over employees, army officers over enlisted personnel, ship captains over their crews, professors over their students. In other relationships, the question of power is less clearly defined and may even shift back and forth, depending on individual personalities and the particular situation: between wife and husband, among sisters and brothers, or among friends in a social clique.

politics The institutionalized process through which decisions that affect a community, a state, or a society as a whole are made and enforced through the state.

power The ability to carry out one person's or one group's will even in the presence of resistance or opposition from others.

authority Power that is regarded as legitimate by those over whom it is exercised, who also accept the authority's legitimacy in imposing sanctions or even in using force.

coercion Power that the people or groups over whom it is exerted regard as illegitimate.

In virtually every modern society, some relatively small group exercises power over the large mass of the population. This dominant group considers it desirable for its political power to be acknowledged as legitimate—as institutionalized authority—by those submitting to it as well as by those implementing their decisions.

Politics and Authority

An individual's authority often will apply only to certain people in certain situations. For example, a professor has the authority to require students to write term papers in a course but no authority to demand the students' votes should he or she run for public office.

Authority depends on the acceptance of the idea that the allocation of power is as it should be and that those who hold power do so legitimately. Max Weber (1957) identified three kinds of authority: charismatic authority, traditional authority, and rational-legal authority.

Charismatic Authority The power that derives from a ruler's force of personality, the ability to inspire passion and devotion among followers, is **charismatic authority.** A charismatic authority can *demand* things of his or her followers. Sitting Bull and Red Cloud, for example, were charismatic leaders of the Sioux Indians. Their people followed them because they led by example and inspired personal loyalty. However, individuals were free to disagree, to refuse to participate in planned undertakings, and even to leave and look for a group led by people with whom they were more likely to agree (Brown, 1974). This was not true in Rome under Julius Caesar, in Russia under Lenin, in Germany under Hitler, or in Iran under the Ayatollah Khomeini. These men all were charismatic rulers but also had the political authority necessary to enforce obedience or conformity to their demands.

Charismatic authorities and rulers typically emerge during times of crisis, when people lose faith in their social institutions. Lenin led the Russian Revolution in the chaos left in the wake of World War I. Hitler rose to power in a Germany that had been defeated and humiliated in World War I and whose economy was shattered: inflation was so bad that money was almost worthless. Khomeini rose to power in a country in which rapid modernization had undercut traditional Islamic norms and values, in which great poverty and great wealth existed side by side, and in which fear of the Shah's secret police left the populace constantly anxious for its personal safety. The great challenge facing all charismatic rulers is to sustain their leadership after the crisis subsides and to create political institutions that will survive their death or retirement.

Traditional Authority Succession is not a problem for **traditional authority.** Its very nature is rooted in the assumption that the customs of the past legitimate the present—that things are as they always have been and basically should remain that way. Usually both rulers and ruled recognize and support the tradition that legitimizes the rulers' political authority. Traditional authority rests on time-honored statuses such as monarch, teacher, or parent. As long as tradition is followed, the authority is accepted.

Legal-Rational Authority Rooted not in tradition, **legal-rational authority** is based on organizational and impersonal principles and rules that define and limit the power exercised by officeholders. Indeed, that is the key: power is vested not in individuals but in particular positions or offices. There usually are rules and procedures designed to achieve a broad purpose. Rulers acquire political power through meeting requirements for office, and they hold power only as long as they themselves obey the laws that legitimize their rule. Legal-rational authority is not necessarily democratic. A society's constitution may invest its president with unlimited powers for life, as Uganda's constitution did under the dictatorship of Idi Amin before he was deposed. Most nations in the modern world claim that their governments follow the legal-rational model rather than a traditional or charismatic authority. In some modern nations, however, such as South Africa, the Israeli-occupied West Bank region, Protestant-dominated northern Ireland, and the current regime in Guatemala, the laws legitimizing the government were imposed by coercion, or force; although technically legal, these governments are not accepted as legitimate by a large number of their subjects. Such governments frequently must use coercion to keep themselves in power.

☐ Government and the State

A society's **government** consists of the particular individuals and groups who control its political power at any given time. In some societies, political power is shared among most or all adults. This is true of the Mbuti pygmies and the !Kung San of Africa, for instance, for which the group is its own authority and decisions are made by a consensus among adults. Among such societies the concept of government is meaningless. But in modern societies, government does exist as an identifiable social entity, and its actions are patterned by a specialized and highly differ-

entiated set of social institutions called the **state**. According to Weber (1949), the state consists of those social institutions that claim "the monopoly of a legitimate use of physical force" within a society. Just as a true government is nonexistent in some societies, so too is the state limited to certain societies. Its presence indicates a particular level of social and political development.

Modern thought regarding the nature of government and its forms is derived directly from the ideas of three Greek philosophers: Socrates, his student Plato, and Plato's student Aristotle. In the *Republic*, written around 365 B.C., Plato was concerned with the form of government that would be most just. It is important to know that when Plato was writing, Athens had been through a period of political upheaval. For that reason Plato was concerned with the problem of maintaining social order. Hence he rejected **democracy**, or rule by the majority, because he believed that this form of government would lead to chaos. He also rejected **autocracy**, or rule by one person, because he thought that no single person could be wise or competent enough to make decisions for a whole society. Rather, he favored what he called **aristocracy**, a form of **oligarchy**, or rule by a select few.

Modern thought about the nature of government is derived directly from the ideas of Socrates, Plato, and Aristotle. The bust depicts Plato.

- **charismatic authority** The power that derives from a ruler's force of personality—the ability to inspire passion and devotion among followers.
- **traditional authority** Power that is rooted in the assumption that the customs of the past legitimize the present—that things are as they always have been and will remain that way.
- **legal-rational authority** Authority that is based on organizational and impersonal principles and rules that define and limit that power exercised by officeholders.
- **government** The particular individual and groups who control a society's political power at any given time.
- **state** Social institutions that claim the monopoly of the legitimate use of physical force within a society.
- **democracy** A political system characterized by representative government, accountability to an electorate, civilian rule, and civil liberties.
- **autocracy** A political system in which the ultimate authority lies with a single person.
- **aristocracy** The rule by a select few; a form of oligarchy.
- **oligarchy** Rule by a select few, as in an aristocracy.

Plato called his proposed ruling class the guardians of society. The guardians, he argued, should be bred from the most exemplary parents but then separated from them at birth. They should live in poverty for 30 years while being trained in mind and body, and then they should fill positions of government in which they would execute their responsibilities wisely and without favoritism. (It is important not to confound Plato's use of the term *aristocracy* with the modern usage. Plato explicitly rejected the ideal of inherited political power, which he believed inevitably results in power falling to unqualified individuals—leading to an unjust society.)

Aristotle (384–322 B.C.) was the tutor of Alexander the Great and a political scholar. Unlike Plato, he recognized that even in just societies, social-class interests produce class conflicts, which are the business of the state to control. Aristotle favored centering political power in the middle class (consisting of merchants, artisans, and farmers), but he insisted on defining the rights and duties of the state in a legal constitution (Laslett and Cummings, 1967).

Forms of Government

Different types of government exist side by side and must deal with one another constantly in today's shrinking world. To comprehend their interrelationships, it is helpful to understand the structure of each main form of government—autocracy, totalitarianism, and democracy.

Autocracy In an autocracy the ultimate authority and rule of the government rest with one person, who is the chief source of laws and the major agent of social control. For example, the pharaohs of ancient Egypt were autocrats. More recently the reigns of Francisco Franco of Spain, Emperor Haile Selassie of Ethiopia, Francois "Papa Doc" Duvalier of Haiti, and the Perons of Argentina have been autocratic.

In an autocracy the loyalty and devotion of the people are required. To ensure that this requirement is met, dissent and criticism of the government and the person in power are prohibited. The media may be controlled by the government, and terror may be used to prevent or suppress dissent. For the most part, however, no great attempt is made to control the personal lives of the people. A strict boundary is set up between people's private lives and their public behavior. Individuals have a wide range of freedom in pursuing such private aspects of their lives as religion, the family, and many other traditional elements of life. At the same time, it should be pointed out that virtually all present-day autocracies have witnessed exploitation of the poor by the rich and powerful—a situation supported by the respective governments.

Totalitarianism In a **totalitarian government**, one group has virtually total control of the nation's social institutions. Any other group is prevented from attaining power. Religious institutions, educational institutions, political institutions, and economic institutions all are managed directly or indirectly by the state. Typically, under totalitarian rule, several elements interact to concentrate political power.

1. *A single political party* controls the state apparatus. It is the only legal political party in the state. The party organization is itself controlled by one person or by a ruling clique.
2. *The use of terror* is implemented by an elaborate internal security system that intimidates the populace into conformity. It defines dissenters as enemies of the state and often chooses, arbitrarily, whole groups of people against whom it directs especially harsh oppression (for instance, the Jews in Nazi Germany or minority tribal groups in several of the recently created African states).
3. *The control of the media* (television, radio, newspapers, and journals) is in the hands of the state. Differing opinions are denied a forum. The media communicate only the official line of thinking to the people.
4. *Control over the military apparatus.* The military and the use of weapons are monopolized by those who control the political power of the totalitarian state.
5. *Control of the economy* is wielded by the gov-

ernment, which sets goals for the various industrial and economic sectors and determines both the prices and the supplies of goods.

6. *An elaborate ideology*, in which previous sociopolitical conditions are rejected, legitimizes the current state and provides more or less explicit instructions to citizens on how to conduct their daily lives. This ideology offers explanations for nearly every aspect of life, often in a simplistic and distorted way (Friedrich and Brzezinski, 1965).

Two distinct types of totalitarianism are found in the modern world. Though they share the same basic political features described above, they differ widely in their economic systems. Under **totalitarian socialism**, in addition to almost total regulation of all social institutions, the government controls and owns all major means of production and distribution: there is little private ownership or free enterprise. This political-economic system is usually labeled **communism** and is typified by the government of the Soviet Union. **Totalitarian capitalism**, on the other hand, denotes a system under which the government, while retaining control of social institutions, allows the means of production and distribution to be owned and managed by private groups and individuals. However, production goals usually are dictated by the government, especially in heavy industry. Hitler's Germany is a good example of totalitarian capitalism. The mammoth Krupp industrial complex was owned and managed by the family of that name, but the government had the company gear its efforts toward producing munitions and heavy equipment to further the nation's political and militaristic aims. We know this form of totalitarianism as **fascism**.

One of the problems faced by totalitarian governments is that because their total control over their citizenry allows no organized independent opposition, they are never sure whether the populace's conformity to the laws is based on its acceptance of the government's legitimate authority or is motivated primarily by fear of coercion by a ruling power it considers illegitimate. This inability to judge ac-curately its citizens' perceptions of its legitimacy is considered by many observers to be a source of great anxiety to the Soviet government and explains some of its oppressive actions, such as imprisoning artists and intellectuals.

Democracy Modern democracy emerged as a form of government along with the Industrial Revolution and the rise of capitalism during the eighteenth and nineteenth centuries. Its tenets were embodied in the American Declaration of Independence and later became law under the Constitution of the United States. Soon thereafter its values provided the rallying cries for the French Revolution (1789–1799).

A basic feature of democracy is that it is rooted in **representative government**, which means that the authority to govern is achieved through, and legitimized by, popular elections. Every government officeholder has sought, in one way or another, the support of the **electorate** (those citizens eligible to vote) and has persuaded a large enough portion of that group to grant its support (through voting). The elected official is entitled to hold office for a specified term and generally will be reelected as long as that body of voters is satisfied that the officeholder is adequately representing its interests.

totalitarian government The total control of the nation's social institutions by one group.

totalitarian socialism A political-economic system in which the government controls and owns all major means of production and distribution as well as the major social institutions.

communism The name commonly given to totalitarian socialist forms of government.

totalitarian capitalism A political-economic system under which the government retains control of the social institutions but allows the means of production and distribution to be owned and managed by private groups and individuals.

fascism A political-economic system characterized by totalitarian capitalism.

representative government Government whose authority to govern is achieved through and legitimized by popular elections.

electorate Those citizens eligible to vote.

Representative institutions can operate freely only if certain other conditions prevail. First, there must be what sociologist Edward Shils (1968) calls **civilian rule**. That is, every qualified citizen has the legal right to run for and hold an office of government. Such rights do not belong to any one class (say, of highly trained scholars, as in ancient China), caste, set, religious group, ethnic group, or "race." These rights belong to every citizen. further, there must be public confidence in the fact that such organized agencies as the police and the military will not intervene in, or change the outcome of, elections (as happened in Greece during the "rule of the colonels" in the 1960s, in Chile with the overthrow of President Salvadore Allende in 1973, and in Pakistan with the overthrow and eventual execution of President Ali Bhutto in 1979). In addition, **public liberties** must be maintained. This means that people must be free to assemble, to express their views and seek to persuade others, to engage in political organizing, and to vote for whomever they wish.

Democratic societies contrast markedly with totalitarian societies. Ideally, they are open and culturally diverse; dissent is not viewed as disloyalty; there are two or more political parties; and terror and intimidation are not an overt part of the political scene.

The economic base of democratic societies can vary considerably. Democracy can be found in a capitalistic country like the United States and in a more socialistic one like Sweden. However, it appears necessary for the country to have reached an advanced level of economic development before democracy can evolve. Such societies are most likely to have the sophisticated population and stability necessary for democracy (Lipset, 1960).

Democracy and Socialism Critics of capitalism argue that "true" democracy is an impossible dream in capitalist society. They claim that although in theory all members of a capitalist society have the same political rights, in fact capitalist society is inherently stratified, and therefore wealth, social esteem, and even political power of necessity are unequally distributed (see Chapter 10). Because of this, some critics contend, "true" democracy can be achieved only under **socialism**—an economic system under which the government owns and controls the major means of production and distribution (thus avoiding inequality of ownership among its members) and in which there is no social stratification (Schumpeter, 1950).

As we have noted, there is no obvious reason that socialist societies cannot be democratic. In fact, though, many societies whose economies are socialist tend to be communist states. One reason is that historically, socialist societies often have been born in revolution. Political revolutions by definition mean a redistribution of power (see discussion of political change later in this chapter). One group seizes power from another and then tries to prevent the old group from retaking it. Lenin argued that in order to consolidate power, it is necessary for the new group to use strong repressive measures against the old—in fact, to build a **dictatorship.** A dictatorship is a totalitarian government in which all power rests ultimately in one person, who generally heads the only recognized political party, at least until all the economic resources of the old group are seized, its links to all political agencies are broken, and its claims to political legitimacy are wiped out. Lenin (1949) quoted Marx on this point:

> Between capitalist and communist society lies the period of the revolutionary transformation of the one into the other. Corresponding to this is also a political transition period in which the state can be nothing but *the revolutionary dictatorship of the proletariat* [the working class].

Lenin (1949) put it more graphically himself:

> The proletariat needs state power, a centralised organisation of force, and organisation of violence, both to crush the resistance of the exploiters and to *lead* the enormous mass of the population . . . in the work of organising a socialist economy.

In the Soviet Union, Eastern Europe, China, Cuba, and more recently in African and Southeast Asian countries, socialist revolutions all have resulted in dictatorships. Families of the previous ruling classes have been executed, jailed, "reeducated," or exiled, and their properties have been seized and redistributed. In none of these societies has the dictatorship proved to be temporary, nor has the state gradually "withered away," as Marx and Engels predicted it would after socialism was firmly established. Many Marxists claim that this will happen in the future, especially once capitalism has been defeated all around the globe and socialist states no longer need to protect themselves against "counterrevolutionary" subversion and even directly military threats by capitalist nations. However, it is fair to observe that even the ancient Greeks knew that power corrupts and that those groups who have power are unlikely ever to give it up voluntarily. So we may expect that at least in the foreseeable future, socialist states that have emerged through revolution will—despite their disclaimers—remain totalitarian communist dictatorships.

By contrast, in those societies in which socialist reforms of capitalist abuses have been introduced, democracy appears to be firmly rooted and is likely to survive. **Democratic socialism** is a political system that exhibits the three dominant features of a democracy (civilian rule, representative government, and public liberties) but in which much of the control of the economy, its major means of production, is vested in the government. Democratic socialism flourishes to varying degrees in the Scandinavian countries, in Great Britain, and in Israel. These countries all have a strong private (that is, capitalist) sector in their economies, but they also have extensive government programs to ensure the people's well-being. These programs pertain to such things as national health service, government ownership of key industries, and the systematic tying of workers' pay to increases in the rate of inflation. Many observers believe that the American political economy has been moving in this direction.

Our discussion of government and the state prompts us to consider what, in fact, the state actually accomplishes as an institution, what problems it solves, and what it does for people.

Functions of the State

Although a preindustrial society can exist without an organized government, no modern industrial society can thrive without those functions that the state performs: establishing laws and norms, providing social control, en-

suring economic stability, setting goals, and protecting against outside threats.

Establishing Laws and Norms   The state is the focus for the establishment of laws that formally specify what is expected and what is prohibited in the society. The laws often represent a codification of specific norms; for example, one should not steal or commit violent crimes against others. The establishment of laws also brings about the enactment of penalties for violating the laws.

Providing Social Control   In addition to establishing laws, the state also has the power to enforce them. The police, courts, and various government agencies make sure that the violation of laws is punished. In the United States, the Internal Revenue Service seeks out tax evaders, the courts sentence criminals to prison, and the police attempt to maintain order.

Ensuring Economic Stability   In the modern world, no individual can provide entirely for his or her own needs. Large work forces must be mobilized to build roads, dig canals, and erect dams. Money must be minted, and standards of weights and measures must be set and checked; and merchants must be protected from thieves, and consumers from fraud. The state tries to ensure that a stable system of distribution and allocation of resources exists within the society.

civilian rule Rule that establishes the legal right of every qualified citizen to run for and hold an office of government.

public liberties Social liberties that enable people to assemble to express their views and seek to persuade others, to engage in political organizing, and to vote for whomever they wish.

socialism An economic system under which the government owns and controls the major means of production and distribution.

dictatorship A totalitarian government in which all the power rests ultimately in one person who generally heads the only recognized political party.

democratic socialism A political system that exhibits the three dominant features of a democracy (civilian rule, representative government, and public liberties) but in which much of the control of the economy is vested in the government.

Setting Goals   The state sets goals and provides a direction for the society. If a society is to curtail its use of oil, for instance, the government must promote this as a goal. It must encourage conservation and the search for alternative energy sources and must discourage (perhaps through taxation or rationing) the use of oil. But how is the government able to accomplish these tasks? How can it bring about individual and organizational compliance? Obviously, it would be best if the government could rely on persuasion alone, but this course seldom is enough. In the end the government usually needs the power to compel compliance.

Protecting Against Outside Threats   Historic data leave little doubt that the rise of the state was accompanied almost everywhere by the intensification of warfare (Otterbein, 1970, 1973). As early as the fourteenth century, Ibn Khaldun (1958), a brilliant Islamic scholar of the time, noted this connection and even attributed the rise of the state to the needs of sedentary farmers to protect themselves from raids by fierce nomads. His views were echoed by Ludwig Gumplowicz (1899): "States have never arisen except through the subjugation of one stock by another, or by several in alliance." In any event, it is clear that one of the tasks of maintaining a society is to protect it from outside threats, especially those of a military nature. Hence governments build and maintain armies. Although the lack of military preparedness may invite an expansionist attack from a neighboring society, it does not follow that such preparedness necessarily will prevent attack.

Although there is widespread agreement that the functions just described are tasks that the state should and usually does perform, not all social scientists agree that the state emerged because of the need for these functions.

Functionalist and Conflict Theory Views of the State

Functionalists and conflict theorists hold very different ideas about the function of the state. As our discussion of social stratification in Chapter 10 revealed, functionalist theorists view social stratification—and the state that

maintains it—as necessary devices that provide for the recruitment of workers to perform the tasks necessary to sustain society. Individual talents must be matched to jobs that need doing, and those with specialized talents must be given sufficiently satisfying rewards. Functionalists therefore maintain that the state emerged because society began to get so large and complex that only a specialized, central institution (that is, the state) could manage society's increasingly complicated and intertwined institutions (Davis, 1949; Service, 1975).

Marxists and other conflict theorists take a different view. They argue that technological changes resulting in surplus production brought about the production of commodities for trade (as opposed to products for immediate use). Meanwhile, certain groups were able to seize control of the means of production and distribution of commodities, thereby succeeding in establishing themselves as powerful ruling classes that dominated and exploited workers and serfs. Finally, the state emerged as a means of coordinating the use of force, by means of which the ruling classes could protect their institutionalized supremacy from the resentful and potentially rebellious lower classes. As Lenin (1949) explained, "The state is a special organisation of force: it is an organisation of violence for the suppression of some class."

There is evidence to support this view of the state's origins. The earliest legal codes of ancient states featured laws protecting the persons and properties of rulers, nobles, landholders, and wealthy merchants. The Code of Hammurabi of Babylon, dating back to about 1750 B.C., prescribed the death penalty for burglars and for anybody who harbored a fugitive slave. The code regulated wages, prices, and fees to be charged for services. It provided that a commoner be fined six times as much for striking a noble or a landholder as for striking another commoner. And it condemned to death housewives who were proved by their husbands to be uneconomical in managing household resources (Durant, 1954).

Nevertheless, the functionalist view also has value. The state provides crucial organizational functions such as carrying out large-scale projects and undertaking long-range planning, without which complex society probably could not exist. Because it provides a sophisticated organizational structure, the state can—and does—fulfill many other important functions. In most modern societies, the state supports a public school system to provide a basic, uniform education for its members. The health and well-being of its citizens also have become the concern of the state. In our own country, as in many others, the government provides some level of medical and financial support for its young, old, and disabled, at the same time that it sponsors scientific and medical research for the ongoing welfare of its people. Regulating industry and trade to some degree also has become a function of the modern state, and it has devised ways (different for each kind of state) of establishing, controlling, and even safeguarding the civil rights and liberties of its citizens. And certainly one of the most important functions of any state is the protection of its people. Long gone are the days when cavedwellers, lords of the manor, or frontiersmen themselves defended their territories and other members of their groups from attack or encroachment; the state now provides such protection through specialized agencies: armies, militias, and police forces.

When groups in a society develop sufficient dissatisfaction with their present system of government and achieve the strength to influence the direction of that system, changes in government can take place. After such changes the state may perform the same functions, but it may do so in a different way and under different leadership.

☐ Political Change

Political change is a shift in the distribution of power among groups in a society. It is one facet of the wider process of social change, the topic of the last part of this book. Here we shall consider briefly three forms of political change: institutionalized change, rebellion, and revolution.

Institutionalized Political Change

In democracies the institutional provision for the changing of leaders is implemented through elections. Usually, candidates representing different parties and interest groups must compete for a particular office at formally designated periods of time. There may also be laws that prevent a person from holding the same office for more than a given number of terms. If a plurality or a majority of the electorate is dissatisfied with a given officeholder, they are given the opportunity to vote the incumbent out of office. Thus the laws and traditions of a democracy ensure the orderly changeover of politicians and, usually, of parties in office.

In dictatorships and totalitarian societies, if a leader unexpectedly dies, is debilitated, or is deposed, a crisis of authority may occur. In dictatorships, illegal, violent means must often be used by an opposition to overthrow a leader or the government: as there is no democratic means by which legally to vote a person or group out of power. Thus, we should not be surprised that revolutions and assassinations are most likely to occur in developing nations that have dictatorships. Established totalitarian societies, such as the Soviet Union and China, are more likely than dictatorships are to offer normatively prescribed means by which a ruling committee decides who should fill a vacated position of leadership.

Rebellions

Rebellions are attempts—typically through armed force—to achieve rapid political change that is not possible within existing institutions. But rebellions do not change the society's political and class structure. In other words, rebellions typically do not call into question the legitimacy of power but, rather, its uses. For example, consider Shays's Rebellion. Shortly after the American colonies won their independence from Britain, they were hit by an economic depression followed by raging inflation. Soon, in several states, paper money lost almost all its value. As the states began to pay off their war debts (which had been bought up by speculators), they were forced to increase the taxation of farmers,

⸰ **political change** The redistribution of power among groups in a society.

⸱ **rebellions** Illegal attempts to achieve rapid political change that is not possible within existing institutions.

In an effort to reverse unfair tax laws, Connecticut farmers banded together under the leadership of Daniel Shays. A brawl is depicted here between a government supporter and one of the rebels.

A British tax collector is tarred and feathered by American colonists.

many of whom could not afford to pay these new taxes and consequently lost their land. Farmers began to band together to prevent courts from hearing debt cases, and state militias were called out to protect court hearings. Desperate, farmers in the Connecticut Valley region armed themselves under Daniel Shays, an ex-officer of the Continental Army (Blum et al., 1981). This armed band was defeated by the Massachusetts militia, but its members eventually were pardoned and the debt laws were loosened somewhat (Parkes, 1968). Shays's Rebellion did not intend to overthrow the courts or the legislature; rather, it was aimed at effecting changes in their operation. Hence it was a typical rebellion.

Revolutions

Revolutions, if they are successful, result in far greater changes than do rebellions, as revolutions change the society's previously existing power structure. Sociologists further distinguish between political and social revolutions.

Political Revolutions Relatively rapid transformations of state or government structures that are not accompanied by changes in social structure or stratification are known as **political revolutions** (Skocpol, 1979). The American War of Independence is a good example of a political revolution. The colonists were not seeking to change the structure of society nor even necessarily to overthrow the ruling order. Their goal was to put a stop to the abuse of power by the British. After the war they created a new form of government, but they did not attempt to change the fact that landowners and wealthy merchants held the reins of political power—just as they had before the shooting started. In the American Revolution, then, a lower class did not rise up against a ruling class. Rather, it was the American ruling class going to war in order to shake loose from inconvenient interference by the British ruling class. The initial result, therefore, was political, but not social, change.

Social Revolutions **Social revolutions**, by contrast, "are rapid and basic transformations of a society's state and class structures; and

464

The French Revolution was a class-based revolt. In this caricature, members of the ruling class are shown riding on the back of a representative of the people.

they are accompanied and in part carried through by class-based revolts" (Skocpol, 1979). Hence they involve two simultaneous and interrelated processes: (1) the transformation of a society's system of social stratification brought about by upheaval in the lower class(es); and (2) changes in the form of the state. Both processes must reinforce each other for a revolution to succeed. The French Revolution of the 1790s was a true social revolution. So were the Mexican Revolution of 1910, the Russian Revolution of 1917, the Chinese Revolution of 1949, and the Cuban Revolution of 1959—to name some of the most prominent social revolutions of our century. In all these revolutions, class struggle provided both the context and the driving force. The old ruling classes were stripped of political power and economic resources; wealth and property were redistributed; and state institutions were thoroughly reconstructed (Wolf, 1969). Political changes can also come about through a change in the demographic makeup of the population. See Case Study: "The Baby-Boom Generation as a Political Force," for an example of how this group has come to have a major political impact.

Although the American Revolution did not arise from class struggle and did not result immediately in changes in the social structure, it did mark the beginning of a form of government that eventually modified the social stratification of eighteenth-century America.

☐ The American Political System

America is a democratic state rooted in an advanced form of capitalist economy, and it has certain distinctive features that interest sociologists.

The Two-Party System

Few democracies have only two main political parties. Besides the United States, there are Canada, Australia, New Zealand, and Austria. The other democracies all have more than two major parties, thus providing proportional representation for a wide spectrum of divergent political views and interests.

The American two-party political system, however, operates on a "winner-take-all" basis. Therefore, groups with differing political interests must face not being represented if their candidates lose. Conversely, candidates must attempt to gain the support of a broad spectrum of political interest groups, because a candidate representing a narrow range of voters cannot win. This system forces accommodations between interest groups on the one hand and candidates and parties on the other.

Few, if any, individual interest groups (like the National Organization for Women, the National Rifle Association, or the Moral Majority), represent the views of a majority of an electorate, be it local, state, or national. Hence it is necessary for interest groups to ally with political parties in which other interest groups are involved as well, hoping thereby to become part of a majority that can succeed in electing one or more candidates. Each inter-

political revolutions Relatively rapid transformations of state or government structures that are not accompanied by changes in social structure or stratification.

social revolutions Rapid and basic transformations of a society's state and class structures that are accompanied, and in part carried through, by class-based revolts.

CASE STUDY
The Baby-Boom Generation as a Political Force

Some 74 million children—fully 31 percent of the country's population—were born in the years between 1947 and 1964. That group of people, known collectively as the Baby Boom, has had a profound influence on American values, economics, family patterns, and work habits as it grew up. Now this group is poised to make its influence felt in another area: the political arena. Politics promises never to be the same.

As a political force, Baby Boomers have been wielding power since they were barely out of love beads. The massive bulge of people that were born after World War II helped to bring down a President (Lyndon B. Johnson); alter environmental laws in the face of opposing big business interests; and fracture the alliance of minorities, labor, southerners, and ethnic groups that Franklin D. Roosevelt had forged into a united Democratic Party in the 1930s.

Some observers had warned that the counterculture behavior of the 1960s was the beginning of fundamental and unalterable changes in society. They concluded that the changing role of women and the greater acceptance of nontraditional lifestyles and family arrangements would become a permanent part of society.

In a recent study of the baby-boom generation, however, the American Council of Life Insurance (ACLI) has discovered some fairly traditional attitudes toward family and child-rearing among baby boomers—particularly those with children—mixed with some fairly unique points of view.

The ACLI survey asked baby boomers to react to a list of social changes that might occur in the coming years. What emerges is a new brand of traditionalism: a distinct longing for more traditional values in some areas, hard work, strong family and religious ties and respect for authority, coupled with an increasing acceptance of nontraditional ideas in other areas—a tolerance of changing sexual mores and a desire for less materialism.

Marital and childbearing patterns of baby boomers are much different from those of their parents. Baby boomers are marrying later, and they are delaying parenthood until an older age. They anticipate having fewer children, and slightly more expect to remain childless. Despite these changes, only 15 percent of baby boomers who are single, divorced, or separated would prefer a single lifestyle or would rather live with someone without the formality of marriage.

Three out of four baby boomers surveyed by ACLI say that an "equal marriage" of shared responsibility is the most appealing lifestyle.

Attitudes toward women's roles vary significantly by a person's level of education and, to a lesser degree by gender. The more highly educated a person, the greater is his or her support for an independent role for women in marriage. Proportionately about half as many persons without a high school degree as with a college degree think that the traditional role of a husband as breadwinner and a wife as homemaker make a better marriage—36 percent versus 68 percent.

In the area of education and the attitudes that result from it, the baby boom is likely to remain fundamentally different from previous generations. Education remains with a person for life, altering attitudes and behavior. The baby-boom generation is much better educated than previous generations. Only 15 percent of Americans aged 35 and older have completed college, while nearly 24 percent of those aged 25 to 34 have had at least four years of college.

Young women have twice the college experience that older women have—one of the most important ways in which Americans are changing. Only 11 percent of women aged 35 and older have attended at least four years of college, compared to 21 percent of women aged 25 to 34. The generations are defined by their educational differences. And differences in education imply long-lasting changes in political and social behavior.

Women's participation in the labor force is the other key difference that members of the baby boom will carry with them throughout life. Most women under the age of 65 are employed, but the share rises among the younger generation. For example, 59 percent of women aged 35 to 64, but fully 70 percent aged 20 to 34, are working or looking for work.

Until now, younger Americans have been underrepresented in the electorate. In 1982, for example, 21-to-34-year-olds accounted for 33.5 percent of the U.S. population, but for only 25.4 percent of those voting in congressional midterm elections.

But as the boomers move into their forties, the situation should reverse. They will begin to make up a larger share of the voters than they do of the total voter-age population. And that will give the boomers the potential to be the dominant force in American politics well into the 21st century.

Baby boomers espouse many traditional values while at the same time embracing a much more tolerant attitude than previous generations toward social changes. While the work ethic is deeply entrenched in baby boomers, two thirds would like to see less emphasis on money. Also, there is a clear pattern of support for more traditional values in three areas: family ties, respect for authority, and religious beliefs. Politicians of the future will have to reflect a society in which there will be not only an increasing heterogeneity of values and lifestyles, but one which is more tolerant of diversity.

Source: Based on Barbara Price, "What the Baby Boom Believes" and Bryant Robey and Cherly Russell, "The Year of the Baby Boom," *American Demographics,* May, 1984, pp. 19–21 and 31–33.   □

est group then hopes that the candidate(s) it has helped elect will represent its point of view. But for most interest groups to achieve their ends more effectively, they must find a common ground with their allies in the party they have chosen to support. And in doing so they often have to compromise some strongly held principles. Hence party platforms often tend to be composed of mild and uncontroversial issues, and party principles tend to adhere as closely as possible to the center of the American political spectrum.

When either party attempts to move away from the center to accommodate a very strong interest group with left- or right-wing views, the result generally is disaster at the polls. This happened to the Republican party in 1964, when the politically conservative (or right-wing) Goldwater forces gained control of its organizational structure and led it to a landslide defeat: in that year's presidential election the Democrats captured 61.1 percent of the national vote. Eight years later the Democratic party made the same "mistake." It nominated George McGovern, a distinctly liberal (or left-wing) candidate who, among other things, advocated a federally subsidized minimum income. The predictable landslide brought the Republicans and Richard Nixon 60.7 percent of the vote (U.S. Dept. of Commerce, 1984). So, in winner-take-all two-party systems, political-interest groups must compromise, and political parties usually stay close to the political center.

The candidates themselves have other problems. In order to gain support within their parties, they must somehow distinguish themselves from the other candidates. In other words, they must stake out identifiable positions. Yet in order to win state and national elections, they must appeal to a broad political spectrum. To do this, they must soften the positions that first won them party support. Candidates thus often find themselves justly accused of "double-talking" and vagueness as they try to finesse their way through this built-in dilemma. This is most true of presidential candidates. It is no accident that once they have their party's nomination, some candidates may express themselves differently and far more cautiously than they did before.

The Distribution of Power

In the United States, there are two decidedly different views of how political and economic power are held, and by whom.

The Pluralist Theory   As we have already noted, our society's political and economic sectors contain groups representing many interests, based on class, race, ethnicity, religion, demography, and occupation. Such interest groups use money, organization, lobbying, campaigns, and votes to have their political candidates elected. In return, those candidates are expected to reward their supporters by promoting all manner of legislation favorable to the interest groups with which they are aligned. In the United States the two major political parties are viewed as the principal means through which special-interest groups advance their respective causes.

Most interest groups are also in either direct or indirect competition with one another. (For example, management and labor bargain collectively in the private sector and use the Republican and Democratic parties to achieve their political ends.) The **pluralist theory** of power maintains that power is distributed among many different interest groups that compete with one another in the private sector of the economy and within the govern-

pluralist theory The theory that power in society is distributed among many different interest groups that compete with one another in the private sector of the economy and the government.

ment (Rose, 1967). When these rivaling interest groups are relatively equal in strength, then an equilibrium or balance of power exists.

The main problem with the pluralist model of democracy is that all interest groups are not adequately represented in the American political process. The poor, for instance, tend to register and vote in smaller numbers than do other socioeconomic groups. Furthermore, they control neither large resources of money nor well-organized blocs of votes. Therefore, they may be ignored with relative impunity by both the Republican and Democratic parties. The Democratic party, for instance, is much more responsive to the demands of organized labor than to the needs of the lower class, because the major unions control large sums of money and influence the votes of millions of workers. Similarly, Republican politicians tend to be more closely aligned with the demands of industrial lobbyists and well-funded professional associations than with the lower-middle class or with supporters over the age of 50.

David Riesman (1950) does not believe that there is an organized elite that dominates society; instead, he sees two levels of power in the United States. One level consists of veto groups that try to protect themselves from proposals that might encroach on their interests. These veto groups unite with or separate from other groups, depending on the issues involved. On the second level is the unorganized public, which is often sought as an ally of the veto groups. Those who seek power must respond to public opinion in order to be successful.

The Power-Elite Theory The American sociologist C. Wright Mills (1959) wrote that those who control the largest private corporations and the highest political and military positions are the leaders who control the nation. According to this **power-elite theory**, these leaders share similar upper-class origins and social values, are white, Anglo-Saxon, and Protestant. They also share a common world view as to what the goals of the nation should be and work together closely to shape national policy.

What is the evidence for Mills's analysis of power? G. William Domhoff (1967) pointed out that the upper class of American society (about one-half of 1 percent) dominates the boards of directors of the top 15 banks, the top 15 insurance corporations, and the top 20 industrial corporations. A study by the sociologist Peter Freitag (1975) concluded that between 1897 and 1973, 87.8 percent of presidential cabinet officials had been associated with corporations, either as directors and officers or as corporate attorneys. Recent presidential administrations have had just this type of interlock: 85.7 percent of the cabinets of the Eisenhower and Johnson administrations and 95.7 percent of the cabinet in the Nixon administration came from the private sector. For a related discussion see Focus on Research: "The Political Power of the Press."

Among the major criticisms of the power-elite theory are the following (Weissberg, 1981):

1. Public officials may have corporate affiliations or be from the upper class without uniformly being committed to advancing corporate interests. (Franklin D. Roosevelt was just such an individual.)
2. It cannot be categorically maintained that the power elite always works toward a common goal, as there is obviously intense competition within and across the various industries. (For instance, most agricultural industries support free trade, whereas many manufacturers demand protection against the incursions of the foreign-import market.)
3. Over the past 20 years, the government has exerted considerably more power over the private sector than vice versa, forcing corporations to accept many policies that had been vigorously opposed. (Examples are stringent pollution regulations, strengthened consumer-protection laws, prohibitions against discrimination in housing, and increased emphasis on employee safety in industry.)

In conclusion, it should be noted that the proponents of both the power-elite and the pluralist theories of power agree that it is a small segment of the population that makes the decisions that affect people in the cities, towns, and in society itself. And those citizens who are not represented by an active, well-organized, and well-funded interest group are likely to have their welfare and concerns ignored.

Voting Behavior

In totalitarian societies, strong pressure is put on people to vote. Usually there is no contest between the candidates, as there is no alternative to voting for the party slate. Dissent is not tolerated, and nearly everyone votes.

In the United States there is a constant progression of contests for political office, and in comparison with many other countries, the voter turnout is quite low. Since the 1920s the turnout for presidential elections has ranged from about 50 percent to nearly 70 percent of the potential voters casting a ballot. (See Table 17.1 for a summary of voter participation rates in national elections.)

The Democratic party has tended to be the means through which the less privileged and the unprivileged have voted for politicians whom they hoped would advance their interests. Since 1932 the Democratic party has tended to receive most of its votes from the lower class, the working class, blacks, Southern and Eastern Europeans, Hispanics, Catholics, and Jews (Cummings and Wise, 1981). Thus almost all the legislation that has been passed to aid these groups has been promoted by the Democrats and opposed by the Republicans: prounion, social security, unemployment compensation, disability insurance, antipoverty legislation, medicare and medicaid, civil rights, and consumer protection.

The Republican party has tended to receive most of its votes from the upper-middle and lower-middle classes, Protestants, and farmers. Americans under 30 tend to vote the Democratic ticket; and those over 49 tend to vote for the Republican party, even though the Democratic party has been responsible for almost all the legislation to benefit older citizens. The politicians of both parties tend to be most responsive to the needs of the best-organized groups with the largest sources of

TABLE 17.1 Voter Participation in National Elections (%)

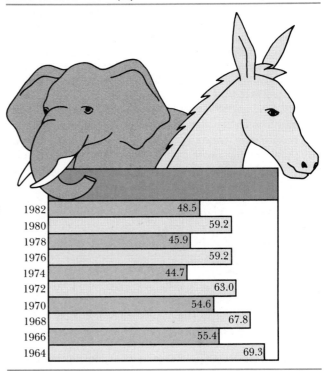

Year	%
1982	48.5
1980	59.2
1978	45.9
1976	59.2
1974	44.7
1972	63.0
1970	54.6
1968	67.8
1966	55.4
1964	69.3

Source: U.S. Department of Commerce, Bureau of the Census, *Statistical Abstract of the United States 1985* (Washington, D.C.: Government Printing Office, 1984), p. 255.

funds or blocks of votes. Thus, we would expect the Republicans to represent best the interests of large corporations and well-funded professional groups (such as the American Medical Association). The Democrats, on the other hand, would be more closely aligned with the demands of unions.

Factors other than the social characteristics of voters and the traditional platforms of parties may affect the way people vote (Cummings and Wise, 1981). Indeed, the physical attributes, social characteristics, and personality of a candidate may prompt some voters to vote against the candidate of the party they usually support. More importantly, the issues of the period may cause voters to vote against

FOCUS ON RESEARCH
The Political Power of the Press

As the following research study reveals by a sociologist working in the political arena, the power of the press in politics goes beyond the function of newspapers as providers of information. The data clearly indicate that the top 24 newspaper companies in the country are closely linked to the nation's power structure and, thus, play a major role in the country's political and governmental processes.

During the past decade, sociologists have developed a growing interest in the upper echelons of business as related to political power, but they have not focused on the press as a special segment. Although a great deal has been written about the "power of the press," little is known about the position of the press within the power structure of the United States. Research has centered on the day-to-day activities of the newsroom itself and the processes of identifying, gathering, writing, and editing the news but has not penetrated the upper echelons of the newspaper hierarchy—the top decision makers or the boards of directors of newspaper-owning corporations. Much of what is known about these individuals comes from official and unofficial biographies of publishers, histories of particular newspapers, and journalistic accounts of the "lords of the press." Though these studies suggest that publishers and board members can have an influence on the general tone of a paper as well as on specific stories, there has been little systematic research on the characteristics of these people and how (or if) they are connected to other sectors of the U.S. power structure. This research represents a systematic examination of the media elites' position in the web of institution affiliations that comprise the U.S. power structure.

For this research, the U.S. power structure is defined as the top institutions in society, including the nation's elite corporations (defined as the 1,000 largest industrial corporations and 50 each of the largest banks, insurance companies, financial companies, utilities, retail companies, and transportation companies in 1979, as listed by *Fortune* magazine), elite business policy groups (defined as the 15 major groups that prior research indicates play a critical role in establishing a common position among the major corporations on important issues), elite universities (defined as the 12 private colleges and universities with the largest endowments), and elite social clubs (defined as the 47 exclusive clubs that draw their membership from a nationwide pool of elites). The newspaper elite is defined as the di-

Elite Affiliations by Newspaper Company

	No. of Directors	Elite Corporations	Business Policy Groups	Elite Universities	Elite Clubs	Total Affiliations
Dow Jones	20	24	19	2	12	57
N.Y. Times	11	23	14	3	7	47
Washington Post	12	12	17	3	9	41
Times Mirror	15	24	7	0	9	40
Field Enterprises	12	15	4	5	12	36
Gannett	21	17	4	1	8	30
Knight-Ridder	18	12	2	2	13	29
Mpls. Star and Tribune	12	6	7	1	12	26
Media General	9	9	7	1	5	22
Hearst	19	3	2	0	15	20
Tribune	11	12	1	3	3	19
Thomson	10	9	4	1	2	16
Harte Hanks	10	13	2	0	0	15
Capital Cities	12	8	2	0	3	13
Affiliated	10	0	1	1	6	8
Scripps	10	1	1	0	6	8
Cox	8	2	1	0	2	5
Copley	11	1	2	0	1	4
Lee	11	3	0	0	1	4
Independent	11	1	0	0	2	3
Central	7	1	0	1	1	3
Evening News	9	0	0	0	1	1
News America	8	0	0	0	0	0
Freedom	12	0	0	0	0	0
Total	290	196	97	24	130	447

rectors of the 24 largest newspaper companies in the United States. After checking a number of sources, a list of 290 directors was drawn up. Standard references, mail questionnaires, and follow-up telephone calls were used to determine the affiliations of these 290 directors with the country's elite institutions.

As may be seen in the preceding table, the data indicate that the nation's major newspaper firms are, in fact, closely linked to the nation's power structure—the 24 newspaper companies have 447 ties with elite organizations, including 196 with *Fortune's* 1,300 largest corporations, 97 with the 15 major business policy groups, 24 with the 12 major private universities, and 130 with the 47 elite social clubs.

The power elite influences government policy not only through lobbying, campaign contributions, and policy groups but also by placing representatives in high-level appointed positions in government, and the newspaper industry is no exception. Thirty-six directors have been appointed to at least one (past or present) high-level federal government position, including cabinet posts, presidential advisory commissions, advisory committees to federal agencies, and regional boards of the Federal Reserve Bank.

One of the mass media's major roles in society is to shape public opinion on crucial issues, to socialize individuals to social roles and behavior, and to legitimate or undermine powerful institutions, individuals, and ideas. The media, in fact, set the agenda of political, social, and economic debate. In so doing, they exert a great deal of political influence, the extent of which is underscored by the close ties among newspaper directors and the country's power structure.

Source: Excerpted and adapted from Peter Dreier, "The Position of the Press in the U.S. Power Structure," *Social Problems* **29** (3) (February, 1982), pp. 298–307. □

---

the party with which they usually identify. When people are frustrated by factors such as war, recession, inflation, and other international or national events, they often blame the incumbent president and the party he or she represents. Considering the emphasis that

Americans place on living in a democratic society, it is interesting that participation in national elections is declining steadily, a cause of grave concern to social scientists and political observers alike.

Voting rates vary with the characteristics of the people. For example, those over 45 years old and with a college education and a white-collar job have high rates of voter participation. People of Spanish origin, the young, and the unemployed have some of the lowest voter participation rates. (See Table 17.2 for voter participation by selected characteristics.)

Recently there have been efforts to increase the number of minority members who register to vote and to improve their voting rate. The greater prominence of minority candidates has helped with this effort, as minority groups are more likely to vote if they feel that the elections are relevant to their lives. (See Using Sociology: "Blacks as a Political Force," for an examination of the political issues that concern blacks.) As minority group members increase their voting rates, they also become successful in electing members of their groups. Figure 17.1 shows the consistent rise, from 1970 to 1982, in the number of black elected officials. There were more than three times as many blacks in office in 1982 than in 1970.

TABLE 17.2 Voter Participation by Selected Characteristics—1982

Characteristic	Percentage Voting
Male	48.7
Female	48.4
White	49.9
Black	43.0
Spanish origin	25.3
18–20 years old	19.8
21–24 years old	28.4
25–34 years old	40.4
35–44 years old	52.2
45–64 years old	62.2
65 and over	59.9
Less than eight years school	35.7
High school graduate	47.1
College graduate	66.5
Unemployed	34.1
White-collar workers	57.8
Blue-collar workers	39.1
Service workers	41.1
Farm workers	51.3

Source: U.S. Department of Commerce, Bureau of the Census, *Statistical Abstract of the United States, 1985* (Washington, D.C.: Government Printing Office, 1984), p. 255.

USING SOCIOLOGY
Blacks as a Political Force

Black Americans always seem to receive attention before major political campaigns, as each candidate attempts to convince them that his or her campaign takes their interests to heart. Black voters have often been skeptical of those preelection promises, sensing that once the election is won, their concerns will once again be given low priority. The following is an examination of the political issues that concern blacks.

Jesse Jackson's 1984 bid for the presidency was effective partly because he made those concerns a focus of his campaign. Voters recognized that even if he were not elected, a strong showing might convince the Democrats that the issues that concern blacks—affirmative action, teenage unemployment, the black underclass—are too important to be dismissed.

Indeed, the statistics on black progress in economic areas are still grim. "Although progress has occurred in recent years," writes William P. O'Hare, a senior research associate at the Joint Center for Political Studies, in Washington, D.C., "the economic gap between whites and blacks remains enormous."

John Reid of Howard University, writing in *Black American in the 1980s*, concurs. "The picture is rosy for education," he stated, "but when one considers the mixed record on fertility and occupation, and the dismal record on mortality rates and income, it becomes clear that a major move by American blacks into mainstream middle-class America is not imminent."

"Statistics from the Census Bureau's latest *Current Population Sur*-veys and the 1980 census show an improvement in income levels of black married-couple families, educational attainment and school enrollment, and home ownership among blacks during the 1970s, say William Matney and Dwight L. Johnson of the Census Bureau. "But the data also reveal setbacks influenced by high black unemployment, sharply increased divorce and separation rates, and a rise in family households maintained by black females."

The Reagan administration has said that the news about black poverty is not as bad as the income statistics suggest, because such benefits as food stamps are not counted as income. But William O'Hare asserts that the income statistics can make blacks look even better off than they are. Black married couples have moved closer to whites in income, but there is a proportionately smaller share of black married couples than there was a decade ago. Even though poverty today may not be as numbing as it was before the government expanded its noncash benefit programs, more blacks are in poverty than a decade ago. In 1981, 11 percent of whites had incomes below the poverty level, but fully 34 percent of blacks did.

Part of the reason for this figure is the continued fragmentation of the black family. The Census Bureau found that the median income of black married couples rose almost 7 percent after inflation between 1971 and 1981, but married couples declined from 64 percent of all black families to 55 percent. As a result, the median income for all types of black families—single-parent combined with married-couple—fell over 8 percent during the decade, and black families, on the average, fell farther behind whites.

As a result of the high divorce rate among blacks, the number of poor black families headed by a woman rose from 834,000 in 1970 to 1.4 million in 1981. In 1981, 70 percent of all poor black families had a woman at the head, up from 56 percent a decade earlier.

During the 1970s, blacks also fell farther behind whites in the accumulation of wealth, according to O'Hare. This was largely because they were not as well positioned as whites were to take advantage of rapidly rising real estate values. Moreover, at every income level, blacks tend to have less wealth than whites do. "Even for blacks who already own a home or eventually manage to purchase a home, the outlook is not entirely positive," says O'Hare, because most blacks' homes are in central cities, which face population losses and deteriorating tax bases.

As politicians court the black vote, they cannot assume that America's blacks are simply another interest group. Indeed, these statistics suggest deep-seated economic differences that may make black voters skeptical of political promises. These differences have made blacks leery of white Democrats, no matter how liberal their voting records are.

Source: Based on Bryant Robey, "Black Votes, Black Money," *American Demographics* **6** (5) (May, 1984), pp. 4–5. □

Women have also been successful in increasing their representation in state and local public offices. Figure 17.2 shows that the number of women holding such offices more than doubled between 1975 and 1981.

Despite these advances, the members of Congress are still overwhelmingly white males over 40 years of age. In 1983 the Senate had only 2 women members and no blacks; the other 98 members were white males. The lack

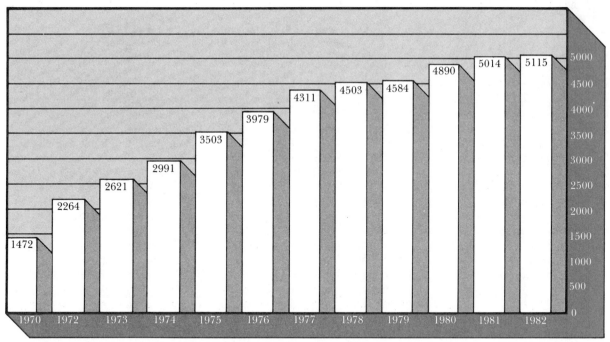

Figure 17.1 Black Elected Officials, 1970–1982

Source: U.S. Department of Commerce, Bureau of the Census, *Statistical Abstract of the United States, 1984* (Washington, D.C.: Government Printing Office, 1983), p. 261.

of women and blacks in the House of Representatives was also striking (see Table 17.3 for a description of selected characteristics of members of Congress).

It would be wrong to conclude from the figures cited that Americans are politically inactive. There is more to political activity than

TABLE 17.3 Selected Characteristics of Members of Congress—1983

	Senators	Representatives
Male	98	413
Female	2	21
White	100	413
Black	0	21
Married	90	366
Unmarried	10	68
Under 40	7	86
40–49 years old	28	145
50–59 years old	39	132
60–69 years old	20	57
70–79 years old	3	13
Over 80 years old	3	1

Source: U.S. Department of Commerce, Bureau of the Census, *Statistical Abstract of the United States, 1984* (Washington, D.C.: Government Printing Office, 1983), p. 258.

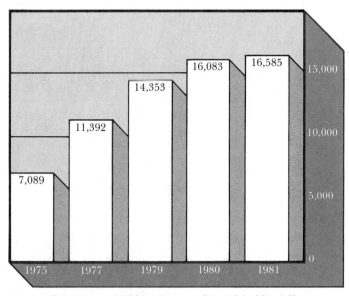

Figure 17.2 Women Holding State and Local Public Offices, 1975–1981

Source: U.S. Department of Commerce, Bureau of the Census, *Statistical Abstract of the United States, 1984* (Washington, D.C.: Government Printing Office, 1983), p. 262

473

POPULAR SOCIOLOGY
What Happened to the Student Radicals?

Many people now find it hard to understand the passions that led student radicals to seize Harvard's University Hall at noon on April 9, 1969. Less than 24 hours after the takeover, as the national press watched, police cleared out the demonstrators, beating many and arresting 184. In the aftermath of the arrests, Harvard's students went on strike and became one of the sixties' leading symbols of student protest. The question that often arises is "What happened to the students who were involved in the radical politics of the late 1960s?" The following examines this question with respect to those who were part of the Harvard Yard takeover.

The Harvard of the 1980s is quiet; the radicals and the student political activities have disappeared. The fervor of those years is now explained away as chiefly a product of an unsettled era. And most assume—as did the makers of *The Big Chill*—that yesterday's radicals have "come home" and are now like everybody else.

In one sense, those assumptions are correct. The students who led the takeover of University Hall do not tend to call themselves revolutionaries anymore. Most have conventional jobs. Norman Daniels, a leading campus radical in 1969, is chairman of the philosophy department of Tufts University; John Berg, who urged the students to fight the police as they were being arrested and served almost nine months in prison for his actions, is an associate professor of government at Suffolk University; Nathan Goldshlag, who

helped throw Dean Archie Epps out of University Hall, designs computer systems. Many of yesterday's radicals now own homes and have teenage children. They jog, take vacations on Cape Cod, and read the latest novels. They no longer cite Karl Marx or C. Wright Mills; instead they ring doorbells for liberal political candidates. The battles they fought—for civil rights, against the Vietnam War, for an open university—ended years ago.

But in another sense, they have not changed. In their odyssey from student dissent to middle age, these radicals have retained many of the ideals of the sixties. And because they have, they may have changed the world more than the world has changed them.

Once gone from Harvard, the student radicals disappeared from view. Some people, like John Berg, acquired criminal records because of the takeover. Nathan Goldshlag and Jonathan Harris, both prominent in the action, were made to leave Harvard and were inducted into the military, although neither went to Vietnam.

Many of the radicals, bolstered by their experience at Harvard, went out into the community to organize for what they saw as the coming revolution. But as the seventies progressed and the country moved to the right, not to the left, the self-professed revolutionaries began to have doubts and to grow weary. Gradually, most drifted away from their work as "revolutionaries." John Berg went back to Harvard to get a

Ph.D. degree. Goldshlag took a conventional job and tried to begin again.

By the late seventies, the former dissidents had left behind their crowded apartments and radical communes. They had gotten married, had children, and bought homes. Some were already divorced. They went to PTA meetings, drove in car pools, and became sports fans. Those who had once rejected the Establishment had apparently come to embrace it.

There have been other changes also. The radical rhetoric has disappeared and, with it, much of the political intensity. Politics is no longer an all-consuming passion. The issues are not as clear-cut, and the commitment no longer seems worth so much effort.

But though these former radicals have joined the society they once rejected, they remain different. In an age of cynicism and political apathy, they persevere. They work in mayoral campaigns, protest U.S. military involvement overseas, and fight nuclear power.

The erstwhile radicals of the sixties do not sigh nostalgically for the old days of community or passively bemoan the swing to the right. Certainly older, and perhaps wiser, they have picked up and moved on, showing that they are the same people now that they were in 1969—society's idealists.

Source: Based on Steven Stark, "The Harvard Strike," *Boston Magazine* **76** (3) (March, 1984), pp. 112–115, 146–149. □

---

voting. A study of American political behavior identified four different modes of participation (Verba, 1972): (1) Some 21 percent of Americans eligible to vote do so more or less regularly in municipal, state, and national elections but do not engage in other forms of political behavior. (2) Roughly 4 percent of the American electorate not only vote but also make the effort to communicate their concerns directly to government officials in an attempt to influence the officials' actions. (3) Some 15 percent of the electorate vote and also periodically take part in political campaigns. However, they do not involve themselves in ongoing local political affairs. (4) Finally, about 20 percent of eligible voters are relatively active in ongoing community politics. They vote but do not get involved in political campaigns.

Mass Political Movements

There is another form of political activism in America, which is important, even though it takes place outside conventional political agencies and institutions. We are referring here to political and social protest movements, such as the civil rights movement of the 1950s and 1960s, the antiwar movement of the 1960s and early 1970s, and the women's rights movements of the 1970s and 1980s. Although the government may attempt to discourage, disrupt, and dissipate these movements through overt and covert means, it is clear that such movements have made critical contributions to the emergence of new social and political climates in this country, which have resulted in an impressive list of political changes. For example, the legal basis for "racial" segregation was eliminated; election reforms were instituted, making it far easier for ethnic minorities and women to take part in party politics; affirmative-action programs were adopted; a president (Lyndon Johnson) was discouraged from seeking a second term in office; the massive American involvement in the Vietnam war was ended; and women not only have become more accepted and visible in traditionally male spheres of activity, they also have succeeded in focusing attention on their need to achieve equal treatment before the law and in job and salary opportunities. In a sense, then, mass political protest movements have become legitimate elements of the American political system. (See Popular Sociology: "What Happened to the Student Radicals?" for an examination of what happened to student activists as they aged and matured.)

One reason for the success of mass political protest movements in effecting change in

After a mass naturalization ceremony some of the nation's newest citizens register to vote.

American society is that they generally have not had revolutionary goals. Never have they posed a realistic threat to state institutions or to established social order. The American government could afford to allow itself (eventually) to be influenced by these movements because its inherent legitimacy was not being called into question, nor was its continued existence at stake. In Europe, however, mass political movements traditionally have been more revolutionary in nature. Therefore, governments have taken more repressive stances against them. Hence the American political system is somewhat unique in the degree to which it allows mass social movements to effect limited political changes, even though at times their tactics involve breaking the law.

Special-Interest Groups

With the government spending so much money and engaged in so much regulating, special-interest groups constantly attempt to persuade the government to support them financially or through favorable regulatory practices. These attempts at influencing government policy are known as **lobbying**. Farmers lobby for agricultural subsidies, labor unions for minimum wages and laws favorable to union organizing and strike actions, corporate and big business interests for favorable legislation and less government control of their practices and power, the National Rifle Association to prevent the passage of legislation requiring the registration or licensing of firearms, consumer-protection groups for increased monitoring of corporate practices and product quality, the steel industry for legislation taxing or limiting imported steel, and so on.

Lobbyists Of all the pressures on Congress, none has received more publicity than the role of the Washington-based lobbyists and the groups they represent. The popular image of a lobbyist is an individual with unlimited funds trying to use devious methods to obtain favorable legislation. The role of today's lobbyist is far more complicated than that.

With the expansion of federal authority into new areas and the huge increase in federal spending, the corps of Washington lobbyists has grown markedly. The federal government now has tremendous power in many fields, and changes in federal policy can spell success or failure for special-interest groups.

Lobbyists usually are personable and extremely knowledgeable about every aspect of their interest group's concerns. They cultivate personal friendships with officials and representatives in all branches of the government, and they frequently have conversations

Many lobbyists believe their most critical and useful role is the research and in-depth information they supply. Here a lobbyist for the United Mine Workers speaks to a member of Congress.

with these government people, often in a semisocial atmosphere, such as over drinks or dinner.

The pressure brought by lobbyists usually has selfish aims, that is, to win special privileges or financial benefits for the groups they represent. On some occasions the goal may be somewhat more objective, as when the lobbyist is trying to further an ideological goal or to put forth a group's particular interpretation of what is in the national interest.

There are certain liabilities associated with lobbyists. The key problem is that they may lead Congress to make decisions that benefit the pressure group but may not serve the interests of the public at large. A group's influence may be based less on the arguments for their position than on the size of their membership, the amount of their financial resources, or the number of lobbyists and their astuteness.

Lobbyists might focus their attention not only on key members of a committee but also on the committee's professional staff. Such staffs can be extremely influential, particularly when the legislation involves highly technical matters about which the member of Congress may not be that knowledgeable. Lobbyists also exert their influence through testimony at congressional hearings. These hearings may give the lobbyist a propaganda forum and also access to key Congress members who could not have been contacted in any other way. The lobbyists may rehearse their statements before the hearing, ensure a large turnout from their constituency for the hearing, and may even give leading questions to friendly committee members so that certain points can be made at the hearing.

Lobbyists do perform some important and indispensable functions, including helping inform both Congress and the public about specific problems and issues that normally may not get much attention, stimulating public debate, and making known to Congress who would benefit and who would be hurt by specific pieces of legislation (*Congressional Quarterly*, 1980). Many lobbyist believe that their most important and useful role, both to the groups they represent and to the government

itself, is the research and detailed information they supply. And in fact, many members of the government find the data and suggestions they receive from lobbyists valuable in studying issues, making decisions, and even in voting on legislation.

Political Action Committees An extremely influential form of special-interest group is the **political action committee (PAC).** These groups are characterized by several important features; they often represent single-issue groups; and most of their actions and political contributions represent corporate, trade, or labor interests. There are thousands of PACs in operation, and between 1981 and 1982, PACs contributed $83 million to congressional campaigns (U.S. Dept. of Commerce, 1984). Local candidates also are supported by PACs. With their rapid growth and abundant resources, PACs have had a significant and substantial influence on politics and policy.

Several criticisms have been leveled at these special-interest groups. Among the most prominent is that they represent neither the majority of the American people nor all social classes. Most members of PACs are affluent, well-educated individuals or big organizations, so that only about 10 percent of the population is in a position to exert this kind of pressure on the government. Disadvantaged groups—those who most need the ear of the government—have no access to this type of political action (Cummings and Wise, 1981).

A sociological perspective of politics allows us to trace the development of political power and structures in the Western world and to form a basis for studying our own political system. With our lives so affected by politics, it is important to understand the rapidly changing political scene—why, how, and which people get elected to office. PACs may

lobbying Attempts by special-interest groups to influence government policy.

political action committee (PAC) A kind of special-interest group that often represents a single-issue business group.

ultimately diminish the role of the individual voter. Part of their power comes from their ability to influence the media, which in turn exert great influence on our political system.

☐ Summary

From a sociologist's point of view, politics is the institutionalized process through which decisions that affect a community, a municipality, a state, or a society are made and enforced. Politics is the process by which people acquire and use power through the state. Power is the ability to carry out one's will even in the presence of resistance or opposition from others. Authority is power that is accepted as legitimate by those over whom it is exercised. There are three principal kinds of authority: charismatic, traditional, and legal-rational.

Our modern concept of government—those individuals and groups who control the political power at any given time—comes from the ancient Greeks. Their ideas have evolved into a variety of forms of government in the world today. These include autocracy, totalitarianism, and democracy. No matter what form of government exists in a particular society, it is expected to perform certain functions: to establish laws and norms, to enforce social control, to provide economic stability, to set goals, and to protect against outside threats.

Political change is the shift in the distribution of power among groups in a society. In a democracy such change is usually institutionalized; that is, it comes about through accepted legitimate channels such as elections. Political change can also emerge from rebellions and revolutions.

Rebellions are attempts to achieve rapid political change that is not possible within the existing institutions. They do not change the society's political and class structure. Revolutions, on the other hand, result in changes in the previously existing power structure of a society. Sociologists distinguish between political and social revolutions.

The American political system has certain distinctive characteristics that are of great interest to sociologists: (1) a winner-take-all two-party system, (2) a democracy in which voter participation is declining steadily, (3) a trend toward voting against, not for, a candidate or issue, (4) a tolerance for political and social protest movements, and (5) well-financed lobbies and political action committees (PACs) that work to influence elections as well as government spending and legislation.

☐ For Further Reading

BAXTER, SANDRA, and MARJORIE LANSING. *Women and Politics: The Invisible Majority*. Ann Arbor: University of Michigan Press, 1980. An examination of the political participation of women since they won the vote.

BRINTON, CRANE. *The Anatomy of Revolution*. New York: Vintage Books, 1962 (orig. 1938). A classic study of revolution. Brinton analyzes the French, American, and Russian revolutions, examining the conditions that led to them and the changes they wrought in their respective societies.

DAHL, ROBERT A. *Dilemmas of Pluralist Democracy: Autonomy Versus Control*. New Haven, Conn.: Yale University Press, 1982. Dahl looks at the problems of pluralism and suggests changes that might improve the current political system.

HAMILTON, RICHARD. *Restraining Myths: Critical Studies of U.S. Social Structure and Politics*. New York: Halsted Press, 1975. A study of the perspectives of pluralism, centrism, and mass society in American politics, which Hamilton argues are "restraining myths" that lead to naive analyses of political processes.

KLEHR, HARVEY. *The Heyday of American Communism: The Depression Decade*. New York: Basic Books, 1984. This exhaustively documented study of the American Communist party during the thirties is the definitive treatment of the subject.

MILLS, C. WRIGHT. *The Power Elite.* New York: Oxford University Press, 1956. One of the most influential studies of power ever written. Mills argues that American society is dominated by three major power centers: economic, political, and military. Each of these is controlled by a small (and interlocking) elite.

NIE, NORMAN H., SIDNEY VERBA, and JOHN PETROCIK. *The Changing American Voter.* Cambridge, Mass: Harvard University Press, 1976. A study of the basic shifts in the attitudes and behavior of American voters since the 1950s.

ORUM, ANTHONY M. *Introduction to Political Sociology: The Social Anatomy of the Body Politic.* 2d ed. Englewood Cliffs, N.J.: Prentice-Hall, 1983. A comprehensive textbook that presents the various theories of political systems.

RENSHON, STANLEY A. *Handbook of Political Socialization: Theory and Research.* New York: Free Press, 1977. A collection of many classic articles on the process by which adults are socialized into political attitudes and behavior.

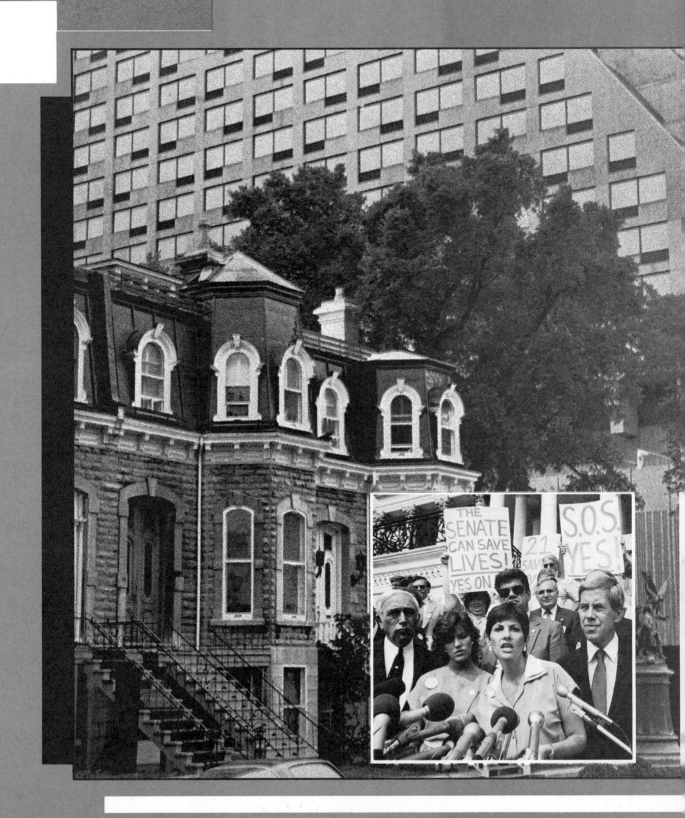

Social Change

□   □   □   □   □   □   □   □

Part Six

18 Social Movements and Collective Behavior

On June 12, 1982, a crowd estimated by police to number 600,000 to 700,000 people inched past a platform in front of the United Nations in New York to protest nuclear arms proliferation.

At a rock concert in Cincinnati, thousands of fans rushed forward as the doors were opened in order to obtain good seats. In the crush, 11 people were trampled to death, and countless others were knocked down and injured.

In July of 1982, Reverend Sun Myung Moon of the Unification church held a mass wedding ceremony for 2,074 couples, many of whom had been paired up only a few days before.

On May 17, 1980, rioters turned Miami, Florida, into a battleground. Angry blacks rampaged through the streets after an all-white jury acquitted 4 white police officers of the brutal killing of a black man. Buildings were looted and set ablaze, and 16 people lost their lives.

We have come to accept phenomena such as these as a natural part of modern existence. But how can they be explained? Where do race riots, panics, protest marches, social movements, and other forms of collective behavior fit into our analysis of society, culture, and subcultures?

Fires spread through parts of Miami as a result of rioting in response to the acquittal of four Miami policemen charged with the beating death of a black insurance salesman.

Throughout much of this text we have looked at the organized side of society—at its social groups, its social interactions, its institutions. We have described the various factors that hold society together, that pattern the interrelationships of peoples' lives in relatively predictable ways. In order to help make the present more understandable, we have traced certain historical developments—the agricultural and urban revolutions, the Industrial Revolution, political movements, social movements—that have left their mark on society as a whole and on the lives of every one of us. In this, the last section of our text, the forces of change themselves come into the spotlight for more intensive investigation.

☐ Collectivities in Social Life

This chapter focuses on **collective behavior** in social life—spontaneous actions by a number of people drawn together for a limited time in relatively unstructured patterns of behavior. Collective behavior may be seen in the form of a crowd watching an auto accident or an audience listening to a lecture. But, it is the more dramatic forms of collective behavior that we tend to remember: riots, lynchings, panics, and social movements. Collective behavior does not necessarily require that people come together in actual groups. They may share common concerns or interests, be physically dispersed, and still be part of a collective unit.

Collective behavior has the potential for causing the unpredictable, and even the improbable, to happen. Collective actions are capable of unleashing surprisingly powerful social forces that catch us by surprise and change our lives in both small and large ways, at times temporarily but at other times even permanently.

Theories of Collective Behavior

The study of collective behavior has fascinated many scholars, and as a result, several theories have been devised to account for crowd behavior. These include the contagion (or "mentalist") theory, the emergent norm theory, the convergence theory, and the value-added theory.

Contagion ("Mentalist") Theory Gustave Le Bon (1841–1931) was a French sociologist whose major interest was the role played by collective behavior in shaping historical events such as the storming of the Bastille in 1789, a turning point in the launching of the French Revolution. In 1895 Le Bon published his classic *The Psychology of Crowds* (1960), in which he argued that once individuals experience the sense of anonymity in a crowd, they are transformed. Hence, they think, feel, and act quite differently than they would alone. They acquire a crowd mentality, lose their characteristic inhibitions, and become highly receptive to group sentiments. Concerns for proper behavior or norms disappear, and individuals give up their personal moral responsibilities to the will of the crowd. When this happens, the crowd becomes a social entity greater than the sum of its individual parts.

Herbert Blumer (1946) explains the contagion that sweeps through a crowd as what he calls the "circular reaction" that typifies crowd behavior. In his view, a crowd begins as a collectivity of people more or less waiting for something to happen. Sooner or later an "exciting event" stirs them, and people react to it without the kind of caution and critical judgment they would ordinarily use if they were experiencing the event alone. Individuals become excited, the excitement spreads, the original event is invested with even greater emotional significance, and people give in to the engulfing "mood, impulse, or form of conduct." In this manner a crowd can spiral out of control, as when a casual crowd of on-lookers observing the arrest of a drunken driver is transformed into an acting crowd of rioters.

There are a number of problems with the contagion theory. Le Bon did not specify under what conditions contagion would sweep through a crowd. In addition, the theory does not account for events that could limit the spread of contagion or for the fact that contagion may affect only one portion of a crowd. Finally, research has not borne out Le Bon's basic premise that the average person can be transformed through crowd dynamics from a civilized being into an irrational and violent person.

Emergent Norm Theory Rather than viewing the formation of crowd sentiments and behavior as inherently irrational, as Le Bon and Blumer did, Ralph H. Turner (1964), as well as other sociologists, espouse the emergent norm theory of collective behavior. This theory implies that crowd members have different motives for participating in collective behavior. They acquire common standards by observing and listening to one another. In this respect, contagion does play a role in establishing the crowd's norms. A few leaders may help in the emergence of these norms by presenting the crowd with a particular interpretation of events. However, even without leaders, the crowd still can develop shared expectations about what behavior is appropriate.

The emergent norm theory provides the basis for analyzing the factors that push a crowd in one direction or another. If people bring with them into a crowd situation a set of expectations about the norms that are likely to be established, then the emergence of such norms will not be just a matter of the collective processes of the moment (Lang and Lang, 1961). Thus, many hockey fans attending the New York Rangers' games in Madison Square Garden expect to vent hostile feelings against opposing players; expect that members of the crowd will throw beer cans and other debris; and expect that management will encourage this fanaticism by playing "Charge!" music on the public address system, by flashing violence-oriented slogans on the scoreboard, and by selling alcoholic beverages. In other words, the fans expect to become frenzied. Predictably, fights often occur in the stands; sportswriters from out of town are subjected to abuse; and players from opposing teams are harassed. As one journalist put it, "A sense of hostility . . . pervades the arena . . ." (Fischler, 1980).

Convergence Theory Whereas contagion theory assumes that a crowd mentality arises when

collective behavior Actions by relatively large numbers of people drawn together for a limited time into noninstitutionalized patterns of behavior that are out of the ordinary in one way or another.

FOCUS ON RESEARCH
Punks, Hippies, and Middle-Class Values: A Comparison

It is the nature of youth to be critical of its elders. When enough young people share a disaffection with the social order as they see it, a social movement may be formed. Such was the case with the beatniks of the 1950s, the hippies of the 1960s, and, most recently, the punks of the 1980s. Each group rebelled in its own way against the values espoused by the dominant culture. Two sociologists have compared the value systems of two of these countercultures with those held by the American middle class, and some of their findings may surprise you.

Punks have not been social or political activists, but they have played a significant role in antinuclear rallies.

The punk movement first came to world attention in Great Britain during the long, hot summer of 1976, a year that had been a particularly bad one for the British. In addition to economic recession, racial violence, and drought, the British public was further distressed to learn that angry mobs of "disaffected" youth from inner-city working-class backgrounds had declared war on contemporary society, its institutions, and its dominant cultural values.

Television news programs and newspapers were filled with the bizarre pictures of costumed, zombie-like, x-rated cartoon characters who stalked the twilight streets of London, hanging out in the rock clubs and shops that catered to their new, adopted lifestyle of punk. Like their idols, the pub-playing punk rock bands, the fans (who were the punks), adorned themselves with safety pins, razor blades, paramilitary garb, and spiked "jewelry"; cropped or feathered their hair and often dyed it shocking colors; and painted their faces in the gaudy and grim starkness suggestive of death.

The movement soon jumped the Atlantic to find converts among the young people of America. Although the British movement had arisen among working-class youth, in the United States, punks usually were from middle-class backgrounds. Despite the difference in their origins, however, their feelings of alienation were the same. The punks vehemently reacted against the norms and values of the dominant culture, which they saw as repressive and inauthentic. They mocked conservative, capitalist big business which dictated what they must wear, buy, and listen to in music. They were cynical about the media, the police, and the entire social system, for which no one (including themselves) wanted to be responsible.

But even though these attitudes may sound very much like those of the hippies of the 1960s, punks never developed the political and social agendas that distinguished their predecessors. Though punks share some of the same contempt for middle-class values that the hippies did, in many ways the groups are very different. Two sociologists, Jack Levin and Philip Lamy, set out to discover just how the two groups differed and also how their values differed from those espoused by the American middle class.

To do this, Levin and Lamy selected for study representative punk lifestyle periodicals (as opposed to the primarily music and art-oriented fan magazines) from several major cities (*NOMAG* from Los Angeles, *The East Village Eye* from New York City, and *Take It!* from Boston). A single issue of each punk periodical from every second month in the year of 1982 was selected on a random basis. Then every second nonfiction article appearing in this sample of issues (for a total of 117 articles), excluding poetry and letters to the editor, was analyzed. In an earlier study, using an identical procedure, Levin and Spates (1970) had examined 316 articles from hippie publications (*Avatar* from Boston, *Distant Drummer* from Philadelphia, *East Village Other* from New York, *Lost Angeles Free Press*, *San Francisco Oracle*, and *Washington Free Press*) during 1967 and 1968.

To provide a comparable sample of articles representing middle-class values, concurrently published issues of the *Reader's Digest*, selected for its variety of middle-class articles from different sources, were analyzed. Excluding fiction and poetry, every second article appearing in every other issue was studied (for a total of 89 articles).

The major value-themes of articles in both the punk and middle-class samples were coded by means of a modified version of Ralph K. White's Value Category, a standardized test that measures values. Because of the presumed violent content of the punk subculture, an additional set of categories examining violence in the punk and middle-class literature was utilized.

Values were measured in four different categories: *Expressive*—articles dealing with such topics as humor, travel, art, sexual expression, friendship, concern for others, new discoveries, or religious themes; *Instrumental*—articles focusing on individual achievement through occupation and hard work, on education as a way of achieving success and happiness, and on discussions of economic issues at the business, state, or national level; *Violence*—articles dealing with physical or psychological injury to oneself, other persons or animals, sexual perversion, destruction of property, or nonviolent articles that had elements that were clearly peaceful, restrained, and respectful; or *Other*—articles exploring topics such as personal fulfillment, independence, and the development of personality; physiologically oriented articles on hunger, sex, health, or other medical topics; or political articles referring to group decision-making processes.

By analyzing the punk press and the *Reader's Digest*, it became clear that expressive concerns occupy a central position in the punk value structure, whereas instrumentalism (an achievement orientation) is virtually nonexistent. Expressive concerns accounted for 80 percent of the value-themes in the punk press, whereas instrumental concerns were the major focus of only 4 percent of these articles. In sharp contrast, instrumental concerns represented the major value theme in the *Reader's Digest* sample (38 percent), whereas expressive concerns were less important.

Although punk detractors often feel that the movement is violent by nature, no significant difference was uncovered between punk and middle-class samples with respect to violent content. Specifically, 35 percent of the articles in the punk sample and 26 percent in the *Reader's Digest* contained violence.

In their earlier study, Levin and Spates found that expressive concerns were the "staple of great magnitude" for readers of the hip underground press and the hippie movement as a whole. Expressive values accounted for 46 percent of their sample. But as high as the expressive content of the hippie movement was, punk expressivism is almost twice as high (80 percent). Moreover, individual and political concerns accounted for 20 percent and 19 percent respectively, of all value categories in the hippie press, but only for 4 percent and 9 percent in the punk press.

Punks are not, nor have they ever been, social and political activists. They have no alternative plan but have resigned themselves to parodying the entire "hopeless" situation that they see as their present and future state of existence. But despite its primary focus on expressive issues rather than political ones, the punk phenomenon in both Europe and America has played a significant role in the antinuclear rallies of recent years. Punks have been prominent among the protesters and have contributed to the apocalyptic "style" of the rallies. The skeletal, white painted "faces of doom" and the mutilated and bloodied bodies of a holocaust scenario are a direct influence of the punk aesthetic. Although the punk philosophy preaches a nihilistic philosophy and calls for the total rejection of society's norms, it is, in its negative way, positively directed. The punk movement succeeds in calling attention to itself and is able to spread its message of discontent, alienation, and uncertainty about humankind's future.

Source: Adapted from Philip Lamy and Jack Levin, "Punk and Middle-Class Values: A Content Analysis." Paper presented at the annual meeting of the American Sociological Association, August, 1984, San Antonio, Texas. □

---

people are gathered in a specific area and interact in ways that produce common perceptions and common behavior, **convergence theory** views collective behavior as the outcome of situations in which people with similar characteristics, attitudes, and needs are drawn together. In contrast with contagion theory, it is not the crowd situation that produces unusual behavior but, rather, that certain kinds of people that are predisposed to certain kinds of actions have been brought together. Consequently, if bizarre or unusual collective behavior takes place during and after a punk music concert, it is because people who are predisposed to this type of behavior have been drawn to the event. (For an interesting comparison of punk and hippie values, see Focus on Research: "Punks, Hippies, and Middle-Class Values: A Comparison.")

convergence theory Collective behavior is the outcome of situations in which people with similar characteristics, attitudes, and needs are drawn together.

PORTFOLIO VI
Persuasion and Protest

*Collective behavior takes many forms and has a wide range
of effects. It may have no formal organization, as in
dispersed collective behavior, when styles of dress are
followed, or as in acting crowds, when riots erupt. Or
collective behavior may be well organized with memberships
and goals and have a long history.*

*The goals of collective action are not always stated,
and in chaotic political times may not even be clear to the
individuals involved. Yet the shape and state of society
are the result of the interaction of many people acting
collectively within a society to influence, to persuade, to
plead, to bargain, to teach, and to force. Some of this
behavior is directed toward changing the present, and some
is directed toward maintaining the status quo.*

*Why are some methods chosen over others? Answers
are as complex as the forces that produce the actions.
Particular currents of history, the types of political systems,
the distribution of power, population growth or decline,
and economic inequities are all factors in determining
which group or movement will push forward, which will be
accepted, and which might resort to illegitimate methods if
its claims are rejected.*

*The pages that follow illustrate the different faces of
collective behavior: the organized and the disorganized, the
legal and the illegal, the peaceful and the violent. Individuals act in groups, and groups act not in isolation but
amid the forces of history, culture, and society.*

Seemingly individual acts can establish an affiliation with a larger group. Signs, symbols, dress, and even participation in a public event underscore shared attitudes and give a social reality to a collective which may not necessarily have any further organization.

IT'S MY RIGHT TO CHOOSE

Meetings, legal procedures of persuasion, and formal organization help to stabilize the ongoing process of influence and change, particularly in a pluralist society. But these types of collective behavior cannot always contain the range of expression generated by controversial issues. And the character of the behavior takes on a less structured tone.

War, revolution, and guerrilla warfare are expressions of unresolved conflicts between social and political forces. These forms of behavior go beyond influence and persuasion to coercion.

Convergence theory is helpful because it stresses the role of the individual and points out that no matter how powerful a group's influence may be, not everyone will respond to it. Therefore, it is unlikely that a group of conservative bankers who may be in attendance at the above-mentioned punk music event will be part of any unusual collective action.

The problem with convergence theory is that it cannot explain why crowds often pass through a number of stages, from disorganized milling to organized action against specific targets. If the participant's characteristics do not change, what does produce the changes in the crowd behavior? Convergence theory also does not tell us which events will ignite a crowd with common characteristics into action and which will thwart collective behavior.

Value-Added Theory Of all the attempts to understand collective behavior, the value-added theory of sociologist Neil Smelser (1962) is in many ways the most comprehensive. It attempts to explain whether collective behavior will occur and what direction it will take. Smelser suggests that when combined, the following six conditions shape the outcome of collective behavior:

1. *Structural conduciveness.* This refers to the conditions within society that may promote or discourage collective behavior. **Structural conduciveness** is tied to the arrangement of the existing social order. For example, in the United States there are many socially isolated inner-city neighborhoods in which poverty and crowding are common and in which people are victimized by highly institutionalized patterns of racial and ethnic discrimination. Watts, in Los Angeles, is such a neighborhood. These conditions have made Watts and similar areas throughout the country susceptible to riots.

2. *Structural strain.* When a group's ideals conflict with its everyday realities, **structural strain** occurs. This condition feeds on racial, ethnic, class, occupational, and other differences that give some groups a clear advantage over others. The race riots of the 1960s, for example, stemmed in part from the frustration that blacks felt over the disparity between the American dream of equality in a land of plenty and their lives of poverty, hunger, unemployment, and discrimination.

3. *Growth and spread of a generalized belief.* People develop explanations for the structural strains under which they must struggle to exist. When these explanations are clearly expressed and widely shared, collective behavior may take the shape of well-organized social movements, such as the civil rights and labor movements. The less clearly these explanations are expressed or the more competing explanations that exist, the more likely it is that collective behavior will emerge in an unstructured form, a riot, for example. In Watts there was no widely shared social or economic analysis other than a strong resentment of the police. Hence, it is not surprising that when collective behavior finally erupted in 1965, it was in the form of a riot rather than an organized social movement.

4. *Precipitating factors.* In all cases of collective behavior there is an event, or a related set of events, that triggers a collective response. For a group of California mothers who organized a campaign against drunk drivers, it was the loss or maiming of their children and other relatives by alcohol-impaired drivers that caused them to unite and take action. In Watts it was a combination of things: the arrest of a drunken driver; the gathering of a casual crowd of onlookers with long-standing antipolice sentiments; the arrival of the arrested driver's mother who began to yell at him, leading to his attempt to break away; the force used by the police to subdue him; the increased tension in the crowd that resulted in a woman spitting on the police; and the police officers' attempts to arrest her, which escalated crowd tensions and led to rumors that the police were beating up an innocent,

---

structural conduciveness One of sociologist Neil Smelser's six conditions that shape the outcome of collective behavior, structural conduciveness refers to the conditions within society that may promote or discourage collective behavior.

structural strain One of sociologist Neil Smelser's six conditions that shape the outcome of collective behavior, structural strain refers to the tension that develops when a group's ideals conflict with its everyday realities.

pregnant woman (Oberschall, 1968). Finally, rocks were thrown, and gangs of youths began to rampage through the streets, breaking into stores and looting.

— 5. *Mobilization for action.* A group of people must be mobilized or organized into taking action. For the women's movement, this mobilization occurred when the National Women's Political Caucus was formed in 1971 with the goal of breaking apart the male-dominated political power structure. The group's coalescence came at the Democratic National Convention in Miami in 1972, which Theodore H. White (1982) describes in the following passage:

> In a single year, from a standing start, the caucus had mastered the mechanics of politics. Women had been observing men practicing politics for years—but usually as handmaidens at conventions and campaign headquarters. They knew how to code names of delegates, how a boiler room operated, how to buttonhole, plead, lobby, threaten—and how to move whips about on the floor of an uncertain convention. These skills were now organized. Every one of the state delegations at the more than 40 Miami Beach convention hotels was circularized with bulletins, leaflets, news. Every night, blue-jeaned volunteers rode the buses to stuff the mailboxes, or slip reports under the door of every delegate. Their sisters on the floor were identified by cause and issue. They installed their own switchboard to link them to key delegations in the rival commands of McGovern and Hubert H. Humphrey.

When there are no previously recognized leaders to take charge, a group is easily swayed by its more boisterous members. In Watts there were no community leaders immediately at hand to direct people into organized, politically channeled social action. Hence, the event with the police mobilized the crowd into unplanned, expressive acts that included stone throwing and destruction of property. By the time community leaders attempted to intervene, the riot had escalated out of control.

6. *Mechanisms of social control.* At this point the course that collective behavior follows depends on the various ways those in power respond to the action in order to reestablish order. In Watts, community response took six days. The police, at first terribly outnumbered, were slow to do anything to suppress the crowd's expressive actions, and days passed before the National Guard was mobilized. Sensing a breakdown in social control, some residents moved to take advantage of the situation by looting stores and burning buildings. In addition, some political activists, hoping that disorder would lead to a widespread rebellion in the black community, helped fan the flames of riot. There is no evidence that the Watts riot was planned—but certainly many individuals took advantage of it to pursue their own ends.

According to Smelser, the final outcome of collective behavior depends on how each of the six determinants has built on the previous one. Each becomes a necessary condition and an important part of the next determinant.

☐ Social Movements

Social movements are perhaps the best-understood of collectivities. A **social movement** is ". . . a conscious, collective, organized attempt to bring about or resist large-scale change in the social order by noninstitutionalized means" (Wilson, 1973). Social movements are not always aimed at changing things. Rather, they may represent attempts to block or to slow down changes that are viewed as undesirable, as the antiequal rights amendment forces did. Because social movements typically have a life span that is measured in terms of years and because they are organized (to a greater or lesser degree), they are relatively easy for sociologists to study through participant observation, by means of selective interviewing, and even through investigation of historical records.

Types of Social Movements

In the previous chapter we discussed rebellions and revolutions, which certainly qualify as social movements; but there are other kinds of social movements as well. Scholars differ as to how they classify social movements, but some general characteristics are well recog-

Social movements sometimes involve attempts to block or slow down changes that are viewed as undesirable. These people have gathered to lend their support to nuclear disarmament.

nized. We shall discuss these characteristics according to William Bruce Cameron's (1966) four social-movement classifications: reactionary, conservative, revisionary, and revolutionary. In addition, we shall examine the concept of expressive social movements first developed by Herbert Blumer (1946).

Although this classification is useful to sociologists in their studies of social movements, in practice it is sometimes difficult to place a social movement in only one category. This is because any social movement may possess a complex set of ideological positions in regard to the many different features of the society, its institutions, the class structure, and the different categories of people within that society.

Reactionary Social Movements **Reactionary social movements** embrace the aims of the past and seek to return the general society to yesterday's values. Using slogans like "the good old days" and "our grand and glorious heritage," reactionaries abhor the changes that have transformed society and are committed to recreating a set of valued social conditions that they believe existed at an earlier point in time. Reactionary groups, such as the neo-Nazis and the Ku Klux Klan (see Case Study: "The Rise and Fall of the Ku Klux Klan"),

hold a set of racial, ethnic, and religious values that are more characteristic of a previous historic period. Their values legitimize prejudice and discrimination based on race, ethnicity, and religion, patterns that are now neither culturally legitimate nor legal.

Conservative Social Movements **Conservative social movements** seek to maintain society's current values. Reacting to change or threats of change that they believe will undermine the status quo, conservative movements are organized to prevent these changes from happening. The Moral Majority holds many conservative views. For example, it is opposed to the forces that promulgate equal rights for women. In order to preserve what it considers traditional values of the family and religion, the Moral Majority has threatened to boycott advertisers that sponsor television programs containing sex and violence

maintain groups

social movement A conscious, collective, organized attempt to bring about or resist large-scale change in the social order by noninstitutionalized means.

reactionary social movement A social movement that embraces the aims of the past and seeks to return the general society to yesterday's values.

conservative social movement A social movement that seeks to maintain society's current values.

CASE STUDY
The Rise and Fall of the Ku Klux Klan

The following study gives a profile of one of the country's best-known reactionary movements. As is true of many social movements, the Ku Klux Klan is not only a reactionary movement but has evolved into an expressive movement as well, particularly in recent years.

. . . Altogether there have been four major periods [in the history of the Ku Klux Klan], the first Klan rode during the troubled times after the American Civil War. The second Klan emerged just before World War I, reached its peak in the mid-twenties, and then suffered a long decline until World War II; gas rationing and back taxes forced its adjournment. Revived again after the war, the fragmented Klan world has not enjoyed the unity and moments of triumph known by its predecessors. It was deadly but not effective in countering the civil rights movement of the 1960s. The rise of black political power in the South, along with changing racial attitudes and an expanded police role of the national government, created formidable barriers to Klan night-riding violence. Nonetheless, after low fortunes for most of the decade of the 1970s, economic uncertainty, black-white confrontation in the smaller industrial towns of the deep South, and new leadership have produced a sporadic renewal of Klan violence and something of a revival. . . .

The Ku Klux Klan has been a vigilante organization, a revitalization movement, a status society, a secret order, a fraternal lodge and, in the twentieth century, a money-maker for its leaders. Its way has been violence. Throughout its history, the Klan has been a conservative, not a revolutionary organization. As a vigilante, it has sought to uphold "law and order," white dominance and traditional morality.

To do this it has threatened, flogged, mutilated and, on occasion, murdered. The main purpose of the Klansmen, Kligrapps, Kludds, and Night Hawks, Cyclopses, Titans, Dragons, and Wizards, assembled in their Dens, Klaverns and Klonvokations, rallying in rented cow pastures and marching in solemn procession through city streets, has been to defend and restore what they conceived as traditional cultural values. The noted anthropologist Anthony F. C. Wallace divides revitalization movements into *revivalism*, which seeks to "revive a previous condition of social virtue," and *nativism*, which attempts to "purge the society of unwanted aliens." Together these have been the sacred missions of the Klan. . . .

As the 1970s ended, Klan fortunes and violence were somewhat on the rise. A pudgy electrical contractor named Bill Wilkinson, wearing large mod glasses and a three-piece blue suit, and surrounded by rifle-carrying guards, organized a rough new Klan which confronted black "justice and job" marchers in the industrial towns of northern Mississippi and Alabama. In black communities across the nation, the Klan—however weak it may be—is the prime symbol of past suffering and present problems. The Southern Christian Leadership Conference (SCLC), seeking a sense of purpose and unity that it had not had since the death of Martin Luther King, Jr., undertook a struggle against the Klan and clashed with it in the streets. While Wilkinson and other Klan leaders recruit from the Klan's traditional world of bourbon and coke and pickup trucks with the rifle on the rack, a handsome, young, college-educated Klansman, David Duke, was downplaying his Nazi background and trying to give klandom a new image via the college campuses and national television.

Behind the revival lies a growing blue collar job anxiety, produced by what the Klans charge is government favoritism toward black peo-

The Ku Klux Klan is an example of a reactionary social movement.

ple in job training, employment and promotion. At a time when the national government seems to be drifting and the economy turning bad, the Klan revival is an expressive form of poor-boy politics. In the American South, the Ku Klux Klan is a traditionally available vehicle. For a limited number of rural-minded, working-class whites, unable to accept and powerless to prevent social change, the deadly game of Klan violence is an emotionally satisfying alternative to the actual power to control larger events.

From a spectator viewpoint, Americans have been fascinated with the Klan. It is seldom out of the newspaper headlines and is widely reported on television. When David Duke announced that his California realm would patrol the Mexican border against illegal aliens, only eight Klansmen, but more than a score of news and TV cameramen showed up.

The best way to see the recent Klans is as a status movement. This is involved in the answers to the question of where the Klans are going now: "What next?" Today's Klansmen are not only unhappy over the social politics of America's postindustrial, pluralistic society, they feel left out. Studies by the sociologist James Vander Zanden, the political scientist William Moore, and my own for the National Violence Commission have found the typical Klansman to be in his middle thirties with no more than a high school education. He has usually been a skilled blue-collar worker (carpenter, bricklayer, mechanic, truck driver), a small independent businessman (the owner-operator of a barber shop, gas station or repair shop), a small-town policeman or a part-time minister. Close to the juncture of the upper-working and lower-middle classes, the Klansman resents his lack of recognition and prestige in society.

By membership in the Klan as a defender of 100 percent American-ism, the white race, school, neighborhood and way of life, the Klansman confers on himself the prestige that society has otherwise withheld from him. In short, membership in the Klan is satisfying in itself, and may well lessen the need for overt action. However, although secrecy and the tradition, aura and talk of violence which generally pervade Klandom may lead to sporadic acts, the Klans lack the community approval and the police permissiveness necessary for a campaign of violence. . . .

And yet the hooded empires peopled by Klansmen, Klanswomen and FBI informants live on. In bygone times, the Klan patrolled the borders of race relations in the South. It was the erosion of those borders which produced a limited, though potentially violent Klan revival. There was an armed clash in Decatur, Alabama, and an anti-Klan rally in Greensboro, North Carolina, which left five dead at the hands of Klansmen and American Nazis. Perhaps the lesson that the revival was to teach again is that the Ku Klux Klan remains the means for the expression of social, economic and racial anxieties of at least a small part of a stratum of society in the American South. The Florida Grand Dragon summed it up with the melancholy explanation that the Klan exists because "the white people has rights just like anybody else."

Source: David Chalmers, "The Rise and Fall of the Invisible Empire of the Ku Klux Klan," *Contemporary Review,* **237** (August, 1980), pp. 57–64. □

---

and has mounted successful campaigns to defeat political candidates who oppose its views.

Conservative movements are most likely to arise when traditional-minded people perceive a threat of change that might alter the status quo. Reacting to what might happen if another movement achieves its goals, members of conservative movements mobilize an "anti" movement crusade. Thus, the conservative forces that opposed the equal rights amendment set up a highly successful anti-ERA campaign, and antigun control groups have waged political war against any group seeking to restrict the public's access to handguns. Although reactive in nature, conservative movements such as these are far different from true reactionary movements, which attempt to restore values that have already changed.

Revisionary Social Movements **Revisionary social movements** accept certain societal values but not others. They seek partial or slight changes within the existing order but do not threaten the order itself. The women's movement, for example, seeks to change the institutions and practices that have imposed prejudice and discrimination on women. The same revisionary goal is still held by the civil rights movement and was described in the following excerpt by Theodore H. White (1982), who traveled to Jackson, Mississippi, in 1964 to meet with members of the Student Nonviolent Coordinating Committee (S.N.C.C.):

In Jackson, the capital, I pass through the black district. Parched lawns littered with trash: shack houses with peeling paint, boards cracked and broken, raggedy children sitting on porches, peering out on nothing. . . . There, next to the Streamline Bar, is 1017 Lynch Street, S.N.C.C. storefront headquarters. It is unmarked but instantly recognizable—two students, one black and one white, are standing outside playing catch, and in the windows are those black and green stickers that say: ONE MAN— ONE VOTE.

Inside, the dominant presence is Bob Moses, the field marshal of the adventure drawing hundreds of students from all over the country. . . . Blinking, soft-spoken, gentle, Moses has been here in Mississippi for three

---

revisionary social movement A social movement that seeks partial or slight changes within the existing order but does not threaten the order itself.

years, trying to rouse his black people to their rights. They must be taught to vote; they must be taught to do things for themselves; they must be taught to be unafraid. He is sweet and stubborn and strong, the stuff of martyrs; he will not kill but will not hesitate to die. Five blacks here in Mississippi have been killed by unknown men since the first of the year; Moses has spent 17 days in solitary confinement in jail; his people are organizing the Mississippi Freedom Democratic Party to challenge the all-white political structure of the state; his people demand their constitutional right to vote. And there is no one authority to whom Moses can talk, no contact. No white official in Mississippi dares have contact with the blacks.

Revolutionary Social Movements **Revolutionary social movements** seek to overthrow all or nearly all of the existing social order and replace it with an order they consider to be more suitable. For example, the black guerrilla movement in Zimbabwe (formerly Rhodesia) was a revolutionary movement. Through the use of arms and political agitation, the guerrillas were successful in forcing the white minority to turn over political power to the black majority and in creating a new form of government that guaranteed that 80 of the 100 seats in the country's legislative body would be held by blacks. The first voting allowing full black participation resulted in the election of Robert Mugabe, a former guerrilla leader, as prime minister.

Although both revolutionary and revisionary social movements seek change in society, they differ in the degree of change they seek. The American Revolution, for example, which sought to overthrow British colonial rule and led to the formation of our own government, differed significantly from the women's movement, which seeks change within the existing judicial and legislative structures.

Expressive Social Movements **Expressive social movements** typically arise to fill some void or to distract people from some great dissatisfaction in their lives. Though other types of movements tend to focus on changing the so-

cial structure in some way, expressive social movements stress personal feelings of satisfaction or well-being. Movements—such as the Hare Krishnas and the "Moonies" of the Unification church—are religious movements of this type. The Yippies of the 1960s typify an expressive movement of a quasi-political nature. Arising in the context of American antiwar movement and the drug counterculture (see Chapter 3), the Yippies were a more or less organized group that sought to convert people to a new lifestyle. Jerry Rubin, one of the movement's founders, tells of its efforts at organization (1970): "We started . . . with an office, a mailing list, three telephone lines, five paid staff organizers, weekly general meetings, and weekly Steering Committee meetings. We were the hardest workers and most disciplined people you ever met, even though we extol [sic] sloth and lack of discipline. . . ." The Yippie lifestyle was pure hedonism, as Abbie Hoffman (1968), another founder, explains: "Our message is always: Do what you want. Take chances. Extend your boundaries. Break the rules. Protest anything you can get away with. Don't get paranoid. Don't be uptight."

The Life Cycle of Social Movements

Social movements, by their nature, do not last forever. They rise, consolidate, and eventually succeed, fail, or change. Armand L. Mauss (1975) suggested that social movements typically pass through a series of five stages: (1) incipiency, (2) coalescence, (3) institutionalization, (4) fragmentation, and (5) demise. However, these stages are by no means common to all social movements.

Incipiency The first stage, **incipiency**, begins when large numbers of people become frustrated about a problem and do not perceive any solution to it through existing institutions. This occurred in the nineteenth century when American workers, desperate over their worsening working conditions, formed the U.S. labor movement. It is a time of some disorder, when people feel the need for something to give their lives direction and meaning or to channel their behavior toward achieving necessary change. Disruption and violence may mark a social movement's incipiency. In 1886 and 1887, for example, as the labor movement grew, workers battled private Pinkerton agents and state militiamen and called nationwide strikes. Although physically beaten, the workers continued to organize.

It is also a time when leaders emerge. Various individuals offer competing solutions to the perceived societal problem, and some are more persuasive than others. According to Max Weber (see Chapter 17), many of the more successful leaders have charismatic qualities derived from exceptional personal characteristics. Samuel Gompers, who launched the American Federation of Labor (AFL) in 1881, was such a leader.

Coalescence In the stage of **coalescence**, groups begin to form around leaders, to promote policies, and to promulgate programs. Some groups join forces; others are defeated in the competition for new members. Gradually a dominant group or coalition of groups emerges that is able to establish itself in a position of leadership. Its goals become the goals of many; its actions command wide participation; and its policies gain influence. This occurred in the labor movement when in 1905, William D. Haywood organized the Industrial Workers of the World (IWW), which led its increasingly dissatisfied members in a number of violent strikes. Labor coalescence continued in 1935 when such militant industrial union leaders as John L. Lewis of the United Mine Workers and David Dubinsky of the International Ladies' Garment Workers founded the Committee for Industrial Organization (CIO), which rapidly organized the steel, automobile, and other basic industries. Thus, through coalescence, the labor movement gradually created several large, increasingly powerful organizations.

Institutionalization During the stage of **institutionalization**, social movements reach the peak of their strength and influence. Their leadership no longer depends on the elusive quality of charisma to motivate followers. Rather, it has become firmly established in formal, rational organizations (see Chapter 6), that have the power to effect lasting changes in the social order. At this point, the organizations themselves become part of the normal pattern of everyday life.

When the institutionalization of the U.S. labor movement became formalized with the legalization of unions in the 1930s, union leaders no longer used the revolutionary rhetoric that was necessary when unions were neither legitimate nor legal. Instead, they talked in pragmatic terms, worked within the political power structure, and sought reforms within the structure of the existing democratic, capitalistic system.

Not all social movements become institutionalized. In fact, social movements fail and disappear more often than they reach this stage. Institutionalization depends, to a great degree, on how the members feel about the movement—whether it reflects their goals and has been successful in achieving them—and on the extent to which the movement is accepted or rejected by the larger society.

Ironically, the acceptance of a social movement may also mark its end. Many members drop out or lose interest once a movement's goals have been reached. It can be argued that a certain amount of opposition from those in power reminds the members that they still must work to accomplish their goals. Movement leaders often hope for a confrontation that will clarify the identity of

revolutionary social movement A social movement that seeks to overthrow all or nearly all of the existing social order and replace it with an order it considers to be more suitable.

expressive social movement A social movement that stresses personal feelings of satisfaction or well-being and that typically arises to fill some void or to distract people from some great dissatisfaction in their lives.

incipiency The period in the life cycle of a social movement in which the movement begins.

coalescence The period in the life cycle of a social movement when groups begin to form around leaders, promote policies, and promulgate programs.

institutionalization The period in the life cycle of a social movement when the movement reaches its peak of strength and influence and becomes firmly established in formal, rational organizations.

the opposition and show the members against what and whom they must fight. Movements that evoke an apathetic or disinterested response from the institutions controlling the power structure have little around with which to unite their membership.

Fragmentation Having achieved their goals, social movements undergo **fragmentation** and gradually begin to fall apart. Their organizational structures no longer seem necessary because the changes they sought to bring about have been institutionalized or the changes they sought to block have been prevented. Disputes over doctrine may drive dissident members out, as when the United Auto Workers (UAW) and the Teamsters left the AFL-CIO. Also, demographic changes may transform a once strong social movement into a far less powerful force. Economic changes have been largely responsible for the fragmentation of the American labor movement. As was pointed out in Chapter 16, unions now represent the smallest share of the labor force since World War II, even though the work force continues to expand. Their lost power is due, in part, to a sharp decrease in the percentage of more easily unionized blue-collar workers in the labor force and a dramatic increase in the percentage of white-collar employees who are largely resistant to unionization.

Demise Eventually many social movements experience a **demise** and cease to exist. The organizations they created and the institutions they introduced may well survive—indeed, their goals may become official state policy—however, they are no longer set apart from the mainstream of society. Transformed from social movements into institutions, they leave behind well-entrenched organizations that guarantee their members the goals they sought. This pattern of social-movement demise has occurred in parts of the American labor movement. The United Auto Workers, for example, is no longer a social movement fighting for the rights of its members from the outskirts of the power structure. Rather, it is now an institutionalized part of society. But all unions have not followed this course. Labor is still very much a social movement,

for it is trying to organize such previously unorganized groups as farm workers, nonunionized clerical and professional workers, and all workers in the traditionally nonunion South. The American Federation of State, County, and Municipal Employees, which tripled in size between 1968 and 1980, is a recent example of the labor movement's continued organizational efforts.

In contrast with the long period of growth, development, and eventual demise usually associated with social movements, the life span of the collectivity called a crowd is always brief.

☐ Crowds: Concentrated Collectivities

A **crowd** is a temporary concentration of people who focus on some thing or event but who also are attuned to one another's behavior. There is a magnetic quality to a crowd: it attracts passersby who often will interrupt whatever they are doing to join. Think, for example, of the crowds that gather "out of nowhere" at fires or accidents. Crowds also fascinate social scientists, because crowds always have within them the potential for unpredictable behavior.

The collective behavior of crowds consists of group action that erupts quickly and often seems to lack structure or direction—either from leaders or from institutionalized norms of behavior. This was well illustrated during the summer of 1979 when the energy crisis hit America's drivers. Gasoline, the life's blood of most Americans' daily existence, suddenly was hard to get. Lines formed at gas stations, snaking back along streets and highways for miles, and motorists waited hours to fill their tanks. Most drivers waited quietly. Many listened to stereos, read, or watched portable TV sets. They bought coffee from youngsters who were quick to spot a lucrative market. But the calm only lasted a few days. Then the mood of some people on many lines changed. In some cases, violence erupted: fistfights, knifings, and shootings were reported; gas was stolen; motorists died. In Levittown, Pennsylvania, for example, some two thousand gas-craving people rioted for three days, destroying property and burning cars. Eventually two hundred people were arrested (*Time*, 1979).

Attributes of Crowds

In his study *Crowds and Power* (1978), social psychologist Elias Canetti attributed to crowds the following traits:

1. *Crowds are self-generating.* Crowds have no natural boundaries. When boundaries are imposed artificially—for example, by police barricades intended to isolate a street demonstration—there is an ever-present danger that the crowd will erupt and spill over the boundaries, thereby creating chaos. So, in effect, crowds always contain threats of chaos, serious disorder, and uncontrollable force.

2. *Crowds are characterized by equality.* Social distinctions lose their importance within crowds. Indeed, Canetti believes that people join crowds specifically to achieve the condition of equality with one another, a condition that carries with it a charged and exciting atmosphere.

3. *Crowds love density.* The circles of private space that usually surround each person in the normal course of events shrink to nothing in crowds. People pack together shoulder to shoulder, front to back, touching each other in ways normally reserved for intimates. Everyone included within the body of the crowd must relinquish a bit of his or her personal identity in order to experience the crowd's fervor. With a "we're all in this together" attitude, the crowd discourages isolated factions and detached onlookers.

4. *Crowds need direction.* Many crowds are in motion. They may physically move from place to place as they do in a marching demonstration or psychologically as at a rock concert. The direction of movement is set by the crowd's goals, which become so important to crowd members that individual and social differences lessen or disappear. This constant need for direction contains the seeds of danger: Having achieved or abandoned one goal the crowd may easily seize on another, perhaps destructive one. The direction that a crowd

will take depends on the type of crowd involved.

Types of Crowds

In his essay on collective behavior, Herbert Blumer (1946) classified crowds into four types: acting, expressive, conventional, and casual.

Acting Crowds   An **acting crowd** is a crowd in its most frightening form. It is a *mob*—a group of people whose passions and tempers have been aroused by some focal event, who come to share a purpose, and who feed off one another's arousal and often erupt into spontaneous acts of violence. The student antiwar groups of the late 1960s that stormed college administration offices and battled police were acting crowds, as were the gasoline rioters in Levittown and the militant Iranians who protested in front of the captured U.S. embassy in Teheran.

Acting crowds are a serious problem for the police, especially in cities. A routine arrest has the potential for provoking rage, violence, and full-scale riot, which is what occurred during the Toxteth, Britain, riot in 1981. When police tried to arrest a motorcyclist, a crowd of people attacked them and dragged the young man to safety. Three days of mayhem followed, with hundreds of black and white youths battling police and looting stores until things quieted down: the results—20 buildings gutted and 260 people injured.

A **threatened crowd** is a special form of acting crowd. It is a crowd that is in a state of

---

fragmentation The period in the life cycle of a social movement when the movement gradually begins to fall apart.

demise The period in the life cycle of a social movement when the movement comes to an end.

crowd A temporary concentration of people who focus on some thing or event but who also are attuned to one another's behavior.

acting crowd A group of people whose passions and tempers have been aroused by some focal event, who come to share a purpose, who feed off one another's arousal, and who often erupt into spontaneous acts of violence.

threatened crowd A crowd that is in a state of alarm, believing itself to be in some kind of danger.

USING SOCIOLOGY
Why Do People Join Cults?

Parents and friends of young people who join such cults as the Moonies, Hare Krishnas, or followers of Bhagwan Shree Rajneesh are often hurt, angry, or baffled by the joiner's decision. They seek ways to explain what seems unexplainable. Were the young people brainwashed, hooked on drugs, or coerced by cult members? One researcher, who has studied members of such groups, found a much more benign explanation for what seems to be a radical move.

Every year thousands of young people abruptly turn their backs on family, friends, and future to join one or another of an estimated 2500 communal groups in North America whose values, dress and behavior seem totally alien to everything the joiner has stood for. Such radical departures are a cultural phenomenon that has inspired more fear, agony, anger, disgust—and misinterpretation—than almost any other.

In seeking to account for such behavior, people have resorted to a variety of explanations: the joiners were troubled, academic failures; loners from embattled homes; drug addicts; or simply gullible innocents who had been brainwashed.

But Saul V. Levine, head of the department of psychiatry at Sunnybrook Medical Center in Toronto and author of a book on the subject of cults, found that, by and large, people who joined such ideological groups came right off the cover of *The Saturday Evening Post*. After intensively studying more than 400 subjects in 15 groups, he has concluded that there were no more signs of pathology among joiners than among any group of youngsters. They came from warm, concerned families that had given them every material, social and intellectual benefit. They were, in short, good kids with everything to look forward to.

Why, then, were they prompted to make such a drastic decision? To understand what makes them different, one must examine what normally happens to teenagers in our society.

In our middle-class culture, we strongly believe that during the adolescent years, children must separate from their families and establish their individuality both practically and psychologically. As children become teenagers, parents begin to diminish control. They no longer try to supervise homework or to act as constant chaperones. At the same time, parents also make it clear to high school students that adult responsibilities loom ahead. They are asked to think about college and to make tentative career choices; most are expected to leave home.

As parents withdraw control, their children also withdraw the unconditional love and faith that typify childhood. But because they cannot proceed into adulthood without love and without faith, they seek intimacy with friends and lovers. That is the normal course of events.

Among radical departers, however, the process is especially difficult. Few of these young people are able to separate gradually to everyone's satisfaction. All of them are still so closely tied to their parents that they resemble children, despite their true age. Few have been involved in relationships that were more than exploitive or tentative. None felt committed to a value system at the time they joined an ideological group.

Joiners look to belief as a way to avoid their personal dilemma. Feeling so little self-esteem, they can't shoulder the responsibility of perhaps making the wrong moral choice and thereby feeling even more worthless. They are looking for ideology that will bolster whatever is admirable in them, and purge whatever is bad.

Just at this critical period in their lives, they are offered what seems a magical solution: separation without out the pain, loneliness, self-doubt, and disillusion that usually accompanies the passage to adulthood. It is very common for such a young person to join an ideological group while away from home, sometimes for the first time. These young people wish to be back at home, safe from the frightening freedom of travel, but then how can they be separate? Separate, they feel empty, as if there is not enough to fill them. The departure is a compromise solution to this conflict.

Despite the public perception that teenagers are somehow tricked into joining radical groups, the initial encounter is actually only the beginning of a screening process that will sort out those who do belong from those who might be alien to the group. In fact, only about 5 of every 100 teens approached will agree to a first visit with the group; fewer than 10 percent who are then invited to a two or three day retreat ultimately decide to join. But this screening process is so accurate that, while only 1 in 500 of those originally approached choose to join, those who do usually stay at least six months.

Belonging is the heart of radical departure. The group is a unity, all doing the same things, believing the same beliefs, speaking the same stock phrases, eating the same food, wearing the same clothes, and working for the same cause. For the period of their commitment, joiners give up the usual adolescent struggle to form an independent self and instead participate with relief in a flawless group self.

But one of Levine's most fascinating findings about radical departure is that despite this intense commitment to the group, nine out of ten members leave their group within two years. After a period of some months, subtle but unmistakable changes begin. Dogmatic atti-

502

tudes relax; there are fewer unequivocal opinions and less inflexible faith. This is quickly followed by a siege of doubt about the perfection of the group and its leader, an upwelling of longing for the family, and, finally, a return to the world.

Radical departures, then, may be seen as a rehearsal for separation, practice for the real task of growing up. While the group members appear to be passively frozen into their narrow mold of commitment, they are, in fact, actively rehearsing for their coming out. The group has served its purpose, and the joiner is now psychologically fortified to deal with the conflicts posed by the passage to adulthood.

But some parents, reluctant to wait for this process to naturally run its course, resort to hiring deprogrammers to get their children back. In Levine's estimation, this is a serious mistake. Deprogramming, he says, works against the possibility that the joiners will resolve their conflicts, leave the group, and rejoin their families in the kind of mature relationship that cements generations. Deprogramming interferes with the natural rhythm of a radical departure, and it can drive young people back into their group, or into a pattern of cult-hopping, for years.

When deprogramming works—brings the joiner back to the family—the loss is even greater. Halted before they have been able to utilize the group self in their own behalf, former members are thrown back upon their psychological dependency on parents. The more clearly they perceive their "mistake," the less trust former members have in their own ability to make wise choices and the more dangerous freedom seems to them.

While no one claims that having a child or friend join a cult is a painless experience, Levine suggests that the best approach may be to wait it out. By understanding what it is that joiners seek, why they find commitment gratifying, and—most important—how the experience is of genuine psychological use to them, we are in a better position to judge what we as a society should do to enable our youth to emancipate themselves and find meaning in their lives.

Source: Saul V. Levine, "Radical Departures," *Psychology Today*, August, 1984, pp. 21–27. □

---

alarm, believing there to be some kind of danger present. Such a crowd is in a state of panic, as when a crowded nightclub catches fire and everybody tries to get out, jamming exits and trampling one another in their rush to escape. A threatened crowd created havoc when a busboy accidentally ignited an artificial palm at the Coconut Grove Night Club in Boston on November 28, 1942, spreading fire instantaneously through the rooms of the club. The fire lasted only 20 minutes, but 488 people died. Most died needlessly when panic gripped the crowd. Fire investigators found that the club's main entrance—a revolving door—was jammed by hundreds of terrified patrons. With their escape route blocked, these people died of burns and smoke inhalation only feet away from possible safety (Veltfort and Lee, 1943). In this as well as other threatened crowds, there is a lack of communication regarding escape routes.

Expressive Crowds
An **expressive crowd** is drawn together by the promise of personal gratification for its members through active participation in activities and events. For example, many rock concert audiences are not content simply to listen to the music and watch the show. In a very real sense they want to be part of the show. Many dress in clothing calculated to draw attention to themselves, take drugs during the performance, dance in the aisles and in packed masses up against the stage, scream and chant, sometimes in unison, and delight in giving problems to security personnel. Another type of expressive crowd is the religious cult, and for an examination of the satisfactions gained from joining this kind of crowd, see Using Sociology: "Why do People Join Cults?"

Conventional Crowds
A **conventional crowd** is a gathering in which people's behavior conforms to some well-established set of cultural norms and in which people's gratification re-

expressive crowd A crowd that is drawn together by the promise of personal gratification for its members through active participation in activities and events.

conventional crowd A crowd in which people's behavior conforms to some well-established set of cultural norms and in which people's gratification results from a passive appreciation of an event.

sults from a more passive appreciation of an event than it does in an expressive crowd. Such crowds include the audiences attending lectures, the theater, and classical music concerts, where it is expected that everybody will follow traditional norms of etiquette.

Casual Crowds A **casual crowd** is the inevitable outgrowth of modern society in which large numbers of people live, work, and travel closely together. Any collection of people who just happen, in the course of their private activities, to be in one place at the same time and focus their attention on a common object or event is called a casual crowd. On Fifth Avenue in New York City at noon, many casual crowds gather to watch the construction of a new building, an accident, a purse snatcher, or a theatrical performer. A casual crowd has the potential of becoming an acting crowd or an expressive crowd; the nature of a crowd can change if events change.

The Changeable Nature of Crowds

Although the typology presented is useful for distinguishing among kinds of crowds, it is important to recognize that any particular crowd can shift from one type to another. For example, if a sidewalk musician starts playing a violin on Fifth Avenue, part of the aggregate walking by will quickly consolidate into a casual crowd of onlookers. Or, an expressive crowd at a rock concert will become a threatened crowd if a fire breaks out.

Changing times may also affect the nature of crowds. For example, until the 1970s, British soccer matches generally attracted conventional crowds who occasionally would turn into expressive crowds chanting team songs. In the last decade or so, however, British soccer fans have become active crowds: fighting in the stands is epidemic, charging onto the field to assault players and officials has become common, and near rioting has taken place, as bands of roving fans have terrorized the neighborhoods around stadiums by assaulting passersby and destroying property.

Because they are relatively concentrated in place and time, crowds present rich materials for sociological study (even if much of the data must be tracked down after the dust has settled). However, when collective behavior is widely dispersed among large numbers of people whose connection with one another is minimal or even elusive, the sociologist must then deal with phenomena that are extremely difficult to study, including fads and fashions, rumors, public opinion, panics, and mass hysteria.

☐ Dispersed Collective Behavior

In this age of mass media, with television and other systems of communication spreading information instantaneously throughout the entire population, collective behavior shared by large numbers of people who have no direct knowledge of one another has become commonplace. Sociologists use the term **mass** for such a collection of people who, although physically dispersed, participate in some event either physically or with a common concern or interest.

A nationwide television audience watching a presidential address or a superbowl game is a mass. So are those individuals who rush out to buy the latest best-selling record and the fashion-conscious whose hemlines, lapel widths, and designer jeans always reflect the "in" look. In other words, dispersed forms of collective behavior seem to be universal.

Fads and Fashions

Fads and **fashions** are transitory social changes (Vago, 1980), patterns of behavior that are widely dispersed among a mass but that do not last long enough to become fixed or institutionalized. Yet it would be foolish to dismiss fads and fashions as unimportant just because they fade relatively quickly. In modern society, fortunes are won and lost trying to predict fashions and fads—in clothing, in entertainment preferences, in eating habits, in choices of investments.

Probably the easiest way to distinguish between fads and fashions is to look at their typical patterns of diffusion through society. Fads have a very short life span marked by a rapid spread and an abrupt drop from popularity. This was the fate of the Hula Hoop in the 1950s and the dance "the twist" in the 1960s.

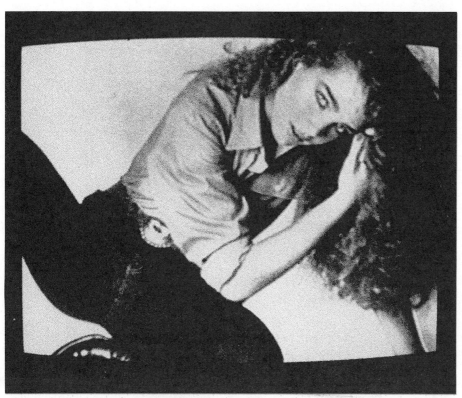

Fashions spread more slowly and last longer than fads.

The roller-skating fad that emerged in 1979 rolled off into the pages of history sometime in the 1980s, as did the Rubik's cube. A fad that is especially short-lived may be called a **craze**. Streaking, or running naked down a street or through a public gathering, was an American craze of the mid-1970s. It seems to have been a descendant of mooning (showing one's bare buttocks), which was a craze among college students in the late 1960s.

At the peak of their popularity, fads and crazes may become competitive activities. For example, when streaking was a craze, individual streaking was followed by group streaking, streaking on horseback, and parachuting naked from a plane. (See Popular Sociology: "The Sports-Crazy Americans," for a discussion of what many considered a fad and which has turned into an important aspect of American society.)

Fashions relate to the standards of dress or manners in a given society at a certain time. They spread more slowly and last longer than fads. In his study of fashions in European clothing from the eighteenth to the present century, Alfred A. Kroeber (1963) shows that though minor decorative features come and go rapidly (that is, are faddish), basic silhouettes move through surprisingly predictable cycles that he correlates with degrees of social and political stability. In times of great stress, fashions change erratically, but in peaceful times they seem to oscillate slowly in cycles lasting about one hundred years.

casual crowd A crowd that is made up of a collection of people who, in the course of their private activities, just happen to be in one place at the same time.

mass A collection of people who, although physically dispersed, participate in some event either physically or with a common concern or interest.

fad A transitory social change that has a very short life span is widely dispersed, and has an abrupt drop from popularity.

fashion A transitory change in the standards of dress or manners in a given society.

craze A fad that is especially short-lived and significantly deviant.

POPULAR SOCIOLOGY
The Sports-Crazy Americans

Sports contests in the United States this year will draw an estimated half-billion fans to everything from peewee football to big-league baseball. Is this just a fad, or is it indicative of a major development in American society? The following examines the extent and implications of this phenomenon.

Richer and with more leisure time than ever, the U.S. has truly become a sports-crazy nation. In every age group, in every region, in every walk of life, a passion for athletics is blossoming.

Professor Charles Prebish of Pennsylvania State University whose field is religious studies, has created a controversy even at sports-minded Penn State by arguing that sport, for an increasing number of Americans has "replaced traditional religion as a means of reaching the ultimate reality."

Religion or not, sport's appeal lies in the sense of freedom and release such activity offers from the monotony and pressures of everyday routine. Taking part in athletics gives people a sense of control and mastery that might not be present in other parts of their lives.

Among the most avid of the nearly 100 million Americans engaging in regular exercise programs are those who hold high-paying jobs. For example, lawyers, accountants, physicians and executives dominate the 22,000 member New York Road Runners Club.

While swimming remains the most popular participant sport, running is the most visible. In a recent survey by the National Park Service, 26 percent of the respondents reported that they jogged, a sport that was too "insignificant" even to be included in a similar survey 20 years ago.

The fastest-growing participant sports, according to a survey by A.C. Nielsen Company, are snow skiing, sailing and soccer. Also gaining in

In every age group, in every region, in every walk of life, a passion for sports continues to be a dominant force.

popularity: Strenuous exercise. Some 34 million people tried physical conditioning—calisthenics and weight lifting—last year.

The sports boom has also had an impact on job opportunities. These days, interest in health, fitness and recreation opens the door to careers that run the gamut from business to medicine to history.

"There has probably never been a time in our society with greater opportunities in sports and recreation than now," says Tony Mobley, dean of the School of Health, Physical Education and Recreation at Indiana University, Bloomington. The American College of Sports Medicine now has 11,000 members, up from 4,000 in 1978. More than a quarter of them are physicians, but there are also exercise biochemists and kinesiologists, among other professionals.

Demand is great enough that many physicians practice sports medicine almost exclusively. The number of sports and cardiovascu-

lar nutritionists belonging to the American Dietetic Association has more than doubled in the past two years.

The expanding opportunities are reflected in rising student interest. This year Penn State turned away 25 qualified applicants to its graduate program in sports psychology because there was no room available. The health-fitness management program at North Texas State has grown from 25 students five years ago to 113 now, and Prof. Bob Patton says: "We can place everyone who graduates."

Sports historians also find a ready audience. Universities offering a course in sports history have grown from a handful a decade ago to easily 100 today.

Hospitals are considered a prime job area because many of them are beginning to offer employee-fitness programs for corporate clients.

Most experts predict that sports will continue to generate an increasing supply of jobs. It is assumed that for the remainder of the 20th century there will be a high interest in all aspects of sports, and there will be thousands of positions available in health, physical education and recreational sports.

Still the sports boom has its drawbacks, such as rising numbers of emergency-room visits by weekend athletes who strain their bodies too far and high pressure parents who turn playgrounds for children as young as 5 years old into arenas of fierce competition.

On balance, though, most observers say that the good outweighs the bad in America's sports craze, which shows no sign of ebbing.

Source: "Sports-Crazy Americans," "Keeping in Shape—Everybody's Doing It," and "New Jobs Blossom in Leisure Field," *U.S. News & World Report*, August 13, 1984, pp. 23–25, 28. □

Georg Simmel (1957) believed that changes in fashion (such as dress or manners) are introduced or adopted by the upper classes who seek in this way to keep themselves visibly distinct from the lower classes. Of course, those immediately below them observe these fashions and also adopt them in an attempt to identify themselves as "upper crust." This process repeats itself again and again, with the fashion slowly moving down the class ladder, rung by rung. When the upper classes see that their fashions have become commonplace, they take up new ones, and the process starts all over again.

Blue jeans have shown that this pattern may no longer be true today. Jeans started out as sturdy work pants worn by those engaged in physical labor. Young people then started to wear them for play and everyday activities. College students wore them to class. Eventually fashion designers started to make fancier, higher-priced versions, known as designer jeans, worn by the middle and upper classes. In this way the introduction of blue jeans into the fashion scene represents movement in the opposite direction from what Simmel noted.

Of course, the power of the fashion business to shape consumer taste cannot be ignored. Fashion designers, manufacturers, wholesalers, and retailers earn money only when people tire of their old clothes and purchase new ones. Thus, they shift hemlines up and down and widen and narrow lapels to create new looks, which consumers purchase.

Indeed, the study of fads and fashions provides sociologists with recurrent social events through which to study the processes of change. Because they so often use concrete and quantifiable objects, such as consumer goods, fads and fashions are much easier to study and count than are rumors, another common form of dispersed collective behavior.

Rumors

A **rumor** is information that is shared informally and spreads quickly through a mass or a crowd. It arises in situations that, for whatever reasons, create ambiguity with regard to their truth or their meaning. Rumors may be true, false, or partially true, but characteristically they are difficult or impossible to verify. Thus, rumors of police brutality and the arrival of troops fanned the flames of riot in Watts. In the midst of such chaos, it was difficult to ascertain anything, and widespread fear made people susceptible to believing any new story that made the rounds.

Rumors are generally passed from one person to another through face-to-face contact, but they can be started through television, radio, and newspaper reports as well. However, when the rumor source is the mass media, the rumor still needs people-to-people contact to enable it to escalate to the point of causing widespread concern (or even panic).

Sociologists see rumors as one means through which collectivities try to bring definition and order to situations of uncertainty and confusion. In other words, rumors are "improvised news" (Shibutani, 1966). Recognizing this, sociologists have been able to help prevent riots in a number of potentially inflammable situations. For example, a national motorcycle race was planned for the Labor Day weekend at Upper Marlboro, Maryland, in the summer of 1965. But earlier that summer, after the national championship motorcycle races in Laconia, New Hampshire, on July 4, the nearby resort town of Weir Beach had erupted into riot. Planners for the Labor Day races were worried that it might happen again—a fear that was strengthened when three Hells Angels motorcyclists (who had been arrested and jailed for disorderly conduct) threatened to "tear up the county." Two sociologists offered their services to law-enforcement officials planning crowd control. Among other things they set up a system for investigating all rumors and quickly disseminating correct information. In their analysis of "the riot that didn't happen" the sociologists credited the continuous flow of accurate information as being one of the major factors in keeping the crowds—which at times were quite unstable—from erupting into serious violence (Shellow and Roemer, 1965).

---

rumor Information that is shared informally and spreads quickly through a mass or a crowd.

Some rumors die more easily than others do. Hard-to-believe rumors usually disappear first, but this is not always the case. In 1975, for example, Eastern Airlines was plagued with a rumor that several of the company's jet liners were haunted by the crew of another Eastern jet that had crashed in the Florida Everglades on December 30, 1972. Pilots and flight attendants reported that the faces of their dead colleagues appeared mysteriously in the cockpits of their planes. Despite its lack of proof and plausibility, the rumor quickly spread among Eastern employees, and passengers and the crews of other airliners heard it as well. It became even more disturbing when reports of grounded planes and passengers seeing ghosts were added onto the original story. "It's kind of a 'flying Dutchman,' " said an executive from Eastern Airlines, referring to the ghost of the legendary sailor sentenced to pilot his ship until Judgment Day. "It's amazing what can happen when a rumor starts" (Perry and Pugh, 1978).

Public Opinion

The term *public* refers to a dispersed collectivity of individuals concerned with or engaged in a common problem, interest, focus, or activity. An *opinion* is a strongly held belief. Thus, **public opinion** refers to the beliefs held by a dispersed collectivity of individuals about a common problem, interest, focus, or activity. It is important to recognize that a public that forms around a common concern is not necessarily united in its opinions regarding this concern. For example, Americans concerned with the issue of abortion are sharply divided into pro and con camps.

Whenever a public forms, it is a potential source of support for, or opposition to, whatever its focus is. Hence, it is extremely important for politicians, market analysts, public relations experts, and others who depend on public support to know the range of public opinion on many different topics. These individuals often are not willing to leave opinions to chance, however. They seek to mold or influence public opinion, usually through the mass media. **Advertisements** are attempts to mold public opinion, primarily in the area of consumption. They may create a "need" where there was none, as they did with fabric

TV newscaster Dan Rather could be considered an opinion leader, a socially acknowledged expert to whom the public turns for information.

softeners, or they may try to convince consumers that one product is better than another when there is actually no difference at all. Advertisements of a political nature, seeking to mobilize public support behind one specific party, candidate, or point of view technically are called **propaganda** (but usually by only those lay persons in disagreement). For example, radio broadcasts from the Soviet Union are habitually called "propaganda blasts" in the American press, but similar "Voice of America" programs are called "news" or "informational broadcasts."

Opinion leaders are socially acknowledged experts to whom the public turns for advice. The more conflicting sources of information there are on an issue of public concern, the more powerful the position of opinion leaders becomes. They weigh various news sources and then provide an interpretation in what has been called the two-step flow of communication. These opinion leaders can have a great influence on collective behavior, including voting (Lazarsfeld et al., 1968), patterns of consumption, and the acceptance of new ideas and inventions. Typically, each social stratum has its own opinion leaders (Katz, 1957), but the mass media have made news anchor people, like Dan Rather and Walter Cronkite before him, accepted opinion leaders for a broad portion of the American public.

When rumor and public opinion grip the public imagination so strongly that "facts" no longer seem to matter, terrifying forces may be unleashed. Mass hysteria may reign, and panic set in.

Mass Hysterias and Panics

On a Wednesday in June, 1962, reports began emerging from a small Southern town of a mysterious illness that had stricken workers in a local clothing plant. According to the 6 P.M. news, at least 10 female employees were hospitalized after complaining of feeling nauseated. While no hard evidence was available, the broadcast blamed the outbreak on "some kind of bug" that may have found its way into the country on a shipment of cloth from England. By the time the 11 P.M. news aired, the stricken workers had narrowed the cause of their illness to the bite of a small insect. They quickly labeled this insect the "June Bug."

Two days later, experts from the U.S. Public Health Service Communicable Disease Center in Atlanta, Georgia, arrived at the plant to investigate the cause of the mysterious outbreak. They set up a task force of community and health service officials to search the plant for the small black bug most employees believed was responsible for the outbreak. Their efforts were fruitless. The only bugs they found in the entire plant were a housefly, a black ant, a mite, and several entirely innocent gnats and beetles. Even though the investigators reported that they could not find the cause of the illness (indeed, no cause was ever found), the outbreak continued. By the time it ended, 62 people were stricken in what sociologists believe was a case of mass hysteria (Kerckhoff and Back, 1968).

When large numbers of people are overwhelmed with emotion and frenzied activity or become convinced that they have experienced something for which investigators can find no discernible evidence, they are suffering from a case of **mass hysteria**. A **panic** is an uncoordinated group flight from a perceived danger, as in the public reaction to the 1938 Orson Welles's radio broadcast of H. G. Wells's "War of the Worlds" and to Joseph Granville's warning to investors to abandon the stock market and "sell everything."

Such bizarre events are not very common, but they do occur often enough to present a challenge to social scientists, some of whom believe there is a rational core behind what at first glance appears to be wholly irrational behavior (Rosen, 1968). For example, sociologist Kai Erikson (1966) looked for the rational core behind the wave of witchcraft trials and hangings that raged through the Massachusetts Bay Colony beginning in 1692, when a group of mostly adolescent girls first pointed their accusing fingers at three "witches": a slavewoman from Barbados, an old and decidedly odd spinster, and a lady of rather high social standing whose chastity had been suspect and the subject of much gossip. Erikson joins most other scholars in viewing this troublesome episode in American history as an instance of mass hysteria (Brown, 1954). He accounts for it as one of a series of symptoms, suggesting that the colony was in the grip of a serious identity crisis and needed to create real and present evil figures who stood for what the colony was not—thus enabling the colony to define its identity in contrast and build a viable self-image.

Mass hysterias account for some of the

public opinion The beliefs held by a dispersed collectivity of individuals about a common concern, interest, focus, or activity.

advertisements Attempts to mold public opinion, usually in the area of consumption.

propaganda Advertisements of a political nature seeking to mobilize public support behind one specific party, candidate, or point of view.

opinion leaders Socially acknowledged experts to whom the public turns for advice.

mass hysteria A condition in which large numbers of people are overwhelmed with emotion and frenzied activity or become convinced that they have experienced something for which investigators can find no discernible evidence.

panic An uncoordinated group flight from a perceived danger.

more unpleasant episodes in history. Of all social phenomena they are among the least understood—a serious gap in our knowledge of human behavior. The potential destructiveness of outbursts of collective violence has risen with the modern expansion of worldwise mass communication. This network provides a means by which collective behavior can sweep swiftly from society to society, across oceans and continents. Americans suffered through a grim version of such continent-hopping mass hysteria in 1979 and early 1980 when the seizure of the U.S. embassy in Iran quickly was followed by mob assaults on American embassies in Pakistan, Libya, and several other countries. Any attempt to understand social change in the modern world will have to deal with this phenomenon.

The perception of danger that causes a panic may come from rational as well as irrational sources. A fire in a crowded theater, for example, can cause people to lose control and trample one another in their attempt to escape. This happened when fire broke out in the Beverly Hills Supper Club on May 28, 1977. In their attempt to escape the overcrowded, smoke-filled room, people blocked the exit doors and 164 people died.

According to Irving Janis and his colleagues (1964), people generally do not panic unless four conditions are met. First, they must feel that they are trapped in a life-threatening situation. Second, they must perceive a threat to their safety that is so large that they can do little else but try to escape. Third, they must realize that their escape routes are limited or inaccessible. Fourth, there must be a breakdown in communication between the front and rear of the crowd. Driven into a frenzy by fear, people at the rear of the crowd make desperate attempts to reach the exit doors, their actions often completely closing off the possibility of escape.

☐ Summary

Collective behavior refers to spontaneous actions by a number of people drawn together for a limited time in relatively unstructured patterns of behavior. There are several theories that have emerged to account for crowd behavior. These include the contagion (or "mentalist") theory, the emergent norm theory, the convergence theory, and the value-added theory.

Neil Smelser devised the value-added theory, suggesting that the following six conditions shape the outcome of collective behavior: structural conduciveness, structural strain, growth and spread of a generalized belief, precipitating factors, mobilization for action, and mechanisms of social control.

A social movement is a conscious, collective, organized attempt to bring about or resist large-scale change in the social order by noninstitutionalized means. Reactionary social movements embrace the aims of the past and seek to return the general society to yesterday's values. Conservative social movements seek to maintain society's current values. Revisionary social movements seek partial or slight changes within the existing order but do not threaten the order itself. Revolutionary social movements seek to overthrow all or nearly all of the existing social order and replace it with an order they consider to be more suitable. Expressive social movements stress personal feelings of satisfaction and well-being and arise to fill some void or to distract people from their problems.

Social movements typically pass through a series of five stages: (1) incipiency, (2) coalescence, (3) institutionalization, (4) fragmentation, and (5) demise.

A crowd is a temporary concentration of people who are focused on some thing or event but who are also attuned to one another's behavior. The behavior of crowds consists of group action that erupts quickly and often seems to lack structure or direction. Canetti (1978) attributed the following traits to crowds: (1) crowds are self-generating; (2) equality exists within the crowd; (3) density is important; and (4) direction is needed.

An acting crowd, often called a mob, frequently erupts into spontaneous acts of violence. A threatened crowd is an acting crowd in a state of alarm, believing itself to be in some kind of danger. An expressive crowd is drawn together by the promise of personal gratification for its members through active participation in activities and events. A conventional crowd is a gathering in which people's behavior conforms to some well-established set of cultural norms, whose gratification results from passive appreciation. A casual crowd is any collectivity of people who just happen to be in one place at the same time. The nature of a crowd does not necessarily remain stable and can change if events change.

Because today's systems of communication spread information quickly among millions of people, collective behavior is often shared by large numbers of people who have no direct knowledge of or contact with one another. Such a collectivity is called a mass. Fads and fashions are patterns of behavior that are widely dispersed among a mass. Rumor is a form of information that spreads quickly and informally through a mass or a crowd. The mass can often be influenced by public opinion: advertisements, propaganda, and opinion leaders. When rumor and public opinion catch the mass imagination so strongly that facts no longer seem to matter, mass hysteria and panic may set in.

☐ For Further Reading

ERIKSON, KAI T. *Wayward Puritans: A Study in the Sociology of Deviance.* New York: John Wiley, 1966.   A penetrating study of the three "crime waves" that swept across the Massachusetts Bay Colony in the seventeenth century. Original insights presented in clear and engaging language.

GARROW, DAVID J. *Protest at Selma: Martin Luther King, Jr., and the Voting Rights Act of 1965.* New Haven, Conn.: Yale University Press, 1978.   King's strategy before, at, and after the 1965 march on Selma, Alabama, to secure the right to vote for blacks. Garrow shows the critical role of the media in creating public and congressional support for direct federal intervention and, five months later, for the passage of the Voting Rights Act of 1965.

KOCH, HOWARD. *The Panic Broadcast: Portrait of an Event.* Boston: Little, Brown, 1970.   The fascinating story of the mass panic that erupted in 1938 from the broadcast of a radio adaptation of H. G. Wells's "War of the Worlds," written by the man who wrote the radio script. Koch recreates vividly the terror and excitement of the night when America believed that the Martians had landed.

PUGH, MEREDITH D. *Collective Behavior: A Sourcebook.* St. Paul, Minn.: West Publishing, 1980.   A collection of papers covering a variety of topics, including collective violence, disaster research, and social movements.

SMELSER, NEIL J. *Theory of Collective Behavior.* New York: Free Press, 1963.   A comprehensive structural-functionalist approach to understanding collective behavior.

TILLY, CHARLES. *From Mobilization to Revolution.* Reading, Mass.: Addison-Wesley, 1978.   A superb analysis of collective political action, from the food riots and land seizures of the sixteenth century to modern-day strikes, demonstrations, and revolutions. Written in an engaging style, the book explains how the growth of the nation-state, capitalism, and modernization have affected such collective behavior.

TOURAINE, ALAIN. *The Voice and the Eye: An Analysis of Social Movements.* (Trans. Alan Duff.) New York: Cambridge University Press, 1981.   A theoretical interpretation of several current social movements.

WOOD, JAMES L., and MAURICE JACKSON. *Social Movements: Development, Participation, and Dynamics.* Belmont, Calif.: Wadsworth, 1982.   An examination of the theories of social movements using a variety of up-to-date examples.

WORSLEY, PETER M. "Cargo Cults." *Scientific American* (May, 1959).   The classic article on Melanesian cargo cults, the conditions that breed them, and the dynamics that operate to sustain them.

ZALD, MAYER N., and JOHN D. MCCARTHY (eds.). *The Dynamics of Social Movements: Resource Mobilization, Social Control, and Tactics.* Cambridge, Mass.: Winthrop Publishers, 1979.   A collection of papers delivered at a symposium, using the resource mobilization theory of social movements.

19 Population and Demography

"Short of nuclear war itself, population growth is the gravest issue that the world faces over the decade ahead. . . . Both can and will have catastrophic consequences. If we do not act, the problem will be solved by famine, riot, insurrection, war."

This view was put forth by Robert S. McNamara, a former secretary of defense and president of the World Bank. Like many other specialists in this field, he believes that overpopulation is now threatening the basic fabric of world order.

The problem is underscored by the increasing speed with which the world's population is multiplying. It took from the beginning of people on the face of the earth until 1960 to reach a world population of three billion, but another two billion have been added just between 1960 and 1986.

During the past decade, the number of people on earth has increased by 770 million, and approximately 80 to 90 million are currently being added each year. The World Bank estimates that in the year 2025, the global population will be 8.3 billion. Of that total, approximately 7 billion will be residents of the poorest and least-developed nations. **Demography** is the systematic study of the dynamics of human populations. Population problems invariably have an impact on the environment. **Ecology** is the study of the relationships between populations and their environment. In this chapter we shall explore several issues that affect human populations.

☐ Population Processes

Population problems become progressively more pressing because of what is referred to as *exponential growth*. The yearly increase in population is determined by a continuously expanding base. Each successive addition of one million people to the population requires less time than the previous addition required. The best way to demonstrate the effects of exponential growth is to use a simple example. Let us assume that you have a job that requires you to work eight hours a day, every day, for 30 days. At the end of that time, your job is over. You are given two choices for how you will be paid for your work. The first choice

is to be paid $100 a day for a total of $3,000 dollars. The second choice is somewhat different. The employer will pay you 1 cent for the first day, 2 cents for the second day, 4 cents for the third, 8 cents on the fourth, and so on. Each day you will receive double what you received the day before. Which form of payment will you choose? The second form of payment will yield a significantly higher total payment, in fact so high that no employer could realistically pay the amount. Through this process of successive doubling, you would be paid $5.12 for your labor on the tenth day. Only on the fifteenth day would you receive more than the flat $100 a day you could have received from the first day under the alternative form of payment: the amount that day would be $163.84. However, from that day on, the daily increase in pay would start to be quite dramatic. On the twentieth day you would be paid $5,242.88, and on the twenty-fifth day your pay would be $167,772.16. Finally on the thirtieth day, you would be paid $5,368,708.80, and your total pay for the month would have exceeded $10 million.

The above example demonstrates how the continual doubling in the world's population produces enormous problems. The annual growth rate in the world's population has declined from 2 percent to 1.7 percent, which means that the world's population now doubles every 42 years instead of every 35 years. Although this is an improvement for the world as a whole, many portions of the world have not seen any improvement in their growth rates; in fact the reverse may be true. In some countries in Africa, the national fertility rates have actually increased in the past decade, and Africa is now the area of the world with the most rapid population growth. For the continent as a whole, the yearly percentage increase in population is 3 percent, which means that the population of the entire continent will double in 23 years and will be ten times the number it is today within 77 years.

demography The systematic study of the dynamics of human populations.

ecology The study of the relationship between populations and the environment.

TABLE 19.1 *Urban Areas with More Than 10 Million Inhabitants: 1950, 1975, and 2000*

1950	(Millions)		(Millions)
New York, northeast New Jersey	12.2	London	10.4
1975			
New York, northeast New Jersey	19.8	Los Angeles, Long Beach	10.8
Tokyo, Yokohama	17.7	Sao Paulo	10.7
Mexico City	11.9	London	10.4
Shanghai	11.6		
2000			
Mexico City	31.0	Cairo, Giza, Imbaba	13.1
Sao Paulo	25.8	Madras	12.9
Tokyo, Yokohama	24.2	Manila	12.3
New York, northeast New Jersey	22.8	Greater Buenos Aires	12.1
Shanghai	22.7	Bangkok, Thonburi	11.9
Beijing	19.9	Karachi	11.8
Rio de Janeiro	19.0	Delhi	11.7
Greater Bombay	17.1	Bogota	11.7
Calcutta	16.7	Paris	11.3
Jakarta	16.6	Tehran	11.3
Los Angeles, Long Beach	14.2	Istanbul	11.2
Seoul	14.2	Baghdad	11.1
		Osaka, Kobe	11.1

Source: United Nations, "Patterns of Urban and Rural Population Growth," Population Studies no. 68 (New York: United Nations, 1980).

In some parts of the world, the growth rate is even beyond what we just described. In Kenya, for example, the average woman now has eight children. When this fact is combined with the declining infant mortality rate, the country's population could balloon from 20 million today to 160 million in the year 2050. Bangladesh and India are two other countries for which enormous growth has been projected.

Most of the world's growth in population in the next few decades will take place in the developing countries. The population of the richer countries will increase by 200 million by the year 2050, and the developing areas will have added about 6 billion (see Figure 19.1).

Symbolizing the shift in population from the developed to the less-developed world is Sao Paulo, Brazil. In 1950, this city was smaller than Manchester, England, but by 2000 Sao Paulo could have a population of 25.8 million

and be one of the largest cities in the world. London, which was the second largest city in the world in 1950, would not be in the top 25 largest cities in 2000 if current growth trends continue (see Table 19.1). Population processes are influenced by three important factors: *fertility, mortality, and migration.*

Fertility

Fertility refers to the actual number of births in the population. One common way of measuring fertility is by means of the **crude birthrate,** a statement of the number of annual births per 1,000 people in the population. The crude birthrate for the United States fell from 24.1 in 1950 to 15.9 in 1980 (U.S. Dept. of Commerce, 1984). Some possible explanations for this trend are discussed in Focus on Research: "Childless Americans."

Another indicator of reproductive behavior is the **fertility rate,** the number of annual births per 1,000 women of childbearing age,

TABLE 19.2   Fertility Rates, 1950 to 1980

Year	Fertility Rate
1980	68.4
1979	68.5
1978	66.6
1977	67.8
1976	65.8
1975	66.0
1974	68.4
1973	69.2
1972	73.4
1971	81.8
1970	87.9
1965	96.6
1960	118.0
1955	118.3
1950	106.2

Source: Adapted from U.S. Department of Commerce, Bureau of the Census, *Statistical Abstract of the United States, 1984* (Washington, D.C.: Government Printing Office, 1983).

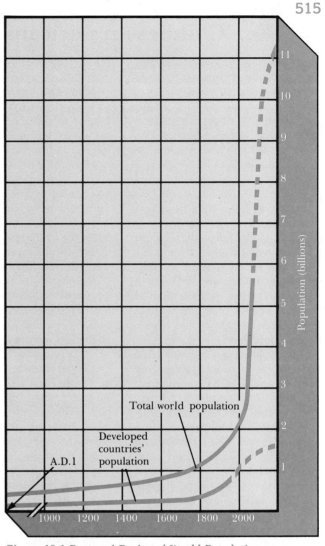

Figure 19.1 Past and Projected World Population, A.D. *1–2150*

usually defined as ages 15 to 44. (Fertility rates for American women between 1950 and 1980 are shown in Table 19.2.)

As you will see later in this chapter, the fertility rate is linked to industralization. Fertility declines with modernization, but not immediately. This lag is a source of tremendous population pressure in developing nations that have benefited from the introduction of modern medical technology, which immediately lowers mortality rates.

Mortality

Mortality is the frequency of actual deaths in a population. The most commonly used measure of this is the **crude death rate,** that is, the annual number of deaths per 1,000 population. Demographers also look at **age-specific death rates,** which measure the an-

fertility The actual number of births in the population.

crude birthrate The annual number of births per 1,000 population.

fertility rate The number of annual births per 1,000 women of childbearing age in a population.

mortality The frequency of actual deaths in a population.

crude death rate The annual number of deaths per 1,000 population.

age-specific death rates The annual number of deaths per 1,000 population at specific ages.

FOCUS ON RESEARCH
Childless Americans

In the following article, Anne R. Pebley, from Princeton University's Office of Population Research, and David E. Bloom, from Carnegie-Mellon University's School of Public and Urban Affairs, apply sociological principles to an analysis of the lowering fertility rate in the United States and its probable effects on society.

As many as 30 percent of today's young women may never have any children. Unprecedented millions of childless women reflect a changing American society: the use of effective contraception, the availability of abortion, the rising expectations of women, changing attitudes about marriage and the family, and the two-income household. . . .

The childless can be divided into four groups: (1) those who are physically incapable of having children; (2) those who could have children, but who choose to remain childless; (3) those who are forced by circumstances beyond their control—such as financial hardship or divorce—to postpone childbearing until they no longer are able or willing to have children; and (4) those who are uncertain about having children, so continue to delay a decision.

Most studies of childlessness concern individuals who are sterile, or who choose not to have children. Researchers understand the causes of sterility better than the reasons people choose not to have children. Research on voluntary childlessness suffers from the difficulty of finding a large and representative sample of the voluntarily childless. In addition, these studies usually examine older women who have already completed their childbearing. But older childless women were making that decision at a time when almost all women had children, and so they are likely to be a select group. Those young women who will remain childless today come from a variety of backgrounds and may have different reasons than previous generations for not having children.

Many childless women may not formally choose to remain childless, but do so only because they have postponed having a child until it is too late. A few researchers have investigated the reasons behind delayed childbearing among today's young women, but because they do not yet know which women will remain childless, it is difficult to distinguish the characteristics of the permanently childless from the majority who will eventually have children.

Despite these limitations, the people who choose to remain childless fit the following rough description: Typically, the voluntarily childless woman is white, lives in an urban area, and is highly educated, employed, not devoutly religious, and more likely than other women to be separated or divorced. Couples with higher incomes also are more likely to remain childless. These are the characteristics of a group whose members are likely to be economically successful and to have many options in life.

Because three-fourths of all Americans live in urban areas, the greater frequency of childlessness among urbanites probably has more to do with the fact that people who live in rural areas today are a select group—more oriented to family life, with greater economic and social incentives to have children. In small rural communities, family ties are important; residents are often involved in church activities, and wives have fewer employment opportunities. Each of these factors encourages childbearing soon after marriage.

The relationship between childlessness and education may be, in part, a matter of definition: Young couples who have a child in their teens or early twenties are often unable to continue in school. However, women who are motivated to finish college or graduate school probably are more likely to postpone childbearing. Once they complete school, these women may further delay having children in order to take a job. After repeated postponements, parenthood may lose its attraction. Demographic research suggests that education is strongly related to low fertility and childlessness in part because it changes a person's perspective on life. The rising educational level of Americans may depress fertility.

Because day-care facilities in this country are inadequate to accommodate the increase in working mothers, and because the burden of child care still falls on mothers, having a child directly conflicts with having a career. It is no surprise, therefore, that women who are interested in careers are most likely to postpone or forgo childbearing. Childless women more frequently hold professional positions and are more likely to be professionally successful. . . .

The relationship between higher income and childlessness is not surprising, because household income is closely associated with the education and employment status of the wife.

Women who marry when they are older are more likely to remain childless. For one thing, they are exposed to the possibility of pregnancy for a shorter time. However, many women postpone marriage for reasons that also increase their chances of never having children: to pursue an education or a career, and to maintain an independent way of life.

Childlessness may change the way Americans live. The cultural draw of the cities is likely to be more attractive to childless couples than to parents, who usually see the suburbs as a better place to raise children. Many two-career childless couples, in particular, prefer cities because the employment opportunities are better. . . .

Growing childlessness will affect consumption patterns. The per capita income of childless households will be higher than that of households with children because there are fewer household members, and in many childless households, the wife has earnings. Despite the fact that they could save more, couples who intend to remain childless have much less incentive to save because they do not face the expense of college tuitions, a large house, or the costs of raising children. Childless couples, particularly two-career couples, are likely to have more money to spend on luxury goods.

Childless couples are more likely to buy evening theater and concert tickets, a sports car, a high quality stereo, and other adult pleasures. Because childless couples are likely to have a less structured schedule and greater discretionary income, they may also travel more extensively than couples with children, both for business and pleasure. Two-career childless couples are also likely to substitute money for time by hiring cleaning help and buying time-saving appliances, eating out, and buying prepared food.

Having children typically interrupts women's education and career. To the extent that such interruptions discourage women from investing in their training or careers, the trend to childlessness may help increasing numbers of women advance upward through organizational ranks and enable more women to participate in the labor force.

In the long run, a rise in childlessness also will change the way we care for the elderly. Although the elderly receive little income from their children, children provide important care and companionship for their elderly parents. Instead of relying on children, the childless elderly and particularly older women, who are likely to survive their husbands by several years, may have to rely on people their own age for care and companionship. Many of them will also be childless.

Because of the changes in women's roles, marriage patterns, and family relationships, a return to higher fertility seems unlikely. Low fertility, however, does not necessarily imply continued increases in childlessness. If day care were more prevalent and work hours more flexible, fewer women might decide to remain childless.

Source: Anne R. Pebley and David E. Bloom, "Childless Americans," *American Demographics* **4**(1) (January, 1982), pp. 18–21.

---

nual number of deaths per 1,000 population at specific ages. For example, one measure used is the **infant mortality rate,** which is the number of children who die within the first year of life per 1,000 live births. In the United States the infant mortality rate dropped from 47.0 in 1940 to 12.6 in 1980 (see Table 19.3). This rate does not apply to all infants, however. In 1940 whites had an infant mortality rate of 43.2 (below the national average), and nonwhites had an infant mortality rate of 73.8. In 1981 the rates were 10.5 for whites and 17.8 for nonwhites. These figures suggest that good infant medical care is not equally available to all Americans. Differing cultural patterns of childrearing may also affect infant mortality.

Mortality is reflected in people's **life expectancy,** the average number of years that a person born in a particular year can expect to live (see Table 19.4). Life expectancy is usually determined more by infant than adult mortality. Once an individual survives infancy, his or her life expectancy improves dramatically. In the United States, for example, only when individuals reach their sixties do their chances of dying approximate those of their infancy (U.S. Dept. of Commerce, 1984).

In developing countries, the proportion of infant and child deaths is quite high, causing there to be a significantly lower life expectancy than that in developed countries. The high proportion of deaths can be attributed to impure drinking water and unsanitary conditions. In addition, the diet of pregnant women and nursing mothers often lacks proper nutrients, and babies and children are not fed a healthy diet. Flu, diarrhea, and pneumonia are common, as are typhoid, cholera, malaria, and tuberculosis. Many children are not immunized against common

infant mortality rate The number of children who die within the first year of life per 1,000 live births.

life expectancy The average number of years that a person born in a particular year can expect to live.

TABLE 19.3 *Infant Mortality Rates, 1940 to 1980*

Year	Whites	Nonwhites	Total
1940	43.2	73.8	47.0
1950	26.8	44.5	29.2
1955	23.6	42.8	26.4
1960	22.9	43.2	26.0
1965	21.5	40.3	24.7
1970	17.8	30.9	20.0
1971	17.1	28.5	19.1
1972	16.4	27.7	18.5
1973	15.8	26.2	17.7
1974	14.8	24.9	16.7
1975	14.2	24.2	16.1
1976	13.3	23.5	15.2
1977	12.3	21.7	14.1
1978	12.0	21.1	13.8
1979	11.4	19.8	13.1
1980	11.0	19.1	12.6
1981	10.5	17.8	11.9

Source: Adapted from U.S. Department of Commerce, Bureau of the Census, *Statistical Abstract of the United States, 1985* (Washington, D.C.: Government Printing Office, 1984), p. 73.

childhood diseases, such as polio, measles, diphtheria, and whooping cough, and the parents' income is often so low that when the children do fall ill, they cannot provide medical care (World Bank, 1984).

TABLE 19.4 *Life Expectancy in the United States, 1900 to 1982*

Year	Whites	Nonwhites	Total
1900	47.6	33.0	47.3
1920	54.9	45.3	54.1
1930	61.4	48.1	59.7
1940	64.2	53.1	62.9
1950	69.1	60.8	68.2
1955	70.5	63.7	69.6
1960	70.6	63.6	69.7
1965	71.0	64.1	70.2
1970	71.7	65.3	70.9
1971	72.0	65.6	71.1
1972	72.0	65.7	71.2
1973	72.2	66.1	71.4
1974	72.8	67.1	72.0
1975	73.4	68.0	72.6
1976	73.6	68.4	72.9
1977	74.0	68.9	73.3
1978	74.1	69.3	73.5
1979	74.6	69.8	73.9
1980	74.4	69.5	73.7
1981	74.8	70.3	74.2
1982*	75.1	70.9	74.5
1983*	75.2	71.3	74.7

*Preliminary.

Source: Adapted from U.S. Commerce, Bureau of the Census, *Statistical Abstract of the United States, 1985* (Washington, D.C.: Government Printing Office, 1984), p. 69.

Migration

Migration is the movement of populations from one geographical area to another. When a population leaves an area, it is said to be **emigrating;** when it enters an area, it is *immigrating.* All migrations, therefore, are both emigrations and immigrations.

Sometimes it is important to distinguish between those movements of populations that cross national boundary lines from those that are entirely within a country. In order to make this distinction, sociologists use the term **internal migration** for movement within a nation's boundary lines—in contrast with **immigration,** in which boundary lines are crossed. For example, the map in Figure 19.2 shows how the center of the U.S. population has shifted westward, reflecting the dominant pattern of internal migration from 1790 onward. Since 1970, population growth in the United States has been greatest in the sunbelt states, reflecting continued migration patterns south and west. Between 1970 and 1980

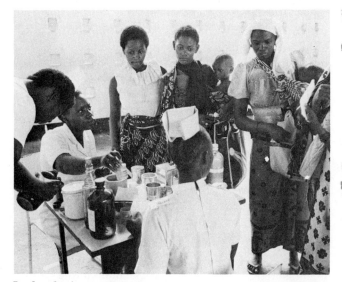

In developing nations the incidence of flu, diarrhea, and pneumonia is high, as is typhoid, cholera, malaria, and tuberculosis.

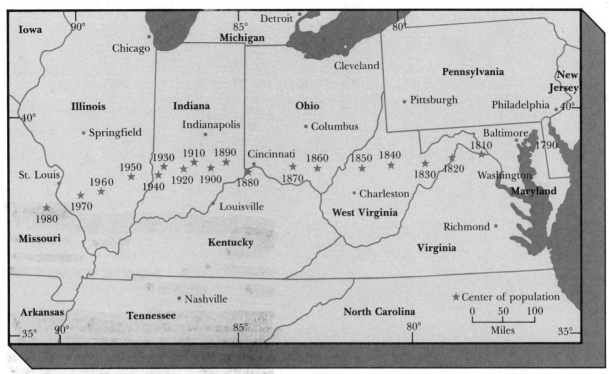

Figure 19.2 Center of United States Population, 1790–1980* **Since the beginning of the United States, its center of population has moved steadily westward. It has also moved southward since 1900.**

*Center of population is that point at which an imaginary flat, weightless, and rigid map of the United States would balance if weights of identical value were placed on it so that each weight represented the location of one person at the date of the census.

Alaska, Florida, Arizona, Nevada, and Wyoming grew by more than 30 percent, and New Mexico, Colorado, Utah, Idaho, Oregon, and New Hampshire grew by more than 20 percent. By contrast, the populations of such eastern states as Rhode Island, New York, and Pennsylvania actually declined (*Time,* 1980).

It is estimated that 10 to 13 million people around the world are being forced to migrate because of war, famine, and political oppression. The Office of U.S. Coordinator for Refugee Affairs estimated that in 1979 alone, close to 600,000 refugees fled Indochina to refugee camps all across Southeast Asia, and it is known that many tens of thousands of so-called boat people drowned at sea or were murdered by pirates. Again, in 1980 many thousands of Cubans left Cuba, including the nearly 125,000 who entered the United States (U.S. Dept. of Commerce, 1981). Once

again, as at the turn of the century, the United States has received hundreds of thousands of the world's homeless (see Table 19.5) who, after arriving on these shores, settle in such states as California (one out of four registered immigrants lives in California), New York, Texas, Florida, and Illinois. As we discussed in Chapter 11, this new wave of immigration has had serious social, economic, and political repercussions both positive and negative, in all the states that attract large numbers of immigrants.

migration The movement of populations from one geographical area to another.

emigration The movement of a population away from an area.

internal migration The movement of a population within a nation's boundary lines.

immigration The movement of a population into an area.

TABLE 19.5 *Immigration to the United States, 1820 to 1980*

Period	Total	
	Number	*Rate**
1820–1830	152,000	1.2
1831–1840	599,000	3.9
1841–1850	1,713,000	8.4
1851–1860	2,598,000	9.3
1861–1870	2,315,000	6.4
1871–1880	2,812,000	6.2
1881–1890	5,247,000	9.2
1891–1900	3,688,000	5.3
1901–1910	8,795,000	10.4
1911–1920	5,736,000	5.7
1921–1930	4,107,000	3.5
1931–1940	528,000	.4
1941–1950	1,035,000	.7
1951–1960	2,515,000	1.5
1961–1970	3,322,000	1.7
1971–1980	4,493,000	2.1

*Annual rate per 1,000 U.S. population.

Source: Adapted from U.S. Department of Commerce, Bureau of the Census, *Statistical Abstract of the United States, 1985* (Washington, D.C.: Government Printing Office, 1984), p. 84.

☐ Theories of Population

The study of population is a relatively new scholarly undertaking, as it was not until the eighteenth century that populations as such were carefully examined. The first person to do so, and perhaps the most influential, was Thomas Malthus.

Malthus's Theory of Population Growth

Thomas Robert Malthus (1776–1834) was a British clergyman, philosopher, and economist who believed that population growth is linked to certain natural laws. The core of the population problem, according to Malthus, is that populations will always grow faster than the available food supply will. With a fixed amount of land, farm animals, fish, and other food resources, agricultural production can be increased only by cultivating new acres, catching more fish, and so on—an additive process that Malthus believed would increase the food supply in an arithmetic progression (1, 2, 3, 4, 5, and so on). Population growth, on the other hand, increases at a geometric rate (1, 2, 4, 8, 16, and so on) as couples have 3, 4, 5, and more children. (A stable population requires that two individuals produce no more than 2.1 children: 2 to reproduce themselves and 0.1 to make up for those people who remain childless.) Thus, if left unchecked, human populations are destined to outgrow their food supplies and suffer poverty and a never-ending "struggle for existence" (a term coined by Malthus that later became a cornerstone of Darwinian and evolutionary thought).

Malthus recognized the presence of certain forces that limit population growth, grouping these into two categories: preventive checks and positive checks. **Preventive checks** are practices that would limit reproduction. These include celibacy, the delay of marriage, and such practices as contraception within marriage, extramarital sexual relations, and prostitution (if the latter two are linked with abortion and contraception). **Positive checks** are events that limit reproduction either by causing the deaths of individuals before they reach reproductive age or by causing the deaths of large numbers of people, thereby lowering the overall population. Positive checks include famines, wars, and epidemics. Malthus's thinking was assuredly influenced by the plague that wiped out so much of Europe's population during the fourteenth and fifteenth centuries.

Malthus refuted the theories of the **utopian socialists,** who advocated a reorganization of society in order to eliminate poverty and other social evils. Regardless of any planning, Malthus argued, misery and suffering are inevitable for most people. On the one hand, there is the constant threat that population will outstrip the available food supplies; on the other, there are the unpleasant and often devastating checks on this growth, which result in death, destruction, and suffering.

Marx's Theory of Population Growth

Karl Marx and other socialists rejected Malthus's view that population pressures and their attendant miseries are inevitable. Rather, they argued, it is industrialism (and in particular, capitalism) that creates the social and economic conditions for population growth. Industrialists need large populations to keep the labor force adequate, available, flexible, and inexpensive. In addition, the capitalistic system requires constantly expanding markets,

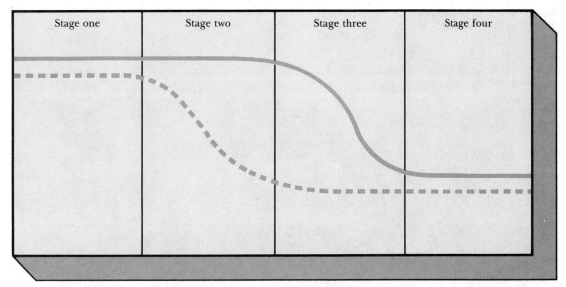

| Stage one | Stage two | Stage three | Stage four |

Figure 19.3 The Demographic Transition The demographic transition theory states that societies pass through four stages of population change. Stage 1 is marked by high birth rates and high death rates. In stage 2, populations rapidly increase as death rates fall, but birth rates stay high. In stage 3, birth rates begin to fall. Finally, in stage 4, both fertility and mortality rates are relatively low.

which can be assured only by an ever-increasing population. As the population grows, large numbers of unemployed and underemployed people compete for the few available jobs, which they are willing to take at lower and lower wages. Therefore, according to Marxists, the norms and values of a society that encourages population growth are rooted in its economic and political systems. Only by reorganizing the political economy of industrial society in the direction of socialism, they contended, is there any hope of eliminating poverty and the miseries of overcrowding and scarce resources for the masses.

Demographic Transition Theory

In 1929, Warren Thompson developed a theory of population dynamics that attempted to explain the rates of population growth in Europe following the Industrial Revolution. According to the **demographic transition theory,** societies pass through four stages of population change. During stage 1, high fertility rates are counterbalanced by a high death rate due to disease, starvation, and natural disaster. The population tends to be very young, and there is little or no population growth. During stage 2, populations rapidly increase as a result of a continued high fertility that is linked to the increased food supply, development of modern medicine, and public health care. Slowly, however, the traditional institutions and religious beliefs that support a high birthrate are undermined and replaced by values stressing individualism and upward mobility. Family planning is introduced, and the birthrate begins to fall. This is stage 3, during which population growth begins to decline. Finally, in stage 4 both fertility and mortality are relatively low, and population growth once again is stabilized (see Figure 19.3).

preventive checks Practices, described by Thomas Robert Malthus, that limit reproduction. Examples: contraception, prostitution, and other "vices."

positive checks Events, described by Thomas Robert Malthus, that limit reproduction either by causing the deaths of individuals before they reach reproductive age or by causing the deaths of large numbers of people, thereby lowering the overall population. Examples: famines, wars, and epidemics.

utopian socialists Theorists who advocated the reorganization of society to eliminate poverty and other social evils.

demographic transition theory. A theory that explains population dynamics in terms of four distinct stages.

The government of India has attempted to reduce population growth by disseminating birth control information.

Applications to Industrial Society   The first wave of declines in the world's death rate came in countries experiencing real economic progress. These declines gradually gained momentum as the Industrial Revolution proceeded. Advances in agriculture, transportation, and commerce made it possible for people to have a better diet, and advances in manufacturing made adequate clothing and housing more widely available. A rise in people's real income facilitated improved public sanitation, medical science, and public education.

Although the preceding explanation applies well to Western society, it does not explain the population trends in the underdeveloped areas of today's world. Since 1920 these areas have had a much faster drop in death rates than Western societies ever experienced. This has happened without a comparable rate of increasing economic development. The rapid rate of decline in the death rate in these countries has been due primarily to the application of medical discoveries made

and financed in the industrial nations. For example, the most important source of death being eliminated is infectious disease. These diseases are conquered through the introduction of medical techniques made possible through personnel and funds from the industrial nations. Those of us who are used to paying high costs for private medical care will find it hard to believe that preventive public health measures in underdeveloped countries can save millions of lives at costs ranging from a few cents to a few dollars per person.

Because the mortality rates in underdeveloped countries have been significantly reduced, the birthrate, which has not fallen as fast or as consistently, has become an increasingly serious problem. Often this problem persists and worsens despite monumental government efforts at disseminating birth control information and contraceptive devices. In India, for example, despite the government's commitment to controlling population size, the population is expected to increase from 717 million in 1982 to 994 million in 2000 (World Bank, 1984). These failures have shown that the birthrate can be brought down only when attention is paid to the complex interrelationships of biological, social, economic, political, and cultural factors (Caldwell, 1976). In this regard, the People's Republic of China stands as a model. Since the formation of the People's Republic some three decades ago, rampant population growth and its associated poverty have been recognized as threats to progress. They have been attacked through a combination of economic incentives, contraception education, and new cultural norms that value small families and stigmatize large ones. China hopes to achieve zero population growth by the year 2000, stabilizing at 1.3 billion (Butterfield, 1979). (For a further discussion of China's progress in this area, see Case Study: "China's Last Word on Children: One.")

☐ World Population Growth

In 1650 there were an estimated 510 million people in the entire world. One hundred years later there were 710 million, an increase of some 39 percent. By 1900 there were 1.6 billion. Only 86 years later the world population had spiraled to 5 billion. As you can see in Table 19.6, the world population has been rising at an ever-increasing rate.

Current Population Trends: A Ticking Bomb?

Right now, the world population is doubling about every 42 years. If it were to continue to expand in this way, by the year 2150 there would be 37.4 billion people crowded onto this planet—a situation in which widespread poverty and famine seem almost assured. In recent years, however, there has been a small but significant slowing in the rate of world

TABLE 19.6 The Population Explosion

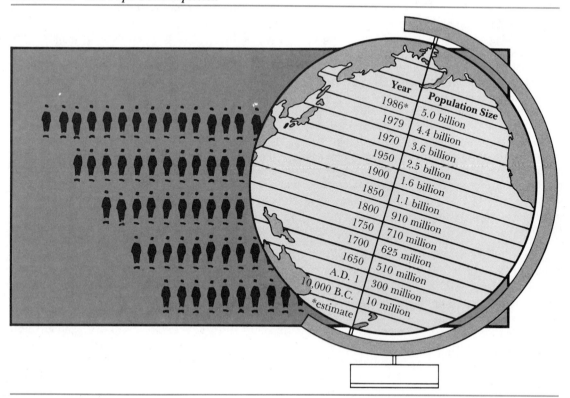

Year	Population Size
1986*	5.0 billion
1979	4.4 billion
1970	3.6 billion
1950	2.5 billion
1900	1.6 billion
1850	1.1 billion
1800	910 million
1750	710 million
1700	625 million
1650	510 million
A.D. 1	300 million
10,000 B.C.	10 million
*estimate	

*estimate

Source: Data through 1970, *The World Almanac* (New York: Newspaper Enterprises, Inc., 1980), p. 734. Data for 1979, U.S. Department of Commerce, Bureau of the Census, *Statistical Abstract of the United States, 1984* (Washington, D.C.: Government Printing Office, 1983).

China's Last Word on Children: One

wan, xi, shao

The Chinese words mean later, longer, fewer.

Later marriage, longer periods of time between pregnancies, and fewer children.

Just a few years ago that slogan launched a birth control campaign—unprecedented in scale in all of history—in the People's Republic of China. Posters proclaiming the message appeared virtually everywhere, even in the smallest village outposts.

At first the goal was not specified, but a three-child family was considered an acceptable limit. Then, two. Now the emphasis is on the last word: shao, *fewer: as few as possible, as fast as possible.*

And shao *has been reinterpreted downward three times from the original "fewer" to "one is best" and finally to "one is enough."*

Today throughout China the one-child family is national policy. In fact, an official policy issued by the Communist party chairman declared: "The state demands that each couple should ideally have only one child and not more than two. To produce a third child is to violate the state regulations." With that pronouncement, China officially set in place the most stringent antibirth program ever adopted in the modern world.

Chinese leaders have given the program top priority, ahead of all other social aims because population size overshadows all other issues. An estimated billion people live in China, a quarter of the world's habitants. For starters, then, there are a billion mouths to feed . . . and that billion must be housed, clothed, educated, medically cared for, and employed.

Never before has the difference between a moderate-sized, three-child family and a one-child family been so startling in terms of impact on population growth. If for the next 100 years, couples were to have an average of only three children, China's population would reach 4.2 billion—the current population of the world—by the year 2080.

But if the planned one-child family were to prevail over that period of time, China could bring its population way down to a socially and economically manageable 370 million by 2080; a number still 150 million greater than the United States today in a land area virtually the same size.

Though it is folly to try to predict any outcome, for the time being it would appear that China's population control program stands a reasonable chance of succeeding. Without question, *shao*—the "one is enough" rule—is the most vital component of the campaign, but *xi* (later marriage) and *wan* (longer periods between pregnancies) still are important.

To promote acceptance of the one-child limit, the government has devised a reward-punishment system that makes daily life easier and richer for those who comply and burdensome for those who do not. A nationwide campaign to promote the one-child family features the Glorious One Child Certificate, under which couples sign an agreement to limit their family to a single child in exchange for extensive benefits.

As long as they only have one child, an urban couple receives a monthly bonus of $5 (Chinese dollars, equal to $3.50 American.) As the average working family income is only $30 to $35 (Chinese dollars) a month, the bonus amounts to an extra 15 percent in income—unearned.

Rural families who work in communes and whose "pay" is largely calculated in work points that are exchanged for supplies rather than money will receive a slightly more generous dividend than the city couple will. The farm couples are awarded four- to six-days worth of extra work points a month, about an extra week's worth.

In China, under the Glorious One Child Certificate plan, a couple may also choose between two other types of preferential treatment. They can opt for child care at no cost at nursery schools until the child is 7 years old or for free medical care for the child until age 14. They also receive preferential treatment in living accommodations, food allowances, and work assignments.

Couples who have two children—spaced over a long period of time—are neither punished nor rewarded. They receive no extra money, no extra work points, and no free education or medical benefits for a second child. They must assume the extra cost of raising the second child themselves, with no help from the state.

But from now on penalties are harsh for those who have a third child. Ten percent of their pay or work points will be deducted from the time of the fourth month of pregnancy until the third child is 14 years old. The same penalties are imposed on couples who have their second child in fewer than four years and on women who have a child out of wedlock.

An additional punishment for the three-or-more-child couple is denial of any job promotion and loss of all work bonuses for at least three years. This is to make sure that couples who exceed the state limit for children do so at the price of personal sacrifice. They cannot prosper by doing extra work.

Little was known about how China could successfully regulate childbearing, or in the Chinese terms, "planned population production." Chinese population scholar H. Yuan Tien, a sociologist at Ohio State University who recently returned from a year in the People's Republic, has shed a great deal of light on this process, in a series of recent reports, including a perspectives analysis.

"There is no question the people in the cities are all for it," he says. "The competition for housing, education, and good jobs creates very conducive circumstances for city dwellers to be very much in favor of having fewer children.

"The problem now is to convince people in the villages that there are advantages in having a small family. They worry that there won't be any young people to care for them in their old age.

"And even now, as in the past, the more hands there are in a household, the greater the amount of money or work points is earned."

Wan, later marriage, remains a significant means to limit family size. The legal age for marriage has repeatedly been raised so that it now is 22 years of age for men and 20 for women, the oldest legal marriage age in the world.

More than 30 percent of China's population is of reproductive age— 15 to 49 years old. But Tien pointed out that in provinces where good population data are available, *married* women of reproductive age account for only 20 percent of the population.

"Since marriage is almost universal among women 23 years of age and older, the fact that married women of reproductive age constitute just 20 percent of the population indicated the impact of *wan* ("late marriage,") as a key ingredient of the Chinese solution to population growth," Tien noted. *Xi*, longer periods between pregnancies or, better yet, only one, can be virtually ensured through universally available contraception and an extraordinary network of reproductive monitoring.

"There exist tens of thousands of provincial and local (planned reproduction group) branches, all the way down to teams in the rural communes and work teams in factories, shops, offices and other places of employment. These grass-roots groups are crucial to the plan," Tien said.

In small teams or cadres in the countryside and on city blocks, workers or volunteers keep well informed about the reproductive practices of the women in their group.

"Each individual woman is represented by a menstrual chart, which makes it easy to detect a missed period and to deter childbearing that does not conform to the national plan," Tien explained.

"For each married woman there is also a Planned Reproduction Card which shows the number of her previous births, by sex, the date of her last birth and the type of contraception she uses. Such individual records make it possible for those in charge of planned reproduction to keep track of all the women on their team, thereby helping to maintain reproductive discipline throughout the whole of China."

On a day-to-day basis, sociologist Tien said, peer and group pressure accomplishes what regulation may fail to do.

"For instance," he said, "in a unit of people, if a couple were to become pregnant for the third time, the cadre leader would visit the house and try to persuade them to agree to an abortion.

"If they didn't agree on the first try, the leader would return again and again, each time taking other members of the unit with her until the couple gave in.

"The couple would be lectured on their selfishness in expecting to receive an unfair share of the food, clothing, education, and so forth, that are available."

The ultimate personal reward is offered to women who practice the most reliable methods of contraception.

Women who have an IUD (intrauterine device) inserted are entitled to 7 days' paid rest.

Those who elect sterilization receive 21 days.

Those who undergo abortion, 14 days.

And those who obtain abortion and sterilization at the same time, a bonanza of 32 days vacation with pay.

Though Tien has little doubt of the effectiveness of China's population control plan and agrees with the need for it, as a sociologist he has second thoughts about some of its long-term social implications.

"When you institute rewards and punishments on birth issues, you, in effect, create two classes of people: one with one child and the rest with more. Those with one child will universally receive preferential treatment, receiving better education, jobs, and living status. Someone with a brother or sister will automatically be denied these advantages. There is a form of injustice built into such a system and one of the problems to be dealt with in the future will be how to resolve this potential injustice."

Source: Excerpted from Loretta McLaughlin, "China's Last Word on Children: 'One,' " *Boston Globe*, September 6, 1980, pp. 1, 2. □

POPULAR SOCIOLOGY
Measuring the Value of Children

Most parents do not explicitly make a calculation of the costs and benefits of having a child, or if they already have children, the values attached to second, third, and fourth children. In the following discussion we will see that the costs and benefits of having a child vary in developed and undeveloped countries. Attempts to limit population growth must take into account a variety of economic, social, and psychological factors.

Potential parents trying to estimate the cost of children would need to consider the following:

Goods and services (food, shelter, clothing, medical care, education, and the like) needed in raising children, and specifically the amount required in each future year.

The amount of time they will put into caring for children, year by year, and the expected wages they will thereby lose.

The amount of time the children would put into earning for the household, and the wages the household can expect to receive.

The probability that children will survive to any given age.

The weight to attach to future costs and benefits from children, such as security in old age, in contrast to immediate costs and benefits.

For a rural sample in the Philippines three-quarters of the costs involved in rearing a third child come from buying goods and services; the other quarter comes from costs in time (or lost wages). But receipts from child earnings, work at home, and old age support offset 46 percent of the total. The remaining 54 percent, the net cost of a child, is equivalent to about 6 percent of a husband's annual earnings.

By contrast, a study of urban areas of the United States showed that almost half the costs of a third child are time costs. Receipts from the child offset only 4 percent of all costs.

Only economic costs and benefits are taken into account in these calculations. To investigate social and psychological costs, other researchers have examined how individuals perceive children. Economic contributions from children are clearly more important in the Philippines, where fertility is higher than in Korea or the United States; concern with the restrictions children impose on parents, on the other hand, is clearly greatest in the United States.

In all three countries, however, couples demonstrate a progression in the values they emphasize as their families grow. The first child is important to cement the marriage and bring the spouses closer together, as well as to have someone to carry on the family name. Thinking of the first child, couples also stress the desire to have someone to love and care for and the child's bringing play and fun into their lives.

In considering a second child, parents emphasize more the desire for a companion for the first child. They also place weight on the desire to have a child of the opposite sex from the first. Similar values are prominent in relation to third, fourth, and fifth children; emphasis is also given to the pleasure derived from watching children grow.

Beyond the fifth child economic considerations predominate. Parents speak of the sixth or later children in terms of their helping around the house, contributing to the support of the household, and providing security in old age. For first to third children, the time taken away from work or other pursuits is the main drawback; for fourth and later children, the direct financial burden is more prominent than the time costs.

These studies focus on the advantages and disadvantages to couples having one or more children. But society as a whole bears many of the costs of population growth. Do couples limit their own childbearing for essentially altruistic reasons? One small study, conducted a decade ago in the Phillipines, suggests they might.

This question was posed:

Supposing the government determined that the population was growing too fast and that there were not enough jobs for the adults, not enough schools for the children, not enough hospitals for everyone, and not enough money to pay for these things. Would you be willing to stop having children (and to stop at two children, if you had no children yet) in order to help solve the problem?

Eighty-four percent of the respondents said they would be willing to stop at two children (if they had none to begin with), and 86 percent said they would be willing to stop at the number they had. The social costs of population growth for this sample appeared real enough to generate some sacrifice from almost everyone.

Source: excerpted from World Bank, "Measuring the Value of Children," *World Development Report 1984* (New York: Oxford University Press, 1984), pp. 122–123. □

population growth: Between 1965 and 1970 the annual rate of growth was 2.1 percent, but between 1975 and 1983 it had dropped to 1.7 percent (U.S. Dept. of Commerce, 1984). If this slowing trend continues, by the year 2100 the world population will be twice its present size, some 8.4 billion people—a staggering number in and of itself but far smaller than the 37.4 billion previously predicted. This more hopeful pattern is contingent on the average family size being limited to two children.

We have already seen a significant trend throughout the world toward smaller families. According to the seven-year-long World Fertility Survey, probably the largest social science research project ever undertaken, the world's crude birthrate is declining in 14 of the 15 nations studied (*Science News*, 1979). The developing countries that are cutting their population growth most quickly are Costa Rica, Colombia, Sri Lanka, and Fiji. Not far behind are South Korea, Thailand, Malaysia, Peru, and the Dominican Republic. Young women in these nations have, on the average, about two fewer children than their mothers and grandmothers had. In Costa Rica, for example, women between the ages of 45 and 49 had an average of 7.3 children. When 15-year-old to 44-year-old women were added to this group, the average number of children dropped to 3.8. Researchers credit increased education, government propaganda, the rapid spread of contraceptive devices, mass communications (legitimizing new norms for families in previously isolated, tradition-dominated societies), and the diminishing necessity to have large numbers of children to ensure adequate labor for family agriculture all as being major reasons for this development. (For a discussion of the costs and benefits of having children in developed and developing countries, see Popular Sociology: "Measuring the Value of Children.")

A demographic trend seen throughout the world is the continued migration of rural peoples into cities. Kingsley Davis (1973) estimated that by the year 2000 some 39.5 percent of the world's population will be living in cities of over 100,000 residents, up from 25.9 percent in 1975. By the turn of the century, according to Davis, one out of three people in the less-developed nations and one out of two in the more-developed nations will be urban dwellers. This trend will have serious sociological consequences. On the one hand, urbanization will make it easier to organize the delivery of goods and services and to develop specialized occupations to meet the needs of newly emerging economic institutions. On the other hand, urban crowding will stress many individuals and will severely strain local environmental resources, an issue that we shall discuss shortly.

Problems of Overpopulation

As long as many of the developing nations remain in stage 2 of demographic transition (high fertility but falling mortality), they will continue to be burdened by overpopulation, which slows economic development and creates widespread severe hunger.

Economic Development and Overpopulation

Although modernization is a worldwide process, not all nations share equally in its benefits. In fact, the economic gap between the industrialized and the still-developing nations is growing, not shrinking. For example, in 1958 the more-developed nations produced 82 percent of the world's goods and services. A decade later this figure had risen to 87 percent (Hartley, 1972). With the notable exception of the oil-rich countries, the gap in per-capita income and all other measures of prosperity also continues to widen.

The **dependency ratio** is the number of people of nonworking age in a society for every 100 people of working age. Overpopulation undermines economic growth by raising this ratio disproportionately. Because populations at stage 2 have a high proportion of children, as compared with adults, they have fewer able-bodied workers than they need. For example, Table 19.7 shows that in 1980, 51 percent of Kenya's population was below the age of 15, compared with 22.9 percent in the United States.

dependency ratio The number of people of nonworking age in a society, for every 100 people of working age.

TABLE 19.7   Comparison of Age Structures in Developed and Developing Countries, 1980

Country Group	Age Distribution (percent)					Total Fertility Rate
	0–4	5–14	15–64	Over 65	All Ages	
All developed countries	7.6	15.5	65.6	11.3	100.0	1.9[a]
Japan	7.3	16.1	67.7	8.9	100.0	1.8
United States	7.9	15.0	66.3	10.7	100.0	1.9
Hungary	8.0	13.7	64.9	15.9	100.0	2.1
All developing countries	13.6	25.5	57.0	4.0	100.0	4.2[a]
Korea, Rep. of	10.6	22.7	62.7	4.0	100.0	3.0
Colombia	14.0	25.4	57.1	3.5	100.0	3.8
Bangladesh	17.9	24.9	54.6	2.6	100.0	6.3
Kenya	22.4	28.6	46.1	2.9	100.0	8.0

[a]Weighted average.

Source: The World Bank. (*World Development Report,* 1984), p. 67.

The economic development of countries with high dependency ratios is slowed further by the channeling of capital away from industrialization and technological growth and toward mechanisms for feeding their expanding populations.

Almost one out of every two individuals in the world today is undernourished.

Malnutrition and Overpopulation   Although estimates vary, there are probably between one and two billion undernourished people in the world today. This means that almost one out of every two individuals is currently undernourished (Brown and Eckholm, 1974). In Colombia, Bolivia, and other Latin American nations, more than half of all infants die from malnutrition (Moulik, 1977). Even in the United States—by most measures, still the world's most prosperous nation—an estimated 20 to 30 million men, women, and children are undernourished (Ehrlich and Ehrlich, 1972).

How will these problems be resolved in the future? Neo-Malthusians paint a gloomy picture of what lies ahead, contending that as we head toward the end of this century the population inevitably will outpace the available supply of food. Others believe that we have the technological means to provide all the world's people with food. They speak of a "Green Revolution" in which new breeds of grain and improved fertilizers will raise harvest yields and eliminate the threat of a food shortage. The only thing holding back the revolution is international cooperation in planning the production and distribution of food. However, the Green Revolution, widely proclaimed in the 1970s, has failed to materialize, owing to a number of serious limitations (Brown, 1974; Brown and Eckholm, 1974; Crossen, 1975).

For one thing, there are inherent limits to the land, water, fertilizer, and energy available for food production. The total availability of land, for example, is declining as the climatic drying trend we have seen in recent decades reduces millions of acres of previously arable land to desert. (Hundreds of thousands of people in northern Africa face starvation because of this problem.) In addition, an unhappy paradox links today's increased agricultural production to the possibility of a smaller food production capacity tomorrow. Overfarming and the indiscriminate destruction of forests have increased erosion, and excess fertilization has polluted rivers and lakes, killing fish and threatening the entire food chain. These factors indicate that the problem of widespread hunger is more complicated than the sole fact of a rising world population.

Predictions of Ecological Disaster

A group of some one hundred scientists, businesspeople, and academics known as the Club of Rome created great controversy with their predictions of worldwide economic and ecological collapse due to continuing population growth (Meadows et al., 1972). Using elaborate computer models developed at the Massachusetts Institute of Technology, they concluded that the current worldwide trends in population, production, and pollution were on a direct collision course with the production limits imposed by natural resources and the pollution-absorbing capacity of the environment.

This "doomsday model" of the future asserts that modern technology is inevitably headed toward the exhaustion of the earth's natural resources. It assumes that we will eventually run out of oil, coal, copper, silver, arable land, and other items vital to production. Further, this model argues that modern technology also is heavily dependent on the environment for waste disposal. Eventually the increased waste from the increased production will go beyond the environment's absorptive capacity. At this point we will not be able to live with our own pollution.

The Club of Rome concluded that if current trends continue, the limits of growth on this planet will be reached within the next one hundred years. The result will be a sudden and uncontrollable decline in population and production capacity:

> . . . We have tried in every doubtful case to make the most optimistic estimate of unknown qualities, and we have also ignored discontinuous events such as wars or epidemics, which might act to bring an end to growth even sooner than our model would indicate. In other words, the model is biased to allow growth to continue longer than it probably can continue in the real world. We can thus say with some confidence that under the assumption of no major change in the present system, population and industrial growth will certainly stop within the next century, at the latest. (Meadows et al., 1972)

Sources of Optimism

The gloomy predictions presented by the Club of Rome have sparked a great deal of controversy and criticism. Critics point to a number of logical fallacies in its reasoning.

Some have also questioned the basic assumptions of the "doomsday model," namely, exponential growth in population and production, and absolute limits on natural resources and technological capabilities. The following (McConnell, 1977) are some of these counterarguments.

1. *Wider application of existing technology.* Greater efficiency and wider application of technology on a worldwide basis could continue to supply the world's needs far into the future. For example, it is estimated that greater efficiency in land cultivation would result in increased capacity to feed the world's population for many years. Many poorer countries that now find their agricultural output limited by pest infestation would see rapid improvement if modern technology were applied.
2. *Discovery of new resources.* Some critics also argue that the supply of natural resources is not really as fixed as the doomsday predictors claim. These critics maintain that technological advances can create new uses for formerly worthless substances. In this

way new resources come into play that were not previously anticipated. Therefore technology will stay ahead of resource use, and the doomsday scenario will never be enacted.

3. *Exponential increase in knowledge.* It is further argued that just as the doomsday predictors claim there will be an exponential growth in population and production, there will also be an exponential growth in knowledge that will enable societies to solve the problems associated with growth. New technological information and discoveries, furthermore, will alleviate new problems as they arise.

Slowing Population Growth

The main reason for wanting the population to grow more slowly is to improve people's well-being. The goal is to move toward a balance of low death rates and low birthrates, essentially completing the demographic transition. There are several factors that can help slow population growth. For the most part, our discussion will be concerned with the situation in developing countries. (The World Bank, 1984)

Reducing Infant and Child Mortality High infant mortality promotes high fertility. Parents who expect some of their children will die may give birth to more babies than they really want as a way of ensuring a certain-sized family. This sets in motion a pattern of many children born close together, weakening both the mother and babies and producing more infant mortality.

In the short term, the prevention of 10 infant deaths may produce only 1 to 5 fewer births. Initially, lower infant and child mortality will lead to somewhat larger families and faster rates of population growth than before. However, the long-term effects are most important. With improved chances of survival, parents give greater attention to their children and are willing to spend more on their children's health and education. Eventually the lower mortality rates help parents achieve the desired family size with fewer births and lead them to want a smaller family as well.

Raising Income It is a well-established fact that people with higher incomes want fewer children. Alternative uses of time, such as earning money, developing or using skills, and pursuing leisure activities, become more attractive, particularly to women. The children's economic contributions become less important to the family welfare, as the family no longer needs to think of children as a form of social security in old age. It is not the higher income itself but, rather, the life changes it brings about that lowers fertility.

This relationship between income and fertility holds true only for those with an income above a certain minimum level. If people are extremely poor, increases in income will actually increase fertility. In the poorest countries in Africa and Asia, families are often below this threshold. Above the threshold, though, the greatest fertility reduction with rising income will take place among low-income groups.

Educating Women One of the strongest factors in reducing fertility is the education of women. The number of children that women have declines quite substantially as their level of education increases. The differences can sometimes be quite large; for example, in Colombia, women in the lowest educational group have, on the average, four more children than do women in the highest educational group.

Studies also show that women's level of education has a greater impact on fertility than does that of men. There are a number of reasons for this. In most instances, children have a greater impact on women, in terms of time and energy, than they do on men. The more educated a woman is, the more opportunities she may encounter that conflict with having children. Education also appears to delay marriage, which in itself lowers fertility. In 10 out of 14 developing countries, women with 7 or more years of education marry at least 3.5 years later than do women with no education. Educated women are also more likely to know about and adopt birth control methods. In Mexico, 72 percent of those women with nine or more years of education are likely to use contraception, whereas only 31 percent of those with five or fewer years of education are likely to do so.

Urban Residence Shift Urban dwellers usually have access to better education and health services, a wider range of jobs, and more avenues for self-improvement and social mobility than do their rural counterparts. They are exposed to new consumer goods and are encouraged to delay or limit their childbearing in order to increase their incomes. They also face higher costs in raising children. As a result, urban fertility rates are usually one to two children lower than are rural fertility rates.

The urban woman marries at least one and one-half years later than the rural woman does. She is more likely to accept the view that fertility should be controlled, and the means for doing so are more likely to be at her disposal.

Later Average Age of Marriage We earlier suggested that the later a woman marries, the fewer children she will have. Early marriage provides more years during which conception can take place, and it decreases the level of schooling and limits employment opportunities.

In South Asia and sub-Saharan Africa, about half of all women between 15 and 19 are, or have been, married. In Bangladesh, the mean age for women at marriage is 16, and thus the fertility rates in these areas are extremely high.

Some countries have tried to establish a minimum age for marriage in order to limit fertility. In 1950, China legislated the minimum age for marriage as 18 for women and 20 for men. It also recognized the effect that social controls can have on the marriage age and so increased institutional and community pressures for later marriage. In 1980, China again raised the legal minimum ages to 20 for women and 22 for men, and it is one of the few countries that has been successful in raising the average age of marriage.

Encouraging Breast-feeding Breast-feeding delays the resumption of menstruation and therefore offers some protection against conception. It also avoids some of the considerable health risks connected with bottle feeding, particularly when the powdered milk may be improperly prepared; adequate sterilization is not possible; and families cannot afford an adequate supply of milk powder. These risks have produced an outcry against certain large companies that produce powdered milk and that have been trying to encourage bottle feeding in Third World countries.

In the United States, breast-feeding was relatively unpopular until the late 1960s. As the advantages of breast-feeding became better known, it increased among better-educated women. Today college-educated women are the most likely to start breast-feeding and continue it for the longest periods.

Contraception Apart from the factors already mentioned, fertility rates are eventually tied to the increasing use of contraception. Use of contraception is partly a function of a couple's wish to avoid or delay having children and partly related to its costs. People have regulated family size for centuries, through abortion, abstinence, and even infanticide. However, the costs, whether economic, social, or psychological, in preventing a birth may be greater than the risk of having another child.

Contraception is most likely to be effective when such programs are publicly subsidized. Not only do such programs address the economic costs in spreading contraception, but they also help communicate the idea that birth control is possible. These programs also offer information about the private and social benefits of smaller families, which also helps reduce the desired family size.

☐ Demographics of Health Care in the United States

In this overview of the traits and processes of human populations, on the one hand, and the ways in which populations interact with their environment, on the other, we have looked at large population and ecological patterns as they are expressed throughout the

TABLE 19.8 Reduction of Death Rates in the United States, 1920 to 1980

Indicator	1920	1950	1980
Death rates (per 100,000 population)	1,298.9	963.8	878.3
Life expectancy	54.1	68.2	74.5 (1982)
Infant mortality (per 1,000 live births)	*	29.2	12.6
Maternal mortality (per 100,000 live births)	*	83.3	9.2

*Data not available.

Source: Adapted from *Mortality Statistics 1950*, Department of HEW, National Center for Health Statistics; *Monthly Vital Statistics Report, 22*, (13)(June 27, 1974); Health Statistics from the *U.S. National Health Survey*, Series B-10 and Series 10, No. 95. U.S. Department of Commerce, Census Bureau, *Current Population Reports*, selected issues and *Statistical Abstract of the United States, 1984* (Washington, D.C.: Government Printing Office, 1983).

world. Now it is time to take a closer look at one particular demographic factor—health. Specifically, we shall focus on health care in the United States and consider the fact that such care is not equally distributed throughout the American population.

The United States has the most advanced health care resources in the world. In 1981 we had 7,027 hospitals, 504,700 highly trained physicians, and 1,273,000 nurses, and we are prepared to treat illness and injury with the most modern techniques available (U.S. Dept. of Commerce, 1984). We can scan a brain for tumors, reconnect nerve tissues and reattach severed limbs through microsurgery, and eliminate diseases like poliomyelitis that crippled a president only a little more than four decades ago. (See Table 19.8 for some major medical advances, as reflected by increased life expectancies and drastically reduced death rates.) We can do all this and much more; yet many would consider our health care system wholly inadequate to meet the needs of *all* Americans. These critics maintain that the current U.S. health care system is one that pays off only when the patient can pay.

Poverty and Health

Poverty contributes to disease and a shortened life span both directly and indirectly. It is estimated that some 25 million Americans do not have enough money to feed themselves adequately and as a result suffer from serious nutritional deficiencies that lead to illness and death.

Poverty also produces living conditions that encourage illness. Pneumonia, influenza, tuberculosis, whooping cough, and even rat bites are much more common in poor minority populations, than among white, middle-class ones. Inadequate housing, heating, and sanitation all contribute to these acute medical problems, as does the U.S. fee-for-service system that links medical care to the ability to pay.

Health Insurance   Most people pay for their health services through some form of health insurance. In 1980 nearly 78 percent of all Americans paid almost $59 billion in insurance premiums (U.S. Dept. of Commerce, 1984). Poor people, however, cannot afford these premiums or the out-of-pocket expenses required before insurance coverage begins. They receive coverage through the government-sponsored Medicare and Medicaid programs. Medicare covers many of the medical expenses of those over 65, and Medicaid is designed to pay for medical care for those who are below or near the poverty level. In 1981 more than 2.6 million Americans were covered by Medicare and 19 million were covered by Medicaid (U.S. Dept. of Commerce, 1984).

Even with these forms of government insurance, the care that the poor receive is inferior to that received by the more affluent. Most doctors will not accept Medicare or Medicaid assignments, requiring patients to reimburse them for the difference between the insurance coverage and their bill. Moreover, most doctors will not practice in poor neighborhoods, with the result that the poor are relegated to overcrowded, demeaning clinics. Under conditions like these it is no surprise that the poor generally wait longer before seeking medical care than do more affluent patients, and many seek medical advice only when they are seriously ill and intervention is already too late.

Age and Health

As advances in medical science prolong the life span of most Americans, the problem of medical care for the aged is becoming more acute. Since the turn of the century, the median age of Americans has risen from 22.9 to 30. In 1900 there were only 3.1 million Americans aged 65 or older, a group that constituted a mere 4 percent of the total population. But by 1982 there were 26.8 million Americans aged 65 or older—a full 11.6 percent of the total population (U.S. Dept. of Commerce, 1984). This change in the age structure of the American population has had important consequences for health and health care in the United States.

At the turn of the twentieth century, more Americans were killed by pneumonia, influenza, tuberculosis, infections of the digestive tract, and other microorganism diseases than by any other cause. By comparison, only 8 percent of the population died of heart disease and 4 percent of cancer. Today, this situation is completely reversed. Major cardiovascular diseases cause 37.8 percent of all deaths in this country, and cancer 20.6 percent. These diseases, which are now the leading causes of death in the United States, are tied to the bodily deterioration that is a natural part of the aging process (U.S. Dept. of Commerce, 1981).

The result of these changes in health patterns is increased hospitalization for those over 65. Only 1 percent of all Americans are institutionalized in medical facilities. But of those 65 and older, 5 percent are institutionalized in convalescent homes, homes for the aged, hospitals, and mental hospitals. The elderly are 30 times as likely to be in nursing homes than are people under 65 (*U.S. News & World Report,* 1982), and unfortunately their care is often wholly inadequate:

> There is little therapy provided for nursing home residents: only fifteen percent are offered recreational therapy, ten percent

physical therapy, and six percent occupational therapy. For those who have been residents for over a year, thirteen percent had not seen a physician for at least six months, and almost nine percent had not seen a physician for at least a year. (Enos and Sultan, 1977)

(For a discussion of an alternative to the institutionalization of the elderly, see Using Sociology. "Florida: A Trendsetter Faces a New Trend.")

Failings in the U.S. Health Care Delivery System

Are many of the shortcomings of the U.S. health care system due to the way health care is delivered? Many critics who believe this to be true point to the fact that the United States is the only leading industrial nation that does not have an organized, centrally planned health care delivery system. Of the 25,881 inpatient medical facilities in the United States in 1978, only 3,821 (14.8 percent) were government run. The rest were private—14,981 (58 percent) run for profit and 7,079 (27 percent) for nonprofit (U.S. Dept. of Commerce, 1981). In addition, despite attempts to enact some form of comprehensive national health insurance that would guarantee all Americans access to medical care, no plan as yet exists.

The American Medical Association has been a leading opponent of national health insurance and has failed to deal with such other health care delivery problems as the very uneven geographic distribution of doctors and the overabundance of specialists. In 1979, for example, only 12.8 percent of the nation's physicians were in general practice, even though many more general practitioners are needed to treat the total population, especially the poor and the elderly.

In essence, because of pressures from the American Medical Association and other sectors of the medical establishment, the United States' health care system focuses primarily on benefits received by doctors. The fee-for-service system of remuneration gives doctors a vested interest in pathology rather than in good health. Instead of emphasizing preventive medical care, the American health care system emphasizes cure (Friedman and Fried-

USING SOCIOLOGY
Florida: A Trendsetter Faces a New Trend

The lifecare community concept took hold in Florida in response to a need that few anticipated when swarms of retirees collected their gold watches and moved to Florida's Gold Coast 20 years ago. At that time Florida led the nation in providing the services that brought the over-sixties set to the South. It promised a balmy climate free of income and inheritance taxes. Mrs. Large will tell you that when she and her husband bought their waterfront retirement home, they planned to "stay forever." But as it turned out, they could not. The lifecare concept has helped people in this position.

Ask former fashion model Sarah Large what it is like to live in a complex of 950 elderly people who have checked in until they die, and she will tell you that there is nothing more secure and enjoyable.

"You would think that it's depressing, but for us, it is very, very happy here," says the effervescent 87-year-old. "We are peers, we went to school together, got married together, had children at the same time. We shared experiences."

The experiences they are sharing now, at the John Knox Village of Florida lifecare community near Fort Lauderdale, Florida, is the experience of growing too old to care for themselves. Not surprisingly, those who are able to afford care have the least to worry about. Private developers who watched prohibitive interest rates stem condominium sales have pegged the frail elderly as a potential market. They are moving strongly into providing services previously provided by churches and nonprofit organizations: developing and managing lifecare communities.

Lifecare offers the elderly the medical and personal care they need. It costs them an initial "endowment," ranging anywhere from about $21,000 to $200,000, depending on the size of the living unit desired. That endowment, along

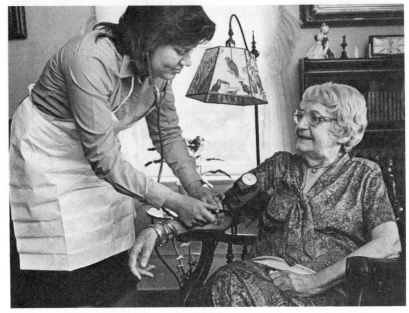

Lifecare centers offer the elderly the medical and personal care they need.

with a monthly maintenance fee, buys them a contract for lifelong care in a comfortable or—depending on the unit—luxurious complex.

The communities provide an apartment or cottage in a campus-like environment, in-home nursing and personal care for as long as the person can live alone, meals, transportation, recreation, and a guaranteed bed in the campus nursing home when the person is unable to live alone. When the person dies, as 10 percent do each year, their apartment or villa reverts to the company to be sold for another endowment.

Though the lifecare concept was born in Philadelphia, it is reaching maturity in Florida, where 17.3 percent of the population is age 65 and over, compared with a national average of 11.3 percent. With 33 lifecare communities, Florida has the highest per-capita concentration of such facilities in the nation, according to a University of Pennsylvania study of 208 lifecare communities nationwide.

Florida courted and won vast populations of the nation's retirees. Real estate developers churned out condominium complexes, luring retirees to the area with offers of country club living on a retirement income. The retirees played golf at the communal course and shuffleboard at the communal court. They took in cut-rate matinees at surrounding theaters, dined on "early bird specials" at nearby restaurants, and socked their pensions into the state's banking system.

Today, the once-active 60-year-olds are in their less-active eighties, a group that has come to be known as the "frail elderly." Just 3.1 percent of Florida's population in 1980, the group grew a full percentage point in 1981 and is expected to account for 4.9 percent of the state's population by the year 2000, according to the University of Florida's Bureau of Economic and Business Research.

Florida's challenge will be to provide shelter and care for this growing group from now until the end of the century. And the rest of the nation is watching. "The whole country is waking up to the fact that they have a tremendous long-term care bill due on a tremendous aging population," says Ann Raper, a Washington-based consultant on gerontology. "Florida has just had the situation longer."

Florida crossed its first hurdle in 1976, when Governor Bob Graham, then a state senator, pushed the legislature to fund programs for the elderly. Known as Community Care Elderly Core Services, the programs are aimed at keeping the elderly out of nursing homes by giving them the help they need shopping, driving, and caring for themselves at home. Those involved with the programs say they have been very successful.

Governor Graham has continued his commitment to the elderly, and today the state that stepped out

to meet the needs of retirees is pioneering public and private sector programs designed to provide a comfortable and satisfying life for the frail.

"Florida is way ahead of all other states in terms of noninstitutional living arrangements for the frail elderly," says a staff member of the state's Department of Health and Rehabilitative Services. "We don't have a perfect system, but we have a network of facilities out there geared to community rather than institutional living."

Whether those facilities will be adequate is the question that public and private gerontological groups are asking themselves. "There will be those who cannot afford care but still need it. There will be those who can afford care but can't find it," predicts Ms. Raper. Those elderly people who cannot find lifecare facilities or who cannot afford them

will have to rely on public transportation and health care services.

Anticipating this problem, in the last half of the 1970s, Florida set about developing a network of health, transportation, and personal services designed to keep the elderly living at home instead of in nursing homes.

Each elderly person living at home saves the taxpayer $5,932 in state and federal money that would be paid to a nursing home, says Karl Dalke, program research and development director with the state's Aging and Adult Services Program.

"They are more cost effective than a nursing home," he points out, "and they are quite important in saving Florida from economic disaster."

Source: Adapted and excerpted from Elizabeth Roberts, "Florida: A Trendsetter Faces a New Trend," *Advertising Age,* August 29, 1983, pp. N-22. □

---

man, 1980). A change in direction is needed in order to make the health system work for all Americans, no matter what their ages or socioeconomic status.

□ Summary

Demography is the systematic study of the dynamics of human populations, and ecology is the study of the relationships between populations and their environment.

Population processes are influenced by fertility, mortality, and migration. Fertility refers to the actual number of births in the population and is measured by the crude birthrate and the fertility rate. Mortality refers to the frequency of actual deaths in a population and is measured by the crude death rate and age-specific death rates. Migration is the movement of populations from one geographic area to another.

Theories of population growth include the Malthusian theory, propounded by Thomas Robert Malthus, which states that populations will always grow faster than the available food supply will; the Marxist theory, which links industrialism and capitalism to population growth; and demographic transition theory, which states that societies have four distinct stages of population change.

The population of the world is doubling every 42 years. However, a slowing trend is now being seen as increased education, government propaganda, contraception, and changing societal norms influence families to have fewer children. Overpopulation channels the capital of underdeveloped nations away from industrialization and technological growth into mechanisms for feeding expanding populations. Despite huge government efforts to feed the masses, between one and two billion people are currently undernourished. Citing these staggering statistics, neo-Malthusians argue that as we head toward the year 2000, the population inevitably will outpace the available food supply. Others see a "Green Revolution" in which new and improved agricultural techniques will eliminate the threat of a food shortage.

There are many factors that can help slow population growth, including lower infant and child mortality rates, higher incomes, better-educated women, urban residence patterns, later average ages of marriage, the renewed popularity of breast-feeding, and the wider use of contraception.

The U.S. health care system does not serve all people equally. Even though the United States has the most advanced health care system in the world, the poor and the elderly are underserved and often receive inferior care. Critics charge that a health care system that is oriented toward care rather than health maintenance serves the needs of the nation's doctors rather than its citizens.

☐ For Further Reading

EASTERLIN, RICHARD A. *Birth and Fortune: The Impact of Numbers on Personal Welfare.* New York: Basic Books, 1980. Easterlin considers the different life chances of people who are part of large and small birth cohorts.

HAUPT, ARTHUR, and THOMAS T. KANE. *Population Handbook.* Washington, D.C.: Population Reference Bureau, 1978. A concise introduction to basic demographic terms and measures.

KRAUSE, ELLIOT, A. *Power and Illness: The Political Sociology of Health and Medical Care.* New York: Elsevier, 1977. A conflict perspective critique of the American health care system.

MCINTOSH, C. ALISON. *Population Policy in Western Europe: Responses to Low Fertility in France, Sweden, and West Germany.* Armonk, N.Y.: M. E. Sharpe, 1983. McIntosh analyzes the responses of political elites and governments to the low fertility rates and low population growth that characterized these nations during the 1970s and early 1980s.

SIMON, JULIAN L. *The Economics of Population Growth.* Princeton, N.J.: Princeton University Press, 1977. A stimulating, scholarly review of the various competing theories that attempt to explain the economic effects of population growth.

20

Social Change

Twenty-five centuries ago the Greek philosopher Heraclitus lectured on the inevitability of change. "You cannot step into the same river twice," he said, "for . . . waters are continually flowing on." Indeed, he observed, ". . . everything gives way and nothing stays fixed" (Wheelright, 1959). Social change is an important topic for sociological study, as in the last three hundred years its pace and pervasiveness have escalated enormously.

☐ Society and Social Change

But what, exactly, is social change? The best way to analyze how sociologists define social change is through example. The invention of the steam locomotive was not in itself a social change, but the acceptance of the invention and the spread of railroad transportation were. Martin Luther's indictments of the Catholic church nailed to the door of Wittenberg Cathedral in 1517 were not in themselves social change, but they helped give rise to one of the major social changes of all time, the Protestant Reformation. Adam Smith's great work *An Inquiry into the Nature and Causes of the Wealth of Nations* (first published in 1776) was not in itself social change, but it helped initiate a social change that altered the world, the Industrial Revolution. Thus, individual discoveries, actions, or works do not themselves constitute social change, but they may lead to alterations in shared values or patterns of social behavior or even to the reorganization of social relationships and institutions. When this happens, sociologists speak of social change. Hans Gerth and C. Wright Mills (1953) define social change as whatever happens "in the course of time to the roles, the institutions, or the orders comprising a social structure, their emergence, growth and decline." To put it simply, using terms we defined in Chapter 5, social change consists of alterations in a society's social organization, statuses, institutions, and social structure.

Some social changes are violent and dramatic, like the French Revolution of 1789 or the 1917 Russian Revolution. However, not all cases of violent social or collective behavior are instances of social change. Thus, the United States' race riots of the late 1960s and early 1970s were not in themselves examples of social change. For that matter, not all social change need be violent. For example, the transformation of the family into its modern forms over the last two hundred years represents an enormous social change that has profoundly affected both the general nature of society and each person's childhood and adult experiences. Similarly, the rise of technology and mass communication over the last century has resulted in the emergence of what sociologist Edward Shils (1971) described as "mass society," in which vast numbers of individuals share collectively in the community and in a common tongue.

It would be a mistake to think of social change only in terms of the social structure. Morris Ginsberg (1958) observed that the "term social change must also include changes in attitudes and beliefs, in so far as they sustain institutions and change with them." In addition, individual motivation always plays a real but immeasurable role in social change.

☐ Sources of Social Change

What causes social change? Sociologists have linked several factors to social change. These factors, which we shall consider here, are categorized as internal and external sources of change.

Internal Sources of Social Change

Internal sources of social change refer to those factors that originate within a specific society and that singly or in combination produce significant alterations in its social organization and structure. The most important internal sources of social change are technological innovation, ideology, cultural conflicts, and institutionalized structural inequality.

Technological Innovation Technological change in industrial society is advancing at a dizzying pace, carrying social organizations and institutions along with it. According to a report commissioned by the National Science Foundation, computer and communications-based electronic information technology will transform American life as we know it in the

Computers are becoming a pervasive influence in American society.

home, family, workplace, and school by the turn of the twenty-first century.

These changes will be accomplished by way of two-way home information systems called teletext and videotex, which experts predict will be found in 40 percent of American homes by the year 2000. The implications of these systems are enormous. To use futurist Alvin Toffler's (1970) phrase, homes will be transformed into "electronic cottages" in which people both work and live. Receiving and sending information through computer terminals, workers will have little need to establish a base of work operations in a separate office. As a result, parents will become more available to their children, traffic and zoning patterns will change, husbands and wives will spend greater amounts of time with each other, and today's patterns of workplace and school socialization will give way to electronically determined relationships that are based on interest and skill rather than on age, proximity, and social class. In addition, the elderly who can earn a living through electronic homework might once again become part of an extended family.

Already, signs of these trends are plentiful. We can deposit funds and pay bills through electronic banking centers without ever handling money. Home computers are already in hundreds of thousands of American homes. Even crime patterns have been changed by the computer. Clever thieves have diverted funds using computer codes in banks and made long-distance calls without charge using computerized "black boxes." In fact, so much about society is changing so quickly as a result of advanced computer technology that scholars are beginning to worry whether humans have the psychological resilience to adapt to the social changes that must follow.

Ideology The term **ideology** is used in many ways. Most often it refers to a set of interrelated religious or secular beliefs, values, and norms that justify the pursuit of a given set of goals through a given set of means. Throughout history, ideologies have played a major role in shaping the direction of social change.

social change Alterations in society's social organization, statuses, institutions, and social structure.

internal sources of social change Those factors that originate within a specific society and that singly or in combination produce significant alterations in its social organization and structure.

ideology A set of interrelated religious or secular beliefs, values, and norms justifying the pursuit of a given set of goals through a given set of means.

Conservative (or traditional) **ideologies** try to preserve things as they are and indeed may slow down social changes that technological advances are promoting.

Liberal ideologies seek limited reforms that do not involve fundamental changes in the social structure of society. Affirmative-action programs, for example, are intended to redress historical patterns of discrimination that have kept women and minority groups from competing on an equal footing with white males for jobs. Although far-reaching, these liberal ideological programs do not attempt to change the economic system that more radical critics believe is at the heart of job discrimination.

Radical (or revolutionary) **ideologies** reject liberal reforms as mere tinkerings that simply make the structural inequities of the system more bearable and therefore more likely to be maintained. Like the socialist political movement described in Chapter 17, radical ideologists seek major structural changes in society. Interestingly, radicals sometimes share the objectives of conservatives in their opposition to liberal reforms that would lessen the severity of a problem, thereby making major structural changes less likely to occur. For example, conservative as well as many radical groups bitterly attacked President Franklin D. Roosevelt's New Deal policies in which federal funds were used to create jobs and bring the country out of the Depression. Conservatives attacked the New Deal as "creeping socialism," and radicals saw it as a desperate (and successful) attempt to save the faltering capitalist system and stave off a socialist revolution.

Cultural Conflicts and Institutionalized Structural Inequality Structural conflict promotes social change as society attempts to accommodate itself to a wide variety of demands for social, economic, political, and cultural reforms. These demands stem from cultural conflict and institutionalized structural inequality.

Cultural conflict exists in America in a variety of forms. Blacks and Hispanics, for example, are often the victims of institutionalized inequality. As these groups have asserted

their rights to equality, the institutions have been forced to change. (Federal, state, and local laws have been passed to make it illegal to discriminate against minorities in voting, the schools, the labor force, housing, and in other sectors of American life.) Cultural conflicts that are institutionalized in the form of structural inequality have caused a strong movement toward change. The labor and civil rights movements, for example, arose because of structural inequalities in American society.

External Sources of Social Change

Every society exists in an environment or, more accurately, in a setting composed of its natural and sociocultural environments. No society fits its environments perfectly because both are constantly changing. What kinds of changes does the sociocultural environment produce? We shall take a close look at one of the **external sources of social change**—the process of diffusion—which occurs when groups with differing cultures come into contact and exchange items and ideas with one another. As we described in Chapter 3, diffusion is the transmission of traits from one culture to another. It does not take the diffusion of many culture traits to result in profound social changes, as the anthropologist Lauriston Sharp (1952) demonstrated with regard to the introduction of steel axes to the Yir Yoront, a Stone Age tribe inhabiting southeastern Australia.

Before European missionaries brought steel axes to the Yir Yoront, these tools were made by chipping and grinding stone, a long, laborious process. Axes were very valuable, had religious importance, and also were the status symbol of tribal leaders. Women and young men had to ask permission from a leader to use an ax, which reinforced the patriarchal authority structure. However, anybody could earn a steel ax from the missionaries simply by impressing them as being "deserving." With women and young men thus having direct access to superior tools, the symbols representing status relations between male and female as well as young and old were devalued, and the norms governing these traditional relationships themselves were upset. In addition, introducing into the tribe valuable tools that did not have religious sanctions governing their use led to a drastic rise in the incidence of theft. In fact, the entire moral order of the Yir Yoront was undermined because their myths explained the origins of all important things in the world—but did not account for the arrival of steel axes. This, as Sharp observed, caused conditions fertile for the introduction of a new religion, a happy circumstance for the missionaries.

Diffusion occurs wherever and whenever different cultures come into contact with one another, though contact is not essential for traits to diffuse from one culture to another. For example, Native American groups below the Arctic smoked tobacco long before the arrival of the Europeans. But in Alaska the Inuit (Eskimos) knew nothing of its pleasures. European settlers brought tobacco back to Europe, where it immediately became popular and diffused eastward across Central Europe and Eurasia, up into Siberia, and eventually across the Bering Strait to the Inuit. (See Case Study. "Rise of the Third World Junkies" for another example of diffusion without cultural contact.)

Today, of course, when so many of the world's peoples increasingly are in contact with one another through all forms of mass communication, cultural traits spread easily from one society to another. But the *direction* of diffusion rarely is random or balanced among societies. In general, traits diffuse from more powerful to weaker peoples, from the more technologically advanced to the less so. When social change is imposed by might or conquest on weaker peoples, sociologists speak of **forced acculturation.**

Why do these internal and external social changes occur? Different theories offer some important insights into the process of social change.

☐ Theories of Social Change

The complexity of social change makes it impossible for a single theory to explain all its ramifications. Because each theory views social change from an entirely different perspective, contradictions are common. For example, functionalist and conflict theories are diametrically opposed, but this does not make one theory "right" and the other "wrong." Rather, they are complementary views that must be analyzed together in order to understand the total theoretical framework of social change.

Evolutionary Theory

By the middle of the nineteenth century, the concept of **evolution**—the continuous change from a simpler condition to a more complex state—was the dominant concern of European scholars in a variety of disciplines. The most influential evolutionary theorist was Charles Darwin who in his 1859 volume, *On the Origin of Species,* described what he believed to be the biological evolutionary process that moved populations of organisms toward increasing levels of biological complexity.

Darwin's evolutionary theory influenced the work of sociologist Herbert Spencer, who used terms like "survival of the fittest" and "struggle for existence" to explain the superiority of Western cultures over non-Western ones. In Spencer's view, Western cultures had reached higher levels of cultural achievement because they were better adapted to compete for scarce resources and to meet other difficult challenges of life.

Late nineteenth-century and early twentieth-century philosophers continued to be influenced by what has come to be known as social-evolutionary thought. Although using different names, the theories they developed

conservative ideologies Ideologies that try to preserve things as they are.

liberal ideologies Ideologies that seek limited reforms that do not involve fundamental changes in the structure of society.

radical ideologies Ideologies that seek major structural changes in society.

external sources of social change Changes within a society produced by events external to that society.

forced acculturation The situation that occurs when social change is imposed by might or conquest on subordinate peoples.

evolution The continuous change from a simpler condition to a more complex state.

CASE STUDY
Rise of the Third World Junkies

Cultural diffusion occurs through a variety of ways. Sometimes the effects are positive, other times negative. Illegal drug traffic, which once was a one-way stream into the Western countries has now changed into a bidirectional flow. The following describes the influence that the United States and Europe have had in the expanded illegal use of drugs throughout the Third World.

Once the drug boom was seen as one-way traffic to the West, fueled by the opium poppy and the coca leaf of the developing world. Now it is a two-way trade, with the expanded use of so-called mood-shaping drugs, or psychotropics. These chemical compounds are manufactured on a massive scale, largely in the great drug laboratories of the industrial world, and are consumed increasingly in the Third World.

Checking the rapid expansion of the underworld trade and abuse of these drugs is one of the toughest challenges facing drug control authorities in the West and the developing world.

There are hundreds of different kinds of drugs in this category. They range from tranquilizers such as valium and librium, to hallucinogens such as LSD, barbiturates (downers), and stimulants (uppers) such as amphetamine (widely known as "speed").

Although many are legal and legally prescribed, several are banned or in heavily restricted official use in most countries, notably the hallucinogen family (mainly LSD), and hypnotics (often sleep aids such as Mandrex). All of them figure in widespread abuse in the Third World, often in tandem with traditional home-grown drugs such as cannabis or opiates.

The extent of the drug problem was underlined by the Vienna-based International Narcotics Control Board (INCB) in its last report: "The drug abuse situation continues to deteriorate in most parts of the world. The number of drug abusers is further increasing; abuse is spreading geographically; the number, variety, and potency of drugs illicitly used are growing. Illicit production is expanding and trafficking thrives."

The INCB says the major international control problem now is the diversion of amphetamines and methaqualone, because of huge overproduction. In the United States, methaqualone is the most widely used illegal drug next to marijuana and causes more injuries and psychic trauma than heroin or cocaine. A former director of the U.S. Drug Enforcement Administration (US-DEA) described the diversion of prescribed drugs as a much greater health hazard than the use of any illegal drug, including heroin. Illicit trade in these drugs in the U.S. is put at a retail value of up to $21 billion annually, considerably more than twice the retail value of the heroin trade.

Psychotropics are manufactured in hundreds of clandestine laboratories in the U.S., as well as being diverted in huge amounts from legal production in Europe. Overprescription and thousands of pharmacy burglaries each year add to the problem.

Although a convention on psychotropic substances, aimed at controlling the manufacture and trade of some of the most dangerous substances, was adopted in Vienna in 1971, many important manufacturing countries, including Britain, Switzerland, Italy, and Japan, have not yet signed it. The pharmaceutical industry has often lobbied against curbs, and drug control agencies have been reluctant to identify and blacklist companies that do not adequately police the distribution of their products.

One conservative estimate by a former chief of the USDEA is that up to 250-million dosage units of controlled drugs production in the U.S. are diverted to the illicit trade. The U.S. has been accused of dumping enormous quantities of amphetamines on the European market at cheap prices, triggering widespread abuse after the Second World War.

The INCB reports that in the Middle East, psychotropic substances, diverted from legal trade, are on the rise. In Egypt, amphetamines, barbiturates, and, in particular, methaqualone, are most frequently found in the illicit traffic. In Iran, opiates are often abused in combination with barbiturates, and in Pakistan, abuse of psychotropic substances, especially methaqualone, remains a serious problem.

"Large quantities of a preparation of amphetamine compounded with aspirin continue to be diverted from the licit trade and are available for abuse in many African countries," it says.

Psychotropics are a major new threat—but the rapid spread of heroin addiction in the Third World is another grim trend. This situation is partly due to the pressure U.S. narcotics agents have put on governments in poppy growing areas. With poppy crops under constant surveillance, it made sense to process the raw opium locally into more easily concealed and transportable heroin. With opium supplies reduced and penalties threatened by new legislation, opium users turned to the new cheap fix—heroin.

Hong Kong's heroin addict population has risen to at least 40,000; Thailand has 500,000 addicts and Iran between 2 million and 3 million. Malaysia reports roughly 400,000 opiate addicts in a population of 13 million, while in Pakistan there may be 30,000 addicts in Karachi alone, chiefly students, poor people and upper-class women.

In sheer trade value, cannabis is even more significant than heroin.

It has become one of the important commodities of the world. As long ago as 1961, before "pot" was fashionable in the West, the World Health Organization estimated that there were 300 million cannabis users around the world. Even in the countries where use of the drug has been endemic for many years, consumption is increasing.

There is also evidence that the number of cocaine users has risen substantially since the early 1970s. The amounts seized more than doubled between 1978 and 1980. Bolivia, Peru and Colombia are the main sources.

The real value of this vast underworld traffic in illicit narcotics and psychotropics is unknown. But the retail value of illicit drugs to the U.S. market in 1980 was estimated at U.S. $80 billion, and the figure for Western Europe could be similar—equal to 8 or 9 percent of all world merchandise trade.

Source: "Mind-Benders: New Menace," and "A Fix to Face the New" *South,* February, 1984, pp. 11–12, 16. ☐

proposed similar stages through which societies progress. Two of the more influential social-evolutionary theorists during this period were Emile Durkheim and Ferdinand Tönnies. In addition to having historical importance, their theories are still considered useful by contemporary sociologists.

Durkheim argued that evolutionary changes affect the way society is organized, particularly with regard to work. Small, primitive societies whose members share a set of common social characteristics, norms, and values come together in a bond of solidarity Durkheim called *mechanical solidarity*. These people tend to be of the same ethnicity and religion and share similar economic roles. As society grows larger, it develops a more complex division of labor. People play different economic roles; a more complex class structure develops; and members of the society increasingly do not share the same beliefs, values, and norms. However, they must still depend on one another's efforts in order that all may survive. Durkheim called the new advanced form of cohesion *organic solidarity*.

Ferdinand Tönnies's views of social evolution parallel those of Durkheim. In his view societies shift from the intimate, cooperative relationships of small societies, characterized by Gemeinschaft to Gesellschaft—the specialized impersonal relationships typical of large societies. Tönnies did not believe that these changes always brought progress (a feeling shared by Durkheim). Rather, he saw social fragmentation, individual isolation, and a general weakening of societal bonds as the direct results of the movement toward individualization and the struggle for power that characterize urban society.

Much of early evolutionary theory has been harshly criticized by contemporary sociologists, who charge that it uses the norms and values of one culture as absolute standards for all cultures. In response to these problems, modern evolutionists propose sequences of evolutionary stages that are much more flexible in allowing for actual historical variation among societies. Anthropologist Julian H. Steward (1955) proposes that social evolution is "multilineal," by which he means that the evolution of each society or cultural tradition must be studied independently and must not be forced into broad, arbitrary, "universal" stages. Marshall D. Sahlins and Elman R. Service (1960) distinguish between "general" evolution (the trend toward increasing differentiation) and "specific" evolution (social changes in each specific society that may move either in the direction of greater simplicity or greater complexity). But all evolutionary theories suffer to a greater or lesser degree from an inability to give a convincing answer to the question, Why do societies change? One approach that attempts to deal with this question is conflict theory.

Conflict Theory

According to the conflict theory, conflicts rooted in the class struggle between unequal groups lead to social change. This, in turn, creates conditions that lead to new conflicts.

Modern conflict theory is rooted in the writings of Karl Marx, whose theory of society and social conflict we introduced in Chapter 1. In *Das Kapital,* first published in 1867, Marx argued that social-class conflict is the most basic and influential source of all social change. The classes are in conflict because of the unequal allocation of goods and services. Those with money may purchase these; those without cannot. To Marx, it is a division between the exploiting and exploited classes.

Europe's transition from a feudal to a capitalistic society gave Marx the source of his model for social change. "Without conflict no progress: this is the law which civilization has followed to the present day" (Marx, 1959).

Several modern conflict theorists have modified Marx's theories of class conflict in light of recent historical events. Ralf Dahrendorf (1959), one of the foremost contemporary conflict theorists, sees as too simplistic the view that all social change is the outgrowth of class conflict. He believes that conflict and dissension are present in nearly every part of society. For example, nonsocial-class conflict may involve religious groups, political groups, or even nations. Dahrendorf does accept, however, the basic principle of conflict theory that social conflict and social change are built-in structural features of society.

Conflict theory accounts for some of the major sources of social change within a society: the changing means of production and class conflict. Marx believed that social change within capitalist society would occur through a violent revolution of the workers against the capitalists. However, Marx did not foresee that those who controlled the means of production would tolerate the legalization of unions, collective bargaining, strikes, and integration of the less privileged into legal, reform-oriented parties of the Left. Marx also did not foresee that those who controlled the means of production would accept government regulation of corporations, welfare legislation, civil rights legislation, and other laws aimed at protecting employees and consumers.

Functionalist Theory

Functionalists view society as a **homeostatic system,** that is, an assemblage of interrelated parts that seeks to achieve and maintain a settled or stable state (Davis, 1949). A system that maintains a stable state is said to be in equilibrium. Because society is inherently an open system subject to influence from its natural and social environments, complete equilibrium never can be achieved. Rather, func-

tionalists describe society as normally being in a condition of dynamic or *near equilibrium,* constantly making small adjustments in response to shifts or changes in its internal elements or parts (Homans, 1950).

Probably the best-known spokesman for functionalist theory in America was Talcott Parsons (1951, 1954, 1966), who saw society as a homeostatic "action system" (see Chapter 3) that seeks to "integrate" its elements and whose patterns of actions are "maintained" by its culture. According to Parsons, it is the role of society to fulfill six basic needs: (1) member replacement, (2) member socialization, (3) production of goods and services, (4) preservation of internal order, (5) provision and maintenance of a sense of purpose, and (6) protection from external attack. These needs are in a constant state of equilibrium with one another, and when one changes, the others must accommodate. For example, when industrialization shifted the burden of socializing young people from the family to the school, schools enlarged their educational function to include the education of the whole child. Parent–teacher associations were established, and guidance counselers were hired to coordinate the function of the school with those of the family and other institutions. Thus, when the family became more specialized, the schools stepped in to fill the vacuum. In this case, as in all others, argued Parsons (1951, 1971), change promotes adaptation, equilibrium, and eventual social stability.

As functionalist theory developed, it began to trace the cause of social change to people's dissatisfactions with social conditions that personally affect them. Consider the area of medicine. Technological advances in medical science have made the practice of general medicine all but impossible and encouraged the development of medical subspecialties. Patients, who were forced to see a different specialist for almost every one of their health care needs, quickly became dissatisfied, even though the technical ability of each subspecialist was greater than that of the general practitioner. Responding to this dissatisfaction and to patients' conviction that their all-around health care was suffering as a result of the system of medical subspecializations,

According to functionalist theory, the Civil Rights Act of 1964 was an attempt by the government to achieve equilibrium in a society that had become unstable because of civil rights protests. Martin Luther King is shown here leading a protest in Selma, Alabama, in 1963.

the medical profession created the "new" specialty of family medicine. Thus, the needs met by the old "family doctor" are once again being addressed by the new "family medicine specialist."

Another example of the functionalist view of social change is the American civil rights movement of the 1960s, which gained strength outside the normal channels of political action. Hundreds of thousands of individuals joined in street protests, and many thousands were arrested. Occurring against the backdrop of race riots in Watts and other inner-city neighborhoods (see Chapter 18), the civil rights movement threatened the society with widespread rebellion and chaos. In response, political and social leaders launched a series of important adjustments that functioned to reform the society's institutional structure. These structural changes included the passage of the Civil Rights Act of 1964, which was intended to eliminate discrimination in public accommodations and in the labor force. Affirmative-action programs were established to integrate blacks into the labor force and provide equal access to higher education. The Voting Rights Act of 1965 was passed to at-

tack discrimination in voting, in particular in the registration procedures in the South. In 1968 Congress passed the first laws to attack discrimination in housing. Institutions that did not comply with these new federal rulings faced the possible withdrawal of all federal funds. Hence, though American society was pushed toward disequilibrium in the 1960s and early 1970s, greater equilibrium was reestablished through selected institutional adjustments that diminished organized expressions of discontent.

Functionalist theory successfully explains moderate degrees of social change, such as the adjustments that diffused the civil rights movement in America. The concepts of equilibrium and homeostasis are not very helpful, however, in explaining major structural changes (Bertalanffy, 1968). This criticism was summed up by Gnessous (1967) when he said that an "equilibrium theory like that of Parsons can neither explain the occurrence of radical changes in society nor account for the

homeostatic system An assemblage of interrelated parts that seeks to achieve and maintain a settled or stable state.

phenomena that accompany them; it says nothing about what happens when a social system is in disequilibrium . . . it is tied to the image of a society whose historical development holds no surprises."

William F. Ogburn's concept of cultural lag (1964) attempts to deal with these criticisms and explain social change in functionalist terms (see Chapter 3). Although all elements of a society are interrelated, Ogburn asserted, some elements may change rapidly and others "lag" behind. According to Ogburn, technological change typically is faster than is change in the nonmaterial culture, that is, the beliefs, norms, and values that regulate people's day-to-day lives in friendship and kinship groups and in religion. Therefore, he argued, technological change often results in culture lag. New patterns of behavior may emerge, even though they conflict with traditional values. When the birth control pill was developed, for example (a product of our material culture), orthodox religious norms forbade its use. Catholic women who wanted to limit their family size thus were on the horns of a dilemma. If they took the pill, they would violate the dictum of the church. If they did not, they would face additional pregnancies and the concomitant economic and family stress. Thus, even though Ogburn adopts a functionalist approach to social change, his theories incorporate the idea that stresses and strains or lack of "fit" among the parts of the social order are inevitable.

Popular during the 1940s and 1950s, the functionalist theory of social change has been criticized widely in recent times. Aside from the criticisms that we have mentioned, critics argue further that functionalism is a conservative theory that overestimates the amount of consensus in society and underestimates the effects of social conflict.

Cyclical ("Rise and Fall") Theory

Inherent in cyclical theories of social change is the assumption that the rise and fall of civilizations is inevitable and the notion that social change may not be for the good. Shocked by the devastation of World War I, people began to see social progress as the decline of society rather than as its enhancement. These feelings were crystallized in the works of Oswald Spengler, Arnold Toynbee, and Pitirim Sorokin.

In his controversial work *The Decline of the West* (1932), German historian Oswald Spengler theorized that every society moves through four stages of development: childhood, youth, mature adulthood, and old age. Spengler felt that Western society had reached the "golden age" of maturity during the Enlightenment of the eighteenth century, and since then had begun the inevitable crumbling and decline that go along with old age. Nothing, he believed, could stop this process. Just as the great civilizations of Babylon, Egypt, Greece, and Rome had declined and died, so too would the West.

British historian Arnold Toynbee (1946) theorized that the rise and fall of civilizations were explicable through the interrelated concepts of societal *challenge* and *response*. Every society, he observed, faces both natural and social challenges from its environments. Are its natural resources plentiful or limited? Are its boundaries easy or difficult to defend? Are important trade routes readily accessible or difficult to reach? Are its neighbors warlike or peaceful? When a society is able to fashion adequate responses to these challenges, it survives and grows. When it cannot, it falls into a spiral of decline. According to Toynbee, as each challenge is met, new challenges arise placing the society in a constant give-and-take interaction with its environments.

In his book *Social and Cultural Dynamics* (1937), Pitirim A. Sorokin (1889–1968) theorized that cultures are divided into two groups: **ideational cultures,** which emphasize spiritual values; and **sensate cultures,** which are based on what is immediately apparent through the senses. In an ideational culture, progress is achieved through self-control and adherence to a strong moral code. In a sensate culture, people are dedicated to self-expression and the gratification of their immediate physical needs.

Sorokin believed societies are constantly moving between the two extremes of sensate and ideational cultures. The main reason for this back and forth movement is that neither sensate nor ideational culture provides the basis for a perfect society. As one culture begins to deteriorate, its weaknesses and excesses become apparent, and there is a movement in the opposite direction. Occasionally, however, a culture may reach an intermediate place between these extremes. Sorokin called this the **idealistic point,** at which sensate and ideational values coexist in a harmonious mix.

Although cyclical, or "rise and fall," theories offer an interesting perspective on social change, they assume social change cannot be truly controlled by those who experience it. There is a supposedly inevitable cycle that all societies follow. The actions of people all are part of an elaborate, predetermined cyclical progression of events that has a life of its own. This may well be true of the ways in which many individuals experience social changes. However, such changes are clearly rooted in concrete decisions made by many individuals. The study of modernization allows us to examine the dominant form of social change in the world today and reveals both social and intrapersonal dynamics at work.

□ Modernization: Global Social Change

Modernization refers to a complex set of changes that take place as a traditional society undergoes industrialization. Modernization as we know it today is a phenomenon that first began with the Industrial Revolution some two centuries ago. Whereas the modernization of Western society evolved steadily over that time, the modernization of the Third World developing nations is proceeding at a much more rapid pace.

Modernization: An Overview
As modernization progresses from the first stages onward, many different changes occur. In the first stages of modernization, farmers move beyond subsistence farming to produce surplus food, which they sell in the market for money instead of bartering them for goods and services. In addition, a few limited cash crops and natural resources are exploited, bringing a steady flow of money into the economy. Simple tools and traditional crafts are replaced by industrialized technology and applied scientific knowledge. And whenever possible, human physical power is replaced by machines.

Work becomes increasingly specialized. New jobs—often requiring special training—are created, and people work for wages rather than living from the products of their labor. The economic system is freed from the traditional restraints and obligations rooted in kinship relations, and money becomes the medium of exchange. Educational institutions become differentiated from family life, and the population becomes increasingly literate. Cities rise as industrial and commercial centers and attract migrants from rural areas. Thanks to modern medicine, the death rate of the population falls, but the birthrate stays the same (at least in the early stages of modernization), creating excessive overcrowding.

The role of the family in social life is narrowed to the socialization of young children. Nuclear families are cut off from extended kinship networks, and many traditional constraints on behavior, such as notions of family pride and religious beliefs, lose their potency. Frequently, social equality between men and women increases as new social statuses and roles allow for changes in institutionalized behavior. Wealth is unequally distributed between the upper and lower classes (Dalton, 1971; Moore, 1965; Smelser, 1971). As you may have noted, many of these developments are separate facets of the overall pattern of increasing differentiation, which is a key trait of modernizing societies.

Modernization in the Third World
Whereas modernization was indigenous to most of Europe, it was forced on Third World nations by conquering armies, missionaries,

ideational culture According to Pitirim A. Sorokin, a culture in which the spiritual has the greatest value.

sensate culture According to Pitirim A. Sorokin, a culture in which people are dedicated to self-expression and the gratification of their immediate physical needs.

idealistic point According to Pitirim A. Sorokin, the intermediate place between the sensate and ideational cultures.

modernization The complex set of changes that take place as a traditional society becomes an industrial society.

plantation managers, colonial administrators, colonist groups, and industrial enterprises. Colonial administrators did not hesitate to destroy existing political structures whenever they seemed to endanger their rule. Missionaries used the threat of military force, bribery, and even good deeds (such as the construction of hospitals and schools) to draw people away from their traditions. They stamped out practices of which they did not approve (such as polygamy) and arbitrarily imposed European customs. Occasionally these missionary activities had comic consequences, as when women, unaccustomed to covering their breasts, simply cut holes in the fronts of their missionary-issued T-shirts. Other results were less humorous: People in tropical climates suffered skin infections after missionaries convinced them to dress in Western clothes but neglected to introduce soap.

Until recently, modernization and "Westernization" were thought of as more or less the same thing. A developing country that wanted to adopt Western technology had to accept its cultural elements at the same time. However, as Third World nations have gained

Modernization can produce abrupt social changes in third world countries. The rapid replacement of traditional institutions can create a variety of social problems.

some measure of economic control over their resources, many have asserted political independence and insisted that modernization be guided by their own traditional values. One need only think of the oil-rich Islamic countries to realize the different directions that the modernization of developing countries is now taking.

The goals and methods of modernization in the Third World vary widely from region to region and even from one nation to another. Nevertheless, because of the extreme abruptness and pervasiveness of the social changes created by modernization, certain common problems confront many of the developing nations.

Modernization and the Individual

Modernization has given people in developed countries improved health, increased longevity, more leisure time and affluence. Poverty, malnutrition, and disease, which were problems of Western nations as recently as 1890, have been eliminated or reduced dramatically for the bulk of the population. Life expectancy at birth increased from 47.6 years in 1900 to 73.8 years, and the workweek has been reduced from about 62 hours in 1890 to about 37 hours today. Indeed, modernization has given many in Western society the "luxury" of turning their attention to the problems of affluence, including anxiety, obesity, degenerative diseases, divorce, high taxes, inflation, and pollution.

The positive psychological effects of modernization were demonstrated by sociologists Alex Inkeles and David H. Smith (1974), who interviewed factory workers in Argentina, Bangladesh, Chile, India, Israel, and Nigeria. These researchers found that attending school and going to work in a factory had been a valued, liberating experience for many of these workers. They had improved their standards of living, overcome their fears of new things and foreign people, become more flexible about trying new ways of doing things, and adopted a more positive and action-oriented attitude toward their own lives.

Despite these benefits, modernization is not without its costs. Max Weber, who valued modernization as a means for making society more rational and efficient, nevertheless was painfully aware of its emotional costs, of its damaging impact on the spirit of the individual:

> Already now, throughout private enterprise in wholesale manufacture, as well as in all other economic enterprises run on modern lines . . . rational calculation . . . is manifest at every stage. By it, the performance of each individual worker is mathematically measured, each man becomes a little cog in the machine and, aware of this, his one preoccupation is whether he can become a bigger cog. (Weber, 1956)

Anthropologists and others have documented the severe psychological dislocation suffered by many peoples around the world as a result of modernization. The collapse of traditional cultures under the pressures of modernization has left individuals emotionally adrift in a world they do not understand and cannot control. Probably the most horrifying account is Colin Turnbull's (1972) of the Ik, a hunting and food-gathering people of Uganda who were relocated and forced to become farmers. Within five years their society, including its basic family unit, had disintegrated. Unable to feed themselves or their families in their traditional way, individuals starved, became demoralized, and lost their ability to empathize with one another.

Thus, it is clear that modernization has a profound psychological effect on people's lives. The *degree* of personal stress and dislocation that individuals experience as their society modernizes depends on many things, including the historical traditions of the culture, the conditions under which modernization is introduced, and the degree to which the masses are allowed to share in the material benefits of the change.

☐ Social Change in the United States

There is virtually no area of life in the United States that has not changed in some respect since the relatively simple days of the 1950s. In addition, the pace of change will quicken even more as the turn of the century approaches. The following are some of the major forces that are shaping future life in the United States.

A Maturing Society

For the first time in our history, there are more people aged 65 and over in the population than there are teenagers, and by 1990 the number of older citizens is expected to surpass 31 million, whereas the teenaged population will shrink to 23 million.

Relatively stagnant birthrates and big jumps in life expectancy have been the causes for this trend. In addition, the enormous baby-boom generation, born between 1946 and 1964, is now moving into middle age. By 1990, the number of people between the ages of 30 and 44 is expected to surge by 20 percent and total 60 million. Some people worry about the potential for conflict between the generations, as the elderly and young battle over spending priorities.

There will be a 60 percent increase in the number of 35- to 44-year-olds in the work force during the next decade, a situation that will produce some problems in the workplace, as large numbers of middle-aged workers compete for advancement. Young people coming into the work force after 1990 can look forward to expanding job opportunities, and they will face less competition for jobs than their older brothers and sisters did.

The Computer Revolution

The computer was born in World War II but perfected in the 1970s to a point that it has dramatically changed business operations and lifestyles.

Although computer technology touches all facets of life, the greatest impact has been in the workplace. The service sector, consisting of banks, insurance companies, and utilities, has been revolutionized by the computer. The reason is that these types of concerns specialize in the collection, analysis, and dissemination of information—tasks uniquely suited to the computer's capabilities. Working at home will also become more common, as computer networks spread: see Popular Sociology: "Working at Home: The Growth of Cottage Industry."

POPULAR SOCIOLOGY
Working at Home:
The Growth of Cottage Industry

One of the major developments in work is that more and more people are now doing their jobs at home instead of at traditional work settings. The following is an examination of this trend and the impact it may have on our society.

Twelve years ago, when Coralee Smith Kern started her own small business, she was ashamed to tell people that she worked from her home. In fact, she went so far as to rent downtown office space, which she never used, in order to have a "legitimate" business address.

Then one day, a chance conversation with a repairman changed her thinking. After the repairman had fixed her typewriter, Kern commented that he was no doubt headed back downtown. He told her that he was staying right in the neighborhood, because there were over 200 typewriters like hers within walking distance of her home. Amazed by that fact, she began to wonder about what was really going on in her neighborhood.

The people she approached did not want to talk about their businesses. It became evident that concerns about zoning laws, the underground economy, and fears of jeopardizing their conventional jobs were among the reasons for their reluctance. But Kern eventually learned enough to make her realize that the United States was experiencing a rebirth of the cottage industry. As she began to speak publicly about working from home, the mail she received reaffirmed her belief that a nationwide movement was under way.

Although there are no hard statistics, the U.S. Chamber of Commerce reports that 10 million businesses list home addresses as their place of business. Jack Nilles of the University of Southern California predicts that by 1990 as many as 15

million people will be telecommuting. And Nilles's figure does not include the people working with products and services not involved with electronic communications. These figures indicate that without question, cottage industries in America have not only reached significant proportions but also will continue to expand.

The size and impact of the work-at-home movement have been largely overlooked, possibly because cottage industries have been lumped together with other small businesses. As a result, their importance to the economy was mistakenly viewed as insignificant, and only in the last few years have cottage industries received serious attention from the government and the media.

Home workers are people who have made certain decisions regarding their careers and lifestyles. Tired of wasting time commuting, they want more time to spend with their families. Many want to take a more active role in raising their children. Others are disenchanted with big corporations and their way of doing things.

Home workers speak of the many advantages of working at home.

They save money on clothes, gasoline, parking, retaurant lunches, and other expenses associated with working in a traditional setting. Child care is less of a problem. Such workers have more freedom to arrange their own schedules and more time for the things they really want to do. And for many, the responsibility and challenge of being one's own boss is the most rewarding aspect.

One of the most frequently cited problems of working at home is the psychological problem of isolation. However, for some, the isolation can be seen as a benefit, as one has fewer interruptions and one's time can be more productive.

Although many people believe otherwise, the work-at-home movement is not a women's movement. Certainly, many women work at home, but a large portion of home workers are men. And all ages are represented in the movement, from young adults to retirees.

There are many "traditional" types of cottage industries, such as making crafts or running beauty salons, funeral parlors, or kennels. But they represent only a small percentage of the types of work now being done at home. Today, cottage industries include such diverse occupations as psychologists, lawyers, consultants, accountants, fabric designers, vehicle testers, publishers, and upholsterers. The increased demand for services has spurred the growth of all types, from cleaning and secretarial to exercise instruction and pet grooming. In addition, advances in microcomputers have opened information-related fields to home workers.

Most futurists recognize that technological advances in mini- and microcomputers and telecommunications are revolutionizing work. Microcomputers and telecommuting will no doubt prove to be the most significant factors in the work-at-home movement. Until now, the decentralization of business was simply not a practical alternative to centralized work sites; effective communication was seriously hampered. Now, it is not only possible but also economically advantageous to have workers at decentralized work stations. In an age in which time and fuel are both precious commodities, telecommuting makes sense.

For people working at home, the major issues of the 1980s will be zoning, labor laws, and licensing. As the number of people who work at home continues to increase, some government and business factions are showing resistance to these changes.

Some labor unions, for example, perceive home businesses as a threat to job security and other gains they have made. They fear that the current growth of the work-at-home movement may undermine union strength or signal a new era of sweatshop labor. Consequently, they have become a primary force behind legislation aimed at making illegal many types of home labor.

A number of states have laws that make it illegal to run crafts businesses from the home. Further, many states and cities that have such laws are beginning stricter enforcement. Some cottage industries have already been shut down, and a ground swell of support is developing among home workers to end overly restrictive legislation.

Because of the difficulty in monitoring home businesses, government officials fear that many home businesses will not pay their share of taxes. Although the "underground economy" no doubt exists, more and more home businesses are run above ground, paying their taxes and taking their legitimate write-offs. Licensing of home businesses will become a greater concern, as a larger percentage of the gross national product is generated by people who work at home.

Despite the negative reactions of some in government, many see the cottage industry as an area for economic growth and are doing whatever they can to encourage cottage industries in their states and communities.

"The work-at-home movement is already much larger than most people realize," says Coralee Smith Kern, who is now executive director of the National Association for the Cottage Industry. "We can expect cottage industries to have a far-reaching impact on our society in the next 20 years. How far-reaching? Well, it is highly improbable that businesses as we know them will cease to exist, but they may well change dramatically as more and more people discover that when it comes to working or running a business, there's really no place like home."

Source: Excerpted and adapted from Tammara H. Wolfgram, "Working at Home," *The Futurist* **18**(3) (June, 1984), pp. 31–34. □

Work

Many of the social changes we see occurring in the workplace involve attempts to create more satisfying working conditions for the majority of American workers, who are no longer content to perform repetititive tasks on an assembly line. (This discontent is especially acute among young workers.) A special task force to the secretary of health, education and welfare (now health and human services) drew the following conclusion in its report (1973):

Simplified tasks for those who are not simple-minded, close supervision by those whose legitimacy rests only on a hierarchical structure, and jobs that have nothing but money to offer in an affluent age are simply rejected. For many of the new workers, the monotony of work and scale of organization and their inability to control the pace and style of work are cause for a resentment which they, unlike older workers, do not repress.

Studies have shown that workers who are given some degree of control over their working conditions have much greater job satisfaction and achieve higher levels of productivity, which may in turn prompt higher levels of investment in these companies (see Using Sociology: "Social Investing: Doing Good While Doing Well"). Corporations like General Foods, Texas Instruments, Motorola, and

USING SOCIOLOGY
Social Investing:
Doing Good While Doing Well

Many investors want their money to bring good to society as well as profit to themselves. A Boston College sociologist explains how this is done and how these investment decisions may, in fact, bring about positive changes in the workplace.

A bank trust officer and a socially conscious investor were discussing what it means to make investments with the aim of effecting social change.

"Investing is *solely* for profit," the trust officer said. "Hell, I'd invest in a whorehouse if it made money and provided a desired service."

The investor thought for a moment, then replied, "Maybe I would, too, if the whorehouse were worker-managed or a cooperative."

The investor's attitude illustrates a trend that is gaining momentum in the investment world. Simply put, more people are now putting their money where their morals are.

Social investing has received increased attention as a result of well-publicized corporate disasters such as Firestone's faulty radial tires, Ford's Pinto, Hooker Chemical Company and the pollution of Love Canal, and the nuclear accident at Three Mile Island. More and more people are questioning the wisdom of investing in companies that look only for short-term profit, at the expense of long-term social good.

Reflecting the changes in Americans' investment concerns, more investment advisers are specializing in socially conscious investments for their clients. And many of these new counselors are doing well. . . .

Such investing could prove to be a force of growing importance in the future, for evidence also indicates that socially responsive corporations are having more success than companies that begrudge attention to issues (such as workers' welfare and the environment) that concern many investors. . . .

Social investors use traditional economic standards for investment decisions, but they use other measures as well. In addition to the return to the investor, they require economic and social return to others. For example, the investment should provide needed jobs for workers, improve the quality of working life, protect the environment, or help resolve major social problems. While traditional investors typically focus on present return, social investors tend to be future-oriented. They look for present return, but social investors also want future benefits for others, an economic and social return that will eventually improve the quality of life for all. . . .

One of the traditional criticisms of social investing is that mixing "soft" social judgments with "hard-headed" economic ones leads to economic failure. Evidence indicates that this is not only a myth but that combining social and economic judgments can actually lessen risk and increase economic return. . . .

An examination of the philosophy of social investors helps explain why economic success and social concern tend to go hand-in-hand. This philosophy is based on the assumption that to do well, one must do good, and vice versa. . . . It sees social responsibility and economic success as necessarily related. When social and economic judgments in business are separated, or when they are considered antithetical, the social and economic costs to corporations, to consumers, and to society as a whole can be great.

In Japan, the guarantee of life-time employment for workers led to their willingness to accept robotization, which in turn led to higher productivity and quality control. The Japanese worker's commitment to the employing corporation, a sense

that one's company was a kind of larger family, was an important factor. Japanese companies involved every worker in quality control. And while Japanese managers were responding to consumer demands for fuel-efficiency and safety, American managers were resisting any attempts to discuss these issues publicly. General Motors' initial response to Ralph Nader's accusations that they were marketing an inherently unsafe automobile was to send private detectives to investigate Nader's personal life.

Alternative forms of social organization in the Swedish Saab and Volvo automobile factories, implemented in the 1960s, contributed to high productivity and product quality. The traditional assembly line in these plants was redesigned to improve the quality of working life. Teams of three to four workers assembled car engines at a rate of up to eight per hour, and team members decided among themselves who would work on what part of the engine. Factories were reported to be safer, cleaner, cooler, and better lighted than American counterparts, and they contained more work space per person. Workers felt autonomous and could communicate freely with each other and with their supervisors.

The point is not that Japanese or Swedish organization and technology should or could be wholly implemented in American automobile plants. What these cases do illustrate is that at a time when foreign executives were responding to the desire of workers for a better quality of working life, of consumers for more efficient and safe automobiles, and of society for pollution control, American executives had a disappointing record of ignoring or opposing social concerns while concentrating only on short-term profits. The resulting decline of the American auto industry should come, therefore, as no surprise. It would appear that those who do not combine economic and social judgments may, indeed, do very badly. What about those who do combine these judgments? Can they do well while doing good?

One of the most striking examples of a marriage between economic success and social awareness can be found in Worthington Industries, which produces steel, steel castings, low-pressure gas containers, metal and plastic pipe fittings, and energy-saving coated glass.

Many years ago, Worthington started a profit-sharing program for workers, who were paid their profits directly on a quarterly basis in order to make the rewards more visible. In addition, all employees were paid a salary, eliminating the invidious distinction between salaried and hourly-wage workers. By 1980, the corporate staff numbered only 17 people, compared with 4,900 employees and 8,600 shareholders. Therefore, Worthington was not a firm top-heavy with unproductive executives utilizing many costly perks, typical of so many American industries.

The results? Worthington's employee absenteeism and turnover are extremely low, and productivity and efficiency are very high by industry standards. In 1980, the company's annual steel sales per employee averaged $180,000, compared with just $65,000 for the steel-processing industry as a whole. Worthington's pollution-control systems have been typically ahead of requirements, avoiding the financial cost and social ill-will of forced compliance with governmental standards.

From 1970 to 1980, Worthington's total sales increased by more than 1,000 percent, its earnings per share by more than 2,500 percent, and its net profit by more than 3,400 percent. These economic rewards were also shared by stockholders as dividends increased from 1 cent to 48 cents per share (4,700 percent), and the average yearly stock price went from 63 cents to $18.38 (2,817 percent). Meanwhile, other U.S. steel-related industries, especially giants like U.S. Steel Corporation, were experiencing major operating problems from higher costs for production and old, unreliable plants.

As the social investment movement attracts more adherents, it will effect a number of important changes. As more brokerage firms and banks respond to the interests of social investors, and as more corporations form ethics committees, there will be a need to train social scientists, business students, and humanities graduates in the new economic and social skills required for investment counseling.

The movement will alter relationships between shareholders, pension fund participants, corporate executives, fund managers, and local community interest groups. Companies will have to reexamine the value of policies of maximum return to shareholders at the expense of worker or public interests (for example, General Motors' insistence on paying dividends throughout a year of losses in 1981).

Finally, the rise of social investing reflects a withering of the old Protestant or Puritan ethic. The early ethic assumed that maximum individual gain would automatically bring about the greatest benefits for all. In an age of conglomerate corporations, controlled and manipulated markets, social commitment to leisure rather than work, and emphasis upon immediate spending rather than future saving, this ethic is no longer viable.

No economic system can continue to prosper without a solid moral base. The social investing movement reflects a search for new moral principles that show a concern for *both* individual and collective gain and well-being.

Source: Excerpted from Ritchie P. Lowry, "Social Investing: Doing Good While Doing Well," *The Futurist* **16**(2) (April, 1982), pp. 22–28. □

---

the Traveler's Insurance Company have responded to these studies by instituting a more humanized, less institutionalized workplace.

At the General Foods Corporation, for example, a new plant was constructed to deal with the problem of worker alienation, which had reached the point of serious vandalism and sabotage. In consultation with workers as well as researchers, the new plant was designed around work teams that took responsibility for large sections of the production process. Tasks were made more challenging and interesting, and the usual status symbols that are built into many industrial plants—like preferential parking lots and separate entrances and cafeterias for management—were eliminated. In addition, management introduced a policy of informing workers about the plant's profitability. It also gave workers greater opportunities to apply for and get job promotions and substituted "team leaders" for "work supervisors." Worker productivity rose dramatically as a result of all these changes, but more importantly, alienation seemed to

FOCUS ON RESEARCH
Wives Who Earn More Than Their Husbands

Recent studies have shown that in America today, six million wives earn more than their husbands do. Who are these women? Are they the media superstars whose lives are often profiled in glossy magazines, or do they fit another, less glamorous, profile?

In recent years, the public has been bombarded with various statistics regarding working women. We now know that more than 50 percent of married women work, that half of today's mothers of preschoolers are in the labor force, and that full-time working women earn 59 cents for every dollar earned by men.

But statistics can distort as well as inform. The subject of the wives who earn more than their husbands is just such as case. Although the popular media have focused on high-earning female doctors, lawyers, and businesswomen, most women in this category do not fit that rarified description.

In 1981, wives who brought home the larger paycheck in a dual-earner marriage earned a median income of $13,000. In over half of these marriages, the husband worked less than full time. Although some of these husbands were retired, disabled, or temporarily laid off, a significant proportion worked part time simply because they wanted to.

This was true of only about one-fourth of husbands whose wives were not in the paid labor force. Secondary-earner husbands were more likely than either the primary or sole male earners to have spent some weeks unemployed or out of the labor force entirely: 49 percent of secondary earners were out of work for some time in 1981, compared with 17 percent of primary earners and 24 percent of sole earners.

Did these husbands who were secondary earners work less than other husbands during 1981 because they were constrained by poor economic conditions or because they were under less economic pressure, given the earnings of their wives? This is a key question, because its answer may suggest how family roles are changing. The answer is mixed: around 30 percent of husbands who were secondary earners worked part time in 1981 because they wanted to. This figure is more than twice that for husbands who were primary earners in dual-earner couples. Fully 70 percent of secondary earners worked part time for involuntary or partially involuntary reasons, however, suggesting that in some families, wives are the primary means of support because the husbands cannot be.

Other demographic factors also have a significant influence on the profile of primary-earning wives. For example, in 1981, black couples were more likely than were either white or Hispanic couples to have the wife in a primary-earning role, either as the sole earner or the higher-earning spouse in a dual-earner couple. In 20 percent of black couples, compared with 11 percent of white couples and 10 percent of Hispanic couples, the wife was the primary earner.

Historically, black wives have had higher rates of labor force participation than white wives, although these differences have narrowed in recent years, as white wives have joined the labor force at greater rates than black wives. Black men have faced serious employment barriers and low earnings, and so black couples are least likely to fit the traditional pattern in which the husband works for pay and the wife is not employed.

Hispanic couples are the most likely to fit the traditional pattern, reflecting their higher fertility and the greater concentration of Hispanic wives in child-rearing roles. Among blacks and Hispanics, as among whites, however, the most common arrangement today—accounting for over 40 percent of all couples—is the dual-earner couple in which the husband is the primary earner.

Dual-earner couples in which the husband is the primary earner have the highest incomes. In 1981, such families had a median income of $30,112, and only 3 percent were below the poverty level. Next to couples without any earnings, those that relied on only the wife's earnings were the worst off. The median income for such families in 1981 was $17,122, and 10 percent lived in poverty.

Though they are less common than the newspapers and magazines would lead us to believe, the ranks of the professionally trained women who earn more than their husbands are growing. In 1981, there were about 860,000 such women, comprising only 15 percent of the 6 million wives who earned more than their husbands did, and a mere 1.8 percent of all couples. More common (and thus less alluring to the public eye) are the wives who work at a nonprofessional job to provide primary support of their families because their husbands have employment problems.

Do the superior earnings of a wife put a strain on the marital relationship? Findings have been mixed. If the husband remains unemployed or underemployed for longer than the couple expects and the wife's earnings are not adequate to support the family, or if both expect the husband to be the primary breadwinner but he does not fulfill that role, problems may well occur. On the other hand, if husbands and wives have chosen similar occupations, received the same amount of education, and have no strong preferences about which one should earn more, there is no particular reason to believe those marriages in which the wife earns more will be less stable.

Many couples are successful in adjusting to the wife as a primary earner, although there are as yet no statistics that measure this relatively new type of arrangement. As women continue to gain in education and employment and their wages catch up to men's, women will be as likely as men to earn high salaries.

Source: Adapted and excerpted from Suzanne M. Bianchi, "Wives Who Earn More Than Their Husbands," *American Demographcis* **6**(7) (July, 1984), pp. 19–24. ☐

---

disappear. Sabotage was eliminated, waste drastically reduced, and plant shutdowns avoided (Special Task Force, 1973).

This kind of work restructuring has already been adopted by many other companies. In many factories, time clocks have been replaced by **flexitime,** which allows workers to adjust their work schedules each day to meet personal needs as long as they put in the required number of working hours per week. Flexitime gives workers more responsibility for arranging when and how their tasks are completed. It also considerably improves workers' morale and decreases morning and evening traffic congestion. In 1980, approximately 7.6 million workers, representing 12 percent of the labor force holding full-time nonfarm jobs, were on a flexitime schedule.

Women in the Work Force

In 1950 only one-third of American women held jobs outside the home. Today, more than 65 percent of women between 25 and 44 are employed. About 57 percent of all married women with children work outside the home, up from 31 percent 20 years ago. (See Table 20.1 for the percentage of the total female population in the labor force) These jobs are often the mainstay of the family's livelihood. The Census Bureau claims there are nearly six million homes in which wives earn more than their husbands (see Focus on Research: "Wives Who Earn More Than Their Husbands").

A continuing sore point for women in the work force is the economic disparity between the sexes. Despite strides in breaking down job barriers, job equality for women has been slow in coming. There are few major firms that have women as the chief executives. Statistics also show that the majority of people living in poverty are female. One out of every 7 families is headed by a woman, up from 1 in 10 families in 1960, and roughly 40 of such families are below the poverty level.

The Rise of Minorities

As their numbers grow, minorities are gaining power and influence. The 28.6 million blacks in the United States now constitute 12.1 percent of the population. Many of them live in states such as New York, Florida, California, and Illinois, where they could play a key role in political contests.

People of Spanish origin, whose numbers increased by 61 percent in the 1970s, now total 16 million. It is expected that in another decade they will overtake blacks and become the largest minority.

The number of Asian Americans jumped 128 percent in one decade, to total 3.5 million in 1980.

The result of these increases has been that congressional seats are now held by 20 blacks, 9 Hispanics, and 4 Japanese Americans, and 19 cities of 100,000 or more population have a black mayor.

TABLE 20.1 *Percentage of Female Population in Labor Force: 1940–1984*

Year	Percentage
1940	27.4
1950	31.4
1955	33.5
1960	34.8
1965	36.7
1970	42.6
1975	46.0
1984	53.2

Source: U.S. Department of Commerce, Bureau of the Census, *Statistical Abstract of the United States, 1984* (Washington, D.C.: Government Printing Office, 1983), p. 413.

flexitime A plan in which workers are allowed to adjust their work schedules each day to meet personal needs as long as they put in the required working hours weekly.

TABLE 20.2 Degrees Conferred: 1950–1982

Year	Bachelors	Masters	Doctorates
1950	434,000	58,000	6,600
1955	288,000	58,000	8,800
1960	395,000	75,000	9,800
1965	539,000	112,000	16,500
1970	833,000	209,000	29,900
1975	988,000	294,000	34,100
1981	1,007,000	296,000	32,900
1982	953,000	295,546	32,707

Source: U.S. Department of Commerce, Bureau of the Census *Statistical Abstract of the United States, 1985* (Washington, D.C.: Government Printing Office, 1984), p. 158.

A Highly Educated Society

Americans have long believed that everyone has a right to a good education. In fact, people are so convinced of this idea that colleges are turning out more graduates than the job market can accommodate. From Table 20.2 we can see that the number of college degrees conferred has been increasing steadily since 1950. It is estimated that 20 occupations will account for 35 percent of the new jobs during this decade, but only two of them, elementary-school teaching and accounting, require college degrees.

The U.S. Bureau of Labor Statistics sees the biggest growth in jobs that require little education. It predicts that by 1995, there will be nearly 800,000 new jobs for janitors—almost twice the number as that for computer specialists—and 600,000 for fast-food workers. The bureau also suggests it is possible that 20 percent of college graduates will find jobs that do not require a degree and that another 14 percent will not be able to get work that matches their qualifications.

Medical Developments

Significant advances will continue to be made on the medical front. In 1983, 3,285 children contracted mumps, compared with 152,209 in 1968. Cases of measles fell from 481,530 in 1962 to 1,436 in 1983. Polio, a disease that crippled many children in the 1950s, has virtually been wiped out. Progress has also been made with heart disease and stroke; deaths from these causes since 1970 have declined 25 percent and 40 percent, respectively.

In vitro fertilization, a process in which an egg is taken from a woman, fertilized in a laboratory dish, and then transferred back to her womb, is no longer science fiction. In addition, experiments are now being done with surrogate *in vitro* fertilization, in which another woman carries and delivers a child that genetically is the product of two other individuals.

The negative side of the medical advances is runaway health care costs. Spending on health care rose from $27 billion in 1960 to $356 billion in 1983, an increase from 5 percent to 11 percent of the gross national product. Medical care costs are rising more than twice as fast as the inflation rate.

☐ Summary

Social change consists of alterations in a society's social organization, statuses, and social structure. Social change is caused by such internal factors as technological innovation, ideology (which may be conservative, liberal, or radical), and cultural conflicts and institutionalized structural inequality. Diffusion—the transmission of traits from one culture to another—is the primary external source of social change.

No one theory of social change explains all its ramifications, as each theory views social change from an entirely different perspective. The evolutionary theory of social change is based on the assumption that Western cultures have reached higher levels of cultural achievement because they are better adapted to compete for scarce resources and to meet other difficult challenges. Conflict theory is rooted in the assumption that the class struggle between unequal groups leads to social change, which in turn creates conditions that lead to new conflicts. Functionalist theory describes society as being in a condition of near equilibrium, constantly making small adjustments in response to shifts or changes in its elements or parts.

Modernization is the complex set of changes that take place as a traditional society experiences the processes of industrialization. Modernization first occurred in Western society after the Industrial Revolution. It was forced on Third World nations by conquering armies, missionaries, and other representatives of Western societies who believed that modernization and Westernization were the same thing. Modernization has been a mixed blessing to both developed and developing nations. On the one hand, it has provided improved health, increased longevity, leisure time, and affluence. On the other, it has generated many strains as people have had to cope with industrialization, urbanization, secularization, and rapid changes.

There is virtually no area of life in the United States that has not undergone considerable change since the 1950s. There are many forces that will shape life in the United States in the future. These include the increasing average age of our population, the computer revolution, more women in the work force, the increase in the number of minority groups in society, the increasing level of education, and major medical developments.

☐ For Further Reading

APPLEBAUM, RICHARD. *Theories of Social Change.* Chicago: Markham, 1970.   An excellent introduction to many of the leading sociological theories of social change.

BLACK, CYRIL E. (ed.). *Comparative Modernization.* New York: Free Press, 1976. A cross-national look at modernization. The book's 21 articles consider the theory of modernization and some of its applications and problems.

DIRENZO, GORDON J. *We, the People: American Character and Social Change.* Westport, Conn.: Greenwood Press, 1977.   A collection of essays explaining how social changes affect American character.

LIPSET, SEYMOUR MARTIN. (ed.). *The Third Century: America as a Post-Industrial Society.* Stanford, Calif.: Hoover Institution Press, 1979.   An analysis of social change in a wide variety of areas.

OGBURN, WILLIAM F. *Social Change.* New York: Viking, 1950.   In this functionalist classic, Ogburn discusses the effects of technological change on social organization and introduces his concept of "cultural lag."

TOFFLER, ALVIN. *The Third Wave.* New York: Morrow, 1980.   A popularized look at the changes that are taking place in our society.

References

ABERLE, D. F., A. K. COHEN, A. K. DAVIS, M. J. LEVEY, JR., and F. X. SUTTON. 1950. "The functional prerequisites of a society." *Ethics,* **60,** pp. 100–111.

ANTHONY, JAMES E., and THERESE BENEDEK (eds.). 1970. *Parenthood: Its Psychology and Psychopathology.* Boston: Little, Brown.

ARENSON, KAREN W. 1982. "Services: Bucking the slump." *New York Times,* May 18, p. D1.

ASCH, SOLOMON. 1955. "Opinions and social press." *Scientific American,* **193,** pp. 31–35.

———. 1951. "Effects of group pressure upon the modification and distortion of judgements." In H. Guptzkow (ed.), *Groups, Leadership and Men.* Pittsburgh: Carnegie Press.

BALES, R. F. 1958. "Task roles and social roles in problem-solving groups." In E. E. Maccoby, T. M. Newcomb, and E. L. Hartley (eds.), *Readings in Social Psychology.* 3d ed. New York: Holt, Rinehart and Winston.

———, and F. L. STRODBECK. 1951. "Phases in group problem solving." *Journal of Abnormal and Social Psychology,* **46,** pp. 485–495.

BANDURA, A. 1969. *Principles of Behavior Modification,* New York: Holt, Rinehart and Winston.

BARDWICK, JUDITH W., and ELIZABETH DOUVAN. 1971. "Ambivalence: The socialization of women." In Vivian Gornick and Barbara K. Moran (eds.), *Woman in Sexist Society: Studies in Power and Powerlessness.* New York: Basic Books.

BARON, SALO W. 1976. European Jewry before and after Hitler." In Yisrael Gutman and Livia Rothkirchen (eds.), *The Catastrophe of European Jewry.* Jerusalem: Yad Veshem.

BASKIN, BARBARA H., and KAREN HARRIS. 1980. *Books for the Gifted Child.* New York: R. R. Bowker.

BAUMRIND, DIANE. 1975. "Early socialization and adolescent competence." In Sigmund E. Dragastin and Glen H. Elder, Jr. (eds.), *Adolescence in the Life Cycle.* New York: Halsted Press.

BECKER, HOWARD. 1963. *Outsiders: Studies in the Sociology of Deviance.* New York: Free Press.

BELL, ALAN P., MARTIN S. WEINBERG, and SUE KIE-

FER HAMMERSMITH. 1981. *Sexual Preference, Its Development in Men and Women.* Bloomington Ind.: Indiana University Press.

BELL, D. 1973. *The Coming of the Post-industrial Society: A Venture in Social Forecasting.* New York: Basic Books.

BEM, SANDRA L., and DARYL J. BEM. 1976. "Case study of a nonconscious ideology: Training the woman to know her place." In Sue Cox (ed.), *Female Psychology: The Emerging Self.* Chicago: Science Research Associates (SRA).

BENDIX, R. 1962. *Max Weber: An Intellectual Portrait.* Garden City, N.Y.: Doubleday/Anchor.

BENEDICT, RUTH. 1961 (1934). *Patterns of Culture.* Boston: Houghton Mifflin.

———. 1938. "Continuities and discontinuities in cultural conditioning." *Psychiatry,* **1,** pp. 161–167.

BENNIS, W. 1971. "Beyond bureaucracy." In S. G. McNall (ed.), *The Sociological Perspective.* 2d ed. Boston: Little, Brown, pp. 225–233.

BEQUAI, AUGUST. 1977. "Wanted: The white-collar ring." *Student Lawyer,* May 5, p. 45.

BERGER, PETER. 1967. *The Sacred Canopy.* New York: Doubleday.

———. 1963. *Invitation to Sociology: A Humanistic Perspective.* New York: Doubleday.

BERNARD, L. L. 1924. *Instinct.* New York: Holt, Rinehart and Winston.

BERRY, BREWTON, and HENRY TISCHLER. 1978. *Race and Ethnic Relations.* 4th ed. Boston: Houghton Mifflin.

BERTALANFFY, LUDWIG VON. 1968. *General System Theory.* New York: George Braziller.

BETTLEHEIM, B. 1967. *The Empty Fortress.* New York: Free Press.

BIERSTADT, ROBERT. 1974. *The Social Order.* 4th. ed. New York: McGraw-Hill.

BLAU, PETER M. 1964. *Exchange and Power in Social Life.* New York: John Wiley.

———, and M. W. MEYER 1971. *Bureaucracy in Modern Society.* 2d ed. New York: Random House.

———, and O. D. DUNCAN. 1967. *The American Occupational Structure.* New York: John Wiley.

BLUM, JOHN M., EDMUND S. MORGAN, WILLIE LEE ROSE, ARTHUR M. SCHLESINGER, JR., KENNETH M. STAMP, and C. VAN WOODARD. 1981. *The National Experience: A History of the United States.* 5th ed. New York: Harcourt Brace Jovanovich.

BLUMBERG, PAUL. 1980. *Inequality in an Age of Decline.* New York: Oxford University Press.

BLUMER, HERBERT. 1946. "Collective behavior." In Alfred McClung Lee (ed.), *Principles of Sociology.* New York: Barnes & Noble.

BLUMSTEIN, PHILIP, and PEPPER SCHWARTZ. 1983. *American Couples.* New York: Morrow.

BOTTOMORE, T. B. 1966. *Classes in Modern Society.* New York: Pantheon.

BRENNER, M. HARVEY. 1977. "Personal stability and economic security." *Social Policy,* May–June, pp. 2–5.

1984 Britannica Book of the Year. 1983. Chicago: Encyclopaedia Britannica Inc.

BRONFENBRENNER, U. 1970. *Two Worlds of Childhood.* New York: Russell Sage Foundation.

BROWN, DEE. 1978. *Bury My Heart at Wounded Knee.* New York: Holt, Rinehart and Winston.

BROWN, LESTER R. 1974. *In the Human Interest.* New York: Norton.

———, and ERIK P. ECKHOLM. 1974. *By Bread Alone.* New York: Praeger.

BROWN, ROGER W. 1954. "Mass phenomena." In Gardner Lindzey (ed.), *Handbook of Social Psychology.* Cambridge, Mass.: Addison-Wesley.

BULLOUGH, VERN L. 1973. *The Subordinate Sex.* Chicago: University of Chicago Press.

BURCHINAL, LEE G., and LOREN E. CHANCELLOR. 1963. "Survival rates among religiously homogamous and interreligious marriages." *Social Factors,* **41,** pp. 353–362.

BURNS, JAMES MACGREGOR, J. W. PELTASON, and THOMAS E. CRONIN. 1981. *Government by the People.* 11th ed. Englewood Cliffs, N.J.: Prentice-Hall.

BUTTERFIELD, FOX. 1979. "In the new China, 1 + 1 can = 4—No more." *New York Times,* November 11, p. E7.

BYRNE, D. 1971. *The Attraction Paradigm.* New York: Academic Press.

CAFFEY, J. 1946. "Multiple fractures to the long bones of infants suffering from chronic subdural hematoma." *American Journal of Roentgenology,* **56,** pp. 163–173.

CALDWELL, JOHN C. 1976. "Toward a restatement of demographic transition theory." *Population and Development Review,* **2.**

CAMERON, WILLIAM BRUCE. 1966. *Modern Social Movements: A Sociological Outline.* New York: Random House.

CANETTI, ELIAS. 1978 (1960). *Crowds and Power.* New York: Seabury Press.

CANTRIL, HADLEY. 1940. *The Invasion from Mars: A Study in the Psychology of Panic.* Princeton, N.J.: Princeton University Press.

CAPDEVIELLE, P., and D. ALVAREZ. 1981. "International comparisons of trends in productivity and labor costs." *Monthly Labor Review,* December, p. 15.

CARNEGIE COUNCIL ON POLICY STUDIES IN HIGHER EDUCATION. 1979. "Giving youth a better chance: Options for education, work, and service." *Chronicle of Higher Education,* December 3, pp. 11–13.

CARNEGIE FOUNDATION. 1979. *Report.* Berkeley, Calif.: Carnegie Foundation.

CARSTENS, KENNETH. 1978. "The churches in South Africa." In Ian Robertson and Phillip Whitten (eds.), *Race and Politics in South Africa.* New Brunswick, N.J.: Transaction Books.

CHERLIN, ANDREW. 1981. *Marriage, Divorce and Remarriage.* Cambridge, Mass.: Harvard University Press.

CHOMSKY, N. 1975. *Language and Mind.* New York: Harcourt Brace Jovanovich.

CLAYTON, RICHARD B., and HARWIN L. VOSS. 1977. "Shacking up: Cohabitation in the 1970s." *Journal of Marriage and the Family,* **39**(2), May, pp. 273–283.

COHEN, ALBERT K. 1955. "A general theory of subculture." In *Delinquent Boys: The Culture of the Gang.* New York: Free Press.

COHEN, YEHUDI A. 1981. "Shrinking households." *Society,* **18**(2), January–February, p. 51.

———. 1974. "Pastoralism." In Y. A. Cohen (ed.), *Man in Adaptation: The Cultural Present.* 2d ed. Chicago: Aldine.

COLE, STEWARD G., and MILDRED WIESE COLE. 1954. *Minorities and the American Promise.* New York: Harper & Row.

COLEMAN, JAMES S. 1977. *Parents, Teachers, and Children.* San Francisco: San Francisco Institute for Contemporary Studies.

———. 1966. *Equality of Educational Opportunity.* Washington, D.C.: U.S. Government Printing Office.

COLLINS, RANDALL. 1979. *The Credential Society: An Historical Sociology of Education and Stratification.* New York: Academic Press.

———. 1975. *Conflict Sociology: Toward an Explanatory Science.* New York: Academic Press.

Common Cause Magazine. 1981. Washington, D.C.: Common Cause Publishers, February, p. 11.

———. 1981. Washington, D.C.: Common Cause Publishers, April, p. 12.

COMTE, AUGUSTE. 1968 (1851). *System of Positive Policy.* Vol. 1. Trans. John Henry Bridges. New York: Burt Franklin.

CONGER, J. J. 1980. "A new morality: Sexual attitudes and behavior of contemporary adolescents." In P. Mussen, J. Conger, and J. Kagan (eds.), *Readings in Child and Adolescent Psychology: Contemporary Perspectives.* New York: Harper & Row.

Congressional Quarterly. 1980. 2d. ed. Washington, D.C.: U.S. Government Printing Office.

COOLEY, C. H. 1909. *Social Organization.* New York: Scribner.

COSER, L. A. 1977. *Masters of Sociological Thought.* 2d ed. New York: Harcourt Brace Jovanovich.

———. 1967. *Continuities in the Study of Social Conflict.* New York: Free Press.

———. 1956. *The Functions of Social Conflict.* Glencoe, Ill.: Free Press.

CRANO, WILLIAM D., and JOEL ARONOFF. 1978. "A cross-cultural study of expressive and instrumental role complementarity in the family." *American Sociological Review,* **43,** August, pp. 463–471.

CRESSEY, D. R. 1969. *Theft of the Nation: The Structure and Operations of Organized Crime in America.* New York: Harper Torchbooks.

CROSSEN, PIERRE R. 1975. "Institutional obstacles to expansion of world food production." *Science,* **188,** pp. 519–524.

CUMMINGS, MILTON C., and DAVID WISE. 1981. *Democracy Under Pressure: An Introduction to the American Political System.* 4th ed. New York: Harcourt Brace Jovanovich.

CURTISS, S. 1977. *Genie: A Psycholinguistic Study of a Modern-Day "Wild Child."* New York: Academic Press.

CUZZORT, R. P., and E. W. KING. 1980. *Twentieth Century Social Thought.* 3d ed. New York: Holt, Rinehart and Winston.

DAHRENDORF, R. 1959. *Class and Conflict in Industrial Society.* Stanford University Press.

———. 1958. "Out of Utopia: Toward a reorientation of sociological analysis." *American Journal of Sociology,* **64,** September.

DALTON, GEORGE. 1971. *Modernizing Village Economics.* Toronto: Addison-Wesley Module.

D'ANDRADE, ROY G. 1966. "Sex differences and cultural institutions." In Eleanor Emmons Maccoby (ed.), *The Development of Sex Differences.* Stanford, Calif.: Stanford University Press.

DANZIGER, SHELDON. 1976. "Explaining urban crime rates." *Criminology* **14,** August, pp. 291–296.

DARWIN, CHARLES. 1964 (1859). *On the Origin of Species.* Cambridge, Mass: Harvard University Press.

DAVIDSON, LAURIE, and LAURA KRAMER GORDON. 1979. *The Sociology of Gender.* Chicago: Rand McNally.

DAVIS, F. JAMES. 1979. *Understanding Minority-Dominant Relations.* Arlington Heights, Ill: AHM Publishing.

DAVIS, KINGSLEY. 1976. *America's Children.* Washington, D.C.: National Council of Organizations for Children and Youth.

——— (ed.). 1973. *Cities: Their Origin, Growth and Human Impact.* San Francisco: W. H. Freeman.

———. 1966. "The world's population crisis." In Robert K. Merton and Robert Nisbet (eds.). *Contemporary Social Problems.* 2d ed. New York: Harcourt Brace Jovanovich.

———. 1949. *Human Society.* New York: Macmillan.

———. 1940. "Extreme social isolation of a child." *American Journal of Sociology,* **45,** pp. 554–565.

———, and W. E. MOORE. 1945. "Some principles of stratification." *American Sociological Review,* **10,** pp. 242–249.

DE BEAUVOIR, S. 1972. "Old age: End product of a faulty system." *Saturday Review of Society,* April 8.

DEVORE, I. (ed.) 1965. *Primate Behavior: Field Studies of Monkeys and Apes.* New York: Holt, Rinehart and Winston.

DOLAN, EDWIN G. 1980. *Basic Economics.* 2d ed. Hinsdale, Ill.: Dryden Press.

DOMHOFF, G. WILLIAM. 1983. *Who Rules America Now?* Englewood Cliffs, N.J.: Prentice-Hall.

———. 1967. *Who Rules America?* Englewood Cliffs, N.J.: Prentice-Hall.

DUBERMAN, LUCILE. 1976. *Social Inequality.* New York: Harper & Row.

DUMANOSKI, D. 1981. "Youth unemployment: Who's to blame?" *Boston Globe,* January 11, p. C2.

DURANT, WILL. 1954. "Our oriental heritage," *The Story of Civilization.* Vol. I. New York: Simon & Schuster.

———. 1944. *Caesar and Christ.* New York: Simon & Schuster.

DURKHEIM, EMILE. 1961 (1915). *The Elementary Forms of Religious Life.* New York: Collier Books.

———. 1960a (1893). *The Division of Labor in Society.* Trans. G. Simpson. New York: Free Press.

———. 1960b (1893). *Montesquieu and Rousseau.* Ann Arbor: University of Michigan Press.

———. 1958 (1895). *The Rules of Sociological Method.* Glencoe, Ill.: Free Prress.

———. 1954 (1917). *The Elementary Forms of Religious Life.* Trans. J. W. Swain. New York: Free Press.

———. 1951 (1897). *Suicide: A Study in Sociology.*

Trans. J. A. Spaulding and G. Simpson. New York: Free Press.

———. 1950 (1894). *Rules of Sociolgical Method.* New York: Free Press.

EHRLICH, PAUL. 1974. *The End of Affluence.* New York: Ballantine.

———, and ANN H. EHRLICH. 1972. *Population, Resources, Environment.* San Francisco: W. H. Freeman.

———, and S. SHIRLEY FELDMAN. 1978. *The Race Bomb: Skin Color, Prejudice, and Intelligence.* New York: Quadrangle.

ELDER, GLEN H. 1975. "Adolescence in the life cycle: An introduction." In Sigmund E. Dragastin and Glen H. Elder, Jr. (eds.), *Adolescence in the Life Cycle.* New York: Halsted Press.

ELLUL, J. 1964. *The Technological Society.* New York: Knopf.

EMBER, CAROL R., and MELVIN EMBER. 1981. *Anthropology.* 3rd ed. Englewood Cliffs, N.J.: Prentice-Hall.

ENGELS, FRIEDRICH. 1942 (1884). *The Origin of the Family, Private Property and the State.* New York: International Publishing.

ENOS, DARRYL D., and PAUL SULTAN. 1977. *The Sociology of Health Care: Social, Economic, and Political Perspectives.* New York: Praeger.

ERIKSON, ERIK H. 1968. *Identity, Youth and Crisis.* New York: Norton.

———. 1964. *Childhood and Society.* New York: Norton.

ERIKSON, KAI T. 1966. *Wayward Puritans: A Study in the Sociology of Deviance.* New York: John Wiley.

FARB, PETER. 1978. *Humankind.* Boston: Houghton Mifflin.

FEDERAL COMMITTEE ON STANDARD METROPOLITAN STATISTICAL AREAS. 1979. *The Metropolitan Statistical Area Classification.* Washington, D.C.: U.S. Department of Commerce, Bureau of the Census, pp. 33–36, 38, 39, 44, 336, 351, 355.

FERHOLT, J. B., D. E. HUNTER, and J. M. LEVENTHAL. 1978. "Longitudinal research on the causes and effects of child maltreatment." Unpublished manuscript.

FESTINGER, LEON, HENRY W. RIEKEN, and STANLEY SCHACTER. 1956. *When Prophesy Fails.* New York: Harper Torchbooks.

FIRTH, RAYMOND. 1963. *Elements of Social Organization.* Boston: Beacon Press.

FISCHLER, STAN. 1980. "Garden security and return of the Bruins." *New York Times,* March 2, p. 25.

FISHER, JEFFREY D., and D. BYRNE. 1975. "Too close for comfort: Sex differences in response to invasions of personal space." *Journal of Personality and Social Psychology,* **32,** pp. 15–21.

FISKE, EDWARD. 1982. "Rising tuitions signal shift in education costs." *New York Times,* May 16, p. A1.

FLANNERY, KENT V. 1968. "Archaeological systems theory and early Mesopotamia." In Betty J. Meggars (ed.), *Anthropological Archaeology in the Americas.* Washington, D.C.: Anthropological Society of Washington.

———. 1965. "The ecology of early food production in Mesopotamia." *Science,* **147,** pp. 1247–1256.

FOGEL, WALTER A. 1979. *Mexican Illegal Alien Workers in the United States.* Los Angeles: Institute of Industrial Relations, University of California.

———. 1975. "Immigrant Mexicans and the U.S. work force." *Monthly Labor Review,* **98,** May, pp. 44–46.

Forbes. 1980. "The 100 largest U.S. multinationals." *Forbes,* July 7, p. 102.

FORD, CLELLAN S. 1970. "Some primitive societies." In Georgene H. Seward and Robert C. Williamson (eds.), *Sex Roles in Changing Society.* New York: Random House.

FORTES, M., R. W. STEEL, and P. ADY. 1947. "Ashanti survey, 1945–46: An experiment in social research." *Geographical Journal,* **110,** pp. 149–179.

Fortune. 1982. "Fortune's directory of the 500 largest industrial corporations." May 3, p. 258.

FRANKFORT, H. 1956 (1951). *The Birth of Civilization in the Near East.* Garden City, N.Y.: Doubleday/Anchor.

FREDRICKSON, GEORGE M. 1971. *The Black Image in the White Mind.* New York: Harper & Row.

FREEMAN, JAMES M. 1974. "Trial by fire." *Natural History,* January.

FREITAG, PETER. 1975. "The cabinet and big business: A study of interlocks." *Social Problems,* **2,** December 23, pp. 137–152.

FREUD, SIGMUND. 1930. "Civilization and its discontents." *Standard Edition of the Complete Psychological Works of Sigmund Freud.* Vol. 29. London: Hogarth Press.

———. 1928. *The Future of an Illusion.* New York: Horace Liveright and the Institute of Psycho-Analysis.

———. 1923. "The ego and the id." *Standard Edition of the Complete Psychological Works of Sigmund Freud,* Vol. 19. London: Hogarth Press.

———. 1920. "Beyond the pleasure principle." *Standard Edition of the Complete Psychological Works of Sigmund Freud,* Vol. 14, London: Hogarth Press.

———. 1918. *Totem and Taboo.* New York: Moffat, Yard & Co.

FRIED, MORTON. 1967. *The Evolution of Political Society.* New York: Random House.

FRIEDL, ERNESTINE. 1962. *Vasilika: A Village in Modern Greece.* New York: Holt, Rinehart and Winston.

FRIEDMAN, MILTON, and ROSE FRIEDMAN. 1980. *Free to Choose: A Personal Statement.* New York: Harcourt Brace Jovanovich.

FRIEDRICH, CARL J., and ZBIGNIEW BRZEZINSKI. 1965. *Totalitarian Dictatorship and Autocracy.* Vol. 2. Cambridge, Mass.: Harvard University Press.

FRIEZE, IRENE H., J. E. PARSONS, P. B. JOHNSON, DIANA N. RUBLE, and GAIL L. ZELLMAN. 1975. *Women in Sex Roles: A Social Psychological Perspective.* New York: Norton.

FRISCH, K. VON. 1967. *The Dance Language and Orientation of Bees.* Cambridge, Mass.: Belknap.

GALDIKAS, BIRUTÉ M. F. 1980. "Living with the great orange apes." *National Geographic,* June.

GALLUP OPINION INDEX. 1976. *Religion in America.*

GALLUP ORGANIZATION. 1982. "Religion in America, 1981." *Gallup Opinion Index.* Princeton, N.J.: Gallup Organization and Princeton Research Center.

GANS, HERBERT J. 1979. "Deception and disclosure in the field." *The Nation,* **17,** May, pp. 507–512.

———. 1977. Why exurbanites won't reurbanize themselves." *New York Times,* February 12, p. 21.

———. 1968. *People and Plans.* New York: Basic Books.

———. 1962. *The Urban Villagers.* New York: Free Press.

GARDNER, HOWARD. 1978. *Developmental Psychology.* Boston: Little, Brown.

GARFINKEL, HAROLD. 1972. "Studies of the routine grounds of everyday activities." In David Snow (ed.), *Studies in Social Interaction.* New York: Free Press.

———. 1967. *Studies in Ethnomethodology.* Englewood Cliffs, N.J.: Prentice-Hall.

GEERTZ, C. 1973. *The Interpretation of Cultures.* New York: Basic Books.

GERSICK, KELIN E. 1979. "Fathers by choice: Divorced men who receive custody of their children." In George Levinger and Oliver C. Moles (eds.), *Divorce and Separation: Context, Causes, and Consequences.* New York: Basic Books.

GERTH, HANS, and C. WRIGHT MILLS. 1953. *Character and Social Structure.* New York: Harcourt Brace Jovanovich.

GESMONE, J. 1972. "Emotional neglect in Connecticut." *Connecticut Law Review,* **5**(1), pp. 100–116.

GIBB, G. A. 1969. "Leadership." In G. Lindzey and E. Aronson (eds.), *The Handbook of Social Psychology.* Reading, Mass.: Addison-Wesley.

GINSBERG, MORRIS. 1958. "Social change." *British Journal of Sociology* **9**(3), pp. 205–229.

GIST, NOEL P., and SYLVIA FLEIS FAVA. 1974. *Urban Society.* 6th ed. New York: Crowell.

GLAZER, NATHAN, and DANIEL P. MOYNIHAN (eds.). 1975. *Ethnicity: Theory and Experience.* Cambridge, Mass.: Harvard University Press.

GLICK, PAUL C. 1984. "How American families are changing." *American Demographics* **6**(1), January.

———. 1979. "The future of the American family." *Current Population Reports* Series P-23, no. 78. Bureau of the Census, Special Studies. Washington, D.C.: U.S. Government Printing Office.

———, and EMMANUEL LANDAU. 1950: "Age as a factor in marriage." *American Sociological Review,* **15,** August, pp. 517–529.

———, and ARTHUR J. NORTON. 1977. "Marrying, divorcing, and living together in the United States today." *Popular Bulletin,* **32,** October, pp. 1–39.

GLUECK, S., and E. GLUECK. 1956. *Physique and Delinquency.* New York: Harper & Row.

GNESSOUS, MOHAMMED. 1967. "A general critique of equilibrium theory. In Wilbert E. Moore and Robert M. Cooke (eds.), *Readings on Social Change.* Englewood Cliffs, N.J.: Prentice-Hall.

GOFFMAN, E. 1971. *Relations in Public.* New York: Basic Books.

———. 1963. *Behavior in Public Places.* New York: Free Press.

———. 1961a. *Asylums: Essays on the Social Situation of Mental Patients and Other Inmates.* Chicago: Aldine.

———. 1961b. *Encounters: Two Studies in the Sociology of Interaction.* Indianapolis: Bobbs-Merrill.

———. 1959. *The Presentation of Self in Everyday Life.* Garden City, N.Y.: Doubleday.

GOLDBERG, PHILLIP. 1968. "Are women prejudiced against women?" *Transaction,* **5,** pp. 28–30.

GOODE, W. J. 1960. "A theory of role strain." *American Sociological Review,* August 25.

———. 1963. *World Revolution and Family Patterns.* New York: Free Press.

GOODMAN, P. 1962. *Growing Up Absurd.* New York: Random House.

GORDON, M. M. 1947. "The concept of sub-culture and its application." *Social Forces,* **26,** pp. 40–42.

GORDON, MILTON M. 1975 (1961). "Assimilation in America: Theory and reality." In Norman R. Yetman and C. Hoy Steele (eds.), *Majority and Minority: The Dynamics of Racial and Ethnic Relations.* Boston: Allyn & Bacon.

———. 1964. *Assimilation in American Life.* New York: Oxford University Press.

GOUGH, KATHLEEN. 1961. "Nayar: Central Kerela." In David M. Schneider and Kathleen Gough, (eds.), *Matrilineal Kinship*. Berkeley and Los Angeles: University of California Press.

———. 1952. "Changing kinship usages in the setting of political and economic change among the Nayars of Malabor." *Journal of Royal Anthropological Institute of Great Britain and Ireland,* **82,** pp. 71–87.

GOULD, H. 1971. "Caste and class: A comparative view." *Module,* **11,** pp. 1–24.

GOULD, STEPHEN JAY. 1976. "The view of life: Biological potential versus biological determinism." *Natural History Magazine,* **85,** May.

GOULDNER, ALVIN W. 1970. *The Coming Crisis of Western Sociology.* New York: Avon.

GREELEY, ANDREW M., WILLIAM MCCREADY, and KATHLEEN MCCOURT. 1975. *Catholic Schools in a Declining Church.* New ed. Mission, Kans.: Sheed Andrews & McMeel.

GREENBERG, J. 1980. "Ape talk: More than 'pigeon' English?" *Science News,* **117**(19), pp. 298–300.

GUMPLOWICZ, LUDWIG. 1899. *The Outlines of Sociology.* Philadelphia: American Academy of Political and Social Sciences.

HALL, EDWARD T. 1974. *Handbook for Proxemic Analysis.* Washington, D.C.: Society for the Anthropology of Visual Communication.

———. 1969. *The Hidden Dimension.* New York: Doubleday.

HALL, R. H. 1963–1964. "The concept of bureaucracy: An empirical assessment." *American Journal of Sociology,* **69,** pp. 32–40.

HARE, PAUL A. 1976. *Handbook of Small Group Research.* 2d ed. New York: Free Press.

HARLAN, JACK R. 1971. "Agricultural origins: Centers and noncenters." *Science,* **174,** pp. 468–474.

HARLOW, HARRY F. 1975. "Review" *Science News,* **108,** December 20, pp. 389–390.

———. 1959. "Love in infant monkeys." *Scientific American,* June, pp. 68–74.

———, and M. HARLOW 1962. "The heterosexual affectional system in monkeys." *American Psychologist,* **17,** 1–9.

HARRIS, C. D., and E. L. ULLMAN. 1945. "The nature of cities." *Annals of the American Academy of Political and Social Science,* **242,** p. 12.

HARRIS, MARVIN. 1980. *Cultural Materialism: The Struggle for a Science of Culture.* New York: Random House.

———. 1975. *Culture, People, and Nature: An Introduction to General Anthropology.* 2d ed. New York: Crowell.

———. 1966. "The cultural ecology of India's sacred cattle." *Current Anthropology,* **7,** pp. 51–63.

HARRIS, SARAH. 1971. *Father Divine.* New York: Macmillan.

HART, C. W. M., and ARNOLD R. PILLING. 1960. *The Tiwi of North Australia.* New York: Holt, Rinehart and Winston.

HARTLEY, SHIRLEY FOSTER. 1972. *Population: Quantity versus Quality.* Englewood Cliffs, N.J.: Prentice-Hall.

HENRY, J. 1963. *Culture Against Man.* New York: Random House.

HERBERS, JOHN. 1981. "Census finds more blacks living in suburbs of nation's large cities." *New York Times,* May 31, pp. 1, 48.

———. 1981. "1980 census finds sharp decline in size of American households." *New York Times.* May 5, pp. A1, A18.

HILLER, E. T. 1941. "The community as a social group." *American Sociological Review,* 6, pp. 189–202.

HILLERY, G. A., JR. 1955. "Definitions of community: Areas of agreement." *Rural Sociology,* **20,** pp. 111–123.

HODGE, R. W., P. M. SIEGEL, and P. H. ROSSI. 1964. "Occupational prestige in the United States." *American Journal of Sociology,* **70,** pp. 286–302.

———, D. J. TREIMAN, and P. H. ROSSI. 1966. "A comparative study of occupational prestige." In R. Bendix and S. M. Lipset (eds.), *Class, Status and Power.* 2d ed. New York: Free Press.

HOEBEL, E. ANDAMSON. 1960. *The Cheyennes: Indians of the Great Plains.* New York: Holt, Rinehart, and Winston.

HOFFMAN, ABBIE. 1968. *Revolution for the Hell of It.* New York: Dial Press.

HOLLINGSHEAD, AUGUST B. 1951. "Age relationships and marriage." *American Sociological Review,* **16,** August, pp. 492–499.

———. 1949. *Elmtown's Youth.* New York: John Wiley.

HOLLINGSHEAD, A. B., and F. C. REDLICH. 1958. *Social Class and Mental Illness.* New York: John Wiley.

HOLT, JOHN. 1972. "The little red prison." *Harper's,* **244,** pp. 80–82.

HOMANS, G. C. 1950. *The Human Group.* New York: Harcourt.

HORNER, MATINA S. 1972. "Toward an understanding of achievement-related conflicts in women." *Journal of Social Issues,* **28,** pp. 157–175.

HOROWITZ, L. I. 1976. *The Rise and Fall of Project Camelot.* Cambridge, Mass.: MIT Press.

HOSTETLER, J. A., and G. E. HUNTINGTON. 1967. *The Hutterites in North America.* New York: Holt, Rinehart and Winston.

HOWE, IRVING. 1976. *World of Our Fathers.* New York: Simon & Schuster.

HOYT, H. 1943. "The structure of American cities in the post-war era." *American Journal of Sociology,* **48,** pp. 475–492.

HUMPHREY, J. A., and M. E. MILAKOVICH. 1981. *The Administration of Justice.* New York: Human Sciences Press.

HUNTER, D. E. 1975. "To find a community." In D. E. Hunter and P. Whitten (eds.), *Anthropology: Contemporary Perspectives.* Boston: Little, Brown.

INKELES, ALEX, and DAVID H. SMITH. 1974. *Becoming Modern: Individual Changes in Six Developing Countries.* Cambridge, Mass.: Harvard University Press.

ITARD, J. 1932. *The Wild Boy of Aveyron.* Trans. G. Humphrey and M. Humphrey. New York: Appleton-Century-Crofts.

JACOBS, J. 1961. *The Death and Life of Great American Cities,* New York: Vintage.

JACOBSON, PAUL. 1959. *American Marriage and Divorce.* New York: Holt, Rinehart and Winston.

JANIS, I., and L. MANN. 1976. *Decision Making.* New York: Free Press.

———, DWIGHT W. CHAPMAN, JOHN P. GILLIN, and JOHN P. SPIEGEL. 1964. "The problem of panic." In Duane P. Schultz (ed.), *Panic Behavior.* New York: Random House.

JEFFRIES, V., and H. E. RANSFORD. 1980. *Social Stratification: A Multiple Hierarchy Approach.* Boston: Allyn & Bacon.

JENCKS, C., M. SMITH, H. ACLAND, J. J. BANE, D. COHEN, H. GINTIS, B. HEYNS, and S. MICHELSON. 1972. *Inequality: A Reassessment of the Effect of Family and Schooling in America.* New York: Holt, Rinehart and Winston.

JENSEN, A. R. 1969. "How much can we boost I.Q. and scholastic achievement?" *Harvard Educational Review,* 39(1), Winter, pp. 1–123.

JOHNSON, NICHOLAS. 1971. "Television and violence: Perspectives and proposals." In Bernard Rosenberg and David Manning White (eds.), *Mass Culture Revisited.* New York: Van Nostrand.

JORGENSON, JOSEPH G. 1971. "Indians and the metropolis." In Jack O. Waddell and O. Michael Watson (eds.), *The American Indian in Urban Society.* Boston: Little, Brown.

KAHL, J. A. 1960. *The American Class Structure.* New York: Holt, Rinehart and Winston.

KASARDA, J. D., and M. JANOWITZ. 1974. "Community attachment in mass society." *American Journal of Sociology,* 48, pp. 328–339.

KATZ, ELIHU. 1957. "The two-step flow of communication: An up-to-date report on an hypothesis." *Public Opinion Quarterly,* 21, pp. 61–78.

KEMPE, C. H. 1978. "Child abuse: The pediatrician's role in child advocacy and preventative pediatrics." *American Journal of the Diseases of Childhood,* 132, pp. 255–260.

———, F. N. SILVERMAN, B. B. STEELE, W. DVORG-MUELLER, and H. K. SILVER. 1962. "The battered child syndrome." *Journal of the American Medical Association,* 181, pp. 17–24.

KEMPE, R. S., and C. H. KEMPE. 1978. *Child Abuse.* Cambridge, Mass.: Harvard University Press.

KENNEDY, JOHN F. 1961. "Introduction." In William Brandon (ed.), *The American Heritage Book of Indians.* New York: Dell.

KENNEY, MICHAEL. 1980. *Boston Globe,* January 7.

KERCKHOFF, ALAN C., and KURT W. BACK. 1968. *The June Bug.* New York: Appleton-Century-Crofts.

KERLINGER, F. N. 1973. *Foundation of Behavioral Research.* 2d ed. New York: Holt, Rinehart and Winston.

KHALDUN, IBN. 1958. *The Mugaddimah, Bollingen Series XLIII.* Princeton, N.J.: Princeton University Press.

KLEIMAN, DENA. 1979. "New York: Suburbs have trouble too." *New York Times,* October 23, p. 6E.

KOHLBERG, LAWRENCE. 1969. "Stage and sequence: The cognitive-developmental approach to socialization." In David A. Goslin (ed.), *Handbook of Socialization Theory and Research.* Chicago: Rand McNally.

———. 1967. "Moral and religious education in the public schools: A developmental view." In T. Sizer (ed.), *Religion and Public Education.* Boston: Houghton Mifflin.

KOHN, HANS. 1956. *Nationalism and Liberty: The Swiss Example.* London: Allen and Unwin.

KOHN, M. L. 1969. *Class and Conformity.* Homewood, Ill.: Dorsey Press.

KOTELCHUK, D. 1976. *Prognosis Negative: Crisis in the Health Care System.* New York: Vintage.

KRAUSE, AUREL. 1956. *The Tlingit Indians.* Seattle: University of Washington Press.

KRAUSE, MICHAEL. 1966. *Immigration: The American Mosaic.* New York: Van Nostrand Reinhold.

KROEBER, ALFRED A. 1963 (1923). *Anthropology: Culture Patterns and Processes.* New York: Harcourt Brace Jovanovich.

KROEBER, T. 1961. *Ishi in Two Worlds.* Berkeley and Los Angeles: University of California Press.

KUMMER, H. 1971. *Primate Societies: Group Technologies of Ecological Adaptation.* Chicago: Aldine.

KUPER, HILDA. 1963. *The Swazi: A South African Kingdom.* New York: Holt, Rinehart and Winston.

LAING, R. D. 1967. *The Politics of Experience.* New York: Ballantine.

LANCASTER, JANE B., and PHILLIP WHITTEN. 1980. "Family matters." *The Sciences,* 20.

LANG, KURT, and GLADYS LANG. 1961. *Collective Dynamics.* New York: Crowell.

LANTZ, HERMAN R. 1982. "Romantic love in the premodern period: A sociological commentary." *Journal of Social History,* Spring.

LASCH, CHRISTOPHER. 1979. *The Culture of Narcissism.* New York: Warner Books.

———. 1977. *Haven in a Heartless World: The Family Besieged.* New York: Basic Books.

LASLETT, P. 1965. *The World We Have Lost: England Before the Industrial Age.* New York: Scribner's.

———, and PHILLIP W. CUMMINGS. 1967. "History of political philosophy." In Paul Edwards (ed.), *The Encyclopedia of Philosophy.* Vols. 5, 6. New York: Macmillan.

LASSWELL, THOMAS. 1965. *Class and Stratum.* Boston: Houghton Mifflin.

LATANÉ, B., K. WILLIAMS, and S. HARKINS. 1979. "Many hands make light the work: The causes and consequences of social loafing." *Journal of Personality and Social Psychology,* **37,** pp. 822–832.

LAZARSFELD, PAUL F. 1971. "Introduction." In Bernard Rosenberg and David Manning White (eds.), *Mass Culture Revisited.* New York: Van Nostrand.

———, BERNARD BERELSON, and HAZEL GAUDET. 1968. *The People's Choice.* 3d ed. New York: Columbia University Press.

LEAKEY RICHARD E. 1981. *The Making of Mankind.* New York: Dutton.

———, and ROGER LEWIN. 1977. *Origins.* New York: Dutton.

LEBON, GUSTAVE. 1960 (1895). *The Crowd: A Study of the Popular Mind.* New York: Viking.

LEE, ALFRED MCCLUNG. 1978. *Sociology for Whom?* New York: Oxford University Press.

LEE, GARY R. 1981. "Marriage and aging." *Society,* **18**(2), January–February, pp. 70–71.

LEE, M. 1966. *Multi-valent Man.* New York: George Braziller.

LEE, RICHARD BORSHAY. 1980. *The !KungSan.* Berkeley and Los Angeles: University of California Press.

———. 1969a. "Kung bushmen subsistence: An input-output analysis." In A. P. Vayda (ed.), *Environment and Cultural Behavior.* Garden City, N.Y.: Natural History Pess.

———. 1969b. "A naturalist at large: Eating Christmas in the Kalahari." *Natural History,* December.

LEMERT, EDWIN. 1972. *Human Deviance, Social Problems and Social Control.* 2d ed. Englewood Cliffs, N.J.: Prentice-Hall.

LENIN, VLADIMIR I. 1949 (1917). *The State and Revolution.* Moscow: Progress Publishers.

LENSKI, GERHARD. 1966. *Power and Privilege: A Theory of Social Stratification.* New York: McGraw-Hill.

LEONARD, IRA M., and R. D. PARMET. 1972. *American Nativism, 1830–1860.* New York: Van Nostrand-Reinhold.

LESLIE, GERALD R. 1979. *The Family in Social Context.* 4th ed. New York: Oxford University Press.

LEVIN, JACK, and WILLIAM C. LEVIN. 1980. *Ageism: Prejudice and Discrimination Against the Elderly.* Belmont, Calif.: Wadsworth.

LEVINE, ADELINE, and JANICE CRUMRINE. 1975. "Women and the fear of success: A problem in replication." *American Journal of Sociology,* **80,** pp. 964–974.

LEVINE, IRVING M., and JUDITH HERMAN. 1974. "The life of white ethnics." In Charles H. Anderson (ed.), *Sociological Essays and Research.* Homewood, Ill.: Dorsey Press.

LEVINSON, DANIEL J., with CHARLOTTE N. DARROW, EDWARD B. KLEIN, MARIA H. LEVINSON, and BRAXTON MCKEE. 1978. *The Seasons of a Man's Life.* New York: Ballantine.

LEWIN, KURT. 1948. *Resolving Social Conflicts.* New York: Harper.

LEWIS, MICHAEL. 1972. "Culture and gender roles: There's no unisex in the nursery." *Psychology Today,* **5,** pp. 54–57.

LEWIS, O. 1960. *Tepotzlan: Village in Mexico.* New York: Holt, Rinehart and Winston.

———. 1951. *Life in a Mexican Village: Tepotzlan Revisited.* Urbana: University of Illinois Press.

LIEBERT, R. M., and R. W. POULOS. 1972. "TV for kiddies—Truth, goodness, beauty, and a little bit of brainwash." *Psychology Today,* November.

LINDESMITH, ALFRED R., and ANSELM L. STRAUSS. 1956. *Social Psychology.* New York: Holt, Rinehart and Winston.

LINK, R. 1980. "The Literary Digest poll: Appearances can be deceiving." *Public Opinion,* February–March, p. 55.

LINTON, R.. 1936. *The Study of Man.* New York: Appleton-Century-Crofts.

———. 1915. *The Cultural Background of Personality.* Westport, Conn.: Greenwood Press.

LIPSET, SEYMOUR M. 1960. *Political Man.* Garden City, N.Y.: Doubleday.

LIPSEY, R. G., and P. D. STEINER. 1975. *Economics.* New York: Harper & Row.

LOMBROSO-FERRERO, GINA. 1972. *Criminal Man.* Reprint ed. Montclair, N.J.: Patterson Smith.

LONGFELLOW, CYNTHIA. 1979. "Divorce in context: Its impact on children." In George Levinger and Oliver C. Moles (eds.), *Divorce and Separation: Context, Causes and Consequences.* New York: Basic Books.

Los Angeles Times. 1980. "Dear Abby," August 23, p. 2–3.

LOULS, ARTHUR M. 1982. "The bottom line on ten big mergers." *Fortune,* May 3, p. 89.

LYNCH, K. 1960. *The Image of the City.* Cambridge, Mass.: MIT Press.

LYNN, DAVID B. 1969. *Parental and Sex Role Identification: A Theoretical Formulation.* Berkeley, Calif.: McCutchan.

MACCOBY, ELEANOR EMMONS, and CAROL NAGY JACKLIN. 1975. *The Psychology of Sex Differences.* Stanford, Calif.: Stanford University Press.

MACMURRY, V. D., and P. H. CUNNINGHAM. 1973. "Mormons and Gentiles." In Donald E. Gelfand, and Russell D. Lee (eds.), *Ethnic Conflicts and Power: A Cross National Perspective.* New York: John Wiley.

MADSEN, WILLIAM. 1973. *The Mexican-Americans of South Texas.* 2d ed. New York: Holt, Rinehart and Winston.

MALINOWSKI, BRONISLAW. 1954. *Magic, Science and Religion.* New York: Free Press.

———. 1922. *Argonauts of the Western Pacific.* New York: Dutton.

MANDLE, JOAN D. 1979. *Women and Social Change in America.* Princeton, N.J.: Princeton Book.

MANN, J. 1981. "Marshall's asset's relatively meager—But he's 'having fun.' " *Los Angeles Times,* May 17, p. 1–5.

MARCUSE, H. 1955. *Eros and Civilization: A Philosophical Inquiry into Freud.* New York: Vintage Books.

MARTIN, H. P. (ed.). 1976. *The Abused Child: A Multidisciplinary Approach to Developmental Issues and Treatment.* Cambridge, Mass.: Ballinger.

MARTIN, K. M. 1976. "The evolution of social forms." In D. E. Hunter and P. Whitten (eds.), *The Study of Anthropology.* New York: Harper and Row.

———. 1974. "The foraging adaptation: Uniformity or diversity?" *Addison-Wesley Modular Publication No. 56.* Reading, Mass.: Addison-Wesley.

———, and B. VOORHIES. 1975. *The Female of the Species.* New York: Columbia University Press.

MARX, KARL. 1967 (1867). *Capital: A Critique of Political Economy.* Ed. Friedrich Engels. New York: New World.

———. 1967 (1867). *Das Kapital.* 3 vols. Ed. Friedrich Engels. New York: International Publishing.

———. 1964 (1844). *The Economic and Philosophical Manuscripts of 1844.* New York: International Publishers.

———. 1959 (1847). In Ralf Dahrendorf (ed.), *Class and Class Conflict in Industrial Society.* Stanford, Calif.: Stanford University Press.

———, and FRIEDRICH ENGELS. 1961 (1848). "The communist manifesto." In Arthur P. Mendel (ed.), *Essential Works of Marxism.* New York: Bantam Books.

MAUSS, ARMAND L. 1975. *Social Problems of Social Movements.* Philadelphia: Lippincott.

MCCONNELL, J. V. 1977. *Understanding Human Behavior.* 2d ed. New York: Holt, Rinehart and Winston.

MCFEE, MALCOLM. 1976. "Social organization I: Marriage and the family." In David E. Hunter and Phillip Whitten (eds.), *The Study of Anthropology.* New York: Harper & Row.

MCNEILL, WILLIAM H. 1976. *Plagues and People.* New York: Anchor/Doubleday.

MEAD, G. H. 1934. *Mind, Self, and Society.* Ed. C. W. Morris. Chicago: University of Chicago Press.

MEAD, MARGARET. 1970. *Culture and Commitment.* New York: Doubleday.

———. 1943. "Our educational emphases in primitive perspectives." *American Journal of Sociology,* **48,** pp. 633–639.

———. 1935. *Sex and Temperament in Three Primitive Societies.* New York: Morrow.

MEADOWS, DONELLE H., DENNIS L. MEADOWS, JORGAN RANDERS, and WILLIAM W. BEHRENS, III. 1972. *The Limits of Growth: A Report of the Club of Rome's Project on the Predicament of Mankind.* New York: Universe Books.

MEGGARS, B. J. 1972. *Prehistoric America.* Chicago: Aldine.

MERTON, R. K.. 1968 (1949). *Social Theory and Social Structure.* 2d ed. New York: Free Press.

———. 1938. "Social structure and social action." *American Sociological Review,* **3,** pp. 672–682.

———, LEONARD BROOM, and LEONARD S. COTTRELL, JR. 1959. *Sociology Today: Problems and Prospects.* New York: Basic Books.

METRAUX, RHODA. 1955. "Implicit and explicit values in education and teaching as related to growth and development." *Merrill-Palmer Quarterly,* **2,** pp. 27–34.

MICHELS, R. 1966 (1911). *Political Parties.* Trans. Eden Paul and Adar Paul. New York: Free Press.

MILLS, C. WRIGHT. 1963. *Power, Politics and People.* New York: Ballantine.

———. 1959. *The Sociological Imagination.* New York: Oxford University Press.

———. 1956. *The Power Elite.* New York: Oxford Unviersity Press.

MILLS, T. M. 1967. *The Sociology of Small Groups.* Englewood Cliffs, N.J.: Prentice-Hall.

Money Magazine. 1982. "Robots and your job." May, p. 196.

MONTAGU, ASHLEY. (ed.). 1973. *Man and Aggression.* 2d ed. London: Oxford University Press.

————. (ed.). 1964a. *The Concept of Race.* New York: Collier Books.

————. 1964b. *Man's Most Dangerous Myth: The Fallacy of Race.* New York: Meridian.

MOORE, WILBERT E. 1965. *The Impact of Industry.* Englewood Cliffs, N.J.: Prentice-Hall.

MORRIS, DESMOND. 1970. *The Human Zoo.* New York: McGraw-Hill.

MOSKOS, C. C., JR. 1975. "The American combat soldier in Vietnam." *Journal of Social Issues,* **31,** 25–37.

MOULIK, MONI. 1977. *Millions More to Feed.* Rome: Food and Agriculture Organization of the United Nations.

MURDOCK, GEORGE P. 1949. *Social Structure.* New York: Macmillan.

————. 1937. "Comparative data on the division of labor by sex." *Social Forces,* **15,** pp. 551–553.

MUSON, H. 1979. "Moral thinking—Can it be taught?" *Psychology Today,* February.

MYRDAL, GUNNAR. 1969. *Objectivity in Social Research.* New York: Pantheon.

————. 1944. *An American Dilemma.* New York: Harper.

NATIONAL OPINION RESEARCH CENTER (NORC). 1977. *Cumulative Codebook for the 1972–77 General Social Surveys.* Chicago: NORC, University of Chicago.

NICKELS, M. K., D. E. HUNTER, and P. WHITTEN. 1979. *The Study of Physical Anthropology and Archeology.* New York: Harper & Row.

NISBET, R. A., and R. G. PERRIN. 1977. *The Social Bond: An Introduction to the Study of Sociology.* 2d ed. New York: Knopf.

NOVAK, MICHAEL. 1972. *The Rise of the Unmeltable Ethnics.* New York: Macmillan.

NOVIT-EVANS, BETTE, and ASHTON WESLEY WELCH. 1983. "Racial and ethnic definition as reflections of public policy." *Journal of American Studies,* **17**(3) pp. 417–435.

OBERG, KALERNO. 1973. *The Social Economy of the Tlingit Indians.* Seattle: University of Washington Press.

OBERSCHALL, ANTHONY. 1968 (1965). "The Los Angeles Watts riot of August 1965." *Social Problems,* **15** (Winter), pp. 297–341.

OGBURN, WILLIAM F. 1964. *On Culture and Social Change.* Chicago: University of Chicago Press.

————. 1964 (1950). *Social Change: With Respect to Culture and Original Nature.* Magnolia, Mass.: Peter Smith.

ORTNER, SHERRY. 1974. "Is female to male as nature is to culture?" In Michelle Zimbalist Rosaldo and Louise Lampheres, (eds.), *Woman, Culture and Society.* Stanford, Calif.: Stanford University Press.

ORWELL, G. 1954. *Animal Farm.* New York: Harcourt Brace.

OTTERBEIN, KEITH. 1973. "The anthropology of war." In John J. Honigmann (ed.), *Handbook of Social and Cultural Anthropology.* Chicago: Rand McNally.

————. 1970. *The Evolution of War.* New Haven, Conn.: Human Relations Area Files.

OUCHI, WILLIAM G. 1981. *Theory Z: How American Business Can Meet the Japanese Challenge.* Reading, Mass.: Addison-Wesley.

PARK, R., E. BURGESS, and R. MCKENZIE (eds.). 1925. *The City.* Chicago: University of Chicago Press.

PARKE, R. D., and C. W. COLLMER. 1975. "Child abuse: An interdisciplinary analysis." In E. M. Hetherington (ed.), *Review of Child Development Research.* Vol. 5. Chicago: University of Chicago Press.

PARKES, HENRY BAMFORD. 1968. *The United States of America: A History.* 3rd ed. New York: Knopf.

PARKINSON, C. NORTHCOTE. 1957. *Parkinson's Law.* Boston: Houghton Mifflin.

PARMET, IRA M., and ROBERT D. PARMET. 1971. *American Nativism, 1830–1860.* New York: Van Nostrand.

PARSONS, TALCOTT. 1971. *The System of Modern Societies.* Englewood Cliffs, N.J.: Prentice-Hall.

————. 1966. *Societies: Evolutionary and Comparative Perspectives.* Englewood Cliffs, N.J.: Prentice-Hall.

————. 1954. *Essays in Sociological Theory.* Rev. ed. New York: Free Press.

————. 1951. *The Social System.* New York: Free Press.

————. 1937. *The Structure of Social Action.* New York: McGraw-Hill.

————, and ROBERT F. BALES. 1955. *Family Socialization and Interaction Process.* New York: Free Press.

————, and E. A. SHILS. 1951. *Toward a General Theory of Action.* Cambridge, Mass: Harvard University Press.

PAULSEN, MONRAD. 1967. "Role of juvenile courts." *Current History,* **53,** August, p. 72.

PAVLOV, I. P. 1927. *Conditioned Reflexes.* Trans. G. V. Anrep. New York: Oxford University Press.

PERRY, JOSEPH B., JR., and M. D. PUGH. 1978. *Collective Behavior: Response to Social Stress.* St. Paul, Minn.: West Publishing.

PETER, L. F., and R. HULL. 1969. *The Peter Principle.* New York: Morrow.

PETERSEN, WILLIAM. 1975. "On the subnations of Western Europe." In Nathan Glazer and Daniel P. Moynihan (eds.), *Ethnicity: Theory and Experience.* Cambridge, Mass.: Harvard University Press.

PETTIGREW, THOMAS F., and ROBERT C. GREEN. 1975.

"School desegregation in large cities: A critique of the Coleman 'white flight' thesis." *Harvard Educational Review,* **46** (1), pp. 1–53.

PIAGET, J., and B. INHELDER. 1969. *The Psychology of the Child.* New York: Basic Books.

PILEGGI, N. 1981. "Open city." *New York Magazine,* January 19.

PIPES, RICHARD. 1975. "Reflections on the nationality problems in the Soviet Union." In Nathan Glazer and Daniel P. Moynihan (eds.), *Ethnicity: Theory and Experience.* Cambridge, Mass.: Harvard University Press.

PROVENCE, SALLY. 1972. "Psychoanalysis and the treatment of psychological disorders of infancy." In S. Wolman (ed.), *A Handbook of Child Psychoanalysis: Research, Theory, and Practice.* New York: Van Nostrand.

———, and R. LIPTON. 1963. *Infants in Institutions.* New York: International University Press.

Public Opinion. 1980. December–January, p. 35.

———. 1978. November–December, p. 33.

QUINNEY, RICHARD. 1974. *Critique of Legal Order.* Boston: Little, Brown.

RACHMAN, DAVID J., and MICHAEL H. MESCON. 1982. *Business Today.* 3rd ed. New York: Random House.

REDFIELD, R. 1960. *The Little Community.* Chicago: University of Chicago Press.

———. 1947. "The folk society." *American Journal of Sociology,* **52,** pp. 293–308.

———. 1941. *Folk Culture of Yucatan.* Chicago: University of Chicago Press.

———. 1934. "Culture changes in Yucatan." *American Anthropologist,* **36,** pp. 57–59.

———. 1930. *Tepotzlan: A Mexican Village.* Chicago: University of Chicago Press.

REICHEL, P. L. 1975. "Classroom use of a criminal activities checklist." *Teaching Sociology,* **3**(1), October, pp. 85–86.

REID, S. T. 1979. *Crime and Criminology.* 2d ed. New York: Holt, Rinehart and Winston.

REISS, IRA L. 1980. *Family Systems in America.* 3rd ed. New York: Holt, Rinehart and Winston.

RIESMAN, D. 1950. *The Lonely Crowd.* New Haven, Conn.: Yale University Press.

ROBINSON, JACOB. 1976. "The holocaust." In Yisrael Gutman and Livia Rothkirchen (eds.), *The Catastrophe of European Jewry.* Jerusalem: Yad Veshem.

ROBINSON, JOHN P. 1979. "Toward a postindustrious society." *Public Opinion,* August–September, pp. 41–46.

ROSALDO, MICHELLE ZIMBALIST. 1974. "Woman, culture and society: A theoretical overview." In Michelle Zimbalist Rosaldo and Louise Lamphere (eds.), *Woman, Culture and Society.* Stanford, Calif.: Stanford University Press.

ROSE, A. 1967. *Power Structure: Political Process in American Society.* New York: Oxford University Press.

ROSEN, GEORGE. 1968. *Madness in Society.* New York: Harper Torchbooks.

ROSENBERG, BERNARD, and DAVID MANNING WHITE (eds.). 1971. *Mass Culture Revisited.* New York: Van Nostrand.

ROSENTHAL, R., and L. JACOBSON. 1966. "Teachers' expectancies: Determinants of pupils' I.Q. gain." *Psychological Reports,* **18,** pp. 115–118.

ROSSI, ALICE. 1977. "A biosocial perspective on parenting." *Daedulus,* **106,** pp. 1–31.

ROSSIDES, D. W. 1976. *The American Class System.* Boston: Houghton Mifflin.

ROSZAK, T. 1969. *The Making of a Counterculture.* Garden City, N.Y.: Anchor/Doubleday.

RUBIN, JERRY. 1970. *Do It!* New York: Simon & Schuster.

RYAN, WILLIAM. 1971. *Blaming the Victim.* New York: Pantheon.

SAGARIN, EDWARD. 1978. *Sociology: The Basic Concepts.* New York: Holt, Rinehart and Winston.

SAHLINS, MARSHALL D. 1972. *Stone Age Economics.* Chicago: Aldine.

———, and ELMAN R. SERVICE (eds.). 1960. *Evolution and Culture.* Ann Arbor: University of Michigan Press.

SALZMAN, P. C. 1967. "Political organization among nomadic peoples." *Proceedings of the American Philosophical Society,* **3,** pp. 115–131.

SAMOVAR, LARRY A., RICHARD PORTER, and NEMI C. JAIN. 1981. *Understanding Intercultural Communication.* Belmont, Calif.: Wadsworth.

SAMUELSON, PAUL A. 1976. *Economics.* 10th ed. New York: McGraw-Hill.

SAPIR, EDWARD. 1961. *Culture, Language and Personality.* Berkeley and Los Angeles: University of California Press.

SCARPITTI, FRANK. 1980. *Social Problems.* 3rd ed. New York: Holt, Rinehart and Winston, p. 368.

SCHMID, CALVIN F., and CHARLES E. NOBBE. 1965. "Socioeconomic differentials among nonwhite races." *American Sociological Review,* **30,** December, pp. 909–922.

SCHUMPETER, JOSEPH A. 1950. *Capitalism, Socialism and Democracy.* 3rd ed. New York: Harper Torchbooks.

SCHUR, EDWIN M., and HUGO A. BEDAU. 1974. *Victimless Crimes: Two Sides of a Controversy.* Englewood Cliffs, N.J.: Prentice-Hall.

Science News. 1979. "World population decline documented." 116, August.

SECORD, PAUL F., and CARL W. BACKMAN. 1974. *Social Psychology*. New York: McGraw-Hill.

SELIGMAN, DANIEL. 1984. "Pay equity is a bad idea." *Fortune*, **109**(10), May 14, pp. 133–140.

SELZNICK, P. 1948. "Foundations of the theory of organization." *American Sociological Review,* **13,** pp. 25–35.

SERVICE, ELMAN R. 1975. *Origins of the State and Civilization,* New York: Norton.

SHARP, LAURISTON. 1952. "Steel axes for stone-age Australians." *Human Organization,* **11,** pp. 17–22.

SHATTUCK, R. 1980. *The Forbidden Experiment.* New York: Farrar, Straus & Giroux.

SHAW, CLIFFORD R., and HENRY D. MCKAY. 1942. *Juvenile Delinquency and Urban Areas.* Chicago: University of Chicago Press.

———. 1931. "Social factors in juvenile delinquency." Vol. 2. In National Committee on Law Observance and Law Enforcement, *Report on the Causes of Crime.* Washington, D.C.: U.S. Government Printing Office.

SHELDON, W. H., E. M. HARTL, and E. MCDERMOTT. 1949. *The Varieties of Delinquent Youth.* New York: Harper.

———, and S. S. STEVENS. 1942. *The Variety of Temperament.* New York: Harper.

———, and W. B. TUCKER. 1940. *The Varieties of Human Physique.* New York: Harper.

SHELLOW, ROBERT, and DEREK V. ROEMER. 1965. "The riot that didn't happen." *Social Problems,* **14,** pp. 221–233.

SHEPARDSON, MARY. 1963. *Navajo Ways in Government.* Manasha, Wis.: American Anthropological Association.

SHIBUTANI, TAMOTSU. 1966. *Improvised News: A Sociological Study of Rumor.* Indianapolis: Bobbs-Merrill.

SHILS, EDWARD. 1971 (1960). "Mass society and its culture." In Bernard Rosenberg and David Manning (eds.), *Mass Culture Revisited.* New York: Van Nostrand.

———. 1968. *Political Development in the New States.* The Hague: Mouton.

———. 1950. "Primary groups in the American army." In R. K. Merton and P. F. Lazarsfeld (eds.), *Continuities in Social Research.* New York: Free Press.

SILBERMAN, C. E. 1978. *Criminal Violence—Criminal Justice: Criminals, Police, Courts and Prisons in America.* New York: Random House.

———. 1971. *Crisis in the Classroom: The Remaking of American Education.* New York: Random House.

SIMMEL, GEORG. 1957. "Fashion." *American Journal of Sociology,* **62,** pp. 541–588.

———. 1955. "The web of group affiliations." In *Conflict: The Web of Group Affiliations.* Glencoe, Ill.: Free Press.

SIMPSON, GEORGE E., and MILTON YINGER. 1972. *Racial and Cultural Minorities: An Analysis of Prejudice and Discrimination.* 4th ed. New York: Harper & Row.

SJOBERG, GIDEON. 1965. *Preindustrial City: Past and Present.* New York: Free Press.

SKINNER, B. F. 1971. *Beyond Freedom and Dignity.* New York: Knopf.

SKOEPOL, THEDA. 1979. *States and Social Revolutions.* New York: Cambridge University Press.

SKOLNICK, ARLENE. 1973. *The Intimate Environment: Exploring Marriage and the Family.* Boston: Little, Brown.

SLATER, P. 1970. *The Pursuit of Loneliness: American Culture at the Breaking Point.* Boston: Beacon Press.

———. 1966. *Microcosm: Structural, Psychological, and Religious Evolution in Groups.* New York: John Wiley.

SMELSER, NEIL J. 1971. "Mechanisms of change and adjustment to change." In George Dalton (ed.), *Economic Development and Social Change.* Garden City, N.Y.: Natural History Press.

———. 1962. *Theory of Collective Behavior.* New York: Free Press.

SMITH, ADAM. 1969 (1776). *An Inquiry into the Nature and Causes of the Wealth of Nations.* 2 vols. Chicago: University of Chicago Press.

SNYDER, Z. 1971. "The social environment of the urban Indian." In Jack O. Waddell and O. Michael Watson (eds.), *The American Indian in Urban Society.* Boston: Little, Brown.

SOLECKI, RALPH. 1971. *Shanidar: The First Flower People.* New York: Knopf.

SOLHEIM, W. G. 1972. "An earlier agricultural revolution." *Scientific American,* April, pp. 34–51.

SOROKIN, PITIRIM A. 1937. *Social and Cultural Dynamics.* New York: American Books.

SPANIER, GRAHAM B. 1983. "Married and unmarried cohabitation in the United States: 1981." *Journal of Marriage and the Family,* **45**(2), May, pp. 277–288.

SPECIAL TASK FORCE TO THE SECRETARY OF HEALTH, EDUCATION AND WELFARE. 1973. *Work in America.* Cambridge, Mass.: MIT Press.

SPENGLER, OSWALD. 1932. *The Decline of the West.* New York: Knopf.

SPICER, EDWARD H. 1962. *Cycles of Conquest.* Tucson: University of Arizona Press.

SPINDLER, GEORGE D. 1955. "Education in a transforming American culture." In George D. Spindler, (ed.), *Education and Culture: Anthropological*

Approaches. New York: Holt, Rinehart and Winston.

SPIRO, MELFORD E. 1960. "Addendum, 1958." In Norman W. Bell and Ezra F. Vogel, (eds.), *A Modern Introduction to the Family.* Glencoe, Ill.: Free Press.

SPITZ, RENÉ A. 1945. "Hospitalism: An inquiry into the genesis of psychiatric conditions in early childhood." In Anna Freud et al. (eds.), *The Psychoanalytic Study of the Child.* New York: International Universities Press.

STAIRES, GRAHAM L., ROBERT P. QUINN, and LINDA J. SHEPARD. 1976. "Occupational sex discrimination." *Industrial Relations,* **15,** pp. 88–98.

STARK, RODNEY, and CHARLES Y. GLOCK. 1968. *American Piety: The Nature of Religious Commitments.* Berkeley and Los Angeles: University of California Press.

STEWARD, JULIAN H. 1955. *The Theory of Culture Change: The Methodology of Multilineal Evolution.* Urbana: University of Illinois Press.

STOLLER, R. J. 1967. "Effects of parents' attitudes on core gender identity." *International Journal of Psychiatry,* p. 57.

STONER, JAMES A. F. 1982. *Management.* 2d ed. Englewood Cliffs, N.J.: Prentice-Hall.

STRAUS, MURRAY A., RICHARD J. GELLES, and SUZANNE K. STEINMETZ. 1980. *Behind Closed Doors.* New York: Anchor/Doubleday.

SULLIVAN, JOSEPH F. 1979. "New Jersey: Assaults are a daily occurrence." *New York Times,* October 23, p. 6E.

SUMNER, W. G. 1906. *Folkways: A Study of the Sociological Importance of Usages, Manners, Customs, Mores, and Morals.* Boston: Ginn.

SURGEON GENERAL'S SCIENTIFIC ADVISORY COMMITTEE ON TELEVISION AND SOCIAL BEHAVIOR. 1972. *Television and Growing Up: The Impact of Televised Violence.* Washington, D.C.: U.S. Government Printing Office.

SUTHERLAND, EDWIN H. 1961. *White Collar Crime.* New York: Holt, Rinehart and Winston.

———. 1940. "White collar criminality." *American Sociological Review,* **40,** pp. 1–12.

———. 1924. *Criminology.* New York: Lippincott.

———, and D. R. CRESSEY. 1978. *Principles of Criminology.* 10th ed. Chicago: Lippincott.

SUTTER, LARRY E., and HERMAN P. MILLER. 1973. "Income differences between men and career women." *American Journal of Sociology,* **78,** January, p. 965.

SUTTLES, G. 1972. *The Social Construction of Communities.* Chicago: University of Chicago Press.

———. 1968. *The Social Order of the Slum.* Chicago: University of Chicago Press.

SUTTON, W. A., and J. KOLAJA. 1960. "The concept of community." *Rural Sociology,* **25,** pp. 197–203.

TERRACE, H. S., L. A. PETITTO, R. J. SANDERS, and T. G. BEVER. 1979. "Can an ape create a sentence?" *Science,* **206,** pp. 891–902.

THOMAS, W. I. 1928. *The Child in America.* New York: Knopf.

THOMPSON, LAURA. 1950. *Culture in Crisis.* New York: Harper.

THOMPSON, WARREN S. 1929. "Population." *American Journal of Sociology,* **34,** pp. 959–975.

TIGER, LIONEL, and ROBIN FOX. 1971. *The Imperial Animal.* New York: Holt, Rinehart and Winston.

Time Magazine. 1980. March 31.

———. 1979. December 31, p. 63.

———. 1979. December 10, pp. 29–34.

———. 1979. September 10.

———. 1979. August 6.

———. 1979. July 17.

———. 1979. July 9, pp. 29–31.

———. 1977. December 26.

TOFFLER, ALVIN. 1970. *Future Shock.* New York: Random House.

TÖNNIES, FERDINAND. 1935 (1887). *Gemeinschaft und Gesellschaft: Grundbegnffeder reinem Soziologie.* Leipzig.

TOYNBEE, ARNOLD. 1946. *A Study of History.* New York and London: Oxford University Press.

TRACHTENBERG, JOSHUA. 1961. *The Devil and the Jews.* New York: Meridian Books.

TREIMAN, DONALD J. 1977. *Occupational Prestige in Comparative Perspective.* New York: Academic Press.

TUMIN, M. 1953. "Some principles of stratification: A critical analysis." *American Sociological Review,* **18,** pp. 385–394.

TURNBULL, COLIN. 1972. *The Mountain People.* New York: Simon & Schuster.

TURNER, RALPH H. 1964. "Collective behavior." In R. E. L. Faris (ed.), *Handbook of Modern Sociology.* Chicago: Rand McNally.

———, and LEWIS M. KILLIAN. 1972. *Collective Behavior.* 2d ed. Englewood Cliffs, N.J.: Prentice-Hall.

TYLOR, E. 1958 (1871). *Primitive Culture: Researches into the Development of Mythology, Philosophy, Religion, Art and Custom.* Vol. 1. London: John Murray.

———. 1889. "On a method of investigating the development of institutions applied to laws of marriage and descent." *Journal of the Royal Anthropological Institute,* **18,** pp. 245–269.

UDY, S. H., JR. 1959. " 'Bureaucracy' and 'rationality' in Weber's Organizational Theory: An empirical study." *American Sociological Review,* **24,** pp. 791–795.

ULC, OTTO. 1975 (1969). "Communist national minority policy: The case of the Gypsies in Czechoslovakia." In Norman R. Yetman and C. Hoy Steele (eds.), *Majority and Minority: The Dynamics of Racial and Ethnic Relations.* Boston: Allyn & Bacon.

U.S. BUREAU OF THE CENSUS. 1982. "Money income and poverty status."

———. 1981a. "Households and family characteristics." *Current Population Reports,* Series P-20, no. 371. Washington, D.C.: U.S. Government Printing Office.

———. 1981b. "Marital status and living arrangements." *Current Population Reports,* Series P-20, no. 366. Washington, D.C.: U.S. Government Printing Office.

———. 1981c. *Money Income of Households in the United States.* Washington, D.C.: U.S. Department of Commerce.

———. 1981d. *1980 Census of Population.* Washington, D.C.: U.S. Department of Commerce.

———. 1981. *U.S.A. Statistical Brief 1981: A Statistical Abstract Supplement.* Washington, D.C.: U.S. Bureau of the Census.

———. 1977. *Statistical Abstracts for States and Metropolitan Areas.* Washington, D.C.: U.S. Government Printing Office.

———. 1976. *Historical Statistics of the United States: Colonial Times to 1970.* Washington, D.C.: U.S. Government Printing Office.

U.S. DEPARTMENT OF COMMERCE, BUREAU OF THE CENSUS. 1984. *Statistical Abstract of the United States, 1983.* Washington, D.C.: Government Printing Office.

———. 1981. *Statistical Abstract of the United States, 1981.* Washington, D.C.: Government Printing Office.

———. 1980a. *Social Indicators III.* Washington, D.C.: Government Printing Office.

———. 1980b. *Statistical Abstract of the United States, 1980.* Washington, D.C.: Government Printing Office.

———. 1979. *Statistical Abstract of the United States 1979.* Washington, D.C.: Government Printing Office.

———. 1978. *Statistical Abstract of the United States, 1978.* Washington, D.C.: Government Printing Office.

U.S. DEPARTMENT OF JUSTICE. 1983. *Report to the Nation on Crime and Justice.* Washington, D.C.: Government Printing Office.

———. *Uniform Crime Report, 1980 Preliminary Annual Release.* Washington, D.C.: Government Printing Office.

———. 1980. *Uniform Crime Report,* 1979. Washington, D.C.: Government Printing Office.

U.S. DEPARTMENT OF LABOR, BUREAU OF LABOR STATISTICS. 1980. *Perspective on Working Women: A Databook.* October, Bulletin 2080, Table 62.

U.S. News and World Report. 1982a. "Why the cost of healthcare won't stop rising." March 8, p. 67.

———. 1982b. "The ever-present hand of government." April 26. pp. 43–45.

VAGO, STEVEN. 1980. *Social Change.* New York: Holt, Rinehart and Winston.

VANFOSSEN, BETH E. 1979. *The Structure of Social Inequality.* Boston: Little, Brown.

VAN LAWICK-GOODALL, J. 1971. *In the Shadow of Man.* Boston: Houghton Mifflin.

VEBLEN, THORSTEIN. 1899. *The Theory of the Leisure Class.* New York: Macmillan.

VELTFORD, HELENE, and GEORGE E. LEE. 1943. "The Coconut Grove fire: A study in scapegoating." *Journal of Abnormal and Social Psychology,* Clinical Supplement, **38,** April, pp. 138–154.

VERBA, SIDNEY. 1972. *Small Groups and Political Behavior: A Study of Leadership.* Princeton, N.J.: Princeton University Press.

WALKER, ALICE. 1952. *The Color Purple.* New York: Harcourt Brace Jovanovich.

WALKER COMMISSION. 1968. *Rights in Conflict: The Violent Confrontation of Demonstrators and Police in the Parks and Streets of Chicago During the Week of the Democratic National Convention of 1968.* Washington, D.C.: U.S. Government Printing Office.

WARNER, W. L. and P. LUNT. 1941. *The Social Life of a Modern Community.* New Haven, Conn.: Yale University Press.

WARREN, R. L. 1972. *The Community in America.* 2d ed. New York: Rand McNally.

WATSON, J. B. 1925. *Behavior.* New York: Norton.

WEBER, MAX. 1962. *Basic Sociology.* Secaucus, N.J.: Citadel Press.

———. 1958a (1921). *The City.* New York: Collier.

———. 1958b. "Class, status, and party." In Hans H. Gerth and C. Wright Mills (eds.), *Max Weber: Essays in Sociology.* New York: Oxford.

———. 1957. *The Theory of Social and Economic Organization.* New York: Free Press.

———. 1956. "Some consequences of bureaucratization." In J. P. Mayer (trans.), *Max Weber and German Politics,* 2d ed.

———. 1949. *Max Weber on the Methodology of the Social Sciences.* Trans. and ed. Edward A. Shils and Henry A. Finch. New York: Free Press.

———. 1947. *Max Weber: Essays in Sociology*. New York: Oxford University Press.

———. 1930 (1920). *Protestant Ethic and the Spirit of Capitalism*. Trans. Talcott Parsons. New York: Scribner.

———. 1922. *Economy and Society*. Trans. Ephraim Fischoff. New York: Bedminster Press, 1968.

WEISS, ROBERT S. 1979a. *Going It Alone: The Family Life and Social Situation of the Single Parent*. New York: Basic Books.

———. 1979b. "Issues in the adjudication of custody when parents separate." In George Levinger and Oliver C. Moles, (eds.), *Divorce and Separation: Context, Causes, and Consequences*. New York: Basic Books.

WEISSBERG, ROBERT. 1981. *Understanding American Government*. Alternate ed. New York: Holt, Rinehart and Winston.

WEITZMAN, LENORE J., and RUTH B. DIXON. 1980. "The transformation of legal marriage through no-fault divorce." In Arlene S. Skolnick and Jerome H. Skolnick (eds.), *Family in Transition: Rethinking Marriage, Sexuality, Child Rearing and Family Organization*. 3rd ed. Boston: Little, Brown.

WESTOFF, CHARLES F., and ELISE F. JONES. 1977. "The secularization of Catholic birth control practice." *Family Planning Perspectives, 9*, September–October.

WHEELWRIGHT, PHILIP. 1959. *Heraclitus:* Princeton, N.J.: Princeton University Press.

WHITE, THEODORE H. 1982. *America in Search of Itself: The Making of the President, 1956–80*. New York: Harper & Row.

WHITE, W. F. 1943. *Street Corner Society*. Chicago: University of Illinois Press.

WHORF, B. 1956. *Language, Thought, and Reality*. Cambridge, Mass.: MIT Press.

WHYTE, W. H. 1956. *The Organization Man*. New York: Simon & Schuster.

WICKMAN, PETER, PHILLIP WHITTEN, and ROBERT LEVEY. 1980. *Criminology: Perspectives on Crime and Criminality*. Lexington, Mass.: Heath.

WIEBE, GERHART D. 1971. "The social effects of broadcasting." In Bernard Rosenberg and David Manning White (eds.), *Mass Culture Revisited*. New York: Van Nostrand.

WILLIAMS, R. 1970. *American Society: A Sociological Interpretation*. 3rd ed. New York: Knopf.

WILLMOTT, PETER, and MICHAEL DUNLOP YOUNG. 1973. *The Symmetrical Family*. New York: Pantheon Books.

WILSON, EDMUND. 1969. *The Dead Sea Scrolls 1947–1969*. Rev. ed. London: W. H. Allen.

WILSON, EDWARD O. 1979. *Sociobiology*. 2d ed. Cambridge, Mass.: Belknap.

———. 1978. *On Human Nature*. Cambridge, Mass.: Harvard University Press.

———. 1975. *Sociobiology: The New Synthesis*. Cambridge, Mass.: Harvard University Prerss.

WILSON, JAMES Q. 1980. *American Government*. Lexington, Mass.: Heath.

WILSON, JOHN. 1973. *Introduction to Social Movements*. New York: Basic Books.

WIRTH, LOUIS. 1944. "Race and public policy." *Scientific Monthly, 58*(4), March, p. 303.

———. 1938. "Urbanism as a way of life." *American Journal of Sociology, 64,* pp. 1–24.

WISSLER, CLARK. 1911. *The Social Life of the Blackfoot Indians*. Anthropological Papers of the American Museum of Natural History, 7(1). New York: American Museum of Natural History.

WOLF, ERIC. 1969. *Peasant Wars of the Twentieth Century*. New York: Harper & Row.

WOLFE, LINDA. 1981. "The good news." *New York Magazine,* December 28, pp. 33–35.

WOLFGANG, MARVIN, ROBERT M. FIGLIO, and THORSTEN SELLIN. 1972. *Delinquency in a Birth Cohort*. Chicago: University of Chicago Press.

WORLD BANK. 1984. *World Development Report, 1984*. New York: Oxford University Press.

———. 1984. *The Development Data Book*. Washington, D.C.: World Bank.

YINGER, J. MILTON. 1970. *The Scientific Study of Religion*. New York: Macmillan.

———. 1960. "Contraculture and subculture." *American Sociological Review, 25,* pp. 625–635.

ZEITLIN, I. M. 1981. *Social Condition of Humanity*. New York: Oxford University Press.

ZELNIK, MELVIN, and KANTNER. 1979. "Probabilities of intercourse and conception among U.S. teenage women 1971 and 1976." *Family Planning Perspectives, 2,* May–June, pp. 177–183.

———. 1972. "Sexuality, contraception and pregnancy among young unwed females in the United States." In U.S. Commission on Population Growth and the American Future, *Demographic and Social Aspects of Population Growth*. Washington, D.C.: U.S. Government Printing Office.

ZIMBARDO, P. G. 1972. "Pathology of imprisonment." *Society,* April 9.

Credits

Photo Credits

Part I
Center: Barbara Pfeffer, Photo Researchers; insert left, ©1981 Robert Houser, Photo Researchers; insert right ©Alice Kandell, Photo Researchers

Chapter 1
p. 10, ©Will McIntyre, Photo Researchers
pp. 14, 16, 20, The Bettmann Archive
p. 23, The Granger Collection
p. 25 (top and bottom left), The Bettmann Archive
p. 25 (top right), courtesy of Robert K. Merton
p. 28, Daniel S. Brody, Stock, Boston
p. 30, March Riboud, Magnum

Chapter 2
p. 36 (top left), © 1976, Esaias Baitel, Photo Researchers
p. 36 (top right), © Phyllis Graber Jensen, Stock, Boston
p. 48, © Teri Leigh Stratford, 1982, Photo Researchers
p. 51, UPI/Bettmann Newsphotos
p. 54, UPI/Bettmann Newsphotos

Part II
Center: James R. Holland, Stock, Boston; insert left, © Bruce Roberts, Photo Researchers; insert right, Peter Southwick, Stock, Boston

Chapter 3
p. 65, © Rene Burri, Magnum
p. 66, © Ray Ellis, 1984, Photo Researchers
p. 68, courtesy of Napoleon Chagnon
p. 70, Bruno Barboy, Magnum
p. 71, Van Bucher, Photo Researchers
pp. 76, 77, The Bettmann Archive
p. 78, Philip Jones Griffiths, Magnum
p. 81, Photo Researchers
p. 84, Paul Fusco, Magnum
p. 87, © Cornell Capa, Magnum
p. 88, Peter Simon, Stock/Boston
p. 89 (left), © Geoffrey Gove, Photo Researchers
p. 89 (right), UPI/Bettmann Newsphotos
p. 90, © 1982, Jan Lukas, Photo Researchers

Chapter 4
p. 98, Jerry Howard, Positive Images
p. 103 (left), courtesy of Henry L. Tischler
p. 103 (right), © 1975, Erika Stone, Photo Researchers
p. 109, The Bettmann Archive
p. 111, UPI/Bettmann Newsphotos
p. 112, courtesy of Henry L. Tischler
p. 113, The Bettmann Archive
p. 116, James Foote, Photo Researchers

p. 117, © F. B. Grunzweig, 1982, Photo Researchers
p. 120, Children's Television Workshop, Photo Researchers
p. 121, Museum of Modern Art/Film Stills Archive

Chapter 5
p. 130, Peter Southwick, Stock, Boston
p. 132, Atoz Images
p. 134, Mimi Forsyth, Monkmeyer Press Photo
p. 135, Jerry Howard, Positive Images
p. 137 (left), © Jim Anderson, 1981, Woodfin Camp & Associates
p. 137 (right), © Alex Webb, Magnum
p. 138, UPI/Bettmann Newsphotos
p. 145, Rhoda Sidey, Monkmeyer Photo Press

Part III
Center: Peter Simon, Stock, Boston; insert left, Kenneth Murray, Photo Researchers; insert right, © Alon Reininger, Contact Stock Images

Chapter 6
p. 154 (top), Christa Armstrong, Photo Researchers
p. 154 (bottom), © Jill Cannefax, EKM–Nepenthe
p. 158, Wide World Photos
p. 162, Omikron, Photo Researchers
p. 163, Wide World Photos

Chapter 7
p. 186, Alan Carey, The Image Works
p. 187, Frederiks D. Bodin, Stock, Boston
p. 188, UPI/Bettmann Newsphotos
pp. 193, 194, The Bettmann Archive
p. 197, Minoru Aoki, Photo Researchers
p. 204, (bottom left), © 1977 Jan Lukas; (top right), © 1976, George E. Jones III, Photo Researchers
p. 205, Peter Vandermark, Stock, Boston
p. 207, J. R. Eyerman, Life Magazine, © Time, Inc. 1953
p. 210, © F. B. Grunzweig, Photo Researchers

Chapter 8
p. 216, © Leonard Freed, Magnum
p. 220, Dr. Robert Carneiro, Magnum
p. 224, © Paolo Koch, Photo Researchers
p. 225, Jean Claude Lejeune, EKM–Nepenthe
p. 226, The Bettmann Archive

Chapter 9
p. 237, Michael Suler/Woodfin Camp & Associates
p. 238, © Jerry Howard, 1984, Positive Images
p. 253, © Sepp Setiz, 1978, Woodfin Camp & Associates
p. 254, © Jim Anderson, 1980, Woodfin Camp & Associates
p. 257, © Barbara Alper, Stock, Boston

p. 260, Michael Hayman, Stock, Boston
p. 263, © Cornell Capa, Magnum

Part IV

Center: ©Ray Ellis, Photo Researchers; insert left, Getsug/Anderson, Photo Researchers; insert right, Jean Claude Lejeune, Stock, Boston

Chapter 10

p. 270, Toga Fujihira, Monkmeyer Press Photo
p. 271, © Alon Reininger, 1978, Contact Stock Images
p. 273 (left), Hiroji Kubota, Magnum
p. 273 (right), Henri Cartier-Bresson
pp. 275, 285, UPI/Bettmann Newsphotos

Chapter 11

p. 300, David Evans, Stockton Record Library
p. 304, © Elizabeth Hamlin, Stock, Boston
p. 307, Ruth Silverman, Stock, Boston
p. 309, UPI/Bettmann Newsphotos
p. 313, The Bettmann Archive
p. 315, Museum of Modern Art/Film Stills Archive
p. 316, The Bettmann Archive
p. 321, UPI/Bettmann Newsphotos
p. 322, Michal Heron, Monkmeyer

Chapter 12

p. 327, © Craig Aurness, 1983
p. 333 (left), David Strickler, Monkmeyer Press Photo; (right), courtesy of Henry L. Tischler
p. 337, Peter Southwick, Stock, Boston
p. 343, The Bettmann Archive
p. 345, © Bruce Roberts, 1977, Photo Researchers

Part V

Center: Toga Fujihira, Monkmeyer Press Photo; insert left, © Elizabeth Crews; insert right, © John Chao, 1980, Woodfin Camp

Chapter 13

p. 353, Owen Franken, Stock, Boston
p. 355 (top), Stock, Boston; (bottom) © Anthony Howarth, Woodfin Camp & Associates
p. 358, The Bettmann Archive
p. 362, © Jerry Howard, Positive Images
p. 367, © Bohdan Hrynewych, Stock, Boston
p. 373, Richard Sobol, Stock, Boston
p. 376, © Jerry Howard 1984, Positive Images

Chapter 14

p. 380, Joe Munroe, Photo Researchers
p. 381, Stephen Feldman, Photo Researchers
p. 384, © 1980 Steve Kagan, Photo Researchers
p. 387, René Burri, Magnum
p. 390, Wide World Photos
p. 397, © Barbara Alper, Stock, Boston
p. 399, Rohn Eng, Photo Researchers
p. 400, © David M. Grossman, Photo Researchers
p. 402, Beryl Goldberg

Chapter 15

p. 411, © Elizabeth Crews
p. 412, courtesy of Henry L. Tischler
p. 416, Ann Holmes, Photo Researchers
p. 418, Constance Manos, Magnum
p. 426, © George W. Gardner, Stock, Boston
p. 427, © Elizabeth Crews

Chapter 16

p. 435, Burk Uzzle, Magnum
p. 437, © George Gerster, Photo Researchers
p. 441, Catherine Ursillo, Photo Researchers
p. 444, Elizabeth Hamlin, Stock, Boston
p. 446, Les Mahon, Monkmeyer Press Photo
p. 447, Owen Franken, Stock, Boston
p. 451, © Robin Lawrence, Photo Researchers

Chapter 17

pp. 457, 464, 465, The Bettmann Archive
p. 475, Wide World Photos
p. 476, Art Stein, Photo Researchers

Part VI

Center: Mike Mazzaschi, Stock, Boston; insert left, Wide World Photos; insert right, Ray Solomon, Monkmeyer Press Photo

Chapter 18

p. 484, Wide World Photos
p. 486, © Jerry Howard, 1982, Positive Image
p. 495, © Jerry Howard, 1984, Positive Image
p. 466, © John Marmara, 1980, Woodfin Camp & Associates
p. 505, Peter Schaaf, © Time Inc.
p. 506, © Barbara Rios, Photo Researchers
p. 508, © Jim Anderson, 1980, Woodfin Camp & Associates

Chapter 19

p. 518, Bernard Pierre Wolff, Photo Researchers
p. 522, Toga Fujihira, Monkmeyer Press Photo
p. 528, © Thomas Hopker, 1983, Woodfin Camp & Associates
p. 534, Alan Carey, The Image Works

Chapter 20

p. 539, © Christina Thomson, 1982, Woodfin Camp & Associates
p. 545, Bruce Davidson, Magnum
p. 548, Dominique Roger, Photo Researchers
p. 550, Alan Carey, The Image Works

Portfolios

Portfolio I

1a (top), John Mass, Photo Researchers; (bottom left), Cary Wolinsky, Stock, Boston; (bottom right), L. L. T. Rhodes, Taurus Photos
1b (top), © Giansanti, Sygma; (center), J. S. Larsen, Photo Researchers; (bottom), John Ficara, Woodfin Camp & Associates.

1c (top left), Burk Uzzle, Woodfin Camp; (top right), Jack Fields, Photo Researchers; (center right), George E. Jones, Photo Researchers; (bottom), ©E.Williamson, The Picture Cube

1d (top left), J. P. Laffont, Sygma; (top right), William Pivelli, The Image Bank; (bottom), Burk Uzzle, Magnum

Portfolio II

p. 105 (top), Jane Latta, Photo Researchers; (bottom), John Launois, Black Star

p. 106 (top), Michael Philip Manheim, Photo Researchers; (bottom), Robert Miller, Black Star

p. 107 (top), Robert Miller, Black Star; (bottom), John Launois, Black Star

p. 108 (top), John Launois, Black Star; (center), John Launois, Black Star; (bottom), Jane Latta, Photo Researchers

Portfolio III

p. 173 (top left), Jeff Rotman, The Picture Cube; (top right), T. McCarthy, The Image Cube; (center), Stan Ries, The Picture Cube; (bottom), Joh Lei, Stock, Boston

p. 174 (top left), Sisee Brimberg, Woodfin Camp & Associates; (middle left), Jeff Lowenthal, Woodfin Camp & Associates; (top right), Taurus Photos; (center right), M. Philippot, Sygma; (bottom), M. Austin, Photo Researchers

p. 175, (top left), Junebug Clark, Photo Researchers; (bottom), Will McIntyre, Photo Researchers; (top right), Joel Gordon;

p. 176 (top left), Jean Louis Attan, Sygma; (top right), Allen Green, Photo Researchers; (bottom left), Gable Palmer, The Image Bank; (bottom right), Michael Rizza, The Picture Cube.

Portfolio IV

p. 4a (top), Georg Gerster, Photo Researchers; (center), John Running, Black Star; (bottom), Buddy Mays, Black Star

p. 4b (top left), Buddy Mays, Black Star; (top right), Douglas M. Wilson, Black Star; (bottom), Porterfield Chickering, Photo Researchers

pp. 4c and 4d, Paul Fusco, Magnum

Portfolio V

p. 5a (top left), Matt Herron, Black Star; (bottom left), Constance Manos, Magnum; (right), Bill Ross, Woodfin Camp & Associates

p. 5b (top left), Alon Reininger, Contact Press Images; (top right), John Neubauer, International Stock Photo; (bottom left), Dan Miller, Woodfin Camp & Associates; (bottom right), Nobu Arakawa, The Image Bank

p. 5c (top left), Christopher Springmann, Black Star; (top right), Martin Adler Levick, Black Star; (center), Jack Pottle, Design Conception; (bottom), Arnold Zann, Black Star

p. 5d (top left), Paul Fusco, Magnum; (bottom left), Burt Glinn, Magnum; (bottom right), Andrew Sacks, Black Star

Portfolio VI

p. 489: (top left), Bill Ross, Woodfin Camp & Associates; (top right), Tomas D. W. Friedmann, Photo Researchers; (bottom left), Susan Berkowitz, Taurus Photos; (bottom right), Lionel Jim Delevigne, Stock Boston

p. 490 (top left), Bohdan Hrynwych, Stock, Boston; (center left), Owen Franken, Stock, Boston; (bottom right), Joel Gordon

p. 491: (top), Rick Smolan, Contact Press; (middle), Jerry Berndt, The Picture Cube; (bottom), Owen Franken, Stock, Boston

Figure Credits

Chapter 6

Fig. 6.1, p. 159: Solomon E. Asch, "Studies of Independence and Conformity: A Minority of One Against a Unanimous Majority," *Psychological Monographs,* Vol. 70, No. 9, 1956.

Fig. 6.2, p. 170: K. K. White, *Understanding the Company Organization.* New York: American Management Association, 1963, p. 112.

Chapter 9

Fig. 9.1, p. 234, adapted from Graeme Newman, *Comparative Deviance: Perception and the Law in Six Cultures.* New York: Elsevier, 1967, p. 116, Table 4.

Fig. 9.2, p. 238, David E. Hunter and Phillip Whitten, *The Study of Anthropology.* New York: Harper & Row, 1976, p. 238.

Fig. 9.4, p. 242, Adapted from Robert K. Merton. *Social Theory and Social Structure* 1968, Enlarged Edition. New York: Free Press, 1968, p. 194.

Fig. 9.5, p. 251, Peter Wickman and Phillip Whitten, *Criminology: Perspectives on Crime and Criminality.* Lexington, Mass.: D.C. Heath, 1980, p. 246.

Indexes

Name Index

Subject Index

Terms in boldface type are defined in the running glossaries on the text pages indicated by boldface numbers.